Bord Fáilte
Irish Tourist Board

Ireland
G u i d e

Moorland Publishing Co Ltd

Published in Ireland by
Gill and Macmillan Ltd
Goldenbridge
Dublin 8
with associated companies throughout the world
0 7171 1976 9

Published in Great Britain by
Moorland Publishing Co Ltd
Moor Farm Road
Ashbourne
Derby DE6 1HD
086190 473 7

Published in North America by
St. Martin's Press Inc.
175 Fifth Avenue
New York
NY 10010–7848
0–312–09584–8
First U.S. Edition: September 1993
"A Thomas Dunne Book"

© Bord Fáilte Eireann-Irish Tourist Board 1993
Designed by
Identikit Design Consultants
Index compiled by Helen Litton
Print origination by
Seton Music Graphics Ltd, Bantry, Co. Cork, Ireland
Printed by Colour Books Ltd, Dublin, Ireland

A catalogue record is available for the Gill and Macmillan edition of this book
from the British Library.

Every care has been taken to ensure accuracy in the compilation of this book. Bord Fáilte and
Gill and Macmillan cannot, however, accept responsibility for errors or omissions but where such
are brought to our attention, future editions will be amended accordingly.
Population figures shown in this guide are those currently available at the time of printing.

Based on the Ordnance Survey by permission
of the Government (Permit No. 5703)

Based upon the Ordnance Survey map with the
sanction of the Controller of HM Stationery Office,
Crown Copyright reserved (Permit No. 553)

Contents

Acknowledgments

*Gill and Macmillan wish to thank the following for their
contributions to this new edition of* Ireland Guide.

*The revision and updating of the text was undertaken
by Paddy Meagher for the Republic of Ireland
and by Ian Hill for Northern Ireland.*

*The cover design, internal layout and maps were conceived
and prepared by Mark Loughran.*

*The photographs were supplied by the Libraries of Bord Fáilte-Irish Tourist Board and
the Northern Ireland Tourist Board. In each case, requests for photographs were
met with unfailing courtesy and efficiency.*

*Gill and Macmillan are also grateful to the specialist contributors who have written
sections of the introduction. The essay on Archaeology and Architecture
is by Laurence Flanagan; that on Literature by Joseph McMinn;
that on folklore by Dáithí Ó hÓgáin; and that on Landscape
and Natural History by Tony Whilde.*

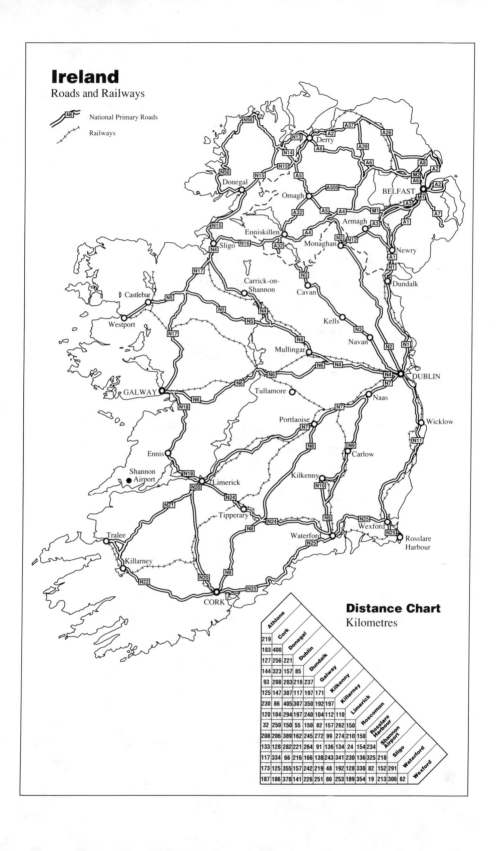

Ireland
Roads and Railways

N6 National Primary Roads

Railways

Distance Chart
Kilometres

Athlone	Cork	Donegal	Dublin	Dundalk	Galway	Kilkenny	Killarney	Limerick	Roscommon	Rosslare Harbour	Shannon Airport	Sligo	Waterford	Wexford
219														
183	400													
127	256	221												
144	323	157	85											
93	208	203	218	237										
125	147	307	117	197	171									
230	86	405	307	350	192	197								
120	104	294	197	240	104	112	110							
32	250	150	55	150	82	157	262	210	150					
208	206	389	162	245	272	99	274	210	150					
133	128	282	221	264	91	136	134	24	154	234				
117	334	66	216	166	138	243	341	230	136	325	218			
173	125	355	157	242	219	48	192	128	330	82	152	291		
187	186	370	141	226	251	80	253	189	354	19	213	306	62	

Introduction

The River Fergus,
near Corofin, Co. Clare

Ireland is small enough to be visited in its entirety within a couple of weeks. It is only a fraction smaller than Austria, although significantly larger than the three Benelux countries combined. In American terms, it is not much bigger than the state of Maine. Into this relatively small area, however, is packed a wide variety of land-scape and people. Although the visitor can *see* everything in a relatively short visit, it is difficult to experience the full variety of Ireland and the Irish without taking a little more time.

Ireland is the last island outpost of the great European land mass. Among its natural advantages is 5,600 km of coastline,

Belvedere House, Co. Westmeath

so indented that you are never more than 110 km from the sea. It is possible to take a day trip to the coast even from the most centrally located inland town. Moreover, you can choose between the long, gently sloping beaches of the east and south-east or the magnificent Atlantic coast to the west, where the sea has a straight run of over 3,200 km from America.

Although the mountains and beaches of the Irish coast are well known, less so are the 800 lakes and rivers that are the delight of inland Ireland. For example, on the 135 km journey from Mullingar to Sligo you hardly ever lose sight of them. This alternation of land and water gives travelling in Ireland its particular variety.

Historically, Ireland has principally been an agricultural country. Apart from the Lagan valley area around Belfast, there has been little tradition of heavy industry. The scenery is seldom marred by industrial wasteland and the rivers and lakes remain, for the most part, clear and unpolluted. Consequently, Ireland remains one of the world's leading venues for angling holidays. Outside the large urban conurbations of greater Dublin and Belfast, population density is low and even in high summer traffic levels are light compared with western Europe in general.

It is this slower pace of life that makes Ireland such a relaxing holiday venue. This is a country where it really is possible to unwind and enjoy the kind of holiday that sends you home feeling renewed, refreshed, and looking forward to your next visit.

Facts about Ireland

Ireland

Ireland is an island of 84,288 sq km (32,544 square miles). Its greatest length is 485 km (302 miles), its greatest width 304 km (189 miles), and its coastline extends for over 5,631 km (3,500 miles). The highest mountain is Carrantuohill (1,040 metres/3,414 feet), near Killarney in County Kerry. The longest river is the Shannon (370 km/230 miles, including estuary). The largest lake is Lough Neagh (396 sq km/153 square miles) in the north-east.

The country is divided into the four historic provinces of Ulster (9 counties) in the north; Munster (6 counties) in the south; Leinster (12 counties) in the east; and Connacht (5 counties) in the west.

The population of the 32 counties of Ireland is approximately 5 million.

Climate

Winters in Ireland are mild and summers temperate due to the prevailing south-westerly winds and the influence of the warm waters of the North Atlantic Drift. Average temperatures during January and February, the coldest months, range from 4°C in some coastal areas. During July and August, the warmest months (and consequently the peak holiday months), average temperatures range from 14° to 16°C but the average maximum temperatures are from 17° to 20°C. May and June are the sunniest months with an average of between 5 and 6½ hours of sunshine a day over most of the country. The extreme south-east is the sunniest area with an average of over 7 hours of sunshine per day during July and August.

The driest area of the country is the coastal strip near Dublin where average annual rainfall is less than 750 mm. Rainfall in the west generally is between 1,000 mm and 1,300 mm though in mountainous areas the rainfall can be over 2,000 mm per year.

The temperature of the water off the coast ranges from 10°C off the south-west coast to less than 7°C off the south-east coast in winter and early spring, and from 15° to 13°C in the same areas in later summer.

Government

The Constitution of Ireland, approved by a referendum in 1937, declares Ireland to be a sovereign, independent, democratic state. The parliament (*Oireachtas*) consists of the President of Ireland (*An tUachtaran*) and two houses: a house of representatives (*Dáil Éireann*) and a senate (*Seanad Éireann*).

The president is elected by direct vote of the people for a seven-year term. Dáil Éireann's 166 members are elected on the system of proportional representation by means of the single transferable vote. Of Seanad Éireann's 60 members, 11 are nominated by the prime minister (*Taoiseach*) and 49 are elected—three by the National University of Ireland, three by the University of Dublin and 43 from panels of candidates established on a vocational basis. Irish citizens become eligible to vote in presidential, parliamentary and local elections at the age of 18.

Northern Ireland comprises six counties of the province of Ulster (Antrim, Down, Armagh, Derry, Tyrone and Fermanagh). This area did not become independent with the rest of Ireland, and remains part of the United Kingdom.

Northern Ireland came into being under the Government of Ireland Act 1920. It has its own parliamentary system until March 1972 when the Parliament was prorogued and the executive powers were transferred temporarily to the United Kingdom Parliament and Government, which have ultimate power over Northern Ireland affairs. The existing arrangements for governing are vested in the Secretary of State for Northern Ireland, who holds legislative power in respect of commerce and industry, agriculture, education, health and welfare. These arrangements are subject to annual review. The Government departments concerned with enforcing these powers remain located in Northern Ireland.

Northern Ireland sends 17 members to the House of Commons, which is the lower house of the United Kingdom Parliament at Westminster. On 1 January 1973 the United Kingdom of Great Britain and Northern Ireland became a member of the European Community. Northern Ireland sends three members to the European Parliament.

Information for visitors

Money

The Irish punt (IR£) is divided into 100 pence (100p). Currency notes are issued in values of £100, £50, £20, £10 and £5. Coins are issued to the value of 100p (£1), 50p, 20p, 10p, 5p, 2p, 1p. In Northern Ireland the pound sterling is divided in a similar way. Irish currency should only be used in the Republic and sterling currency in Northern Ireland.

Banks

Most banks in Ireland are open from Monday to Friday from 10.00 to 12.30 and from 13.30 to 15.00 hours. Of these, some branches are open through lunchtime. In Northern Ireland the opening hours are 10.00 to 15.30 Monday to Friday. In the Republic there is extended opening until 17.00 on one day per week (the choice varying from place to place; it is Thursday in Dublin). The opening hours of the TSB Bank are slightly different: 10.00–16.00 Monday, Tuesday, Wednesday and Friday; 10.00–19.00 Thursday; no lunchtime

closing. In Northern Ireland in some places, the banks close for lunch 12.30–13.30. In the Republic and Northern Ireland, in very small villages, banking services may be provided only on two or three days per week, so it is advisable for the visitor to make arrangements to get cash in the bigger centres. Cash dispensers have become more widely available in recent years and post offices can also provide limited cash services.

Public Holidays

Public holidays in the Republic of Ireland are New Year's Day (1 January); St Patrick's Day (17 March) (if St Patrick's Day falls on a Sunday, the following Monday is a public holiday); Good Friday (though this is not a statutory public holiday); Easter Monday, first Mondays in June and August, last Monday in October; Christmas Day (25 December); St Stephen's Day (26 December). In Northern Ireland St Patrick's Day and Good Friday are not public holidays but 12 July is.

Postage Stamps

Irish postage stamps must be used on letters posted in the Republic and British postage stamps on letters posted in Northern Ireland. Details of stamps available for sale for philatelic purposes may be obtained from the Controller, Philatelic Section, G.P.O., Dublin 1, or equivalent in Northern Ireland.

Maps

A comprehensive series of maps covering Ireland is produced by the Ordnance Survey of Ireland in Dublin and the Ordnance Survey of Northern Ireland in Belfast. Holidaymakers will find useful a new series of four 'Holiday maps' covering all Ireland (scale at 1:250,000 or ¼ inch to 1 mile) which are jointly published by both Ordnance Surveys. Maps are on sale at Tourist Information Offices and most booksellers.

Telephones

Tones
Telephone tones and their significance vary from country to country. These are the tones used throughout the island:
Dial Tone A continuous high pitched tone;
Ringing Tone A repeated double beat tone—burr-burr;
Engaged Tone A high pitched, broken tone beep-beep-beep.

Public Phones in Ireland
There are public telephones in many outdoor locations all over Ireland as well as in Telecentres, public buildings including rail and bus stations, shops, pubs, restaurants and hotels. Local, trunk and international calls can be dialled direct from these phones. Telecom Éireann has introduced Cardphones in cities and towns throughout Ireland. Cards can be purchased in Telecentres and in post offices and retail outlets displaying the Callcard sign. Cards can be purchased in 10, 20, 50 and 100 unit denominations. Operating instructions are displayed in each kiosk or on the payphone itself.

For locations of Cardphones and Callcard Agents ring Freefone 1800 250 250.

A list of all Irish regional codes and International direct dialling codes is contained in the front of each telephone directory.

Emergency Numbers
Dial 999 and ask the operator for the emergency service you require: Fire, Gardaí (Police), Ambulance, Boat and Coastal Rescue, Mountain and Cave Rescue. When the emergency service answers, state the address or location at which help is needed. Calls to these services are free of charge.

International Operator Service
If you cannot direct dial the number you want or if you do not know the number of the person you wish to call, contact the international operator on 114, or 10 if you are ringing from oldstyle A/B coinboxes.

International Advice of Duration and Charge
To know the duration and charge for an international call made through the operator, dial 114 and ask the operator when booking the call for 'advice of duration and charge'. The operator will call you back with this information when the call is finished. The charge for this service is 30p.

International Credit Cards
Countries from which credit cards are accepted by the international telephone exchange for calls back to issuing country:

Australia	Greece	New Zealand
Bahamas	Hawaii	Norway
Brazil	Hong Kong	Singapore
Bulgaria	Hungary	South Africa
Canada	Italy	Taiwan
Columbia	Japan	Thailand
Cyprus	Korea,	Uganda
Denmark	Republic of	USA
Egypt	Kuwait	Yugoslavia
France	Netherlands	

International Reverse Charge Calls or Collect Calls
You may have the charge for an international call transferred to the called number (not a payphone) in most countries if the charge is accepted when the operator offers the call. To use this service, dial 114, or 10 if you are ringing from oldstyle A/B coinboxes.

International Personal Calls
You may book a call to a designated person. A personal fee is, however, charged in addition to the standard charge. This fee varies with the call destination— dial 114, or 10 if you are ringing from oldstyle A/B coinboxes.

Serious Difficulties
If you have serious difficulties in making an international call please contact the Chief Supervisor (Continental and Overseas) on Freefone 1800 680000.

Near Camlough, Co. Armagh

Directory Enquiries

If you cannot find the number of the person you wish to call, contact the Operator.

Dial 1190 for numbers within Ireland.
Dial 1197 for numbers within Great Britain.
Dial 114 if you require an international
    number.
Dial 10 for the local operator (when
    ringing from oldstyle A/B coinboxes).
    Give the person's name and address
and any other information that may help to
identify the number.

Operator-assisted Trunk Calls

For internal and cross-channel calls which cannot be dialled direct, contact the operator on '10'. Give the operator the number from which you are calling and the number you require. Please dial direct if you can—it saves you time and money.

Northern Ireland Telephones

Public telephones will take either Phonecards, which you can buy in post offices or shops displaying the Phonecard sign, or cash. Booths give instructions on the use of both. Most coinboxes will take £1, 50p, 20p and 10p coins. If you are outside Belfast and wish to telephone the city the dialling prefix is 0232; for central London it is 071, for outer London 081 and for Dublin it is 010 353 1.

Dial 100 to obtain the operator.
Dial 155 for the international operator.
Directory enquiries for the UK—dial 192.
International directory enquiries—dial 153.

Tourist Information Offices and Centres

Basic tourist information on Ireland can be obtained from the Irish Tourist Board (Bord Fáilte) and from the Northern Ireland Tourist Board offices as follows:

Irish Tourist Board (Bord Fáilte)

Head Office
Bord Fáilte—Irish Tourist Board
Baggot St Bridge
Dublin 2
Tel. (01) 765871/616500
Telex 93755
Fax (01) 764764

Northern Ireland
Belfast
53 Castle St BT1 1GH
Tel. (0232) 327888
Fax (0232) 240201

Derry
Foyle St
Tel. (0504) 369501
Fax (0504) 369501

Europe
London
150 New Bond St
London W1Y 0AQ
Tel. (071) 473 3201
Telex 266410
Fax (071) 493 9065

All–Ireland Travel Desk
British Travel Centre
12 Regent St
Picadilly Circus
(personal callers)

Paris
33 Rue de Miromesnil
75008 Paris
Tel. (1) 47 42 03 36
Fax (1) 47 42 01 64

Frankfurt
Irische Fremdenverkehrszentrale
Untermainanlage 7
W 6000 Frankfurt Main 1
Tel. (069) 23 64 92
Telex 414628
Fax (069) 23 46 26

Milan
Via S. Maria Segreta 6
20123 Milano
Tel. (02) 8690541
Telex 312179
Fax (02) 8690396

Brussels
Avenue de Beaulieu 25
1160 Brussels
Tel. (02) 673 9940
Telex 23071
Fax (02) 672 1066

Amsterdam
Leidsestraat 32
1017 PB Amsterdam
Tel. (020) 6 22 31 01
Fax (020) 6 20 80 89

Copenhagen
Box 104
1004 Kobenhavn k
Tel. (033) 15 8045
Fax (033) 93 6390

Stockholm
Box 5292
102 46 Stockholm
Tel. (08) 662 8510
Fax (08) 661 7595

North America
New York
757 Third Avenue
New York NY 10017
Tel. (212) 418 0800
Telex 422234
Fax (212) 371 9052

Toronto
160 Bloor Street East
Suite 934
Toronto
Ontario M4W 1BN
Tel. (416) 929 2777
Telex 06–22084
Fax (416) 929 6783

Australia
Sydney
5th Level
36 Carrington St
Sydney NSW 2000
Tel. (02) 299 6177
Fax (02) 299 6323

Northern Ireland Tourist Board
Head Office
Northern Ireland Tourist Board
St Anne's Court
59 North St
Belfast BT1 1ND
Tel. (0232) 231221
Telex 748089
Fax (0232) 240960

Ireland
Dublin
16 Nassau St
Dublin 2
Tel. (01) 6791977
Fax (01) 6791863

Europe
London
11 Berkeley St
London W1X 5AD
Tel. (071) 493 0601
Fax (071) 499 3731

All–Ireland Travel Desk
British Travel Centre
12 Regent St
Picadilly Circus
(personal callers)

Paris
Office de Tourisme d'Irlande du Nord
3 Rue de Pontoise
78100 Saint Germain
Tel. (01) 39 21 9380
Fax (01) 39 21 9390

Frankfurt/Main
6000 Frankfurt/Main
Taunusstrasse 52–60
Tel. (069) 234504
Fax (069) 2380717

North America
New York
5th Floor
Suite 500
276 5th Avenue
New York NY 10001
Tel. (212) 686 6250
Fax (212) 686 8061

In addition, offices of the British Tourist
Authority (BTA) in many countries carry
tourist information on Northern Ireland.

The information supplied at these offices is designed to help the potential visitor to plan his visit to Ireland either personally or through a travel agent or tour operator. When the visitor arrives in Ireland, he can obtain more detailed information on the areas in which he is staying from the local tourist inform-ation offices. The local offices are run by the regional tourism organisations and, in the case of the Shannon region, by the Traffic and Tourism Division of Shannon Development. A list of the local offices of these information offices run by them and by Shannon Development is appended. The tourist information offices also provide a nationwide rooms reservation service. They charge a small booking fee and the visitor is also asked to pay a 10 per cent booking deposit refundable when paying the bill.

Appended also is a list of the local tourist offices in Northern Ireland. Apart from the offices operated by the Northern Ireland Tourist Board, many of these offices are based in local District Council offices or in shops, post offices, libraries, caravan parks or visitor or leisure centres in the towns listed.

Regional Tourism Organisations
Dublin (Dublin City and County)
Dublin Tourism, 1 Clarinda Park North,
Dun Laoghaire, Co. Dublin
Tel. (01) 808571. Fax (01) 802641

South East (Carlow, Kilkenny, South Tipperary, Waterford, Wexford)
South East Tourism
41 The Quay, Waterford
Tel. (051) 75823. Fax (051) 77388

South West (Cork, South Kerry)
Cork/Kerry Tourism
Grand Parade, Cork
Tel. (021) 273251. Fax (021) 273504

West (Galway, Mayo, Roscommon)
Ireland West Tourism
Aras Fáilte, Eyre Square, Galway
Tel. (091) 63081. Fax (091) 65201

North West (Cavan, Donegal, Leitrim, Monaghan, Sligo)
North West Tourism
Aras Reddan, Temple Street, Sligo
Tel. (071) 61201. Fax (071) 60360

Midlands East (Kildare, Laois, Longford, Louth, Meath, North Offaly, Westmeath, Wicklow)
Midlands East Tourism
Dublin Road, Mullingar, Co. Westmeath
Tel. (044) 48761. Fax (044) 40413

Note: There is no Regional Tourism Organisation in the Shannon Region. RTO functions are carried out by the Traffic and Tourism Division of Shannon Development, Shannon Town Centre, Shannon, Co. Clare.

Shannon (Clare, Limerick, North Kerry, North Tipperary, South Offaly)
Tel. (061) 361555. Fax (061) 361903

Tourist Information Offices: Republic of Ireland

Watch out for this sign that marks a Tourist Information Office. Their Tourist Advisers are experts on the surrounding areas and on all aspects of Irish holidays. They can help you with:

• Booking your accommodation
• Places to visit
• Places to eat
• Things to do
• Routes to take
• National and local events
• Maps, guides and books

Normally offices are open from 9.00 a.m. to 6.00 p.m. Monday to Friday and 9.00 a.m. to 1.00 p.m. on Saturday. These hours may vary to suit local circumstances during summer.

Location	Telephone	Open
Achill The Sound Achill Island, Co. Mayo.	(098) 45384	July–Aug
Adare The Thatch Cottage, Main St Adare, Co. Limerick.	(061) 396255	April –Oct
Aran Islands Kilronan Inishmore, Co. Galway.	(099) 61263	May –Sept
Arklow The Parade Ground Arklow, Co. Wicklow.	(0402) 32484	June –Aug
Athlone The Castle, Market Square Athlone, Co. Westmeath.	(0902) 94630	April –Nov
Athy Town Hall Athy, Co. Kildare.	(0507) 31859	June–Sept
Ballina Cathedral Rd Ballina, Co. Mayo.	(096) 70848	June–Aug
Ballinasloe Keller's Travel Agency Ballinasloe, Co. Galway.	(0905) 42131	July–Aug
Bantry The Square Bantry, Co. Cork.	(027) 50229	June–Sept
Birr Rosse Row Birr, Co. Offaly.	(0509) 20110 (0509) 20660 Fax	May–Sept
Boyle Market St Boyle, Co. Roscommon.	(079) 62145	June–Aug
Bray Unit 2, Florence Rd Bray, Co. Wicklow.	(01) 2867128	June–Aug

Bundoran Main St Bundoran, Co. Donegal.	(072) 41350	June–Sept
Bunratty Folk Park, Bunratty, Co. Clare.	(061) 360133	April–Sept
Cahir Castle St Cahir, Co. Tipperary.	(052) 41453	May–Sept
Carlow Traynor House, College St Carlow.	(0503) 31554	June–Sept
Carrick-on-Suir The Clock Tower Carrick-on-Suir Co. Tipperary.	(051) 40726	May–Sept
Carrick-on-Shannon The Quay Carrick-on-Shannon Co. Leitrim.	(078) 20170	May–Sept
Cashel Town Hall, Co. Tipperary.	(062) 61333	March–Sept
Castlebar Linen Hall St, Castlebar Co. Mayo.	(094) 21207	July–Aug
Cavan Farnham St Cavan.	(049) 31942	**All year**
Clifden Market St Clifden, Co. Galway.	(095) 21163	May–Sept
Cliffs of Moher (Liscannor) Co. Clare.	(065) 81171	March–Oct
Clonakilty 9 Rossa St Clonakilty, Co. Cork.	(023) 33226	June–Sept
Clonmacnois, Co. Offaly. via Shannon Bridge.	(0905) 74134	April–Oct

Clonmel Chamber Buildings Clonmel, Co. Tipperary.	(052) 22960	June–Sept
Cork Tourist House Grand Parade, Cork.	(021) 273251 (021) 273504 Fax	**All year**
Cork Ferryport (Ringaskiddy)		June–Sept
Dingle Main St Dingle, Co. Kerry.	(066) 51188	May–Oct
Donegal Town Quay St Donegal.	(073) 21148	May– Sept
Drogheda West St Drogheda, Co. Louth.	(041) 37070	June –Aug
Dublin Airport	(01) 376387 (01) 425886 Fax	**All year**
Dublin (O'Connell St)	(01) 747733 (01) 743660 Fax	**All year**
Dublin College Green (Foster Place) Dublin 2.	(01) 711488	March–Sept
Dublin Baggot St Bridge Dublin 2.	(01) 765871	Jan–Dec
Dublin North Wall Ferryport (B & I Terminal).	To meet evening arrivals	June–Sept
Dundalk The Market Square Dundalk, Co. Louth.	(042) 35484 (042) 38070 Fax	**All year**
Dungarvan Mary St Dungarvan, Co. Waterford.	(058) 41741	June–Sept

Dungloe Main St Dungloe, Co. Donegal.	(075) 21297	June–Aug
Dun Laoghaire St Michael's Wharf Dun Laoghaire, Co. Dublin.	(01) 2806984 (01) 2806459 Fax	**All year**
Ennis Clare Rd Ennis, Co. Clare.	(065) 28366	**All year**
Enniscorthy The County Museum The Castle, Co. Wexford.	(054) 34699	June–Sept
Galway Victoria Place Eyre Square Galway.	(091) 63081 (091) 65201 Fax	**All year**
Galway Airport	(091) 55252	June–Sept
Glengarriff Main St, Glengarriff Co. Cork.	(027) 63084	July–Aug
Gorey Main St Gorey, Co. Wexford.	(055) 21248	July–Aug
Kenmare Main St Kenmare, Co. Kerry.	(064) 41233	June–Sept
Kilkee Main St, Co. Clare.	(065) 56112	May–Sept
Kilkenny Shee Alms House Rose Inn St, Kilkenny.	(056) 21755 (056) 63955 Fax	**All year**
Killaloe The Bridge Killaloe, Co. Clare.	(061) 376866	May–Sept
Killarney (Town Hall) Killarney, Co. Kerry.	(064) 31633 (064) 34506 Fax	**All year**

13

Kilrush Main St, Kilrush Co. Clare.	(065) 51577	June–Aug
Kinsale Emmet Place Kinsale, Co. Cork.	(021) 772234	June–Sept
Knock Village Co. Mayo.	(094) 88193	May–Sept
Knock Airport Horan International–Kilkelly Co. Mayo.	(094) 67247	**All year**
Lahinch Main St Lahinch, Co. Clare.	(065) 81474	May–Sept
Laragh Laragh, Co. Wicklow.		July–Aug
Letterkenny Derry Rd, Co. Donegal.	(074) 21160 (074) 25180 Fax	**All year**
Limerick Arthur's Quay Limerick.	(061) 317522 (061) 315634 Fax	**All year**
Listowel St John's Church Listowel, Co. Kerry.	(068) 22590	May–Sept
Longford Main St Longford.	(043) 46566	June–Aug
Monaghan Market House Monaghan.	(047) 81122	**All year**
Mullingar Dublin Rd Mullingar, Co. Westmeath.	(044) 48650	**All year**
Nenagh Connolly St Nenagh, Co. Tipperary.	(067) 31610 (067) 33418 Fax	May–Sept

Newbridge Main St Newbridge, Co. Kildare.	(045) 33835	June–Aug
Newgrange via Slane Co. Meath.	(041) 24274	April–Oct
New Ross The Quay New Ross, Co. Wexford.	(051) 21857	June–Sept
Portlaoise James Fintan Lawlor Ave Portlaoise, Co. Laois.	(0502) 21178	May–Sept
Roscommon Harrison Hall Roscommon.	(0903) 26342	June–Aug
Rosslare Harbour (Kilrane) Co. Wexford.	(053) 33232	April–Sept
Rosslare Terminal	(053) 33622 (053) 33421 Fax	**All year**
Salthill Promenade Salthill, Co. Galway.	(091) 63081	May–Aug
Shannon Airport, Co. Clare.	(061) 61664	**All year**
Skerries (Community Office) Skerries, Co. Dublin.	(01) 490888	Jan–Dec
Skibbereen (Town Hall) Skibbereen, Co. Cork.	(028) 21766 (028) 21353 Fax	**All year**
Sligo Aras Reddan Temple St, Sligo.	(071) 61201 (071) 60360 Fax	**All year**
Thoorballylee (Yeats Tower) Gort, Co. Galway.	(091) 31436	March–Sept
Tipperary Town Community Office Tipperary.	(062) 51457	Jan–Dec

Tralee Ashe Memorial Hall Tralee, Co. Kerry.	(066) 21288	**All year**
Tramore Railway Square Tramore, Co. Waterford.	(051) 81572	June–Sept
Tuam The Mill Museum Tuam, Co. Galway.	(093) 24463	July–Aug
Tullamore Williams St Shopping Centre Tullamore, Co. Offaly.	(0506) 52141	June–Aug
Waterford 41 The Quay, Waterford.	(051) 75788 (051) 77388 Fax	**All year**
Westport The Mall Westport, Co. Mayo.	(098) 25711 (098) 26709 Fax	**All year**
Wexford Crescent Quay, Wexford.	(053) 23111	**All year**
Wexford Heritage Park	(053) 41911	**All year**
Wicklow Rialto Centre, Fitzwilliam Square, Wicklow.	(0404) 69117	**All year**
Youghal, Market House Market Square Youghal, Co. Cork.	(024) 92390	June–Sept

Tourist Information Points

Below is a list of manned Tourist Information Points at which you will be assisted with information on local attractions and services. These units carry tourist literature.

County Clare
Aillwee Cave (The Burren)
Corofin (Village Hostel)
Doolin (Doolin Hostel)
Dysert O'Dea (Archaeology Centre)
Ennistymon (KAM Knitwear)

Inagh (Ceol Agus Ol)
Kilfenora (Burren Display Centre)
Killimer Ferrypoint (The Closh Bar)
Lisdoonvarna (Spa Wells)
Scarriff (Mrs Bane, Gift Shop)
Tulla Business Centre (Main Street)

County Cork
Blarney
Castletownbere
Cobh
Dunmanway
Fermoy

Ireland

Provinces and Counties

- – – – – Boundry between Republic of Ireland and Northern Ireland
- —— Provincial boundaries
- — County boundaries

Donegal

Derry

Antrim

Tyrone

Ulster

Fermanagh

Down

Sligo

Armagh

Monaghan

Leitrim

Cavan

Louth

Mayo

Roscommon

Longford

Meath

Connacht

Westmeath

Galway

Offaly

Kildare

Dublin

Leinster

Laois

Wicklow

Clare

Carlow

Kilkenny

Tipperary

Limerick

Wexford

Munster

Kerry

Waterford

Cork

Macroom (The Square)
Mallow (Bridge St)

County Donegal
Bunbeg
Ballybofey
(Daniel McIntyre, Newsagent)
Dunfanaghy (McAuliffe's Shop)
Glencolumbkille (Holiday Village)
Glenties (General Store)
Killybegs (Cunningham's, Main St)

County Galway
Athenry (Fields of Athenry)
Cleggan (Oliver Coyne)
Furbo (Filling Station)
Glenamaddy (Mannion's)
Gort (Michael Cunningham, Bridge St)
Inishmaan (Mrs Angela O'Fatharta)
Letterfrack (Kylemore Abbey, Mother Magdalena)
Loughrea (Sweeney Travel)
Oughterard (Monaghan's Craft Shop)
Portumna (Development Office)
Spiddal (Forbaort Pobal Teo)

North Kerry
Abbeydorney (Post Office)
Ballybunion (Post Office)
Ballyheigue (Post Office)
Crag Cave, Castleisland
Tarbert (Murphy's Restaurant)

South Kerry
Ballyferriter (Heritage Centre)
Cahirciveen
Glenbeigh
Kells
Killorglin
Sneem
Waterville

County Leitrim
Ballinamore (Mrs S. Smyth, High St)
Drumshanbo (Mrs E. Mooney, Carrick Rd)

County Limerick
Foynes GPA Flying Boat Museum
Kilfinane (Educational Centre)

County Louth
Dromad (Ravensdale, Dundalk)

County Mayo
Achill (Teddy Lavelle)
Ballinrobe (Ferrick Travel)
Ballycastle
Bangor Erris
Belmullet (Noone's Filling Station)
Charlestown (P. Colleran, The Square)
Crossmolina
Foxford
Killala
Louisburgh
Newport (Darac Handcrafts)
Swinford (Mellet Travel)

County Meath
Enfield (Mr Carey)
Trim (Castle St)

County Offaly
Banagher (Crank House)

County Roscommon
Arigna
Ballaghaderreen (John Casey)
Strokestown (Heritage Centre)

County Sligo
Tubbercurry (Killoran's)

County Tipperary
Ballinderry (Lakeshore Cottage)
Roscrea (Damer House)
Thurles (Centrefield)

Tourist Information Offices:
Northern Ireland
Apart from the main tourist information
centres and other offices listed here,
visitors can often obtain leaflets and help
from the local library. The village post
office is also a mine of information!
Opening times are usually from 9.00 a.m.
to 5.00 p.m. Monday to Friday, although
the closing time varies from place to place.
A few of the bigger offices also open on
Saturdays.

Location	Telephone	Open
Annalong (Corn Mill) Co. Down.	(039 67) 68736	June–Aug
Antrim (Council Offices).	(084 94) 63113 (084 94) 64469 Fax	**All year**
Pogue's Entry, Church St Antrim.	(084 94) 63113	**All year**
Armagh (Bank Building) Co. Armagh.	(0861) 527808 (0861) 524246 Fax	**All year**
Library at Market House Armagh, Co. Armagh.	(0861) 524072	**All year**
Ballycastle Sheskburn House, 7 Mary St Ballycastle, Co. Antrim.	(026 57) 62024 (026 57) 62515 Fax	**All year**
Ballymena Council Offices 80 Galgorm Rd Ballymena, Co. Antrim.	(0266) 44111 (0266) 46296 Fax	Nov–April
Morrow's Shop Bridge St Ballymena, Co. Antrim.	(0266) 653663	May–Oct
Ballymoney Council Offices 14 Charles St, Ballymoney Co. Antrim.	(026 56) 62280	**All year**
Riada Centre 33 Garryduff Rd Ballymoney, Co. Antrim.	(026 56) 65792 (026 56) 65150 Fax	**All year**
Banbridge (Leisure Centre) Banbridge, Co. Down.	(082 06) 62799 (082 06) 62595 Fax	**All year**
Bangor (Tower House) 34 Quay St Bangor, Co. Down.	(0247) 270069 (0247) 271370 Fax	**All year**
Belfast St Anne's Court, 59 North St Belfast BT1 1NB	(0232) 231221 (0232) 240960 Fax	**All year**

Belfast city (City Hall) Co. Antrim.	(0232) 320202 ext 2227 (0232) 438075 Fax	**All year**
Belfast City Airport	(084) 457745 ext 132 (084) 459198 Fax	**All year**
Belfast International Airport Belfast, Co. Antrim.	(084 94) 22888 ext 3009 (084 94) 52084 Fax	**All year**
Benone Tourist Complex Magilligan, Co. Derry.	(050 47) 50555	**All year**
Carnlough Post Office Carnlough, Co. Antrim.	(0574) 885210	**All year**
Carrickfergus Town Hall Carrickfergus, Co. Antrim.	(096 03) 51604 (096 03) 66696 Fax	**All year**
Caravan at Castle Green Carrickfergus, Co. Antrim.	(096 03) 51604	June–Aug
Castlerock (Swimming Pool) Castlerock, Co. Derry.	(0265) 848258	July–Aug
Coleraine (Council Offices) 41 Portstewart Rd, Coleraine Co. Derry.	(0265) 52181	**All year**
Railway Rd Coleraine, Co. Derry.	(0265) 44723 (0265) 53489 Fax	**All year**
Cookstown (Council Offices) 12 Burn Rd, Cookstown Co. Tyrone.	(064 87) 62205 (064 87) 64360 Fax	**All year**
48 Molesworth St Cookstown, Co. Tyrone.	(064 87) 66727	April–Sept
Cranagh (Sperrin Heritage Centre), 274 Glenelly Rd Cranagh, Co. Tyrone.	(066 26) 48142	Easter–Sept
Cushendall Carpark 24b Mill St Cushendall, Co. Antrim.	(026 67) 71180	**All year**

Cushendun 1 Main St Cushendun, Co. Antrim.	(026 674) 506	April–Sept
Derry City 40 Foyle St, Derry City.	(0504) 267284	**All year**
Waterside Derry City, Co. Derry.	(0504) 49331	July–Aug
Donaghadee (Town Hall) Donaghadee, Co. Down.	(0247) 882087	**All year**
Downpatrick (Leisure Centre) Market St, Downpatrick Co. Down.	(0396) 613426	**All year**
(Council Offices) 24 Strangford Rd, Downpatrick, Co. Down.	(0396) 614331	**All year**
Dungannon (Council Offices) Circular Rd Dungannon, Co. Tyrone.	(086 87) 25311 (086 87) 22541 Fax	**All year**
Enniskillen Lakeland Visitor Centre Shore Rd, Enniskillen Co. Fermanagh.	(0365) 323110/325050 (0365) 325511 Fax	**All year**
Fivemiletown Library, Main St Fivemiletown, Co. Tyrone.	(036 55) 21409	**All year**
Giant's Causeway Visitor's Centre, Bushmills Co. Antrim.	(026 57) 31855	June–Sept
Hillsborough (Council Offices) The Square, Hillsborough Co. Down.	(0846) 682477 (0846) 689016 Fax	**All year**
Kilkeel Mourne Esplanade Kilkeel, Co. Down.	(069 37) 64666 (069 37) 63495	**All year**
Killymaddy On A4 2m west of Parkanaur Forest Park Co. Tyrone.	(086 87) 67259 (086 87) 22541 Fax	May–Sept

Larne (Harbour)	(0574) 70517	**All year**
Council Offices	(0574) 72313	
Victoria Rd, Larne		
Caravan in car park	(0574) 72313	June–Aug
at Murrayfield Shopping Centre		
Larne, Co. Antrim.		
Limavady (Council Offices)	(050 47) 22226	**All year**
7 Connell St	(050 47) 22010	
Limavady, Co. Derry.		
Lurgan (Library), Carnegie St	(0762) 323912	**All year**
Town Hall, 6 Union St	(0762) 323757	**All year**
Lurgan, Co. Armagh.		
Magherafelt (Council Offices)	(0648) 32151	**All year**
43 Queen's Avenue	(0648) 31240 Fax	
Magherafelt, Co. Derry.		
Bridewell Centre	(0648) 32151	May–Sept
Magherafelt, Co. Derry.	(0648) 31240	
Newcastle	(039 67) 22222	**All year**
Newcastle Centre		
Central Promenade		
Newcastle, Co. Down.		
Newry	(0693) 66232	**All year**
Arts Centre, Bank Parade	(0693) 66177 Fax	
Newry, Co. Down.		
Newtownards (Council Offices)	(0247) 812215	**All year**
2 Church St	(0247) 819628 Fax	
Newtownards		
Co. Down		
Regent St	(0247) 812215	June–Aug
Newtownards	(0247) 819628 Fax	
Co. Down.		
Newtownstewart (Main St)	(066 26) 61560	June–Sept
Newtownstewart, Co. Tyrone.		
Omagh	(0662) 247831/2	**All year**
1 Market St, Omagh	(0662) 243888 Fax	
Co. Tyrone.		

Portadown Library, Edward St Portadown, Co. Armagh.	(0762) 332499	**All year**
Portaferry (Shore St) Co. Down.		June–Aug
Portrush (Town Hall) Portrush, Co. Antrim.	(0265) 52181	April–Sept
Portstewart (Town Hall) Portstewart Co. Derry	(026 583) 2286	July–Aug
Sion Mills (Melmount Rd) Sion Mills, Co. Tyrone.	(066 26) 58027	June–Sept
Strabane (Abercorn Square) Strabane, Co. Tyrone.	(0504) 883735 (0504) 382264 Fax	June–Sept
Warrenpoint (Boating Pool) Warrenpoint, Co. Down.	(069 37) 52256	July–Aug

Accommodation

The range of accommodation available in Ireland covers the following categories:

Hotels—graded A*, A, B*, B and C
Guesthouses—graded A, B*, B and C (the Northern Ireland Tourist Board grades guesthouses A and B only)
Town and Country Houses, Farm Houses
Caravan and Camping Sites
Self-catering Accommodation
Youth Hostels, Holiday Hostels

Tullybawn beach, Co. Mayo

Premises included in these categories are listed in the official guides which are published each year by the tourist boards. The prices listed in the guides are maximum prices and cannot be exceeded without prior consent in writing from the tourist board concerned. All these accommodations must meet minimum standards requirements; the bases for the various gradings of hotels and guesthouses are explained in the forewords to the accommodation guides and are generally related to levels of comfort and service provided by an individual premises and the experience and competence of the management and staff. Guesthouses, town and country houses (the country houses are usually similar to the town houses except for location) and farm houses being smaller are usually family run and while lovely and comfortable would not provide the service or facilities of a hotel.

Self-catering accommodation is for those who wish to come and go as they please and range from apartments to cottages, bungalows, houses and even castles. Rentals are normally from Saturday to Saturday but they are often available for rental at weekends outside the main summer season.

Each tourist board produces a guide listing a range of premises which provide meals for the visitor. These guides in many cases set out the type of food served which can range from haute cuisine to simple bar food and give an indication of the price the visitor can expect to pay. A 'Special Value Tourist Theme Guide' is also published listing restaurants which have undertaken to provide special value meals—three-course meals at a fixed price.

In Northern Ireland, restaurants guaranteeing to use mainly local produce are listed in the Guide with 'A Taste of Ulster' symbol.

Anyone who is dissatisfied with any aspect of the accommodation, service, food or prices charged while on holiday should first complain to the management of the premises concerned. If the visitor is dissatisfied with the response, he should take the matter up with the local tourist information office or in writing direct with the Customer Relations Unit of Bord Fáilte at its Baggot St Bridge office in Dublin 2 or if in Northern Ireland with the Northern Ireland Tourist Board at St Anne's Court, 59 North St, Belfast BT1 1NB.

Transport

Access Transport

Ireland is served by a range of regular and comfortable surface and air services which require advance booking especially in the peak holiday season when many services operate to full or near full capacity. During the Easter and Christmas periods early advance booking is essential. The main sea and air service areas are as follows:

By Sea

Direct from Britain

Services provided by	*Service*
B & I Line	From Holyhead to Dublin Ferryport
	From Pembroke to Rosslare Ferryport
Sealink	From Holyhead to Dun Laoghaire Ferryport
	From Fishguard to Rosslare Ferryport
	From Stranraer to Larne Ferryport
Hovercraft SeaCat	From Stranraer to Larne Ferryport
Norse Irish Ferries	From Liverpool to Belfast
Swansea/Cork Car Ferries	From Swansea to Cork
P & O European Ferries	From Cairnryan to Larne
Isle of Man Ferries	From Douglas to Dublin
	From Douglas to Belfast

Direct from Mainland Europe

Irish Ferries	From Le Havre to Cork
	From Le Havre to Rosslare
	From Cherbourg to Rosslare
Brittany Ferries	From Roscoff to Cork

By Air

To Dublin Airport	From Britain, Europe and N. America
To Shannon Airport	From Britain, Europe and N. America
To Knock Airport	From Britain
To Cork Airport	From Britain and Europe

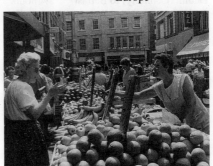

Shopping in Moore Street, Dublin

To Galway Airport	From Britain via Dublin
To Kerry Airport	From Britain via Dublin
To Sligo Airport	From Britain
To Waterford Airport	From Glasgow
To Belfast International Airport	From Britain, Europe
To Belfast City Airport	From Britain
To Derry Airport	From Britain and Dublin

Internal Transport

Rail

Mainline trains run between Dublin and cities and towns throughout Ireland. On the principal inter-city routes express trains operate at average speeds of 60 mph and most of these longer distance trains have catering facilities ranging from bar service and light refreshments to à la carte meals.

Express train times from

Dublin (Heuston) to Cork	2½ hours
Dublin (Heuston) to Galway	3 hours
Dublin (Heuston) to Killarney/Tralee	
	3 hours
Dublin (Heuston) to Limerick 1½–2 hours	
Dublin (Heuston) to Westport	4 hours
Dublin (Heuston) to Waterford	2½ hours
Dublin (Connolly) to Belfast	2¼ hours
Dublin (Connolly) to Wexford/Rosslare	
	2¼/2½ hours
Dublin (Connolly) to Sligo	3½ hours

In Northern Ireland there are three main rail routes out of Belfast Central Station; north to Derry via Ballymena and Coleraine, east to Bangor along the shores of Belfast Lough, and south to Dublin via Lisburn, Portadown and Newry. The journey time to Dublin is just over 2 hours.

Trains from York Rd station connect with the Larne/Scotland ferries. A bus service links both stations.

DART (Dublin Area Rapid Transit), an electric rail service, serves the coastal commuter belt around Dublin from Howth on the northside to Bray on the southside. The Belfast commuter belt is served by Northern Ireland Railways diesel services.

Various types of incentive or conces-sionary fares are available on nearly all rail services.

Express Bus

An express bus service network serves all the cities and most of the towns and villages outside Dublin; in Dublin, Cork, Galway, Limerick and Waterford there are local bus services which connect the city centres with their suburbs. Similarly in Northern Ireland, express buses from Belfast serve all the main towns and villages and there are excellent local bus services serving the cities and towns and their surroundings. In both parts of Ireland, there are half-day, day and extended coach tours available. As with the trains there are many cheaper excursion, day return or other incentive or concessionary fares available on the buses.

Internal Air Service

There are a limited number of internal air services (including helicopter) available and these are mainly during the holiday season. However it is advisable to check the services out in advance as in most cases they are not scheduled.

Taxi Services

Taxi services are available in Dublin, Cork, Galway and Limerick. Prices are controlled and are based on metered mileage with special extra charges for specific factors; a minimum fare applies. Outside these cities, hackney services are available to provide transport on request. In all cases, the visitor is advised to check out the approximate fare in advance with the driver. In Northern Ireland there is also an adequate service; in Belfast, London-type black taxis are available in two distinct systems: at railways stations and city centre ranks, they ply trade just as London-style cabs; at other ranks they run 'mini-bus' services to eastern and western areas of the city.

Island Boat Services

Licensed boat services operate to some of the islands off the coast but it is advisable for visitors to make advance arrangements as these services are often dependent on weather conditions.

Car Hire

There are a number of car hire companies operating throughout the country and in most cases these companies are members of the Car Rental Council of Ireland which operates a Code of Standards to which it expects its members to conform. The visitor is advised to check insurance and other complications in relation to car hire before signing the contract to hire. It is also advisable to check in advance the approximate cost for a specific type car, period of hire, petrol etc. before completing the agreement. Most companies operate a pick-up and set-down arrangement which enables the visitor to hire a car at his point of entry and complete the hire at another departure point; it is advisable to check whether this service is subject to surcharge.

Argus Rent-a-Car Ltd
Argus House, 59 Terenure Rd East,
Dublin 6
Tel. (01) 904444 Fax (01) 906328

Atlas Car Rentals Ltd
Desk 1, Arrivals Hall, Dublin Airport
Tel. (01) 8444859 Fax (01) 8407302

Avis/Johnson & Perrott
Emmet Place, Cork
Tel. (021) 273295
Telex 76077
Fax (021) 272202

Budget Rent-a-Car
Ballygar, Co. Galway
Tel. (0903) 24668/24678/24777
Telex 53914
Fax (0903) 24759

Cahills Car Rentals Ltd
36 Annesley Place, North Strand,
Dublin 3
Tel. (01) 747766
Fax (01) 742160

Capitol Car Hire
Jet Station, Woodquay,
Headford Rd, Galway
Tel. (091) 65296/66778
Fax (091) 61221

Cara Rent-a-Car Ltd
Coonagh Cross, Ennis Rd,
Limerick
Tel. (061) 55811
Fax (061) 55369

Casey Auto Rentals Ltd
Turlough Rd, Castlebar,
Co. Mayo
Tel. (094) 21411
Fax (094) 23823

Dan Dooley/Kenning Rent-a-Car
Knocklong, Co. Limerick
Tel. (062) 53103
Telex 70209
Fax (062) 53392

Deasy Rent-a-Car
Commons Rd, Cork
Tel. (021) 395024/5
Fax (021) 397658

Diplomat Cars Ltd
Knock International Airport,
Charlestown, Co. Mayo
Tel. (094) 67252
Fax (094) 67394

Hamills Rent-a-Car
Dublin Rd, Mullingar, Co. Westmeath
Tel. (044) 48682/40508
Fax (044) 41374

Hertz Rent-a-Car
Head Office, PO Box 23,
Ferrybank, Wexford
Tel. (053) 23511
Telex 80124
Fax (053) 22405

Killarney Autos Ltd
Park Rd, Killarney, Co. Kerry
Tel. (064) 31355
Fax (064) 32053

Motor World Rent-a-Car Ltd
Carrigrohane Rd, Cork
Tel. (021) 542344

Telex 75517
Fax (021) 342696

Murrays Europcar Car Rental
Baggot St Bridge, Dublin 4
Tel. (01) 681777
Telex 93784
Fax (01) 602958

O'Mara's Rent-a-Car Ltd
Galway Rd, Athlone,
Co. Westmeath
Tel. (0902) 92325
Fax (0902) 94310

Payless/Bunratty Car Rentals
Coonagh Cross, Ennis Rd, Limerick
Tel. (061) 52781
Telex 70013
Fax (061) 52516

South County Car Rentals
Rochestown Avenue, Dun Laoghaire,
Co. Dublin
Tel. (01) 2806005
Fax (01) 2857016

South East Budget Rent-a-Car
Shannon Motors, New Ross, Co. Wexford
Tel. (051) 21550
Fax (051) 21235

Thrifty Irish Car Rentals
Maxol Station, Ennis Rd, Limerick
Tel. (061) 53049
Telex 70349
Fax (061) 53433

Tom Mannion Travel
71 O'Connell St, Ennis, Co. Clare
Tel. (065) 24211
Telex 70728
Fax (065) 24166

Treaty Rent-A-Car
37 William St, Limerick
Tel. (061) 416512
Fax (061) 412266

Windsor Car Rentals
South Circular Rd, Rialto, Dublin 8
Tel. (01) 540800
Telex 90901
Fax (01) 540122

Northern Ireland
Belfast
Avis Rent-a-Car
69 Great Victoria St
Tel. (0232) 240404

Bairds Rentals
7 Boucher Rd
Tel. (0232) 247770

Belfast Rent-a-Car
188a Saintfield Rd
Tel. (0232) 401344

CC Economy Car Hire
2 Ballyduff Rd
Carnmoney
Tel. (0232) 840366

Carriageway Cars and Car Hire
21 Holywood Rd
Tel. (0232) 652000

Godfrey Davis Europcar
J. E. Coulter Ltd
58 Antrim Rd
Tel. (0232) 757401/2

Howards Car Hire
6a Bloomfield Avenue
Tel. (0232) 452567

Knockdene Garage
397 Upper Newtownards Rd
Tel. (0232) 654687

Loopland Car Hire
81 Loopland Drive
Tel. (0232) 452024 *and*
150 Castlereagh Rd
Tel. (0232) 453850

McCausland Car Hire
27 Grosvenor Rd
Tel. (0232) 333777

McCay Car Hire
2 Limestone Rd
Tel. (0232) 747377

Moley's Self Drive
38 Great Patrick St
Tel. (0232) 233123

Practical Used Car Rental
6 Agincourt Avenue
Tel. 331922 *and*
Holywood Rd
Tel. (0232) 656866

Sam Holmes Motors
102 Beersbridge Rd
Tel. (0232) 451850

Sydney Pentland
17 Ravenhill Rd
Tel. (0232) 451422

Woodstock Car Hire
192 Woodstock Rd
Tel. (0232) 451441

Belfast International Airport
Avis Rent-a-Car
Tel. (084 94) 22333

Cosmo-Eurodollar
181 Airport Rd
Tel. (084 94) 52565

Dan Dooley Vehicle Rentals
175 Airport Rd
Tel. (084 94) 52522

Europcar Ltd
Terminal Building
Tel. (084 94) 23444

Hertz Rent-a-Car
Terminal Building
Tel. (084 94) 22533

McCausland Car Hire
171 Airport Rd
Tel. (084 94) 22022

Belfast Harbour Airport
Avis Rent-a-Car
Sydenham Bypass
Tel. (0232) 452017

Europcar Ltd
Sydenham Bypass
Tel. (0232) 450904

Hertz Rent-a-Car
Airport Rd, Tel. (0232) 732451

Antrim
Town Parks Car Sales
Ballymena Rd
Tel. (084 94) 62506

Ballygawley
Practical Used Car Rental
9 Richmond Lane
Tel. (066 253) 8932

Ballykelly
B. Mullan Motors
8a Loughermore Rd
Tel. (050 47) 22164

Ballymena
Delta Hire
144 Ballymoney Rd
Tel. (0266) 659136

General Motor Works
197 Ballymoney Rd
Tel. (0266) 652171

Peugeot Talbot Rentals
409 Cushendall Rd, Rathkenny
Tel. (0266) 73591

Ballymoney
Model Car Hire
Model Rd
Tel. (026 56) 63275

Ballynahinch
R. Gibb & Sons
41 Main St
Tel. (0238) 562519

Bangor
Ballyrobert Cars
402 Belfast Rd
Tel. (0247) 852262

McCausland Car Hire
8 Quay St
Tel. (0247) 270622

Practical Used Car Rental
4b Holborn Avenue
Tel. (0247) 271562

Castlederg
Practical Used Car Rental
52 Strabane Rd
Tel. (066 26) 70047

Coleraine
Avis Rent-a-Car
Dunmore St
Tel. (0265) 43654
(Serves Eglinton Airport)

Coleraine Cars
Castle Lane, Waterside
Tel. (0265) 56221

Europcar Ltd
2 Castlerock Rd
Tel. (0265) 44944

Lindsay Cars
80 Bushmills Rd
Tel. (0265) 55921

Practical Used Car Rental
Unit 1, The Marina
Tel. (0265) 52800

Comber
Strickland Bros
2 Newtownards Rd
Tel. (0247) 872512

Cookstown
Bell's Car Hire
52 Church St
Tel. (064 87) 62353

McNicholl Car Hire
47 Chapel St
Tel. (064 87) 63210

R.A. Patrick
21 Orritor Rd
Tel. (064 87) 63601

Donaghadee
APM Car Hire
207 Millisle Rd
Tel. (0247) 883704

Downpatrick
DSC Cars
10 Church St
Tel. (0396) 614322

Dromore
Practical Used Car Rental
2 Hillsborough Rd
Tel. (0846) 693620

Dungannon
Corrigan Vehicle Rentals
1 Park Rd
Tel. (086 87) 24929

Morgan Car Hire
Fork Service Station, 57 Moy Rd
Tel. (086 87) 22499

Enniskillen
Lochside Garage
Tempo Rd
Tel. (0365) 324366

Practical Used Car Rental
Kilmacormick Rd
Tel. (0365) 324712

Larne
Practical Used Car Rental
41 Belfast Rd
Tel. (0574) 78200

Limavady
Practical Used Car Rental
Cannings Complex
Tel. (050 47) 68525

Lisburn
Garvey Car Hire
3 Thornleigh Park
Tel. (0846) 676478

Lindsay Cars
20 Market Place
Tel. (0846) 673121

Lisburn Car Hire
56 Railway St
Tel. (0846) 663617

Practical Used Car Rental
77a Causeway End Rd
Tel. (0846) 676369

Saville Motors
70 Belfast Rd
Tel. (0846) 665270

Derry
Eakin Bros
Maydown
Tel. (0504) 860601

Hertz Rent-a-Car
173 Strand Rd
Tel. (0846) 360420

Lurgan
Practical Used Car Rental
235 Gilford Rd
Tel. (0762) 323650

Roadside Motors
1 Dromore Rd, Dollingstown
Tel. (0762) 321038

Moneymore
Practical Used Car Rental
32 Turnaface Rd
Tel. (064 87) 48811

Roadside Motors
Magherafelt Rd
Tel. (064 87) 48631

Newry
Hollywood Bros
48 Monaghan St
Tel. (0693) 62208

Practical Used Car Rental
Bank Parade
Tel. (0693) 67245

Newtownards
Lyle Motors
Portaferry Rd
Tel. (0247) 813376

MS Motorworld
118 Donaghadee Rd
Tel. (0247) 812626

Omagh
Johnston King Motors
82 Derry Rd
Tel. (0662) 242788

Omahire
62 Gortin Rd
Tel. (0662) 246521

Tattyreagh Car & Van Hire
110 Tattyreagh Rd, Fintona
Tel. (0662) 841731

Portadown
Edwin May
128 Bridge St
Tel. (0762) 332238

Francis Neill Motors
7 Cecil St
Tel. (0762) 338873

Practical Used Car Rental
2 Druminally Rd
Tel. (0762) 338309

Portstewart
Coastal Self Drive
112 Station Rd
Tel. (026 583) 4088

Tintern Abbey, Co. Wexford

Practical Used Car Rental
35a Burnside Rd
Tel. (026 583) 2599

Rostrevor
Practical Used Car Rental
Shore Rd
Tel. (069 37) 38691

Sion Mills
P. G. McGillion (Motors)
132 Melmount Rd
Tel. (066 26) 58275

Motoring

Most visitors to Ireland who wish to tour the country either regionally or otherwise bring their own cars. Ireland is especially attractive to the motorist because of its scenic beauty and the comparative absence of traffic on its roads even on the main trunk routes between the cities and towns. Before going on tour it is advisable to check speed limits, parking regulations, petrol prices and grades, repair and maintenance services. The staff at the tourist information office at the point of entry to the country will be pleased to help with these details.

Whether hiring a car or travelling in his own car, the visitor is advised to take normal precautions in relation to any property which he is bringing with him and to ensure that he is parking his car (especially in the cities) where it is unlikely to be broken into or vandalised.

A number of recommended motoring tours are included on p. 441 of the Guide. These will be helpful to the motorist who wishes to get the 'feel' of the country especially if he has only a limited time to enjoy his visit here.

Entertainment

Theatre and Cinema

Theatre and cinema programmes of high quality are available throughout Ireland. However it is in Dublin and Belfast and other cities that the visitor is assured of a continuity, professionalism and variety of especially theatrical productions, which compare with the best available elsewhere. Dublin is the home of the Abbey Theatre (the National Theatre of Ireland), famous the world over for its association in its early days with W. B. Yeats, J. M. Synge and Sean O'Casey. The Abbey is committed to presenting the works of these and later dramatists and has the special function of presenting the works of new Irish dramatists where these are judged to meet the levels of its standards and tradition. The Gate Theatre is mainly concerned with the production of international classics and for famous comedies by Irish writers such as Goldsmith, Sheridan, Shaw and Wilde. The Gaiety and Olympia Theatres present programmes of drama, concerts, musicals and revue; the Gaiety is also the venue for the Dublin Grand Opera Society's grand opera season. The Project Arts Centre presents drama, poetry readings and recitals at lunchtime and in the evenings, and because of the innovative nature of its productions is very popular with the youth. In Cork the Opera House provides a frequent change of programme during the summer. Irish plays are more usual though there are occasional musical comedy, ballet or opera productions. Galway has the Druid Theatre and Punchbag Companies which have both lunchtime and evening entertainment and also Taibhdhearc na Gaillimhe which offers evenings of Irish traditional music, song and dance in a theatrical setting. Cultur, Galway's Folk Theatre, has performances

of traditional music, dance, song and drama during the tourist season.

Limerick's Belltable Arts Centre presents a special programme for visitors during July and August; supper and theatre commencing at 6.30 p.m. or theatre and dinner afterwards at 10.45 p.m. are available. In Sligo, the Hawkswell Theatre produces a continual programme of drama and concerts throughout the year. Waterford Theatre Royal provides similar entertainment and hosts a Light Opera Festival at the end of September/beginning of October. Wexford is internationally famous for its Opera Festival held each year in October. It represents a triumphal blending of top operatic talent with local resources and commitment. The Siamsa Tire in Tralee is a folk theatre entertainment based on the music, folklore and dance of an age when Irish was the spoken language. It recaptures on stage with the music of pipes, flute and fife, the spirit of the rural life of the period in lively and colourful productions.

In Belfast the Grand Opera House puts on a wide variety of shows from opera to pantomime throughout the year. The Arts Theatre stages popular productions including musicals, while the Lyric Theatre is known for its productions of Irish and international drama and for promoting the work of new playwrights.

The Old Museum Arts Centre features experimental work, the Crescent Arts Centre mainly youth theatre and dance, and the Golden Thread Theatre a mix of community and *avant-garde* work. Outside Belfast, the Audhaven Theatre in Enniskillen and the Riverside Theatre in

Roundstone, Co. Galway

Coleraine have continuous programmes throughout the year.

Cinema programmes are available throughout the country and especially in the cities. It is possible for the visitor to catch up with the latest releases within a short period of their release on the international market.

Cabaret

Irish cabaret is a popular entertainment for visitors which in Dublin's main venues can be enjoyed over drinks and/or dinner. Top-class performers provide a range of entertainment with an Irish flavour which the visitor can enjoy in an amusing and friendly atmosphere. The medieval banquets which are put on by Shannon Free Airport Development Company in Bunratty, Knappogue and Dunguaire Castles are known worldwide. Visitors are greeted on arrival, wined, dined and entertained in the lavish style of a nobleman of the fifteenth century whose standing was judged not only on his possessions or conquests but on the level of his hospitality to friends and strangers alike. 'A Taste of Irish' is a cabaret staged in a

number of hotels in the Shannon region during the season which is very popular. In other parts of the country cabaret is available in selected hotels or bars and details can be obtained at the local tourist offices.

Pubs

Pub entertainment has become widespread and popular in the last decade or two and no matter to what part of the country the visitor travels he is likely to be able to experience music, singing and dancing of a mainly Irish character in happy and convivial surroundings. The pub is an integral part of the Irish social scene where the visitor is as welcome as the regular customer. Nowadays most pubs serve tea, coffee and sandwiches and an increasing number provide good and economical lunches which many visitors find more suitable to their needs especially if they are touring and staying in bed and breakfast accommodation.

Traditional Entertainment

Apart from the traditional type entertainment which is theatre based as in the

Siamsa Tire at Tralee or Cultur in Galway mentioned above and the traditional music to be heard in a pub atmosphere, Irish traditional music, song and dance is performed at many other venues throughout the country. The 'ceili', an evening of Irish music and dancing, has become more popular with the greater level of interest in Irish music. Comhaltas Ceoltoiri Éireann is the central organisation for the promotion of traditional music, song and dance and it organises national and local events where performers of all ages can compete before an appreciative audience of visitors and residents alike. The All-Ireland Fleadh held in the last weekend of August is the most important event in the traditional music calendar. It is a three-day music and song festival which takes place in a different town each year where there are music and singing competitions for all grades and ages. Teach Ceoil ('Houses of Music') are to be found around Ireland and in those houses in an oldtime Irish kitchen atmosphere, traditional music can be enjoyed at its best.

Food & Drink/Shopping

Ireland is a leisurely land where there is still time for everything—including the time to enjoy one's food. In terms of calories consumed per head, it is one of the best-fed countries in the world. To experience the unique flavour and texture of Irish food is one of the major pleasures of a visit to Ireland. Here there is an abundance of fresh food, such as meat, fish, butter, eggs, bread and vegetables. With basic ingredients of the highest quality, no appetizing sauces or elaborate presentation are necessary to tempt the palate. Simplicity is the keynote of native Irish cooking, though international haute cuisine is naturally to be found in leading hotels and restaurants.

Ireland's lush pastures are rich and extensive, making it possible to raise animals to full maturity, thereby producing some of the finest quality meat in Europe. Here you will be well advised to choose a juicy fillet or sirloin steak in preference to an escalope of veal.

Of equally high quality are Irish mutton and lamb—delicate in flavour, lean and firm in texture. Limerick and Ballymoney hams have an international reputation, and Irish pork is so good that an unpretentious dish of roast pork and apple sauce will delight the most exacting palate. And there are few simple meals to beat Irish stew, bacon and cabbage, or fresh eggs accompanied by home-baked wholemeal bread.

Where seafood is concerned, Ireland occupies a particularly high place. An outstanding speciality is smoked salmon. The fresh, wild salmon, poached or grilled, is second to none; so also are the sea and brown trout. Galway Bay and Strangford Lough oysters are small, succulent and delicately flavoured, usually taken with home-made wheaten bread and a bottle of stout. Irish lobsters are also hard to equal, and Dublin Bay prawns are internationally famous.

To sample food representative of the country, some of the dishes to look for are: smoked salmon, oysters, prawns, grilled sole on the bone, lobster *au naturel*, spring chicken and Limerick ham, fillet steak cooked on an open grill, lamb cutlets, grilled or poached salmon, trout—and last but not least, game when in season.

When it comes to drink, there is much on offer that is distinctively Irish. Most famous of all the wide range of Irish ales, beers and lagers is, of course, the dark stout that is exported all over the world. Ireland also produces excellent whiskey, gin and vodka. Whiskey has been drunk here for more than five centuries, the word itself being derived from the Irish *uisce beatha* ('water of life'). Irish whiskey is generally a pure pot-still product, made from malted and unmalted barley with a small proportion of other native cereals—wheat, oats, and occasionally a pinch of rye. To bring the flavour and bouquet to full richness, the whiskey is matured in wooden casks for at least seven years.

Whiskey is drunk neat or with a little water. Its international reputation has been increased in recent years by the popularity of Irish Coffee, which is made with a small measure of whiskey, one or two teaspoons of sugar, and black coffee—the mixture being topped with a thick layer of cream. There is also an Irish whiskey liqueur, Irish Mist. Irish cream liqueurs have become enormously popular in recent years.

Dining Out

There are eating places in Ireland to suit all palates from the most sophisticated to the simplest. Visitors, especially those who would prefer to eat inexpensively, should know at the outset that more than 360 restaurants throughout the country have a special 'tourist menu' which offers wholesome food at a reasonable price. Those who are not confined to a strict budget will have an opportunity to sample Irish and international cuisine in a wide variety of restaurants. They may even indulge themselves in a medieval banquet if they so wish, sampling food and drink as it was served in the castles of fifteenth-century Ireland.

Shopping in Ireland

Ireland has many exciting and distinctive products to offer the visitor ranging from the highly sophisticated and contemporary to the traditional. The Crafts Council of Ireland and its equivalent in Northern Ireland has a wide range of promotional activities which helps increase awareness of the range and quality of Irish craftworks.

The Irish Craft, Gift and Fashion Fair
This major trade fair takes place in Dublin in January each year and is the international shop window for the Irish craft industry.

The Crafts Council HQ Gallery at the Powerscourt Centre in Dublin provides a national showplace for craftwork of excellence. The Gallery Shop offers an extensive range of quality goods.

The Crescent Gallery in Kilkenny provides a retail outlet and shows work by the young craftworkers at the Council's Crescent Workshops.

Craftworks in Belfast provides a further outlet for craft workers and designers.

What to buy in Ireland

Irish handwoven tweed, a traditional craft, has been acclaimed world wide for its quality, individuality, versatility and colour blends. It makes up into a wide range of clothing as well as soft furnishings.

Linen weaving is one of Ireland's earliest crafts and Irish linen and damasks are world renowned. However, the industry has expanded as linen has become high fashion and clothing has now been added to the more traditional bed and table linenware.

Lace as well as hand-painted silk items are also widely available.

Knitwear has undergone a revolution in Ireland in recent years and has fast become one of our flagship small industries. The intricate stitchwork of the traditional Aran sweater has been incorporated into a wide variety of stylish designs and patterns. The patterns of the original bainin sweater (so called because of the undyed wool from the Aran Islands which was used to knit them) were unwritten and handed down from family to family, emerging today as one of our most fashionable and versatile items of clothing.

Glass factories existed in many parts of Ireland until the early nineteenth century when heavy duties were imposed and the industry was crushed. The present industry is a restoration of the old craft and there are now glass-cutting industries producing fine crystal and cut-glass in Waterford, Cork, Cavan, Galway, Kilkenny, Tipperary, Tyrone, Sligo and Dublin. Handblown glass is being produced at Jerpoint in Kilkenny as well as in Kerry, Dublin and Tipperary.

Pottery The ceramic industry is flourishing in Ireland with factories as well as

Dalkey, Co. Dublin

studio potteries all over the country producing a whole variety of designs in ovenware, tableware and other decorative items. Belleek Pottery was started in County Fermanagh as early as 1857 and their china is world famous. Irish porcelain is being made increasingly and is now manufactured in Cork, Clare, Galway, Leitrim, as well as in Kilkenny.

Silver The working of precious metals in Ireland started about the year 2000 B.C. The tradition of Celtic ornamentation has inspired the jewellery and silverwork of present-day craft workers and today this tradition is continued in the Kilkenny silver workshop where a variety of pieces including jewellery is handwrought.

There is much else of interest for the discerning visitor to buy in Ireland from food products like hand-made chocolates, smoked salmon and preserves to ready-to-

wear clothing. All share a common hallmark, however, and that is quality.

VAT Shopping Rebate for Visitors

Certain retail outlets (mainly large department stores) in Ireland have a scheme whereby visitors to the country may claim relief from VAT (Value Added Tax) on purchases made while visiting the country. Rebate is subject to certain conditions.

Visitors from the EC (including Northern Ireland) will be allowed relief on the purchase of individual items to the value of IR£460 or more (including VAT). This limitation does not apply to non-EC residents.

Refunds may be claimed at points of departure from the country or after returning home, but anyone hoping to avail of the scheme should enquire about it when making their purchase.

Sport and Recreation

Ireland is renowned as a land of sport and it has much to offer the visitor either as a spectator or participant. Perhaps the most important feature of the country's sporting life is the number and variety of activities associated with the horse which has a special place in Irish life going back to antiquity. It is said that Ireland's temperate climate which in turn provides grassland of a special quality creates the circumstances where horses can be bred, nurtured and developed into top performers in international competition.

Horses

Horse-racing is a favourite sport in Ireland and there are over 233 days of racing in the year spread over the 27 racing tracks all over the country including two in Northern Ireland. For the enthusiast, there is ample opportunity to watch great horses and top-class riders in action. At the Curragh, Co. Kildare, where all the Irish flatrace classics are held, the visitor can rub shoulders with the great names in racing from all over the world and if he's lucky, perhaps recover some of the cost of his holiday, while enjoying himself among the racing crowd who will make him welcome and let him in on any 'inside information' to help him pick a winner. During the April to August period evening meetings are held at a number of venues and an interesting feature in recent years has been the introduction of Sunday racing. National Hunt or racing over jumps is especially enjoyed by Irish racing crowds (the first steeplechase is reputed to have been run in south Co. Cork in 1752); the meetings at Punchestown (Co. Kildare) and Fairyhouse (Co. Meath)

Connemara Pony Show, Clifden, Co. Galway

are the highlights of the jumping season and attract large enthusiastic crowds.

Hunting The hunting season in Ireland begins in October and ends in March. Visitors are welcome but it is necessary to make advance arrangements for participation. These can be made through a riding stable, the hunt secretary or the master of the hunt.

Trail riding is the most popular form of Irish equestrian holidays. The variety is in line with the different types of terrain in which the trail rides are located but these generally tend to be located in the most scenic parts of the country. Usually the trail rides are designed for riders who wish to stay at one accommodation but daily transfers to different starting and finishing points ensure that a new route is covered each day.

Riding centres There are many centres offering horse-riding holidays in a range of accommodation from farmhouse to manor style country house. Some specialise in hunting; others offer tuition and cross-country riding through scenic areas.

Showjumping Ireland is noted for its showjumpers and some of the most noted horses on the international scene, if not actually owned and trained in Ireland, were bred in Ireland. The Dublin Horse Show is the highlight of the year and horses and riders from all over the world compete.

Horse-drawn caravans A holiday in a horse-drawn caravan provides both transport and accommodation for a holiday in a slow, relaxed manner which offers the best opportunity to enjoy seeing the country and meeting its people. The holiday provides clean accommodation and adequate cooking facilities. The horse has been chosen for its suitability and the visitor will be instructed on harnessing and horse care and on selected routes and overnight stops.

Fishing

I reland is noted for the quality and variety of its fishing and enthusiasts have been coming here for a long time to enjoy their sport in its teeming waters.

In many countries owing to industrialisation and consequent pollution, rivers, lakes and the sea no longer hold the numbers of fish that were once available but Ireland's lack of industry has ensured that its waters still carry enough fish to provide good and exciting sport for both the dedicated angling holidaymaker and the amateur who may just want to while away a few hours during a touring or based holiday.

Salmon and Sea Trout Angling on rivers and lakes is possible from as early as New Year's Day but angling opens on most rivers and lakes between February and

Brackley Lake, Co. Cavan

April. A State, or in Northern Ireland, a Fishing Conservancy Board or Foyle Fisheries Commission licence covering salmon and sea trout is required plus a permit from the Department of Agriculture or owner of the water. It can be obtained from most tackle shops and from the regional fisheries boards. In the west of Ireland, the Connemara and Mayo fisheries are the most well known and for generations have attracted the expert game angler to pit his expertise against the elusive salmon and sea trout in the area.

Brown Trout River and Lake Angling centres are much more widely distributed through the country and it is much more a late spring and summer month activity. No State licence is required in the South but reasonably priced permits are required on club-controlled brown trout waters or those controlled, stocked and managed by the fishery boards. Many Irish rivers and lakes do not require any permit but in Northern Ireland the FCB or FFC licence and a permit from the Department of Agriculture or the owner of the water or a club is required.

Coarse Fishing or angling for pike, bream, rudd, tench, roach and perch is available all over the country and except in Northern Ireland does not require a licence or a permit. Ireland is famous for the size and the fighting qualities of its pike and it is a favourite catch for the Continental fisherman. The dace is only present in the Blackwater but provides great sport for those fishing with light tackle. Lough Melvin on the border between Counties Fermanagh and Donegal has brown trout, the separate trout species of ferox, gillaroo and sonaghan, and an Ice Age predecessor of the trout called the char.

Sea Fishing Ireland is the outstanding sea angling holiday centre of Europe and has successfully hosted most of Europe's top sea angling competitions. All around the coast there are well-developed sea angling centres which have all the facilities required by even the most dedicated competition angler or the ordinary holidaymaker who just wants to fish or to help his children to do so. In Ireland sea fishing can be divided into 3 categories: (1) shore angling which the complete beginner can enjoy from rocks, beaches or piers; (2) inshore angling which is carried out from small boats within bays and inlets; (3) deep sea angling which calls for small motor vessels and heavy tackle to cope with the bigger fish that one is likely to encounter.

For all types of fishing there are numerous competitions held through the year at which it is possible for even the newcomer to win a good quality prize. For salmon, sea trout and brown trout fishing there are angling schools and seminars during the season at which the techniques of trout fly casting and fishing are explained.

Golf

Ireland has nearly 200 uncrowded golf courses about half of which are 18-hole. These courses are spread throughout the country; every town and village with a population of more than 1,000 is likely to have its own course. Visitors are always welcome though in the courses near the cities, it is best to try to get a game outside the weekend when members are more free to play and the tees can become rather crowded.

Whether the visitor is an accomplished golfer or only playing the game for relaxation and enjoyment he will find most of the golf courses not only testing in golfing terms but he will be able to play in spectacularly scenic surroundings. He will be welcome not only to play golf but also in the clubhouse, the dining-room, bars and lounges where he can meet the members and fellow guests socially and convivially. Green fees in Ireland are generally very reasonable, ranging from IR£15–IR£30. Golf is playable all year round though it is best in the April to September period.

Most clubs rent clubs and other equipment to the visitor who would like a game and who may not have brought his own golfing bag. The committed golfer can on a circuit of Ireland visit those championship links courses which have been praised for their quality by some of the leading players in the game—courses such as Portmarnock, Royal Co. Down, Royal Portrush, Rosses Point, Lahinch, Ballybunion, Killarney and Royal Dublin.

In recent years there has been an expansion of smaller 9-hole and par 3 golf courses which have opened up the game to large numbers of new players. Green fees at these courses are even more reasonable than those for a full 18-hole course and they may be very attractive to the visitor who is not a golfer and who may want to try something new when on holiday. These short courses are often more suitable for children or the elderly.

Walking and Cycling

There has been a great increase in the number of visitors to Ireland who want to get away from it all and to view the country from an aspect that is not possible for the more mobile tourist to obtain. To cater for this demand, many areas of the country have been opened by the provision of waymarked trails through the loveliest areas in Ireland. It is hoped eventually to create a walking route all round the country; to date 12 trails totalling 200 km have been completed and another 9 are in the making or planned. The trails are clearly waymarked at all junctions and are provided with stiles and footbridges as necessary. They give the visitor the chance to sample every aspect of the Irish countryside; walks along canal towpaths, tracks through woods, rambles over uplands and hills which provide glorious views of the countryside. This type of holiday is most suitable for youthful visitors who will have the strength and stamina for a long trek. However many of these walks can be taken in stages and in this way can appeal to young and old alike.

Some of the more scenic walks are: the Wicklow Way from Marley Park, Co. Dublin, to Clonegal, Co. Carlow (132 km); the Kerry Way, a circuit of 200 km round the Ring of Kerry; the Slieve Bloom Way, a circular walking trail of 50 km; the Ulster Way in Northern Ireland which is one of Europe's great long-distance footpaths. The Mourne Wall walk used to bring walkers from far afield every June to walk the length of the 35 km wall surrounding the Silent valley in the Mourne Mountains in Co. Down until the walk was suspended due to the erosion caused by the large numbers of walkers, a hazard that is unlikely to be repeated on the walking routes referred to above whose attraction is the peace and quiet and the small numbers of people that are likely to be encountered on the route.

Cycling is another way of seeing Ireland which has been popular since the country opened up to tourists. Cyclists may travel as individuals, as couples or in small and large groups and special holidays are being sold to cater for the demand. Ireland is traffic free compared with Britain or the Continent and for this reason is attractive to cyclists who also enjoy the scenic beauties of the countryside and the friendliness of the people they meet. The road surfaces, particularly in the main tourist areas, are good and there are adequate facilities for spares and repairs in even the most remote areas. Some visitors who come here on holiday by sea or air and who are taking a based holiday may wish occasionally to do some cycling. Cycle rental facilities are fairly general and prices are reasonable. The tourist information offices will provide a list of recommended cycling tours which can embrace the whole country if that is what the cycling visitor requires.

Hurling and Football

The visitor to Ireland is hardly likely to return home without having had some contact with the activities promoted and fostered by the Gaelic Athletic Association which was founded in 1884. All round Ireland, the visitor is likely to come across crowds of people either going to or coming from a hurling or gaelic football game in which the crowds' village, town, county or province is engaged. The games which are amateur and highly organised are played

Hurling, probably the fastest field sport in the world

by all ages from school child to adult. While gaelic football is played country-wide, hurling, which is the more traditional and whose roots go back to pre-Christian times, is played in a smaller number of counties. Efforts to extend hurling to a wider playing fraternity have to date not been successful; it seems that the traditional feel for the 'caman', the stick with which the game is played, is difficult to pass on. While gaelic football is a game which combines aspects of soccer and rugby and is very like Australian football, which may or may not have derived from it, hurling is distinctively Irish. It is a spectacular game calling for speed, skill, fitness and commitment, and the Munster and Leinster Finals and the All-Ireland Semi-finals and Final are when the game is seen at its best. These games are played throughout the summer and the visitor who takes in a hurling game during the holiday is assured of an experience he will not easily forget.

Archaeology and Architecture

The Irish countryside is liberally supplied with traces of the people who have inhabited it over the past 9,000 years. In some instances the 'trace' may consist of a lost or discarded flint or bronze implement or a scatter of broken pottery, sometimes constituting the first perceived evidence of the existence of a dwelling-site or a grave. Some sites are instantly recognisable as ancient monuments: a cluster of stone buildings, including a Round Tower, grouped around a High Cross, immediately suggests the remains of an Early Christian monastery. Others, however, are not so easily recognised or interpreted: a collection of large stones in the corner of a field is not always immediately to be identified as the remains of a megalithic tomb of prehistoric times. Some sites have no surface indications at all, or at best only a few humps or bumps, whose significance may be revealed only by ploughing or other disturbance. It is not necessarily the age of the site or monument that dictates its state of preservation; the materials of which it was originally made are much more influential: structures of organic materials such as wood decay quite rapidly, often leaving little or no trace; structures of earth can be eroded—literally washed away—in the course of time; structures of stone can, of course, be thrown down—literally delapidated—but the stones themselves endure, unless deliberately removed from the site. Much of the time the monuments we see in the countryside, like many of the artefacts we see in museums, are incomplete—the more vulnerable elements have disappeared: the stone axe lacks its wooden haft, the earthen rampart its timber palisade, the stone castle its wooden floors, the Georgian house its roof. Throughout Irish history and prehistory structural materials have dictated the preservation of sites, monuments and artefacts, though later human interference in the form of ploughing, quarrying or other forms of 'development', as well as simple neglect or acts of war, has often accelerated the pace of destruction.

Mesolithic

(Middle Stone Age)

The earliest settlers to arrive in Ireland came about 7000 B.C. They pursued a life-style dependent on hunting, fishing and food-gathering. The most durable material they used was flint, from which they fabricated tools and implements. Until about twenty-five years ago it was only from the mute testimony of their flint tools that their existence was inferred; it seemed that they inhabited only the north-east of the country, where their tools and implements appeared mainly in the raised beaches of the Early Post-Glacial Period. Because their dwellings were flimsy huts of wood no traces were visible on the surface and it was only as a result of carefully planned research programmes that an important Mesolithic campsite was discovered at Mount Sandel, Co. Derry (1), overlooking the estuary of the River Bann. Since then other sites of this period have been discovered throughout the country, notably at Lough Boora in Co. Offaly (2), demonstrating that our earliest inhabitants were not restricted to the north-east, but were present throughout the country, mainly along the river valleys.

Neolithic
(Late Stone Age)

With the arrival of the first farmers, about 4000 B.C., monuments were erected which have, to a greater or lesser extent, endured. These are megalithic (i.e. built of large stones) tombs of several different types—quite probably intended to survive as monuments to those buried within them.

Creevykeel Court Cairn, Co. Sligo

Considered generally to be the earliest are the so called Court Tombs, consisting of a series of rectangular burial chambers opening off a ritual 'court', often a complete oval but frequently reduced to an open semicircle, set in a long cairn of stone, such as examples at Creevykeel, Co. Sligo (3), or Ballyglass, Co. Mayo (4), where indeed the foundations of one of the few timber-built Neolithic houses so far found in Ireland was discovered under such a tomb. Some of the tombs show architectural pretensions, such as the tomb at Shalwy, Co. Donegal (5), which boasts a double lintel reminiscent of a Greek pediment. The greatest incidence of these tombs is in the northern half of the island, with concentrations in Donegal, Sligo and Mayo (where, indeed, extensive walled field systems of the period have been observed under the covering of bog). Probably derived from the Court Tombs are the Portal Tombs (sometimes described as Dolmens), consisting of large erect stones supporting an often enormous capstone which, usually denuded of the long cairns of stone with which they were originally enveloped, stand dramatically on skylines throughout the country. The most spectacular of these Neolithic burial

Newgrange, the most spectacular Neolithic passage tomb in Europe

monuments, however, are the Passage Tombs—so called because in the classic examples a long passage, lined with great slabs, often elaborately decorated, and ending in a cruciform chamber, penetrates

Maeve's Cairn, on Knocknarea, Co. Sligo

an enormous circular mound or cairn (in the largest examples as much as 100 m in diameter). They are frequently found in groups as at Carrowmore, Co. Sligo (6), or Loughcrew, Co. Meath (7). The best-known and most spectacular examples are both in Co. Meath, at Newgrange (8) and Knowth (9). The most spectacularly sited example is Maeve's Carn, on Knocknarea,

Co. Sligo (10)—a massive landmark dominating much of the surrounding countryside. Some of the Stone Circles found throughout the country, possibly including the large example at Grange, Co. Limerick (11), probably date from this period, as may some of the solitary Standing Stones. Several Axe-Factories for the production of the raw-material for stone axes existed, with one near Portrane, Co. Dublin (12); the most spectacular, however, is at Tievebulliagh, Co. Antrim (13), where a hard stone known as *porcellanite* was extracted and traded over much of the British Isles.

Newgrange (top and above) showing the entrance stone with its spiral patterns and the interior of the tumulus

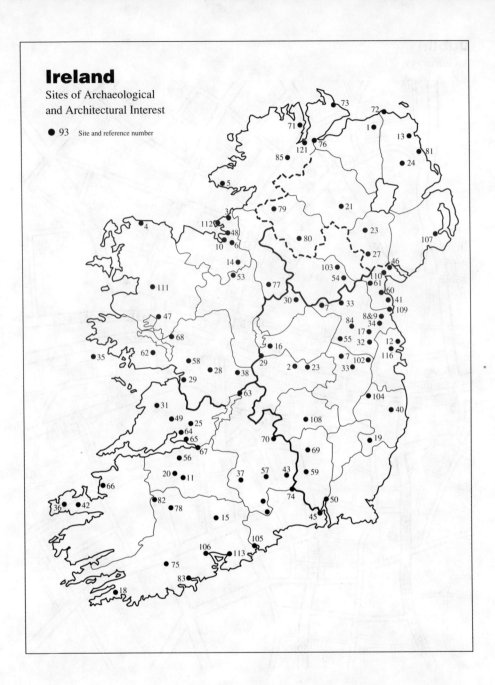

Ireland
Sites of Archaeological
and Architectural Interest

● 93   Site and reference number

73
72
71
1
13
76
121
81
85
24
5
79
21
3
112
4
23
107
48
80
6
27
46
10
103
110
14
54
61
53
60
77
41
111
30
33
109
7
84
8&9
47
34
68
17
12
62
55
32
116
35
58
16
29
7
104
28
2   23   102
40
38   63
33
31
108
49
70
19
25
64
69
65
56   67
43
59
20   11
37   57
74
50
66
82
45
36   42   78
15
105
106   113
75
83
18

47

Dublin
Archaeology

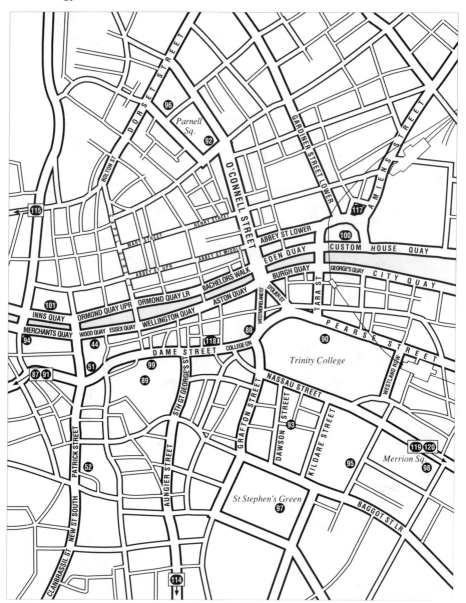

Earlier Bronze Age

Around 2000 B.C. an important new concept was introduced to Ireland, probably by new settlers known as the Beaker People, whose characteristic pottery, Beakers, is known from all over Europe. They are credited with being itinerant metallurgists and it was the concept of making tools and weapons from copper that they introduced, with the necessary skills of finding and processing the needed raw materials. The type of megalithic tomb with which their pottery is most frequently associated in Ireland is the so called Wedge Tomb, consisting of a slightly tapering chamber with an ante-chamber, or porch, at the entrance, set in an elongated D-shaped cairn. These tombs occur all over the island, though most densely in the west; a tomb at Moytirra, Co. Sligo (14), was one of the first to yield Beaker pottery, while a particularly well-preserved example is at Labbacallee, Co. Cork (15). The practice of burial in collective, megalithic tombs was replaced by a preference for burial in single graves—usually a stone-lined hole in the ground, known as a *cist*, often detected by a ploughshare's catching on the covering stone; often these graves were assembled in a cemetery and covered with a round cairn of stone, as at Knockast, Co. West-meath (16), where around forty burials were covered by the same low mound. Often an existing mound was reused, as at Tara, Co. Meath (17), where an earlier Passage Tomb had some forty burials inserted in it. Sometimes no mound or cairn was used and the burials, often without even the stone lining of the burial pit, grouped to form a flat cemetery. Such cemeteries, understandably, are exceedingly difficult to detect except by luck or accident. Many of the Stone Circles, particularly common in Cork and Kerry, where they are sometimes accompanied by burials, are likely to date from this period, as are many of the solitary Standing Stones, which at this time seem sometimes to have been used as simple grave-markers. Perhaps the most appropriate monuments of this period are the copper mines, located predominantly in the south-west: at Mount Gabriel (18), in the Mizen Peninsula of Co. Cork, extensive copper workings, with shafts up to 9 m long, have been dated to between 1700 and 1500 B.C.

Later Bronze Age

About 1200 B.C. great and radical changes took place in the industrial and social structures of Ireland: the most striking was in the great variety of novel types of tools and weapons produced by a bronze industry that appears to have undergone basic reorganisation, with, perhaps a change to mass-production of implements at fixed workshop sites. Such workshops have been found, for example, at Rathgall, Co. Wicklow (19), on a hilltop site where traces of a large wooden structure were also found at Knockadoon, Co. Limerick (20), associated with a rectangular building with stone footings, and at Lough Eskragh, Co. Tyrone (21), in association with a timber-piled lakeside settlement. Such lakeside, timber-piled settlements seem one of the features of this later part of the Bronze Age, as at Ballinderry, Co. Offaly (22), while hilltop locations are preferred not only at Rathgall (where one of the very few Later Bronze Age burials yet identi-fied was also found), but at Navan, Co. Armagh (23), where extensive traces of successive wooden buildings were uncover-ed. It is possible that the preference for hilltop or lakeside locations was dictated by the desire for protection, which would accord with the increased manufacture of defensive and offensive equipment such as swords, spears and shields.

Earlier Iron Age

Traditionally this is regarded as the period when 'Celtic' culture arrived in Ireland, and certainly from about 200 B.C. objects, usually of bronze, though sometimes associated with the remains of iron weapons, decorated in La Tène style (an art style combining elements and motifs from various European cultures—Greek, Etruscan, Roman—and turning them into a specifically 'Celtic' style) appear in Ireland, represented by the famous site at Lisnacrogher, Co. Antrim (24). At this time too there begin to appear true Hill Forts, such as the enormous and impressive Mooghaun, Co. Clare (25), where some 12.5 ha of hilltop are defended by three massive concentric walls of limestone rubble. As well as such spectacularly defended sites, 'Royal' sites, probably dedicated more to ritual than to defence, appear such as Navan, Co. Armagh (23) (the centre, indeed, of the Ulster Cycle of tales and regarded as the 'capital' of the Ulaid, or Ulstermen), Dun Ailinne, Co. Kildare (26), and even Tara, Co. Meath (17). Coinciding precisely with the date of timbers felled for the construction of the ritual site at Navan (94 B.C.) are timbers used in the construction of the enormous, albeit rather enigmatic, enclosure known

Turoe Stone, Co. Galway

as the Dorsey in Co. Armagh (27) (some 120 ha in extent). Examples of La Tène art on field monuments are to be found on several superbly ornamented pillar-stones such as that at Turoe, Co. Galway (28). Burials of the period are sometimes to be found enclosed in small ring-barrows such at that at Grannagh, Co. Galway (29), accompanied by characteristic bronze brooches and glass beads. Some of the wooden trackways found in the bogs, such as that at Corlea, Co. Longford (30), date from this period.

Later Iron Age

(Early Christian/Early Medieval Period)

Towards A.D. 400 the Roman Empire, as a result of internal dissension and attacks from without, came under stress, culminating in the withdrawal of Roman legions from Britain in A.D. 406. Meanwhile a new social and political order emerged in Ireland. Oddly enough contacts with the mainland of Europe improved, and many of the tools, weapons and even ornaments produced in Ireland show clear derivation from Roman originals. The dominant domestic sites, for the most part defended farmsteads, were the Ring Forts, usually consisting of a circular area about 30 m across, defined by an earthen rampart with an external ditch, known generally in the east and north by the Irish terms *Rath* and *Lios*; in the west and south-west, where the defences were normally of stone, the terms used were more usually *Caher* and *Cashel*. These sites, quite frequently with as many as three surrounding ramparts, are the most common monuments to be encountered in the Irish countryside, some 40,000 existing or recorded. Surviving examples, of course, are bereft of the wooden buildings (of several different types) with which the enclosed space was equipped, though among the stone examples, as at Caher-commaun, Co. Clare (31), clear evidence survives of stone buildings. Often associated with such Ring Forts are stone-lined underground passages known as Souterrains. Crannogs—artificial islands at the edges of, sometimes in the middle of, lakes—were common; some examples have produced very rich finds, such as Lagore (32) and Moynagh Lough (33), both in Co. Meath.

The most dramatic innovation of this period, however, was the introduction of Christianity, which, while it made little difference to, for example, the kinds of pottery used, or not used, by the ordinary people, it did have a great effect on the Irish landscape and the kinds of monuments that have survived in and on it. Although St Patrick was not the first Christian missionary to arrive in Ireland, from his arrival in A.D. 431 the Church in Ireland really became established; he himself is credited with the founding of some sixty churches, in the care of bishops, throughout the country. These earliest churches were of wood, so that examples do not survive above ground. The erection of stone churches was obviously such a novelty that a foundation by St Ciana, who died in A.D. 489 is still known as *Daimh Liag* (house of stones), or Duleek, Co. Louth (34), where indeed a stone church known as St Ciana's Church survives, in which the saint is reputed to be buried. The earliest stone churches were built of unmortared stone, which necessitated the use of a corbelled roof (of courses of slabs, each course projecting a little more inwards than the last, until they meet in the middle and provide mutual support); often the side walls project beyond the gables, forming a feature known as *antae* which is probably a relic of their timber predecessors. Such churches, usually consisting of a single compartment not divided into nave and chancel, can be seen at, for example, St MacDara's Island, Co. Galway (35); an example of an even more primitive style of corbelled building in unmortared stone is the Oratory of Gallarus in Co. Kerry (36). Most surviving examples of early churches are remarkably

Gallarus Oratory, Co. Kerry

small, and there seems to have been a tradition of building a number of small churches rather than one large one, except, possibly at some of the more important sites: the use of such placenames as 'Kilmore' or 'Donaghmore'—each meaning 'large church'—would suggest that large church buildings were a novelty. Until about 1130 Irish churches were relatively unadorned; with the building of Cormac's Chapel at Cashel, Co. Tipperary (37)—the first closely dated example of Romanesque architecture in Ireland—and the introduction of round-headed arches and vaulting, elaborate decoration of churches made its appearance, with distinguished examples of doorways at places like Clonfert Cathedral, Co. Galway (38). Other buildings frequently associated with ecclesiastical sites are the typically Irish Round Towers, a frequent feature of both large (as at Clonmacnois, Co. Offaly (39), or Glendalough, Co. Wicklow (40)), and small (as at Monasterboice, Co. Louth (41)), monastic sites, often enclosed inside quite massive ramparts; as their name in Irish *cloigtheach* ('bell-house') would suggest, these were probably primarily bell-towers, but in view of the position of their entrances, usually well above ground level, were used as strongrooms and refuges as well. Other specifically Christian monuments include a succession of crosses, beginning, probably, with examples simply inscribed on a convenient stone or pillar, sometimes with an ogham inscription such as one at Arraglen, Co. Kerry (42), through

Rock of Cashel, Co. Tipperary

a whole series of grave-slabs exemplified by the splendid collection at Clonmacnois, Co. Offaly (39), and culminating in the range of High Crosses, many with sculpted biblical scenes, with superb examples at Ahenny, Co. Tipperary (43), Clonmacnois, Co. Offaly (39), and Monasterboice, Co. Louth (41). While the Vikings, whose raids on Ireland began at least by A.D. 795, influenced the art styles even of the High Crosses, and are credited with the foundation of non-ecclesiastical towns in Ireland, no specifically Viking monuments exist above ground level, though at places like Dublin (44*) and Waterford (45) large areas of Viking settlements have been revealed by excavation.

Anglo-Norman (Medieval) Period

Although the Franks, as contemporary Irish sources rightly describe them, or Anglo-Normans, as they are commonly dubbed today, did

not arrive in force in Ireland until 1170, the introduction some thirty years earlier of Continental religious orders such as the

High Cross, Moone, Co. Kildare, west face

Cistercians paved the way for new styles of religious and military architecture in Ireland. The first Cistercian foundation was at Mellifont, Co. Louth (46), in 1142, where there is a unique and spectacular

Mellifont, Co. Louth

lavabo or bath-house: the regular Continental plan of this monastery, with buildings arranged systematically around a rectangular court or quadrangle, with the church usually on the northern side, the other sides being occupied by ancillary buildings, was in sharp contrast to the less formal layout of Irish monastic foundations. Other Continental orders arrived in Ireland, such as the Augustinian Canons, with houses at, for example, Cong, Co. Mayo (47), where some fine features are preserved. Dominican Friars

did not arrive until 1224: one of the most noteworthy Dominican foundations is Sligo 'Abbey' (48)—strictly the Priory of the Holy Cross—with some original features and many superb additions. While Franciscan Friars may have been in Ireland from 1224, one of the most interesting Franciscan friaries was founded in about 1240, at Ennis, Co. Clare (49), which retains many noteworthy features. In addition to monastic churches, of course, there were parish churches, such as St Mary's Church in New Ross, Co. Wexford (50), possibly the largest medieval parish church in Ireland, and cathedrals of which the two in Dublin, Christ Church (51*) (the Cathedral of the Holy Trinity) and St Patrick's (52*) are worth citing, not only because of the (not unparalleled) unusual existence of two cathedrals in the same diocese and in close proximity. In the course of this period the style of architecture in vogue made a gradual transition from Romanesque to Gothic. Boyle Abbey in Co. Roscommon (53), established in 1161, is one of the finest examples of Transitional architecture in the country, displaying both round-headed and blunt-pointed arches.

While many of the medieval ecclesiastical foundations were established by the Anglo-Norman invaders, as it was

Clonmacnois, Co. Offaly

Trim Castle, Co. Meath

said 'to ensure their position in the next world', they also cannily built castles throughout the country 'to ensure their survival in this world'. The earliest of these castles were great mounds of earth, shaped like truncated cones, known as *mottes*, often with defensive outer works, known as *bailies*, which would have contained such ancillary wooden buildings as stores and stables, while the motte itself would have carried a palisade and wooden tower. Many examples exist, but that at Granard, Co. Longford (54), is said to be the largest in Ireland. Often the temporary wooden tower was later replaced by a stone one, as at Clonmacnois, Co. Offaly (39). More often, however, because of the limitations of space, an entirely new stone castle was erected, often in close proximity to the earlier motte. Basically these great stone castles followed the layout of the earlier temporary structures: a central stronghold, known as the *keep*, with, inside a strong *curtain wall*, one or more *wards*, approached usually through a strongly defended gatehouse, and which contained ancillary buildings such as halls and

kitchens. Examples of good medieval castles may be seen throughout the country—notably at Trim, Co. Meath (55) (with a moat fed from the River Boyne), or Adare, Co. Limerick (56).

Under the protection of many of these great stone castles, towns with the additional protection of town walls grew up: often, as at Trim (55), the only vestiges of these walls are the defensive gatehouses; at Fethard, Co. Tipperary (57), however, parts of the wall and one gatehouse survive, while at Athenry, Co. Galway (58), one gate and five flanking towers as well as substantial lengths of the wall still stand. Parts of the bridge over the River Boyne at Trim, Co. Meath (55), are probably of Medieval date—as so often in Ireland to facilitate troop movement as much as trade. Representations of the people who built the castles, founded the towns and funded the churches can sometimes be seen, as for example in the church at Kilfane, Co. Kilkenny (59), where there is an effigy, of about 1320, of Thomas de Cantwell.

Late Medieval Period

During the fourteenth century various factors, including expense, inhibited extensive building in stone, and towards the end of the century a new, smaller and less costly type of fortified house emerged, the so called 'Tower House', consisting of a great stone tower, usually rectangular and of four or five storeys, like that at Roodstown, Co. Louth (60), often with at least one storey with a vaulted stone ceiling to reduce the risk of fire, and a battlement to protect a wall-walk at roof level. Those built in isolation usually had an outer yard or bawn, while those in urban contexts, such as Ardee, Co. Louth (61), appear to have been bawnless. The building of such strong houses continued until the sixteenth and even seventeenth century. The most splendid example is at Aughnanure, Co. Galway (62), built about 1500, with two bawns, or at Pallas, Co. Galway (63), also dating from around 1500, which has been described as one of the best-preserved tower-houses in a county with many well-preserved examples. In others such as Urlanmore, Co. Clare (64), the rather stark interiors were relieved by outline animal paintings, while at Bunratty, Co. Clare (65), there is a chapel with an elaborate stucco ceiling.

In addition to the ongoing alterations and improvements carried out on existing ecclesiastical buildings, as at Ardfert Cathedral, Co. Kerry (66), where a south transept with an east chapel was added in the fifteenth century, or at St Mary's Cathedral, Limerick (67), where a unique set of misericords (carved projections on the undersides of the hinged seats in choir-stalls), in black oak, were installed around 1489, other monasteries were built, in the Gothic style now predominant, as at Ross, Co. Galway (68), founded for Franciscan Observantine Friars in 1498, of which the ruins are exceptionally well preserved. One of the great surviving glories of this period are the effigial tomb-sculptures of Rory O'Tunney with examples in St Canice's Cathedral at Kilkenny (69) and, thought to be his greatest work, at Kilcooley Abbey, Co. Tipperary (70), of Pierce Butler, dating from 1526. Towards the end of this period, however, the ferocity of the Elizabethan wars and the zeal with which the Suppression was conducted led to the destruction not only of many of the monasteries as, for instance, in 1552 when the English from Athlone reduced Clonmacnois, Co. Offaly (39), to total ruin, or in 1595 when the Carmelite Priory of St Mary's at Rathmullan, Co. Donegal

Elizabethan manor house at Carrick-on-Suir, Co. Tipperary

(71), was pillaged, but to the destruction of statues within churches, under an Act of 1552.

It was, of course, to this period that the most notable shipwreck sites belong—the wrecks of the unsuccessful Spanish Armada, some twenty of which occur along the north and west coasts of Ireland, most notably the treasure-laden wreck of the *Girona*, at Lacada Point, Co. Antrim (72), or that of *La Trinidad Valencera*, with its fantastic burden of bronze guns cast by the foremost Renaissance gun-founders, at Glenagiveny, Co. Donegal (73).

As a kind of compensation for the loss of so many fine ecclesiastical buildings there began to appear some good examples of Elizabethan manor-houses: the best example is at Carrick-on-Suir, Co. Tipperary (74), where a house, complete with long gallery and stucco armorial medallions, including one of Elizabeth flanked by Justice and Equity, was erected beside a fifteenth-century Butler castle. (Here, too, is a bridge much of which dates from the sixteenth century.) In Kilkenny (69) is a fine example of the town-house of a rich merchant, with an arcaded ground-floor front, built in 1594 and known after its builder as the Rothe House.

The Plantation Period

While the Plantation of Munster had begun in 1593 with the defeat and death of the Earl of Desmond, it was not until after the resounding English victory at Kinsale in 1601, followed by the Flight of the Earls in 1607, that it and the Plantation of Ulster were successfully put into effect. The main visible effects were the creation of planned Plantation towns. The best surviving example of such a town in Munster is probably Bandon (properly Bandonbridge), Co. Cork (75), founded in 1608 under the patronage of Richard Boyle, Earl of Cork, with a town wall built in the 1620s. In contemporary plans and descriptions it is described as a large and beautiful town

consisting of about 250 houses, of 'English' type—of two storeys, with slate roofs and stone or brick chimneys. A Protestant parish church, built in 1610, still survives in part. In Ulster similarly planned towns were erected, notably 'Londonderry' (76) itself, founded on the site of a church and monastery founded by St Colm in 546 and known as *Doire Cholm Cille*, on which work began in 1610, with a stout wall pierced by four gates, and with streets laid out on a grid pattern and the Protestant Cathedral constructed between 1628 and 1633, which, ironically, is now one of the finest examples of Gothic survival buildings in these islands. Other walled towns were created outside these official Plantation areas, such as Jamestown, Co. Leitrim (77), built to protect the Shannon crossing in 1622, of whose defences only a gate survives.

To protect the great estates of the new English landlords, a new generation of castles or tower-houses was initiated, because, by and large, their presence was not exactly welcomed by the native Irish. One of the most notable was at Mallow, Co. Cork (78), 'a goodly, strong and sumptuous house' built by Sir Thomas Norreys about 1598 on the site of a Desmond Castle, but others were built throughout the country. In Ulster examples such as Castle Archdale (79) (1618/9) and contemporary Castle Balfour (80), both in Co. Fermanagh are

Kanturk Castle, Co. Cork

defended houses rather than tower-houses, while at Ballygalley, Co. Antrim (81), a tower-house in the rather mean Scottish Baronial style was erected in 1625 by James Shaw of Greenock. Such castles were not restricted totally to the colonialising English. At Kanturk, Co. Cork (82), a large fortified house was built by the Mac Donaghs about 1609, only to have work stopped on the orders of the Privy Council because of complaints from the local English settlers that the house was 'much too large for a subject'. To protect the realm from invasion, because the memory of the Spanish attempt in 1588 was all too fresh, great 'star' forts were built at the most vulnerable ports. At Kinsale, Co. Cork (83), are the impressive remains of the best preserved of them all, with outer defences still standing to a height of over 12 m.

In the longer settled areas, such as the Pale, existing tower-houses such as Athlumney, Co. Meath (84), had Tudor mansions with mullioned windows built on to them. In other areas such ruined buildings as the Carmelite Priory in Rathmullan, Co. Donegal (71), were converted into fortified houses; indeed again in Co. Donegal, in 1636/7 Bishop John Leslie constructed a great fortified house at Raphoe (85), using the demolished Round Tower for building material. The most remarkable domestic building of the period, however, is undoubtedly Jigginstown House in Co. Kildare (86); it was one of the earliest brick buildings in Ireland, begun in 1636/7. Had it been finished (building work came to a halt when its builder was beheaded in 1641) it would have been—at a total length of 120 m—the largest unfortified residence in the country. The outstanding building of the period, and the oldest surviving fully classical building in Ireland, is the Royal Hospital, Kilmainham (87), modelled on the similarly purposed Les Invalides in Paris, on which work began in 1680.

The Eighteenth Century

The defeat of James II at the Battle of the Boyne in 1690 saw not only the total subjugation of Ireland but the emergence of Dublin as the true political centre of the country which resulted in building and rebuilding on an enormous scale. Two of the most important, for a capital city, were the provision of Houses of Parliament (88*), of which the first stone was laid in 1729, and of which a portion still survives, including the House of Lords. The other was the refurbishment of the Castle (89*), of which the whole of Upper Castle Yard was rebuilt during the first half of the century, in brick with stone dressings. Another institution to undergo extensive rebuilding at the start of the century was Trinity College (90*), including the Library, conceived on a heroic scale and begun in 1712, the west front from 1751 and the elegant Provost's House of 1759. Among other noteworthy public buildings in Dublin of this period were St Patrick's Hospital (91*) of 1747/8, which closely resembled a large private house and the more grandiose Lying-in Hospital known as the Rotunda (92*) of 1757. Among the Dublin churches of this period was St Anne's (93*) of 1720 and of standard Protestant type, rectangular with galleries on three sides and a short sanctuary at the east end. To these public buildings might be added the Brazen Head (94*) in Bridge Street, a purpose-built hotel of the very early years of the century.

Private houses of the earlier years of the century that have survived, mainly town houses of rich landowners, include Leinster House (95*), built in 1745 (by Richard Cassels) for the Earl of Kildare, which is now the seat of the Irish Government, and Charlemont House in Parnell Square (96*), once one of the finest of the Dublin Mansions built in 1761 for the Earl of Charlemont, but now, rather mutilated, serving as the Municipal Gallery of

Castletown House, Co. Kildare

Modern Art. The earliest of the famous Dublin squares, St Stephen's Green (97*), contains many houses—some with good original stucco—of the middle of the century, while Merrion Square (98*), laid out in 1762, retains the Georgian elevations of its brick houses in varying degrees. The establishment of a body known as the Wide Streets Commissioners in 1757 had brought fresh impetus—and a degree of town planning—to Dublin. In its wake there came many important buildings such as the Royal Exchange (99*) (now the City Hall), a superb design with a copper dome; this was followed by the Custom House (100*) of 1781 to 1791, and at the very end of the century the magnificent Four Courts (101*) (now sadly mutilated), both by the English architect James Gandon.

Outside Dublin too there was also intensive building activity: among the earliest and most splendid examples of Early Georgian mansions is Castletown, Co. Kildare (102), begun between 1719 and 1722 for William

Conolly, Speaker of the Irish House of Commons and reputedly one of the richest men in Ireland; only slightly later is Bellamont Forest, Co. Cavan (103), of about 1730, remarkable for being faced entirely in red brick. Russborough, Co. Wicklow (104), a vast house built about 1750 has been described as 'a piece of theatrical scenery flung across the Wicklow landscape facing the mountains'. Many less ostentatious mansions and houses were built throughout the country, of which a considerable number survive.

In the provincial towns there was a spate of buildings, notably of courthouses, as at Kinsale (83), of 1706 (near to which are preserved the eighteenth-century stocks) or, quite frequently, combined Town Halls and Market Halls, as in the unusually attractive 'Tholsel' at Kilkenny (69). At Youghal, Co. Cork (105), is the 'Clock Gate' of 1771 whose upper storeys contained the town gaol. An attractive Custom House of this period can be seen at Limerick (67), dating from 1769. Almshouses are a fairly common feature of

The Tholsel, Kilkenny

provincial towns and survive at Cork (106) (Skiddy's Almshouses, of 1718), arcaded on two of three sides; the most attractive, however, are those of the Southwell Charity in Downpatrick, Co. Down (107), dating from 1733.

There was a considerable volume of church building during the century; in Waterford (45) both the Church of Ireland Cathedral of 1770 to 1779 (on the site of the earlier medieval Christchurch) and the Roman Catholic Cathedral of 1793 to 1796 were designed by the same architect, John Roberts. Among the Church of Ireland churches surviving, unaltered, without the 'benefit' of later restoration, is the church at Timogue, Co. Laois (108), with half-heartedly pointed windows in the nave, while the church of St Peter in Drogheda, Co. Louth (109), is acknowledged to be the finest built in a provincial town in the middle years of the century. The oldest surviving Roman Catholic church of the period is at Grange, Co. Louth (110), of the T-shaped plan that was equally popular

with Presbyterians (mainly on economic grounds since this was the plan that could accommodate the largest congregation at the lowest price). The finest Roman Catholic church in any Irish town is generally deemed to be St Patrick's in Waterford (45) of 1764, with a rectangular plan and galleries around three sides. A fairly regular feature, particularly of non-conformist churches, was the provision of living accommodation for the pastor beneath the same roof as the chapel or meeting house, as at Castlebar, Co. Mayo (111) (1785 and Methodist).

The Nineteenth Century

The Act of Union of 1800 was for Ireland a salutary introduction to the new century. While certain trends may be discerned—Gothic was for provincial Protestant churches, Classical for Roman Catholic churches, and for courthouses, gaols and hospitals—such was the diversity of buildings, many with quite novel applications, that it is possible only to mention a few of the most notable examples. Of country houses Lissadell, Co. Sligo (112), near the end of the classic tradition, in 1830, is one obvious choice—but for literary associations rather than architectural merit—while the vast and castellated Ashford Castle, near Cong, Co. Mayo (47), built for the Guinness family in 1873, is another.

The Catholic Emancipation Act of 1829 made possible the erection of new Roman Catholic cathedrals (but oddly none was built in Dublin, Belfast or Cork), usually in the new growing centres of population rather than on the sites of Medieval cathedrals. Thus the Catholic Cathedral for the diocese of Killaloe is at Ennis (49), and, commenced in 1831, is an interesting example of the style known as 'carpenter's Gothic'. The cathedral at Cobh, Co. Cork (113), begun in 1868, but which took fifty years to build, is the work of the son of one of the most celebrated nineteenth-century Irish architects A. W. N. Pugin.

Among the most memorable nineteenth- century structures in Ireland are, of course, the Martello towers, constructed in the fear of a Napoleonic invasion: building of the towers near Dublin commenced in 1805, and while the fifty or so built show a general similarity they are by no means identical. Other novelties of this innovative

Queen's College (now University College), Cork

century included railway stations, the termini mainly in classical styles, such as those at Galway and Sligo, the wayside stations often Gothic or 'Tudor'. Other distinguished examples of public architecture were the three Queen's Colleges, at Belfast, Galway and Cork, all opened in 1849, and all, apart from accretions of more recent buildings, more or less as they were built. As the population of Dublin expanded, so did the city: charming, middle-class suburbs (frequently of houses with basements) such as Rathmines (114*) developed in the period 1830 to 1840; towards the end of

A mid-Victorian house in Ballsbridge, Dublin

the century the need for more modest accommodation led to formations such as the Dublin Artisans' Dwelling Company, which in 1870 created such model inner suburbs as the mini-village at Stoneybatter (115*) on the north side of the river, consisting of small 'two-up, two-down' houses, forming a pleasant if low-cost pattern of terraces. Among the most charming and characteristic of the relics of the nineteenth century in Ireland, of course, are typical Irish public houses, both in the country and in the cities—or at least the relatively small numbers that have not been 'modernised'. Probably the majority of the single-storey 'peasant' houses, some of which retain their original roofing of thatch, which are such a feature of scenic views of Ireland, date from the nineteenth century. While they are frequently described as 'cottages'—a word which seems intended to conjure up a more romantic image—they are more properly described simply as 'houses'.

The Twentieth Century

Modern architecture did not reach Ireland until the 1930s; at first the use of mass concrete was restricted to avant-garde private houses. Its clean, functional appearance, however, made it seem particularly suitable to hospital buildings, such as those at Cashel, Co. Tipperary (37), of 1937, and Kilkenny (69), of 1942. What has been described as 'a particularly adventurous example of its use is to be seen at Collinstown (116) in the form of Dublin Airport—the rightful successor to the railway termini of the previous century—completed in 1941, with a curved central block flanked by great curved wings, forming a convex arc on the operational side, to service the greatest possible area. Also to serve the needs of travellers was the central bus-station, or Busaras (117*), of 1953, by Michael Scott, one of the most distinguished twentieth-century Irish architects, with a strongly sculpted quality, and contrasting great

Busarus, Dublin

areas of glass with the mass concrete, but given relief by the use of mosaic, wrought iron and perforated brick.

Almost inevitably most of the most striking buildings in this material have been public buildings: by and large the recent suburbs—both in Dublin and the provinces—have totally lacked the grace of their predecessors. While few of the branches of the Irish banks have attracted much attention, such imposing edifices as the Central Bank in Dame Street, built in 1978 (118*), incurred criticism because of its deemed lack of respect for the scale and proportions of adjacent buildings. The Group Headquarters of Allied Irish Banks in Ballsbridge (119*) of 1980, was reputed to be at the time the most expensive building ever erected in Dublin.

Among the other Dublin buildings to excite general admiration are the United States Embassy, again at Ballsbridge (120*), of 1964, and the New Library at Trinity College (90*), built by Paul Kovalek in 1960, after a competition, and, notwithstanding its being mainly in raw concrete, with only the façade clad with granite, achieving a romantic air and a surprising compatibility with its neighbours. Another of the most respected Irish architects of this century has been Liam McCormick whose churches give a new architectural interest not only to many provincial towns, but also to the open countryside, as does the elegant Church of St Aengus at Burt, Co. Donegal (121), built in 1967.

Literature

The international achievement and reputation of Irish literature seem quite disproportionate to the size of the country. Situated at the western edge of Europe, with the neighbouring shadow of England on one side, and the Atlantic reaches on the other, this island has created a literature which has been translated and celebrated throughout the world. Today especially, there seems something about the historical role of Irish literature in helping to shape a sense of cultural and national identity which strikes the observer and the visitor as quite exceptional.

Ireland has a literary history stretching back to the fifth century A.D., the oldest vernacular tradition in Europe. Literary composition in Gaelic began shortly after the arrival of Christianity, practised by the monks in their schools of learning. Their simple, lyrical verses on nature often appeared in the margins of the elaborate, illuminated versions of the gospels which they produced in those schools.

This monastic culture also recorded and preserved the mythological and legendary tales of pagan Ireland, the most famous and enduring of which is *Táin Bó Cuailnge* (the Cattle Raid of Cooley), about a heroic, aristocratic society which existed around 300 B.C. The dominant character of the *Táin* is Cúchulainn, a warrior-hero whose exploits fascinated many twentieth-century writers, especially W. B. Yeats. Indeed, one of the remarkable features of modern Irish writing is its continued attraction to ancient mythology, its sense that the past still offers the present some imaginative wisdom.

For over a thousand years, Irish was the dominant language of literature on the island. This tradition was sustained by the 'filí', the poets of the bardic schools, men who formed a privileged and learned elite which chronicled and commemorated the life and times of the Gaelic chieftains who protected them. After the Battle of Kinsale (1601), in which those chieftains were defeated by English forces, the rapid and systematic colonisation of the country soon destroyed the Gaelic order upon which the poets depended.

At the end of the seventeenth century, with the victory of King William of Orange at the Battle of the Boyne (1690), the surviving poets had virtually lost their audience and were reduced to beggary and despair. The voice of protest at invasion and dispossession is heard in the verse of such distinguished poets as Dáibhí Ó Bruadair (1625–1698), Aodhagán Ó Rathaille (1670–1726) and Eoghan Rua Ó Suilleabháin (1748–1784), and the characteristic form of that protest came to be known as the *Aisling*, a dream or vision in which Ireland was imaged as a beautiful woman in distress, calling out to her young men to free her from slavery and exile. Politically, this was a Jacobite verse, based on the increasingly slender hope that the Stuarts would return to the English throne, and that the native Irish would he restored to their earlier independence and glory.

During the eighteenth century a strong folk tradition in verse survived these calamities, and showed the resourcefulness and tenacity of the oral tradition. Two outstanding poems, both influenced by this tradition, merit special attention. *Cúirt an Mheán Oíche* (The Midnight Court) is an elaborate burlesque of the *Aisling*, and, though bawdy, is about sexual equality. It was written by Brian Merriman (1749–1805), a County Clare schoolmaster, about whom very little else is known. It has seen many modern translations, has been adapted for the stage, and continues to intrigue today's readers and scholars.

Caoineadh Art Uí Laoghaire (The Lament for Art O'Leary) was written by Eibhlín Dubh Ní Chonaill, an aunt of the famous Catholic politician, Daniel O'Connell. This is one of the greatest elegies in the Irish tradition, in which Ní Chonaill grieves for and praises a husband shot dead by the English forces while on a visit home from Austria, where he served in the Imperial Army as an exile. These classic poems, one comic, the other tragic, combine the political and the personal in ways which still resonate for a contemporary audience.

The Protestant minority in eighteenth-century Ireland came to be known as the 'Anglo-Irish', many of whom were born in Ireland, descendants of English and Scottish settlers. For most of the century this colonial society ruled the country for England, but they also began to develop and assert their own cultural identity. The 'Georgian' style of Dublin is their architectural legacy: they also created a new sense of a 'Protestant nation' in Ireland.

Foremost amongst those who helped forge this new dimension to the Irish

Jonathan Swift

cultural identity was Jonathan Swift (1667–1745), born in Dublin, schooled in Kilkenny, and eventually famed as Dean of St Patrick's Cathedral. Unsuccessful in his early ambition to find a clerical post in England, he committed himself to the public good of his birthplace, and wrote many pamphlets, including *The Drapier's Letters* (1725) and *A Modest Proposal* (1729), to expose the injustice of English rule and the appalling misery of the native population. His most famous work, *Gulliver's Travels* (1726), was as much influenced by the Irish landscape as by English politics. He is buried in St Patrick's, where the visitor may read his famous epitaph which refers to him as an 'earnest and dedicated champion of Liberty'.

Other important figures in the rhetoric of eighteenth-century Ireland are Henry Grattan (1746–1820), who led the 'Patriot Parliament' of the 1780s which secured legislative independence for a short period, and Edmund Burke (1729–1797), whose oratorical skills were repeatedly engaged with the need for political consensus in Ireland.

The modern Irish novel begins with the work of Maria Edgeworth (1767–1849), whose *Castle Rackrent* (1800) satirised the chaotic world of the Big House, and thereby introduced one of Irish literature's most haunting and enduring symbols of decay and disorder. William Carleton (1794–1869), born into the Gaelic-speaking world, went on to master English and produce *Traits and Stories of the Irish Peasantry* (1830–1833), a collection of hilarious and sensational sketches of rural Ireland, hugely popular in its day. Carleton also wrote several novels, the last of which, *The Black Prophet* (1849), appeared just after the Great Famine, a national catastrophe which decimated much of the Irish-speaking population, left over a million dead from starvation and disease, and began a massive wave of emigration to North America.

Richard Lovell Edgeworth, eighteenth-century landowner and a man of letters and father of Maria Edgeworth

he tragedy of the Great Famine had important political, cultural and literary consequences for Ireland. A new spirit of political separatism and cultural resurgence developed, which tried to preserve a distinctive national inheritance and inspire a new generation of writers with images of a heroic and proud legacy. A Celtic Revival emerged, pioneered by linguists, antiquarians and translators such as Standish O'Grady (1846–1928), who revealed a rich hoard of epic and legendary narrative which was still part of the folklore of the peasantry, but was inaccessible to those who understood only English. Douglas Hyde (1860–1949), who later became the first president of Ireland, founded the Gaelic League, and produced several important and influential works which introduced the older tradition to a new and much wider audience. These works included *A Collection of Irish Gaelic Folk Stories* (1890), and the renowned *Love Songs of Connaught* (1893).

Contemporaneous with this Revival, Irish writers continued the tradition of a dramatic intervention on the London stage. Oscar Wilde (1854–1900) delighted and scandalised audiences with his satirical plays about the Victorian upper classes, most notably in *Lady Windermere's Fan* (1892) and *The Importance of Being Earnest* (1895). George Bernard Shaw (1856–1950) began his long career in English theatre with *Arms and the Man* (1894), but also wrote about the continuing Anglo-Irish crisis, as in his ironic version of inherited stereotypes, *John Bull's Other Island* (1904). Shaw was one of three modern Irish writers to be awarded the Nobel Prize for Literature.

George Bernard Shaw

he Irish Literary Revival of the early twentieth century was deeply inspired by the vision of W. B. Yeats (1865–1939), perhaps the country's greatest modern poet. Along with Lady Augusta Gregory (1852–1932) and John Millington Synge (1871–1909), he founded Ireland's first National Theatre Company, the Abbey Theatre, which opened in 1904 with Synge's *Riders to the Sea*, and which promised to create and encourage a poetical drama drawing upon the folk tradition and the ancient mythologies. Among its most

W. B. Yeats

Thoor Ballylee, Yeats's home in Co. Galway where he wrote some of his most enduring poetry

successful, and controversial, productions was Synge's *Playboy of the Western World* (1907). The Abbey also produced the early work of Sean O'Casey (1880–1964), including *Juno and the Paycock* (1924) and *The Plough and the Stars* (1926), plays which reflected on the political crises of the 1916 Easter Rising and the subsequent Civil War, events which led, in 1922, to Partition. Parallel to his work in the theatre, W. B. Yeats achieved national and international recognition for his poetry, becoming a Senator in the new Irish Free State and being awarded, in 1923, the Nobel Prize for Literature.

Ireland has made a major, pioneering contribution to the literature of Modernism in this century, most significantly through the fiction of James Joyce (1882–1941). There is now as much critical literature about Joyce as about Shakespeare. Although he spent most of his life in Europe, mainly in Italy and France, Joyce wrote about nowhere but Ireland, especially its ancient capital, as can be seen throughout his work, *Dubliners* (1914), *A Portrait of the Artist as a Young Man* (1916) and, of course, *Ulysses* (1922). Samuel Beckett (1906–1989) also revolutionised the nature of modern literature in both the novel and the theatre. Like Joyce, he settled in France, but often drew upon an

A cartoon of James Joyce, the great novelist

65

imaginative Irish landscape for his writing, as in the radically experimental *Waiting for Godot* (1953) and the novels *Murphy* (1938) and *Malone Dies* (1951). In 1969 Beckett was awarded the Nobel Prize for Literature.

Sean O Faolain

The contemporary scene in Ireland shows an inherited enthusiasm for the literary imagination, as well as a recognition of the subtle ways in which tradition continues to influence current innovation and aspiration. Writing in the Irish language, for example, is going through a rich period of revival and translation, epitomised in the work of poets such as Nuala Ni Dhomhnaill and Gabriel Rosenstock: new bi-lingual editions of modern Irish verse, such as *An Crann Faoi Bhláth: The Flowering Tree*, embody and celebrate this continuity with the past.

The Irish short-story, building upon the legacy of writers such as Frank O'Connor and Sean O Faolain, continues its distinctive craft in the work of John MacGahern, Mary Lavin and William Trevor. Developments in the contemporary Irish novel, realistic and experimental, may be viewed in the fiction of Brian Moore, Jennifer Johnston, John Banville and Dermot Bolger.

The political conflict in the north of Ireland has deeply influenced, but does not entirely explain, the remarkable achievement of the two most important writers of today, the poet Seamus Heaney, and the dramatist, Brian Friel. Since his first collection, *Death of a Naturalist* (1966), up to his latest, *Seeing Things* (1991), Heaney has tried to explore and understand the complex relation between the personal and the political, the present and the past. In 1980, Brian Friel helped to establish the Field Day Theatre Company which, like Yeats's earlier project with the Abbey, tried to confront and interpret the fundamental issues of cultural inheritance and political mythology. Plays such as *Translations* (1980) and *Dancing at Lughnasa* (1990) have met with world-wide acclaim and success.

An energetic and self-critical debate about identity and tradition has been generated by much contemporary Irish writing. The most significant result of that debate has been the publication of the *Field Day Anthology of Irish Writing*, a monumental achievement which tries to show the range, complexity, diversity and promise of the various literary traditions in Ireland.

The extraordinary success of the Summer Schools in Ireland ensures that the exchange of ideas about literature is not limited to enclosed academics and scholars. There are over forty such events throughout the country, each one devoted to the work and influence of an Irish writer associated with that region of the country. Some of the best known include that on Yeats in Sligo, Merriman in Clare, and Swift in Kildare. The Irish Summer School is as much a social event as a literary gathering, one which is open to all, local and visitor alike, and which insists that a tradition as rich as this is cause for celebration as well as examination.

Folklore

Despite the tempestuous history of Ireland, basic cultural forms have changed, but slowly, and as a result this is one of the more important countries in Europe in terms of folklore. Centralisation has come late, which means that small local communities have until recently relied on their own resources for education and entertainment. This, and the particular taste for style in Irish speech, can be counted as the major reasons for the elaborate nature of our storytelling. A comparison with the culture of other countries will show that Irish storytellers have a special and quite unique tendency to lengthen and to ornament their narratives.

The main divisions of folk stories in Ireland are native hero-tales, adaptations of international folk-tales, and oral legends of famous persons and things. As well as these, shorter forms of narrative have been much cultivated, such as jokes, verse-anecdotes and accounts of personal experiences. The hero-tales and the longer types of folk-tales are told almost exclusively in the Irish language, whereas the other genres thrive to an equal extent in English as in Irish. Due to the influence of commercial entertainment and the mass media in recent generations, there has been a decline in storytelling as a social phenomenon. There is now, however, a resurgence of interest in folklore, and particularly in its relevance to environmental and communal matters and to the study of local and family history. There is also a growing awareness of the artistic importance of storytelling, and of the treasures of imagery and imagination which it contains.

Few of the mythological stories of old Irish literature are found in the folklore of recent times, but there are some significant exceptions. Especially notable is the lore concerning the champion, Lugh, who survives the schemes of his tyrant grandfather, Balar 'of the destructive eye', and slays that formidable opponent. This epical story evolved from ancient sources in the Middle East, where the Continental Celts picked it up and applied it to their god, Lugus. It can still be heard told in the north and west of Ireland, this being but one of many examples of how early European culture is mirrored in living Irish tradition. Other divine personages who survive in folk stories are the smith-god, Goibhniu, who is popularly known as the Gobán Saor, 'the finest tradesman who ever lived'; and the land-goddess called the Hag of Beare (Cailleach Bhéarra) who we are told was a great lady-farmer and lived longer than any other person.

People everywhere love stories of great heroes. In Ireland, our hero-tales have been reinforced through the centuries by written texts. This is true of all versions of stories from the Ulster Cycle, or 'Rúraíocht', which have been current in folklore. Their sources were manuscript retellings which were read out at get-togethers in the evenings. Most dramatic are the deeds of the youthful super-hero, Cú Chulainn, who while still a boy and unarmed slew a massive and savage hound, and went on to fight whole armies single-handedly. Also very popular was the story of the tragic life of the beautiful but ill-fated Deirdre, who was

Glencar Lake, Co. Sligo

Inisbofin, Co. Galway

deprived of her true love and made to marry the vengeful King Conchubhar Mac Neasa instead.

Folk accounts of Fionn Mac Cumhaill are much more varied and numerous, combining tragedy, comedy and simple curiosity. The special popularity of Fionn-lore is due to the simple and catchy form of his adventures and also to the large number of late literary texts which focus on him and his warriors. The account of his fugitive youth, and of how he gained prophetic wisdom through tasting a mystical salmon, was known to Irish speakers in every part of the country. Another widely known story tells of an adventure which he and some of his warriors (called 'Fianna') had in a strange house where they encountered time in the person of an old man, youth as a beautiful maiden, and energy in the form of an aggressive ram. Despite his great knowl-edge, Fionn was puzzled until all was explained to him. This story resembles the literary allegories which scholars were so fond of writing in medieval Europe. That the ordinary people in Ireland appreciated its meaning and developed the characteri-sation in it shows how sophisticated folklore can be.

The companions of Fionn are equally colourful. Pre-eminent is Oisín, the hero's son, who is claimed by tradition to have lived on into the Christian era and to have debated the ancient epics with St Patrick himself. Then there is Diarmaid Ó Duibhne, the handsome young warrior with a love-spot on his forehead, and all women who see this spot fall hope-lessly in love with him. There is the great runner, Caoilte, who can race across Ireland from shore to shore in a few minutes and who shows his speed and agility by herding all the hares and rabbits in the country. There is also the great Goll Mac Morna, rival of Fionn, but famous for his strength and integrity, and his uncouth brother, Conán Maol, who torments the Fianna warriors with his greed and his vicious tongue. Late folklore has added its own dimensions to the myth of Fionn, often describing him as an outwitter of hostile giants and attributing to him wise proverbs concerning social and economic life.

Versions of hundreds of international folk-tales have been collected in Ireland. The medieval literature shows that several of these stories have been told in the Irish language for a long time, but others have entered the country in more recent centuries. One very popular genre was the short animal tale, which attributes fanciful experiences and often human-like intelligence to the various creatures. Some of these tales purport to explain origins, such as how the wren became king of the birds or how the plaice got its crooked mouth, but especially popular were the imagined deeds of the clever fox. Wonder tales were in great demand in many countries in olden times and were most popular with Irish storytellers and their audiences. These narratives were long and elaborate, telling of fantastic events in a world of 'long ago' where the ordinary confines of nature were superseded. For instance, the dragon-slayer who rescues a princess and upstages his dishonest rival, the widow's son who can only save a princess from a giant by finding out where the giant's heart resides outside of his body, or the young man who is sent on the dangerous mission of plucking three hairs from the devil's beard!

Since medieval times, people have been accustomed to select and develop material which they heard in church sermons. Thus many stories tell of adventures in search of salvation, of tussles with demons, and of various other ways in which man acts out his moral dilemma in concrete terms. There are many artistic touches to these, such as a man who does penance in a river, and his tears of remorse are so bitter that they cut their way through the water and leave holes in the bed of the river beneath. There are also strange but striking circumstances, such as the wild cow-herd who lives alone on a mountain and never commits a sin, or a bird which sings so sweetly that hundreds of years pass for those who listen to it for what

seems a short while. Several other tales of international origin relate circumstances of coincidence and chance in real-life situations, while a wide range of humorous anecdotes were told about tricksters and rogues, about stupid characters who were not always so stupid, and especially about how fortune could sometimes turn and smile upon the poor and oppressed.

An oral legend is a story to which a significant amount of belief is attached, and various examples of this genre are found in Ireland. Again demonstrating its importance in international cultural studies, Irish folklore has many fine examples of 'migratory' legends, which were once current in other parts of Europe as well. Instances are the legend of a river which periodically claims a victim, or that of a sleeping army of old which waits at a hidden location for the appropriate time to return. The rich fairy lore of Ireland contains some migratory legends also, such as that of a midwife who assists at a birth in the fairy world or a changeling who is discovered by a wise individual with the result that an abducted child is restored. Some sea legends are within the same category, for example the account—prevalent along the north and west coasts—of how a mermaid married into a human family but finally returned to her watery realm.

Otherwise, Irish fairy lore, like that of Europe generally, is a combination of ancient ideas of the otherworld with explanations loosely derived from Christian literature. The most prevalent explanation is that the fairies were a section of the fallen angels after the great battle in heaven, who were allowed by God to inhabit land, sea and air. Most lore of the fairies has them inhabiting a world which is a mirror-image of human society, and engaging in agricultural and household chores in much the same way as humans do. Some elements are survivals from ancient times, such as the belief that the fairies reside in the barrows, tumuli and raths, and that they could be inspirers of wisdom and art. A common type of legend has a man falling asleep on a fairy rath, and in his dream he receives a mystical book which enables him to become a brilliant poet.

Local dedications and the custom of praying at holy wells has led to a large number of stories concerning the saints from Ireland's 'golden age'. The saint is portrayed as a kindly person who possesses astounding miraculous powers, such as in the common legend which has the holy man or woman banish a ferocious monster into one or other of the many Irish lakes. Traditions of the great trio of saints, Patrick, Brigid and Colmcille, had wide provenance. Patrick is represented as the original missionary who overcame druids and banished demons; Brigid functions in the role of protective goddess, though presented as a kindly Christian; whereas the image of Colmcille probably preserves something of the druid in his portrayal as a strong-willed and powerful figure with a high social profile.

The major figures of Irish political history occur in legends which have varied origins according to the aura appropriate to each of them. Those with particularly developed narratives are the quasi-historical King Cormac Mac Airt, who is said to have ruled with great wisdom and generosity at Tara, and his historical counterpart, Brian Boru, victor over the Vikings at the great Battle of Clontarf in A.D. 1014. No less important are figures of more recent vintage such as the oppressor Oliver Cromwell who, we are told, sold his soul to the devil to gain his power; and the political champion, Daniel O'Connell, whose quick wit and ready replies are celebrated and much exaggerated in popular lore. More localised stories tell of good social leaders, cruel tyrants, brave outlaws, accomplished sportsmen, and individuals to whom extraordinary powers such as healing or prophecy were attributed. Especially popular are short and pithy accounts of poets, which tell of how and why a certain verse was composed. There is a high demand for funny stories about learned individuals, and many such concern the celebrated Dean Swift and his saucy servant who continually tricks and exasperates him.

The natural environment, its flora and fauna, and the climatic and seasonal variations which colour it, have all been favourite subjects for the folk imagination. Many accounts tell of the origins of things

Lough Derg pilgrimage centre, Co. Donegal

and of traits attributed to them. Similarly the passing of time, whether in the life cycle of individuals or the festivals which punctuate the year, have given rise to a rich amalgam of folk belief, practice and narrative. Birth, marriage and death were traditionally the three focal points in human life, and this is strongly reflected in the folk superstitions concerning them. Death is especially marked in folk belief, and unique to Ireland is the 'bean sí', or ghostly lady, whose eerie cry is heard to presage the death of members of old Irish families.

In calendar custom, stress continued to be placed down through the centuries on the four junctures of the year as they were in ancient Ireland—St Brigid's Feast (originally Imbolg), Bealtaine (the May feast), Lughnasa (the harvest feast at the beginning of August), and Samhain (the November feast). Christian festivals have, however, also accumulated a good deal of folklore, especially in the cases of Christmas, Easter and Pentecost. A wide variety of sport and entertainment was, and continues to be, basic to Irish folk life. Preeminent are singing, dancing, music, cardplaying, horse-racing, hurling and football, and various athletic contests. And, of course, storytelling, the one pastime which brings all others into its ambit.

Landscape and Natural History

The Burren, Co. Clare

Ireland has been an island for the past 8,500 years, isolated by rising seas as the glaciers of the last Ice Age melted. Cut off from Britain and the Continent, and abandoned in the face of Atlantic gales and rain, it has been shaped into a unique blend of mountains, bogs, lakes, rivers, and remote wave-lashed islands. Ireland's plant and animal life, although impoverished by its early isolation and continuing remoteness, is still diverse and all the more interesting because of the strange combinations of arctic/alpine and southern species which live side by side on Irish soil.

Shaped very much like a saucer, Ireland's rock framework is composed of a central, low-lying limestone plain, hemmed in by a rim of mountains, with only the occasional break allowing access to the sea. The central plain is, for the most part, covered with a mantle of boulder clay deposited during the Ice Age and overlain in the centre by raised bogs—unique domes of peat covered in their pristine form with sphagnum moss and heather. A flight across Ireland confirms its legendary green mantle, though today this is pock-marked with extensive brown 'deserts' where the raised bogs are being stripped to supply hungry electricity generating stations and the equally demanding domestic fuel and horticulture markets.

Ireland's rich green pastures have been nurtured over the centuries by the steady fall of rain carried on westerly winds. Much of this rain eventually finds its way

Powerscourt Waterfall, Co. Wicklow

into the centre of the 'saucer' from whence the mighty River Shannon carries it back to the Atlantic Ocean. The Shannon is a broad, sluggish river, expanding at intervals to form some of Ireland's largest loughs—Allen, Ree and Derg. It drains an area of about 15,000 square kilometres, almost one-fifth of the area of the country,

and drops only 147 metres on its 336-km journey from source to sea.

To the north, and soon to be linked by canal to the Shannon, the complex and beautiful Lough Erne meanders through 'basket of eggs' drumlin country north-westwards to the coast. Further north and east still, and very different in character, is

Lough Neagh, Ireland's largest lake. Broad, shallow, and almost devoid of islands, this enriched lake is Ireland's premier inland waterbird haunt, and in winter it is host to tens of thousands of ducks.

The River Bann carries the bountiful waters of Lough Neagh to the north coast where they enter the sea not far to the west of the Giant's Causeway, with its famous basalt columns—formed at a time when America was breaking away from Continental Europe. Inland are the tidy picturesque Glens of Antrim, oases in a moorland fastness. Then comes Belfast Lough, industrialised, but still a regular haven for shorebirds, and Strangford Lough, arguably the most outstanding coastal wildlife habitat in Ireland. In autumn it receives the first skeins of brent geese as they return from their breeding grounds in Arctic Canada, and in summer it is host to breeding terns which have travelled northwards from their wintering areas off the coast of Africa. Beneath its waters the sea-life is rich and beautiful.

The Mountains of Mourne, tall and imposing, are part of a granite landscape which cradles Carlingford Lough, well known for its wildlife, too. Further south, granite hills again rise to dominate the coastal scene in Dublin and Wicklow, with Lugnaquilla Mountain (920 m) taking pride of place above this moorland plateau which is dissected by long, forested, eastward-running valleys. Inland, the central plain is broken by the Old Red Sandstone and quartzite mountains of the Slieve Bloom, Knockmealdown, Galtee and Slieve Aughty Mountains.

The coastal lowlands in the south-east of the country boast some of Ireland's most ancient rocks, about 2,000 million years old, and some of its finest coastal wildlife habitats. The Wexford Slobs, Ladies Island Lake and Tacumshin Lake are internationally significant for their waterbirds, and the Saltee Islands are renowned for their seabird colonies.

To the west, extensive deposits of Old Red Sandstone have been crumpled into a series of east-west running ridges and valleys, the latter descending into broad shallow bays separated by rugged peninsulas which project finger-like into the Atlantic. Carrauntuohil (1004 m), guarded by steep and treacherous crags, is Ireland's highest mountain. It is at the northern edge of the Old Red Sandstone and not far from the Lakes of Killarney, with their neighbouring oak woodlands and herds of native red deer. The mild climate in the south-west brings flowers into bloom earlier than anywhere else in the country, and allows plants such as the strawberry tree, which is usually found only much further south in Europe, to flourish.

Offshore, standing firm against the Atlantic breakers, the Skellig and the Blasket Islands are home to many thousands of breeding seabirds, among them gannets, puffins and manx shearwaters. The rich waters off the south-west coast are a busy thoroughfare, too, for whales, dolphins and porpoises on their seasonal migrations.

To the north, beyond the broad estuary of the Shannon, rise the stark, grey limestone terraces of the Burren. Deceptive in its barrenness, the Burren is one of the most fascinating areas in Ireland for the naturalist. Growing side-by-side are arctic/alpine plants such as the mountain avens and warmth-loving species such as the maidenhair fern. The limestone is permeated with caves which carry water away from the surface to the lowland rivers to the south, or down to the coast where it sometimes emerges again only below sea-level.

To the west, the Aran Islands are an extension of the Burren limestone and have many features in common with it. However, to the north, across Galway Bay, there is a very different landscape— blanket bog, lakes and steep rocky ridges of ancient, unyielding quartzite. This is Connemara, another area of contrasts and conundrums. Heathers more typical of southern climes and mountain plants more at home in the Arctic grow in this exposed and inhospitable outpost of Ireland. And in winter geese come from Greenland to feed in its soggy bogs and whooper swans from Iceland to find sustenance in its small, infertile loughs.

Wind-swept open spaces are the essence of west Mayo, with its vast expanse of blanket bog pressed up against the sinuous quartzite ridge of the Nephin Mountains. The bogs, though, come to an abrupt end at the spectacular, contorted cliffs of the north Mayo coast, from which there is a

panoramic view across Donegal Bay of the limestone buttress of Benbulben to the east, in Sligo, and the stupendous cliffs of Slieve League and the mountains of Donegal to the north-east.

Barnes Gap, Co. Tyrone

Dublin

The Custom House

Dublin Bay, with its great sweep of coast from the rocky brow of Howth in the north to the headland of Dalkey in the south, is a fitting introduction to one of Europe's finest capitals. The city is spread over the broad valley of the River Liffey, with the Wicklow Hills sheltering it on the south. In addition to its splendid public buildings, Dublin is particularly rich in domestic architecture of the eighteenth century. Fine Georgian mansions, many of them with historical associations, lend sober beauty to the city's wide streets and spacious squares. There is a wealth of interest for the visitor to Dublin in its architecture, its

fashionable shopping centres, its wide range of entertainments and important events. The beautiful surroundings of the city are very easy to get to; a short journey brings one to a pleasant beach or to the Dublin Mountains.

Dublin City

Baile Atha Cliath
(The Town of the Hurdle Ford)

Pop. 477,675.
(Dublin *city* 1991 CSO figures)

Tourist offices:
14 Upper O'Connell St, Dublin 1.
Tel. (01) 747733, Fax (01) 743660.

St Michael's Wharf, Dun Laoghaire.
Tel. (01) 2806984, Fax (01) 2806459.

Airport, arrivals area
Tel. (01) 8445387, Fax (01) 8425886.

i Northern Irish Tourist Board Office:
16 Nassau St, Dublin 2.
Tel. (01) 6791977.

American Express:
116 Grafton St, Dublin 2.
Tel: (01) 772874, Fax (01) 713752.

✉ Post Office:
General P.O. O'Connell St, Dublin 1.
Tel. (01) 728888, Fax (01) 734498.
Open: 09.00 – 18.00

Dun Laoghaire: Marine Rd.
Tel. (01) 2859346.

Ⓟ Parking Regulations:
Meter parking; disc parking

Railway Stations:
Heuston Station, Islandbridge, Dublin 8.
Tel. (01) 366222/365421.

Connolly Station, Dublin 1.
Tel. (01) 363333.

Westland Row (Pearse).
Tel. (01) 7033633

🚌 Bus Depot: Busarus, Store St,
Dublin 1. Tel. (01) 302222/366111.

🚗 Car Hire: Argus Rent a Car Ltd,
Argus House, 59 Terenure Rd East,
Dublin 6.
Tel. (01) 904444, Fax (01) 906328.

Avis Rent a Car Ltd,
1 Hanover St East, Dublin 2.
Tel. (01) 774010, Fax (01) 776642.

Budget Rent a Car, Dublin Airport.
Tel. (01) 370919.

Dan Dooley Rent a Car, 42/43 Westland
Row, Dublin 2. Tel. (01) 772723.

Hertz Rent a Car, Leeson St Upper,
Dublin 2. Tel. (01) 602255.

Murrays Europcar Rental,
Baggot St Bridge, Dublin 4.
Tel. (01) 681777.

Windsor Car Rentals,
33 Bachelors Walk, Dublin 1.
Tel. (01) 730944.

🚲 Bicycle Hire: Rent a Bike,
58 Lower Gardiner St, Dublin 1.
Mike's Bikes, Unit 6, St George's Mall,
Dun Laoghaire Shopping Centre,
Dun Laoghaire. Tel. (01) 2800417.

Dates of principal cultural
events/festivals: Dublin Traditional Music
Festival (June), Dublin Street Carnival
(June), Dublin Horse Show (July/August),
Dublin Theatre Festival (October).

Dublin is the capital of the Republic of Ireland and Ireland's principal port.
From Dublin Airport, 6 miles (10 km) north of the city centre, there are regular flights to and from Britain, Europe and North America. The Car Ferry terminal from Liverpool is at Alexander Road, North Wall Quay, on the north side of the city.
Irish Rail (the national transport company) provides rail connections from Dublin to Waterford, Cork, Tralee, Galway and Westport from Heuston Station (off Parkgate Street); to Belfast, Sligo and Wexford from Connolly Station (Amiens Street) and to Wexford from Pearse Station (Westland Row). DART (Dublin Area Rapid Transit) provides a frequent and

efficient electric train service every day covering the coastal area of Dublin from Howth on the north side of the city to Bray on the south side.

Dublin Bus city and suburban services operate from the city centre, while Bus Éireann operates provincial services which depart from Busarus (bus station), Store Street. Metered taxis may be hired throughout the city.

Things to do

Dublin has all the attractions of a modern European capital, including facilities for most major sports. The national hurling and Gaelic football finals (September) and the Dublin Horse Show (July/August) are outstanding among the city's sporting events. There is horse-racing at Leopardstown, County Dublin, and the headquarters of Irish racing at the Curragh, County Kildare (where all the Irish Classics are run), is within easy reach; greyhound racing takes place for most of the year on six evenings a week at one of the two Dublin tracks. The golfer has a large number of excellent courses to choose from, and in season there are frequent hunting meets near the city. Sea bathing is available at nearby resorts, and there are municipal indoor heated pools in the city and suburbs.

A full programme of sightseeing tours of Dublin all year and surrounding areas in summer is operated by Dublin Bus. Walking tours are signposted in the city centre. These interesting tours are contained in a special booklet giving maps and background information on points of interest along the routes. Approved Dublin and National Guides are available from Dublin Tourism office. Principal theatres are the Abbey, Peacock, Gate, Gaiety, Olympia and Eblana; for details of these and the many other evening entertainments, see the daily newspapers or enquire at the information office of Dublin Tourism.

Dublin's many public parks offer havens of relaxation for the visitor. Chief among them is the Phoenix Park at the western edge of the city, one of the finest public enclosed parks in the world. It has a circumference of 7 miles (11 km) and covers 1,760 acres. There is a network of roads through it and many quiet walks. Near the main entrance are the Zoological Gardens, founded in 1830.

Near by is the People's Park and at the other side of the main road the 205-feet high Wellington Monument. The official residence of the President of Ireland, Aras an Uachtarain, lies to the right of the main road; on the left is the space called 'The Fifteen Acres' (but actually covering about 200) which is laid out in playing fields. It was once the recognised duelling ground of eighteenth-century Dublin. On the north side of the city at Glasnevin, the 50-acre Botanic Gardens are of interest both to the sightseer and the botanist. The Garden of Remembrance, at the north side of Parnell

Bust of James Joyce in St Stephen's Green

Square, commemorates all those who died for Ireland. St Stephen's Green, at the top of Grafton Street, covers 22 acres and is delightfully laid out; it contains several interesting monuments and sculptures.

Dublin's History

The earliest accounts of Dublin go back to A.D. 140 when the geographer Ptolemy (who called it Eblana) mentioned it as a place of note. The name Dublin is derived from the Irish Dubhlinn (Dark Pool), and is more recent than the Irish form in current use Baile Atha Cliath (the town of the Hurdle Ford). Father Mathew Bridge now spans the Liffey at the site of the ancient ford of the hurdles.

St Patrick is believed to have visited Dublin in 448 and converted many of the inhabitants to Christianity. During the next four centuries a Christian community grew around the site of the primitive ford. In 840 a party of Norse sea-rovers landed and set up a fortress as a base for their maritime expeditions; twelve years later a Danish force took possession of the town. The years that followed brought continual warfare between the Irish and Danes, until Danish power in Dublin was finally broken at the Battle of Clontarf in 1014.

In 1169, English power began to assert itself in Ireland. The Earl of Pembroke ('Strongbow') landed in Wexford and, after making himself master of Waterford and a great part of Leinster, took Dublin by storm. In 1171, Henry II came to Dublin to survey his newly acquired domains, received allegiance from some of the Irish chieftains and granted Dublin its first charter.

Inevitable wars followed during the succeeding centuries, 'England never wholly victorious nor Ireland thoroughly subdued'. Historic events crowded one upon the other, Dublin all the time figuring prominently at the scene. Among them were the crowning of the pretender, Lambert Simnel, as King Edward VI, the siege of the city by Owen Roe O'Neill in 1646, and its occupation by Oliver Cromwell three years later.

With the eighteenth century came the most colourful period of Dublin's history. Architecture and other arts found ready encouragement from the wealthy society of the metropolis. New streets and squares were added as the nobility built palatial town residences, and the Parliament House in College Green was the first of a great series of public buildings. In 1783, England

conceded a short-lived autonomy to the Irish Parliament, which ended with the Act of Union in 1800. Even during that period there was growing political unrest, because of the repressive policy of the British Ministry (which still controlled executive government). This unrest culminated in the unsuccessful uprising of 1798. Five years later, Robert Emmet's insurrection began and ended in the streets of Dublin.

More than a century later, the Rising of 1916 took place in Dublin during Easter week. Dublin was again a storm centre in the tragic Civil War which followed the setting up of the Irish Free State in 1922, but her shattered buildings were subsequently restored and the building of a modern European capital city begun.

Cultural History

Dublin has produced an astonishing number of eminent writers. Jonathan Swift, the greatest satirist in English literature, was born in Dublin. Among his contemporaries were Bishop Berkeley and Edmund Burke, both renowned as prose-writers and philosophers. The many literary personalities of

Trinity College

nineteenth-century Dublin included James Clarence Mangan (one of the most noteworthy of the Anglo-Irish poets); Thomas Moore, author of the famous 'Irish Melodies'; and the novelists Charles Lever and J. Sheridan Le Fanu—all natives of the city. In recent times Dublin has inspired works such as George Moore's *Hail and Farewell*, James Stephens' *The Crock of Gold* and James Joyce's *Ulysses*.

In the annals of the theatre, Dublin also occupies an important place. Congreve, Farquhar and Oliver Goldsmith were all educated at Trinity College. Richard Brinsley Sheridan, Oscar Wilde, George Bernard Shaw and W. B. Yeats were all Dublin born.

Towards the end of the nineteenth century, Dublin became the centre of two great cultural movements. The first of these was the Gaelic League (Conradh na Gaeilge), founded in 1893 by Dr Douglas Hyde with the object of restoring the Irish language. The patriotic influence of the league was the main inspiration of the 1916 Rising and the later struggle for independence. Today there are branches of the organisation in Ireland, England, Scotland and the United States; its activities cover such fields as Irish language classes, lectures, debates, music, drama and folk-dancing.

At much the same time as the beginnings of the Gaelic League was the start of the Irish Literary Renaissance, which ushered in the twentieth century with the early writings of Yeats and the foundation of the Abbey Theatre. The Abbey, which first opened in 1904, has played an important part in the development of modern drama. The plays of J. M. Synge, Sean O'Casey and W. B. Yeats made it world famous. Other well-known Abbey dramatists include Lennox Robinson, Padraic Colum, T. C. Murray, George Fitzmaurice, George Shiels, Paul Vincent Carroll and Denis Johnston. The theatre has also been the nursery of many actors and actresses who have achieved world fame on stage and screen. The original theatre was destroyed by fire in 1951; the modern building on the same site (in Abbey Street) was opened in 1966.

Dublin has also produced famous scientists and scholars. Most renowned perhaps is Sir William Rowan Hamilton (1805–1865), who discovered quaternions and whose work in the field of dynamics foreshadowed the quantum theory of the atom. Other famous Dublin-born mathematicians were George Francis Fitzgerald

The Bank of Ireland by night

(1851–1901) and George Salmon (1819–1904). The city has a long-standing reputation as a centre of medical teaching, and Robert Graves (1797–1853) and William Stokes (1804–1878) are famous among its pioneers of medical research.

A mong Dublin's scholars are such great names as Sir James Ware (1594–1666), historian and antiquary; Edmund Malone (1741–1812), the Shakespearian scholar; George Petrie (1789–1866), renowned for his collection of Irish music and his work on Irish ecclesiastical architecture. John Pentland Mahaffy (1839–1918), a versatile scholar with a European reputation, was one of Dublin's most famous 'characters'. Among many historical writers born in the city were W. E. H. Lecky (1838–1903) and the principal historian of the city, Sir John Gilbert (1829–1898).

As a musical centre, Dublin is notable for the first performance of Handel's 'Messiah' which took place at the Musick Hall in Fishamble Street in 1742, Handel himself conducting. Many other eminent figures in the world of music visited the Irish capital during the eighteenth century. In 1856 the Royal Irish Academy of Music was founded. At least two world-famous singers—John McCormack and Margaret Burke-Sheridan—won their first laurels at the annual Dublin Feis Ceoil (Musical Festival).

Dublin's Public Buildings

The Old Parliament House

T his building in College Green is now the Bank of Ireland. It was begun in 1729 from the design of Sir Edward Lovat Pearce, Surveyor-General of Ireland, and is regarded as one of the finest specimens of eighteenth-century architecture. The receding front has finely grouped Ionic columns; the eastern portico, of the Corinthian order, was erected in 1785 after the design of James Gandon; a screen wall connects it with the main building. The western

West front of Trinity College

Dublin

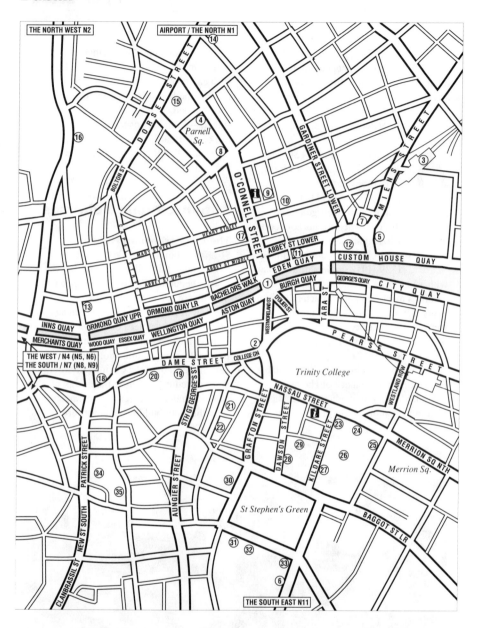

THE NORTH WEST N2

AIRPORT / THE NORTH N1

DORSET STREET

Parnell Sq.

BOLTON ST

O'CONNELL STREET

GARDINER STREET LOWER

AMIENS STREET

HENRY STREET

MARY STREET

ABBEY ST LOWER

ABBEY ST MIDDLE

ABBEY ST UPR

BACHELORS WALK

CUSTOM HOUSE QUAY

EDEN QUAY

BURGH QUAY

GEORGE'S QUAY

CITY QUAY

INNS QUAY

ORMOND QUAY UPR

ORMOND QUAY LR

ASTON QUAY

WESTMORELAND ST

D'OLIER ST

TARA ST

MERCHANTS QUAY

WOOD QUAY

ESSEX QUAY

WELLINGTON QUAY

PEARSE STREET

THE WEST / N4 (N5, N6)
THE SOUTH / N7 (N8, N9)

DAME STREET

COLLEGE GN

Trinity College

WESTLAND ROW

STH GT GEORGE'S ST

GRAFTON STREET

NASSAU STREET

DAWSON STREET

KILDARE STREET

MERRION SQ NTH

Merrion Sq.

PATRICK STREET

AUNGIER STREET

St Stephen's Green

BAGGOT ST LR

NEW ST SOUTH

CLANBRASSIL ST

THE SOUTH EAST N11

82

1. O'Connell Bridge
2. Bank of Ireland
3. Connolly Station
4. Garden of Remembrance
5. Financial Services Centre
6. National Concert Hall
7. Busaras
8. Rotunda Hospital
9. St Mary's Pro Cathedral (RC)
10. Tyrone House
11. Abbey Theatre
12. Custom House
13. Four Courts
14. St George's Church (CI)
15. Municipal Gallery
    of Modern Art
16. King's Inn
17. General Post Office
18. Christ Church Cathedral (CI)
19. City Hall
20. Dublin Castle
21. Powerscourt House
22. Civic Museum
23. College of Physicians
24. National Library
25. National Gallery
26. Leinster House
27. Natural Museum &
    Natural History Museum
28. Mansion House
29. Royal Irish Academy
30. Royal College of Surgeons
31. University Church (CI)
32. Newman House
    (University College)
33. Iveagh House
34. St Patrick's Cathedral (CI)
35. Marsh's Library

portico and screen wall were added between 1792 and 1794. The walls of this building echoed the speeches of men renowned for their oratory—men like Henry Grattan who became a popular idol during the struggle for constitutional independence in the late eighteenth century. In 1782, Lord Charlemont's armed Volunteers paraded in College Green, while Grattan, in the Parliament House, demanded and obtained the removal of restrictions on Irish trade. Independence was conceded to the Irish Parliament the following year.

The most dramatic scene enacted here was the passage, in 1800, of the Act of Union. The Act was opposed with passionate eloquence, but the British Government secured a majority by wholesale bribery of the members. Grattan, an ailing man clad in his old Volunteer uniform, took his leave of the independent parliament in a splendid speech.

Interior alterations have been made since the Bank of Ireland took over the building in 1804, but some of the old features have been retained and a number of objects of historic interest are preserved.

Trinity College

On the east side of College Green, this university was founded in 1592 on the site of a priory that had been suppressed by Henry VIII. The college was a Protestant foundation, designed to further the Reformation in Ireland.

The earliest surviving portion of the buildings dates from 1722. In 1759, the great façade, designed by Keane and Saunders, was erected. Chambers designed the Examination Hall (1787) and the finely proportioned Chapel. In one corner of the New Square stands the Printing House (1726–1734), designed by Cassels in the style of a Doric temple. Opposite is the Museum Building (1857) which has stone carving by the famous O'Shea brothers. The Provost's House, facing Grafton Street, was erected in 1760.

Trinity College Library dates from 1601 and is housed in two fine buildings: the Old Library (completed in 1732) and the New Library (1967). It contains over half a million printed books and over 2,000 manuscripts. By an Act of 1801 it has the right to a copy of every book printed in Ireland or Britain. Egyptian papyri and some Greek and Latin manuscripts are the oldest of its treasures. There are over 140 Irish manuscripts, some dating from the sixth century.

The library's greatest treasure is the *Book of Kells*, a wonderful illuminated manuscript of the gospels (probably eighth century). Other ancient Irish manuscripts here include the Books of *Dimma* and *Durrow*, the *Book of Armagh*, the *Liber Hymnorum*, the *Book of Leinster* and the *Yellow Book of Lecan*. The library also contains the finest collection of early printed books in Ireland and there are numerous rare editions.

Trinity College Historical Society, founded in 1770, is the oldest university debating society in Ireland or Britain. It was the direct successor of the Club, founded by Edmund Burke in 1747, and the Historical Club, founded in 1753. Wolfe Tone was auditor in 1785, and Robert Emmet and Thomas Moore became members in 1797; Thomas Davis was auditor from 1838 to 1840, a period during which another member was Isaac Butt, afterwards the leader of the Irish Party at Westminster. In more recent years prominent members have included Bram Stoker, author of *Dracula*, Edward Carson, the great lawyer and politician, and Douglas Hyde, founder of the Gaelic League and first President of Ireland.

University College, Dublin

The city's other university, formerly at Earlsfort Terrace, moved to a new campus at Belfield, beyond Donnybrook in the southern suburbs. This college originated in the Catholic University of Ireland founded in 1854 by Dr John Henry (afterwards Cardinal) Newman, its first rector.

The Literary and Historical Society of University College, founded in 1855 at a meeting presided over by Dr Newman, has been associated with many prominent figures in the intellectual and political history of modern Ireland. Among holders of its auditorship were John Dillon (1873), Francis Sheehy Skeffington (1897), Tom Kettle (1898) and in later years many of the men prominent in the struggle for independence and in the development of the young Irish state.

Newman House
The Catholic University's principal centre at 85–86 St Stephen's Green, later became the university college conducted by the Jesuit Fathers in connection with the Royal University of Ireland. At this period Father Gerard Manley Hopkins (the famous poet) was professor of Greek and James Joyce a student. In 1908 the college became part of the National University of Ireland.

Restoration work on Newman House has been partially completed and the building has been opened to visitors who will experience a range of interiors illustrating the development of the Dublin town house during the course of the eighteenth century. The visitor tour proceeds from the early Georgian entrance hall of No. 85 into its splendid reception rooms, the Apollo Room and the Saloon which overlook St Stephen's Green and then to the impressive Bishop's Room in No. 86 which evokes the spirit of the nineteenth-century Catholic University.

The Custom House
On the north bank of the River Liffey between Butt Bridge and Matt Talbot Bridge, this is Dublin's finest public building. It was designed by James Gandon and completed in 1791. The main front, facing the river, is made up of pavilions at each end, joined by arcades to a central portico of four Doric columns. From the centre rises a superbly graceful dome, surmounted by a figure of Hope. Other exterior decoration includes a symbolic alto-relievo in the tympanum, the arms of Ireland (surmounting the pavilions), and a series of allegorical heads representing the Atlantic Ocean and thirteen Irish rivers. The north front's portico has also four columns, with statues on the entablature representing Europe, Asia, Africa and America. The east and west fronts are similar in design, but less ornate.

The Custom House was burned to a shell in 1921 but was restored, and the present building retains all the beauty of the original.

Dublin Castle
Standing on high ground west of Dame Street, the castle was built between 1208 and 1220. The Upper Castle Yard covers roughly the area enclosed by the original walls. On the southern side are the State Apartments, once the residence of the English viceroys and now the venue for Ireland's presidencies of the European Community, for Irish presidential inaugurations and other important state functions. Most impressive of the apartments is St Patrick's Hall, 82 feet long by 41 feet broad, with a lofty panelled ceiling decorated by paintings.

At the south-western corner of the enclosure is the Bermingham Tower, erected in the fourteenth century and rebuilt in 1777. Only the sloping base of the original tower remains, hidden by later building. This tower was for long used as a prison, and from it young Red Hugh O'Donnell made his historic escape on Christmas Eve 1592.

In the Lower Castle Yard is the massive Record Tower. This, the largest visible fragment of the old Norman building, now houses the State Paper Office, a repository of historical documents. Also in the Lower Castle Yard is the Church of the Most Holy Trinity, formerly known as the

The Four Courts

Chapel Royal and built to the design of Francis Johnston between 1807 and 1814. It was restored in 1989. Noteworthy features inside are the Irish oak carving and the ancient middle portion of the east window. The exterior is decorated with over ninety carved heads representing British monarchs and other historical figures. (Since 1943 this church has been in Catholic ownership.)

The City Hall
This building, adjoining the castle, was erected between 1769 and 1779 and was formerly the Royal Exchange. Designed by Thomas Cooley, it is a square building in Corinthian style, with three fronts of Portland stone. The interior is designed as a circle within a square. Fluted columns support a dome-shaped roof over the central hall, which has a number of statues. In the Muniment Room can be seen the documentary records of the Corporation and the mace and sword of the city.

The Four Courts
This is on the northern quays a half-mile (1 km) west of O'Connell Bridge. It was begun in 1786 from designs by Thomas Cooley, but on his death the plan was recast and the work completed by James Gandon. A magnificent building, it consists of a centre flanked by squares which are connected with the main building by rusticated arcades. The Corinthian portico supports an entablature with a statue of Moses and figures of Justice and Mercy. Above the circular centre hall is a massive dome. The Four Courts was almost completely destroyed in the Civil War of the 1920s, but was later restored. An irreparable loss, however, was the adjoining Public Record Office, where priceless legal and historical documents perished.

The Royal Hospital, at Kilmainham in the western suburbs, was built by the Duke of Ormonde in 1680–82 as a hospital for veteran soldiers. A fine building designed by Sir William Robinson, it is in the form of a quadrangle, with two storeys and dormer windows. From the centre of one façade rises a graceful tower. The spacious hall, with its great roofbeams, is perhaps the finest interior in Dublin. Beautiful carved oak adorns the walls, and there are portraits of Charles II, William and Mary, Ormonde (the founder) and Archbishop Marsh. The chapel has a magnificent stucco ceiling and notable wood carvings.

Extensive restoration of the building began in 1980 and it has been designated by the government as the National Centre for Culture and the Arts. It has received Europa Nostra's Premier Conservation Award.

It has been open to the public since 1986 and it has been the venue for a wide-ranging programme of exhibitions, concerts and lectures. The Irish Museum of Modern Art is housed at the Royal Hospital and it represents in its permanent collection and temporary programmes Irish and international art of the twentieth century with an emphasis on educational and community involvement and development.

Opposite the west entrance to the hospital is Kilmainham Jail, where generations of Irish patriots were imprisoned and the leaders of the 1916 Rising executed. The prison is now a historical museum.

The General Post Office, in O'Connell Street, was finished in 1818 from designs by Francis Johnston. This large granite building has a grand Ionic portico of Portland stone consisting of six fluted columns. On the pediment are statues representing Hibernia, Mercury and Fidelity. During the 1916 Rising the GPO was the headquarters of the Irish Volunteers, and here the Republic was proclaimed. The building was shelled by a British gunboat anchored in the River Liffey and completely gutted by fire. A plaque on the front of the building commemorates the Rising, and in the central hall is a memorial that takes the form of a bronze statue of the dying Cuchulainn (by Oliver Sheppard, R.H.A.).

O'Connell Street, where the GPO stands, is Dublin's principal thoroughfare. Down its centre runs a series of monuments,

O'Connell Street looking north

Christ Church Cathedral

including the O'Connell Monument, the Parnell Monument and the statue of Father Theobald Mathew.

Opposite Cathedral Street is the sculpture popularly known as the 'Floozie in the Jacuzzi'. The Anna Livia Millennium Fountain, to give it its official name, was unveiled in June 1988 as part of the Dublin millennium celebrations and is based on the character Anna Livia, which represents the River Liffey.

The Mansion House, in Dawson Street, is a fine building in Queen Anne style that has been the residence of Dublin's Lord Mayors since 1715. Many important events in Ireland's history took place here, including the adoption of the declaration of independence in 1919 and the signing of the truce that ended Anglo-Irish hostilities in 1921.

Leinster House, a splendid Georgian mansion in Kildare Street, is now the meeting-place of both houses of the Irish Parliament, the Dáil and the Seanad. Built

by the 1st Duke of Leinster in 1745, the house was occupied by his successors until rented by the Royal Dublin Society in 1815. It stands behind a spacious quadrangle, flanked on one side by the National Library and on the other by the National Museum.

Powerscourt Town House in South William Street is a large Georgian house built between 1771 and 1774, designed by Robert Mack for Richard Wingfield, 3rd Viscount, Lord Powerscourt. The house contains fine rococo plasterwork; the wood carving is notable, particularly the mahogany staircase. The courtyard buildings have been refurbished into an interesting shopping and crafts centre.

Marino Casino is situated just off the Malahide Road in the north city. It is a building which ranks with the finest architecture of Classical Europe. It was commissioned by James Caulfield, 1st Earl of Charlemont, who founded the Royal Irish Academy. It was designed by Sir William Chambers and constructed in the garden of Lord Charlemont's house in Marino by the English sculptor Simon Vierpyl. The Casino is small in scale, perfect in detail and proportion. It is open to visitors from mid-June to mid-September 10.00–18.30 every day.

Guinness Brewery is the home of Guinness stout, the famous black beer with the distinctive white head. Brewing began there in 1759 when Arthur Guinness first produced his 'porter' which is now consumed around the world. The Guinness Hop Store, a converted nineteenth-century building, houses an audio-visual show tracing the history of Guinness in Ireland. It includes also a model cooperage and transport museum, a souvenir shop and a bar where Dublin's finest brew can be sampled at leisure. The two top floors of the building are used for art exhibitions throughout the year.

The Electricity Supply Board and the National Museum have combined to restore 29 Lower Fitzwilliam Street as a middle-class house of the late eighteenth century, open to the public except on Mondays.

Dublin's Cathedrals and Churches

Christ Church Cathedral
Standing on high ground at the western end of Lord Edward Street, this is one of the city's finest historic buildings. The original eleventh-century structure was replaced by the great new cathedral founded by Strongbow in 1172, which took fifty years to build. Most of the present structure dates from the nineteenth-century restoration by George Edmund Street, but the transepts and some other parts of Strongbow's church remain.

The cathedral is a very handsome building with little exterior decoration. The interior has magnificent stonework and graceful pointed arches with delicately chiselled supporting columns. Strongbow

was buried in the church, though the effigy representing him is probably not the original monument, which was damaged in 1562 when the roof collapsed. Beside this effigy is the figure of a child, believed to represent Strongbow's son. The twelfth-century crypt has statues of Charles II and James II, some noteworthy sculptured monuments and other interesting historical relics.

Christ Church was the scene in 1394 of the knighting of four leading Irish chieftains by Richard II. In 1487 the imposter, Lambert Simnel, was crowned here as King Edward VI. Archbishop Browne, the first Protestant to occupy the see of Dublin, was the chief instrument of Henry VIII's religious policy in Ireland. In 1551 the Book of Common Prayer was promulgated in the cathedral by the English viceroy— the first time the English liturgy was read in Ireland. The rites of the old faith were briefly restored during James II's stay in Dublin from October 1689 to July 1690, and Mass was celebrated in the cathedral · in the presence of the King.

St Patrick's Cathedral
This is in Patrick Street, a short distance south of Christ Church. Founded in 1190, the building is mainly Early English in style, but its square tower is fourteenth century and the spire an eighteenth-century addition. The original structure was extensively rebuilt towards the end of the fourteenth century after a fire. In 1320, the Pope founded a university which had its home in the cathedral until it was suppressed by Henry VIII. During the seventeenth-century wars Cromwellian troopers stabled their horses in the aisles. The building was in a ruinous state when a thorough restoration was carried out in the 1860s.

The 300-foot long interior (St Patrick's is the longest church in Ireland) has many historical relics. They include a monument erected in 1631 by Richard Boyle, 1st Earl of Cork, and others commemorating the Duke of Schomberg (the Williamite commander at the Battle of the Boyne), the celebrated orator John Philpot Curran, the last of the Irish bards Turlough O'Carolan, and the novelist and poet, Samuel Lover.

St Patrick's is perhaps best known for its associations with Jonathan Swift, who was Dean from 1713 to 1745. The pulpit from which he preached is still to be seen. In the south aisle is his tomb, and over the door of the robing-room is his own poignant epitaph: 'He lies where furious indignation can no longer rend his heart.' Near by is the grave of Hester Johnson ('Stella'), one of Swift's two great loves.

St Werburgh's Church in Werburgh Street (off Christchurch Place) was built towards the end of the twelfth century and repaired and enlarged in 1715. This was, for a long time, the parish church of Dublin, and in it were held many historic functions, including the swearing-in of the viceroys. The pulpit, a fine piece of Gothic sculpture, was transferred in 1877 from St John's in Fishamble Street. An object of great interest is the massive Geraldine Monument. Beneath the church are 27 vaults, one of which contains the body of Lord Edward Fitzgerald. By a strange coincidence, the remains of his captor, Major Sirr, lie in the adjoining churchyard.

St Michan's Church in Church Street (near the Four Courts) is a seventeenth-century structure on the site of an eleventh-century Danish church. It has some very

Mummies in St Michan's Church

fine woodwork, and an organ (dated 1724) on which Handel is said to have played.

The eighteenth-century 'stool of repentance' is an interesting curiosity. In a wall recess near by is the effigy of a medieval bishop.

The strangest feature of St Michan's is its vaults, where bodies have lain for centuries without decomposition—probably because of the dry atmosphere. The skin of the corpses remains soft as in life, but is brown and leather-like in appearance. St Michan's churchyard may contain the unmarked grave of Robert Emmet. Oliver Bond and Charles Lucas were certainly interred there, and in the vaults are the remains of the brothers Sheares, all of them insurgent leaders of 1798. Charles Stewart Parnell lay in state in St Michan's before his burial in Glasnevin.

St Audoen's Church in High Street was founded by the Normans about the end of the twelfth century and dedicated to St Ouen of Rouen. The building is now partly ruined, but some of it is still used for public worship. Features of the interior include the fifteenth-century Portlester Chapel and some interesting tombs and monuments. There is a beautiful Norman font and in the porch is the 'lucky stone' of St Audoen's, which has been venerated for centuries. The tower contains a fine peal of six bells, three of which (cast in 1423) are the oldest in Ireland.

St Audoen's Church is the venue for 'The Flame on the Hill', an audio-visual ten-projector show on a large screen with all-round stereophonic sound which tells the story of Ireland before the coming of the Vikings. Beside the churchyard is St Audoen's Arch (1215), the only surviving gate of the ancient city walls. The tower-room over the arch was the meeting-place of many of the old city guilds. The first issue of the *Freeman's Journal* was printed here in 1763.

The Catholic Pro-Cathedral (St Mary's) in Marlborough Street is in Grecian-Doric style and was completed in 1825. The

IRELAND

OF THE WELCOMES

If you can't make it to Ireland straightaway why not visit us through the pages of
Ireland of the Welcomes magazine.
The magazine's name is derived from the Celtic greeting, 'Céad Míle Fáilte' or
'A Hundred Thousand Welcomes', and our goal is to welcome you to the many facets
of Irish life and culture. And just to give you the flavour here are a few extracts.

The Beauty . . . Connemara. Its
hills rise up like waves from the
pewter sea and sail over the land in
misted ranks, the grey-shawled
granite of the Twelve Bens
stretching up in the midst of them
like Manannan MacLir's wild horses
breaking from the frothing sea;
shaking drops of water from their
shoulders in winding, silvery
rivulets.

The Flora . . . The very best way
to visit St. Anne's Park Rose Garden
in the Dublin suburb of Clontarf, is
to take the 30 or 44A bus to their
terminus. Guided by a trusted
companion, walk along Mount
Prospect Avenue with eyes firmly
shut. The day must be hot, still and
sunny and it must be early July. A
faint roar is heard in the distance,
growing louder as you walk on,
until it attains the level of a small
domestic airport on a busy day. This
is the sound of bees at work.

The Fauna . . . We are noted for
our wildlife. No snakes it's true but
we're possibly one of the few last
sanctuaries in Europe where the
river otter has any measure of
freedom. We still have our own
species of deer in the south-western
part of the country, our wild fowl
stock draws the bird enthusiast, our
dolphin vouches for the clear state
of our coastal waters. Up north . . .
Hold it. A Dolphin?

The Events . . . Punchestown.
Last year in glorious sunshine over
30,000 people enjoyed five days of
dressage, steeple chasing, cross
country and show jumping, all
rolled into one event, palpitating
in a riotous festival atmosphere. It
lured parading celebrities and
politicians, horse-loving clergy,
picnicking urban families and
captains of industry intent on
wooing clients in the tented village
of corporate boxes — all indulging
in plenty of plenty.

The Food . . . Amazed, your
guests will ask if you made this
feather-light thing yourself and the
answer is to strike your forehead
and cry, 'Oh puff-pastry, don't
remind me! Is it worth all the
effort?' Your appreciative guests
assure you that it is and if you have
tailored your reply carefully, you
have not actually told a single word
of a lie.

The Blarney ". . . and an elderly
road worker just past Dooletter
saved me a great deal of trouble by
pointing out, in answer to my
asking, if I was on the right road:
'Merciful hour, not at all. If you
keep on, you'll soon see the birds
flying backward, and you'll know
you have gotten yourself all the way
to Donegal!"

The Tradition . . . Just down the road, on the outskirts of
Durrow town, Cathal and Finbarr O'Brien chip away with their
hammers and chisels at massive limestone slabs and under their
expert hands patterns and interlaced 'ropes' and borders and
'Celtic' rings take shape, just as was done by or for monks of ten
centuries ago.

The Castles . . . Ballybur Castle stands near the tiny village of
Grange or Cuffesgrange about 3.5 miles south of Kilkenny in rich
farming lands — fields of golden corn, Irish meadows, gracious manor
houses. It is a fine example of the type of Tower House built for security
— and status — in the troubled centuries following the Norman
invasion, and which are still such a feature of the Irish landscape.

So, discover Ireland with us. You will
be our fireside guests on our travels
through the country, viewing our
cities and towns, enjoying our
festivals and folklore.

All this by simply subscribing to:
Ireland of the Welcomes.

Annual subscription for six issues (by destination):
Ireland IR£11, Britain STG£11, Other Europe IR£13,
USA US$21, Canada CAN$25, Australia AU$$36,
New Zealand NZ$49, Rest of the World IR£25.
Please send a cheque or money order to:
Ireland of the Welcomes, P.O. Box 84, Limerick, Ireland.

Name:_____

Address:_____

_____

City:_____County:_____

IC

Glendalough, Co. Wicklow

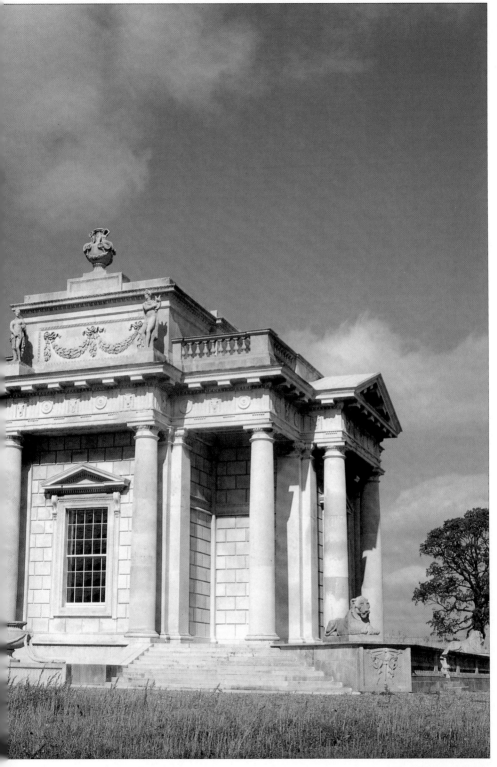

Marino Casino, Dublin

HOUSE of IRELAND
A landmark in Dublin Shopping

For the visitor, Dublin is a treasure chest waiting to be discovered ..... a place crammed with gems of history and beauty ..... Trinity College, St. Stephen's Green, Kilmainham, and of course, House of Ireland, which boasts its own exquisite collection of quality Irish and European products.

Explore a world of Cashmere and Wool Jackets, Capes, Aran Sweaters and Barbour Country Clothing. Discover the classic elegance of pure Irish linen ... or the craftsmanship of Waterford Crystal, Wedgwood China, Belleek, Lladro and hand crafted jewellery.

And all with the added advantage of TAX-FREE shopping. No visit to Dublin would be complete without a trip to House of Ireland, the home of quality. **All major credit cards accepted. All crystal and china mailed home to the U.S. is duty paid by House of Ireland.**

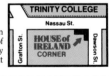

HOUSE of IRELAND

HOUSE OF IRELAND, NASSAU STREET, DUBLIN 2.
TELEPHONE 714543. FAX 6791023.
Open 7 days a week. Mail Order specialists.

building has a portico of six Doric columns supporting an entablature surmounted by statues of the Blessed Virgin, St Patrick and the patron saint of Dublin, Laurence O'Toole. The portico is copied from the Temple of Theseus in Athens, and the interior modelled on the Church of St Philippe du Roule in Paris.

Dublin's Museums, Art Galleries and Libraries

The National Museum comprises three divisions, devoted respectively to Irish antiquities, art and industry, and natural history. The main entrance is from Kildare Street, but part of the natural history division is approached from Merrion Street.

The Irish antiquities division holds one of the most impressive collections of national antiquities in Europe. Every age down to medieval times is represented. Of special interest is the splendid collection of gold ornaments of the Bronze Age, the 'Tara' Brooch, the Ardagh Chalice, the Cross of Cong and many shrines and other precious relics of the Early Christian and medieval periods. A recent addition to the collection was the Derrynaflan Hoard which was found in a bog in County Tipperary in 1980 and was restored in the British Museum. There is also a decorative arts section featuring silver, glass and ceramics, and also a historical section which includes 'The Road to Independence' focusing on the period 1900–1923.

The Natural History Museum contains collections illustrative of wildlife in Ireland, including mammals such as the red deer, the squirrel, otter, hare, badger, and birds: a special feature being the displays of sea birds and kingfishers. There are also displays of butterflies and other native insects and of the various types of fish to be found both in inland and coastal waters. The museum also has an international section and extensive African and Asian exhibitions.

The Dublin Civic Museum is at the City Assembly House, a fine eighteenth-

century building, located in South William Street. It has a permanent collection of antique and historical exhibits relating to Dublin, including newspapers and cuttings, pictures, prints, maps, coins, etc. which inform the visitor of a range of different aspects of Dublin life through the ages. It is operated under the control of the Dublin Public Libraries Committee of the

Dublin Writers' Museum, Parnell Square

Corporation and it has the function of collecting and preserving as much material as possible to provide the visitor with knowledge and understanding of Dublin city and its people.

The National Wax Museum is at Granby Row off Parnell Square, and is a world where fantasy and reality combine. There is a children's section, the World of Fairytale and Fantasy and the main section reflects the historical and cultural development of Ireland including life-size figures of famous personalities. Other entertaining exhibits are the Chamber of Horrors and the Hall of Megastars.

The Dublin Writers' Museum at 18–19 Parnell Square North is essential for the visitor who wishes to explore Dublin's rich literary heritage. Paintings, letters, photographs and artefacts referring to writers such as Swift, Wilde, Yeats, Shaw, O'Casey, Joyce and Behan are on display.

The National Gallery is on Leinster Lawn, Merrion Square West. It was opened in 1864 and has examples of works from all the European schools. Included are major works by Renaissance masters such as Fra Angelico, Paolo Uccello, Mantegna, Cosimo Tura, Signorelli, Perugino, Fra Bartolommeo, Michelangelo, Correggio, Titian and Tintoretto. There is also an unusually representative collection of sixteenth- and seventeenth-century Italian painters, and all the masters of the Dutch seventeenth-century school are well represented with the exception of Vermeer.

Other points of interest are: a fine collection of Flemish and German primitives; examples of the work of Rubens, Van Dyck, Teniers and their contemporaries; a number of Poussins, two of them world famous; a Spanish room, with notable paintings by Goya, El Greco, Ribera, Zurbaran and Murillo; and an English collection that includes ten major works by Gainsborough.

Sir Alfred Chester Beatty's gift of a hundred pictures, donated in 1950, includes several masterpieces by Meissonier, a Boudin, an unusual Corot and a highly representative group of paintings of the Barbizon school.

In the Irish rooms there are works of one of the greatest of modern portrait painters, John Butler Yeats (1839–1922), father of the poet W. B. Yeats; and there are many fine works by Hone, Osborne, Lavery, Orpen and Tuohy, as well as examples of the earlier phases of Irish painting. Irish portraits in the gallery provide a fascinating survey of historical personalities over three centuries.

The Municipal Gallery of Art is housed in a fine Georgian mansion on the north side of Parnell Square. It was founded in 1907, chiefly through the generosity of Sir Hugh Lane, who contributed a number of paintings to the original collection. He also lent to the gallery his collection of European pictures, but later lent them to the National Gallery in London because there were inadequate facilities to house them in Dublin. Lane

was drowned in the sinking of the *Lusitania* in 1915, and a codicil to his will, leaving the pictures to the Dublin Municipal Gallery, was held to be invalid. After more than forty years of negotiations, an arrangement was made in 1959 to divide the collection of 39 pictures into two groups, which are now exchanged between Dublin and London every five years.

The Gallery has a splendid collection of works by well-known artists, and has the distinction of being the first public gallery in Ireland or Britain to possess a representative group of Corot's work. Irish artists are well represented. Among the sculptures are works by Rodin, a head in bronze of Lady Gregory by Epstein, and 24 pieces by the Irish sculptor, Andrew O'Connor, who died in 1941.

The National Library of Ireland, in Kildare Street, is the State Library and the largest public library in the country. It was founded in 1877 with a collection of books donated by the Royal Dublin Society as the nucleus. The library has half a million books, besides many maps, prints and manuscripts. It is particularly rich in the more expensive works on botany, zoology and fine arts, and has an unrivalled collection of maps of Ireland. The Joly Collection includes 70,000 prints, among them a group of 3,000 Irish portraits. The collection of Irish newspapers (comprising 15,000 volumes and constantly being added to), is an invaluable source of historical evidence. The library also has a large collection of historical and literary manuscripts relating to Ireland, which is supplemented by microfilms of documents relating to Ireland from foreign libraries and archives. For Trinity College Library, see page 84.

The Royal Irish Academy Library, in Dawson Street, has one of the most extensive collections of ancient manuscripts in Ireland. The academy was formed in 1785 to promote the study of science, literature and antiquities, and has been in its present premises since 1852. In 1890, the academy's great collection of Irish antiquities was transferred to the National Museum. The many volumes of the academy's Transactions and Proceedings contain papers on science, literature, history and archaeology, and its publications take a leading place among those of learned societies in Europe.

The manuscripts in the library include the *Book of the Dun Cow*, the *Book of Ballymote*, the *Speckled Book* and the *Stowe Missal*. Also there is the *Cathach* or Battle Book, the great O'Donnell heirloom believed to be the actual copy of the psalms made by St Colmcille in the sixth century, and one of the original autograph copies of the *Annals of the Four Masters* compiled between 1632 and 1636.

Marsh's Library, adjoining St Patrick's Cathedral, was founded by Archbishop Marsh in 1707 and is the oldest public library in Ireland. It has over 25,000 volumes, chiefly of theology, medicine, ancient history, maps, Hebrew, Syriac, Greek, Latin and French literature. There are 250 volumes of manuscripts, a number of early printed books and many pamphlets. Also to be seen are a copy of Bellarmine's *Disputationes*, bearing the autograph and annotations of Archbishop Laud; a copy of Baronius' *Annals* with Isaac Casaubon's signature and notes; and a copy of Clarendon's *History of the Great Rebellion*, with the pencilled notes of Dean Swift.

The Royal Dublin Society Library, at Ballsbridge, has more than 150,000 volumes for the use of its members. The society was founded in 1731 for the advancement of agriculture, industry, science and art, and is the oldest society of its kind in these islands. The internationally known Dublin Horse Show, held in July/August, is one of the society's major annual shows.

To the public-spirited efforts of this society Dublin owes its National Library, National Art Gallery, Botanic Gardens, and to some extent the National Museum. Cultural activities of the society today include the reading of scientific papers, the publication of its scientific proceedings

and the holding of music recitals during the winter season.

The Chester Beatty Library, 20 Shrewsbury Road, Ballsbridge, has one of the most valuable private collections of oriental manuscripts and miniatures in the world. It includes manuscripts of the New Testament, unique Manichaean Papyri, and miniatures from all parts of the East, as well as albums, picture scrolls and jades from the Far East.

Other Dublin libraries are: the King's Inns Library, Henrietta Street; University College Library, Belfield; the Worth Library, Steevens' Hospital; the Franciscan Library at the Franciscan House of Studies, Killiney, and the Central Catholic Library in Merrion Square. Twenty-seven municipal libraries are maintained by Dublin Corporation.

Skerries
Sceiri (Sea Rocks)

Pop. 6864.

Tourist information office: Community Office. Tel. (01) 8490888.

Fishing boats at Skerries

This is a resort noted for its dry, bracing climate.

Things to do
There is a good sandy beach as well as bathing places. Other recreations include golf (18), boating, sailing, tennis and sea angling.

Around Skerries
Near the shore are three small islands—St Patrick's Island, Colt Island and Shenick's Island. Shenick's Island can be visited on foot at low tide; the other two are reached by boat. On St Patrick's Island are the ruins of an ancient church. Five miles (8 km) out to sea, Rockabill Lighthouse stands on an isolated rock.

There are pleasant walks in the neigh-bourhood, particularly along the coast on either side of the town. Bernagearagh Bay, 3½ miles (6 km) north-west, is a favourite place for picnics. A walk along the cliffs south of the town leads to Loughshinny, a little fishing village on a pretty bay, and about 2 miles (3 km) south-west are St Mobhi's Oratory and Holy Well. This saint lived in the seventh century.

A well-preserved ruin, 2 miles (3 km) south of Skerries is Baldongan Castle, the scene of a massacre by Parliamentary forces in 1642.

Four miles (6 km) north is Balbriggan, a quiet seaside resort with sheltered sandy beaches on the north and south. Recreations include golf (18), boating and tennis. There is pretty scenery along the adjoining coast.

Malahide
Mullach Ide (Ide's Hilltop)

👪 Pop. 9,940.

Malahide, on the southern shore of a narrow estuary, is a popular sea-side resort with a good sandy beach and golf courses (9 and 18). Malahide Castle, open to the public every day, is one of Ireland's oldest and most historical castles, dating back to the fourteenth century. The castle contains one of the finest collections of Irish period furniture together with a collection of Irish portrait paintings from the National Gallery and others, covering the period from the seventeenth century.

Boswell, biographer of Samuel Johnson, was related to the Talbots of Malahide Castle and the discovery of some of his papers in the castle some years ago created a literary sensation at the time.

Fry Model Railway Museum based at Malahide Castle features a rare and unique collection of hand-made models of Irish trains from the beginning of rail travel to modern times. The collection was built by Cyril Fry, a railway engineer and draughts-man in the late 1920s and early 1930s. The working layout measuring 32 feet by 72 feet is not just a model railway but a grand trans-port complex which includes models of stations, bridges, trains, buses, barges, boats, the River Liffey and the Hill of Howth.

Around Malahide
A town 3 miles (5 km) west of Malahide is Swords, the site of a sixth-century monas-tery founded by St Colmcille (no trace remains). Swords Castle, a large irregular pentagon built about 1200, is at the northern end of the town. Also of interest is the 75-foot high round tower in the grounds of the Protestant church. An old church tower near by is all that remains of a medieval church.

At the village of Lusk, 5 miles (8 km) north of Swords, is a round tower and an ancient church. About 2 miles (3 km) east is Rush, a quiet family seaside resort and market-gardening centre. Facilities include golf (9), at Rush and golf (18) at Corballis. Lambay Island, 3 miles (5 km) offshore, is a noted bird sanctuary (for permission to visit apply to the Steward, Lambay Island, Rush, County Dublin).

Donabate

Newbridge House near Donabate in north County Dublin is an important eighteenth-century house designed by Richard Castle for the then Archbishop of Dublin, Dr Charles Cobbe. The house was completed in 1740 and a wing added in 1756 contains the important large drawing-room; the house has one of the finest Georgian interiors in Ireland with plasterwork attributed to Richard Williams.

The house is set on 350 acres of parkland and has been fully restored. Each room open to the public has its own style of antique furniture. Downstairs there is an antique kitchen and laundry, a craft shop and a restaurant. Facilities also include a 29-acre traditional farm stocked with native Irish animals.

Howth

Beann Eadair (Edar's Peak)

Pop. included in Dublin city.

Howth is a popular beauty spot and health resort, 9 miles (15 km) from the centre of Dublin city. Howth Harbour was the scene of the dramatic landing of arms for the Irish Volunteers from the *Asgard* in 1914.

Things to do

There is golf (18) and two other courses near by; bathing from a number of beaches, coves and rock pools. Motorboats and rowing boats are available for trips in the harbour and to Ireland's Eye, a little island a mile (2 km) offshore—a favourite picnicking haunt.

Points of interest

In the town are the interesting ruins of Howth Abbey and the sixteenth-century Howth College. Howth Castle, a baronial mansion dating from 1654, incorporates part of an earlier building. The beautiful gardens attract many visitors, especially when the rhododendrons and azaleas are in bloom. In the demesne (which is open to the public) is a massive dolmen called 'Aideen's Grave' and the ruined square tower of Corr Castle (probably sixteenth century).

The Hill of Howth (560 feet) forms the northern horn of the crescent of Dublin Bay. Buses run to the summit of this rocky promontory, and the hill is encircled by pleasant pathways. A cairn on the summit is the reputed burial ground of Criffan, High King of Ireland at the beginning of the Christian era. There are fine views from the path above the cliffs which bound the hill on three sides. On the north side is the Baily Lighthouse, on the site of an ancient fortress. Walking from Sutton to the Baily the visitor passes the tiny church of St Fintan (possibly ninth century or later).

Around Howth

Five miles (8 km) north of Howth (9 miles/ 15 km from Dublin) is the popular little seaside resort of Portmarnock, which has a magnificent 3-mile (5 km) sandy beach and a championship golf course.

Two miles (3 km) west of Portmarnock is St Doulagh's Church, an interesting building on the site of the anchorite cell of St Doulagh (seventh century). The present building includes the last anchorite cell built on the site. Next in date comes the chapel, with its high-pitched roof of stone. The tower, with its stepped battlements, is probably fourteenth century.

From early times the Catholic parish church was built against the north side of the cell and chapel. The present parish church (Church of Ireland), a rebuilding of 1864, occupies the same position and is still in use. A short distance north is the bapistery, a two-storey octagonal building with a vaulted stone roof, built over a well. Adjoining this is a small subterranean chamber covering a curious sunken bath (formerly called St Catherine's Pond) which remains permanently filled with water to a depth of about three feet.

Near by is St Doulagh's Lodge, which was the home of the landscape and seascape painter, Nathaniel Hone (1831–1917).

Dun Laoghaire

Dun Laoghaire (Leary's Fort)

Pop. 54,715 (borough).

Tourist information office: St Michael's Wharf.
Tel. (01) 2806984. Fax (01) 2806459.

D un Laoghaire (universally pronounced as 'dunleary') is a large residential town, shopping area and holiday resort, beautifully situated on the southern shore of Dublin Bay. Its magnificent harbour, terminus of the car ferry services from Holyhead, is sheltered by two fine piers.

Things to do

Bathing at the municipal baths, at Seapoint and Sandycove (1 mile/2 km), and at Killiney (3 miles/5 km). Golf (18), and other courses near by. Dun Laoghaire is Ireland's chief yachting centre and races are held regularly from May to September. The National Maritime Museum is situated at the Mariners' Church. Leopardstown racecourse, driving range and short golf course is 3 miles (5 km) away. Other entertainment includes the Lambert Mews Puppet Theatre and the Irish Cultural Institute, Culturlann na hÉireann, which presents a variety of traditional entertainment at Monkstown. Sport includes tennis, bowls and sea angling, and at Stillorgan ten-pin bowling.

History

Dun Laoghaire's name is derived from the fortress built there by a fifth-century king of Ireland. At the beginning of the last century it was a small fishing village. In 1834 the Dublin–Dun Laoghaire railway was opened, and with the completion of the harbour (in 1859) and the establishment of the mailboat service with Holyhead, the town developed rapidly. In 1821 its name was changed to Kingstown to commemorate the visit of George IV, but in 1920 the name of

Dalkey Island

Dun Laoghaire was restored. The town became a borough in 1930.

Around Dun Laoghaire

Two miles (3 km) north of Dun Laoghaire is Blackrock, with fine open-air seawater baths. At Sandycove, just south of Dun Laoghaire, is the Martello Tower where James Joyce once lived. Today it is open to the public as a Joyce museum. Two miles (3 km) south of Dun Laoghaire is the secluded and pleasant town of Dalkey. There are very fine views of Dublin Bay from Sorrento Terrace and Sorrento Park. The park contains a monument to the Elizabethan lutanist and composer, John Dowland, who was born at Dalkey. There are remains of two of the seven castles which guarded the town and harbour in medieval times. Dalkey Island, the largest of a group of rocky islands offshore, is crowned by a Martello tower and fragments of St Begnet's Oratory. Torca Cottage, on Dalkey Hill, was the home of George Bernard Shaw from 1866 to 1874.

Beyond Dalkey is Killiney. Killiney Bay, especially when viewed from the summit of Killiney Hill, is one of Ireland's most beautiful panoramas. Behind the crescent-shaped sweep of beach rises Bray Head and the pointed peaks of the Big and Little Sugarloaf overlooking the wooded Shanganagh Vale. Northwards the valley of the River Liffey can be seen, together with Dublin city and the bold headland of Howth. The summit of Killiney Hill is crowned by an obelisk erected in 1741. On the south side of the hill are the remains of the very ancient Killiney Church and near by is a curious collection of stones known as the 'Druid's Chair'. On the western slopes is Killiney golf course (18). Inland, at Sandyford, Fernhill Gardens are open to visitors in summer.

Wicklow

Powerscourt Waterfall

The county of Wicklow, just south of Dublin, has a great variety of scenery within its borders. It is known as the 'Garden of Ireland'. In the east the coastal area is low and sandy, except in a few places where it crops out in headlands; two of the country's main resorts, Arklow and Bray, are along this coast. Central Wicklow is a mass of domed granite mountains, penetrated by deep glens and wooded valleys; it contains some of the finest scenery in Ireland. To the west, the mountains give way to gentler country on the edge of the central plain.

Bray

Brí Cualann (The Hill of Cuala)

Pop. 25,101 (urban district).

Tourist information office (seasonal): Tel. (01) 2867128.

Bray is one of Ireland's biggest and longest-established seaside resorts. It has a safe beach of sand and shingle over a mile (2 km) long, and a setting dominated by Bray Head which spectacularly overlooks the town. Fronting the length of the beach is a spacious esplanade—a favourite strolling place during both day and evening. Between this esplanade and the road is a green sward that has facilities for mini-golf, a bandstand and other amusements. Bray is an excellent centre for touring the beauty spots of County Wicklow, and is near the cross-channel ferries at Dun Laoghaire and Dublin from Holyhead and Liverpool. The town is within the Dublin commuter belt and is served by the DART electric train service and a regular bus service from the city.

Things to do

Apart from the main beach, there is bathing at the North Strand. Rowing boats are for hire along the esplanade. Four golf courses are easily reached: a 9-hole course near the town, and 18-hole courses at Woodbrook (1 mile/2 km), Greystones (4 miles/ 6 km) and Delgany (5 miles/8 km). There is a new par-3 public golf course at Bray Head, and a bowling green at Failte Park a short distance from the beach. There is horse-racing at Leopardstown (6 miles/ 10 km). In the holiday season evening entertainments include dancing, cinemas and concerts. A feature of Bray is the variety of amusement centres offering games and carnival attractions.

The new National Aquarium on the esplanade has a wonderful variety of native and tropical fish on display. There is also a fine new bowling centre in the town.

The Bray Heritage Centre in the Town Hall contains many artefacts, records, maps and photographs dealing with the history of the town and its neighbourhood.

Bray Head

The resort's most prominent landmark rises steeply from the sea to a height of 791 feet. It is a colourful sight, as its covering of heather and gorse changes hue during the summer, and it provides splendid panoramic views for the visitor. The side of the head facing the town is a public park that covers 75 acres. The summit is reached from the end of the esplanade on foot by a path known as 'The

Dargle Glen Gardens

Powerscourt Gardens and the Great Sugarloaf

Great White Way', but the easiest way to reach the top is on the inland side, from the Greystones Road.

Also interesting is the cliff walk to Greystones, around the seaward side of the head. Ireland's oldest plant fossil, Old-hamia, is found along here.

Around Bray

About 2½ miles (4 km) west of Bray is a thickly wooded valley of great beauty, the Glen of the Dargle. A narrow pathway runs beside the River Dargle, a winding road follows the glen higher up, and the scenery alternates between wild grandeur and wooded beauty. A romantic feature is the Lover's Leap, a massive rock jutting out over the valley. Water from the Vartry Reservoir at Roundwood is carried across the glen in an aqueduct, supported at either end by castellated towers.

About 2 miles (3 km) south of Bray, at the foot of the Little Sugarloaf Mountain (1,120 feet), is Hollybrook, the estate of

the dashing eighteenth-century sportsman who is immortalised in the song 'Robin Adair'. The Brennanstown Riding School is at Hollybrook estate.

A mile (2 km) further on is the village of Kilmacanogue, under the Great Sugarloaf Mountain (1,654 feet). A road goes to within a short way of the summit, from which there are fine views over a wide area.

Enniskerry

Ath na Scairbhe (The Rugged Ford)

 Pop. 1,229.

Enniskerry, one of the prettiest villages in Ireland, lies in a wooded hollow among the hills west of Bray. Near by are Powerscourt demesne and the Glen of the Dargle.

Powerscourt

The 14,000-acre demesne lies astride the upper course of the River Dargle. The

Powerscourt Gardens

main drive runs by the river through plantations, rare shrubberies and a deer park with some fine herds of deer. The celebrated Powerscourt Waterfall, which tumbles obliquely over a cliff 400 feet high, is seen in its full magnificence after a rainy spell; it is the highest waterfall in these islands.

Powerscourt House itself was on the site of the former castle of the O'Tooles, Irish lords of Glencullen. The mansion, an imposing eighteenth-century building of hewn granite, was gutted by fire in 1974. The site is reached by a fine avenue nearly a mile (2 km) in length, and is on high ground with its sloping gardens adorned with statuary, tessellated pavements and ornamental lakes; in season there is a splendid display of rhododendrons. The demesne, gardens and armoury at Powerscourt are open daily from Easter to October. The waterfall may be visited all year, through its own gate which is 4 miles (6 km) from Enniskerry.

Glencree

West of Enniskerry, is a valley of rugged beauty that curves for 7 miles (11 km) from near the base of the Great Sugarloaf to the foot of Glendoo Mountain. Flowing through it is the Glencree River, which later becomes the Dargle. The glen was formerly covered by a primeval forest of

oak, and at one time was preserved by the English sovereign as a royal park.

The Glencree road runs west from Enniskerry for about a mile (2 km), then forks south-west along the northern slopes. At the head of the valley, about 1,100 feet above sea level, are the buildings which house a reconciliation centre for promoting understanding between the religious communities in Northern Ireland and between North and South. These were one of a series of barracks put up by the British Government along the Military road after the 1798 Rising. Near by, in a beautiful setting, is a small cemetery for German servicemen who died in Ireland during two World Wars.

About 2 miles (3 km) north of Enniskerry, the main road to Dublin passes through the Scalp—a spectacular rocky defile rising steeply on either side of the road, with huge granite boulders strewn about in wild confusion. It is a good example of a 'dry gap' formed at the end of the Ice Age, when streams from glaciers cut deep drainage channels.

The Wicklow Way

For the long-distance walker the well-signposted Wicklow Way stretches over the Dublin and Wicklow Mountains from the edge of the Dublin suburbs at Marlay Park, Ballinteer, to Moyne in County Wicklow, a distance of 57 miles (92 km).

Much of the route lies above 1,600 feet and follows rough sheep tracks, forest firebreaks and old bog roads. Raingear, windproof clothing and stout footwear are essential.

Greystones

Cloch Liath (Grey Stone)

Pop. 8,455.

Greystones is a seaside resort lying in a pleasantly wooded part of the Wicklow coast, south of Bray. It is also within the Dublin commuter belt which accounts for the large population increase in recent years.

Things to do

There is safe bathing from the long sand and shingle beach. Motorboats and rowing boats are for hire, and other activities include a cinema, tennis and badminton. There is golf (18) at Greystones itself, at Delgany (1½ miles/2 km) and a par-3 public course and driving range close to the South Beach. The Bray Harriers hunt in the surrounding district.

Around Greystones

Delgany, 1½ miles (2 km) to the south-west, is a pretty village in wooded surroundings. Near to it is the Glen of the Downs, where a nature trail has been laid out through the state forest. On the road south to Wicklow from Greystones are two quiet little villages, Kilcoole, home to the popular Irish TV series 'Glenroe', and Newcastle, each about a mile (2 km) from the sea. The shingle beaches south of Greystones provide excellent shore-angling. Newcastle was named after a fortress erected there in the thirteenth century to guard the Dublin–Wicklow highway and protect the English colony from raids by the O'Tooles and O'Byrnes.

Newtownmountkennedy, a few miles inland, is a village in attractive hilly country.

Ashford

Baile Mhic Cathaoir
(MacCathaoir's Town)

Ashford is a pretty village on the Dublin–Wicklow road. Close by is another village called Newrathbridge.

On the Newrathbridge side of Ashford along the valley of the River Vartry are the Mount Usher Gardens, with many varieties of trees, plants and shrubs, including subtropical species. The gardens are open to the public every day during the tourist season.

Around Ashford

About a mile (2 km) to the north-west is the Devil's Glen. This well-known beauty spot is a deep chasm whose craggy sides are covered with trees and shrubs. On entering the glen the Vartry River falls nearly a hundred feet into the 'Devil's Punchbowl', a deep basin in the rock below. Walks have been built at a considerable height, and there are fine views from them and from the winding pathways around the glen. In the 1798 Rising an insurgent group led by Joseph Holt took refuge here. The Tiglin Adventure Centre at Devil's Glen offers training in a variety of outdoor activities. Among the many other glens and mountain hollows of the district, the most notable is Dunran Glen. It has several fantastic rock formations, including the 'Bishop's Rock' which is in the shape of a mitre.

Horse-riding can be enjoyed at a number of equestrian centres in the area.

Wicklow

Cill Mhantain
(The Church of St Mantan)

Pop. 5,847 (urban district).

Tourist information office: Tel. (0404) 69117.

Wicklow, a seaside resort that is also the county town, stands on the lower slopes of Ballyguile Hill. It overlooks a wide bay fringed by a crescent curve of coast.

St Mantan, after whose church the town is named, lived at the time of St Patrick (fifth century). Long after him the town was occupied by the Danes, who called it Wykinglo and made it one of their main maritime bases on the east coast. After the Anglo-Norman invasion in the twelfth century, Wicklow was included in the large grants of land made by Strong-bow to Maurice Fitzgerald. From then until the seventeenth century the town was repeatedly attacked, as the O'Tooles and O'Byrnes contended with the English for it.

The old town of narrow streets has been considerably modernised, but still keeps much of its old-world atmosphere.

Things to do
A sand and shingle beach stretches for several miles north from the town. It is backed by a fine stretch of sward called the Murrough. The nearest golf course (9) is on the south side of the town; Blainroe golf course (18) is 4 miles (6 km) south of Wicklow. There are facilities for indoor sports and games provided by a number of clubs, and a cinema. The bay has good sea fishing, and some streams in the area hold small brown trout. Sailing is a popular pastime with Wicklow people, and a regatta is held early in August. Wicklow Sailing Club provides facilities for visiting yachtsmen.

The Black Castle
Is a ruin standing on a rocky promontory at the eastern end of the town. The castle was begun by Maurice Fitzgerald when he was granted the district in 1176, but his death a year later delayed its completion. In 1375 the castle was strengthened by William Fitzwilliam, whose decendants held the constableship for several generations. The castle was frequently attacked by the Irish and sometimes occupied by them. Early in the sixteenth century it was held by the O'Byrnes, but they had to surrender it, with the town, to the forces of the Crown in 1543. Luke O'Toole invested the fort-ress in 1641, but was forced to raise the siege when the army of Sir Charles Coote arrived.

Other points of interest
Some remains of a Franciscan Friary may be seen in the grounds of the parish priest's house. Founded by one of the Fitzgeralds

in the thirteenth century, it later came under the patronage of the O'Byrnes. After the dissolution of the monasteries at the time of the Reformation, the building became a courthouse; later it was used as a store for war equipment. The heritage centre in the modern courthouse provides a genealogical service and has some interesting artefacts relating to the history of the town.

The Church of Ireland parish church, though itself a late structure, has an interesting Norman doorway in the south porch and an ancient stone font. In Market Square, the 1798 Memorial remembers Wicklowmen who fought in this and later struggles; it consists of a life-size figure of a pikeman. On Kilmantan Hill is Wicklow Gaol (now disused); Billy Byrne of Ballymanus, a leader of the 1798 Rising, was among those imprisoned in it (see Aughrim, County Wicklow). In Fitzwilliam Square is the Halpin Monument, an obelisk of polished granite. This commemorates Captain Robert C. Halpin (1836–1894), a Wicklowman who commanded the *Great Eastern*, the ship that laid the first cable across the Atlantic.

Around Wicklow
Two miles (3 km) south is Wicklow Head, which has fine views; its three lighthouse towers are a curious feature. A little further on, the Silver Strand is a popular sandy beach surrounded by cliffs. Six miles (10 km) to the south of Wicklow is Jack's Hole, a secluded little seaside place with wide smooth sands. Just beyond is Brittas Bay, where there is a 3-mile (5 km) stretch of sandy beach backed by dunes, very popular with Dubliners.

Arklow
Inbhear Mor (Broad Estuary)

Pop. 7,992 (urban district).

Tourist information office (seasonal): Tel. (0402) 32484.

Arklow, one of the main seaside resorts on the east coast, is beautifully situated at the mouth of the River Avoca, in the extreme south of County Wicklow. Fishing and shipping are traditional here. The yacht that Sir Francis Chichester brought around the world, Gipsy Moth III, was built in an Arklow shipyard. The town's famous pottery products are exported worldwide.

Things to do

Splendid beaches stretch north and south of the town. There is a swimming pool and a well-equipped sport and leisure centre. There is a golf course (18) beside the South Strand, and at Woodenbridge (9) (5 miles/ 8 km). There is a cinema and dancing available. Conducted tours of the potteries take place at 3 p.m. on weekdays, or by appointment. Arklow Maritime Museum is open every day during the summer months.

History

The first Christian missionary to Ireland, Palladius, landed in the Arklow area in A.D. 430, and there is also a tradition that St Patrick landed here. Later the town became an important centre in the coastal territory held by the Danes of Dublin, and the present English name is a relic of this period. After the Anglo-Norman invasion in the twelfth century, Arklow was included in land granted to the invaders by Henry II. Later it was granted by King John to Theobald Fitzwalter, Lord Butler of Ireland. During the wars of 1641 the Wicklowmen captured and held the castle of Arklow, which Cromwell seized on passing through the town in 1649. In 1798 the decisive battle of the Rising was fought at Arklow, when the insurgents were defeated by British forces under General Needham.

Points of interest

The 1798 Memorial, in front of the Catholic parish church, is a statue of Father Michael Murphy, who was killed while leading the insurgents at the Battle of Arklow. In a field adjoining the parish priest's house are remains of a Dominican Friary founded in 1264. St Saviour's Church (Church of Ireland) was built in 1900 and is a fine example of Gothic Revival architecture. It has a good three-light window by Harry Clarke, one of Ireland's best-known stained-glass artists of this century. Along the South Strand past the golf course is Arklow Rock (415 feet), which has fine

Window at St Saviour's Church, Glendalough

views; on it is Our Lady's Well, which has a long tradition of veneration.

Around Arklow

Two miles (3 km) to the north-west is Shelton Abbey, formerly the residence of the Earls of Wicklow and now a state forestry school. The demesne is noted for its rhododendrons.

The Vale of Avoca and the Croghan valley are easily reached from Arklow.

The Military Road

The Wicklow Mountains were for centuries the strongholds of the unsubdued O'Tooles and O'Byrnes, and even down

Lough Dan

until 1803 a leader of the 1798 Rising, Michael Dwyer, was able to remain at large among them. It was to make these mountain strongholds accessible to the British Army that the Military road was

View from the Military Road near the Sally Gap

built after 1798. It runs from Rathfarnham, just south of Dublin, to Aghavannagh, and today it opens up the beauties of the central Wicklow area to the visitor. Relics of the road's original purpose are the

block-houses that can be seen at several points along the route.

From Rathfarnham the road rises steeply, with fine views back over the city of Dublin, until it levels out to pass across the boggy plateau of the Featherbed. As it approaches Kippure Mountain (2,475 feet), the road looks down on two mountain tarns, Upper Lough Bray and Lower Lough Bray. A little beyond is the source of the River Liffey, which meanders down the mountain slopes into County Kildare and then flows northwards to enter County Dublin near the County Kildare village of Leixlip. The length of its winding course to the sea at Dublin is 80 miles (129 km).

From the source of the River Liffey the road climbs upwards to Sally Gap (1,631 feet), a watershed in the hills between Kippure and Djouce Mountain (2,385 feet). From here the Military road continues for several miles through bleak moorland. From this wilderness it suddenly turns into Glenmacnass, a beautiful valley walled in by towering mountains through which the Glenmacnass River flows to join the Avonmore. The waterfall at the northern end of the glen is best seen when approached from the direction of Laragh.

An alternative way to Laragh from Sally Gap is through Roundwood. There is an ESB power station on the right-hand side of the road at Turlough Hill. The road follows the Cloghoge River which joins Lough Tay and Lough Dan. Lough Tay (or Luggala), with its wooded shores and precipitous mountain walls, has the air of a romantic retreat. Lough Dan, fed by several streams, is a long sheet of water in a hollow between mountains. In the hills near by a 1798 leader called Joseph Holt evaded capture long after the defeat of the insurgent forces.

A few miles east of Lough Dan is Roundwood, an attractive village, a horse-riding and angling centre on the banks of the Vartry River; it is claimed that it is the highest village in Ireland. Between Roundwood and Laragh is the pretty village of Annamoe, in pleasant wooded surroundings on the banks of the Annamoe River. Annamoe is associated with a remarkable adventure of the youthful Laurence Sterne. 'It was in this parish during our stay that I had the wonderful escape of falling through a mill-race whilst the mill was going, and of being taken out unhurt. The story is incredible, but known for truth in all that part of Ireland, where hundreds of people flocked to see me.' The ruins of the mill are still to be seen. At the Annamoe Leisure Park and Trout Farm there is fun for all the family, with the possibility of catching a trout for tea.

At Laragh, several glens converge and roads from north, south, east and west meet. Westward stretches Glendalough. South of Laragh the Military road again climbs into the hills, and then drops into the valley of Glenmalure at Drumgoff,

where the ruin of one of the military block-houses stands.

Glenmalure is a place of wild beauty, flanked by mountains which culminate on the western side in the great mass of Lugnaquilla (3,039 feet), the second highest mountain in Ireland. There is a fine drive up the valley for about 9 miles (14 km). The Avonbeg River, which rises on Table Mountain at the head of the valley, flows through Glenmalure to join the Avonmore at the 'Meeting of the Waters' near Avoca.

Glendalough

Glenmalure was once the heart of resistance to British rule in this region. Fiach MacHugh O'Byrne, the Wicklow chief who routed the army of Lord Deputy Gray here in 1580, had his stronghold at the eastern end of the glen at Ballinacor. The traditional site, marked by the remains of a series of stone walls, is still seen high on the side of Ballinacor Mountain.

The young Red Hugh O'Donnell was sheltered here after his escape from Dublin Castle in 1592. Glenmalure was also for a time the headquarters of Michael Dwyer. In the glen is a large boulder bearing inscriptions commemorating Fiach Mac-Hugh O'Byrne and Michael Dwyer.

From Glenmalure the Military road continues across the hills for 5 miles (8 km) to Aghavannagh, a wild and desolate valley hemmed in by mountains. Another of the military block-houses built here was later used as a shooting box by Charles Stewart Parnell. After Parnell's death, another political leader, John Redmond, bought it and used it as a residence. It is now a youth hostel.

Glendalough
Gleann Da Locha
(The Glen of the Two Lakes)

Glendalough is a valley celebrated equally for its beauty and for its historical and archaeological interest. The area also provides excellent rock-climbing, rough scrambling and ordinary hill walking. A visitor centre, located at the mouth of the valley, provides a unique opportunity to interpret the lives and times of the monks of Glendalough.

History
In the sixth century St Kevin came to Glendalough in search of solitude. For years he lived here as a hermit, sleeping sometimes in the hollow of a tree. In time, however, his sanctity and learning attracted many disciples to join him; Glendalough became a famous school of learning, inhabited by thousands of students from Ireland, Britain and Europe. When Kevin died at a great age in A.D. 618, Glendalough was only at the beginning of its fame. In the ruins lying around the shores of the two lakes, the history of the glen can be traced— its settlement by Kevin, its period of European renown, its vicissitudes in the plundering raids of the Danes and later in the strife between Wicklow chiefs and Anglo-Norman invaders, its final burning in 1398.

In the long line of abbots after Kevin, St Laurence O'Toole is an outstanding figure. Born in 1128, he became Abbot of Glendalough at the age of 25. In 1161 he was made Archbishop of Dublin, a position he held during the troubled period of the Anglo-Norman invasion. He was an able administrator who carried out a programme of reforms and set an example by the austerity of his life. In 1180 he fell ill during a journey to France to mediate between the English monarch and the deposed High King of Ireland. He died at Eu in Normandy, and was canonised in 1226.

Upper Lake
The earliest oratory mentioned in the life of Kevin is Teampall na Skellig (the Church of the Rock). It is on the south shore of the Upper Lake and has to be reached by hired boat. It stands on an artificially levelled platform that is approached by a flight of stone steps.

The building is about 25 feet by 14 feet on the inside. The west doorway is of large granite blocks, with inclined jambs, and the double-light east window is cut from a single stone. To the east of this oratory, in the cliff about 30 feet above the lake, is St Kevin's Bed. This is a tiny hole in the rock probably used by St Kevin during his period of solitude in the glen.

At the south-east corner of the Upper Lake, near the Glenealy River is the important ruin of Reefert Church (righfheart means Kings' burial place). This was a cemetery for the O'Tooles and for the ancient chiefs before them. The church consists of a nave and chancel joined by an arch. There are two small round-headed windows in the south wall of the nave, and a similar one in the east gable of the chancel. The foundations of the altar are still visible. A little to the west of this church is St Kevin's Cell—the ruin of a 'beehive' cell used by St Kevin after he built Reefert.

Beside the eastern shore is the ruin of a Bronze Age or even earlier stone fort, the Caher, which was long disused before St Kevin's time. Between Reefert and the

Round Tower and Cemetery, Glendalough

Lower Lake are five crosses which marked the boundary of the monastic lands. Later, when Glendalough was one of the four main pilgrimage centres of Ireland, they became station crosses on the pilgrim's way.

Lower Lake

The most important remains at Glendalough are the main group just east of the Lower Lake, together with those which are further east towards the mouth of the valley. This was the setting of the monastic city that grew up after St Kevin's time. The Gateway, chief entrance to the city, is the only surviving example in Ireland of an entrance to a primitive establishment. It has two round-headed arches of plain granite blocks. A flagged causeway leads through the enclosure. The Round Tower, still almost perfect after more than a thousand years is 103 feet high and 52 feet around the base.

To the west of the tower is what is perhaps the oldest church in this part of the valley, the Church of Our Lady (or St Mary's Church). Its main feature is the massive west doorway. St Kevin was buried here and his tomb was venerated until the eighteenth century.

Within the ancient cemetery is the Priest's House, so named because it was used during the Penal times as a burial place for local clergy. This attractive Hiberno-Romanesque building of the twelfth century has been partly reconstructed. There is some fine sculpturing on the arched recess on the outside of the east wall, and over the door is an interesting carving of great antiquity. Between this building and the cathedral is St Kevin's Cross, a plain granite structure dating from the sixth or seventh century.

The largest of the ruins at Glendalough is the Cathedral, which has many noteworthy architectural features. It consists of a nave and a chancel, with a small sacristy attached to the south side of the chancel. A gravestone in the chancel's north wall bears inscriptions in Irish and features carved crosses; another similar slab has a beautiful design of scroll foliage branching from its stem.

An interesting example of an Early Irish barrel-vaulted oratory is St Kevin's Church. It has a high-pitched stone roof, and some of the building may date from the time of St Kevin. However, the small round-tower belfry belongs to around the eleventh century. Originally a single-cell church, it was extended by the erection of a chancel (since destroyed), and a sacristy. It is now used to store the large number of carved slabs, capitals, bases, fragments of arches and other remains gathered from all over the valley.

Just outside the stone wall enclosing the chief group of buildings are the remains of the tiny St Ciaran's Church, discovered beneath a mound of earth and stones in 1875. It commemorates the founder of Clonmacnois. The remains are of a nave (19 feet by 4½ feet) and a chancel (9 feet by 9 feet).

Nearly a mile (2 km) east of the cathedral is the latest and most ornate of the Glendalough churches, St Saviour's Priory. It is said to have been founded by St Laurence O'Toole, but may in fact be even earlier. The buildings, reconstructed around 1875, consist of a nave and chancel with a small block of domestic buildings attached to the north side. The church contains many features of the Hiberno-Romanesque style of the twelfth century, notably the decorated chancel arch and the ornamental east window.

A short distance north-east of the cathedral, beside the road, is Trinity Church, said to have been the church of St Mocherog, grandson of Brachan, the King of Britain. It has a nave and chancel and, at the west end, the remains of a small vaulted chamber.

Rathdrum
Rath Droma (The Rath of the Ridge)

 Pop. 1,307.

This little town stands high on the western side of the beautiful Avonmore valley. It lies at the joining of several roads and so is a good touring centre. The Avonmore and Avonbeg Rivers hold numerous small brown trout. The Clara Funpark provides family entertainment.

Around Rathdrum
A mile (2 km) to the south is Avondale, best-known as the residence of Charles Stewart Parnell. The house was built in 1779 for Samuel Hayes, and many of the trees he planted on the 550-acre estate still stand. Today Avondale is a forestry school of the Department of Lands, and the house has been restored; it is open to the public during the season. A nature trail in the grounds is open daily all the year. On the outskirts of the town is the Parnell Memorial Park which includes a magnificent bronze sculpture of Parnell.

Three miles (5 km) south of Rathdrum is Whaley Abbey, residence in the eighteenth century of a noted Dublin 'blood' called Buck Whaley. He made a famous bet, which he won, that he would walk to Jerusalem and back within two years.

To the north-east, on the Wicklow road 5 miles (8 km) from Rathdrum, is the pretty village of Glenealy. Rising above it on the west side is Carrick Mountain (1,256 feet). An agriculture museum of old farm machinery is open during normal working hours.

The Vale of Avoca
Abhainn Mhor (Great River)

 Pop. 490.

There is not in this wide world a valley so
sweet
As that vale in whose bosom the bright
waters meet;
Oh! The last rays of feeling and life must
depart
Ere the bloom of that valley shall fade
from my heart.

Thomas Moore

Going south from Rathdrum, the Avonmore and Avonbeg Rivers join to form the Avoca River, about 3 miles (5 km) north of Avoca village; this is the famous Meeting of the Waters. Overlooking the scene is Castle Howard, from its imposing position on a cliff over the river's eastern bank. Near by is Tom Moore's tree, where the poet is said to have spent long hours in contemplation. Now it is a stark skeleton, railed off to save it from souvenir-hunters.

The Vale of Avoca is especially lovely in late spring, when drifts of white blossom from the wild cherry trees show bright against the green foliage. On either side of the valley the ground rises in little hills, culminating on the western side in a background of mountains. In the valley are valuable deposits of pyrites which were known in pre-Christian times; they contain ores of copper, lead, zinc and sulphur (no longer mined). In Avoca village a weaving centre is open to the public; its products are internationally renowned.

Around Avoca

Among the many walks or short drives from Avoca village are:

1. Go past the Catholic church and out via Sulphurbrook and Kilmacoo; turn left at Kilmacoo Cross, through Conary village; turn left at next crossroads to the Motte Stone, a glacial boulder of granite about 10 feet high by 14 feet by 10 feet,

Vale of Avoca

perched on the summit of a hill over 800 feet high. From the top of the stone there is an extensive view of the valley.

2. From Avoca village turn left at Ballygahan Garage up Red Road via Ballygahan and Ballymurtha. Keep right at Ballymurtha and follow Mines Road, meeting the main road again at Kilcashel (opposite White Bridge). The enormous Bell Rock gets its name from the bell that was rung there to call the miners to work.

Two miles (3 km) south of Avoca is Woodenbridge, a village prettily situated at the junction of three river valleys. It is where the Aughrim and Avoca Rivers form a second 'Meeting of the Waters'. There is golf (9) and a trout farm that is open to the public.

The Croghan Valley

The Croghan valley is a tranquil area of leafy glens, mountain streams and gentle rivers at the southern end of County Wicklow. The goldsmiths of ancient Ireland got much of their material from Croghan Mountain (2,000 feet), at the head of the Gold Mines River a few miles south-west of Woodenbridge. In 1796 a nugget was found there and this led to a gold rush in which 2,000 ounces were found within a few months.

Aughrim

Known as the Granite Village (because many of its buildings are of Wicklow Granite), 9 miles (14 km) south-west of Rathdrum and the same distance north-west of Arklow, is beautifully situated at the junction of several mountain valleys. There is fine scenery along the valley of the River Ow, which extends north-west of Aughrim for about 10 miles (16 km) to the foot of Lugnaquilla Mountain (3,039 feet). On the western slope of this valley, at Ballymanus, is the birthplace of Billy Byrne, an insurgent of 1798 (see Wicklow Town). The Rivers Aughrim, Ow and Derry hold numerous small brown trout.

Tinahely

Tinahely is 8 miles (13 km) south-west of Aughrim among the hills in the valley of the River Derry. The area was once part of the estates granted to Thomas Wentworth, Earl of Strafford, and near the village are the ruins of a mansion built by him. The village was destroyed in the 1798 Rising, but rebuilt shortly afterwards.

Shillelagh

This village, 5 miles (8 km) south of Tinahely, lies in a wooded valley almost surrounded by hills. The district was once covered by the extensive Shillelagh Wood, which was famous for its oaks (the oak roofing in St Patrick's Cathedral in Dublin came from here). To the east of the village is Coolattin Park, once the large estate of the Fitzwilliam family with its golf course (9). Near by also, at Aghowle, is an ancient church with a twelfth-century doorway and two small round-headed windows with Romanesque ornamentation. The Tinahely horse fair and agricultural show takes place in August each year.

Carnew

Situated 4 miles (6 km) beyond Shillelagh, Carnew is near the County Wexford border. Here you can see a seventeenth-century castle which is still used as a residence. In 1798 it was garrisoned by the British when the insurgents captured and set fire to the town. A monument commemorates 36 insurgents who were executed within the castle walls.

Blessington

Cros Bhaile Choimin
(Cross of Comyn's Town)

Pop. 1,322.

Blessington, a pleasant village of one wide tree-lined street, was built in the second half of the seventeenth century. It was granted a charter by Charles II and was once a place of importance on the mail coach route from Dublin to Waterford.

Around Blessington

On the eastern edge of the town is the northern arm of the large Pollaphuca Lake of the River Liffey hydroelectric scheme. In addition to supplying energy, the lake also provides Dublin with water. At high water the reservoir covers 5,320 acres. With its wooded promontories and background of mountains, it presents many beautiful views. The lake has excellent angling for large brown trout. Fishing passes may be had at tackle shops in Dublin, or Blessington. Right on the lakes and within a short distance of the town is the Lakeside Outdoor Pursuits Centre, which offers canoeing, hill walking, orienteering, pony-trekking and other activities. Two miles (3 km) south of Blessington is Russborough, a fine example of Georgian architecture housing the Sir Alfred Beit Art Collection (open to the public Sundays and public holidays Easter to October and additional days in summer).

Four miles (6 km) south of Russborough, Hollywood Glen stretches for about 1½ miles (2 km) between Church Mountain (1,789 feet) and lesser hills to the west. The glen is traditionally associated with St Kevin, who is said to have had his first hermitage here. There are fine panoramic views from the summit of Church Mountain.

About 3 miles (5 km) west of Hollywood Glen, on the Naas–Baltinglass road, is Dunlavin. This pleasant village is situated where the County Wicklow hill-country meets the limestone plain of County Kildare. On the County Kildare border, 4 miles (6 km) to the south-west, is an ancient cemetery called Cillin Chormaic (Cormac's burial-place).

Approached from Hollywood Glen by the village of Donard is the Glen of Imaal. This is a military training ground and the

Russborough House

notices erected by the Department of Defence should be observed. The River Slaney, rising on Lugnaquilla Mountain at the eastern end, is fed by numerous tributary streams as it winds through the glen.

On the southern side of the glen at Derrynamuck is the Dwyer-MacAllister Cottage, where Michael Dwyer and four companions were trapped by British forces on a night in 1799. After the attackers has set the cottage on fire, Sam MacAllister sacrificed his life to let Dwyer escape by opening the door and drawing the fire of the soldiers. The cottage has been restored and is preserved as a national monument.

To the west of the glen and 3 miles (5 km) south of Donard the Castleruddery Transport Museum is open to the public.

Baltinglass

Mainistir an Bhealaigh (Abbey of the Pass)

 Pop. 1,089.

Baltinglass is in a pleasant part of the Slaney valley, with Baltinglass Hill (1,258 feet) rising steeply above it on the east and slightly lower hills beyond the river to the west. On the summit of the hill are the remains of a large cairn containing a group of Bronze Age burial chambers. From the summit there is a very fine view over the surrounding country.

To the north are some remains of the Cistercian Abbey of Vallis Salutis. This was founded in the twelfth century by the King of Leinster, Dermot MacMurrough, who is said to have been buried here. When the abbey was suppressed its estates were given to Viscount Baltinglass, but they were lost by one of his descendants who participated in the unsuccessful Desmond Revolt during the reign of Queen Elizabeth I. A noteworthy feature of the abbey are the six Gothic arches on either side of the nave, supported by alternate round and square pillars.

There is brown trout fishing, mostly free, on the Slaney. Outside the town is a golf course (9).

Wexford

Dolmen at the Irish National Heritage Park, Ferrycarrig

ounty Wexford is in the south-eastern corner of the country, with a long coastline on both the Irish Sea and the Celtic Sea. On the north it is bounded by the hills of County Wicklow and on the west by the River Barrow and the Blackstairs Mountains. Its fertile central plain is watered by the River Slaney. Wexford's history goes back to pre-Christian times. Above all, the county is rich in memories of the 1798 Rising, when insurgent pikemen fought heroically against overwhelming odds. For the holidaymaker in Wexford there are the sandy beaches of many resorts, angling and canoeing on the River Slaney, climbing in the Blackstairs Mountains, and golf and hunting in several parts of the county.

Gorey

Guaire (Ancient pagan king)

Pop. 2,445.

Tourist information office (seasonal): Tel. (055) 21248.

orey, which is situated midway between Dublin and Wexford, is an ideal centre for the holiday-maker who wishes to gain easy access to the numerous beaches of the area. The town has a modern layout and is an ideal shopping centre. Molumney Art Centre is open daily in summer. At the western end of the town is Gorey Hill (418 feet), a camping place of the 1798 insurgents before their march on Arklow. At the end of the town near the hill is the 1798 Memorial, a granite cross of Celtic design. A few miles to the north-east is Tara Hill (833 feet), another good vantage point for views of the surrounding country. Three miles (5 km) east of Gorey is Ballymoney, a little holiday resort with an excellent sandy beach. About 6 miles (10 km) south of Gorey are the secluded coves of Ardamine and Pollshone. At Ardamine is a little church by George Edmund Street, who designed the London Law Courts and restored Christ Church Cathedral in Dublin. Further south is Cahore, a small village with an extensive sandy beach.

Courtown Harbour

Courtown, 4 miles (6 km) from Gorey, is a popular family resort with a fine sandy beach 2 miles (3 km) long with amuse-ments and golf (18) on a wide sweep of coast called Courtown Bay. The village has grown up around the harbour, which was completed about 1830. There are many charming walks in the surrounding countryside.

Bunclody

Bun Clóidí (The mouth of the River Clody)

unclody is a small picturesque town nestling in the foothills of Mount Leinster and is a convenient starting point for climbing in the Blackstairs Mountains. It is here that the River Slaney enters County Wexford and is joined by the little River Clody. There is excellent fishing in the Slaney. Tennis and an open-air swimming pool are available to visitors.

In 1577 the town's name was changed to Newtownbarry, after a sheriff of Dublin who was its patron, but in recent times the original name has been restored. In 1798 insurgents under Father Kearns attacked Bunclody in an unsuccessful attempt to open communications with their comrades in Carlow and Wicklow.

Around Bunclody

At Kilmyshall, 2 miles (3 km) to the south, is the grave of Eileen Booth of Clonmullen Castle, who is said to have inspired the song 'Eileen Aroon', which Handel said he would rather have written than all his oratorios.

Ferns

This village was once the capital of Leinster. The see of Ferns was founded in the sixth century by St Maodhog (or Mogue). The religious settlement and the town which grew around it were often plundered by the Danes. In the twelfth century the King of Leinster, Dermot MacMurrough, made Ferns his capital and founded the abbey there. After the Anglo-Norman invasion the town declined, and in 1406 the episcopal see was transferred to New Ross.

Ferns Castle, the finest of its kind in Ireland, is a large rectangular keep with circular towers at three of the angles. The main part of the building measures 80 feet by 60 feet, and the towers (there were originally four) are nearly 30 feet across. The windows in the upper parts of the walls have graceful trefoil pointed heads.

On the first floor of the south-eastern tower is the remarkable circular chapel, a beautiful example of thirteenth-century architecture. It is covered by a vault carried by moulded ribs that spring from corbels in the form of capitals with short shafts. There are three single windows. It is not known when the castle was erected, or by whom. There was a manor and castle here in 1232, but the architecture of the chapel and the windows of the keep belong to later in the thirteenth century, when the castle was held by William de Valence.

The castle is on the site of the ancient fortress of the kings of Leinster, and was for a long time the residence of the bishops of the diocese. It suffered severely from attacks made by the Irish, and was finally dismantled by Sir Charles Coote in 1641.

The Augustinian Abbey was founded by Dermot MacMurrough, probably on or near the site of the primitive oratory of St Mogue. The abbey was burned down in 1154, but MacMurrough rebuilt it in 1160 and died there in 1171. The remains consist of a tower built in two stages (the lower stage square and the upper stage round), the north wall of the church and the priests' residential apartments.

The only remains of the Cathedral are the ruined chancel and some fragments of the piers of a nave arcade, which are built into the walls of the modern building now used as a parish church and cathedral. On each side of the chancel is an arcade of five lancet windows. The interior has interesting sculptures. In the graveyard is part of the decorated shaft of a cross that is said to mark the grave of Dermot MacMurrough.

Around Ferns
In the graveyard on the high ground outside the village is St Peter's Church, probably of the sixteenth century. The ruins consist of nave and chancel. There is a Romanesque window in the south wall of the chancel, with a round-headed arch internally and a lancet arch externally. The internal part appears to have been taken from the Augustinian abbey, the outer part—and the two lancets in the east gable—from the ruins of the cathedral.

About 5 miles (8 km) south-east of Ferns is the village of Boolavogue, where the burning of a Catholic chapel precipitated the insurrection in Wexford in 1798. Father John Murphy, the curate, took command of a body of the insurgents and led them in various engagements until the defeat at Vinegar Hill, after which he was captured and executed.

Enniscorthy
Inis Córthaidh (Rock Island)

Pop. 4,127 (urban district).

Tourist information office (seasonal): Tel. (054) 34699.

Enniscorthy, a thriving market town (pottery is a speciality of the area), is in a very picturesque part of the Slaney valley, on steeply sloping ground on both banks of the river. The River Slaney is navigable up to this point, and there is much river traffic with Wexford. Enniscorthy was the object of many attacks in the centuries following the Anglo-Norman invasion. It was also a storm centre of the 1798 Rising. Vinegar Hill offers a wonderful view of the surrounding countryside and the river. The annual Strawberry Fair takes place in late June/early July. Golf (18).

Enniscorthy Castle

Points of interest
Enniscorthy Castle, a square towered keep rebuilt about 1586, is in perfect preservation

and is now a folk museum which is open to the public. The original castle here may have been erected by Raymond le Gros. Later it came into the hands of the Mac-Murrough Kavanaghs, who granted it to the Franciscan monastery. After the suppression of the monasteries the castle and lands were held by a succession of owners, including the poet Spenser. The castle was damaged by Cromwell's guns in 1649. During the 1798 Rising it was used as a prison, and in the nineteenth century it was restored for use as a residence.

On a commanding site overlooking the Slaney is St Aidan's Cathedral, a Gothic Revival building of the 1840s designed by Pugin. In Market Square is the 1798 Memorial by Oliver Sheppard, R.H.A.—a bronze representation of Father Murphy and a pikeman. In Abbey Square is a memorial to Seamus Rafter, a commandant of 1916.

At the eastern edge of the town is Vinegar Hill (390 feet), where the Wexford pikemen made their last stand in June 1798 against the British generals Lake and Johnson. The insurgents' defeat ended major resistance in Wexford.

Around Enniscorthy
The journey to Wexford by road or river has many pleasant views, and some bends of the river are particularly fine. The last stages lie through the Barony of Shelmalier, which has always had a population of net-fishermen and fowlers. The 'bold Shelmalier' with his long-barrelled duck-gun was a formidable marksman in the Wexford insurgent army. He is commemorated in many ballads. West of Enniscorthy are the Blackstairs Mountains (highest point Mount Leinster, 2,610 feet), which form part of the boundary between the counties of Wexford and Carlow. There is interesting climbing and ridge-walking. At the foot of the mountains is the village of Killann, home of the youthful insurgent Captain John Kelly who is celebrated in the ballad 'Kelly, the boy from Killann'. His monument in Killann graveyard is a cross of Celtic design.

Crannog, Irish National Heritage Park, Ferrycarrig

Wexford

Loch Garman (The Loch of Garman)

 Pop. 9,537 (borough).

i Tourist information office:
Crescent Quay, Wexford.
Tel. (053) 23111.

National Heritage Park, Ferrycarrig,
Wexford (seasonal): Tel. (053) 41911.

✉ Post Office:
Anne St, Wexford. Tel. (053) 22123.

Ⓡ Parking Regulations: Disc parking.

🚉 🚌 Railway Stations/Bus Depot:
O'Hanrahan Station, Wexford.
Tel. (053) 22522.

🚗 Car Hire: Avis Rent a Car,
Rosslare Harbour, Co. Wexford.
Tel. (021) 965045.

Hertz Rent a Car, P.O. Box 23, Ferrybank,
Wexford. Tel. (053) 23511.

South East Budget Rent a Car, Terminal
Building, Rosslare. Tel. (053) 33318.

🚲 Bicycle Hire: Rent a Bike,
Goulding St, Rosslare Harbour.

The Bike Shop, 9 Selskar St, Wexford.
Tel. (053) 22514.

Hayes Cycle Shop, 108 South Main St,
Wexford. Tel. (053) 22462.

🎭 Dates of principal cultural
events/festivals:
Wexford Opera Festival (October).

Wexford, the county town, is
picturesquely situated where the
River Slaney enters Wexford
Harbour. It is an ancient town of narrow,
winding streets.

Things to do
Fishing and boating may be enjoyed in the
harbour, with golf (18), tennis and other
sports provided for by local clubs. There is
a cinema and dancing in the hotels. There
is horse-racing at Bettyville Racecourse.
Walking tours each evening in summer are
conducted by members of the Old
Wexford Society, starting from the local
hotels. The annual Wexford Festival at the
end of October is an international operatic
occasion. The Wexford Arts Centre has
year-round exhibitions, recitals and poetry
readings.

West Gate Heritage Centre in the
restored thirteenth-century gate tower (part
of the Viking/Norman walls) provides an
audio-visual display of the history of
Wexford during the season.

History
On the second-century map of Ptolemy the
site of Wexford is marked Menapia, after a
Belgic tribe which is believed to have
settled here in prehistoric times. The Irish
name, Loch Garman, is so old that its
origin was disputed even in early Christian
times. The modern English name comes
from Waesfjord ('the harbour of the mud
flats'), which was what the Viking sea-
rovers called the settlement they
established here.

Wexford was taken by the Normans
soon after their landing in 1169 at Bannow
some 20 miles (32 km) away. In 1649
Cromwell captured it and massacred the
inhabitants. In 1798 it was taken by the
insurgents and held for nearly a month.

Points of interest
There were originally five fortified
gateways in the town walls—only one of
them, Westgate Tower, still stands. Near
by is the ruin of Selskar Abbey, dedicated
to St Sepulchre. The present Protestant
church of St Selskar is on the site of the
old abbey choir, and the ancient
battlemented tower is now used as a vestry
room and belfry.

Wexford

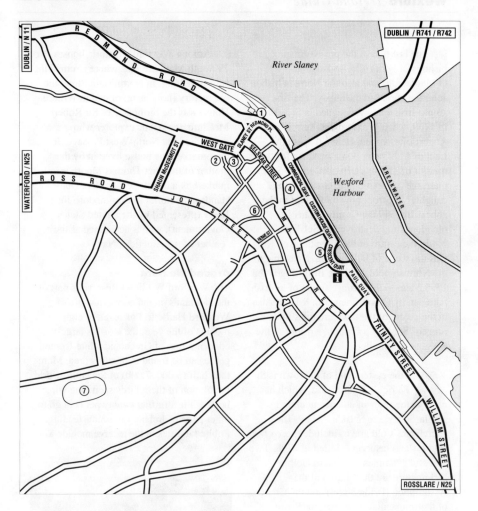

1. O'Hanrahan Station
2. Westgate Tower
3. Selskar Abbey
4. Bull Ring
5. Maritime Museum
6. Town Hall
7. Wexford Park

The last two of the pre-Norman bishops of Ferns (O hAodha and O Maolaoidh) and also the Norman bishop John are buried in the abbey. The first Anglo-Irish treaty was signed in St Selskar's in 1169, when Wexford was surrendered to Robert Fitzstephen. Henry II spent the Lent of 1172 here, doing penance for the murder of Thomas à Becket. In 1175 the marriage of Raymond le Gros and the daughter of Strongbow took place in the abbey. In 1649 the Cromwellians plundered and destroyed St Selskar's.

In the centre of the town the Bull Ring was the scene of bull-baiting, a pastime of the Norman nobles. In the Bull Ring is the 1798 Memorial, a bronze figure of an Irish pikeman by Oliver Sheppard, R.H.A. Also in the centre of the town are the slight ruins of St Mary's Church, a priory of the Knights Hospitallers.

At the eastern end of the town is St Patrick's Churchyard, which has the ruins of an ancient church similar in style to Selskar Abbey. The churchyard's old graves include those of soldiers and insurgents killed in 1798. Two graceful examples of modern Gothic architecture are the Church of the Assumption (Bride Street) and the Church of the Immaculate Conception (Rowe Street). The foundation stones of these twin churches were laid on the same day in 1851. Their spires are 230 feet high.

In John Street the Franciscan church is on the site of the first Franciscan friary in Wexford, founded in the year 1230. The ceiling has some fine stucco work and beneath the altar is the reliquary of St Adjutor, a boy martyr of ancient Rome. In a glass case is a wax figure containing the remains of the saint, and there is also a phial of his blood. (Visitors may apply to see the reliquary at the door of the Friars' convent.) St Adjutor was brought up in the Christian faith by his mother, unknown to his pagan father. When the father did find out, he killed his son with an axe.

Among Wexford's historic houses, No. 29 South Main Street is where Cromwell stayed in 1649. In North Main Street the old rectory (now incorporated in White's Hotel) was the birthplace of Sir Robert McClure, the Arctic explorer who discovered the North-West Passage. In Cornmarket, the house lived in by the mother of the poet Thomas Moore is marked by a tablet. On Crescent Quay stands a memorial to Commodore John Barry (presented by the United States Government), who is acclaimed as the 'Father of the American Navy'.

Around Wexford

The Wexford Wildfowl Reserve is part of the sloblands on the northern shore of Wexford Harbour. For seven to eight months of the year, the world's largest concentration of Greenland white-fronted geese can be found in this tiny area. More than half (6,000–7,000) of the entire world population of these birds spend the winter here, while a further twenty per cent go to other parts of Ireland for winter feeding. Public facilities in the reserve include a

Johnstown Castle

screened approach, car park and picnic area, observation tower, lecture hall, laboratory and library. Close to this reception area a collection has been established of a variety of species of duck, geese and swans which frequent the slobs.

Three miles (5 km) south of Wexford is Johnstown Castle, built in the thirteenth century by the Anglo-Norman Esmonde family. It was dismantled by Cromwell and sold by one of his soldiers to John Grogan of Yorkshire in 1683. In 1944 it was presented to the nation for use as an agricultural college and soil research centre. The Irish Agricultural Museum at Johnstown has a fine collection of Irish agricultural tools and farming implements on display. The gardens and museum are open to visitors on weekdays throughout the year.

The 'English Baronies' of Forth and Bargy extend south from Wexford, taking in the whole of the coast from Wexford Harbour to Bannow Bay. This was the first area in Ireland to be settled by the Anglo-Normans, and it has many well-preserved castles as well as ruined abbeys and churches. Until comparatively recent times the people of the baronies spoke a dialect (Yola) in which many Early English words and forms were preserved. The men of Forth and Bargy were a formidable contingent in the Wexford insurgent army of 1798.

On the north bank of the Slaney 3 miles (5 km) from Wexford is Ferrycarrig, where the river narrows from a wide and calm lake into a rapid torrent passing through wooded heights. High on a rocky spur is a massive fifteenth-century keep that was built on the site of a castle of Robert Fitzstephen, the first Norman invader of Ireland. On the opposite bank is a modern round tower that commemorates Wexford men killed in the Crimean War.

The National Heritage Park at Ferrycarrig, on a 30-acre site overlooking the Slaney, depicts life in Ireland from Stone Age times, including full-size replicas of a mesolithic site, a dolmen, cist burial, ogham stone, early Christian site, crannog and Viking boathouse. There is also a replica of a Norman motte and bailey and a nature trail.

Seven miles (11 km) north-east of Wexford is the pretty seaside village of Curracloe, set on a wide bay backed to the north by low hills. There is a splendid

Agricultural Museum, Johnstown Castle

6-mile (10 km) long sandy beach, which shelves gently and is perfectly safe. A feature of the district is its neat whitewashed cottages with thatched roofs.

Rosslare

Ros Láir (The Middle Peninsula)

Pop. 704.

Tourist information office (seasonal): Rosslare Harbour (Kilrane). Tel. (053) 33232; Rosslare Terminal. Tel. (053) 33622. Fax (053) 33421.

Rosslare is a well-known seaside resort 11 miles (18 km) south-east of Wexford. Its wide bay is fringed by a 6-mile (10 km) arc of firm sand and shingle, with safe bathing at all stages of the tide. Golf (18). Five miles (8 km) south of Rosslare is Rosslare Harbour, terminus of car ferries from Fishguard and Le Havre, Cherbourg and Pembroke.

Around Rosslare

Four miles (6 km) to the west on the road to Wexford is the neat village of Killinick. At Mayglass, 3 miles (5 km) further south-west, are the ruins of a church built in 1798; on the north wall is a plaque commemorating the insurgent leader, Bagenal Harvey, who was buried there.

Near Carnsore Point to the south is the sea inlet called Lady's Island, which is joined to the mainland by a causeway. It has been a place of pilgrimage for centuries

Mesolithic campsite, Irish National Heritage Park, Ferrycarrig

and was the site of an ancient monastery dedicated to the Blessed Virgin. On the island are the ruins of an Augustinian priory and a twelfth-century Norman castle whose tower leans at a greater angle than the Tower of Pisa. Out to sea is the Tuskar Rock, where a lighthouse was erected in 1815. The light is visible for 19 miles (31 km).

Also near Carnsore Point are the remains of the ancient church and holy well of St Vogue (or Veoc), an Irish saint who died in Brittany in A.D. 585. At Carne there is an excellent sandy beach.

A short distance west of Lady's Island, at Ballysampson, Tacumshane is the birth-place of Commodore John Barry, 'father' of the American Navy. It has the only surviving working windmill in Ireland.

Kilmore Quay

This picturesque seaside village of thatched cottages is noted for its fishing industry. From the harbour there is a pleasing view over the flat coast stretching for miles eastwards. Kilmore has a

flourishing sea angling club and the waters in the area offer mackerel, sole, gurnard, ray and flatfish. The Maritime Museum is housed on board the lightship 'Guillemot', which is the last Irish Light vessel, complete with original cabin furniture, generators and fittings, while housing many original and unusual artefacts.

Around Kilmore Quay

The village is the point of departure for the Saltee Islands, Ireland's largest bird sanctuary. In a cave on one of the islands the insurgent leader Bagenal Harvey of

Cottage at Kilmore Quay

Bewley's Coffee Shop, Grafton Street, Dublin

Cheekpoint, in Waterford Harbour

St Canice's Cathedral, Kilkenny

Bargy Castle was captured after the Battle of Vinegar Hill.

North-west of Kilmore Quay is Cullenstown, a quiet little seaside place with an excellent sandy beach. Further along the coast is Bannow (scene of the first Norman landing in 1169), which was part of the original area granted by Dermot MacMurrough to Hervey de Monte Marisco, and the first corporate town built by the Normans. It was an important town even as late as the seventeenth century, but life eventually deserted it because of the sands which silted up the channel. It continued to return MPs representing a church and a chimney to the Irish Parliament until 1798. Today little remains of this lost Norman town.

Near the head of Bannow Bay is Clonmines, the site of an ancient town which is said to have had its own mint in Danish times (silver and lead were mined near by). Beside the river are the tower and walls of a fourteenth-century Augustinian church and the remains of Black Castle, a fortress of the Fitzhenrys. Another ruin near by is called the Cowboy's Chapel, built by a cowherd who became rich, as a memorial to his mother. North of Clonmines are the villages of Clongeen and Foulksmills, the scenes of encounters during the 1798 Rising. Longgraigue House near Foulksmills was the site of Sir John Moore's camp; from it he advanced to intercept fugitives from the Battles of New Ross and Enniscorthy.

A few miles south-west of Clonmines is Tintern Abbey, a residence incorporating remains of the abbey founded about 1200 by the Earl of Pembroke, William le Mareschal, who was shipwrecked here, in thanksgiving for his escape. It was occupied by monks from the Cistercian abbey of the same name in Wales. The present church and a bridge near by were built with masonry from the original abbey.

Fethard-on-Sea
Fiodh Ard (The High Wood)

This is a quiet little resort on the eastern side of the Hook Peninsula, convenient to many fine sandy beaches. The Hook Tower is probably the oldest lighthouse in Europe, built in the twelfth century. Amenities include all types of sea fishing, sub aqua and water sports. It was once a town of some importance, being made a borough in the reign of James II. Although the place was almost deserted at the time of the Act of Union in 1800, its owners received £15,000 to compensate for its disenfranchisement.

Around Fethard
There are some interesting remains of castles and churches in this district. About a mile (2 km) to the south is the rocky promontory of Baginbun, scene of the Anglo-Norman landing which preceded the main invasion force of 1170. The head is joined to the mainland by a narrow isthmus on which are earthworks which are probably the remains of an ancient fort.

Duncannon
Dun Conan (Conan's Fortress)

This is a pleasant seaside resort with a good sandy beach, on the eastern shore of Waterford Harbour.

On a rocky headland guarding the approach to the estuary is Duncannon Fort, covering an area of about three acres. This was the site of the prehistoric dun of Conan, after which the town was named. In the twelfth century it was selected for defensive purposes by the Anglo-Normans, and in 1588 the English government strengthened the fortifications as a precaution against the Spanish Armada. During the wars of the seventeenth century the fort was taken by the Confederate Catholics after a two-month siege. It was later defended against a Cromwellian force, and only surrendered in 1650 after the capitulation of Waterford.

From Duncannon, after his defeat by William at the Battle of the Boyne, James II took ship in 1690 for Kinsale, County Cork, before his final departure from Ireland. Two months later, William III also spent some days here before leaving for England.

Around Duncannon

On the Waterford shore of the harbour, opposite Duncannon, are the ruins of Geneva Barracks (see Tour of Waterford coast). About 2 miles (3 km) north of Duncannon are the two small fishing villages of Arthurstown and Ballyhack. Ballyhack Castle, once a preceptory of the Knights Templars, is an interesting ruin. There is a ferry between Ballyhack and Passage East on the Waterford shore.

New Ross

Ros Mhic Treoin
(The Wood of the Son of Tream)

Pop. 5,021 (urban district).

Tourist information office (seasonal): Tel. (051) 21857.

New Ross, on a steep hill overlooking the River Barrow, is one of the oldest towns in County Wexford. Its narrow winding streets give it a medieval appearance, and in some places they are stepped and so negotiable only by pedestrians. A long bridge across the river connects the main town with its suburb on the County Kilkenny side, Rosbercon. New Ross is an important inland port, connected with Dublin and the interior by the Barrow navigation and the Grand Canal.

Ballyhack

The Galley, New Ross

History

A monastery may have been founded here by St Abban in the sixth century, but the place was of little importance until the Anglo-Norman invasion. A new bridge across the river was built about 1200, and a little later the town was walled. About this time it became known as New Ross—Old Ross, to the east, was then a town of some significance.

New Ross was granted many royal charters and letters patent, and rivalled Wexford as a commercial centre. In 1643 it withstood a siege by the Duke of Ormonde, but fell to Cromwell six years later. In 1798 insurgent forces under Bagenal Harvey attacked it from Corbett Hill, after their peace envoy had been shot by the British garrison. Lord Mountjoy, who came to pacify the insurgents, was shot as a reprisal for the envoy's death. The insurgents triumphed after a fierce battle, but were surprised, as they celebrated their victory, by a relief force under General Johnson. They were driven from the burning town and suffered heavy losses.

Points of interest

St Mary's Abbey, founded in 1212 on the site of the sixth-century church of St Abban, was used for religious services until 1811. The nave was then taken down to make room for the present Protestant church. In the graveyard is a cenotaph of Isabella de Clare (died 1220) and the tomb of Peter Butler (died 1599). In the modern church

are some mural monuments to the Tottenham family, several of whom represented the town in the Irish Parliament.

Housing the municipal offices is the Tholsel, erected in 1749 and rebuilt because of subsidence in 1806. It is on the site where the market cross of the medieval town was erected in 1320. A clock tower with a fine cupola rises from the centre of the building, and inside are preserved the maces of Edward III and Charles II, the original charter of James II and three volumes of the minutes of the old corporation. At the Tholsel is the 1798 Memorial, a statue of a 'croppy boy'.

Around New Ross

New Ross is an excellent centre for exploring the fine river scenery of the Nore and Barrow valleys, by land or water. The River Nore may be ascended to Woodstock and Inistioge, and the Barrow to St Mullins and Graiguenamanagh. Another interesting trip is down the estuary to Waterford, or to Dunbrody. Lunch and dinner are served on board cruisers which serve these routes.

Golf (9) at Tinnerany, 1 mile (2 km) west of town.

At Dunganstown near New Ross is the cottage which was the birthplace of the great-grandfather of John Fitzgerald Kennedy, President of the United States from 1961 to 1963. Near by on Slieve Coilte is the John F. Kennedy Memorial Arboretum and Forest Park (open to visitors). It is a tribute to the life-work of President Kennedy from United States citizens of Irish origin.

Near the village of Campile, 8 miles (13 km) south of New Ross, is Dunbrody Abbey. This was built in 1182 by the monks of St Mary's Abbey in Dublin. The abbey had the right of sanctuary and became known as the Monastery of St Mary of Refuge. It became an important house whose abbot was a lord of parliament. The last abbot was

Alexander Devereux, who was made Bishop of Ferns in 1537.

The extensive ruins are among the finest in Ireland. The church is of the usual cruciform type, with nave, aisles, choir and transepts, with a low tower rising from the intersection. It is 200 feet long and 140 feet broad at the transepts. Joining each transept are three chapels, vaulted and groined, each having a narrow one-light window. Adjoining the south transept is a vaulted chamber that was probably the sacristy; another dark chamber off it may have been the repository of the church plate.

Other interesting features include the fine lancet east window of three lights, the lavishly ornamented west door, and the rows of early pointed arches which separate the nave from the aisles. There are also some remains of the monastic buildings. Of the approaches to the abbey, a small square tower on the east side and a Gothic archway on the west still remain.

Five miles (8 km) east of New Ross is the tiny village of Old Ross. Though important in ancient times, its development was checked by the growth of New Ross near by. The old castle of Ross was one of those seized by 'Silken Thomas' Fitzgerald during his rebellion against Henry VIII.

Two miles (3 km) south-east of Old Ross is Carrickbyrne Hill (769 feet), an insurgent camp for some days before the Battle of New Ross. At the foot of it was Scullabogue House, where about a hundred prisoners of the insurgents perished by fire after the defeat at New Ross.

Near Carrickbyrne, at Carrigadaggin, is a granite column memorial to Sir Ralph Abercromby, British commander-in-chief in the period before the 1798 Rising. He was forced to resign after protesting to his government against the cruelty and licentiousness of the soldiery.

Kilkenny

Kilkenny Castle

The central part of County Kilkenny is undulating limestone plain, bordered in some areas by gently sloping hills. In the north are the attractive uplands of the Castlecomer district, and the Slieveardagh Hills and Booley Hills extend across the County Tipperary border on the west. There are many pleasant landscapes, especially in the Rivers Nore and Barrow valleys, and the historic county town has numerous points of interest. Kilkenny is also an excellent sporting county, with good opportunities for hunting, angling, shooting and golf. Kilkenny is famous for its hurling teams; the ancient Irish game is regarded and practised almost as an art-form in the county.

Kilkenny

Cill Choinnigh (Canice's Church)

Pop. 8,513 (borough).

Tourist information office: Rose Inn St, Kilkenny. Tel. (056) 21755. Fax (056) 63955.

Post Office: 73 High St, Kilkenny. Tel. (056) 21879. Open 9.00–18.00.

Parking Regulations: Pay and display parking (disc bought in car park).

▦ ⓑ Railway Station/Bus station: MacDonough Station, Carlow Road, Kilkenny. Tel. (056) 22024.

🚗 Car Hire: (nearest depot is Rosslare Harbour or Waterford).

🚲 Bicycle Hire: J. J. Wall, 88 Maudlin St, Kilkenny. Tel. (056) 21236.

🎭 Dates of principal cultural events/festivals: Kilkenny Arts Week (August)

A side street in Kilkenny

Kilkenny is finely situated on both banks of the River Nore. Its narrow winding streets and old buildings add an old-world aspect to a busy modern city.

Things to do
The golf course (18) is one mile (2 km) to the north, at Newtown. There is brown trout and pike fishing on the River Nore, and several streams in the area also have brown trout. The Kilkenny Foxhounds hunt the district. In the city itself there is a walking tour of medieval Kilkenny, which commences from the Tourist Office, and also a cinema, dancing and greyhound racing.

Among the fine walks near by is one along the south bank of the Nore, from the bridge at the foot of Rose Inn Street.

Kilkenny Arts Week takes place annually during August, with concerts, lectures, theatre, recitals and exhibitions.

History
The city is named from the sixth-century church founded by St Canice. It was the capital of the Kingdom of Ossory in pre-Norman times, and after the invasion it passed into the hands of William le Mareschal, Strongbow's son-in-law. In 1391 the Earl of Ormonde bought the lordship from Mareschal's descendants.

Kilkenny was the venue of many parliaments during the fourteenth century, including that of 1366 which passed the infamous Statute of Kilkenny. This statute

St Canice's Cathedral

Kilkenny

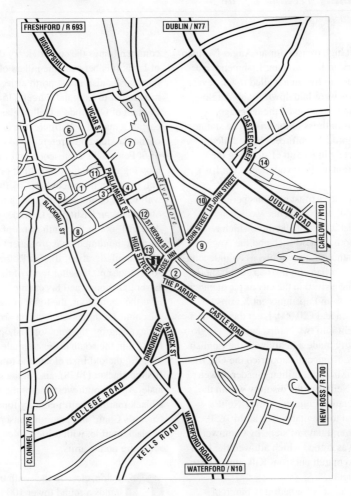

1. Abbey Street
2. The Castle
3. Rothe House
4. Courthouse
5. Black Abbey
6. St Canice's Cathedral
7. St Francis' Abbey
8. St Mary's Cathedral
9. Kilkenny College
10. St John's Church and Priory
11. Black Freren Gate
12. Kyteler's Inn
13. Town Hall (Tholsel)
14. McDonagh Station

made it high treason for an Anglo-Norman to marry an Irishwoman; Irishmen were forbidden to live in a walled town; severe penalties were laid down for an Anglo-Norman who adopted the language, customs or dress of the Irish. The statute was rigorously enforced, but it failed completely in its aim of stopping the absorption of the invaders into the Irish way of life.

The city's most glorious period was from 1642 to 1648. This was when the Confederation of Kilkenny, which represented both the Old Irish and the Anglo-Irish Catholics, functioned as an independent Irish Parliament. In 1645 Archbishop Rinuccini arrived in the city as papal nuncio, bringing from Pope Innocent X arms for 6,000 men and £20,000. Later the confederation split into two camps, and the Anglo-Irish Party made a treaty with the English Viceroy. Rinuccini supported the Old Irish and their brilliant military leader, Owen Roe O'Neill, but the disunity within the confederation coupled with O'Neill's death led to inevitable defeat. In 1650, after several days of siege by Cromwell, a treaty was signed which allowed the Irish Army to march out from Kilkenny with full honours.

St Canice's Cathedral (Church of Ireland) dates from the thirteenth century and may be on the site of the sixth-century church of St Canice. Much repair and restoration has been carried out over the centuries—especially after the havoc wrought by Cromwell's soldiers, who left it a roofless ruin. Despite these depredations the cathedral, with its massive squat tower and stepped battlements, retains its original austere lines. Notable features are the fine Early English west window, the east window, the beautiful groining of the central tower and the quatrefoil windows of the clerestory.

The interior has many fine medieval monuments, carrying effigies and other sculptures. Among them are the earliest dated monument (1285) which commemorates the son of Henry de Ponto of Lyra; it is between the pillars of the north aisle; also in the north aisle, the monument to Edmund Purcell (1549), Captain of Ormonde's Gallowglasses: this carries a mailed half-figure, the emblems of the Passion and a reference to the denial of St Peter—the representation of a cock crowing on the edge of the high priest's pot, in which it was cooking; by the north wall of the choir, a tomb bearing the figure of Franciscan Bishop de Ledrede, who died in 1360; in the south transept of the choir, a monument to a prominent member of the confederation, Bishop Rothe; in the south transept, the altar tomb of the 8th Earl of Ormonde and his countess (1539); near the south door, the tomb of the 1st Viscount Mountgarrett, with an armoured effigy; near by, the tomb of Bishop Walsh (1585); in the south aisle, a female effigy wearing the old Irish cloak; the tomb of Bishop Hacket (1478), also in the south aisle. At the south-west end of the nave is a black marble twelfth-century font. 'St Ciaran's Chair' in the north transept is also of black marble, with thirteenth-century sculpture on the arms.

Outside, close to the south transept, stands a round tower 100 feet high and 46½ feet in circumference at the base. This is a relic of the ancient church which occupied the site, though the original conical cap has been replaced by a slightly domed roof. The top storey has six windows instead of the usual four, and each of the other five storeys has an unusually wide single window. To the north-west of the cathedral is St Canice's Library, which has 3,000 volumes of the sixteenth and seventeenth centuries. Leading to the cathedral from Irishtown are St Canice's Steps (1614) with fragments of old sculptures set in the walls.

Kilkenny Castle, at the south-eastern end of the city, is a magnificent building on high ground beside the river. It was built in the thirteenth century in place of an earlier motte fortress erected by Strongbow. Though much altered, the structure retains the lines of a medieval fortress. Today it forms three sides of a quadrangle, and three of the four original round corner-towers remain.

From the fourteenth century the castle was the main seat of the Butlers, the Earls and Dukes of Ormonde, who play a large part in Irish history. Today the castle is in state care, having been handed over to the city of Kilkenny by the Marquess of Ormonde, prior to restoration and opening to the public. In the old castle stables is the Kilkenny Design Centre where an exhibition hall is open to visitors.

Across the river from the castle is Kilkenny College, the successor of St John's College (founded in 1666) whose

Butler tomb, St Canice's Cathedral

notable pupils included Swift, Congreve, Berkeley and Farquhar; the present building dates from 1780. It is no longer used as a college. About 150 yards north of the college is St John's Church (Church of Ireland), which incorporates the Lady Chapel of a priory of the Knights Hospitallers, founded in the thirteenth century.

Other points of interest

Off Blackmill Street, the Dominican Church incorporates the slender tower and some fine fourteenth-century windows of the Black Abbey, built in 1225 by William le Mareschal. On the left of the path from the street are monumental slabs and stone coffins which were found during excavations in the vicinity. Near by is St Canice's Well, covered by a stone well-house. In the thirteenth century Bishop Geoffrey de Turville gave the Dominicans of Black Abbey the right to take water to their house from this well, by a conduit not wider than his episcopal ring.

In Abbey Street, which runs eastwards from the Dominican Church, is the only remaining gate of the medieval town walls, Black Freren Gate. Continuing along Abbey Street and across Parliament Street to the Bull Ring leads to the ruin of the Franciscan Grey Friary (1234), located in the yard of Smithwick's Brewery. The remains consist of a graceful belfry tower and a beautiful east window of seven graduated lights.

Parliament Street, running southwards from Irishtown towards the centre of the city, was named from the Confederation Parliament House, which was pulled down in the 1860s, but a tablet marks the site. In this street also is Rothe House, home of Bishop Rothe at the time of the confederation and now the museum and library of the Kilkenny Archaeological Society. A slab in the front wall carries the Rothe arms and the date 1594; a well-house in the inner courtyard is dated 1604.

Near by in St Kieran's Street is the oldest house in Kilkenny, Kyteler's Inn, now a restaurant. This was the home of Dame Alice Kyteler. Born in 1280 a lady of great wealth who carried on a lucrative business as a banker and moneylender, she was accused in 1324 of witchcraft and of poisoning her four husbands. Dame Alice escaped, but her maid Petronilla was convicted and burned at the stake.

Dunmore Caves

St Mary's Hall (formerly St Mary's Church) behind the Tholsel, is believed to date from the thirteenth century and is the oldest parish church in Kilkenny. It is now a parish hall. In the monument room are preserved the medieval tombs removed from the church, commemorating Rothe, Butler, Shee and other families prominent in the history of Kilkenny. In the burial ground is the fine Shee altar tomb with carved figures of the twelve apostles, the

Rothe House

tomb of John Rothe Fitzpiers, founder of Rothe House, and an interesting collection of eighteenth-century carved tombstones.

In High Street is the Tholsel (also called the Town Hall and the City Hall). This was the old toll-house or exchange. The present building, erected in 1761, has a curious clock-tower and a front arcade over the pavement. About 100 yards south-east, in Rose Inn Street, is the Shee Almhouse. Founded in 1594 by Sir Richard Shee, it houses the Kilkenny Tourist information office, and the City Scope exhibition which is a 20 minute-presentation of the history of the city and the everyday life of its inhabitants.

A prominent feature of the city is St Mary's Cathedral (Catholic), a fine nineteenth-century limestone building with a tower 200 feet high. The church has a statue of the Blessed Virgin by Benzoni.

Thomas Moore had many associations with Kilkenny, where he first met his future wife, and where at George Bryan's country seat at Jenkinstown he wrote the 'Last Rose of Summer'.

Shee Almhouse

Around Kilkenny

Seven miles (11 km) north of the city is one of the finest natural limestone caves in the country. Dunmore Cave, now a national monument and open to visitors, has a number of large chambers with magnificent dripstone formations. Most spectacular is the 'Market Cross' stalagmite which is over 20 feet high. The cave is known to have been the scene of a massacre in Viking times, and numerous bones and coins have been found there.

Castlecomer

Caislean an Chumair
(The Castle of the River Confluence)

Pop. 1,490.

This attractive little town in the hilly northern part of Kilkenny lies in a wooded valley where the River Dinin is joined by a tributary from the

west. Though the centre of the country's largest coalfield (now worked out) the neighbourhood has a scenic charm not usually associated with colliery areas. The district was once part of the territory of the O'Brenans, who were finally dispossessed in the seventeenth century, but are still numerous in the area. A biennial Brennan family rally has been held here.

Around Castlecomer

Seven miles (11 km) to the west is a little town on the River Nore, Ballyragget, where there are remains of a large Ormonde castle dating from the fifteenth century.

In 1600 Ballyragget was the scene of the capture of the Lieutenant-General of Queen Elizabeth's forces by Owen MacRory O'More.

Six miles (10 km) south-west of Bally-ragget, in a gap of the Slieveardagh Hills, is Freshford. A twelfth-century church was built here on the site of the original foundation by St Lachtain (died 622); though since rebuilt, a beautifully sculptured Hiberno-Romanesque doorway and porch remain. At Fertagh, 10 miles (16 km) to the north-west (via the village of Johnstown), there is a ruined church and round tower on the site of a monastery founded by St Ciaran.

Callan

Pop. 1,266.

Callan, in the centre of a fertile plain, is an ancient market town which was strongly fortified in medieval times. Corporate rights were granted to the town in 1271. In 1408 there was a battle here in which the Prince of Ossory and 800 of his men were slain by the English. There are some remains of the fifteenth-century Augustinian priory founded by Sir James Butler, and traces of the castle which was bombarded by Cromwell in 1650. In the main street stands a handsome memorial in Kilkenny limestone to Edmund Ignatius Rice (1762–1844), founder of the Irish Christian Brothers. James Hoban, architect of the White House at Washington, D.C., was born near Callan in 1762. Robert Fulton, designer of the first steamship was born here in 1765.

Around Callan

At Westport, outside the town, is the neat thatched farmhouse, now fully restored, where a plaque marks the birthplace of Brother Rice. Six miles (10 km) east of Callan is the village of Kells, an important place in the ancient kingdom of Ossory. After the Anglo-Norman invasion it was granted to Geoffrey FitzRobert. There are extensive remains of a fortified Augustinian priory that FitzRobert founded about 1193. The ruins include parts of the church and the surrounding wall with its defensive towers.

Jerpoint Abbey

At Kilree, 2 miles (3 km) to the south of Kells, is a round tower 96 feet high which has lost its conical cap. Also here is an uninscribed monolithic cross which is popularly believed to mark the burial-place of a ninth-century High King of Ireland, Niall Caille.

Thomastown

Baile Mhic Anndain
(FitzAnthony's Town)

Pop. 1,465.

This town, in beautiful surroundings in the Nore valley, is named after Thomas FitzAnthony Walsh, Seneschal of Leinster, who built a wall around it early in the thirteenth century and erected a castle. The castle was destroyed by Cromwell in 1650. There are some interesting monuments among the ruins of a large thirteenth-century church and the present Catholic church contains the old high altar of Jerpoint Abbey (see below).

Around Thomastown

On the west bank of the Nore, half a mile (1 km) to the south-east, are the ruins of Grianan Castle, also built by FitzAnthony and again captured by Cromwell.

One and a half miles (2 km) to the south-west is one of the finest monastic ruins in Ireland, Jerpoint Abbey. This Cistercian abbey was founded in 1158 by the King of Ossory, Donagh MacGilla-patrick. In 1387 the abbot was fined for violating the Statute of Kilkenny, which forbade the admission of Irishmen as members of the community. In 1540 the abbey was suppressed and its lands given to the Ormonde family.

The oldest parts of the ruins are the Hiberno-Romanesque chancel and transepts. The rough barrel vault and stone roof of the original chancel are preserved, but the east window is a fourteenth-century insertion. There is a square central tower (fifteenth century) with distinctively Irish stepped battlements, and a row of six wide pointed arches between the nave and the north aisle. The three-light west window and the clerestory windows are round headed. In the fifteenth-century cloisters, which have been restored, there are many interesting sculptures. Many fine monuments are preserved, including Walsh and Butler tombs of the fifteenth and sixteenth centuries. In the chancel is the tomb of the first abbot, Bishop Felix O'Dullany (died 1202), whose effigy holds a crosier gnawed by a serpent.

Three miles (5 km) past Jerpoint Abbey is the village of Knocktopher, where the tower and doorway of a fourteenth-century Carmelite priory founded by the Earl of Ormonde are still standing.

Two miles (3 km) to the north of Thomastown is Kilfane. In the ruins of its medieval church is a thirteenth-century effigy of a knight in full armour, with a shield bearing the Cantwell family arms. Tullaherin, a mile north of Kilfane, is the burial ground of St Ciaran. There is a round tower 73 feet high and the ruins of a church, together with a small local museum.

Inistioge

Inis Tíog (Tíog's Island)

Pop. 267.

This is a charming village with a tree-lined square, lying in a pretty part of the Nore valley where the river winds between wooded banks flanked by hills.

An Augustinian priory was founded here in 1210 by Thomas Fitzgerald, and the nave, tower and adjoining Lady Chapel remain. Some monuments of the Tighe family are in the tower, including an effigy by Flaxman of Mrs Mary Tighe (died 1810), the authoress of *Psyche*.

The former home of the Tighes, Woodstock House, is in a wooded demesne south of the village. The house was damaged by fire in 1922, but the fine formal gardens can still be enjoyed.

On a rock above the river at the village are the remains of a Norman motte-and-bailey castle.

Graiguenamanagh

Graig na Manach (Village of the Monks)

Pop. 1,485.

Graiguenamanagh, east of Kilkenny on the Carlow border, has a fine situation at a bend of the River Barrow, overlooked by Brandon Hill (1,694 feet) on the south. The approach to the town from the west gives beautiful views, with the long ridge of the Blackstairs Mountains in the background.

Graiguenamanagh was at one time a place of ecclesiastical importance; it is now a prosperous market town. Salmon and trout fishing is available on the River Barrow and there is also excellent coarse fishing.

The Abbey of Duiske was a place of great ecclesiastical significance, founded in the early thirteenth century by the Earl of Pembroke, William le Mareschal. Its extensive buildings occupied much of the present town area. The abbey was suppressed in 1536, but continued to be occupied by monks for many years afterwards. In 1774 the tower of the ruined abbey church collapsed. The abbey has now been restored to much of its former splendour.

Around Graiguenamanagh

There is delightful scenery on the River Barrow, north and south of the town. Brandon Hill, an easy ascent, is worth climbing for the fine views from the summit. At Ullard, 3 miles (5 km) to the north, are the ruins of an ancient church and a tall sculptured cross. Ullard was a foundation of St Fiachra (seventh century), who later settled in Breuil in France as a hermit.

Between Graiguenamanagh and Kilkenny is the village of Gowran, once a seat of the kings of Ossory. After the Anglo-Norman invasion, the lands here came into the possession of Theobald FitzWalter, ancestor of the Ormonde family. Edward Bruce and his army took

Gowran in 1317, and a century later the place was burned in a battle between the Irish and the Anglo-Normans. In 1608 James I granted a new charter to Gowran and made it a parliamentary borough. After a brief siege in 1650 Gowran Castle surrendered to the Cromwellians, who then burned the castle and shot the garrison.

There are some interesting remains of Gowran Old Church, parts of which have been incorporated into the present Protestant church. There is an effigy of the 1st Earl of Ormonde (died 1327) and an ancient font of black marble.

In the modern Gowran Castle demesne which adjoins the village stands the keep of Ballyshawnmore Castle, also taken by the Cromwellians in 1650.

Meetings are held at Gowran Park Racecourse throughout the year.

Carlow

Browne's Hill Dolmen

Carlow is a tiny inland county in the shape of an upside-down triangle, south of County Kildare and south-west of County Wicklow. The River Slaney flows through its eastern part, which is an extension of the granite area of County Wicklow. West of this lies the fertile lime-stone land of the Barrow valley, and beyond to the north-west is pleasant upland country. The county has much to offer the sightseer, the sportsman and the climber.

Carlow
Ceatharlach (Fourfold Lake)

Pop. 11,275 (urban district).

Tourist information office: Tel. (0503) 31554.

Carlow, the county town is pleas-antly situated on the River Barrow. Its thriving industries include a beet sugar factory, flour milling and malting.

Muine Bheag (formerly Bagenalstown)

Things to do
There is salmon, trout and coarse fishing on the Barrow. The golf course (18) is in the beautifully wooded Oak Park north of the town. River cruising, tennis, pitch and putt, swimming (outdoor heated pool), cinema.

History
Carlow was a stronghold of the Anglo-Normans. It was frequently a storm centre because of its strategic position on the border of the English Pale. The earliest record relating to the town is the charter of William le Mareschal, Earl of Pembroke. Between 1361 (when the town was walled) and 1650, its history is a series of struggles for possession, sieges and burnings. In the 1798 Rising, Carlow was again a scene of battle, and 640 of the attacking insurgents were killed.

Points of interest
The keep of the thirteenth-century Norman Castle was a rectangular structure with a circular tower at each of the angles. The west wall and its two flanking towers still stand, near the bridge across the Barrow. The Cathedral of the Assumption (Catholic) is a cruciform building of Gothic design with a lantern tower 151 feet high, containing Hogan's fine monument to Bishop Doyle. Other interesting buildings are St Mary's parish church (Church of Ireland) and St Patrick's College. The Doric portico of the court house is modelled on the Parthenon at Athens. The County Museum operated by the Old Carlow Society is in the Town Hall.

Around Carlow
In Browne's Hill demesne, 2 miles (3 km) east, is a fine dolmen whose 100-ton capstone is the largest in Ireland. The doorway of Killeshin Church (in ruins), 3 miles (5 km) west of Carlow, is a fine example of Hiberno-Romanesque architecture. In the Barrow valley, 7 miles (11 km) south of Carlow, is Leighlinbridge, where the ruined Black Castle beside the river dates

from 1181. Old Leighlin, 2 miles (3 km) to the west, has a twelfth-century cathedral, now Protestant, which was much rebuilt in the sixteenth century.

Three miles (5 km) south of Leighlinbridge, also on the River Barrow, is the pleasant town of Muine Bheag (formerly Bagenalstown), a fishing and hunting centre. Two miles (3 km) east of the town is the substantial ruin of Ballymoon Castle. Eight miles (13 km) downriver from Muine Bheag is the little town of Borris. It has golf (9) and is a good point from which to explore the Blackstairs Mountains to the east (highest point Mount Leinster 2,610 feet). The beautiful Borris House demesne lies between the town and the river. At Clashganna on the Barrow outside Borris a cultural village for the handicapped is being developed.

Another place of interest in the Barrow valley is the village of St Mullins, 9 miles (14 km) south of Borris, where there are both Early Christian and medieval remains. The monastery was founded by St Moling, who later became Bishop of Ferns, and was the burial-place of the kings of Leinster. The *Book of Moling*, a Latin copy of the Gospels of very ancient date, is now in Trinity College, Dublin.

Tullow

Tulach O bhFeilim
(The Hill of the O'Felimy Territory)

Pop. 2,324.

Tullow, the main town in the east of the county, is a centre for anglers fishing the Slaney and other nearby rivers. In the market square stands a statue of Father John Murphy, the insurgent leader, who was captured near Tullow and executed in the Market Square on 2 July 1798.

Around Tullow

The town is conveniently placed for exploring the beauty spots of south Wicklow and north Wexford, as well as those of Carlow itself. Three miles (5 km) east of Tullow is the ancient stone fort of Rathgall. This is a structure of four ramparts, and the outer ring is about 1,000 feet across. There is a fine example of a dolmen in Tobinstown. Along the picturesque Slaney valley is Aghade a few miles south of Tullow. Further south is Clonegal, with Huntingdon Castle and demesne near by. There is an art gallery and craft centre in the courtyard. Myshall, 6 miles (10 km) west of Clonegal, has a fine memorial church.

North of Tullow is the neat village of Rathvilly, which has some interesting ruins. Hacketstown, the scene of a battle in 1798, is 6 miles (10 km) further east, in the foothills of the Wicklow Mountains. At Eagle Hill, south of the town, there are panoramic views from the summit of the county spread out below.

The Altamont Gardens off the Tullow–Bunclody road are worth a visit.

Ardattin

Kildare

National Stud

The inland county of Kildare is famous as a sporting, racing and hunting region. Bordering Dublin to the west, it is situated on the edge of the central plain. The county's main features are big open grasslands, lush green pastures and large tracts of ancient bogland—all interspersed with trees and gentle rolling hills. This charming countryside can be seen when travelling from Dublin to Galway, Limerick, Cork and Waterford.

Naas

Nás na Rí
(Assembly-place of the Kings)

Pop. 11,140 (urban district).

Naas, the county town, is on the main road from Dublin to Cork, Limerick and Waterford. In early times it was the seat of the kings of Leinster, and the North Mote is the site of the ancient royal palace. St Patrick visited here and is said to have camped on the site of the present Protestant parish church. The town was fortified by the Normans, and plundered in 1316 by Robert and Edward Bruce. A Norman castle, once part of the town's fortifications, has been converted into the modern Church of Ireland rectory.

Things to do

Naas racecourse, at the Dublin side of the town, is a popular venue; so too is Punchestown racecourse, 3 miles (5 km) to the south-east, which is famous for its steeplechases. There is golf (9) near Sallins, 3 miles (5 km) to the north, and motor racing at Mondello Park (5½ miles/9 km).

Around Naas

A mile (2 km) away is the shell of Jigginstown House, a seventeenth-century building noted for its fine brickwork. It was built by Thomas Wentworth, Earl of Strafford and Viceroy of Charles I, but never completed owing to Strafford's execution in 1641.

Five miles (8 km) north of Naas is Clane, now just a small village but an important place in medieval times. Near by are the ruins of a Franciscan friary founded in 1258 by Sir Gerald Fitzmaurice, as well as Bodenstown churchyard, the burial place of Theobald Wolfe Tone (see around Letterkenny).

Two miles (3 km) north of Clane is Clongowes Wood College, a splendid building incorporating the old castle of the Wogan-Brownes, several of whom were distinguished soldiers in European armies. Clongowes was opened as a boys' college by the Society of Jesus in 1814.

For a time in the 1890s James Joyce was a pupil and re-created his experience of student life there and at Belvedere College in his *Portrait of the Artist as a Young Man.*

Some remains of the Pale, the fortification that once marked the boundary of English influence in Ireland, can be seen in the grounds. The chapel has several works by modern Irish artists: the Stations of the Cross are by Sean Keating and the stained-glass windows by Evie Hone and Michael Healy. The college museum contains interesting antiquities.

Three miles (5 km) west of Clane is the Grand Canal-side village of Robertstown where canal cruisers can be hired. Close by is the village of Prosperous which is a well-known coarse-angling centre.

Three miles (5 km) from Naas, to the north-west of the village of Straffan, is the ruin of Rathcoffey Castle. This was once the residence of the Wogan family, of whom the most famous was Sir Charles Wogan (born about 1698). He was a prominent Jacobite who was imprisoned in London for his part in the Scottish 'Fifteen' Rising: in 1716 he escaped to France and served in Dillon's regiment of the Irish Brigade.

Straffan Steam Museum is worth a visit.

Twelve miles (19 km) north-east of Naas is Celbridge, a picturesque village on the River Liffey. Celbridge Abbey was the home of Esther Vanhomrigh, the ill-fated 'Vanessa' of Jonathan Swift. The Dean often visited her here, and a seat beneath the rocks at the river's edge was their favourite retreat.

Adjoining Celbridge is Castletown, a magnificent Palladian-style mansion which is open to the public. It was built in 1722 for William Conolly, the speaker of the Irish House of Commons, and designed by the Italian architect Alessandro Galilei. The interior contains some magnificent plasterwork, a long gallery painted in the Pompeian manner and hung with Venetian chandeliers, with an eighteenth-century print room. It is now the headquarters of the Irish Georgian Society, who have restored the building and furnished it with Irish furniture and paintings of the period. Castletown is a venue for a great variety of functions throughout the year.

Downriver from Celbridge, in a prettily wooded part of the Liffey valley and on the main Dublin–Galway road, is

Carton House

the village of Leixlip. Here the battlements of the twelfth-century Leixlip Castle overlook the salmon leap which gave the place its name (Danish, lax-hlaup). A hydroelectric dam forms a narrow lake stretching for about 2 miles (3 km) upriver. A fish pass in the dam, based on the principle of a canal lock, allows fish to go upstream. The Liffey Descent, an international canoeing event, takes place here in September each year.

A mile south-west of Leixlip on private property is the 'Wonderful Barn', built in 1743 for Lady Conolly of Castletown House. The building, a conical structure of bricks and stone, has five storeys of single rooms with domed ceilings. Goods stored in it were hauled up by a winch through circular openings in the centre of the floors. A spiral stone staircase winds around the outside of the building.

On the Lyons estate now owned by the Faculty of Agriculture of UCD, there is the 645-feet high Lyons Hill which was an

Iron Age hill-fort and from which there is a panoramic view of the Wicklow Mountains and the Liffey and Barrow valleys.

Maynooth

Maigh Nuad (Nuat's Plain)

Pop. 4,768.

At the northern end of the county, on the Dublin–Galway road, is the village of Maynooth beside the Royal Canal. Maynooth Ecclesiastical Museum and Maynooth Castle are open to visitors by arrangement.

St Patrick's College is the centre for the training of Catholic diocesan clergy in Ireland, and also a constituent college of the National University. It was established in 1795 on the site of an earlier college founded by the Earl of Kildare in the sixteenth century, but soon suppressed by Henry VIII. The college library has some rare manuscripts and old printed books (admission on written application to the librarian). A museum contains exhibits illustrating the history of the Church in Ireland.

Beside the main gateway of the college are the remains of Maynooth Castle, ancient seat of the Fitzgeralds. The oldest part is the keep, dating probably from the thirteenth century; there is also a fine gate-tower. The castle had an eventful history as the stronghold of the Kildare Geraldines, until it was dismantled by the forces of Owen Roe O'Neill in 1647.

Carton House, at the east end of the town, was the residence of the dukes of Leinster. The house is an imposing mansion in classic style designed by Richard Castle about 1740; it is no longer open to the public. In the grounds is a stone table which was the council table of Gerald, the sixteenth-century 9th Earl of Kildare. Also in the grounds is the 'shell house', with an interior decorated entirely with sea shells; this work is said to have been carried out by the 6th Duchess.

Droichead Nua (Newbridge)

Droichead Nua (New Bridge)

👪 Pop. 5,983.

ℹ️ Tourist information office (seasonal): Tel. (045) 33835.

Droichead Nua, also known as Newbridge, is 7 miles (11 km) beyond Naas on the road from Dublin to Cork and Limerick. This former garrison town on the River Liffey now has some thriving industries and the research centre of Bord na Mona, the national authority for peat development.

Golf (9) and (18), greyhound racing, horse-riding and outdoor swimming pool.

On the bank of the river is an ancient motte about 40 feet high and 180 yards across.

Around Droichead Nua

At Great Connell, 1½ miles (2 km) to the east, are the remains of an Augustinian abbey founded by Myler FitzHenry in 1202. Some sculptured stones from the tomb of Walter Wellesley, a bishop of Kildare who was prior of the abbey in the sixteenth century, are built into the wall of the graveyard. Near by, in the old burial ground called 'The Religeen', is the recumbent effigy of another bishop.

Five miles (8 km) north-west of Droichead Nua is the Hill of Allen, rising 676 feet from the plain. It was the site of one of the three royal residences of Leinster in early times. Here, too, lived Fionn Mac Cumhaill, commander of the legendary Fianna in the third century and hero of many folk-tales. A battlemented stone tower stands on the summit, from which there is a fine view over the surrounding country. The tower, erected in 1859 for Sir Gerald Aylmer of Donadea Castle, carries Latin inscriptions on its face and the names of the workmen who built it on the steps of the spiral staircase. On the western side of Droichead Nua is the Curragh, a vast plain that has been a horse-racing venue from the earliest times. It is the headquarters of Irish racing today, and here the Irish Derby and other classic races are decided. For nearly a century the Curragh Camp has been an important military station and training centre: it was handed over to the Irish Army in 1922. East of the camp is the Curragh Golf Club (18). At Donnelly's Hollow, on the eastern end of the Curragh, a small obelisk commemorates a celebrated boxing match in 1815. Dan Donnelly, a giant Irishman, defeated the English champion George Cooper. Donnelly's footprints on leaving the hollow have been preserved by being retrodden by countless visitors since. Four miles (6 km) south of Droichead Nua is the little town of Kilcullen beside the River Liffey. Near by at New Abbey is the Portlester tomb, which carries sculptured effigies of the fifteenth-century Baron

Portlester and his wife. At Old Kilcullen, 2 miles (3 km) to the south, are the remains of a round tower and three ninth-century figured high crosses in granite; the west cross has panels of figured scenes. Also near Kilcullen is Dun Ailinne (now Knockaulin), once a residence of Leinster kings.

Kildare
Cill Dara (The Church of the Oak)

Pop. 4,268.

K ildare, on the opposite edge of the Curragh plain to Droichead Nua, is the centre of Ireland's horse-breeding and training industry. St Brigid founded a religious establishment here in the fifth century, and St Brigid's Cathedral (Church of Ireland) is a beautiful building incorporating part of a thirteenth-century structure and a tenth-century round tower.

Near Kildare
Outside the town are the slight remains of Grey Abbey, a Franciscan friary founded by William de Vesci in 1260. At Tully, three quarters of a mile away (1 km), are the remains of a preceptory church of the Knights Hospitallers.

Also at Tully are the Japanese Gardens, open to the public, founded by Lord Wavertree and designed by the Japanese landscape designer Eida in 1906. The delightful gardens are renowned for their symbolism of 'The Life of Man'. Guided tours are provided. Visitors may visit the Irish National Stud across the road which has produced many famous race-horses and incorporates a horse museum.

Seven miles (11 km) west of Kildare is the market town of Monasterevan, on the River Barrow. Moore Abbey, a mansion built on the site of an ancient Cistercian foundation near the town, was at one time the residence of the celebrated Irish tenor, Count John McCormack.

St Brigid's Cathedral, Kildare

Athy
Baile Átha Í (The Ford of Ae)

Pop. 5,205 (urban district).

A thy, in the south of the county on the Dublin–Waterford road, is County Kildare's largest town. There is fishing on the Grand Canal and River Barrow. Tennis, indoor swimming pool, and golf (9). Overlooking the bridge across the River Barrow is White's Castle, built in the sixteenth century by the Earl of Kildare to defend this strategic crossing. Downriver from the castle is a striking example of modern church architecture, the fan-shaped Dominican church.

Near Athy
About half a mile (1 km) to the north is the ruined Woodstock Castle (thirteenth century). Three miles (5 km) north is a moss peat factory at Kilberry. Four miles (6 km) to the north-east is the Motte of Ardscull, where Edward Bruce defeated an English army in 1315. A few miles east of Ardscull is Ballitore, once a flourishing

Quaker settlement. Its famous school, founded by Abraham Shackleton, was attended by Edmund Burke in his early years. At the outskirts of the village is Crookstown Mill and Heritage Centre which is open to visitors. At Moone, south of Ballitore, is an ancient Celtic cross 17½ feet high; it carries 51 sculptured panels of scriptural scenes. At nearby Timolin is the Irish Pewter Mill and Craft Centre where the craft of pewter was restored in Ireland; it is open daily to visitors.

Nine miles (14 km) south-east of Athy is Castledermot, which has a group of remains that include a round tower, two high crosses and the ruins of a Franciscan friary. Three miles (5 km) away is Kilkea Castle, once the residence of the Duke of Leinster, but now a hotel and health farm.

The castle was built by Hugh de Lacy in 1180, and later passed to the Fitzgeralds. Garrett Og Fitzgerald, 11th Earl of Kildare, is said to have practised magic in Kilkea Castle. The castle was restored in 1849, but some of the old work remains.

Castledermot

Laois

Ballyfin House

Laois is an inland county to the south-west of County Kildare. It forms part of the central plain, though the Slieve Bloom Mountains (highest point Arderin, 1,734 feet) are a prominent feature in the north-west of the county. There is much of interest and beauty in the quiet byways of this area, away from the main roads that lead from Dublin to Limerick and Cork. Sporting attractions include fishing, hunting, shooting and golf.

Portlaoise

Port Laoise (The Fort of Laois)

👪 Pop. 3,773.

ℹ️ Tourist information office (seasonal): Tel. (0502) 21178.

Portlaoise, the county town, was once called Maryborough. In the reign of Philip and Mary it was fortified as part of a plan to subdue the local chiefs, the O'Mores, but nothing remains apart from the outer wall of the tower. Golf (18) at 'The Heath', tennis. A jazz festival is held at the beginning of June each year.

Around Portlaoise

Four miles (6 km) to the east is the prominent Rock of Dunamase. On its summit is a ruined castle which was a

Rock of Dunamase

fortress of the twelfth-century King of Leinster, Dermot MacMurrough. It was the scene of many conflicts in the centuries after the Anglo-Norman invasion, and was demolished in 1650 by the Cromwellians.

A mile (2 km) further to the east is Dysart, the birthplace of Dr Bartholomew Mosse, founder of the Rotunda Hospital in Dublin. Seven miles (11 km) east of Portlaoise is Stradbally, birthplace of the historian John Conor O'Hanlon. The Stradbally Steam Museum may be visited in the town. Timahoe, 5 miles (8 km) south of Stradbally, has a well-preserved round tower. At Killeshin, near to the border with County Carlow, the ancient church has a fine Hiberno-Romanesque doorway. On the Stradbally–Carlow road, Windy Gap has a famous view of the Barrow valley. Vicarstown, north-east of Stradbally, is a pretty inland port on the Barrow canal; it is a cruising and coarse-angling centre.

North of Portlaoise, for many miles, runs an esker, a great ridge of sand and gravel that is a relic from the Ice Age. Seven miles (11 km) to the north is Mountmellick, a small town almost encircled by the Owenass River. It was founded by the Society of Friends (Quakers), and 4 miles (6 km) north-west is the oldest Quaker burial ground in Ireland, at Rosenallis.

To the west, the many roads crossing the Slieve Bloom Mountains provide a variety of interesting drives. At the foot of the mountains is the town of Mountrath, which also offers fishing and golf (9). At Borris-in-Ossory are the ruins of a castle built to defend the main highway into Munster (Ballaghmore Castle is now open to the public) and at Aghaboe are the ruins of a fourteenth-century Dominican abbey.

The author and traveller Richard Hayward wrote of the Slieve Bloom Mountains: 'They are both as sweet and delightful as their names and at any season of the year they fill the eye with beauty and the lungs with their fragrant delicious air.' Excellent roads traverse this mountain range providing delightful views and enjoyment.

Portarlington
Cúil an tSúdaire (The Tanner's Nook)

Pop. 3,295.

Until fairly recently Portarlington had a Huguenot colony, and today the 'French Church' and other relics of the colony remain. There is an attractive golf course (9) at Garryhinch and a fine indoor heated swimming pool in the town.

Around Portarlington
A landmark is the cooling tower of the power station, which was the first to be built in Ireland to generate electricity from peat. Its capacity is nine million units a year, and its intake of 120,000 tons of peat is produced by machinery on the 4,000-acre Clonsast Bog, 4 miles (6 km) north of the town.

Five miles (8 km) south of the town is Emo Court with extensive gardens, open to the public at weekends, May to mid-October, containing specimen trees and flowering shrubs. The house, which is not open, was built in 1795 to designs of James Gandon who also designed the nearby Georgian Inn and the church at Coolbanagher which has an elaborately carved font of the fourteenth or fifteenth century.

Two miles (3 km) to the east is the ruined Lea Castle, once a stronghold of the Fitzgeralds, built around 1250 as a frontier post of the Normans.

At Ballybrittas, 4 miles (6 km) south-east of Portarlington, a fine example of modern Hiberno-Romanesque architecture is the Adair Memorial Church. There are forest walks at Rathdeire (1 mile/2 km) and riverside walks at Garryhinch (4 miles/6 km).

Vicarstown

Abbeyleix
Mainistir Laoise (The Abbey of Laois)

 Pop. 1,468.

Abbeyleix, 9 miles (14 km) south of Portlaoise, takes its name from a Cistercian abbey founded here in 1183 by Conor O'More. Today it is an attractive town with tree-lined streets. Golf (9), tennis, game fishing. In the grounds of the de Vesci demesne (which is not open to the public) is the tomb of a Laois chieftain, Malachi O'More.

Around Abbeyleix
Two miles (3 km) north at Corbally is an interesting craft centre. Six miles (10 km) north-east on the Stradbally road is the Pass of the Plumes, so called because of the plumed helmets that were strewn there in 1599 after Owen MacRory O'More defeated the English forces under Essex. On the banks of the Erkina River is Durrow, sheltered by the woods of Castle Durrow demesne; there are forest walks near by at Capponellen. Nine miles (14 km) further west is the main town of south-west Laois, Rathdowney. Thomas Prior, the philanthropist and one of the founders of the Royal Dublin Society, was born here in 1679.

Offaly

Birr Castle

Offaly lies near the centre of Ireland. In the south-east of the county are the heathery Slieve Bloom Mountains, among which there are pretty valleys to be explored. The rest of the county is largely level plain and bogland, with occasional elevations. In the west the River Shannon separates the county from Counties Galway and Roscommon. There are numerous points of interest in the towns and countryside of Offaly, including one of the most important historic sites in Ireland—Clonmacnois.

Tullamore

Tulach Mhór (Great Assembly Hill)

Pop. 8,623 (urban district).

Tullamore is the county town and the marketing centre of a fertile agricultural district. Among the imposing buildings are the Catholic Church of the Assumption, the Court House, and the modern County Hospital. There is an outdoor swimming pool, and golf (18) about 2 miles (3 km) away, pitch and putt, tennis. The whiskey liqueur Irish Mist is made in Tullamore.

Around Tullamore

South-west of the town is the demesne of Charleville, with a splendid early nineteenth-century baronial mansion (open to the public by appointment). North of Tullamore on the Durrow Abbey estate is the site of the Monastery of Durrow founded by St Colmcille. The famous *Book of Durrow*, now in Trinity College, Dublin, was written here in about the seventh century. Apart from a high cross, few traces of the ancient monastery remain.

Five miles (8 km) west of Tullamore, close to the Grand Canal at Rahan, are the remains of two churches on the site of a sixth-century monastery founded by St Carthach.

Nine miles (14 km) east of Tullamore is Daingean, which was the seat of the chiefs of Offaly, the O'Conors, and was also for a time the county town. It was once called Phillipstown after Philip II of Spain, consort of Henry VIII's daughter, 'Bloody Mary'. Croghan Hill (769 feet) to the north, is a prominent feature of the landscape, and has good views. At Geashill, 5 miles (8 km) south of Daingean, are the remains of a castle of the O'Dempseys.

To the south-west of Tullamore, on the River Brosna, is the town of Clara. Five miles (8 km) further west on the road to Clonmacnois is Boher, where the twelfth-century shrine of St Manchan is preserved in the Catholic church. It is a yew box covered in embossed and enamelled metalwork, and was built to contain the relics of the saint around the year 1130.

Edenderry

Eadan Doire (Oakwood Hill-Brow)

 Pop. 3,539.

Edenderry, located on the Grand Canal, is a picturesque market town on the Enfield–Tullamore road.

Fishing: coarse and trout, golf (9), tennis, indoor swimming, parachute club.

Around Edenderry

The River Boyne has its source near the town. On a hill south of the town are the ruins of Blundell's Castle. A mile (2 km) to the west are the remains of Monasteroris Monastery, founded in the fourteenth century by Sir John De Bermingham.

Birr

Biorra (Spring Wells)

 Pop. 3,257 (urban district).

i Tourist information office (seasonal): Tel. (0509) 20110. Fax (0509) 20660.

Birr is a prosperous market town on the Camcor River with tree-lined malls and quiet Georgian streets. Birr Castle withstood many a siege in the wars of the sixteenth and seventeenth centuries. It later became the residence of the earls of Rosse, and the 3rd Earl

Birr

maintained a famous observatory there, with a telescope made to his own design. For eighty years this was the largest telescope in the world. At St John's Mall there is a statue of the famous astronomer.

The display area at the site in the gardens contains astronomical artefacts, drawings, photographs, a scale model of the original telescope and a tape-recorded 'History of Astronomy at Birr'.

The gardens which cover one hundred acres are open daily to the public, contain over one thousand catalogued trees and are noted for their spring flowering and autumnal colouring. The box hedges feature in the *Guinness Book of Records* as the tallest in the world.

Birr Castle gardens

There is good fishing for brown trout on the Little Brosna. There is an indoor heated swimming pool and an outdoor education centre and golf (18). Horse-riding is available at Belmont.

Birr Vintage Week, held in August each year, is a very successful festival.

Around Birr

On the road to Tullamore is the village of Kilcormac, where a beautifully carved wooden pietà is in the Catholic church; it is believed to be the work of a sixteenth-century artist.

On the road to Mountmellick is the pretty village of Kinnitty, at the foot of the Slieve Bloom Mountains; near by is a lovely little valley between the hills, Forelacka Glen. There is a Slieve Bloom Display Centre at Birr. Four miles (6 km) south-west of Kinnitty is Seirkieran, named after St Ciaran who founded a

monastery here in the fifth century. There are interesting antiquities in the vicinity, and a curiosity is a whitethorn called 'St Ciaran's Bush', which grows in the middle of the road about half a mile (1 km) south of Clareen crossroads. A few miles to the south is the fifteenth-century Leap Castle, an ancient stronghold of the O'Carrolls of Ely. The castle was burned in 1922, but many interesting features remain. It was reputed to have been one of the most haunted castles in Ireland.

Banagher

Beannchar na Sionna
(Pinnacled Rocks beside the Shannon)

Pop. 1,465.

Banagher, a pretty village on the east bank of the River Shannon, is a good centre for exploring the western part of the county. The banks of the Shannon north of Lough Derg, known as the Shannon Callows, are noted for the number and variety (87 species) of birds. In 1990 a sanctuary for corncrakes was opened in the area. The Rivers Shannon and Brosna have fair brown trout fishing, and there are large deep pools in the Shannon with numerous pike, perch and bream. There are excellent cruiser mooring facilities beside the bridge which spans the river and cruisers and rowing boats for hire. Adventure canoeing and camping holidays are available. A river bus provides a scenic tour from Banagher. Visitors are welcome at the squash and tennis courts. On the west bank is an outdoor swimming pool. The local Crannog Pottery is well worth a visit. The remains of the batteries built in the seventeenth century to command the crossing of the river can still be seen. Anthony Trollope wrote his first two novels in Banagher while working as a post office surveyor in 1841.

Around Banagher

South of the town, 1½ miles (2 km), are the ruins of Garry Castle, a stronghold of the

Clonmacnois from the air

MacCoghlans. Near Cloghan village, 5 miles (8 km) to the north-east, is the imposing ruin of Clonony Castle. A flagstone marks the graves of two cousins of Queen Ann Boleyn. Near Lusmagh is the twelfth-century Cloghan Castle, the oldest inhabited castle in Ireland, currently being restored and open to the public. Four miles (6 km) further north, just before the village of Ferbane, is Gallen Priory, now a house of the Sisters of St Joseph of Cluny. A monastery was founded here by St Gallen in 492, and many interesting finds have been made during attempts to discover the exact site.

Eight miles (13 km) north-west of Cloghan is the village of Shannonbridge, where a fine bridge of 16 arches crosses the river. A 5½-mile (9 km) circular tour by narrow gauge railway traverses the bog near Shannonbridge with a pre-tour slide show at the visitor centre during the season.

Clonmacnois

Cluain Mic Nois
(Meadow of the Son of Nos)

i Tourist information office (seasonal). Tel. (0905) 74134.

Clonmacnois, one of the most celebrated of Ireland's holy places, is beside the River Shannon, 4 miles (6 km) north of Shannonbridge. St Ciaran founded a monastery here in 548 which became the most famous of all the monastic cities of Ireland. It flourished under the patronage of many kings; the last High King, Rory O'Conor, was buried here in 1198.

Down the centuries, however, Clonmacnois was the object of many plundering raids—by native chiefs and by the Danes and the Anglo-Normans. In 1552 the settlement was despoiled by the English garrison of Athlone, who carried off even the glass in the windows.

The site at Clonmacnois contains a cathedral, eight church ruins, two round towers, three sculptured high crosses and parts of two others, over 200 monumental slabs and the remains of a castle. The Crosier of Clonmacnois, now in the Royal Irish Academy at Dublin, is one of the best-preserved Irish crosiers in existence. A pilgrimage to Clonmacnois is held each year on the feast of St Ciaran (9 September) and on the following Sunday. Guided tours are conducted in season.

Temple Ciaran (or Eaglais Bheag: 'The Little Church') is a ninth-century cell, 12½ feet long. Part of the slanting walls, deep antae and inclined jambs of the original building remain. It may stand on the site of St Ciaran's own clay-and-wattle oratory. The saint's grave is said to be in the east end of the church.

Temple Doulin (or Dowling) is of similar construction to Temple Ciaran but much bigger (31½ feet long). It is named after Edmund Dowling who repaired it for Protestant worship in 1689.

Temple Hurpain (or MacLaffey's Church) was added to the east end of Temple Doulin in the seventeenth century; it fell into ruin shortly afterwards. Temple Hurpain was the ancient name of Temple Doulin.

The Cathedral (or Daimhliag Mhor: 'Great Stone Church') was founded in 904 by Abbot Colman and King Flann Sinna. It was a simple oblong 62 feet long, but only the antae at the east and west ends belong to the original structure. In the north-east corner of the chancel is the grave of Rory O'Conor, and in the south-east corner that of his father, Turlough, King of Connacht.

Temple Conor, now used as a Protestant church, was founded in 1010 by Cathal O'Conor, King of Connacht. The round-headed doorway and small round-headed windows are features of the original building that have survived.

Temple Ri, 'The King's Church' (or Melaghlin's Church), is a rude oblong building of the early twelfth century. The most interesting feature is the east window of two round-headed lancets deeply splayed internally.

Temple Kelly, founded in 1167 by Conor O'Ceallaigh, was 32½ feet long; only the foundations remain.

Temple Finian (twelfth century) replaced an earlier church dedicated to St Finian. It has an almost totally ruined nave, a well-formed chancel and a round tower belfry 56 feet high. This church was assigned to the MacCarthys as a burial-place, and is also known as MacCarthy's Church.

The Nun's Church, a short distance east of the cemetery where the other churches stand, was built in the tenth century. It is one of the finest examples of Hiberno-Romanesque, despite being just 50 feet in length and having a nave and chancel only. The west doorway and chancel arch, both of great beauty, were built in 1167 by the penitent Dervorgilla, wife of Tiernan O'Rourke of Breifne.

O'Rourke's Tower, named from the tenth-century Fearghal O'Rourke, was originally higher than its present height of 60 feet. In 1135 the cap was struck by lightning, and the present masonry at the top may date from the subsequent restoration. The doorway is 12 feet above ground level, so that in time of danger the community could withdraw into the tower and draw up the gangway.

The Cross of the Scriptures (or King Flann's Cross), which stands in front of the cathedral's west door, was erected by Abbot Colman over the grave of King Flann Sinna (died 914). This magnificent high cross carries a wealth of illustrative and ornamental carving on both faces and sides, as well as two inscriptions in Irish.

The South Cross faces the entrance gate of the cemetery. Nine feet high, it is carved in low relief in imitation of metalwork. The principal feature of this eleventh-century cross is a representation of the Crucifixion.

High Cross at Clonmacnois

The North Cross appears to be the earliest of the Clonmacnois crosses (ninth century). Only the shaft remains, covered with interlacing patterns and abstract human and animal figures.

Clonmacnois contains the largest and most important collection of inscribed sepulchral slabs of the Christian period in Ireland. A selection is displayed in an arcade near the entrance. Numbering over 200, they date probably from the sixth to the eleventh century. They carry crosses, and in many cases memorial inscriptions in Irish, and show a development from simple to more elaborate designs. Some of the most beautiful slabs were executed about the end of the ninth century and are ascribed to the sculptor Turcan of Clonmacnois.

The Castle, the only non-ecclesiastical building at Clonmacnois, was erected in 1214. It was destroyed by being blown up, probably in Cromwell's time. The remains are of a strong keep and a small courtyard with domestic quarters.

The Pilgrims' Road was the only road to Clonmacnois in ancient times. Still in use, it extends from the cemetery towards Ballinahown. Fragments of the eleventh-century causeway connecting the road with the cemetery are still to be seen.

The decorated prehistoric Clonfinlough Stone is to be seen 2 miles (3 km) east, near Clonfinlough church.

Westmeath

Tyrellspass

Westmeath is an inland county that contains some delightful scenery— chiefly near the centre of the county, where a number of lakes with wooded shores and surrounding hills provide many charming views. There are other lakes on the northern border and in the west is Lough Ree, a large expansion of the River Shannon, where the boundaries of Counties Westmeath, Longford and Roscommon meet. Much of County Westmeath is flat, and its highest point rises to little more than 850 feet.

Mullingar

Muileann Cearr (Carr's Mill)

Pop. 8,077.

Tourist information office: Dublin Road. Tel. (044) 48650. Fax (044) 40413.

Mullingar, on the Brosna River midway between Lough Ennell and Lough Owel, is the county town and the centre of a cattle-raising area. The town, almost encircled by the Royal Canal, is dominated by the Cathedral of

Christ the King, with its adjoining ecclesiastical museum. There is also a historical museum in Market Square open during the summer.

Mullingar was one of the ancient palatinate settlements established by the English settlers of Meath. Important Augustinian and Dominican priories were founded here, but no trace of either remains. During the Williamite wars Ginkel fortified the town and made it the main rendezvous for his forces before the siege of Athlone in 1691.

Mullingar is a good centre for the Westmeath lakes, most of which hold brown trout. Visitors are welcome at the squash and tennis courts.

Around Mullingar

Three miles (5 km) south is the picturesque Lough Ennell, 6 miles (10 km) long and 3 miles (5 km) wide. On the north-eastern shore is the ancient ruin of Lynn Church. There is a championship golf course (18) and a pitch and putt course (18) overlooking Lough Ennell. There is a fully developed caravan park by the lakeshore at Tudenham and horse-riding is also available at Ladestown House on the lake.

Lough Ennel

Castletown Geoghegan was named after the MacEochagains, ancient rulers of Westmeath. The family's extensive territories, known as Cineal Fiacha, remained intact down to Cromwellian times, when they were reduced to the immediate district of Castletown. At the southern end of the village is a fine example of a motte. To the south-east is Middleton Park, an imposing classic-style residence. A chair-shaped rock near by is said to be the ancient inauguration stone of the MacEochagains.

From Castletown the road runs northeast to Dysart, a village on the Mullingar–Moate road. To the east, near the western shore of Lough Ennell, is the conspicuous mound of Dun na Sciath (Fort of the Shields), a seat of the great King Malachy who died in 1022 on nearby Cro-Inis (Hut Island) in a bay of Lough Ennell. From Dysart the route continues north for 3 miles (5 km) to join the Mullingar–Athlone road, Mullingar being to the right.

Three miles (5 km) north of Mullingar is Lough Owel, which occupies an area over 2,200 acres. It was in this lake that King Malachy I drowned the Danish chief, Turgesius (see around Nenagh, County Tipperary). Among the islands in the lake is Inis Mor (also called Church Island) which contains the ruined oratory of St Loman. The ruins of an old abbey are in the grounds of Portloman, on the western shore.

Lough Owel is the base for the Mullingar sub aqua and sailing clubs and outdoor swimming facilities are also available. An indoor heated pool is located at Annebrook Park, in the centre of the town.

About 3 miles (5 km) north of Lough Owel is the village of Multyfarnham, one-time Tidy Towns winner. The modern Franciscan college is on the site of an early monastic foundation, and the tower of the adjoining church probably dates from the sixteenth century, and has recently been extensively restored. On the lawns around the church and college are elaborate life-size Stations of the Cross, one of the finest outdoor shrines in Ireland. There are horse-riding facilities available.

On the Delvin road 2 miles (3 km) north-east of Mullingar is the conspicuous

Hill of Rathconnell, the scene of many battles in pre-Norman times. The Pass of Rathconnell was fortified by Irish forces in 1642 in an attempt to cut off an English army retreating from Athlone. About a mile (2 km) from the village of Crooked-wood is the ruin of ancient Taghmon Church. Knockdrin Castle, a mile (2 km) further south, is a nineteenth-century castellated mansion with the ruins of an Anglo-Norman castle in the extensive and well-wooded grounds.

Also north of Mullingar is Lough Derravaragh, an irregularly shaped lake with thickly wooded shores and a number of delightful views. It is associated with the most tragic of Irish legends, the fate of the children of Lir. Lir was a chief of the legendary Tuatha De Danann, supposed to have inhabited Ireland in pre-Christian times, whose second wife, Aoife, was jealous of her four step-children. Using her skills as an enchantress, she turned them into swans and decreed that they remain so for 900 years—300 years each on Lough Derravaragh, the Sea of Moyle and the Bay of Erris. The children kept their human faculties and were also endowed with the gift of song. During the centuries of their enchantment, they endured much suffering, but brought joy to all who heard their singing. The end of the spell coincided with the coming of Christianity, and when they were restored to human form, the children were converted and baptised by St Mochaomhog. The legend tells that the jealous Aoife was punished for her crime by her father, who turned her into a hideous air-demon.

There are fine views of the lake and the surrounding country from Knockeyon (710 feet) near the south-eastern end, and also from Knockross (567 feet) on the opposite shore.

Four miles (6 km) east of Ballymore is the prominent Hill of Uisneach (602 feet), a place of religious importance in pagan times; the view extends over much of the central plain. On the south-west of the summit is Aill na Mireann (the Stone of the Divisions), where the boundaries of the ancient provinces of Ireland are said to have met.

Castlepollard
Cionn Torc (The Hill of the Boars)

 Pop. 803.

Castlepollard, in a district of low hills east of Lough Derravaragh, is a good angling centre for the West-meath lakelands and a base for exploring this part of the county.

Around Castlepollard
Tullynally Castle, the residence of Lord Longford, is 1¼ miles (2 km) west of the village. The gardens are open to the public during the summer season. A large castel-lated mansion, it is mentioned several times under its former name of Pakenham Hall in the memoirs of the eighteenth-century novelist, Maria Edgeworth, whose father was a frequent guest there.

North of Castlepollard are Lough Kinale (mainly in County Longford) and Lough Sheelin, in whose waters the boundaries of Counties Westmeath, Meath and Cavan meet. Lough Sheelin is a noted 'dapping' lake and holds brown trout.

Finea, a village between the two lakes, is where Myles 'The Slasher' O'Reilly made his epic stand during the confederate wars. In 1646, an Irish company of horse under O'Reilly defended the bridge of Finea against a larger English force. All the Irish were killed in the engagement, which ended with the arrival of Irish reinforcements from Granard. They were just in time to witness O'Reilly's heroic death. A Celtic cross in the main street commemorates the event.

Three miles (5 km) east of Castle-pollard, between prominent hills, lies the village of Fore, an ancient place with a group of interesting antiquities. In the graveyard is the partly restored St Fechin's

Church (seventh century), a fine example of early church architecture. The west doorway has a massive lintel weighing over two tons. An ancient cross discovered in 1912 has been re-erected in the grave-yard. Close by the church is the Anchorite's Cell. The eastern section, consisting of a tower of two storeys, is ancient; the western part is a mausoleum erected in the nineteenth century by the Greville-Nugent family. Keys for both the cell and mau-soleum can be had at Fore post office.

A short distance from Fore is a thirteenth-century Benedictine abbey whose square towers and loophole windows resemble a castle rather than a monastery; it is well preserved and has a number of interesting features, notably the cloister arcade. Among the ruins in the abbey grounds is a circular columbarium or pigeon house.

Other antiquities at Fore are St Fechin's Mill, St Fechin's Well and a ruined church near the present Catholic church. There are nine ancient crosses within a radius of 1 mile (2 km) from the village. Near the foot of the Ben of Fore (713 feet) is a large motte which is reputed to be an early Anglo-Norman fortification. There are also some slight remains of the walls and gateways which fortified the medieval town of Fore.

To the north are Loughs White, Ben and Bane, strung along the border with County Meath. Lough Lene, to the south, is a good brown trout lake (preserved) and provides excellent outdoor swimming. Five miles (8 km) from Collinstown, a little crossroads village near the shore of Lough Lene, is the well-preserved Kilpatrick Church, which has a fine barrel-vaulted ceiling.

Seven miles (11 km) south-east of Collinstown is Delvin, a picturesque village in wooded surroundings. The Dysart lakes near by are good for angling. Delvin Castle (thirteenth century), a well-preserved ruin, was erected by the Nugents. They later abandoned it to move to Clonyn Castle,

west of the village. The present Clonyn Castle is a nineteenth-century building which replaced the original one that stands in ruins in the grounds. Brinsley MacNamara, the writer, was born at Ballinvalley near Delvin and some of his works are set in the neighbourhood. There is an 18-hole golf course in the grounds of Clonyn Castle. About 6 miles (10 km) north-east of Delvin is the village of Clonmellon, adjoining the estate of a fine eighteenth-century mansion, Killua Castle, once the home of Sir Benjamin Chapman. Near by stands an obelisk to commemorate the introduction of the first potato to Ireland by kinsman, Sir Walter Raleigh.

Kinnegad
Ceann na nGad (Head of the Withes)

Pop. 433.

K innegad, on the Dublin–Galway road, is a village in the flat border country of Counties Westmeath and Meath. The fine altar in the Catholic church is attributed to Willie Pearse, the brother of Padraig Pearse, with whom he was executed for his part in the 1916 Rising.

Around Kinnegad
Fifteen miles (24 km) from Kinnegad is the attractive village of Tyrellspass, where Irish forces under Captain Richard Tyrell defeated an Elizabethan army in 1597. The Tyrells were an Anglo-Norman family who held this area until Cromwell dispossessed them. Tyrellspass was an award winner in the 1976 European Architectural Heritage Year.

Kilbeggan
Cill Bheagain (The Church of Becan)

Pop. 603.

Kilbeggan is a pleasant little place once noted for its distillery. Near the Catholic church at the east end of the village is a fine statue of Christ the King.

Around Kilbeggan

A green mound known as the Church of the Relic, half a mile (1 km) south of the village, is said to mark the site of a Cistercian abbey founded in the thirteenth century on the site of St Becan's settlement.

Four miles (6 km) to the south-east, there are good views from the summit of the motte at Rathugh, the site of an Early Christian settlement. Part of the Eiscir Riada sand and gravel ridge runs through the Kilbeggan district.

The small village of Horseleap, 4 miles (6 km) to the west, is named from the tradition that an Anglo-Norman called Hugh de Lacy leaped his horse over the drawbridge of Ardnurcher Castle, when pursued by a party of the MacGeoghegans. Of the castle only the drawbridge pillars remain.

Moate

Mota (Motte)

Pop. 1,659.

Moate, on the Dublin–Galway road, is an important market town in the centre of a rich cattle-raising area. The town takes its name from the remarkable mound near by, Mota Ghrainne Oige. Grainne Og (Young Grace) was the wife of the chief of the district, O'Melaghlin. Two miles (3 km) to the north-west are the ruins of a sixteenth-century castle of this family.

Around Moate

There is a 9-hole golf course 2 miles (3 km) east of Moate. The prominent Garbh-Eiscir (Esker Ridge) runs almost parallel with the Moate–Mount Temple road. The district around Moate has a number of interesting antiquities, including ruined castles and souterrains. In 1932 the Harvard expedition excavated crannog sites in the area and found many important archaeological remains which are now in the National Museum in Dublin. Near Mount Temple, 3 miles (5 km) from Moate, is another remarkable mound—over 60 feet high, with a peculiar conical shape. A few miles west of Mount Temple at Bealin Twyford, is a sculptured cross nearly seven feet high which is believed to date from the ninth century. Its panels carved with spiral and interlaced designs resemble the crosses of Clonmacnois. About a mile (2 km) from Moate is Dun-na-Si, a traditional Irish music and dancing centre.

Athlone

Ath Luain (The Ford of Luan)

Pop. 8,158 (urban district).

i Tourist information office: Athlone Castle. Tel. (0902) 94630.

Athlone is on the River Shannon, which marks the boundary between the provinces of Leinster and Connacht. A busy road and rail junction and a harbour on Ireland's inland navigation system, Athlone has a number of light industries and is the main marketing and distribution centre for the surrounding country.

Things to do

There is an 18-hole pitch and putt course in town and a fine indoor heated swimming pool at Retreat Heights. Lough Ree near by offers game fishing and sailing. Rowing and sailing events are arranged by local clubs, and international teams compete in the annual regatta. There is golf (18) 4 miles (6 km) from the town, and the South West-meath Harriers hunt the area. There are cinema, drama and variety shows, tennis, boat hire and pleasure cruises. Athlone

Athlone Castle and the River Shannon

Bust of John McCormack in Athlone

Castle includes an interpretative centre which in an audio-visual display features the history of the area and the famous siege, the life and times of John McCormack, the world famous tenor who was born in the town, the flora and fauna of the Shannon basin and also a military museum. In the restored keep of the castle, there is a museum of antiquarian and historical items relating to Athlone and district.

History

The old name for Athlone was Ath Mór (Great Ford). Turlough O'Connor built a wattle bridge here and fortified the banks. Brian Boru, High King of Ireland, convened a great hosting at Athlone in 1001. Two centuries later the Anglo-Normans occupied it and built a castle to guard the crossing. The settlement grew rapidly and in 1257 the first walls were erected. During the succeeding centuries the possession of Athlone was constantly disputed and the castle and walls were often repaired and refortified. The powerful Clanricardes, who held the district during the Wars of the Roses, increased its importance so much that Queen Elizabeth later made the town the seat of the presidency of Connacht. The Cromwellian Court of Claims which dealt with the lands of dispossessed Irish families had its headquarters in the castle of Athlone.

After their defeat at the Boyne in 1690 the Irish Jacobite army withdrew to the west and made the Shannon their first line of defence. Colonel Grace held the castle of Athlone for King James and withstood a week's siege. The following year the Williamite commander, Ginkel, advanced from Mullingar and again laid siege. The Irish retreated to the Connacht side of the river, destroying the bridge behind them. Attempts to repair the bridge were thwarted by the heroic Sergeant Custume and a handful of Irish soldiers, who broke down the improvised structure in the face of heavy fire. The town fell ten days later and the Irish withdrew further into Connacht.

Points of Interest

Near the present bridge on the Connacht side is the Church of Saints Peter and Paul, an impressive building in Roman Renaissance style with prominent twin spires and a graceful dome. Overlooking the bridge, almost opposite the church, is King John's Castle, a fortified thirteenth-century building (see above). Within the 40-foot high curtain wall that surrounds the castle are the governor's apartments. The interior is small and confined, but the loopholes in the wall and castle give good views over the town. Fragments of the old town walls, which were repaired and strengthened in the sixteenth and seventeenth centuries, are near St Mary's Church (Church of Ireland). This nineteenth-century building incorporates the tower of an older structure, and according to tradition the tower bell is one of those removed at the despoiling of Clonmacnois. St Anthony's Friary, a modern building in Hiberno-Romanesque style, has an unusual round tower belfry.

In the Bawn, off Mardyke Street, a bronze plaque marks the birthplace of John Count McCormack, the celebrated tenor. A bust in his memory may be seen at the

The Shannon, Lough Ree and Athlone

promenade. The Genoa Café at the end of Church Street is believed to be the house occupied by Ginkel during the siege of 1691. Athlone was one of the towns linked by the famous Bianconi cars—Ireland's first public transport, established in 1815— and the stopping place was at the Royal Hotel in Mardyke Street. T. P. O'Connor (died 1929), the journalist and politician, was born in the Square; the house is marked by a plaque. Tradition holds that Colonel Grace, the Jacobite defender of the town in 1691, was interred in St Mary's in Church Street.

Around Athlone

Athlone is an excellent centre for exploring the shores and islands of picturesque Lough Ree. This lake, 15 miles (24 km) long and between 1 mile (2 km) and 6 miles (10 km) wide, is an expansion of the River Shannon. It is bordered on the west by County Roscommon and on the east by Counties Longford and Westmeath. The irregular shoreline varies from deep bays to shallow inlets; much of it is pleasantly wooded.

Several of the larger islands have remains of ancient churches. Near the Westmeath shore, 4 miles (6 km) north of Athlone, is the wooded Hare Island, with the ruins of a church said to have been founded by St Ciaran (sixth century) before Clonmacnois. Hodson's Bay is a picturesque formation on the opposite shore. Further north are Inchmore, Inchbofin and Saints Island, which all contain church remains. On a point of land jutting into the narrow middle part of the lake is Rindown Castle (thirteenth century), also called St John's Castle from its occupation at one time by the Knights of St John. Inchcleraun, in the northern half of the lake, is named after a sister of Queen Maeve, Clothra, who is said to have been killed

here by an enemy while she was bathing. This island is the site of a monastery founded by St Diarmait in 540, and on it today are remains of six churches.

Bordering Lough Ree north of Athlone is the Poets' Country of Oliver Goldsmith and John Keegan Casey. Goldsmith's boyhood home, Lissoy or Auburn, is 3 miles (5 km) north of the pretty village of Glasson. He was born in 1729 at Pallas in County Longford, but came here at the age of two when his father became rector of Kilkenny West. Goldsmith went to school at Lissoy, and describes it and the surrounding district in 'The Deserted Village' (see County Longford).

Two miles (3 km) north-east of Glasson, on a hill which is said to be the geographical centre of Ireland, is a round tower-like structure with a domed roof erected in 1769. Near the shore of Lough Ree is Portlick Castle, once a stronghold of the Dillons. The greater part of the building is seventeenth century, but the left wing is fourteenth century Norman.

Six miles (10 km) north of Auburn is Gorteen, where John Keegan Casey ('Leo') lived; it is in County Longford. Six miles (10 km) east of Auburn is Ballymore, scene of a battle in which Owen Roe O'Neill defeated the forces of Ormonde. There are some slight remains of Ballymore Castle, a fourteenth-century Anglo-Norman fortress. There is a well-preserved Mass rock east of Ballymore village.

Near Drumraney, 3 miles (5 km) west of Ballymore, is Bryanmore Hill. On it are remains of a circular earthwork said to be the site of a first-century house of hospitality, Bruidhean-da-Choga.

Longford

Longford Town

Longford is an inland county of quiet farmlands and brown bog, with occasional low hills and pleasant views of lake and river. It is bounded by Counties Leitrim, Cavan, Westmeath and Roscommon—being separated from County Roscommon on the west by the River Shannon and its lakes. The highest point in Longford is Carn Clonhugh (916 feet), one of a range of low round hills extending south-west from Lough Gowna on the County Cavan border. The county offers angling, hunting and shooting, and should interest the lover of literature in the associations with Oliver Goldsmith, Maria Edgeworth, John Casey and Padraic Colum.

Longford

Longphort (Fortress)

Pop. 6,393 (urban district).

Tourist information office (seasonal): Tel. (043) 46566.

Longford, the county town, is on the south bank of the little Camlin River and on the Dublin–Sligo road. It was named after the ancient castle of the princes of Annaly, the O'Farrells, who also founded a Dominican priory here in 1400. Neither building has survived, but there are slight remains of the castle erected by the 1st Earl of Longford in 1627 incorporated in the old military barracks. During the Confederate Wars of

Post office, Granard

1641 the castle was captured by the English, and later it withstood a siege of several weeks by Owen Roe O'Neill.

Near the centre of the town is St Mel's Cathedral, a nineteenth-century Renaissance-style building of grey limestone. The saint's crosier is preserved in the diocesan museum at the rear of the cathedral. St Mel's College, the diocesan seminary, contains part of the library of Edgeworthstown House. The County museum containing many artefacts and providing a genealogical service is located in the old post office in the main street.

Around Longford
At Ballinakill, 8 miles (13 km) south-west, there are five cross-inscribed grave slabs mounted on a modern stand of cement. Here also is the 'Bishop's Grave', possibly that of the Bishop of Ardagh, William MacCasey, who died in 1373.

Three miles (5 km) north-west is the village of Newtownforbes, on the road to Carrick-on-Shannon. Between the village and Lough Forbes lies the demesne of Castle Forbes, a fine seventeenth-century castellated mansion. Permission to view the grounds must be obtained in advance. Lough Forbes, 2 miles (3 km) from the village, is one of the Shannon lakes, containing trout, pike and perch.

The village of Drumlish lies west of a ridge of low hills running north-eastwards from Newtownforbes to Arva in County Cavan. Carn Clonhugh (916 feet), the county's highest point, is 2 miles (3 km) south-east of Drumlish. From the summit, which is crowned by a cairn, there are good views. Ballinamuck, 4 miles (6 km) north of Drumlish, was where a French and Irish force under General Humbert was defeated in 1798 by the English army of General Lake. A statue near the village, of a pikeman holding a broken pikeshaft, commemorates the battle. A new monument to all who died in the battle was erected in 1983.

At Tubberpatrick, 3 miles (5 km) north of Ballinamuck, the old cemetery has memorials to General Blake, an Irish officer in the French Army, who was executed by the English after the Battle of Ballinamuck. Another monument is to Gunner Magee who fired one of Humbert's guns, loading it with broken pots and pans when the ammunition ran out. When a wheel of the gun broke towards the end of the battle, two of Magee's cousins supported the axle with their backs while he fired the last shot. Their backs were broken by the recoil. The Cashel Museum at Newtowncashel, a village that features in the annual Tidy Towns Competition, is a restored nineteenth-century cottage with the typical utensils etc. of the period.

Near Keenagh, at Corlea Bog, a preserved oak pathway across the bog over 5,000 years old was revealed.

Granard

Granard (Ugly Height)

👫👫 Pop. 1,338.

Granard, a market town and angling centre, stands on high ground near the Longford-Cavan border. Horse-riding is available and the County Longford Harriers hunt the district.

The prominent Motte of Granard, at the south-western end of the town, is said to be the site of the royal residence of Cairbre, eldest son of Niall the Great. The Anglo-Normans fortified the motte about 1200 to aid in the defence of the northern marches of Leinster. On top of the motte stands a statue of St Patrick, erected in 1932 to mark the fifteenth centenary of his coming to Ireland.

In 1315 Edward Bruce sacked and burned Granard after being refused winter quarters there. In 1798 a party of insurgents, who had withdrawn to Granard to regroup, was defeated here and most of them were executed on the spot. During the War of Independence the district witnessed many engagements.

Around Granard

Beside the village of Abbeylara (2½ miles/ 4 km) and near the shore of Lough Kinale are the slight remains of a thirteenth-century abbey founded by an Anglo-Norman, Richard Tuite. It was plundered by Edward Bruce after the sack of Granard, but it survived until the Dissolution and two of its abbots became bishops of Clonmacnois. A semicircular earthwork north of the village is regarded locally as the site of the original church founded here by St Patrick about 460. From the shore of Lough Kinale, 1 mile (2 km) north-east of Abbeylara, parts of the ancient defensive earthwork known as the Black Pig's Race extend north-westwards for 6 miles (10 km) to the shore of Lough Gowna.

Seven miles (11 km) west of Granard is the village of Ballinalee. This is where the commander of the English forces, Lord Cornwallis, stayed for two days after the Battle of Ballinamuck in 1798. During that time 130 insurgent prisoners were executed and buried in the old graveyard called 'Bully's Acre'.

About 4 miles (6 km) north of Granard is Lough Gowna, which lies partly in County Cavan. This lake provides fine views and holds very large trout. The River Erne, which has its source here, flows from an extension of the lake to the east (in County Cavan). On the 25-acre Inchmore Island, near the south-western corner of the lake, are some ancient church remains on the site of a monastery founded by St Columcille in the sixth century. A bronze bell from this church is preserved in the Catholic church at Aughnacliffe, west of the lake; beside the village a large dolmen can be seen.

Edgeworthstown

Mostrim – Meathas Truim
(Elder-tree Fruit)

👫👫 Pop. 806.

This neat village on the Dublin–Sligo road has a long association with the Edgeworth family, who first settled here in 1583. The best-known Edgeworths were Richard Lovell Edgeworth (1744–1817), an author and inventor; his daughter Maria (1767–1849), the novelist and essayist; the Abbé Edgeworth de Firmont (1745–1807), confessor to Louis XVI, whom he attended on the scaffold; and Michael Pakenham-Edgeworth (1812–1881), botanist and author.

Edgeworthstown House, at the eastern end of the village, was the family residence. Notable visitors here during the nineteenth century were Sir Walter Scott and William Wordsworth. The Edgeworth family vault, where Richard Lovell and Maria are interred, is in the churchyard of St John's.

Visitors are welcome to join the Longford Harriers hunt.

Around Edgeworthstown

Two miles (3 km) to the north-west, at Moatfarrell, is the ancient motte said to have been the inauguration mound of the O'Farrell chiefs. The tiny village of Ardagh is in a wooded area south-west of Edgeworthstown. The see of Ardagh, of which St Mel became the first bishop, was founded by St Patrick in the fifth century. Near the present St Patrick's Church are the ruins of an early church which may have been built on the site of the original cathedral where St Mel is reputed to have professed St Brigid.

The convent school beside the village was formerly Ardagh House, the residence of a landlord called Fetherstone. It was this house Goldsmith mistook for an inn one night in 1744, and his amusing experience inspired the comedy *She Stoops to Conquer*. The ornamental clock-tower in the village commemorates a member of the Fetherstone family.

About a mile (2 km) to the south-west is the Hill of Ardagh (659 feet) and 3 miles (5 km) to the west is the ruin of an O'Farrell fortress, Castlereagh Castle.

Lanesborough

Ballymahon

Baile Mathuna (Mahon's Town)

ŤŴŤ Pop. 859.

Ballymahon is on the Inny River, near the heart of the Goldsmith country. The river, spanned here by a bridge of five arches, holds brown trout—fishing being partly free.

Around Ballymahon

About 3 miles (5 km) to the east is Pallas, according to an entry in the family bible, the birthplace of Oliver Goldsmith 1729. Close to the village of Abbeyshrule are the ruins of a Cistercian abbey founded in 1150. At Gorteen, west of Ballymahon, lived John Keegan ('Leo') Casey (1846–1870) who wrote 'Maire, My Girl', 'The Rising of the Moon' and other patriotic ballads. On the Ballymahon–Longford road, 2 miles (3 km) north-west of Kenagh village, are the partially restored ruins of an Augustinian friary called Abbeyderg.

Twelve miles (19 km) from Ballymahon is Lanesborough, at the northern end of Lough Ree. A peat-fired electric power station is situated on the east bank of the River Shannon near the town. Lanesborough is a noted coarse-fishing centre. Horse-riding is available and boats may be hired to visit the ancient monastery of Inchcleraun on an island on Lough Ree. It is also the base for barge cruising.

Meath

Newgrange

County Meath consists almost entirely of a rich limestone plain, with occasional low hills. 'Royal Meath' was for centuries a separate province which included the area of County Westmeath. It was ruled by the kings of pagan and Early Christian Ireland. There is much to interest the visitor by way of scenic beauty and of historic sites, particularly in the Boyne valley. There are also seaside resorts along the county's coastline.

Navan

An Uaimh (The Cave or Grotto)

Pop. 3,411 (urban district).

Navan, the county town, is in pleasant undulating country at the meeting of the Boyne and Blackwater Rivers, with a recently developed industry deriving from mineral deposits. Navan is now one of the major centres for furniture manufacture in the country.

Things to do

There is tennis on grass courts, a horse-riding school and two cinemas in the town.

Greyhound racing is held every Wednesday and Thursday. Horse-racing is at Proudstown Park 2 miles (3 km) away. Golf (18) is 4 miles (6 km) from the town. Both the Rivers Boyne and Blackwater hold salmon, trout and perch. The Meath Foxhounds and the Tara Harriers hunt the area.

History

Navan is of great antiquity, but it was as a palatinate town of the English settlers that it became important. It was walled and fortified by Hugh de Lacy, and became an outpost in the defences of the Pale. Charters of incorporation were granted by English kings down to the seventeenth century. The town began to decline after the wars of 1641 which hit it hard, and the corporation was finally dissolved at the time of the Act of Union in 1800.

Around Navan

West of the town is the great Motte of Navan, a favourite vantage point. At Athlumney, 1½ miles (2 km) south, is the striking ruin of a sixteenth-century fortified mansion near the east bank of the River Boyne. Also at Athlumney is a souterrain, consisting of a large passage branching at right angles into two smaller passages, each with a 'beehive' chamber.

Beside the Boyne, 5 miles (8 km) south of Navan, are the extensive ruins of the twelfth-century Bective Abbey of the Cistercians. This was an important establishment whose abbot in later centuries was a lord of Parliament. The cloisters are well preserved. Another monastery site is at Ardbraccan, 3 miles (5 km) west of Navan. Here St Brecan (died 650) founded an establishment, and St Ultan added, in 656, a hospital for children whose mothers had died in a plague.

North-west of Navan is the mutilated Nevinstown Cross, whose inscription commemorates a Michael Cusack who died in 1589. Further along the River Blackwater, about 2 miles (3 km) from Navan, is Rathaldron Castle. This is a fifteenth-century quadrangular tower, partly modernised and incorporated in a nineteenth-century castellated mansion.

The Blackwater at Kells

On the opposite bank of the river is another quadrangular fortress, Liscartan Castle, which was held in 1633 by Sir William Talbot. Near by are the ruins of a church with some fine windows. Three miles (5 km) beyond is Donaghpatrick, on the site of a fifth-century church which was built for St Patrick by Conall, brother of King Laoghaire. Near the church are the remains of an ancient rath which consisted of a mound surrounded by four ramparts.

Near Donaghpatrick is Rathcairn, the centre of an Irish-speaking colony where there is a holiday hostel for children. To the west is the Hill of Tailte, and on it the Rath Dubh (Black Fort) which was the site of one of the four ancient royal residences built by King Tuathal. This was the venue of the Aonach Tailteann, the Olympic Games of Ireland, a festival established in prehistoric times and held here until the twelfth century. The Hill has fine views of the meandering Rivers Boyne and Blackwater.

One and a half miles (3 km) north-east of Navan on the Slane road is Donaghmore, site of an Early Christian settlement. A fine round tower (probably tenth century) remains. The doorway, twelve feet from the ground, has inclined jambs and a semicircular head; on the keystone is sculptured a figure of the crucified Christ, and on each side of the architrave is a sculptured human head. There are also some remains of a fifteenth-century church near by. About a mile (2 km) further east on a height overlooking the Boyne is the fifteenth-century Dunmoe Castle, which was burned in 1799. Many good views are to be had along this stretch of the river.

Six miles (10 km) south of Navan is the Hill of Tara, the religious and cultural capital of Ireland in ancient times. Every three years there was a great national assembly (feis) where laws were passed, tribal disputes settled and matters of peace and defence arranged. By the end of the sixth century the Tara monarchy had become the most powerful of Ireland's five kingdoms, but the importance of Tara itself waned with the spread of Christianity. Nevertheless it was the residence of Mael Shechlainn who abandoned it in 1022.

On the crest of the hill is a pillar-stone which is said to be the Lia Fail, coronation

Hill of Tara

stone of the ancient kings. Little else is to be seen today, apart from some low mounds and earthworks. The systematic scientific investigation of the site began in 1952 with the excavation of the Rath of the Synods.

Sixteen miles (26 km) south-east of Navan, on the Dublin–Slane road, is the village of Ashbourne. This was the scene of a notable engagement in the 1916 Rising which resulted in the surrender of British forces to Volunteers led by Thomas Ashe. Beside the village are the kennels and deerpark of the Ward Union Hunt.

To the south-west of Ashbourne (near Ratoath) is Fairyhouse racecourse, venue of the Irish Grand National.

Trim
Baile Atha Truim
(Town of Elder-tree Ford)

Pop. 1,781 (urban district).

Charmingly situated on the River Boyne, Trim is one of the oldest ecclesiastical centres in Ireland. Fishing, golf (18), riding. A town tourist trail is signposted.

History
The town takes its name from a small ford where the first inhabitants settled; the ford can still be seen above the town bridge. St Loman was first bishop of the see established here in the fifth century by St Patrick; in 1152 it was united with others to form the see of Meath. When the Anglo-Normans came, Trim and the area around were granted to Hugh de Lacy. Edward Bruce halted his army at Trim on the retreat from Munster, and later Richard II imprisoned the young Lords Gloucester and Henry of Lancaster (afterwards Henry V) in Trim Castle. The town was walled in 1359 and the fortifications strengthened. Several parliaments were held here in the fifteenth century. The inhabitants supported Lambert Simnel in

his attempts to claim the English throne from Henry VII, and in the sixteenth century 'Silken Thomas' Fitzgerald occupied the town during his brief insurrection against Henry VIII.

Confederate forces occupied the town in 1642 but were dislodged by Sir Charles Coote, who was afterwards killed here. The town fell to Cromwell in 1649.

Trim Castle, on the east side of the town overlooking the Boyne, is the largest Anglo-Norman fortress in Ireland. Originally constructed by Hugh de Lacy, it was later rebuilt. The well-preserved ruins cover two acres and consist of a keep with 70-foot high turrets, flanked by rectangular towers abutting on each side. The outer wall is almost 500 yards long and was strengthened by ten circular towers, including the gate-towers. The five surviving towers and one of the two gate-towers date from 1220; the South Gate (unique in Ireland) is later. The barbican is well preserved, but the portcullis and drawbridge have disappeared. A moat which could be filled from the River Boyne surrounded the fort and completed its isolation. Trim had two other fortresses, Nangle's Castle and Talbot's Castle. The latter, off High Street, was built in 1415 by the Lord Lieutenant of Ireland, Sir John Talbot. It was later converted into a school where the Duke of Wellington and Sir William Rowan Hamilton received their early education. The Duke lived in Dublingate Street (now Patrick Street), where a statue on a pillar commemorates him.

The Yellow Steeple, the most prominent of Trim's many ruins, overlooks the town from a ridge opposite Trim Castle. Once part of the thirteenth-century Augustinian abbey of St Mary's, the steeple dates from 1368. On the suppression of the abbey the buildings were reserved for the use of the Lord Deputy. By 1648 the abbey had decayed but the steeple was maintained as a watch-tower. It was deliberately destroyed in 1649 to prevent its falling into

Cromwellian hands, and today only the east wall remains. It is 125 feet high and is buttressed by fragments of the south and north walls. The floor levels of each of the five storeys may be clearly seen.

Other points of interest

St Patrick's Church of Ireland Cathedral was built early last century and may be on the site of a church founded by St Patrick. The square castellated tower belonged to an earlier structure, and dates from 1449. The tower's vaulted ground floor is used as a vestibule of the church.

In Market Street the Courthouse is said to be on the site of the medieval Grey Friary dedicated to St Bonaventure. The records of Trim Corporation, dating from 1659, are preserved in the Town Hall in Castle Street. There are some remains of the old town walls still to be seen. These include the ruined Sheepgate, a semi-circular-headed arch about 15 feet high, and fragmentary remains at the Watergate.

Around Trim

About a mile (2 km) downstream from Trim Castle is Newtown Trim, where there are the ruins of the Abbey of the Canons Regular of St Victor. It was founded in 1206 by the first English bishop of Meath, Simon de Rochfort, and the church served as cathedral for the see of Meath for over 300 years until the confiscation of the abbey in 1536. Some distance east is the ruined St John's Priory, founded in the thirteenth century for Crouched Friars of St John the Baptist.

About 2 miles (3 km) south of Trim is Laracor, where Dean Swift was rector from 1700 to 1713. Near by, on the Trim road, are the remains of the cottage occupied by 'Stella' (Hester Johnson). Further south in the wooded demesne of Summerhill is the sixteenth-century Lynch Castle, destroyed in 1649.

On the Dublin–Mullingar road, 4 miles (6 km) from Trim, is the tiny village of Clonard. The great monastic school of

Clonard, founded in the sixth century by St Finian, attracted thousands of pupils from all over Ireland as well as from Britain and Europe. Despite repeated plunderings, the school flourished for centuries after Finian's death, but no trace remains of it nor of the Augustinian monastery built on the site in 1175. A large body of insurgents was defeated at Clonard in one of the last major engagements of the 1798 Rising.

Three miles (5 km) west of Trim on the way to Athboy is Trimblestown Castle. It was strongly garrisoned and fortified during the Cromwellian wars, and eventually surrendered to General Jones in 1647.

Athboy

Baile Atha Buidhe
(The Town of the Yellow Ford)

 Pop. 1,055.

This is a small agricultural town on the Athboy River, in wooded country near the County Westmeath border. In medieval times it was a walled stronghold of the Pale. Owen Roe O'Neill took it in 1643, and six years later Cromwell camped his army on the Hill of Ward near by.

The tower of the Protestant church is a remnant of a fourteenth-century Carmelite priory. Behind the church are remains of the town walls.

Around Athboy

A mile (2 km) east is the Hill of Ward, site of the ancient palace of Tlachtga and the venue of an oenach or festival like that of Tailteann. Three miles (5 km) north of the hill, on the Athboy–Navan road, are the ruins of Rathmore Church (fifteenth century) and Rathmore Castle. The church, disused since the seventeenth century, has some interesting sculpture.

At Ballyfallon, 1½ miles (3 km) south of Athboy, is the house which was the boyhood home of a pioneer of the Irish language revival, Father Eoghan O

Gramhna. At Kildalkey, 4 miles (7 km) south of Athboy, are the remains of a medieval church said to be on the site of the seventh-century abbey of St Dympna. Further south is the village of Ballivor, on the edge of the extensive Clonycavan bog.

Kells

Ceanannus Mor (Great Residence)

Pop. 2,187 (urban district).

This ancient town is in a wooded part of the River Blackwater valley. Golf (18) and angling.

History

Kells reached its greatest importance when St Columcille founded a monastic settlement there in the sixth century. The foundation survived repeated raids by Danish and Norse invaders, and was strengthened in the ninth century by a colony of monks who took refuge at Kells after being expelled from Iona by the Danes.

An illuminated Latin manuscript of the four gospels, the *Book of Kells*, was produced here about the beginning of the ninth century. It is one of the greatest triumphs of illuminated art that the world has seen. During the Cromwellian invasion the book was removed to Dublin and was later presented to Trinity College Library, where it is on view today. A facsimile is in St Columba's Church in Kells. The Cumhdach or Shrine of Kells, an elaborately ornamented book shrine, is now lost, but another of the Kells treasures, a crosier made in the monastery, is in the British Museum.

The monastic settlement was sacked many times during the tenth and eleventh centuries, but was rebuilt each time. In 1152 Cardinal Paparo attended a synod at Kells as papal legate and presented palls to the four archbishops of Ireland. De Lacy built a castle here in the twelfth century, and later the place was walled and fortified. In 1315 Edward Bruce burned the town, but it

was rebuilt and granted a charter by Richard II. Kells maintained its importance until the dissolution of the monastery in 1551.

Points of interest

St Columcille's House is a high-roofed building similar to St Kevin's church at Glendalough and Cormac's chapel at Cashel. It measures about 24 by 21 feet, with walls nearly four feet thick; the height is 38 feet. The roof is a continuation of the side walls, which incline inwards until they meet in a ridge; the gable walls are therefore almost in the shape of a half ellipse. There are two storeys, and the upper one seems to have been divided into three rooms. The ceiling of the lower storey is barrel vaulted. The original doorway, eight feet from the ground, has been walled up and another door opened at ground level.

The Round Tower nearly 100 feet high is a perfect specimen, though it has lost the original conical cap. The top storey is unusual for having five windows, each of which points to an ancient entrance to the town. Near the round tower is the largest and probably the oldest of the Kells high crosses. It carries a wealth of sculptured

High Cross and Round Tower at Kells

ornament. There are three other crosses in the graveyard. In the market place is a fifth cross, also richly sculptured, which was used as a gallows in 1798. The upper part of the shaft and the top portion of the wheel are missing.

Around Kells

A prominent feature on the road to Virginia is the Hill of Lloyd (428 feet). On the top is a tower resembling a lighthouse, a folly erected to the memory of the Earl of Bective by his son. Outside the town on the north-east is the wooded estate of Headfort and a fine golf course (18). Two miles (3 km) to the north is the ruin of Dulane Church, which has a fine early doorway with massive lintel and slightly sloping jambs. Nine miles (14 km) north-east of Kells is the village of Nobber, near which (at Spiddal) the last of the Irish bards, Turlough O'Carolan, was born in 1670.

About 4 miles (6 km) west of Kells, on the south side of the River Blackwater, is the ruin of the fourteenth-century St Kieran's Church. The remains include a number of the termon crosses that marked the boundary of sanctuary around a church.

Oldcastle

Sean-chaislean an Fhasaigh
(The Old Ruined Castle)

Pop. 869.

This neat little town is on the broad plain that extends from Loughcrew to the hills of County Cavan.

Around Oldcastle

Three miles (5 km) south-east of Oldcastle is a range of hills called Slieve na Caillighe (also known as the Loughcrew Hills). A remarkable group of about 30 neolithic chambered cairns is spread over the three peaks, making the area one of the most important archaeological sites in the country. Many of the cairns' structural

stones are decorated in the same style as those at Newgrange, and there is similar decoration on the huge stone that stands a few feet north of the summit cairn of Sliabh na Caillighe. There is a cemetery or collection of passage-graves situated on the neighbouring peaks which are called Cairnbane East and Cairnbane West.

St Oliver Plunkett, the martyred Archbishop of Armagh, was born at Loughcrew in 1625. He was canonised as a martyr saint in Rome in 1975.

Slane

Baile Shláine (Slaine's Town)

This pleasant village is in one of the loveliest parts of the Boyne valley. There is fishing on the Slane Estate Fishery by permit from the secretary. Slane was the birthplace of Francis Ledwidge, the poet whose promising career was cut short by his death in the First World War. A folk and transport museum has a collection of vehicles and memorabilia.

Around Slane

A mile (2 km) to the north is Slane Hill (500 feet), where St Patrick proclaimed Christianity in 433 by lighting the paschal fire. The fine view embraces much beautiful countryside, including the whole of the Boyne valley from Trim to Drogheda. On the hill are remains of a sixteenth-century church on the site of the ancient church founded by St Patrick, and of the

Francis Ledwidge's cottage at Slane

The Hermitage of St Erc, near Slane

monastic school which became a noted seat of learning in later centuries. In the graveyard near by are some interesting

tombs, and on the west side of the hill the remains of an ancient circular fort.

To the west beside the river is Slane Castle, beautifully situated in a demesne which contains the ruins of a Gothic church called the Hermitage of St Erc. Erc was the first Bishop of Slane.

Along the north bank of the River Boyne, a few miles to the east, is the remarkable pre-Christian cemetery Brugh na Boinne, legendary burial-place of the kings. It is a series of neolithic tumuli of which the three principal mounds are at Knowth, Newgrange and Dowth, about 1 mile (2 km) apart from one another. The Newgrange tumulus has a passageway leading to a central chamber with side recesses for burials. During the winter solstice, the rays of the sun reach the central chamber. Newgrange has been developed as a major tourist attraction and has its own tourist information office (seasonal). Tel. (041) 24272. At all three sites there are interestingly decorated stones.

Newgrange

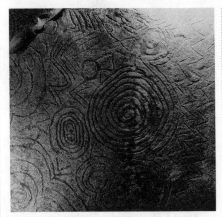

Detail of spiral rock patterns, Newgrange

About a mile (2 km) west of New-grange on the further bank of the Boyne is Rosnaree, where the third-century King Cormac Mac Airt was buried, according to legend. Against his wishes, attempts were made to inter him with the pagan kings at Brugh na Boinne—but this was foiled by the sudden rising of the river, which carried his bier down to Rosnaree.

Duleek
Daimhliag Chianain
(The Churchstone of St Cianan)

This little village is 5 miles (8 km) south-west of Drogheda in the valley of the River Nanny. Its name comes from an ancient stone church—one of the first in Ireland—said to have been founded in the fifth century by St Patrick for his disciple St Cianan; no trace of the church remains. The remains of St Mary's, an Augustinian priory founded in 1182 by Hugh de Lacy stand on the site.

In a cemetery overlooking the village is the belfry of the ruined Priory of the Blessed Virgin (twelfth century). Grave slabs of the sixteenth and seventeenth centuries can be seen in the ruins, and the graveyard has two interesting crosses. On a pedestal in the village is an unusual pillar cross, the Dowdall Cross, erected in 1601 as a memorial to the Bathe family.

South-east of the village an inscribed plaque bearing the date 1587 is set in the parapet of the bridge; this is reputedly the same bridge over which the Irish Jacobite Army retreated from the Boyne in 1690.

Around Duleek
Four miles (6 km) north of Duleek is the little village of Donore, near which is the site of the Battle of the Boyne. From Donore Hill the ground slopes down to the river, and here on 1 July 1690 (12 July by the modern calendar), William III defeated the exiled James II for the crown of England. James had his headquarters in the medieval church ruin on the summit of Donore Hill. The Williamite army crossed the Boyne at several points, forcing the Jacobites to fall back on Donore and eventually to Duleek. The Williamite commander, General Schomberg, was killed while leading an attack across the principal ford at Oldbridge, and William himself received a shoulder wound during reconnaissance before the battle. On the County Louth bank of the river is the ravine called King William's Glen.

Three miles (5 km) south of Duleek is Athcarne Castle, a massive Elizabethan mansion originally built in 1587.

Bettystown and Laytown
Baile an Bhiadhtaigh
(Town of the Hospitaller)
Port na Hinse (The River-meadow Fort)

Pop. 3,321.

These are twin seaside resorts on the short strip of coastline which is County Meath's only outlet to the sea. A magnificent sandy beach stretches 6 miles (10 km) from south of Laytown to the mouth of the Boyne at Mornington. The eighth-century Tara Brooch, one of the finest examples of the goldsmith's art in Early Christian Ireland, was found on the beach at Bettystown in 1850. It is now pre-served in the National Museum in Dublin.

Golf (18) Laytown/Bettystown G.C. Fishing, brown and sea trout, on the River Nanny. Tennis at Bettystown.

Around Bettystown and Laytown

The Maiden Tower at Mornington, a beacon for ships entering Drogheda, dates from Elizabethan times. Near by is a small obelisk called 'The Lady's Finger'.

Near the village of Gormanston, 4 miles (6 km) south of Laytown, is Gormanston Castle, now the property of the Franciscan Order. Built in 1786 by Sir Jenico Preston, 12th Viscount Gormanstown, it is on the site of a castle built in 1372. The castle chapel dates from 1687. On the lawn at the east end of the castle

are fine cloistral walks made up of yew trees in the form of a triangle with sides 100 yards long; near by is a spherical tea house of yews.

On the border with Dublin is the important prehistoric site of Fourknocks (near Naul, a village 5 miles (8 km) west of Balbriggan). The site dates from the Early Bronze Age (about 1800 B.C.) and three earthen mounds have been excavated. In one is a passage-grave of cruciform plan, with decorated uprights and lintels resembling the Newgrange designs.

On the coast, north of Balbriggan, is the Mosney Holiday Centre which has modern amenities for family holidays.

Louth

Cooley Peninsula

L outh, the smallest county in Ireland, covers an area of only 317 square miles. It runs northwards from the River Boyne to Carlingford Lough, consisting mainly of fertile undulating country with a coastline of wide sandy bays and occasional rocky headlands. In the north, however, between Dundalk Bay and Carlingford Lough, is the mountainous Cooley Peninsula. The territory now known as County Louth figures prominently in the epic tales of ancient Ireland. It was also the scene of important events, and many chapters of Ireland's history are illustrated by the county's numerous relics of the past.

The Cooley Peninsula

The Cooley Peninsula, between Dundalk Bay and Carlingford Lough, is one of the finest scenic areas on the east coast. Carlingford Lough is particularly beautiful, with the Cooley Mountains on its south side and the Mourne Mountains rising steeply from the northern shore. This peninsula was the scene of the *Táin Bó Cuailgne* ('The Cattle Raid of Cooley'), a famous legend of ancient Ireland.

Approaching the peninsula from Dundalk, there is a fine example of a dolmen (Proleek Dolmen) near Ballymascanlon. About 3 miles (5 km) beyond Riverstown, the road divides. Straight ahead is Greenore; to the left is Carlingford.

Carlingford

Carlingford is at the foot of Slieve Foye (1,935 feet), on the southern shore of Carlingford Lough. Tradition says that St Patrick landed near here on his return from Rome. Later the Norsemen established a settlement, which they used as a base for plundering the rich hinterland. After the Anglo-Norman invasion, King John ordered the erection of a castle to guard the harbour. Although not walled until the sixteenth century, the town was always strongly fortified and had at one time 32 castellated buildings.

The ruin of King John's Castle, a massive fortress overlooking the harbour, may occupy the site of a much older structure. A high wall running north and south divides the castle into two; the west section is the older. Off Dundalk Street is the fourteenth-century Dominican Abbey; a long high building of stone, it is divided into nave and chancel by a square tower over a beautiful Gothic arch. Taaffe's Castle (probably sixteenth

century) is a large square keep near Newry Street; the building is in good preservation. Just off the Square is the Mint, a fortified house of the fifteenth century. Near by, forming an arch over the roadway, is the Tholsel. This was originally a gate-tower in the town walls; during the eighteenth century it was used as a gaol.

The tower of the Protestant church was originally part of the town's fortifications— the church being later built against it. Other remains of the town walls can also be seen. The Church of Ireland Rectory and Ghan House are notable eighteenth-century residences. Carlingford was the birthplace of Thomas D'Arcy McGee (1825–1868), the poet and Canadian statesman.

Greenore is a container ferry port in beautiful surroundings near the entrance to Carlingford Lough, with a shingle beach extending over 3 miles (5 km). It has an 18-hole golf course. South-west of Ballagan, 3 miles (5 km) to the south, is the ruin of the fifteenth-century Ballug Castle. Near by is another fifteenth-century ruin, Kilwirra Church, which may have belonged to the Knights Templars who gave their name to the surrounding district, Templetown.

Omeath is another beautifully situated little resort, near the head of Carlingford Lough. In the hills near by, Flagstaff Cairn and the Long Woman's Grave are good vantage points for fine views across the lough. A novel feature of the village on Sundays in summer is that jaunting cars may be hired to take trips from the strand to the open-air Calvary and Stations of the Cross at the Charity Fathers' Monastery which are much visited; some of the statues were smuggled from France during the persecutions there.

Dundalk
Dun Dealgan (Delga's Fort)

👫 Pop. 25,842 (urban district).

ℹ️ Tourist information office: Market Square. Tel. (042) 35484. Fax (042) 38070.

Dundalk, a busy manufacturing centre at the head of Dundalk Bay, is the county town of Louth.

Things to do
Dundalk racecourse is 1½ miles (2 km) to the north. There is greyhound racing twice weekly. Salmon and trout fishing is available on the River Fane and other streams, and there is golf (18) at Blackrock, horse-riding instruction and pony-trekking. Louth Foxhounds and Dundalk Harriers hunt the district. Tennis, squash, dancing, cinemas and other entertainments are available. An international theatre festival takes place every year. The forest park at Ravensdale has walks and nature trails.

History
The area is associated with Cuchulainn, a hero of the legendary Red Branch Knights who are associated with the Early Christian

period. In 929, when Norse sea-rovers held many bases on Ireland's east coast, one of their fleets was captured in Dundalk Bay by the Prince of Aileach, 'Murtagh of the Leathern Cloaks'. In the same century another Norse naval force was defeated in the bay by the Munster fleet.

In 1177 the Anglo-Norman John de Courcy took possession of Dundalk on his way north to subdue Ulster. Henry II granted the town eight years later to Bertram de Verdon, who walled and fortified it; King John later made the place a royal borough. Dundalk was burned in 1253 by Brian O'Neill and again in 1315 by Edward Bruce, who was crowned King of Ireland on a hill near the town. His army was defeated and Bruce himself slain three years later at Faughart (see below).

During the next 300 years, Dundalk was the object of repeated attacks as a frontier town of the English Pale. In 1600 it was garrisoned by Lord Mountjoy in his campaign against Hugh O'Neill. It changed hands several times in the wars of the seventeenth century—down to 1690, when the Williamite army entered as James II withdrew southwards to the River Boyne. Most of the fortifications were removed during the eighteenth century, and few traces of the town's historic past now remain.

Points of interest
The Catholic St Patrick's Church, a fine building in Newry granite, has an exterior modelled on King's College Chapel, Cambridge. The high altar and pulpit are of carved Caen stone, and there is good mosaic work in the chancel and side-chapels. Fronting the church is a memorial to a sea tragedy in 1858, when four members of a rescuing party lost their lives.

Among Dundalk's nineteenth-century buildings are the Town Hall and the Courthouse. In Market Square is the 1798 Memorial. In Clanbrassil Street, north of the Market Square, is St Nicholas' Church (Church of Ireland). Its records date back to 1207, though only the tower of the present structure is ancient. Among the tombstones in the churchyard is that of Agnes Galt, sister of the Scottish poet Robert Burns. Burns is commemorated by a pillar to the right of the church entrance.

The Arctic explorer Admiral Sir Francis Leopold McClintock (1819–1907) was born in Kincora House, Seatown Place. Also in Seatown Place is the old Windmill, an immense structure of seven storeys which dominates the view from Roden Place. In Castle Street is the ruin called the Castle, which is actually the bell-tower of a thirteenth-century Franciscan friary; the tower was repaired early in the nineteenth century.

Around Dundalk

To the north-east of Dundalk is the Cooley Peninsula. Near the village of Kilcurry, 3½ miles (6 km) north of the town, is the birthplace at Rosskea of the celebrated Gaelic poet, Peadar Ó Doirnín (1704–1768). He taught at Kilkerley (3 miles/5 km) west of Dundalk and at other places in the county before settling as a schoolmaster at Forkhill, County Armagh. Faughart, 4 miles (6 km) north of Dundalk, is the reputed birthplace of St Brigid; her shrine here is a place of pilgrimage. Edward Bruce, killed in battle at Faughart Hill in 1318, was buried in Faughart cemetery.

At Castletown, 1½ miles (2 km) west of Dundalk is the ancient Dun Dealgan—a mound rising over 60 feet high that is said to be the birthplace of the legendary hero Cuchulainn. On the summit is the ruin of a house built in 1780. Castletown Castle, not far distant, is a well-preserved building of four storeys, with angular corner-towers. This was a fortress of the Bellew family, who also owned Castle Roche, an imposing structure standing on a precipitous rock 4 miles (6 km) further north-west.

At the old church at Ballybarrack, 2 miles (3 km) south of Dundalk, the

shrine of St Oliver Plunkett is a place of pilgrimage. Five miles (8 km) south-west of Dundalk is the village of Knockbridge, where the Catholic church is unusual in that the high altar is in the middle of one of the long walls. The bronze crucifix over the tabernacle is a copy of the ancient Cross of Clogher. A mile (2 km) from Knockbridge, at Ratheddy, is the conspicuous landmark of 'Clochafermor' or 'Cuchulainn's Stone'.

According to legend the mortally wounded Cuchulainn threw away his sword and bound himself to this stone, so that even in death he would face his enemies standing. It was not until a bird perched on his shoulder that his adversaries could be sure he was dead and dared to approach. A bog near by is said to be the site of 'Lochan an Chlaiomh' (The lakelet of the Sword), into which Cuchulainn's sword fell.

Eight miles (13 km) south-west of Dundalk is the village of Louth. Though now only a cluster of houses, it was once important enough to give its name to the county. St Patrick is said to have built the original church here and to have appointed St Mochta first Bishop of Louth. St Mochta's House, beside the village, is a small building dating probably from the twelfth century. It is in excellent preservation and has a high-pitched roof of stone. The lower storey is vaulted and the upper is reached by a stairway built into one of the walls. Also beside the village is St Mary's Abbey. Built long before Anglo-Norman times, it was reconditioned in 1148 by Donough O'Carroll, the Prince of Oriel, who also endowed Mellifont. In 1242 an important synod was held here. The abbey was destroyed by fire in 1312 but rebuilt. The ruins (probably fourteenth century) are of a large church about 150 feet by 50 feet.

A mile (2 km) to the east of Louth is the height called Ardpatrick, site of a church founded by St Patrick. St Oliver Plunkett lived here for some years and ordained many priests in the area.

Blackrock
Creagacha Dubha (Black Rocks)

Blackrock is a small but popular resort on the shore of Dundalk Bay 3 miles (5 km) south of the town and near the mouth of the River Fane.

Things to do
Attractions include bathing, golf (18), tennis and other seaside amusements. The River Fane holds some salmon, sea trout and brown trout.

Around Blackrock
Three miles (5 km) to the west is Heynestown Castle, a ruined sixteenth-century tower, and not far distant from that is another ruin, Dunmahon Castle. South of Dunmahon, on the banks of the River Fane, is the ruin of a medieval Franciscan foundation, Rossmakea Abbey.

Four miles (6 km) from Blackrock is Dromiskin, site of a monastery said to have been founded by St Patrick. It suffered much in the tenth century from raids by the Norsemen, who were strongly established on the nearby coast. In the fourteenth century the primates of Armagh had their residence here. The graveyard is the site of the ancient monastery, and there are some remains of a medieval church, a round tower and a sculptured cross.

A mile (2 km) north-west of Dromiskin is Milltown Castle, which was used as a dwelling down to recent times. A well-preserved structure that is remarkably narrow in proportion to its height, the building has round corner-towers and unusually high-pitched stepped battlements.

A few miles west of Dromiskin, is the modernised Darver Castle, originally a square keep with corner turrets. Killin-coole Castle, a mile (2 km) further north, is also in good preservation. A native of Darver was Dr Nicholas Callan (1799–1864), professor of natural philosophy and mathematics at Maynooth for 38 years. He was an outstanding pioneer in the field of electricity, and published works on mathematics, science and religion.

Five miles (8 km) south of Blackrock is Castlebellingham, a village formerly called Garlandstown or Gernonstown after an Anglo-Norman family who occupied the castle until their estates were confiscated by the Cromwellians and granted to Henry Bellingham. The old castle of the Gernons was burned in 1690. A wayside shrine at the entrance to the Bellingham demesne commemorates a deceased member of the family. Colonel Thomas Bellingham was aide-de-camp to King William at the Battle of the Boyne. Two miles (3 km) south of the village, a number of Bronze Age implements were found during excavations at Greenmount Motte.

Three miles (5 km) south-east of Castle-bellingham is the fishing village of Annagassan, the site of one of the east-coast settlements established by the Danes. The Rivers Dee and Glyde, both of which hold salmon and trout, unite about half a mile (1 km) to the south and flow into Dundalk Bay at the village.

Ardee
Baile Atha Fhirdiadh
(The Town of Ferdia's Ford)

👪👪 Pop. 3,253.

Ardee is an ancient town on the River Dee near the border with County Meath. There is golf (18) at the northern end of the town, and the Dee has salmon, trout and pike fishing. Louth Foxhounds hunt the district.

History
Even in pre-Christian times this was a place of importance as a strategic crossing on the main road to the north. It formed part of the ancient territory of Muirtheimhne, and was the scene of one of the most famous of Ireland's ancient epics—the four-day hand-to-hand combat in which Cuchulainn finally slew his friend Ferdia (from whom the place gets its name).

In 943 Murtagh of the Leathern Cloaks, Prince of Aileach, was killed at Ardee in a battle with the Norsemen. After the Anglo-Norman invasion the district came into the hands of Roger de Pippard, who founded the Trinitarian monastery and hospital of St John at Ardee in 1207. The town which grew around these establishments became an important outpost of the English Pale.

In 1641 Sir Phelim O'Neill took the town on his way to Drogheda, but on the retreat was overtaken here by English forces and his rearguard defeated. Ardee was occupied by James II in 1689, and in the following year both James and William passed through on their way to the Boyne. The Corporation of Ardee was dissolved in 1800, but the silver maces and the minute book (earliest entry 1661) are preserved.

Points of interest

In the main street is Ardee Castle, a square keep of the early thirteenth century, possibly built by Roger de Pippard. It was frequently a mustering point for attacks on Ulster by the English. At the Restoration the castle was given to Theobald Taaffe, Earl of Carlingford. In the nineteenth century the building was repaired and converted to use as a courthouse (to enter, apply to the town clerk). Hatch's Castle, in Market Street, is also believed to date from the thirteenth century; it differs from Ardee Castle in that its corners are rounded and not square (not open to the public).

The Protestant St Mary's Church in the main street includes part of an ancient Carmelite church said to have been founded by Roger de Pippard. The church was burned by Edward Bruce in 1315 but later rebuilt, except for the north aisle which the present building still lacks. Some features of the old church have been uncovered, including the piers of the chancel. Here also is a staircase built in the wall, possibly to lead up to the rood screen and serve as a pulpit. The church contains a beautifully carved font which was discovered in Mansfieldstown graveyard,

near Castlebellingham. At the church entrance is an ancient stone cross, with ornamentations.

The pier of the east gate ('Cappocks Gate') is all that remains of the medieval wall.

Around Ardee

Two miles (3 km) south-east of Ardee at Kildemock is the 'Jumping Church', so called because the gable (which is the only remaining wall) stands three feet inside its foundation. Tradition states that the wall jumped inwards to exclude the grave of an excommunicated person who had been buried within the church.

Near by is the ancient earthen Fort of Garret Iarla. According to legend, Garret Fitzgerald and his soldiers sleep enchanted in a cave here—waiting for a six-fingered man to break the spell by drawing from its scabbard a sword that hangs in the cave.

Near the slight remains of the old church of Stickillin, 2 miles (3 km) east of Ardee, are three interesting souterrains, one of which has two entrances and is almost large enough for a person to walk upright inside.

About 4 miles (6 km) south of Ardee is Smarmore Castle, a square keep probably dating from the fourteenth century. Modern wings have been added and the castle operates an adventure centre. It was occupied by a branch of the Taaffe family. Among the members of this family were Theobald Taaffe (1639–1677), general of the Catholic Confederation forces in Connacht and Munster; Francis Taaffe (1639–1704) and Nicholas Taaffe (1677–1769), both of whom became field-marshals of the Austrian Army; and John Taaffe (1787–1862), a poet who is best known as a commentator on Dante.

At Dromin, 3 miles (5 km) from Ardee on the Dunleer road, are the remains of an ancient church. In 1678 Dunleer was given a charter by Charles II, and the borough returned two members to the Irish Parliament down to 1800. In the Catholic churchyard is the grave of Father Laurence Murray (died 1941), a former parish priest who was a prominent figure in the Irish language revival. In the porch of the Protestant church are three ancient cross-inscribed stones. John Foster, the last Speaker of the Irish House of Commons, is buried in the adjoining graveyard.

South from Dunleer, 1½ miles (2 km) on the west side of the main road, is Athclare Castle, a well-preserved fortified mansion, with a square battlemented tower. Three miles (5 km) east of Dunleer is Barmeath Castle, a castellated mansion incorporating parts of an ancient castle.

On the other side of Ardee, 2 miles (3 km) to the north-west, was the Ford of Aclint (where Aclint bridge now spans the River Glyde). This was the scene of parleys between Hugh O'Neill and the Earl of Essex in September 1599. These meetings resulted in the signing of a truce at the castle of Captain Garret Fleming at Lagan Ford, 2 miles (3 km) to the south-west. Captain Fleming was the father of a celebrated Franciscan priest, Patrick Fleming, who was born at Lagan Castle in the year of the truce. He was martyred in what is now Czechoslovakia in 1631.

Monasterboice
Mainistir Buithe (St Buite's Abbey)

Monasterboice, a secluded place 6 miles (10 km) north-west of Drogheda, is noted for its remains of the monastic settlement founded by St Buite as early as the fifth century. Little is known about the life of this saint, but he is said to have studied in Wales and to have been a missionary among the Picts before returning to Ireland and founding a monastery here on land granted by the local chief. St Buite is said to have died in 521, but there is no definite evidence to support this.

Points of interest
The remains, surrounded by the old grave-yard, consist of two churches, a round tower, three sculptured crosses, two early grave slabs and a sundial. The South Church (probably ninth century) is the older of the two. It consists of a rectan-gular nave roughly 39 by 22 feet. There are some slight remains of the chancel arch (now blocked). The present west wall is of later date than the rest of the building.

The smaller North Church, beside the round tower, is a rectangular building with no trace of a chancel. The west door, pointed on the outside, is continued through the wall by a round-headed vault. There is another larger door in the south wall. The

Detail from High Cross at Monasterboice

Round Tower, Monasterboice

east gable has collapsed, leaving no trace of the east window; but each of the side walls has two windows.

The Round Tower, 51 feet across and about 100 feet high, must have been the tallest in Ireland when complete with now missing upper part and conical cap. The door, six feet above the present ground level, is approached by a modern flight of steps (removable ladders were used in ancient times). The door has a round-headed arch made from a single stone.

The cross nearest the graveyard entrance is Muireadach's Cross, an outstanding example of the high crosses of the Early Christian period in Ireland. It is a monolith 17 feet 8 inches high, with almost every inch of the surface ornamented with sculptured panels of excellent design and workmanship. The bottom panel on the west face of the shaft bears the inscription Or do Muireadach las ndearnad in Chros ('a prayer for Muireadach who caused the Cross to be made'). This was probably the Muireadach, Abbot of Monasterboice, who died in 922.

Also richly ornamented is the West Cross, 21 feet 6 inches high. Between the shaft and the head is a separate stone that shows much less weathering, and so was probably inserted at a later date. Some of the scenes on this cross resemble those on Muireadach's Cross, but the others are generally much more difficult to interpret.

The North Cross, which was about 16 feet high, consists of the head supported on a modern stem (in place of the original one which lies broken inside the enclosing railings). The only carvings on this cross are a simple representation of the Crucifixion on the west face, and a beautiful circular pattern of spirals on the east face.

A grave slab, inside the railings around the West Cross, bears a cross with triangular expansions of the arms. Another grave slab, which lies inside a low railing

Muireadach's Cross, Monasterboice

to the north of the North Cross, is inscribed with a Latin cross and the words 'Or do Ruarcan' (a prayer for Ruarcan). The sundial, now inside the protecting railings around the North Cross, is a granite block 6 feet 8 inches in height. Sundials are common on ancient monastic sites in Ireland, but this one is more ornate than most of its kind.

Around Monasterboice

About a mile (2 km) north of Monasterboice is a good example of a Bronze Age 'gallery grave' at Paddock, near Tenure. This is locally called 'the Cailleach Beara's House'—the Cailleach (or Hag) Beara being a noted figure in Irish folklore.

Drogheda

Droichead Atha (The Bridge of the Ford)

Pop. 23,845 (borough).

Tourist information office (seasonal): Tel. (041) 37070.

- IRELAND -
A TRADITION OF CREATIVITY AND QUALITY

Travelling through Ireland most visitors are struck by the unspoilt nature of the countryside. From the stark beauty of the Cliffs of Moher in County Clare to the gently rolling Shannon, much of Ireland's strikingly beautiful countryside remains unchanged since pre-Celtic times. To some it can appear that an unseen hand has been responsible for preserving this for modern generations. And in some ways this may be true. There has been no "grand plan" over the centuries, no particular resistance to industrialisation, and certainly no element of backwardness. In fact, Ireland stands out as one of the most technologically advanced nations in Europe.

Galway gave birth to the legendary Claddagh Ring and now plays host to Digital, one of the largest computer corporations in the world. Surprisingly there is a common element in these two seemingly very different traditions. Modern high-tech industries are known for their emphasis on quality, innovation and creativity.

Irish craftsmanship, whether in textiles, jewellery, crystalware, knitwear or art is based on the same principles.

Irish design and craftsmanship has always been known to impress. The Tara Brooch has been a symbol of these qualities for centuries. This and other similar works made Irish metalwork famous throughout the world before Caesar first set foot in Britain. And its fame continues. Today, that spirit of craftsmanship has found a whole new range of expression. While remaining distinctly Irish and unchanged, it is undoubtedly modern and its most enduring facet is its quality. This reflects a commitment to quality inbred in the Irish and given its greatest expression in the magnificent Book of Kells - which can only be said to speak for itself.

On holiday people's minds usually turn to gifts and souvenirs. But souvenirs and gifts are only part of the story. Almost everything you will see, apart from the country itself, can be bought almost anywhere in the world. In fact, in many cases more are sold outside of Ireland than inside. But why wait to return? Why not buy them in their home? The quality alone is reason enough to buy, and the value here makes it even more compelling. Take fabrics and textiles for example. These did not come out of thin air. They came out of the land and the people. The Aran sweater was born out of the wild Atlantic seaboard of Ireland's western shores. Handmade to patterns passed on from generation to generation, you won't find any better insulation from Ireland's soft rain. The Aran sweater itself has evolved to take modern tastes into account. You can now buy this most traditional of Irish clothing in a range of stunning styles and colours which make not only a warm functional garment but an exciting fashion accessory as well. Irish tweed is nothing short of legendary. Anyone who has worn the real thing will accept no substitute. The combination of this fabric and the talents of Irish designers has brought about a beautiful new array of styles. Then there is the whole range of Irish knitwear. Using a variety of natural fibres, both home grown and imported, the range of stylish, high quality sweaters, cardigans, jackets and so on, from small and large firms throughout the country, will surprise even the most experienced traveller. Almost every town you visit will have its own range, whether from small producers preserving the great hand knitting tradition and styles of an older Ireland, or from modern sophisticated factories producing the most modern styles but still adhering to that tradition of quality.

If Irish clothing and fabric have done much to make this small country world famous, then what can be said of Irish crystal? From the White House to the Elysee Palace toasts are drunk from Irish glassware, rooms are lit from it, and punch is served from it. The traditions of Irish glass blowing and cutting go back almost as far as

the first use of glass in this country and survive today as the world's best. Visitors have been so impressed with the standard of Irish glassware that their first visit to Ireland started them on a lifetime hobby, collecting crystal. These same people created such a demand for it that now it can be bought in most leading department stores in most cities in the world. The same standard of care and craftsmanship which goes into the creation of Irish crystal also goes into Irish jewellery. From the traditional Claddagh Rings and Tara Brooches to highly innovative pieces by young Irish artists, Irish jewellery is distinctive, exciting and above all - beautiful.

This is only a small foretaste of what awaits travellers through Ireland. Our designs and products have been forged with much more than human hand and mind, like that strange quality 'Irishness' which has been a hallmark of our people wherever they have travelled in the world. It is a unique bridge between past and present, between what we were, still are, and have become.

Ireland's Trade Board, ITB have been helping people all over the world experience this tradition for many years. Most of the goods you will find throughout the country are also available in almost every corner of the world thanks to them. If you want to find out where you can "buy Irish" when you go home, why not write to them at Irish Trade Board, Merrion Hall, Strand Road, Sandymount, Dublin 4.

And before you go, there are a few other things which you might like to sample which you may not be able to get at home. Irish breakfasts, draught stout, potato bread, Irish stew....

An Bord Tráchtála
The Irish Trade Board

Bank of Ireland, College Green, Dublin

Take a Cruising Holiday with the people who know the Shannon best

A relaxing Shannon Cruise - no other Irish holiday is quite like it! Discover out-of-the-way villages and islands, visit historic sites and enjoy the breath taking beauty of Europe's most scenic waterway... all at your own leisurely pace. And nobody knows the Shannon better than Emerald Star. With nearly 200 superbly equipped Cruisers for hire - a choice of 10 different classes

accommodating up to 8 people. Plus a choice of two cruiser stations - Carrick-on Shannon on the upper river with direct access to the Shannon/Erne link, and Portumna on the lower.

When it comes to Cruising Holidays Ireland, you're better off going First Class with Emerald Star! Take the first step to holiday you'll treasure always, call or writ for our colour brochure today.

Emerald Star

The ancient and historic town of Drogheda is situated on the River Boyne, which at this point separates the counties of Louth and Meath. It is an important industrial centre. Although 4 miles (6 km) from the coast, Drogheda is also a notable port with a fine harbour formed by the estuary of the River Boyne.

Things to do

Recreations at Drogheda include tennis, dancing, dramatic and variety programmes. There is excellent salmon and trout fishing on the Boyne; details of preserved stretches may be had locally. There is golf (18) at Baltray (4 miles/6 km) and Bettystown (5 miles/8 km). The Louth Foxhounds and Littlegrange Harriers hunt the district. A booklet is available of the town's signposted tourist trail.

History

The ancient name of Drogheda was Inver-Colpa (Estuary of Colpa), and a colony existed here from early times. In 911 the Danes established a permanent fortified settlement which grew in importance during that century until it ranked with Dublin and Wexford as a trading centre.

The Anglo-Normans built a bridge at the site of the ancient ford. At first two towns evolved, one on either bank of the river, but they were united by a charter of Henry IV. During the fourteenth century Drogheda, now walled and fortified, further improved its position as a commercial centre and became one of Ireland's four principal towns. In 1394 Richard II held court here to receive the submissions of the princes of Leinster and Ulster. Later, Drogheda Corporation was granted the right to coin its own money and given permission to set up a university with privileges similar to those of Oxford. Sometimes meetings of Parliament were held in Drogheda. The most notable was the assembly of 1494 which passed Poynings' Law, decreeing that future laws made by the Irish Parliament would be valid only when ratified by the English Privy Council.

In 1641 Phelim O'Neill attempted to capture the town, but failed. Eight years later Cromwell took it by storm and massacred 2,000 of the garrison and inhabitants. On the outbreak of the Williamite wars, the town was held for King James, but surrendered to William the day after the Battle of the Boyne.

Points of interest

Of the ten gates originally set in the town walls only St Lawrence's Gate survives. It is one of the most perfect specimens now extant in Ireland, and has two high drum towers and a loop-holed connecting wall. The slight ruins of the thirteenth-century Augustinian Abbey of St Mary d'Urso consist of a central tower with a fine pointed arch that spans Abbey Lane; this abbey was on the site of an earlier foundation associated with St Patrick and St Columba. The Magdalen Steeple, a two-storey tower springing from a pointed arch, is all that remains of a thirteenth-century Dominican friary.

The Tholsel, now a bank, is a fine square building with a cupola. In the southern part of the town is a large mound called Millmount, said to have been erected over the grave of a son of Milesius (eleventh century B.C.). The fourteenth-century fort built on the mound was stormed by Cromwell in 1649. Millmount Museum is housed in the eighteenth-century military barracks and illustrates the history of Drogheda. It is open to the public for a small entrance charge.

In West Street is the Gothic-style St Peter's Church. This was erected as a memorial to St Oliver Plunkett, the Archbishop of Armagh who was martyred at Tyburn (London) in 1681. His head is preserved here in a special shrine, and pilgrims come from many parts of Ireland to venerate the relic.

Drogheda has another St Peter's Church, belonging to the Church of Ireland, which

Mellifont Abbey

stands on a height in the town. In its
graveyard the tombstones include those of
Isaac Goldsmith, uncle of the poet (died
1769), and Bartholomew van Homrigh
(died 1785), father of Swift's 'Vanessa'.

Around Drogheda
Drogheda is a convenient base for exploring
the scenery and antiquities of the Boyne
valley. The large wooded estate of
Townley Hall, on the north bank of the
River Boyne about 4 miles (6 km) west of
Drogheda, includes on its eastern edge
King William's Glen, which extends for
about a mile (2 km) from Tullyallen south-
wards to the river. In 1690 a body of
William's army made use of this glen to
conceal their approach to the Boyne. The
Williamite general, the Duke of
Schomberg, was killed at its mouth.

Four miles (6 km) downriver from
Drogheda, near the mouth of the Boyne, is
the quaint little village of Baltray, where
there is a championship golf course and a
3-mile (5 km) long beach. Two miles
(3 km) north of here is Termonfeckin, which
grew around the sixth-century monastic
settlement of St Fechin. A convent for
nuns was founded here and confirmed by a
papal bull of Pope Celestine III in 1195. In
the village cemetery is a high cross, probably of the tenth century, which is richly
ornamented with sculptured figures and
interlaced designs. In the porch of the
Protestant church is a stone that bears an
ancient commemorative inscription in
Irish. On a hill east of the village is
Termonfeckin Castle, a well-preserved
square tower of the fifteenth century, with
a fine spiral stairway. Near by An Grianan,
the residential centre of the Irish Country-
women's Association, offers adult education courses in crafts and horticulture.

Nine miles (14 km) north-east of
Drogheda is Clogher, a fishing village
lying at the south side of Clogher Head
(205 feet). The harbour and pier, called
Port Oriel, are on the north side of the

headland. In the face of the head is the 'Red Cave', so called from the colour of the rock—which is stained by a fungus growth. There are excellent sandy beaches near by and this district has many associations with St Oliver Plunkett. He is said to have ordained many priests at Glasspistol, a mile (1 km) south of the village.

Mellifont
An Mhainistir Mhór (The Big Monastery)

The ruins of this important foundation—the first Cistercian house in Ireland—stand beside the Mattock River, 6 miles (10 km) west of Drogheda.

History
Mellifont owed its establishment to St Malachy O'Morgair, Archbishop of Armagh, and was built in 1142 on land granted by the Prince of Oriel, Donogh O'Carroll. The Irishmen of the original community were trained in the Cistercian rule by St Bernard at Clairvaux. In 1157 the Abbey Church was consecrated during a synod attended by a papal legate, the Irish primate, seventeen bishops and the chief lay people of Ireland.

Henry II, on his visit to Ireland in 1172, received the submission of O'Neill and other northern chiefs at Mellifont. Dervorgilla, wife of Tiernan O'Rourke of Breffni, retired to Mellifont, and died there in 1193.

Suppressed in 1539, the abbey later came into the possession of Sir Edward Moore, who made the church into a fortified dwelling. Young Red Hugh O'Donnell, on his escape from prison in Dublin Castle in 1592, was kindly treated here by Moore's son, Sir Garret. The house was taken by Sir Phelim O'Neill during the siege of Drogheda in 1641, but the Moores returned and lived at Mellifont until about 1720.

Points of interest
On the approach to the abbey are the remains of the Gate House, a massive

square tower still standing to a height of about 50 feet. The Abbey Church was very large, with a nave 120 feet long by 54 feet wide, transepts 116 feet across by 54 feet wide, and a chancel 42 feet deep by 26 feet wide. There are some remains of the piers of clustered columns which supported the belfry tower. On the south side of the high altar is the piscina, a basin for washing liturgical vessels. Here also are remains of the sedilia, under which was discovered during excavations a tomb containing a skull, other bones and a gold ring. This may have been the tomb of Dervorgilla, or of one of the two archbishops of Armagh who were buried at Mellifont. An arched recess on the north side is probably the site of the founder's tomb. In the north transept were six chapels, and the piscinas are still to be seen in the adjoining piers. There is also, in the transept's north wall, a fine doorway with jambs of clustered columns.

Of the cloisters only the outline remains, but considerable portions of the abbey buildings still stand. The Chapter House is a two-storey building in the Norman or Early English style, which must have been one of the finest examples of its kind in Ireland. Glazed flooring tiles from the abbey church, many of them bearing interesting designs, have been relaid on the floor of this building.

One of the most interesting of the existing buildings is the Lavabo, a curious structure about 30 feet across which was originally octagonal. Now roofless, it has only four sides remaining, each having a wide opening that rises from ground level to a round-headed arch. In this building a fountain issued from a central column in jets, and here the monks washed their hands before entering the refectory for meals.

On high ground near the abbey are the ruins of a church (probably fifteenth century) which may have been a parish church.

Around Mellifont

About 4 miles (6 km) north of Mellifont, on the road from Slane to Ardee, is the quiet village of Collon. The Catholic church here has a beautiful monument in white marble, consisting of an effigy of Dorcas (died 1876), wife of Percy Fitzgerald of Fane valley. Collon House, at the centre of the village, was the birthplace of John Foster (1740–1829), the last Speaker of the Irish House of Commons and a bitter opponent of the Act of Union. He was later raised to the English peerage as Lord Oriel. At the northern end of the village is a house built by Foster which, since 1939, has been a Cistercian monastery called New Mellifont.

Cork

Allihies

Cork is the largest county in Ireland, with an area of 2,880 square miles. In the east and north is undulating limestone land, interrupted by long ridges of sandstone with picturesque river valleys between them. To the west these ridges increase until they mass in peaks along the County Kerry border. The long coastline also has magnificent scenery—especially in the south-west, where rocky peninsulas jutting into the Atlantic enclose deep, island-strewn bays.

Cork City

Corcaigh (Marshy Place)

Pop. 127,024 (borough).

Tourist information office: Tourist House, Grand Parade, Cork.
Tel. (021) 273251. Fax (021) 273504.

American Express:
Heffernan's Travel, Pembroke House, Pembroke St, Cork.
Tel. (021) 271081. Fax (021) 271863.

On the Beara Peninsula

Post Office:
Oliver Plunkett St, Cork.
Tel. (021) 272000. Open 9.00 – 18.00.

Parking Regulations:
Disc parking.

Railway Station:
Kent Station, Cork. Tel. (021) 504422.

Bus Depot:
Parnell Place Bus Station, Cork.
Tel. (021) 506066.

Car Hire: Budget Rent a Car,
Tourist Office, Grand Parade, Cork.
Tel. (021) 274755 Cork (City)
Tel. (021) 314000 Cork Airport

Murrays Europcar Car Rental,
Cork Airport. Tel. (021) 966736.

Bicycle Hire: Rent a Bike 1/2
Redclyffe, Western Road, Cork.

Cycle Repair Centre, 6 Kyle St, Cork.
Tel. (021) 276255.
Cycle Scene, 396 Blarney St, Cork.
Tel. (021) 301183.

Dates of principal cultural
events/festivals: Cork International Choral
Festival (May), Cork Jazz Festival
(October).

Cork, Ireland's third largest city, is
excellently situated for exploring
the Cork coast and river valleys—
and indeed the whole of south-west
Ireland. Spenser wrote:

The spreading Lee, that like an island fayre
Encloseth Corke with his divided flood . . .

But Cork has long since spread out from
the valley floor and crept up the hills lying
above the River Lee to the north and south.
The river now flows in two main channels,
crossed by numerous bridges; along with
quiet backwaters like the Mardyke stream,
they give the city a picturesque air.

Cork is a place of commercial importance, largely due to the excellence of its harbour; the city quays can accommodate the largest vessels. It is an export centre for the agricultural produce of the south, and the many industries in the city include brewing, distilling, hosiery, flour milling, bacon curing, chemical and paint works, clothing and footwear factories.

The city is noted for its cultural societies. The Cork Literary and Scientific Society, founded 1820, is the oldest of its kind in these islands. Cork is also the headquarters of the Cork Historical and Archaeological Society (1891), the Munster Fine Art Club (which holds annual exhibitions) and the Munster Agricultural Society (1857—annual show and exhibition).

History

Cork's history goes back to the sixth century, when St Finbarr founded a church and school on the south bank of the Lee, near the site of the present University College. The area was then a marsh, hence the derivation of the city's name from Corcach (meaning a marshy place). A section of the city is still known as the 'Marsh'.

Finbarr's school flourished for over two centuries, and around it grew a considerable town. But in 820 the Norsemen sailed up the Lee, burned the city and plundered the surrounding country. They returned a few years later, this time to settle down in Cork, fortifying

Inchiquin Lake, Beara Peninsula

the area between the present North and South Gate bridges as their exclusive settlement. Time, however, broke down the barriers and the Norsemen eventually merged with the native population.

At the time of the Anglo-Norman invasion in 1172 Cork was still largely a Danish stronghold, though one native chieftain (Dermot MacCarthy) did hold sway in Desmond (south Munster). After a stubborn fight the Normans broke the power of the Danes. Having induced MacCarthy to take a Norman wife, they prevailed on him to pay homage to Henry II, who established a garrison in Cork and gave the city its first charter. But gradually the Anglo-Norman settlers, like the Danes before them, were absorbed by the native Irish. Although English laws were nominally in force, in practice it was the edicts of Cork's prosperous commercial magnates that were obeyed. The citizens asserted a remarkable independence from outside authority, most notably when the pretender Perkin Warbeck arrived in Cork in 1492. His cause was taken up by the mayor and principal citizens, who went with him to Kent and proclaimed him 'Richard IV King of England and Lord of Ireland'. Like Warbeck himself, the mayor and conspiring citizens were executed at Tyburn, and for a while the city lost its charter.

In the war between Charles I and his parliament, Cork declared for the royal cause, but submitted to Cromwell when he entered the city in 1649. In 1690, the army of William III compelled the garrison to surrender after five days' siege; soon afterwards the walls and fortifications were destroyed. In the nineteenth century 'Rebel Cork' again justified its title as a centre of the Fenian movement. It also figured prominently in the 1919–1921 War of Independence.

Main points of interest

A city tourist trail guide book is available from the tourist information office in Grand Parade (see also next section on city tours).

Cork

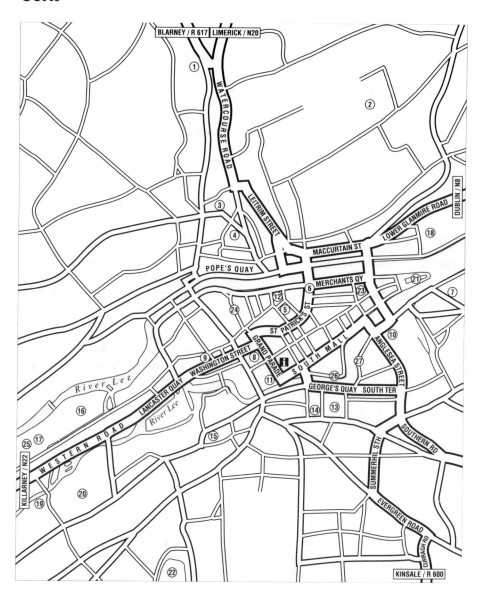

BLARNEY / R 617   LIMERICK / N20

WATERCOURSE ROAD

LEITRIM STREET

POPE'S QUAY

MACCURTAIN ST

DUBLIN / N8

LOWER GLANMIRE ROAD

MERCHANTS QY

ST PATRICK'S ST

GRAND PARADE

WASHINGTON STREET

LANCASTER QUAY

River Lee

River Lee

WESTERN ROAD

KILLARNEY / N22

SOUTH MALL

ANGLESEA STREET

GEORGE'S QUAY   SOUTH TER

SUMMERHIL STH

SOUTHERN RD

EVERGREEN ROAD

CURRAGH RD

KINSALE / R 600

1. Church of the Assumption (RC)
2. Collins Barracks
3. St Mary's Pro Cathedral (RC)
4. St Ann's Church (CI), Shandon
5. Crawford Municipal School of Art
   & Art Gallery
6. Father Mathew Statue
7. Marina
8. Church of the Holy Trinity (CI)
9. Court House
10. City Hall
11. National Monument
12. Opera House
13. St Finbarr's Church (RC)
14. Red Abbey Tower
15. St Finbarr's Cathedral (CI)
16. Mardyke
17. Cork Public Museum
18. Kent Station
19. Gaol Gate
20. University College, Cork
21. Custom House
22. Cork Lough
23. Bus Station
24. Cornmarket Street
25. Fitzgerald Park
26. Father Mathew Quay
27. Union Quay

Shandon Church, Cork city

A short distance from the city centre is the famous Shandon Church, whose giant pepperpot steeple dominates the view of the north side of the city. Built in 1722 to replace an older church destroyed in the 1690 siege, it is a plain structure on classic lines, with walls of great strength. The peculiar feature of its massive tower is that the north and east sides are of red sandstone and the other two of grey limestone. 'Partly coloured like the people, red and white is Shandon steeple': so goes an old Cork jingle. From the top of the tower (120 feet) there is a fine panorama of the city. Many interesting memorial tablets adorn the church's interior walls, but it is the famous bells which attract most visitors—the bells immortalised by Francis O'Mahony ('Father Prout') in his 'Bells of Shandon'. (Father O'Mahony's remains lie in the old cemetery beside the church.) The eight bells were cast by Abel Rudhall of Gloucester.

The Church of Ireland Cathedral of St Finbarre is said to occupy the site of the sixth-century church of that saint. As a result of damage from the 1690 siege, the building was pulled down and a new church erected in 1735. This in turn was replaced by the present building, which dates from 1865–1880. The architecture is in the early French Gothic style, with great height in proportion to its size. The cathedral is highly ornamented and there is some very good mosaic work, particularly in the apse pavement. The bells, a peal of eight, are from the previous church. In the south transept is a cannon ball fired in the siege of 1690 and afterwards found in the tower, 40 feet above the ground.

The Catholic St Mary's Cathedral, a prominent landmark on the north side of the city, was built in 1808 on the site of an older church. The inside decoration is a florid Gothic with a surprising amount of detail. On the north side, near the high altar, is a monument by Turnerelli to the founder, Bishop Moylan (1786–1815). Outside the main entrance is a statue of Bishop Delaney by Lawlor (1889). Opposite the cathedral is the presbytery, once part of an ecclesiastic college, where

St Mary's Dominican Church, Cork city

well-preserved records of baptisms and marriages since 1748 are a valuable source of family history.

On Father Mathew Quay is the Father Mathew Memorial Church (1832), a Gothic-style building with a graceful spire. It commemorates the 'apostle of temperance', who was also renowned for his fearless work among the victims of a cholera epidemic in 1832. Over the high altar is a stained-glass window to Daniel O'Connell.

The Dominicans first came to Ireland in 1224. Five years later they built their church in Cork on the site now occupied by the Convent of Marie's of the Isle, on the south side of the city. The foundations of the present St Mary's Dominican Church (on the north side of the city) were laid in 1832. A flight of steps leads up to the broad portico of stout Ionic columns, crowned by a massive pediment. Within the church is the miraculous statuette known as 'Our Lady of Graces', removed from the friary at Youghal. It is a carved ivory representation of the madonna and child, of Flemish fourteenth-century workmanship.

Since 1845 Cork's old tradition as a seat of learning has been re-established by University College. This is near the site of Finbarr's sixth-century school, and its motto 'Where Finbarr taught, let Munster learn', is a reminder of Cork's heritage. The university has a library with a fine collection of early Cork-printed books, a fine group of ogham-inscribed stones, and natural history, geological and other collections (visitors may examine the exhibits on request). Attached to the college is the Honan Collegiate Chapel, a little architectural gem modelled on the twelfth-century Hiberno-Romanesque style.

In the attractive grounds of Fitzgerald Park is the Cork Public Museum, where the display is a connected history of the Cork region from early prehistoric times. Crawford Municipal School of Art, in Emmet Place, has fine sculpture and picture galleries open to the public.

Beside the Albert Quay railway station on the south channel of the river is the City Hall; its façades of dressed limestone have Doric columns. The main entrance, with marble-paved vestibule and polished marble stairs, leads to a spacious council chamber. An assembly hall, with capacity for 2,000 people, is used for public functions.

The Court House (1835) was built from designs of George Richard Pain. The main front has a broad Corinthian portico raised on a platform of eleven steps. Over the pediment is a bronze group representing Justice supported by Law and Mercy, and backed by a large copper dome. The other façade, overlooking Liberty Street, is in Tudor style.

Tours of the city

Tour 1: Starting point for this tour is the crescent-shaped St Patrick Street, the city's main thoroughfare. It was formed in 1789 by covering in an open channel of the river, and runs from St Patrick's Bridge to the Grand Parade. At the bridge end is Foley's bronze statue of Father Mathew, the 'apostle of temperance' who was superior of the Capuchin Order in Cork up to his death in 1856.

St Patrick's Bridge was opened in 1859 to replace the bridge swept away by a flood in 1853. The bridge leads to the north side of the city and from it St Patrick's Hill is seen, rising steeply. On the right, on going down St Patrick Street, is Academy Street, which leads to Emmet Place and the Municipal School of Art. From here a short walk (via Paul Street) leads to the Church of Saints Peter and Paul, a Gothic building designed by Pugin with a finely proportioned interior. Returning to St Patrick Street and continuing towards the Grand Parade, a turn to the right leads to Cornmarket Street—site of the open-air market known as the 'Coal-Quay'.

Grand Parade is a spacious thoroughfare running from St Patrick Street to the south channel of the river. Halfway along it is the Berwick Fountain. On the right is the Cork Lending Library, which has extensive reading and reference departments. At the end of the Parade is a monument to Irish patriots of the period 1798–1867: under a Gothic canopy is a figure of Erin and, at the angles, statues of Wolfe Tone, Thomas Davis, Michael Dwyer and O'Neill Crowley. Near the monument are some fine eighteenth-century bow-fronted houses.

Near by is the commercial heart of Cork, the South Mall. On the right, at the entrance to the Mall, is the memorial to the Royal Munster Fusiliers who fell in the First World War. On the left is the head office of the Allied Irish Bank; in the interior, six of the marble pillars supporting the roof are from Old St Paul's, London. On the right of the Mall is Father Mathew Street, leading to the Father Mathew Memorial Church. To the left, on the Quay, is the Municipal School of Commerce. Parnell Bridge is reached by continuing down the Quay; near by is the ornate Corinthian edifice of the Allied Irish Bank, and on the opposite side of the channel is the City Hall. Near the Allied Irish Bank is the Cork Savings Bank, which has a statue of William Crawford by John Hogan.

Continuing eastward, the Custom House is soon reached; here the two channels of the river meet. The return to St Patrick Street can be made by Oliver Plunkett Street; halfway up on the left is the General Post Office.

Tour 2: From St Patrick Street to Grand Parade, then turn right up Washington Street. Here is the Augustinian Church and the Court House. Behind the Court House is the fine modern Church of St Francis of Assisi. This area, the 'Marsh', is the oldest part of the city. A short distance west is the Mercy Hospital, once the Mansion House of Cork. A turn to the left from here and the Mardyke is reached; this leads to Fitzgerald Park and the Cork Public Museum. At the top of the Mardyke are the Sacred Heart Church and College. Western Road is entered by turning left, and following this citywards to pass the Cork Greyhound Track and behind it the Bon Secours Hospital. Next are seen the buildings of University College and at Gilabbey, on the limestone cliff above the river, is the Boer War Memorial Cross.

Tour 3: From St Patrick's Bridge, the Dominican Church is reached by a short walk along Camden Quay to the left and then on to Pope's Quay. From the church the north channel of the river is followed west to the North Gate Bridge (Griffith Bridge), which was the site of one of the city gates in the days when Cork was a walled city. Beyond the bridge is the North Mall, prettily lined with trees, and on the opposite side there are some fine old Georgian houses on Bachelor's Quay.

From the bridge, Shandon Street leads to St Mary's Cathedral. Near by are Shandon Church and Skiddy's Almshouse. Above the cathedral is the huge housing scheme of Gurranabraher. Near here also is the Christian Brothers school, North Monastery—which has an industrial museum and a technical school with some unique models and early scientific apparatus. In the graveyard is buried the author Gerald Griffin (see Limerick city and Kilrush, County Clare), who joined the Christian Brothers after abandoning his literary career.

Tour 4: The south side of the city is approached via Parnell Bridge near the City Hall. Walk up Union Quay (to the right) as far as Mary Street, where the South Chapel is one of the oldest parish churches in Cork. Hidden among the houses is the tower (all that remains) of the Augustinian Red Abbey, notable as the Duke of Marlborough's headquarters during the siege of Cork in 1690. At Sullivan's Quay is the hump-backed Parliament Bridge and then the South Gate Bridge. On the heights above the latter (reached via Barrack Street) is Elizabeth Fort, one of the old city fortifications. Beyond is St Finbarre's Cathedral and near it the Municipal Technical Schools. From here one can walk via Clarke's Bridge to Washington Street and on to University College.

Other places of interest on the south side include the Lough, a venue for model-yacht racing, and Christ the King Church at Turner's Cross, one of the finest examples of modern church architecture in Ireland.

Tours on the fringes of Cork

Tour 1: By Washington Street to the Mardyke Walk running parallel with the Lee. Across the river is Sunday's Well, with picturesque residences scattered along the hillside. Beyond the Mardyke, at the Lee Fields, are the municipal baths. On rising ground on the opposite side of the river are the city waterworks and the extensive buildings of the Cork Mental Hospital. This walk can be extended by going from Victoria Cross to Carrigrohane, along a 3-mile (5 km) stretch of road that is used for motor racing and cycling competitions. To the left is the Munster Institute, an agricultural college. Two miles (3 km) further on is Inniscarra, a

lovely spot among the woods that border the River Lee.

An alternative extension of this walk is to the left from Victoria Cross, following the Bandon road for about a mile (2 km) to the gate of the African Mission College, then turning left for St Finbarre's cemetery. Here in the Republican Plot lie the remains of two of Cork's lord mayors—Tomás MacCurtain and Terence MacSwiney—and of others who lost their lives in the War of Independence and the Civil War that followed it. From the cemetery, take the road leading to the right and then by Barrack Street to the city.

Tour 2: Along the Mardyke as before, then turn right over Thomas Davis Bridge and to the right again for Sunday's Well, a picturesque residential district on a hill overlooking the river and the city. The road is then downhill to the North Mall and across North Gate Bridge to the city centre.

Tour 3: By St Patrick's Bridge and MacCurtain Street and straight on past St Patrick's Church and the railway station, then along the Lower Road, passing beneath Montenotte and Tivoli, two residential districts with pretty villas and gardens overlooking the river. Sir Walter Raleigh lived for a while in Tivoli House, and some of the trees in the vicinity are said to have been planted by him. In Tivoli also is Woodhill House, at one time the residence of Sarah Curran, the beloved of Robert Emmet—a tragic romance that inspired Moore's 'She is Far from the Land'. About a mile (2 km) further on is Dunkettle Station, and opposite it (on the bank of the Lee) Blackrock Castle. Take the junction left here through the wooded valley of the Glanmire River to the pretty villages of Glanmire, Riverstown and Sallybrook. At Glanmire is Dunkathel, a fine example of late eighteenth-century architecture, open to view two days a week in summer. Near by is Riverstown House, rebuilt in 1745, with fine plasterwork by the Francini brothers; it is open to the public Thursday to Sunday in summer.

Return to Cork through New Inn and Mayfield.

Tour 4: By the South Mall, Parnell Bridge and Anglesea Street to Douglas, a village suburb of Cork with a golf course (18).

Tour 5: By the South Mall, Parnell Bridge, Albert Quay and the Centre Park Road to the Marina, a fine walk stretching along the south bank of the Lee between rows of fine old trees. Seats and rustic shelters are placed at intervals. Here the river widens into Cork Harbour, and across the river are the heights of Montenotte and Tivoli. On the right are the grounds of the Gaelic Athletic Association, the Cork Show Grounds and Marine Park. At the end of the Marina is Blackrock, a small fishing village suburb of Cork. Blackrock Castle is on a little promontory running out into the Lee, where it begins to expand into Lough Mahon.

Blarney

An Bhlarna (The Plain)

Pop. 1,952.

The village of Blarney is 5 miles (8 km) north of Cork city. Blarney Castle, and the magic Blarney Stone with its traditional power of conferring eloquence on those who kiss it, are world famous.

History

The word 'Blarney' is supposed to have originated in the dealings of Queen Elizabeth's government with the then Lord of Blarney, Cormac MacDermot MacCarthy. Repeatedly he was asked by the Queen's Deputy, Carew, to renounce the traditional system by which the clans elected their chief, and to take the tenure of his lands from the Crown. While seeming to agree to this proposal, he put off the fulfilment of his promise from day to day 'with fair words and soft speech'. At last Carew became the laughing-stock of Elizabeth

Blarney Castle House

and she declared, 'This is all Blarney: what he says he never means.' Thus 'Blarney' came to mean pleasant talk intended to deceive without offending.

The Castle

This is principally a massive square keep or tower, with a battlement parapet 83 feet above the ground. Originally a fortress of the MacCarthys of south Munster, it withstood several sieges from the fifteenth to the seventeenth centuries. Cromwell, Ireton and Fairfax all attacked Blarney, and the army of William III after the Battle of the Boyne was the last to take the castle. Most of the old structure was then demolished.

The castle was built in two sections: the first, a tall, narrow tower with a staircase and small rooms; the second—adjoining and overlapping the earlier work—a massive oblong keep, with battlements that are typically Irish in form. Below them the famous Blarney Stone is set in the wall, and to kiss it one has to lean over backwards from the parapet walk of the battlements.

The view from the top of the castle over the wooded hills of Muskerry is very fine. To the south is the modern Blarney Castle, and in its grounds is the little Blarney Lake that features in many folk-tales. There is a cave beneath the outer wall of the keep, and a staircase within the castle leads to another cave—artificially enlarged— which may have been a dungeon. The castle is open daily throughout the year.

Kissing the Blarney Stone

Other points of interest

North of Blarney, up the valley of the Martin River, is Waterloo Bridge, near which is a modern round tower erected in the nineteenth century by Father Matt Horgan in support of the theory that these towers were used as belfries in ancient times (this tower is now used as a belfry for the Catholic church near by). Four miles (6 km) north-west of Blarney, there is a fine earthen fort at Loughnane East, and a pair of standing stones close by.

Cobh

Cobh (Haven)

Pop. 6,206 (urban district).

Cobh (pronounced 'cove') is a relatively modern town on the eastern side of Cork Harbour, 15 miles (24 km) from Cork city. It is an important Irish port of call for cruise liners; as they enter the harbour, passengers have a fine view of the town, with its houses rising on a terraced hillside beneath the towering form of St Colman's Cathedral.

Daniel O'Connell (the 'Liberator') attended school at Cobh, and his contemporary, the 'apostle of temperance', Father Mathew, died here. In 1849 the place was renamed Queenstown to commemorate a visit by Queen Victoria, but the Irish designation was readopted in 1922. The Royal Cork Yacht Club at Cobh is the oldest of its kind in the world, dating back to 1720.

Things to do

There is seabathing near the town, tennis at Whitepoint, golf (9) at Monkstown which is reached by ferry, and golf (18) and horse-riding at Little Island 8 miles (13 km) away. The harbour provides sea fishing, boat trips and yachting.

Points of interest

Features of the beautiful Gothic Revival Cathedral of St Colman are the blue granite

Roche's Point, at the southern end of Cork Harbour

exterior, the main doorway and the rose window above it, the flying buttresses, the interior columns of polished marble, the mosaic flooring, the diapered wall ornamentation, the elaborately carved capitals, the open triforium with its moulded arches and columns, the apse with its tracery, the rich colouring of the windows and the beautiful detail of the marble reredos. The cathedral carillon of forty-seven bells is one of the finest in the world; regular carillon recitals are held.

The Old Church Cemetery is the burial-place of Tobin, the playwright, Wolfe, author of 'The Burial of Sir John Moore', and more recently, of hundreds of the victims of the *Lusitania*, sunk by a German submarine off Kinsale in 1915. There is a memorial to the disaster on the quayside.

A heritage centre which will feature the history of Cobh and its involvement with sea transport and wartime significance will open in 1993.

Around Cobh

South of the town is Spike Island, an army coastal defence station. West of Spike Island is Haulbowline Island, to the east is the Spit Lighthouse and beyond it can be seen the wooded shores of the harbour around Rostellan and Aghada. Guarding the narrow harbour mouth are the ancient forts of Dun an Daibhisigh and Dun Ui Mheachair.

A short run from Cobh is East Ferry, where a branch of the Lee estuary divides the mainland from Great Island, on which Cobh is situated. The main road from Cork comes on to the island at Belvelly Bridge, near which is the square keep of the fourteenth-century Belvelly Castle; on the mainland side the road passes around the wooded Fota Estate which is an important recreation and amenity park. It includes a wildlife park where most of the animals

Cheetah in Fota Wildlife Park

live in as natural an environment as possible and an arboretum which is one of the best in the country and includes trees imported from all parts of the world. Fota House, a splendid example of Regency architecture, has been restored and includes an important collection of Irish landscape paintings.

Crosshaven
Bun tSabhairne
(Mouth of the River Savairn)

👪 Pop. 1,362.

C rosshaven, on the west side of Cork Harbour, 17 miles (27 km) from Cork city, is a favourite seaside resort of Cork people and an important yachting centre. A frequent bus service connects it with Cork city.

Church Bay, Myrtleville Bay and Grall Bay are bathing places with good cliff scenery and fine views across the harbour mouth. Above Church Bay is the prominent landmark of Templebreedy Church. Along the bays near Crosshaven the pre-glacial raised beach of south Cork is plainly exposed.

Crosshaven may be reached from Cork city by either of two routes. The shorter is through the town of Carrigaline where the road skirts the Owenboy River through delightful woodland scenery; an expansion of this river is known as 'Drake's Pool', where Sir Francis Drake is said to have taken refuge with his ships in 1587 when pursued by the Spanish fleet. On nearing Crosshaven, the wooded hill of Curragh-binny is seen across the water, with its large prehistoric burial cairn crowning the hilltop, known as the Giant's Grave.

The alternative route from the city to Crosshaven is by Passage West, once a famous dockyard. Further on is Monkstown Castle, an Elizabethan fortified house on a commanding height above the water. It was built by Anastasia Gould, who shrewdly stipulated that the workmen should buy all

their food from her; when the final accounts were balanced, the cost to her of building the castle came to a single groat.

Mallow
Mala (Hill-brow)

👪 Pop. 6,244 (urban district).

M allow, on the River Blackwater 22 miles (35 km) north of Cork city, is a sugar-manufacturing centre in the middle of a rich agricultural region. For centuries the place was an important ford on the Blackwater, and up to a century ago its spa (now closed) drew crowds of visitors, some of whom gave the town a certain notoriety, if the popular song 'The Rakes of Mallow' is anything to go by. Mallow was the birthplace of many famous people, including the patriot and poet Thomas Davis and William O'Brien, MP. The writer, Canon Sheehan, went to school here with William O'Brien.

Mallow is well known as an angling and hunting centre; there is also a race-course and golf (18). In the town itself the picturesque half-timbered Clock House, the Spa Well and the old Mallow Castle are worth seeing.

Around Mallow
Of the many walks in the area, the most interesting are those along the Blackwater valley. South-east of the town are the Nagles Mountains, a compact group of hills with fine hill-walks. About 6 miles (10 km) south are the ruins of Mourne Abbey, a preceptory of the Knights Templars founded early in the thirteenth century by Alexander de Sancta Helena. Near by, on the hill west of the River Lee, is the ruined keep of Castlemore Barrett.

North of Mallow, Buttevant has ruins of a thirteenth-century Franciscan abbey and of Ballybeg Abbey, outside the town. The Barry family settled here in the twelfth century and founded the castle, which has now been modernised. The first recorded steeplechase was run in 1752 from the steeple of Buttevant Protestant church to that of Doneraile, 4½ miles (7 km) away. Near Doneraile is the ruin of Kilcolman Castle, where Edmund Spenser lived from 1586 to 1598 and wrote his 'Faerie Queene' and other works. In the cemetery at Rath Luirc (Charleville) is the grave of the celebrated Gaelic poet, Sean Clarach Mac Domhnaill (1691–1754). Charleville has one of the largest milk and cheese processing plants in Ireland.

East of Mallow is Killavullen; here, on a cliff overhanging the river, is the house of the ancestors of Hennessy, the original distillers of brandy. Under the house are caves in which were discovered the remains of extinct Irish animals. About a mile (2 km) away is the house where Nano Nagle (1728–1784), founder of the Presentation Order of nuns, was born. Two castles near the village, Monanimy Castle and Carrigacunna Castle, were strongholds of the Roches.

Other towns in north Cork within easy reach of Mallow include Kanturk, with its old MacCarthy castle, and Newmarket, which was the residence of John Philpot Curran; his daughter Sarah Curran, Robert Emmet's beloved, is buried in the grave-yard here. Millstreet is romantically situated among mountains on the south side of the River Blackwater. It has an international horse show every year, organised at the initiative of a local businessman.

Fermoy
Mainistir Fhear Muighe
(Abbey of the Plainsmen)

Pop. 2,297 (urban district).

Fermoy, on the River Blackwater, 22 miles (35 km) north-east of Cork city, has a charming environment. For the sporting tourist its main attraction is the excellent salmon fishing on the Blackwater, and angling for trout in several of the tributary streams. The coarse fishing is also very good, and the Blackwater River system is the only one in Ireland holding roach and dace. Fermoy Golf Club (18).

Walks in and around Fermoy
1. Along the tree-shaded promenade of Barnane Walk. Opposite, in choicely wooded grounds, is Castlehyde House.
2. From the mill, along the right bank of the river to Carrigabrick railway bridge and the old castle.
3. The road along the north side of the river to Castlehyde House and Cregg Castle (ruin).
4. Along the Rathealy road (with the Blackwater on the right). It is worth keeping on for 2 miles (3 km) to the bridge across the River Funshion, near which this tributary joins the Blackwater.

Tours from Fermoy
1. By the Rathealy road and along the Blackwater valley via Ballyduff to Lismore (County Waterford), where the Blackwater is seen at the height of its beauty. The return to Mallow can be made through the Bride valley via Tallow, Conna and Castlelyons (interesting abbey ruins and old castle).
2. To Glanworth. Near Labbacallee Hill, on the way, is a dolmen of huge proportions. Entering Glanworth village, there is a fine view of the Funshion River with its ancient narrow bridge of 13 arches, and the busy little woollen mill behind. Here also are the ruins of an old Roche castle destroyed by Cromwell's army, and of a thirteenth-century Dominican abbey. West from Glanworth is Castletownroche, on the Awbeg River; here Bridgetown Abbey overlooks a lovely valley where the Awbeg flows into the Blackwater.

Anne's Grove Gardens 2 miles (3 km) north-west of Castletownroche are open to the public. There is a particularly impressive water garden.

Mitchelstown
Baile Misteala

👪 Pop. 3,210.

This town, at the south-west corner of the Galtee Mountains near the County Tipperary border, is the centre of a busy agricultural district. The town's major industry is a creamery noted for its large-scale production of butter and cheese. Mitchelstown Golf Club (9).

Around Mitchelstown
In the former demesne of the earls of Kingston beside the town are the ruins of the ancient Brigown Church. Four miles (6 km) north-east, at Kilbeheny village in County Limerick, are remains of an ancient church and a castle. Kilbeheny was the birthplace of John O'Mahony, co-founder of the Fenian movement.

North-east of Mitchelstown are the Galtee Mountains and in the same direction (in County Tipperary) are the Mitchelstown Caves, open to the public every day (see around Clonmel).

Youghal
Eochaill (Yew Wood)

👪 Pop. 5,532 (urban district).

ℹ️ Tourist information office (seasonal): Tel. (024) 92390.

Youghal (pronounced yawl), 30 miles (48 km) east of Cork city, is one of the county's foremost resorts. It has a fine beach and its situation at the mouth of the River Blackwater makes it an excellent touring centre. Youghal is famous for its point lace (*pointe d'Irlande*) which is distinguished by its vivid patterns.

Things to do
Golf (18), tennis, fishing and boating are available. The Youghal Tourist Trail is a walking guide of the interesting parts of the town. Copies of the booklet are available from the local tourist information office.

History and points of interest
The Danes may have occupied Youghal, but its established history dates from the arrival of the Normans. The town supplied King John with three fighting ships, and in return received its first charter from him. A great deal of the medieval walls and towers still remain and may be seen on the Youghal Tourist Trail. A wall-top walk incorporated in the reconstructed section of wall behind the Church of St Mary gives very good views of the town in its coastal setting. Dating from the same period is one of the finest ancient buildings in the county, the great Church of St Mary (restored in the nineteenth century). Among the interesting monuments in the church is the elaborately sculptured tomb of Richard Boyle (1566–1643), an English lawyer who became the 1st Earl of Cork.

Sir Walter Raleigh was closely identified with Youghal and was once its mayor. According to tradition, it was here he smoked the first tobacco and grew the first potatoes in Ireland. His house, Myrtle Grove, a much-altered Elizabethan building, is open to visitors.

The thoroughfare known as South Abbey commemorates a Franciscan friary founded by Maurice Fitzgerald around 1230; it may have been the first house of the Order in Ireland. Some remains of the Benedictine St John's Abbey are a short distance further north and near by the Dominican St Mary's Abbey. Other interesting features of Youghal are the Clock Gate, the Water Gate (under which Cromwell passed in 1649), and Tynte's Castle.

Around Youghal
About 2 miles (3 km) north on the Cappoquin road are the beautifully situated ruins of Rincrew Abbey, once a preceptory of the Knights Hospitallers. Templemichael Castle ruin is 1½ miles (2 km) further on.

In Ballinatray demesne, Molana Abbey has a statue representing its sixth-century founder, St Molana, and the reputed tomb of one of Strongbow's generals, Raymond le Gros.

Ballycotton
Baile Coitin (Cotton's Town)

Pop. 438.

Situated on a cliff 26 miles (42 km) south-east of Cork city, this fishing village looks out over the wide inlet of Ballycotton Bay. In front is a steep island crowned by a lighthouse, and between this island and the village is the sheltered, boat-filled little harbour. For centuries fishermen have worked the plentiful bay off Ballycotton.

Things to do
There is good bathing in several coves and rock pools along the shore, and to the north a fine beach of level sand stretches 4 miles (6 km) to Garryvoe; there is a scenic cliff walk 200 feet above the sea.

Around Ballycotton
A popular excursion is via Garryvoe to Knockadoon, where there is fine cliff scenery, and to Ballymacoda, a pleasant village overlooking Youghal Bay. Another trip from Ballycotton is to Shanagarry (2 miles/3 km), where an interesting feature is the ruin of the ancient house of the Penn family, one of whom founded the state of Pennsylvania. There is also a local pottery industry. A few miles east is Cloyne, with its well-preserved round tower and its restored fourteenth-century cathedral. In the cathedral is a monument to the celebrated philosopher, Bishop Berkeley (1685–1753); a small building near by is believed to be a reconstruction of the oratory of St Colman, who founded the bishopric of Cloyne in the seventh century. Near the village are extensive limestone caves, and there is a large dolmen in the Castlemary demesne.

Midleton
Mainistir na Corann (Monastery of Coran(n))

Pop. 2,990 (urban district).

Situated on the Cork–Youghal road, this is a market town. There is a very large distillery in the town which produces the bulk of Irish whiskey and gin. An interpretative centre, depicting the history, methods of distillation and other aspects of the industry, is open to the public. There is golf (18) near by.

On the coast, south of Midleton, is the Trabolgan Holiday Village which has modern amenities for family holidays.

Kinsale
Ceann Saile (Tide Head)

Pop. 1,784 (urban district).

Tourist information office (seasonal): Tel. (021) 772234 and (021) 774417. Fax (021) 774438.

Kinsale, overlooking the winding estuary of the Bandon River, has an old-world charm. Most of the present town, with narrow winding streets and interesting ruins tucked away amid Georgian houses, dates from the eighteenth century.

Things to do
Kinsale is one of the best-equipped sea angling centres on the south coast. There is good bathing at Summer Cove, Charles Fort and Oyster Haven; there is golf (9), and boats can be hired. The town is noted for the number and quality of its restaurants; fish is a speciality. Kinsale Gourmet Week in August each year is a highlight. The Kinsale Tourist Trail is a walking tour of the town; guide books are available from the Kinsale tourist information office.

History
At the height of its prosperity Kinsale was one of the chief ports of the British Navy,

but its docks and quays were too small to accommodate the eighteenth-century expansion in the shipbuilding industry. Trade was lost to bigger ports, leaving Kinsale deserted except for the fishing boats from the nearby herring and mackerel grounds.

The Corporation of Kinsale was granted its first charter by Edward III. The corporation archives are still in the possession of the Kinsale Urban Council, and some of the charters are displayed in the town museum. Perhaps the most outstanding event in Kinsale's history was the siege of 1601–1602, when a Spanish force sailed into the harbour, took over the walled town and held it against the English armies of Mountjoy and Carew. Irish forces under the Earls of Tyrone and Tyrconnell marched from the north and joined the local chiefs to raise the siege, but their efforts failed and the Spanish forces surrendered. Kinsale then became a completely English town, and up to the end of the eighteenth century the Irish were not allowed to live within its walls.

In the seventeenth century the Chudleighs of Kinsale made the famous invasion craft which were taken overland to subdue Ross Castle at Killarney, and in 1700 the same family built the royal frigate H.M.S. *Kinsale*. The founder of the state of Pennsylvania, William Penn, was Clerk of the Admiralty Court in Kinsale; his father, Admiral Penn, was governor of the town.

Points of interest

Most interesting of Kinsale's historic buildings is the twelfth-century Church of St Multose, which has a fine west tower, north transept and font. The old town stocks are preserved here, and some curious sixteenth-century gravestones.

Other interesting buildings are the ruined fourteenth-century Carmelite Friary, the Desmond Castle (or 'French Prison'), and the quaint 'new' Courthouse which now serves as a museum, containing many relics of old Kinsale.

Kinsale

Kinsale Harbour

Around Kinsale

A favourite walk is along the road encircling Compass Hill; this gives panoramic views of the town and across the Bandon estuary. Another pleasant stroll is through the fisherman's quarter of Scilly (with its quaint cottages) on the eastern side of the harbour, along to Summer Cove and the Charles Fort which has been restored and where guided tours are available in season.

The trip up the Bandon River to Innishannon (via White Castle, Dunderrow and Shippool Castle) is noted for its fine river and woodland scenery. The route to the Old Head of Kinsale follows the Bandon to the Western Bridge; after crossing it, the road then climbs high above the river to Ballinspittle village. Overlooking the village is the large three-ringed fort of Ballycateen. The cliff scenery of the Old Head is magnificent; an old de Courcy castle spans the narrowest part (on the site of one of the three great forts of ancient Ireland), and at the extreme point is a lighthouse. It was off here in 1915 that the *Lusitania* was sunk by a German submarine, with a loss of over 1,500 lives.

Close to the western side of the Old Head of Kinsale, Garrettstown Strand is a favourite resort for a quiet seaside holiday. The cliff scenery is magnificent in contrast with the well-sheltered beach backed by hills. Places of interest near by include Howe Strand on Courtmacsherry Bay, Kilbrittain (old castle and grounds) and Coolmain Castle, once the home of the writer Donn Byrne. Neither castle is open to the public.

Pleasantly situated on the southern shore of Courtmacsherry Bay is the pretty village resort of Courtmacsherry, with a background of woods. There is bathing, boating, angling and tennis, and many interesting walks in the area. Three miles (5 km) away is Timoleague Abbey, in its day one of the most important religious houses in Ireland. The existing ruins are of the fourteenth-century Franciscan friary founded by a prince of Thomond, Donal Glas MacCarthy; it succeeded an earlier house founded here by St Molaga (Timoleague means House of Molaga). The most interesting features arc the nave, the south transept and the tower. Part of an old

Norman castle is near by. Castle gardens around the castle are open to the public.

Clonakilty

Clanna Chaoilte (O'Keelty's Sept)

Pop. 2,444 (urban district).

Tourist information office (seasonal): Tel. (023) 33226.

Clonakilty, one of the chief towns in west Cork, is in a fertile agricultural district. In the centre of the town the Georgian houses of Emmet Square surround the Kennedy Gardens. Visit the museum and see the post office which was once a church.

Around Clonakilty

In the neighbourhood are several ancient castles. The Irish resistance leader, Michael Collins (1890–1922), was born about 3½ miles (6 km) west of Clonakilty, at Woodfield. Five miles (8 km) from Clonakilty is Ballinascarthy, birthplace of William Ford, father of Henry Ford.

Among the many fine beaches in the area is Inchadoney (3 miles/5 km), a triangular promontory encompassed by narrow inlets that run in off Clonakilty Bay. There is excellent bathing from the sandy beach, and tennis courts are available. There is golf (9) at Dunmore. West of Inchadoney is Rosscarbery Bay, with the picturesque little town of Rosscarbery in an elevated position on the shore. This is a quiet spot with good bathing and sea fishing. In the sixth century St Fachtna founded a monastery here, which became famous for its school. A mile (2 km) to the east are the remains of an establishment of the Knights Templars and the ruins of Benduff Castle; in this direction too is the wooded demesne of Castle Freke. Owenahincha Strand near by is a popular bathing place.

Four miles (6 km) from Rosscarbery, the attractive little resort of Glandore has a beautiful outlook over the waters of Glandore Harbour. The neighbouring coast is strikingly picturesque, especially when viewed from the road leading to Leap and Skibbereen. Glandore is popular for its excellent bathing and the mildness of its climate. There is good trout fishing a few miles away on Ballinlough Lake and Shepperton Lakes.

Across the harbour is the quaint little village of Union Hall, which acquired recognition when Dean Swift lived in Rock Cottage here in 1723, and wrote his poem 'Carberiae Rupes'. Kilfinnan Castle, some of whose walls are 13 feet thick, was the seat of a branch of the Townshend family. Ancient ruins in the area include Raheen Castle and Castle Eyre (both strongholds of the O'Donovans).

Another pretty village is Castletownshend, on a sheltered haven which saw a memorable sea-fight between English and Spanish squadrons in 1602. Three tower-like islands standing out from the shore are known as the 'Stags'. Castletownshend demesne is close to the village, and interesting remains include Glenbarrahane Castle and church, and an ancient stone fort with a souterrain and hut sites. Somerville and Ross, the two Victorian ladies who wrote *Tales of an Irish R.M.* lived most of their lives here.

Skibbereen

Sciobairin (Little Boat Harbour)

Pop. 1,887 (urban district).

Tourist information office: Town Hall, Main Street, Skibbereen. Tel. (028) 21766. Fax (028) 21353.

Skibbereen, one of the main towns in County Cork, is on the River Ilen where it widens to form a creek and unites its waters with an inlet of Baltimore Bay. Skibbereen produced two fighting bishops in the wars against Elizabeth and Cromwell—Owen MacEgan, killed in battle

(1602), and Boetius MacEgan, hanged at Carrigadrohid (1650). Skibbereen suffered particularly badly during the Famine years. O'Donovan Rossa, prominent in the movement for independence, lived here, and a small park on the outskirts of the town commemorates him.

Things to do

There is a golf course (9), river and lake angling, and the beaches at Tragumna, Tralispeen and Sandycove are popular bathing places.

Points of interest

The Pro-Cathedral is a fine Grecian-style building (1826). On the banks of the River Ilen, west of the town, are the ruins of Abbeystrewery (Cistercian).

Around Skibbereen

Four miles (6 km) south-west is Lough Ine (or Hyne), a beautiful land-locked inlet surrounded by hills. On an islet in the centre of the lough are some remains of Lough Ine Castle, a fortress of the O'Driscolls. Lough Ine is also the site of a marine biological research station.

The fishing village of Baltimore (8 miles/13 km south-west) has had a stormy history, of which the visitor is reminded by the ruined castle of the O'Driscolls on a rock overlooking the harbour. The 'Sack of Baltimore' by Thomas Davis is a vivid description in poetry of a raid by Algerian pirates in 1631, when some of the inhabitants were massacred and about two hundred others shipped as slaves to north Africa. There is a sailing school centre near the village.

Lying athwart the bay is Sherkin Island (motorboat from the harbour), an interesting place with numerous coves and the ruins of an old Franciscan abbey and ancient castle. South-west of Sherkin is the larger Cape Clear Island (daily ferry from Baltimore, details available locally). Its inhabitants retain the Irish language and traditions. From its cliffs and headlands

there are striking coastal views. The ruins of Dunamore Castle—a stronghold of the once powerful rulers of the island, the O'Driscolls—stand precariously on a rock on the north-west side of the island. To the south-west is Ireland's most southerly point, the solitary Fastnet Rock with its lighthouse.

The road west from Skibbereen runs beside the River Ilen, and then close to the shore of Roaring Water Bay through Bally-dehob and on to Schull, a small village with a quaint little harbour. Bathing, boating, yachting, water skiing, sea angling and pony-trekking are among the attractions here. There is a planetarium (the only one in the Republic) attached to the Community College in Schull, which is open to visitors during the season. The road onwards to Mizen Head (18 miles/29 km from Schull) sweeps round lovely Toormore Bay to Goleen, with its secluded sandy beach. From here there is a choice of two routes; the slightly longer and more picturesque is through Crookhaven, a charming spot whose safe harbour is much used by yachtsmen. After skirting Barley Cove, with its magnificent sandy beach, Mizen Head is reached. The coastal scenery here and on to Three Castles Head is remarkably fine. The return to Schull can be made along the shore of Dunmanus Bay and via the road behind Mount Gabriel (1,339 feet).

Bantry

Beanntraighe (Descendants of Beann)

 Pop. 2,811.

Tourist information office (seasonal): Tel. (027) 50229.

The town of Bantry is delightfully situated beneath sheltering hills at the head of famous Bantry Bay, one of the most beautiful bays along the Irish coast. Whiddy Island (with its forts and remains of earlier fortifications of

O'Sullivan Beare) is prominent in the view across the bay towards Glengarriff. River and lake angling, deep sea and inshore boats for hire, golf (9), mountain and forest walks.

History

Bantry Bay was twice entered by French fleets aiming at the invasion of Ireland—first in 1689 to aid James II, and again in 1796 when the expedition of General Hoche was dispersed by storms. T. M. Healy (1855–1931), first Governor-General of the Irish Free State, was born in Bantry; his name is commemorated in the Healy Pass leading from Adrigole to Lauragh.

Around Bantry

Bantry House beside the town in beautiful surroundings, has a splendid collection of art treasures (open all year round). Built about 1750, the house was formerly the home of the earls of Bantry, from whom the present owner is descended in the female line. The 2nd Earl of Bantry added the south front to the house in 1840, and filled it with a collection of tapestries and other works of art gathered during his travels in various parts of Europe. In the courtyard of the house there is an exhibition devoted to the French expedition under General Hoche in 1796, which was accompanied by Wolfe Tone. The expedition was abandoned after the fleet was dispersed by storms. The exhibition tells the story of what happened and how it fitted in with the political developments at the time.

South-west of Bantry, the Sheep's Head Peninsula has attractive scenery. Kilcrohane and Ahakista (there is a memorial here in the form of a garden to those who lost their lives in the 1985 Air India disaster off the Irish coast) are two of its villages that have fine beaches. The road from Bantry via Cousane Gap to Bealnablath (Michael Collins memorial) and Macroom is a very scenic route. The road to Glengarriff (11 miles/18 km) has magnificent mountain and sea views.

Glengarriff

Gleann Garbh (Rugged Glen)

👪 Pop. 244.

ℹ️ Tourist information office (seasonal): Tel. (027) 63084.

Glengarriff, though famous as a tourist resort, is just a village lying in the heart of a beautiful glen. It consists chiefly of pleasantly scattered hotels and other places catering for visitors. The valley, though rocky, is thickly wooded with oaks, elms, pines, yew and holly. There is also in the more sheltered spots a luxuriant Mediterranean flora of arbutus, fuchsia, and various flowering plants. Glengarriff Harbour has the appearance of a lovely land-locked estuary or a lake dotted with a hundred wooded islets; its entrance is guarded by the island of Ilnaculin or Garinish Island whose famous and beautiful gardens are open to the public (boats available).

Things to do

Sea bathing, golf (9), boating, sea and river fishing are among the recreations available; there is also good climbing and ridge-walking in the area.

Walks around Glengarriff

1. To Poulgorm (blue pool), about two minutes' walk by a pathway west of the post office. This is an exquisite spot with fine views from several woodland walks.

2. To Cromwell's Bridge, among the trees which overhang the river.

3. To Lady Bantry's Look-out. Return by Shrone Hill (919 feet), a magnificent viewpoint, and along the seashore to Biddy's Cove (good bathing).

4. To the Eagle's Nest, beyond Lady Bantry's Look-out.

5. Over Carrigrour Hill, taking the second road branching to the left east of the village, then turning left again on reaching a dolmen, to come out on the Kenmare Road.

    6. To Leary's point by the Bantry road.

Further afield from Glengarriff

Glengarriff is on the Beara Peninsula, most westerly of the long peninsulas of Cork. For over 30 miles (48 km) it stretches south-westwards between Bantry Bay and the Kenmare River estuary. It is almost entirely mountainous, except for a narrow coastal strip of lowland. The Caha and Slieve Miskish ranges form the mountain massif, and along the Caha range runs the border between Cork and Kerry—the north-west corner of the peninsula belonging to Kerry.

    Leaving Glengarriff, the road along the peninsula skirts Bantry Bay and winds along the rocky coastal strip beneath the Caha Mountains. The Sugarloaf Mountain (1,887 feet) is on the right. At Adrigole Bridge, on the right, is the spectacular Healy Pass road across the mountains.

Continuing along the coast, the long Bere Island comes into view. Between the island and the mainland is Berehaven, a fine sheltered harbour. The town of Castletownbere is an excellent centre for exploring the beautiful south-western tip of the peninsula.

    Less than 2 miles (3 km) from the town is Dunboy Castle; this stronghold of O'Sullivan Bere was the last in Munster to hold out for Philip of Spain against the forces of Carew. It was finally destroyed in 1602, the garrison refusing to surrender until the walls were completely shattered.

    A worthwhile trip is over the Slieve Miskish Mountains to Eyeries, then north-west to Ardgroom and along the shore road to Lauragh (County Kerry) where the beautiful Derreen Garden is open to the public in summer. Near Eyeries is a pillar stone 17½ feet high, with an ogham inscription. Inland from Lauragh, the road ascends to the summit of the Healy Pass (1,084 feet).

West Cork

Spoiled for choice

The centre of a once rich copper district, Allihies, is reached via Charphuca and then over a gap in the hills. The sea-scapes here are magnificent. A by-road through Ballydonegan goes to a narrow part of the peninsula, where a road leads via Garinish (fine bathing) to Dursey Sound. A cable-car operates between Dursey Sound and Dursey Island. On Dursey Island was born in 1590 Don Philip O'Sullivan, soldier and historian, who wrote in classical Latin, his *Catholic History of Ireland of the Elizabethan Period*—a key reference book of that time.

Macroom
Maghcromtha (Sloping Field)

Pop. 2,362 (urban district).

Macroom is an important market-ing centre in the picturesque valley of the Sullane River. On market days the visitor will hear Irish spoken as the vernacular and see the quaint hooded cloaks worn by women of the older generation.

History
The castle in the town was the scene of many a siege, particularly in the sixteenth and seventeenth centuries. The castle and town of Macroom were at one time the property of Admiral Sir William Penn, whose son founded the state of Penn-sylvania. The castle is now demolished.

Around Macroom
West of the town is the Gaeltacht (Irish-speaking district) which embraces Ballin-geary, Ballyvourney and Coolea. In this area lived Seán Ó Riada who contributed so much to Irish music and who is buried in the graveyard in Ballyvourney. One of the most celebrated Gaelic scholars of the language revival, Father Peter O'Leary (1839–1920), was born near Macroom at Liscarrigane.

The routes from Macroom to Killarney, Glengarriff and Cork city are all very beautiful. In fact, the road from Cork to Glengarriff via Macroom is one of the scenic highlights of the county. It traces the Lee valley to its source in Gougane Barra, then crosses the Shehy Mountains by the Pass of Keimaneigh southwards to the shores of Bantry Bay. Points of interest along the way include the vast artificial lakes of the Lee hydroelectric works at Inniscarra, the fishing centre of Inchigeelagh on Lough Allua, and the Gearagh National Nature Reserve, with its ancient forest system, rare plants and large numbers of wildfowl.

A short detour leads to the lake of Gougane Barra, set among magnificent mountain scenery, with brooding cliffs rising above the dark waters. In the lake is a tiny island, connected to the mainland by an artificial causeway; this was the hermitage of St Finbarr, patron saint of Cork. Nothing remains of the early structure, but there is an eighteenth-century church where an annual pilgrimage is made in September. The forest park above the lake is open to visitors.

According to legend, the Pass of Keimaneigh (The Deer's Pass) was once leaped by a deer which was fleeting from hunters. At the head of the pass crags overhang the road; then on rounding the pass, the wide valley of the Ouvane River stretches out in dramatic contrast to the gorge-like pass.

Bandon

Droichead na Banndan
(The Bridge of the Bandon River)

 Pop. 1,943.

Bandon is a large town in a fertile agricultural district, which is also a great region for angling and has much of archaeological interest. There is a golf course (18).

History and points of interest
During the Desmond revolt and later wars, the McCarthys, O'Mahonys, O'Donovans, O'Driscolls, O'Learys and other native septs were ousted from their lands by the Earl of Cork, who obtained grants of the forfeited estates and planted them with English and Scottish settlers. Fragments of the old town walls still remain. Kilbrogan Church (Church of Ireland), built in 1610, has the town stocks and other relics.

Around Bandon
Beyond Bandon, the road westwards skirts Castle Bernard estate (Earl of Bandon) and soon runs through the twin villages of Enniskean and Ballineen. Four miles (6 km) north of Enniskean is the curious round tower of Kinneigh. It is 68 feet high, the lower 18 feet hexagonal in cross-section. There are six storeys inside the tower and the entrance door is ten feet above ground level. From Ballineen westwards to Manch Bridge (a favourite haunt of anglers), the Bandon valley is particularly lovely. Near Manch Bridge are the well-preserved ruins of Ballinacarriga Castle (1585).

Kerry

Lough Acoose, near Killarney

Kerry, in the extreme south-west of Ireland, has two contrasting types of terrain—the mountainous southern part with its three large hilly peninsulas of Beara, Iveragh and Dingle, and the smaller area of undulating plain in the north that stretches as far as the Shannon estuary. Along the coast, sandy bays alternate with cliffs and rocky headlands; inland, too, are regions of outstanding scenic beauty—including Killarney's perfect blend of mountain and island-studded lake, wooded shore and glen. But scenery is by no means Kerry's only attraction: there are many coastal resorts, excellent angling waters, climbing that includes Ireland's highest mountain, good golf courses and a wealth of ancient monuments.

Killarney
Cill Airne (Church of the Sloe)

Pop. 7,253 (urban district).

Tourist information office: Town Hall. Tel. (064) 31633. Fax (064) 34506. Kerry County Airport, Farranfore (seasonal): Tel. (066) 64399.

Killarney, one of Ireland's loveliest districts, is known all over the world. Poets, painters and writers have never fully succeeded in conveying the varied beauty of this wonderland of mountains and lakes.

The three main lakes of Killarney occupy a broad valley stretching south between the mountains. Nearest the town is the Lower Lake, the largest of the three. The peninsula of Muckross separates this from the Middle Lake, which is connected with the Upper Lake by a narrow strait called the Long Range. The lakes are surrounded by luxuriant woods of oak, arbutus, birch, holly and mountain ash, among which grows a profusion of ferns, saxifrages, mosses and liverworts. Besides the three main lakes there are Lough Guitane (4 miles/6 km south-east) and many tarns in corries and folds of the mountains.

Firm old red sandstone and grit make up the surrounding mountain mass, and there is an interesting series of volcanic rocks south of Lough Guitane; on the east side of Bennaunmore Hill these rocks stand out in columns reminiscent of the Giant's

Causeway in County Antrim. Around the Middle and Lower Lakes limestone is seen—fretted and eroded in many places into fantastic shapes and caves by the action of the lake waters. Around Killarney the effects of the Ice Age are everywhere in evidence: ice-smoothed rocks abound in the glens (especially along the Kenmare road and in the Loo valley), also perched boulders, ice striae and deep corries excavated by glacial action (the best examples are the Horses' Glen and the Devil's Punch Bowl). Part of Killarney's lake district is within the 25,000-acre Killarney National Park which consists of woodlands and mountains around the lakes of Killarney. The heart of the National Park is Muckross Demesne centred on Muckross House and gardens. This nineteenth-century manor house is now a folklife centre where blacksmith, weaver, basketmaker and potter demonstrate their skills. The park and house are open all the year.

Muckross House, Killarney

Killarney

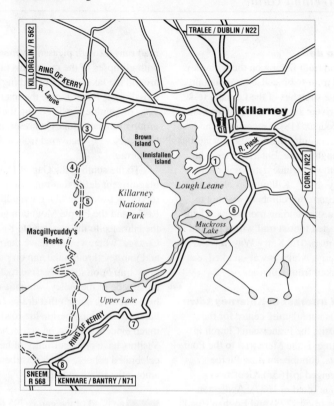

1. Ross Castle
2. Killarney Golf Club
3. Dunloe Castle
4. Kate Kearney's Cottage
5. Gap of Dunloe
6. Muckross House
7. Ladies' View
8. Moll's Gap

Things to do

Salmon and trout fishing on the Killarney lakes, and trout fishing also on mountain lakes (some stretches of the Laune, Flesk and other rivers are preserved). There are two golf courses (18), a racecourse, and excellent canoeing; there is also a waterbus tour of Lough Leane. Entertainments in Killarney town include dancing, cinema and variety shows. Killarney is also an excellent centre for climbers wishing to explore the surrounding mountains. There is a signposted tourist trail with a printed guide and map. The Kerry Way, a walker's Ring of Kerry, which is way-marked, can be undertaken from Killarney.

Points of interest in Killarney town

The town is a marketing centre for the area. Opposite the Franciscan Church in College Street is the Memorial to the Four Kerry Poets, commemorating Pierce Ferriter (hanged in 1653), Geoffrey O'Donoghue (died in 1677), Aodhagán Ó Rathaille (died 1728) and Eoghan Ruadh O'Sullivan (died 1784). The Catholic Cathedral of St Mary in New Street is a fine example of the Early English style, designed by Pugin (1855). The Parish Church of St Mary (Church of Ireland), also in Early English style, has a richly decorated interior. The National Museum of Irish Transport contains a unique collection of vintage cars and over 2,000 other transport-related items.

Tours of the Killarney district

(These tours can be made independently or on an organised basis by arrangement with hotels or tourist agents.)

1. Gap of Dunloe, Upper Lake, Long Range, Middle and Lower Lakes, Ross Castle. (A full day tour, more conveniently made on an organised basis, by pony trap from one's hotel or from the town centre, as cars must otherwise be left at Kate Kearney's Cottage and collected after the boat trip by returning to the cottage by pony trap.) Leaving the town by New Street, the road runs through pleasant avenues of trees with glimpses of the mountains clustering around the lakes. After branching left and crossing the River Laune the road gives a view of Dunloe Castle among the trees. A group of ogham stones is preserved near here; they were recovered from a destroyed souterrain.

To the south is the Gap of Dunloe, a magnificent defile that runs for 4 miles (6 km) between the Macgillycuddy's Reeks and the Purple Mountain group. At the entrance to the gap is Kate Kearney's Cottage, where visitors leave their vehicles and journey through the gap on ponies, pony trap or on foot. Massive rocks rise on either side of the valley, which is traversed by a turbulent stream that drains five small lakes strung along beside the road. There is much evidence of glacial action here. Visitors have an opportunity of hearing the celebrated echoes, which reverberate eerily among the rocks and hills.

The head of the gap is 795 feet above sea level, and on the descent the Upper Lake comes into view, with Cummeenduff or Black Valley stretching into the hills on the right. Beyond Lord Brandon's Cottage a path leads to the head of the lake (3 miles/5 km from the southern end of the gap), where the tour is continued by boat.

On leaving the Upper Lake by the narrow channel known as Coleman's Eye, the strait called the Long Range is entered, passing under the wooded crags of the Eagle's Nest on the left. The boatman will demonstrate the echo of a bugle call against this great crag, where the last eagles of Killarney had their eyrie. In the woods bordering the lakes here are often seen red deer, also Japanese deer and wild goats. Beyond the Eagle's Nest is the Old Weir Bridge; after shooting the rapids here, boats enter a calm stretch at the Meeting of the Waters. On Dinis Island the visitor may admire the sub-tropical plants and shrubs at Dinis Cottage.

On the Dingle Peninsula, Co. Kerry

Following pages: Aerial view of the Blasket Islands, Co. Kerry

Garinish Island, Co. Cork

Leaving the island, the boat crosses the Middle Lake (also called Muckross or Torc Lake). On the north shore are the Colleen Bawn Caves, hollowed out of the limestone by the action of the lake waters. The Lower Lake (or Lough Leane), largest of the Killarney lakes, is entered by rowing under Brickeen Bridge. Many islands are passed (there are thirty in the Lower Lake), of which the boatman will tell many a tale and legend.

The boat ends its journey at Ross Castle, a well-preserved fourteenth-century ruin that is one of the best examples of castle-building in County Kerry. In the Cromwellian wars it was defended by royalist forces under Lord Muskerry against General Ludlow in 1652. Only when armed vessels (brought overland from Kinsale) appeared on the lake to bombard the castle did the garrison eventually surrender.

Near the castle are disused copper mines, a rich source of ore dating back to prehistoric times. Near by at Governor's Rock is a nature preserve (flora). Innisfallen Island, reached by boat from Ross Castle, has the ruins of an abbey founded about 600. In 1215 it became a priory of the canons regular of St Augustine. Here between 950 and 1320 the famous manuscript called the *Annals of Innisfallen* was written (now in the Bodleian Library, Oxford).

2. Muckross Abbey, Dinis Island, Torc Waterfall. (Distance 12 miles (19 km) —this tour can also be made by cyclists and walkers.) The beautifully situated ruin of Muckross Abbey is approached by a short drive along the wooded shore of the Lower Lake, after entering the magnificent 25,000-acre national park at Muckross. The abbey (or friary) was founded by Donal MacCarthy Mor and occupied by Franciscans in 1448. Although it was formally suppressed in 1542, the friars were still in residence in 1589 when the abbey was raided by Elizabethan soldiery.

It came into secular hands in 1595. Later the friars returned, but final destruction came when the abbey was burned by the Cromwellians in 1652. Nevertheless, the Franciscans never left the district and they maintain the tradition of Muckross in their modern friary in Killarney town.

In the church, a massive tower separates the nave and adjoining transept from the choir with its lovely east window, its tombs of the founder and other chieftains of the MacCarthy, O'Donoghue and O'Sullivan clans, and its graves of the Kerry poets. The remarkable cloisters have 22 arches (Gothic on two sides, Norman or Romanesque on the others) enclosing an open court. There is a noon-dial carved under the north centre arch. In the court is a giant yew tree (now reduced by a storm to half its former height), which tradition dates from the abbey's foundation five centuries ago. Three stairways to the upper floor give access to the conventual apartments of the friars—dormitory, refectory, kitchen, scriptorium, infirmary and tower.

On leaving the abbey Muckross House is on the left. The road now winds among woodlands and shrubs, giving enchanting vistas of the lakes and mountains. In a short distance is reached the ruin reputed to have been the house of Danny Mann, the faithful boatman of the 'Colleen Bawn' story. Near by are the caves and the limestone crag known as the Colleen Bawn Rock. At the narrowest part of the Muckross Peninsula the hump-backed Brickeen Bridge is crossed and Dinis Cottage on Dinis Island comes into view. From a path behind the cottage there is a fine view of the Old Weir Bridge and the Meeting of the Waters. Near by is the whirlpool known as O'Sullivan's Punch Bowl.

On resuming the journey along the shore the main Kenmare road is reached beneath Torc Mountain. Soon after turning left to skirt the Middle Lake, the road passes beneath Torc

Jaunting car on the Muckross Estate

Waterfall (on right), which is approached by a short path through a wooded glen. Here the waters of the distant Devil's Punch Bowl on Mangerton Mountain fall more than 60 feet down a series of precipitous sandstone crags, forming one of the prettiest waterfalls in Ireland. Above the fall a winding path leads upwards through tall trees, and from it there are fine views of the lakes and Torc Mountain. (On leaving the fall, the main road is followed back to Killarney town.)

3. Aghadoe, Ross Castle. A journey of about 2½ miles (4 km) brings us to the summit of Aghadoe Hill (400 feet), from which there is a fine view of the Killarney area. At Aghadoe there are also the ruins of a round tower, church and castle. From here you can continue to Ross Castle and Ross Island, along the shore of the Lower Lake.

4. Muckross village, Torc Waterfall, the Tunnel, Derrycunnihy, the Lakes (distance 24 miles/39 km). Leaving Killarney by the Muckross road, the route is as in the latter part of Tour 2. Splendid views of the mountains are unfolded in passing Torc Mountain and the Long

Range. The road then climbs among the rocks, many of which bear scratches of glacial origin. Under Cromaglan Mountain an enormous rib of rock is pierced by a tunnel, and in about a mile (2 km) one of Killarney's prettiest beauty spots is reached—Derrycunnihy. There is a delightful cascade here, set among dense foliage; near by is the Queen's Cottage. From Galway's Bridge above the cascade, the wild valley of the old Kenmare road can be explored. Near this point visitors can embark on the boating tour described in Tour 1.

5. Lough Guitane (distance 15 miles/24 km). This tour gives an opportunity to explore the lesser known eastern part of the Killarney district. Lough Guitane, reached via Castlelough and Abbey Cross, is backed by the peak of Bennaunmore, with Crohane on the east and Eskduff to the west. Further on, the romantic Glenflesk valley is crossed. On the way back by the Flesk valley, a by-road may be followed to Lissivigeen. Here there is a perfect example of a prehistoric stone circle, with two standing stones near by.

Kenmare

The Ring of Kerry

The broad Iveragh Peninsula (also called the Waterville Promontory) stretches south-west from Killarney for nearly 40 miles (64 km) and has an average width of 15 miles (24 km). It has some of the finest mountains in Ireland and the coastal strip around the peninsula carries the famous 'Ring of Kerry' road. The following section traces the 'Ring' from Kenmare to Killorglin (75 miles/121 km), but the tour can just as profitably be made in the opposite direction.

Kenmare

An Neidin (The Little Nest)

Pop. 1,130.

Tourist information office (seasonal): Tel. (064) 41233.

K enmare is charmingly situated at the head of Kenmare Bay, where the Roughty River meets the sea.

It is an excellent centre for exploring both the Iveragh and Beara Peninsulas.

Things to do

There is bathing at sheltered coves west of the town, boat trips on Kenmare River, golf (9), salmon, brown trout and sea fishing. Derreen Gardens near Lauragh on the Beara Peninsula, are worth a visit. The grove of New Zealand tree fern is the central feature.

History

The ancient name Ceann Mara (Head of the Sea) was probably applied to the old site on the south side of the estuary, at the mouth of the River Sheen. It was at Ceann Mara that Papal Nuncio Rinuccini landed in 1645, on his way to Kilkenny. Later the modern town on the north side of the estuary was founded by Sir William Petty, ancestor of the Lansdowne family. Petty also established an iron-smelting works which used the rich woods of the district as fuel. Today Kenmare is noted for its lacemaking (point lace and other varieties) and the homespun woollen industry. A Kenmare heritage centre is in the course of construction.

Points of interest

At the northern end of the New Bridge is Cromwell's Fort. Cromwell himself was never nearer here than Kinsale, but the fort was held by English troops during the Cromwellian wars. Cromwell's Bridge, a small rainbow footbridge across the Finnehy River north-west of the town, probably dates from before the seventeenth century: there is a tradition that it was built to give access to Our Lady's Well.

An abbey once stood on the left bank of the River Finnehy near the bridge. Between this site and the bridge is a fine stone circle, consisting of 15 standing stones making a circle about 50 feet across. In the centre is a dolmen with a large capstone. There are many other stone circles in this district. St Finan's Holy Well at Kenmare Old has a reputation for healing; near by are the ruins of a church traditionally associated with St Finan.

Around Kenmare

Leaving Kenmare, the 'Ring of Kerry' road travels west along the shore of the estuary of the Kenmare River. On the opposite bank are the Caha and Slieve Miskish Mountains. Among the points of interest that are passed on the way to Sneem are Dunkerron Castle and Dunkerron Island opposite it in the estuary, Cappana-cuss Castle, once a residence of the O'Sullivans, the little village of Tahilla, nestling in the tiny Coongar Harbour, and Derryquin Castle, with Rossdohan Island opposite.

Sneem

An tSnaidhm (The Knot)

 Pop. 309.

Sneem village in beautiful scenery is situated on the estuary of the Ard-sheelaun River. The village derives its importance from the proximity to some fine mountain and river scenery. To the north rises a wild ridge of rocky peaks, dominated by Knockmoyle (2,245 feet).

Points of interest

Over the high altar in the Catholic church (1865) is a stained-glass window erected by the poet Aubrey de Vere (1814–1902). In the church is buried Father Michael Walsh (1828–1866), parish priest of Sneem and the 'Father O'Flynn' of the famous song. The Protestant church at Sneem probably dates back to the Eliza-bethan period; it has a tower-like front and a salmon as a weathercock. In the South Square is an abstract memorial to a former President of Ireland, Cearbhall Ó Dalaigh, who is buried in the village graveyard.

Around Sneem

Two miles (3 km) to the south is the beautiful hotel and estate of Parknasilla, on the shore of the Kenmare River. There is a private golf course (9) for hotel residents and good sea fishing in the bay. Beyond Sneem the 'Ring of Kerry' road winds inland for a few miles through wild scenery, meeting the coast again at Castlecove and Westcove, peaceful retreats near a fine sandy beach. About 1½ miles (2 km) north of the road are the imposing ruins of Staigue Fort, one of Ireland's finest archaeological remains. Circular in shape, the fort is constructed of rough stones built into position without mortar of any kind. The space enclosed is about 90 feet across, and the walls are 13 feet wide at the base with an average height of 18 feet. The only entrance is through a little doorway with sloping sides. Along the interior of the walls are several flights of stairs remarkably perfect in construction.

Continuing the journey along the coast, the village of Caherdaniel is beyond West-cove, near the shore of Derrynane Bay. In the vicinity is the curious hermitage of St Crohane, hewn out of solid rock; about a mile (2 km) away is an ancient stone fort, similar in construction though smaller than Staigue. Near by Derrynane House, with its historic park, was once the home of Daniel O'Connell, the 'Liberator' who lived and worked there during his political life. The house, now excellently restored, contains a museum with O'Connell's personal possessions and furniture. It is open to the public all year round.

As the road rises and crosses the Pass of Coomakista, 700 feet above the sea, there are fine views of Ballinskelligs Bay, the Skelligs Rocks and other features of the coast, and inland the mountains rising sharply to 1,600 feet. Beyond the pass, the road winds down to Waterville.

Waterville
An Coirean (The Little Whirlpool)

👫👫 Pop. 475.

Waterville, famous as an angling centre, also has much to offer the general tourist. There is a fine sandy beach on the shore of Ballin-skelligs Bay, and a championship golf course (18).

Around Waterville
The town is on the eastern shore of Ballinskelligs Bay, on a strip of land that separates the sea from Lough Currane, one of the most beautiful lakes in Ireland and a great fishing centre. On the east and south mountains rise from the lake shore, reaching 2,000 feet on the east side; on the lake itself, several islands add beauty to the scene. On Church Island are the remains of a twelfth-century church dedicated to the sixth-century St Finan Cam, and a beehive cell is said to have been that of the saint. In addition to Currane, there are many other smaller lakes in the vicinity.

The little Irish-speaking village of Ballinskelligs is charmingly situated on Ballinskelligs Bay; its attractions include boating, bathing, fishing and fine coastal scenery. A beach outside the village stretches for 4 miles (6 km). A little to the west are the ruins of an ancient castle of the McCarthys, and of an ancient abbey.

From Waterville, the 'Ring of Kerry' road runs inland, with views of the Iveragh Mountains and occasional glimpses of the sea.

Cahirciveen
Cathair Saidhbhin
(The Stone Fort of Sabina)

👫👫 Pop. 1,310.

Cahirciveen is situated at the foot of Bentee Mountain, overlooking Valentia Harbour. The inhabitants of the area earn their living from farming, fishing, turf production and light industry. The town is the main shopping centre for the western end of the Ring of Kerry. River and sea angling. An interpretative centre based in the old RIC barracks is being made ready.

Around Cahirciveen
At Carhan, a short distance from the town on the Glenbeigh road, are the ruins of the mansion where O'Connell was born in 1775; the Catholic church in Cahirciveen itself was built as a memorial to him.

There are interesting rambles in the neighbourhood of the town, particularly in the hills. About 2 miles (3 km) away at Kimego West is Leacanabuaile Fort, standing on a rocky eminence that commands an excellent view of the district. Defended on three sides by steep slopes, the only easy approach is on the east, where the fort's entrance was consequently placed. The massive circular stone rampart has steps at intervals along the inner side; it contains chambers, one of which communicates by a souterrain with a house site at the west side of the enclosure. Three other house sites have been discovered, and finds from

On the Great Skellig

excavations suggest that the fort was occupied in Early Christian times.

Near Cahirciveen, joined to the mainland by a bridge, is Valentia Island, a resort particularly popular with deep sea anglers. The island, about 7 miles (11 km) long by 2 miles (3 km) wide, is one of the most westerly points of Europe. The surface is bold and rocky, two prominent features being Geokaun Mountain (880 feet) on the north and Bray Head (792 feet) on the south; both are splendid vantage points for the sightseer. About 9 miles (14 km) off Valentia Island are the Skelligs Rocks. The Great Skellig, largest of the three, is an enormous mass of rock rising sharply out of the sea to more than 700 feet. On it are the ruins of a settlement built by early Christian monks: a small ancient church, a larger church of later date (probably tenth century), two oratories, six beehive cells, several burial enclosures, crude crosses, and two wells. The climb from the lighthouse to the monastery is by stone steps shaped out of the solid rock. In former times the Great Skellig was visited by crowds of pilgrims who came here doing penance. Above 'Christ's Saddle' is a projecting flake of rock, inscribed with a cross which pilgrims kissed.

The Skellig Experience is a major visitor attraction which includes a visitor centre where audio-visual techniques are used to tell the story of (1) the life and work of the monks who lived on island monasteries; (2) the history of the lighthouses and their keepers who served on the Skelligs from 1820 to 1987; (3) the seabirds of coastal south-west Kerry and the Skelligs; (4) the underwater life in the area. A key aspect of the Skellig Experience is a 1½-hour cruise of the islands in a purpose-built vessel with an onboard commentary by a local expert on the story of the islands.

The road from Cahirciveen north-east to Glenbeigh is one of the highlights of the 'Ring of Kerry'. At first it runs up a broad valley to Kells, where the road comes close to the waters of Dingle Bay and gives fine views across the bay to the peaks of the Dingle Peninsula. From Kells the road hangs high over the bay, hugging the steep Drung Hill and then passing through Mountain Stage (a relic of the coaching days) on its way down to Glenbeigh.

Glenbeigh
Gleann Beithe (Birch Glen)

Pop. 184.

A popular holiday base situated at the entrance to a horseshoe of mountains where the Behy River flows into Dingle Bay, Glenbeigh nestles at the foot of Seefin Mountain (1,621 feet).

Around Glenbeigh
The mountain scenery here is magnificent, and the circuit of the hills from Seefin to Drung Hill, called the 'Glenbeigh Horseshoe', is one of Kerry's finest mountain walks. A feature of the circuit is the series

Reenbeg Point on the Dingle Peninsula

of glacial corries and lakes which lie at the head of the Behy valley. There is trout fishing on Lough Coomasaharn, the largest of the lakes, and the Behy River.

Near Glenbeigh is the ruin of 'Wynne's Folly', a castellated mansion built by Lord Headley Wynne in 1867. About 2 miles (3 km) from Glenbeigh is Rossbeigh beach, under the shadow of Curra Hill. Miles of sandy beach backed by dunes stretch out into the bay. At the north end is a stone tower, built in the nineteenth century as a guide mark for ships entering Castlemaine Harbour.

From Glenbeigh it is 3 miles (5 km) via the Windy Gap, Blackstones Bridge and the course of the Caragh River, with lovely scenery all the way, to the angling and climbing centre of Glencar. Caragh Lake is a beautiful expanse of water 4 miles (6 km) long, set among broom and heather-covered hills with majestic mountains in the background.

Killorglin

Cill Orglan (Orgla's Church)

Pop. 1,304.

The town is situated on a hill overlooking the wide and graceful Laune, a river offering salmon and trout fishing. Dominating the landscape to the south are the Macgillycuddy's Reeks.

Killorglin is the scene of the famous 'Puck Fair and Pattern', which lasts for three days in August and is attended by thousands of people from all parts of Ireland. On the evening of the first day a procession in pageant assembles at the bridge end of the town. A large billy goat, his horns bedecked with ribbons and rosettes, is borne in triumph in a lorry through the streets to a raised platform in the town square at the centre of the town. Here King Puck is enthroned for the next two days, presiding over a great cattle, sheep and horse fair. During the fair, shops

225

and business premises except public houses are open day and night.

It has been suggested that the enthroning of the goat is a custom surviving from pagan times, but there is probably more truth in the tradition which argues that 'Puck' commemorates an occasion when the stampeding of goats gave warning of the approach of English forces.

Around Killorglin

The diversified and undulating character of the surrounding country is largely due to the accumulation of moraines brought down by glaciers in the Ice Age. A great tongue of ice pushed northwards from the mountains and deposited a series of crescentic moulds around Killorglin. Many small lakes lie between the ridges.

Completing the 'Ring of Kerry' circuit, the Laune River is followed to Killarney. Along the road there are magnificent vistas of the Reeks and the other hills of the Killarney district. The complete tour of the Iveragh Peninsula, from Kenmare to Killarney as outlined in this section, covers 90 miles (145 km). A further 20 miles (32 km) is added by continuing to Kenmare, thus returning to the starting point.

Dingle

Daingean Ui Chuis (O'Cush's Fortress)

 Pop. 1,253.

ℹ️ Tourist information office (seasonal): Tel. (066) 51188 and (066) 51241.

The Dingle Peninsula, stretching westwards for 30 miles (48 km) from the low-lying country near Tralee, is the most northerly of the hilly promontories of County Kerry. Between Tralee and Inch runs the Slieve Mish range of mountains; further west, in the centre of the peninsula, is a tract of wild hilly country; then north of Dingle town is the mighty rampart of Brandon (3,127 feet),

and on its western side a coastal plain studded with typical Irish hamlets and villages. This western end of the peninsula has magnificent coastal scenery, and is an Irish-speaking district where the traditional customs, crafts and lore are still very much alive.

Dingle is the chief town of the peninsula and an excellent touring centre. Lying at the foot of a steep slope on the north side of Dingle Harbour, it is bounded on three sides by hills. Dingle was the chief port of Kerry in the old Spanish trading days, and in the reign of Queen Elizabeth was important enough to be a walled town.

Things to do

Dingle has a cinema, and there is golf (18) in the locality at Dun an Oir. There are fine beaches and other natural bathing places near the town, and the sea fishing off Dingle is particularly good. The Dingle Way runs from Tralee practically the length of the peninsula and is fully way-marked.

Tours from Dingle

1. Ventry, Slea Head, Dunquin, Ballyferriter, Kilmalkedar, Gallarus Oratory (30 miles/48 km). From Dingle the road skirts the north shore of the harbour to Milltown. Beyond Milltown Bridge is the 'Milestone', a giant standing stone. Near by are two other standing stones, the 'Gates of Glory', and in the same field is a large boulder bearing cup and circle carvings. At the south-west end of Dingle Harbour are the wooded grounds of Colaiste Ide (formerly Burnham House, residence of Lord Ventry); a group of ogham stones are along the drive up to the house.

Continuing west, the road brings into view Ventry Harbour with the slopes of Mount Eagle (1,696 feet) and Croagh Marhin (1,331 feet) beyond. Ventry is the scene of the ancient romantic tale, Cath Fionntra (The Battle of Ventry Strand). The tale, as told in a fifteenth-century

Slea Head

manuscript now in the Bodleian Library, Oxford, describes how the King of the World, Daire Doon, landed at Ventry with his vassal monarchs in an attempt to invade Ireland, and how they were defeated by the Fianna under Fionn Mac Cumhaill.

A short distance from Ventry village the road turns inland, meeting the sea again 2 miles (3 km) later at Kilvicadowning. From here to Slea Head the road is on the cliffs along the southern slopes of Mount Eagle, with magnificent coastal views. This area has many archaeological remains,

Coumeenoole Strand near Dunquin

most notably the Fahan group which includes 414 clochans (unmortared beehive cells or huts), 19 souterrains, 18 standing and inscribed stones, 2 sculptured crosses, 7 earthen ring forts and 2 fortified headlands.

Dunbeg Fort in this group consists of a fortified stone wall cutting off a triangular promontory. The landward side is protected by an elaborate system of earthen ramparts and trenches. The cliff edge inside the fort shows remains of stone walling. There is a ruined circular building inside the enclosure, and in the great wall (22 feet thick) is a remarkable doorway and an elaborate souterrain.

Cathair na Mairtineach, a stone fort 108 feet across, has a number of souterrains and beehive stone huts. Cathair Murphy is similar, but almost the entire enclosure is covered with buildings. Cathair an da Dhoras is a triple clochan rather than a fort; it is very well preserved.

Off the shore at Slea Head is the group of seven islands and many rocks known as the Blaskets. The Great Blasket is the largest; about 4 miles (6 km) long and ¾ mile (1 km) wide. It had a village settlement at the north-east end (the inhabitants were moved to the mainland in 1953). Many of the islanders were adept at recounting folk-tales, and Blasket islanders have produced such well-known books as *Twenty Years Agrowing* (M. O'Sullivan) and *The Islander* (T. Ó Crohan).

Near Clogher Head the route turns inland. About 2 miles (3 km) north-west of Ballyferriter village are the remains of Ferriter's Castle, birthplace of Pierce Ferriter, a poet, scholar and soldier who was one of the last Irish chiefs to hold out against Cromwell's army. North of Ballyferriter is the broad inlet of Smerwick Harbour, where the old fortress of Dun an Oir (The Fort of Gold) stands on a rock

Blasket Islands

promontory. In 1580 a massacre took place at Smerwick when over 600 Spanish and Irish soldiers surrendered, to be butchered by Lord Grey's troops. A monument to commemorate the massacre was erected in 1980.

Near Ballyferriter is the Riasc Stone and the recently excavated site of the ancient monastery. East of Ballyferriter the road through Emlagh should be followed to reach Kilmalkedar, where the view of the Brandon range to the east is magnificent. Kilmalkedar has a fine twelfth-century Hiberno-Romanesque church. Also of interest are the Alphabet Stone (close to the chancel doorway), ogham stone, sundial, and St Brendan's House. South of the church is the Chancellor's House (fourteenth or fifteenth century).

About 2 miles (3 km) south of Kilmalkedar is Gallarus Oratory, one of the best-preserved Early Christian church buildings in Ireland. The building suggests, in outline, an inverted boat. The doorway is characteristic of Irish Early Christian architecture in that it narrows towards the top. Inside the oratory measures 15 feet by 10 feet, and at the east end is a deeply splayed loophole window. On the summit of each gable is a socketed stone in which a stone cross was inserted. The unique feature of Gallarus is that it is built throughout of unmortared stone, yet is completely watertight after more than a thousand years.

In the vicinity of Gallarus and Kilmalkedar is the Saint's Road, an ancient track said to have been built by St Brendan, to the summit of Brandon Mountain.

2. Milltown, Gallarus, Kilmalkedar, Murreagh, Ardamore, Ballydavid, Brandon Creek (20 miles/32 km). The first part of this tour has been described above. From Kilmalkedar the sea is reached in 2 miles (3 km) at Murreagh, and on the road to Ardamore there are fine views of Smerwick Harbour, with the Three Sisters Head to the west and Ballydavid Head to the north. There are many sea fishing communities along this coast, and at Ballydavid village is a currach-building industry. (Currachs are boats consisting of a wooden framework covered with tarred canvas; peculiar to the west of Ireland, the high prows of these craft are well designed to ride the waves in safety.)

The coast of Brandon Creek north-east of Brandon Head is a succession of mighty cliffs where the peak of Masatiompan (2,509 feet) comes down to the sea.

3. Dingle to Tralee by the Connor Pass (40 miles (64 km) including detours). This journey is one of the finest in the peninsula. Leaving Dingle, the road climbs north-eastwards between the Brandon and central Dingle groups of mountains. Near at hand is Ballysitteragh (2,050 feet), the southern peak of the Brandon group.

At the summit of the Connor Pass (1,500 feet) the bays of Brandon and Tralee are seen below to the north, with the sandy peninsula of Rough Point separating them. To the south there is also a fine view of Dingle Bay and the environs of Dingle town. In the deep valley below the road to the left are a number of lakes. Descending from the top of the pass on the north side, the road winds along the base of great cliffs, while below it the valley slope is a boulder-strewn wilderness. About a mile (2 km) down, the road curves sharply over a deep gorge: here in a small corrie 100 feet above the road is 'Pedlar's Lake' (Lough Doon), so named because of a local tale that a pedlar was drowned here by a companion who robbed him of his money.

At the foot of the pass, a branch road on the left leads to the villages of Cloghane and Brandon. Cloghane, on an inlet of Brandon Bay beneath the eastern slopes of Brandon Mountain, has a fine beach and is a good base for climbing Brandon (3,127 feet). Brandon, 3 miles (5 km) north of Cloghane, is another small coastal village and a good centre for exploring the magnificent coastal scenery between Brandon Point and Brandon Head.

The main road from the Connor Pass continues to Stradbally village, a good starting point for climbing Benoskee and Stradbally Mountains. From the village a

The Magharees

branch road on the left leads to Castle-gregory, at the base of the sandy peninsula that separates the bays of Brandon and Tralee. The place is named after Gregory Hoare, a sixteenth-century chief who built a castle here. West of the village is Lough Gill, and beyond the northern tip of the peninsula are the Seven Hogs or Magharee Islands. One of these, Illauntannig, has the remains of an Early Christian monastery attributed to St Seanach. A wall surrounds the remains of two oratories, three beehive cells, and a small cross. Boats are available at Fahamore for trips to the island.

From Castlegregory, the remainder of the journey to Tralee provides fine views of Tralee Bay. At Camp the Slieve Mish Mountains are again close at hand, and Camp village is the best starting point for the ascent to the fortress of Caherconree. The approach is by the mountain road running south to Beheenagh, where the western spur of the mountain can be climbed. On a triangular plateau at 2,050 feet are the remains of the stone fort of Caherconree. In folklore this was the fortress of Curaoi Mac Daire, a king of ancient Ireland whose wife informed her husband's foes of his presence in the fort by pouring milk into the river; they then came to the fort and killed him.

5. Inch, Annascaul. The head of Dingle Bay is cut off by two narrow sandhill promontories—one an offshoot of the Dingle Peninsula, the other of the Iveragh Peninsula at Rossbeigh; together they enclose the harbour of Castlemaine. On the inner side of the Dingle promontory is the sheltered seaside resort of Inch.

Its magnificent 4-mile (6 km) beach of firm golden sand is backed by dunes which are well known to archaeologists for the kitchen middens and old habitation sites among them.

From Inch the main road back to Dingle can be rejoined at Lougher and then to Annascaul, or the coast road can be followed westward from Inch (via Red Cliff) to reach Annascaul after 5 miles (8 km). In the village is the 'South Pole Inn', once lived in by Thomas Crean (born 1877) who accompanied Scott on his expedition to the South Pole. Minard Castle, 3 miles (5 km) south of Annascaul, is said to have been built by the Knight of Kerry and is the largest fortress in the peninsula. Thomas Ashe, one of the patriots of the 1916 Rising, was born in 1885 in the village of Kinard East.

Tralee

Traigh Li (Beach of the River Lee)

👤👤👤 Pop. 17,206 (urban district).

ℹ️ Tourist information office: Ashe Memorial Hall. Tel. (066) 21288.

F inely situated where the River Lee flows into Tralee Bay, Tralee is the chief town of County Kerry and the gateway to the Dingle Peninsula.

Things to do
There is bathing along the shores of the bay, and a golf course (18), horse-racing, greyhound racing, horse-riding and pony-trekking, and day coach tours in summer. A modern sports centre incorporates many sports including swimming and tennis. See the headquarters of Siamsa Tire, the National Folk Theatre of Ireland, which was founded in 1974 to project Irish traditional customs, song and dance through the medium of the theatre. There

are performances during season in the new theatre in Tralee Town Park. The design of the new theatre is based on the 2,000-year-old Irish stone forts, particularly the one at Staigue (see Dingle).

History
Tralee is closely identified with the history of the Desmond family (a branch of Anglo-Norman Fitzgeralds) and at one time was the chief seat of the clan. Their castle stood where Denny Street joins the Mall, but today only a fragment of its wall remains. The Dominicans were brought to Tralee in 1243 by John, Earl of Desmond, and in the old Dominican grounds (at Abbey Street) thirteen earls are buried. The story of the Desmond Geraldines is told in the 'Medieval Experience', a show put on in the Ashe Memorial Hall, which also houses an exhibition on the Anglo-Normans, their arrival in Ireland and settlements in Kerry. On the forfeiture of the Desmond estates (following the rebellion they led), Tralee was granted to Sir Edward Denny (whose name is remembered in the present Denny Street). After a six-month siege in 1641 by Irish forces under Pierce Ferriter, the garrison of Tralee Castle surrendered. The castle was rebuilt in 1653 after another Irish raid, but it was again laid in ruins during the Williamite wars.

William Mulchinock (1820–1864), who wrote the song 'The Rose of Tralee', lived near the town at Cloghers House, Bally-mullen. The Rose of Tralee Festival, held each year in early September, is known throughout the world. The Rose for the year is selected from girls of Irish descent from countries selecting candidates through competition. Roger Bresnahan, born in Tralee in 1881, became one of the most famous baseball players of his time in the USA. Bresnahan was the inventor of shinguards and was the first to wear them (in 1907).

Points of interest
The Dominican Church of the Holy Cross is a Gothic structure designed in the

Blennerville Windmill

nineteenth century by Pugin. It has some fine stained glass, the work of Michael Healy of Dublin. In the priory attached to the church are many sculptured stones from the old Dominican Holy Cross Abbey.

Around Tralee

A steam train and a ship canal connects Tralee with the bay at Blennerville, where the old windmill tower near the bridge is picturesquely set against the peaks of the Slieve Mish Mountains. The windmill has been restored and houses an exhibition which tells the story of the emigration from Kerry through Blennerville Port in the nineteenth century and also the history of Irish milling including working millstones. About 3 miles (5 km) south of Tralee is Scota's Glen, where a large flagstone marks what is said to be the grave of Scota, widow of Milesius and daughter of a Pharaoh of Egypt. The ancient writers describe how the sons of Milesius and their followers, on landing in Ireland (Anno Mundi 3500), joined in battle with the Tuatha De Danann at the foot of the Slieve Mish Mountains. The Milesians won the day but Scota was among their slain. Another victim of the battle was Fais, wife of Un Mac Uige, who was buried in Glen Aish (about 10 miles/ 16 km south-west of Tralee).

A mile (2 km) east of Tralee is Rathass Church, preserved as a national monument. The principal feature of the ruin is the well-preserved doorway in the west gable, with the sloping jambs characteristic of Irish Early Christian architecture.

Annagh Church, 3 miles (5 km) south-west of Tralee, has an interesting sculptured stone preserved in the ruin. It shows a man on horseback holding a scythe. Spa, 4 miles (6 km) west of Tralee, gets its name from a mineral spring which was popular in the eighteenth century for the curative properties of its waters.

About 8 miles (13 km) west of Tralee is a small port on the bay, Fenit. St Brendan, patron saint of Kerry and famous as Brendan the Navigator (484–577), who, it is suggested, may have discovered America, was born in the neighbourhood.

Near the village is a glacial erratic, a large boulder of sandstone resting on limestone near the water's edge. A natural limestone cave at Lissodigue, 3 miles (5 km) to the north-east, can be explored for over 700 feet. Fenit Castle ruin, on Fenit Island 2 miles (3 km) from the village, was built to guard the entrance to Barrow Harbour, which at one time had a considerable trade with Spain and the Low Countries.

North-west 5½ miles (9 km) from Tralee on the Ballyheigue road is Ardfert, where the imposing cathedral dates mainly from the thirteenth century. The west door and fragments of an arcade on each side are twelfth-century work, the remains of a Hiberno-Romanesque church that was probably the earlier cathedral. A thirteenth- or fourteenth-century effigy of a bishop was unearthed here in 1830 and now stands in a niche in the building. Visitors should also see the twelfth-century Teampall na Hoe, Teampall Griffin and the ogham stone in the graveyard. In the former Crosbie demesne is Ardfert Friary, founded in 1253 by the first Lord Kerry, Thomas Fitzmaurice.

A mile (2 km) west of Ardfert there is a single-rampart earthen fort in a field by the roadside. This is now called Casement's Fort, because Sir Roger Casement (1864–1916) was arrested here in 1916 after landing at Banna Strand with arms for the Easter Rising.

On Ballyheigue Bay the quiet little resort of Ballyheigue has an excellent sandy beach. North of the village is the striking ruin of Ballyheigue Castle, a nineteenth-century mansion. Ballingarry Castle, about 4 miles (6 km) north, was a small fortress built by David Crosbie in 1641. Here is fine coastal scenery especially around the promontory of Kerry Head which shelters Ballyheigue Bay on the north. In the cliffs and rocks of this head are found large numbers of amethysts and 'Kerry diamonds', almost perfectly formed quartz crystals, purple or clear, with six-sided conical ends.

On the other side of Tralee, Castleisland is a thriving market town at the eastern end of the 'Vale of Tralee'. It got its name from a castle built in 1226 by Geoffrey de Marisco. In 1345 it was held for the Earl of Desmond but was taken by Sir Ralph Ufford who killed the entire garrison. Crag Cave, which is open to the public, is superbly lit and has a synchronised sound system commentary.

Ballybunion
Baile an Bhuinneanaigh
(The Town of the Sapling)

Pop. 1,452.

B allybunion is a popular family resort on the north-west coast of County Kerry, near where the River Shannon meets the sea. The surrounding country is comparatively level, but the coastline at Ballybunion, with its sea caves, rugged cliffs, coves and beaches, forms a very fine district for seaside holidays.

Ballybunion has a magnificent golf links (18). A fine sandy beach fronts the town and continues southwards for 2 miles (3 km). Boats for angling or pleasure trips are available. There are dancing, cinema and variety performances during the summer.

Around Ballybunion
On the northern side of Ballybunion is a range of cliffs which alternate with stretches of level beach as far as the Shannon estuary. Many of the caves in these cliffs can be entered on foot during low tide; others can be reached only by boat. A path runs north for 3 miles (5 km) along the cliffs, past the old Fitzgerald fortress of Lick Castle.

Ballybunion Castle, on the headland jutting out between the two sections of the beach, was built by the Fitzmaurices; it was burned in 1583, and all that remains is a lofty wall standing on the Castle Green. South of the town, the coastal path lies past the golf course through the sand dunes.

The Old Course, Ballybunion

Near by is Cashen Fishery, on Cashen Bay, one of the finest salmon fisheries in Ireland. Three miles (5 km) east of the town is Knockanore Hill (880 feet), with a wonderful view of the River Shannon that extends as far as the spires of Limerick city. At Knappoge North, Ballyduff, 7 miles (11 km) from Ballybunion, the Rattoo Heritage Complex, an interpretative museum for north Kerry, houses exhibits from all ages of the history of the area which are displayed in an exciting and original way (open daily during the season).

Listowel
Lios Tuathail (Fort of the Tuathails)

Pop. 3,326 (urban district).

Tourist information office (seasonal): St John's Church. Tel. (068) 22590.

L istowel is a thriving inland town on the banks of the River Feale. In the town are the ruins of a castle which belonged to the lords of Kerry, and was the last to hold out against the Elizabethan forces during the Desmond revolt; in 1600 it was taken by Sir Charles Wilmot, who put the garrison to the sword.

Angling for brown trout on the River Galey and on the River Feale (salmon and sea trout). Teach Siamsa Folk Theatre at Finuge (3 miles/5 km). Day coach tours. Centre for Writers Week, Harvest Festival of Ireland and 'Wren Boys' Championships. Horse-racing Festival meeting in September. There is a heritage centre with a theatre which features Irish traditional music and an exhibition.

Around Listowel
Four miles (6 km) north-west is Gunsborough, birthplace of Earl Kitchener of Khartoum (1850–1916). Lixnaw, 6 miles (10 km) west of Listowel was once the seat of the earls of Kerry, whose ruined castle adjoins the village. On a height a short distance to the east of the village is a monument to the 3rd Earl.

Eight miles (13 km) north of Listowel, on the Shannon estuary, is Ballylongford, and near by is the ruined Lislaughtin Abbey.

Carrigafoyle Castle, on the Shannon shore 2 miles (3 km) north of Ballylongford, was the object of many attacks in the sixteenth and seventeenth centuries. It has been in ruins since its partial destruction by the Cromwellians in 1649. The castle consisted of an oblong tower 80 feet high, placed centrally in a walled courtyard; the wall also enclosed a dock for boats at the foot of the tower.

Four miles (6 km) north-east of Ballylongford is the village of Tarbert on a steep slope overlooking one of the prettiest parts of the Shannon; from here the Shannon car ferry crosses to Killimer, County Clare, every hour on the half-hour. The ferry service provides the opportunity for several attractive circular tours. The 20-minute crossing saves 85 miles (137 km) on the same journey via Limerick. Tarbert House, completed about 1730, has a fine collection of Georgian furniture, including the best example of an Irish Chippendale mirror. The house is open to groups by prior arrangement.

Limerick

King John's Castle, Limerick city

Much of County Limerick is low and undulating, particularly in the east where it forms part of the rich plain known as the Golden Vale. There are, however, considerable elevations towards the west, south and north-east fringes of the county, and in the south-east the Galtee Mountains reach into County Limerick from neighbouring County Tipperary. Limerick city, standing where the River Shannon becomes tidal, is a historic place with many interesting features; it is also an important port and industrial centre. The county is a place of quiet beauty and rural charm, offering good sport to the angler and golfer and some of the finest hunting country in Ireland.

Limerick City

Luimneach (Bare Spot)

Pop. 52,040 (Limerick *city* 1991 CSO figures).

Tourist information office: Arthur's Quay, Limerick.
Tel. (061) 317522. Fax (061) 315634.

American Express: Riordan's Travel Ltd, 2 Sarsfield St, Limerick. Tel. (061) 414666. Fax (061) 414875.

✉ Post Office:
Henry St, Limerick. Tel. (061) 315777.
Open: 9.00 – 18.00

Ⓡ Parking Regulations:
Disc parking.

🚃 Railway Station:
Colbert Station, Parnell St, Limerick.
Tel. (061) 315555.

🚌 Bus Depot:
Shannon Airport. Tel. (061) 361311.

🚗 Car Hire: Tom Mannion Rent a
Car Ltd, 71 O'Connell St, Ennis, Co.
Clare. Tel. (065) 24211.

Budget Rent a Car, Shannon Airport,
Co. Clare. Tel. (061) 61688.

Bunratty Car Rentals Ltd, Coonagh Cross,
Caherdavin, Limerick. Tel. (061) 52781.
Fax (061) 52516.

Treaty Car Rentals Ltd, 37 William St,
Limerick. Tel. (061) 46512.
Fax (061) 42266.

*Hall's Alms Houses, off Nicholas Street,
Limerick city*

🚲 Bicycle Hire: Rent a Bike, 1 Pery
Square, Limerick.

Emerald Cycles, 1 Patrick St, Limerick.
Tel. (061) 46983.

Limerick, the fourth largest city in
Ireland, is attractively laid out with
wide streets. Its strategic position on
the River Shannon makes it an important
port, and Shannon Airport is 15 miles
(24 km) away (in County Clare). Limerick-
cured hams and bacon enjoy a world-wide
reputation, and the making of traditional
Limerick lace is still carried on in the city
by the nuns at the Good Shepherd convent
in Clare Street, open to the public.

Things to do

There is golf (18) at Ballyclough and at
Castletroy, each 3 miles (5 km) from the
city; salmon and trout fishing at Castleconnell (8 miles/13 km), and brown trout
and grilse fishing on the River Mulcair (4
miles/6 km); greyhound racing three times
weekly at the city track; swimming and
boating on the River Shannon. Limerick is
also the centre of good hunting country
which maintains a number of fine packs.
Limerick museum has displays of the city's
heritage. The Gallery of Art has a permanent
collection of Irish art of eighteenth, nineteenth and twentieth centuries. There is
horse-racing at Greenpark outside the city.
There are guided walking tours of the city
during July and August from the tourist
office. For night-time entertainment the
city has the Belltable Arts Centre Theatre,
a *Son et Lumière* show in St Mary's
Cathedral, cabaret shows in local hotels,
and 7 miles (11 km) from the city are the
world-famous Bunratty Medieval Castle
Banquets and Shannon Ceili.

History

Limerick dates from the ninth century,
when the Danes made a base here for

plundering the hinterland. This colony suffered continual attacks by the Irish for more than a century, until Brian Boru finally sacked the town and drove out the settlers. The town was taken by the Anglo-Normans towards the end of the twelfth century, but control was later regained by the O'Briens. King John visited Limerick in 1210 and ordered a strong castle to be built—'to watch towards Thomond'—and a bridge to span the Shannon. More than a century later, Edward Bruce occupied the city for several months.

In later centuries the city walls were extended, and this security fostered a strong allegiance to the English throne. Parliaments were convened at Limerick and the port became a commercial rival to Galway. The Confederate forces occupied the city in 1642; four years later the Papal Nuncio, Rinuccini, stayed here during the siege of Bunratty Castle (County Clare). Ireton laid siege to Limerick in 1651; after six months resistance ended when some of the garrison officers betrayed the city to the Cromwellians.

After the defeat at the Boyne in 1690 the Irish forces retired to Limerick, pursued by William of Orange at the head of a large army. William laid siege to the city and awaited the arrival of his heavy artillery. The Irish leader, Patrick Sarsfield, secretly left the city and intercepted the Williamite siege train at Ballyneety. After three unsuccessful attempts to storm the city, William eventually raised the siege and marched away.

A year later, however, another Williamite army (under General Ginkel) appeared before the walls of Limerick. After nearly two months of siege, the Irish opened the negotiations which led to the Treaty of Limerick being signed (October 1691).

Under the terms, the garrison marched out with full honours, and 11,000 of them later joined the standard of Louis of France. This was the beginning of an exodus almost

Sarsfield Bridge, Limerick city

without parallel in Ireland's history; during the half-century following the treaty, nearly half a million Irish soldiers entered the service of France and Spain. The exclusively Protestant parliament at the time refused to ratify the treaty, however, as it guaranteed religious tolerance.

Points of interest

The Walls of Limerick were seen in the eighteenth century as a hindrance to the city's development, and were knocked down. A few parts escaped the dismantling, however, and the most striking section is at the rear of Lelia Street. Also worth seeing is the 'Devil's Battery' at the end of St John's Hospital grounds; the two massive gateways inside the entrance to the grounds are said to be the town gate and the outer gate of the citadel.

Built in the thirteenth century to dominate the crossing point of the Shannon, King John's Castle is a fine example of medieval architecture, with towers and curtain walls. Some patches of brickwork, seen from Thomond Bridge, show the damage done by Ginkel's guns. A barracks

Matthew Bridge with St Mary's Church of Ireland Cathedral, Limerick

was built inside the castle walls in the eighteenth century and this greatly changed the structure, but the larger part of it remains. The castle was restored and developed in 1990 and now houses a major exhibition and audio-visual show on the history of the castle and of Limerick. On a pedestal at the County Clare end of Thomond Bridge is the Treaty Stone, an irregular block of limestone on which the 1691 treaty is said to have been signed.

At the top of Athlunkard Street is part of a castellated building known as O'Brien's Castle, probably the palace of the royal family of Thomond in the period after 1190. It is said to have been used as a hiding place in penal times by Franciscan priests. In Bridge Street is the site of the old city courthouse (now the Gerald Griffin Memorial Schools) where the trial of John Scanlon for the murder of his wife Ellen took place in 1819. Scanlon, who was defended by Daniel O'Connell, was found guilty and executed. The trial gave a young Limerick newspaper reporter, Gerald Griffin, the motif for his famous novel, *The Collegians,* on which were based the Boucicault drama, *The Colleen Bawn*, and the Benedict opera, *The Lily of Killarney*.

The Church of Ireland St Mary's Cathedral was founded about 1168, when Donal Mor O'Brien donated his own palace for the purpose. Parts of the palace were incorporated in the building, so that in several details it differs from the usual structures of the period. The western front still has its projecting pilasters and a fine Romanesque doorway from the twelfth-century building. Inside there are many interesting monuments; the fifteenth-century misericords, with their grotesque carvings in black oak, are unique specimens in Ireland. The cathedral has just undergone a major restoration. Forming part of the boundary wall of the cathedral grounds is the front of the Exchange, built in 1673 by Alderman William York and remodelled in 1702 after being damaged in the Williamite bombardment. In the Exchange

Limerick

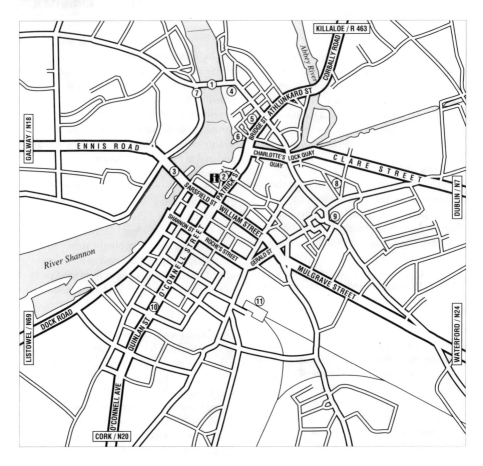

1. Thomond Bridge
2. Arthur's Quay
3. Sarsfield Bridge
4. King John's Castle
5. St Mary's Cathedral
6. Courthouse

7. Treaty Stone
8. City Wall
9. St John's Cathedral
10. O'Connell Monument
11. Colbert Station

stood the pedestal called the 'Nail' on
which the city merchants paid their debts,
a custom which gave rise to the expression
'paying on the nail'.

The Catholic St John's Cathedral, a
nineteenth-century Gothic building
with a tower 280 feet high, has a
fine marble madonna by Benzoni in the
sanctuary and a bronze statue of Patrick
Sarsfield in the grounds; in the presbytery
are the exquisitely worked mitre and
crosier of a fifteenth-century bishop of
Limerick, Cornelius O'Dea. John's Square
dates from the mid-eighteenth century and
is made up of Georgian town houses. The
Square was restored by the Corporation as
Ireland's contribution to the European
Architectural Heritage Year of 1975. The
Redemptorist Church (1862) at Mount St
Alphonsus is a Gothic building with an
impressive interior.

In the Crescent is the O' Connell
Monument, one of the finest works of the
Irish sculptor John Hogan.

Around Limerick

Three miles (5 km) north of the city is the
University of Limerick. The university
houses, in the Hunt Museum, approximately
one thousand items donated to the nation
by the late John Hunt, a noted Celtic
historian (open daily in summer).

The River Shannon is the largest river
in Ireland or Britain. From its source in
County Cavan to Limerick the river is 170
miles (274 km) long, and the estuary
stretches westward for a further 60 miles
(97 km). Below Castleconnell, 8 miles
(13 km) north of Limerick, near an old
castle of the de Burgos, the river suddenly
leaps over a series of limestone shelves,
swirls around the rock promontory of
Doonass and races foaming over a long
stretch of shallows before resuming its
placid course.

Twelve miles (19 km) south of
Limerick among low hills is Lough Gur.

Around its shores is an extraordinary
collection of ancient monuments: stone
circles, stone forts, dolmens and other
megalithic tombs, standing stones, house
sites, etc. Excavations have shown appar-
ently continuous occupation from the
neolithic period down to late medieval times.
The natural caves above the lake have
yielded remains of extinct animals such as
the reindeer, the giant Irish deer and bear.

The Lough Gur Interpretative Centre
near Herbertstown is open from May to
September presenting a visual impression
of the history of this area. There is a fine
view of the lake and the surrounding
countryside.

The road south from Lough Gur passes
the village of Bruff, with its ruined castle
of the de Laceys. A few miles to the east is
Knockainy, only 537 feet high but prominent because of its isolation. It was named
from a Munster princess who lived there in
the second century (Cnoc Aine means
Aine's Hill). In early times it was the venue
of a festival like that of Tailte in County
Meath. Knockainy village, on the east side
of the hill, was a town of importance in
medieval times.

Nine miles (14 km) east of Limerick
city, on the hillside of Murroe village, is the
modern Benedictine establishment, Glenstal
Abbey. It is a castellated nineteenth-century
mansion that was once the family seat of
the Barringtons (who founded Barrington's
Hospital in Limerick city in 1820). The
castle was taken over by the Benedictines
in 1927 and transformed into a modern
college run on traditional Benedictine lines.
Among the beautiful structural features
that have been preserved is a door, a replica
in stone of the Hiberno-Romanesque doorway of Killaloe Cathedral. The priory
grounds are particularly beautiful in
rhododendron time, when the hills are a
blaze of colour.

North of Glenstal and near Newport
(County Tipperary) is a noted beauty spot
called the Clare Glens. The Clare River
flowing through the gorge makes a series

Cottage in Adare

of pretty cascades, and scenic walks are signposted.

East of the village of Mungret, 3 miles (5 km) from Limerick on the road to Glin and Tarbert, is the well-preserved ruin of Mungret Abbey. This is a fifteenth-century structure believed to occupy the site of a Patrician foundation. St Nessan, the first abbot, is said to have been buried here about 550. Close to the abbey are the ruins of two early churches.

The castled crag of Carrigogunnell, 3 miles (5 km) west of Mungret, is a prominent landmark. Erected by the O'Briens in the fourteenth century, it was demolished during the Siege of Limerick in 1691. Further west on the main road to Askeaton is a district with many medieval castles. Near Kildimo is the ancient oratory of Killulta, believed to be the oldest church in the country.

Adare

Ath Dara (The Ford of the Oak Tree)

Pop. 792.

Tourist information office (seasonal). Tel. (061) 396255.

This old-world village of thatched cottages and lichened medieval churches is in wooded surroundings on the west bank of the River Maigue. Adare was adjudged winner of the annual Tidy Towns competition in 1976. Riding, trekking and other equestrian activities are available. There is salmon and trout fishing and golf (18). The washing pool and watering place for horses recalls a way of life that has vanished. Each year during July, Adare Manor hosts the Adare Festival, a major international music festival.

History

Little is known of the ancient town which stood near the castle on the east bank of the river. The Anglo-Normans occupied it during the reign of Henry II and in the thirteenth

Franciscan Abbey, Adare

century it became the property of the Fitzgeralds, earls of Kildare. The town was
incorporated in the fourteenth century, when
a grant was made for the erection of walls.

Points of interest

Finest of the monastic ruins at Adare is the
Franciscan Friary (fifteenth century) in the
middle of the golf club on the Manor
demesne on a slope overlooking the river.
Founded by the Earl of Kildare in 1464,
the building shows later additions. The
transept and belfry were built before the
end of the fifteenth century, but the small
chapels east of the transept, the dormitory
and the infirmary date from the early
sixteenth century. The nave, choir and
south transept of the church remain, and a
tower rising from the intersection; in the
choir are several stalls, niches and fonts of
fine design. Under the window in the
transept are finely wrought sedilia and a
well-carved piscina. The cloisters are well
preserved and around them are arranged
the domestic buildings. Throughout the
architecture is of the later English style.
South of the friary is a fine old gateway,
with a shield of the Geraldine branch of
the Anglo-Norman Fitzgeralds inset,
known as the Kilmallock Gate.

The Trinitarian Abbey (thirteenth
century) was the only Irish house of the
Order for the Redemption of Christian
Captives during the Third Crusade. The
remains are of the tower, nave and part of
the choir of the church (which was restored
to use as a Catholic church in the nineteenth
century). The corbels of the tower and the
cornice along the south wall are noteworthy. Originally part of the monastic
buildings was the nearby Convent of
Mercy: a set of twelve sixteenth-century
carvings is preserved in the vestry of its
church.

The Augustinian Abbey (fourteenth
century) was probably founded by the 1st
Earl of Kildare. The remains, near the
bridge, are of a square tower, and the nave
and part of the choir of the conventual
church; they have been restored for use as
a Protestant church. On the north side are
the cloisters, converted in 1822 into a
mausoleum for the family of Quin, earls of
Dunraven. Over the doorway are shields
with the Kildare and Desmond arms. The
refectory and other parts of the domestic
buildings were also restored in the nineteenth century and converted to use as a
school.

The Desmond Castle, a strongly fortified keep built in the early thirteenth century on the site of an ancient ring fort, was often attacked in later times. The extensive ruins are of an inner ward surrounded by a moat and enclosed by a large courtyard. Within the courtyard are two other buildings. The more ancient is nearer the main gateway and is of two storeys, of which the upper one was the great hall of the castle. Its windows are round headed in pairs, with sandstone mouldings (dating from about 1200). The second building dates from later in the thirteenth century, when it may have replaced the older one.

This castle passed to the Fitzgeralds, earls of Kildare, in 1227 and was partially rebuilt by them early in the fourteenth century. Burned by Turlough O'Brien in the fifteenth century, it was soon restored. Cromwell ordered its dismantling in 1657, but the estates remained in the hands of the Fitzgeralds until 1721, when they were bought by ancestors of the Earl of Dunraven.

Near the castle are the ruins of St Nicholas' Church (eleventh century), and north of that the ruined Desmond Chapel (fourteenth century). Adare Manor, a nineteenth-century limestone building in Neo-Gothic style, was the ancestral home of the earls of Dunraven. It is now a luxury hotel.

Around Adare

The district around Adare and Rathkeale was long known as the Palatine, because early in the eighteenth century it was settled with a colony of German refugees who had been driven from the Palatinate by the French. Brought to Ireland at public expense, they were given leases on generous terms. They preserved many of their national customs until late in the nineteenth century. There is now a museum recalling this era in the Community Centre in Rathkeale.

Five miles (8 km) west of Adare, Curragh Chase was the birthplace of the poet and author Aubrey de Vere (1814–1902). The demesne, one of the finest in Ireland, is open to the public (the house was destroyed by fire in 1941) with nature trails, forest walks, picnic areas, arboretum and caravan park.

Seven miles (11 km) from Adare is the market town of Rathkeale, on the River Deel in the dairy farming district of west Limerick. The town and district were part of the possessions of the earls of Desmond, who erected castles here to guard the passage of the river. One such castle, Castle Matrix, has been restored. The castle and grounds are open to the public on request, and cater for group visits. In 1580 Walter Raleigh, installed in Castle Matrix, was responsible for the defence of the town during the march by English troops to meet the Spanish force then entrenched at Smerwick Harbour (County Kerry). Cromwell disenfranchised the town during his Munster campaign for refusing to provision his army.

The River Deel has salmon and brown trout. In the town are the ruins of St Mary's Priory, a thirteenth-century Augustinian foundation. Four miles (6 km) south of Rathkeale is the ruin of Ballyallinan Castle, a stronghold of the O'Hallinans.

Seven miles (11 km) south-east of Adare is the pleasant little town of Croom, in wooded country on the banks of the River Maigue. Beside the town are the remains of a stronghold of the Fitzgeralds, Croom Castle (1190). The war-cry of the Geraldines (Kildare branch) 'Crom Abu' (Croom to Victory) was taken from here. In the eighteenth century the town was the meeting-place of the 'Maigue Poets': Sean O Tuama, Aindrias Mac Craith and Sean Clarach Mac Domhnaill.

O Tuama (1706–1775), who is buried in the local graveyard, kept open house for his fellow bards in his tavern. An annual literary festival, Feile na Maighe, held in towns in the Maigue district, now commemorates this gathering.

At Manister, 2½ miles (4 km) east of Croom, are the ruins of Monasteranenagh Cistercian Abbey, an important twelfth-century daughter house of Clairvaux whose abbots were lords of Parliament. The church has some good carving, and there are also remains of the chapter house and the abbey mill.

Rathmore Castle, a ruin 1½ miles (2 km) further east, is near the scene of the battle in which Turlough O'Brien defeated the Danes in 1148. (In thanksgiving he founded the abbey at Manister.) The castle is believed to have been built in 1306 by the Earl of Desmond, though the square tower probably dates from the fifteenth century. Near by are the remains of the ancient ring fort of Rathmore from which the castle was named.

Foynes
Faing (Raven)

Pop. 707.

Foynes is a small seaport on a picturesque part of the Shannon, with modern yachting facilities. The first steamship to leave this port was a blockade runner carrying uniforms from a Limerick factory for the Confederate armies in the American Civil War. Later, Foynes became the terminus of a transatlantic seaplane service, which used the sheltered strait between the village and Foynes Island. Foynes Flying Boat Museum recalls this era with great detail using graphic panels and audio-visual aids.

Points of interest
Beside the Catholic church is the tomb of Sir Stephen Edward de Vere (1812–1904), brother of the poet Aubrey de Vere. Sir Stephen, also a poet and writer, was MP for Limerick city from 1854 to 1859. He collaborated with Charlotte Grace O'Brien in investigating the conditions on ships carrying Irish emigrants to America, and to gain firsthand experience, travelled himself to Canada as a steerage passenger on one of them. His account of the voyage played a part in the passage of legislation to eliminate these 'coffin ships'.

Around Foynes
On a hill overlooking the village is a huge limestone cross that is visible for several miles; this is a memorial to Stephen Edmond Spring Rice (1814–1865), brother of the first Baron Monteagle. South of the village rises Knockpatrick (572 feet), from which St Patrick is said to have blessed the people of Thomond. There are some remains of an ancient church in the burial ground on the summit, and adjoining it an inscribed slab marks the grave of Charlotte Grace O'Brien (see entry for Newcastle West).

Four miles (6 km) south-east of Foynes and 2 miles (3 km) east of Shanagolden village are the ruins of Old Abbey, an ancient foundation of Augustinian nuns; the church has a fine Gothic west door, and two footbridges, a fishpond and a corbelled pigeon-house are still to be seen. On a hill 2 miles (3 km) south of Shanagolden are the ruins of Shanid Castle, one of the strongest fortresses of the Fitzgeralds of Desmond. The ruins are of a polygonal keep and part of the curtain wall, on top of a large motte surrounded by a fosse and outer bank; lower down are the rampart and fosse of a D-shaped bailey. The war-cry of the Munster Geraldines 'Seanad Abu' (Shanid to Victory) derived from here.

Seven miles (11 km) east of Foynes is the quiet town of Askeaton, another Desmond stronghold. The castle ruins here are of a fifteenth-century tower and other buildings, which almost entirely cover a rocky islet in the River Deel. Desmond Hall has vaulted rooms underneath and a small chapel at the south end. The hall measures 90 feet by 30 feet and has well-designed windows set in embrasures that are provided with window seats; the traceried window, now incomplete, was one of the most elaborate in an Irish castle.

Glin

Other points of interest at Askeaton include the ruined Franciscan friary (fifteenth century) on the banks of the river. The church consists of a nave, chancel and north transept; the cloister arcade is well preserved, and there are also remains of other buildings in the friary. In the Protestant cemetery are the chancel and belfry of the fifteenth-century St Mary's Church; adjoining the ruin is the grave of the poet Aubrey de Vere.

On the Shannon shore 8 miles (13 km) west of Foynes is Glin, a centre of the dairying industry. Adjoining the village is the beautiful demesne of Glin Castle (open to groups by arrangement). This is the seat of the Knight of Glin, whose family (the Fitzgeralds) has been in almost continuous possession for 700 years. Beside the village is the ruined keep of the ancient Glin castle, destroyed in 1600 by Carew after a fierce battle in which the Knight of Glin was killed.

On a height overlooking the pier is Hamilton's Tower, a nineteenth-century castellated building. Another interesting curiosity is in Kilfergus graveyard, a mile (2 km) south-east of Glin; the tombstone of Timothy Costelloe, a local farmer who composed his own epitaph in verse and carved it himself on the stone.

Newcastle West
An Caislean Nua (The New Castle)

 Pop. 3,370.

Newcastle West, a busy market town, is the centre of prosperous dairy country, with fishing, golf (9) and tennis. The town takes its name from a twelfth-century castle which stands in ruins in the park beside the Square. Built in 1184 for the Knights Templars, it later passed to the earls of Desmond. The building suffered much during centuries of wars, and the ruins show evidence of many rebuildings and alterations. The castle has two halls (both fifteenth century), one of which has been subdivided, but the other, the Desmond Hall, is still complete. It has a vaulted basement. It is now in public ownership and serves as a cultural centre where concerts, recitals, exhibitions and lectures are held.

Around Newcastle West
Three miles (5 km) north of Newcastle West is Ardagh, where in 1868 the famous Ardagh Chalice was discovered in Reevassta Fort, an ancient ring fort. This treasure, now in the National Museum in Dublin, is a perfectly proportioned two-handed cup seven inches high. It is wrought in gold, silver and bronze, with rich settings of enamel, amber, glass and crystal, and dates from the eighth century.

North of Ardagh is Cahermoyle House (1871), which incorporates much of the previous house, the residence of William Smith O'Brien (1803–1864), the Young Ireland leader. His daughter, Charlotte Grace O'Brien (1845–1900), a noted writer and social worker, was born at Cahermoyle. The house is now a novitiate of the Oblate Fathers.

Five miles (8 km) south of Newcastle West is Barnagh Gap with its magnificent views of five counties. Barnagh Gap Gardens and Aviary is a nice place from which to enjoy this view.

Twelve miles (19 km) south-west of Newcastle West is the market town of Abbeyfeale, on the River Feale in hilly country near the border of Counties Limerick and Kerry. There is fishing in the

Feale, much of it free, for salmon, sea trout and brown trout. The town was named after a Cistercian abbey founded here in the twelfth century by Brian O'Brien; the present Catholic church incorporates part of the abbey structure. One-and-a-half miles (2 km) north-west of the town is Portrinard Castle, the ruin of a fourteenth-century Geraldine stronghold which had been erected on the site of an earlier fortress.

Kilmallock

Cill Mocheallog (Mocheallog's Church)

👫👫 Pop. 1,424.

Kilmallock, a small country town in the fertile Golden Vale, was once the headquarters of the earls of Desmond and one of the most important towns in Munster. A small museum features scale models of Stone Age habitations, a model of medieval Kilmallock and a small collection of materials relating to the locality in the eighteenth and nineteenth centuries.

History

Kilmallock was the site of a seventh-century abbey founded by St Mocheallog. From the fourteenth to the sixteenth century the town was the principal stronghold of the Fitzgeralds, and because of this suffered much in the Desmond wars. In 1568 James Fitzmaurice burned the town to prevent it being occupied by English forces. Finally the Fitzgeralds were dispossessed and their estates confiscated by the English Crown. The town, occupied by the Irish, withstood a siege in 1642, but later fell to the Cromwellians (who dismantled the fortifications). The walls were restored by the Corporation, and stood until their final destruction in the Williamite wars in 1690.

Points of interest

North of the town, on the bank of the River Loobagh, is the well-preserved ruin of a thirteenth-century Dominican abbey. This was richly endowed, and became a chapter house of the Order. It was granted to the Corporation by Queen Elizabeth at the dissolution of the monasteries. There is a fine window in the transept, while the 90-feet high tower is supported by unusually narrow arches. The choir has a restored east window and some interesting tombs (including that of Edmund Fitzgibbon (1552–1600), the last 'White Knight', who betrayed the 'Sugan' Earl of Desmond, James Fitzgerald).

The Church of Saints Peter and Paul (probably thirteenth century) consists of an aisled nave and south transept; the tower is part of an ancient round tower. The church has interesting tombs, and in the burial ground beside it is the grave of the eighteenth-century Gaelic poet, Aindrias MacCraith.

The ruined King's Castle was used as an arsenal during the Parliamentary Wars and later by the Cromwellians as a hospital. In Emmet Street is Blossom's Gate, the only survivor of the four gates that once pierced the walls. Kilmallock was formerly noted for its Elizabethan houses, and one of these remains (now used as a store).

Around Kilmallock

Four miles (6 km) north-west is Bruree, a small village on the River Maigue. This was a residence of Munster kings in early times (the Irish name means royal residence). The ruined castle beside the Protestant church is said to have been a de Lacy fortress. A small museum is dedicated to the memory of Éamon de Valera, a former President who went to school here.

About ten miles (16 km) north-east of Kilmallock is Scarteen House, headquarters of the foxhounds called the Scarteen 'Black-and-Tans', which cover this hunting country on either side of the border of Counties Limerick and Tipperary. Northwards 4½ miles (7 km) from Scarteen is the village of Hospital, named after the

house of the Knights Hospitallers established there by Geoffrey de Marisco in
1215, on a site now occupied by the ruins
of a seventeenth-century church.

Kilfinane
Cill Fhionain (St Finan's Church)

Pop. 788.

This small town, a centre of the
dairying industry, is beautifully
situated overlooking the Golden
Vale to the north and backed on other sides
by hills. The main point of interest in the
town is Kilfinane Motte, a great flat-
topped mound encircled by three earthen
ramparts. The town is also the centre for
holidaying in rural Ireland, with farm
trails, horse-riding and walking on the
recently opened Ballyhoura Way.

History
St Finan 'Lobhar' (the Leper) is said to
have founded in the seventh century the
church after which Kilfinane is named. In
976 a brother of Brian Boru, Mahon, was
murdered by the son of the King of
Desmond, Molloy, at the Gap of Red Chair
(6 miles/10 km) south of the town; Mahon's
death was later avenged by Brian in a
battle near the same place.

In 1291 Edward I granted the town a
charter for the holding of fairs. In the
sixteenth century the district shared in the
general devastation of Munster during the
Desmond Wars. In 1602 O'Sullivan Beare
and his men camped at Kilfinane on their
epic march to the north-west. Later in the
century, Kilfinane Castle was stormed and
blown up by a force of Cromwellians.
About the year 1740 a colony of 500
Palatine refugees settled in Kilfinane, and
a few families of Palatine origin still
remain in the district. (See around Adare.)

Around Kilfinane
The hills around Kilfinane, with their
wooded slopes and pretty glens, provide

very fine scenery; a touch of the romantic
is added by placenames that evoke the
legendary and other associations of the
district. The best views are from Slieveragh
(1,531 feet), which overlooks the town on
the north-east.

A mile (2 km) west of the town is the
Palatine's Rock, said to have been used as
an assembly place by the Palatine settlers
in the district. Cush, 2 miles (3 km) north,
has an extensive complex of earthworks,
burial mounds and ancient fields—evidence
of continuous occupation by an agricultural community from about 1000 B.C. to
about A.D. 400. Ornaments and other
articles found here are now in the National
Museum in Dublin.

The tiny village of Ardpatrick is 3 miles
(5 km) south of Kilfinane, beneath the
northern slopes of the Ballyhoura Mountains. The hill above the village is traditionally the site of a church founded by St
Patrick, and there are some remains of a
round tower and a church in the old burial
ground on the summit.

The highest point of the Ballyhoura
Range is Seefin (1,702 feet), one of the
many Irish hills named after the legendary
warrior, Fionn Mac Cumhaill. On the
summit a cairn is said to mark the grave of
Fionn's son, the poet and warrior, Oisin.

Beneath the eastern brow of the
mountain is the beautiful valley of
Glenosheen (Oisin's Glen), birthplace of
the brothers Patrick Weston Joyce
(1827–1914), scholar and historian, and
Robert Dwyer Joyce (1830–1883),
physician and poet. In the heart of the glen,
on the former Castle Oliver estate, is a
large nineteenth-century residence with
towers, battlements and spires, approached
by two long avenues with quaint gate
lodges. 'The Folly', a curious structure in
the grounds, was built to give employment
in a time of famine. Castle Oliver is said to
have been the birthplace of Marie Gilbert
(stage name Lola Montez), the adventuress
and dancer who gained control of the
government of Bavaria during the reign of

Ludwig I. She was banished from Bavaria in 1848.

A pretty village penetrating the south side of Seefin Mountain is Glenanaar, which provided the title and locale of Canon Sheehan's romantic tale of rural Ireland.

At Ballylanders, a small village 7 miles (11 km) east of Kilfinane near the western edge of the Galtee Mountains, an object of interest is the large roofless church of red sandstone beside the village. The tower forming the west end was begun as a castle late in the seventeenth century by the landlord of the district, but was left unfinished. Later the tower was completed, an eastern extension added and the building opened as a Protestant church.

Beside the Tipperary border, 3 miles (5 km) north-east of Ballylanders, is Galbally village. (Near by, in County Tipperary, is Moor Abbey.) West of the village is the hill of Duntryleague (the fort of the three pillar stones), named after the fort built on the summit for Cormac Cas, a second-century Munster king who was buried within the dun. Three pillar stones were put around a well in the centre, and the King's bed laid on these so that his head could be bathed constantly with water from the well. There is a well-preserved megalithic tomb on the summit, and adjoining it an ancient stone fort called 'Brian Boru's Fort'.

Clare

Cliffs of Moher

The River Shannon and Lough Derg form the eastern boundary of County Clare. On the west is the wonderfully varied Atlantic coast, with mighty cliffs, caverns and sandy bays. To the north this rugged coast rises nearly 700 feet above the sea in the sheer Cliffs of Moher; here also is the amazing limestone district called the Burren, with its many caves, underground streams and rare flora. On the south is the broad Shannon estuary, where Ireland's greatest river meets the sea.

Ennis

Inis (River-Meadow)

Pop. 13,746 (urban district).

Tourist information office: Clare Road. Tel. (065) 28366.

Ennis is the county town and the main road junction of County Clare. Although an old town with narrow winding streets, it is a progressive business and marketing centre. There is golf (18), pitch and putt, tennis, heated swimming pool, and brown trout and coarse fishing on the River Fergus and many lakes. A

In the Burren

booklet with signposted walking tours of the town is available from the town's information office. For evening entertainment there is a cinema and 'Cois na hAbhanna' entertainment centre where members of Comhaltas Ceoltóirí Éireann perform traditional Irish music throughout the year. The Ennis Museum displays many mementos from Irish history, especially those with local interest.

Points of interest
Ennis Abbey (1241), founded by Donough Cairbreach O'Brien for the Franciscans, was for long a famous seat of learning. It was finally closed in 1692 (open daily during the season).

Ennis Courthouse (1852) is a good example of classic revival architecture. Outside stands the recently erected statue of Éamon de Valera, former Taoiseach (Prime Minister), who represented the county in the Dáil from 1917 to 1959 when he was elected President. At the town centre is a monument to Daniel O'Connell (the 'Liberator') who was MP for Clare (1828–1831). At the old railway station is

the preserved West Clare railway engine, immortalised by Percy French in his famous song, 'Are you right there, Michael, are you right?'

Around Ennis
About a mile (2 km) south of the town, and a half-mile (1 km) from the road to Clarecastle, are the ruins of Clare Abbey, an Augustinian priory founded in 1195 by Donal O'Brien, last King of Munster. The same king also founded (in 1190) Killone Abbey, on the shore of Killone Lough, 3 miles (5 km) south of Ennis.

At Newmarket-on-Fergus, between Ennis and Limerick, is Dromoland Castle, once the residence of the O'Briens of Thomond (the Lords Inchiquin). It is now a luxury hotel.

i Tourist information office: Tel. (061) 61664.

Twelve miles (19 km) south-east of Ennis on the Limerick road, a road leads west to Shannon Airport, the

Bunratty Castle

first customs-free airport in the world and now also the site of a large industrial estate and centre of Ireland's aerospace industry.

A new town called Shannon was created to house those working in the industrial estate and their families. It now has about 8,000 inhabitants, making it the second largest town in County Clare.

i Tourist information office (seasonal): Tel. (061) 360133.

Back on the Limerick road, Bunratty Castle was once the residence of the O'Briens of Thomond. It was restored in 1960 and furnished with fifteenth-and sixteenth-century furnishings. It is open daily to the public and medieval banquets are held there each evening. Beside the castle is a folk-park where visitors may see farmhouses, fishermen's and labourers' cottages, a forge, a reconstructed country town street and a growing agricultural museum. Within the folk-park is another superb night-time entertainment, the Shannon Ceili.

A few miles beyond Bunratty is Cratloe Castle, a square tower built by the Mac-Namaras in 1610. The woods of Cratloe furnished oaks for the roof of Westminster Hall in London and Amsterdam City Hall (now the royal palace); the woods were once also the haunt of a highwayman

Bunratty Folk Park

named Freeney. Cratloe Woods House, the last inhabited example of an Irish longhouse, is near by and is open to the public during the summer.

Six miles (10 km) east of Ennis, beside the village of Quin, is Quin Abbey. This well-preserved ruin is of a Franciscan friary founded in 1402 by Sioda MacNamara. Remains of a Norman castle on the site were used in the building, and three of the castle's corner towers still stand at the angles of the friary buildings. The church consists of a nave and chancel with a tower between, and has tombs of the MacNamaras.

At another MacNamara castle, Knappogue, about 3 miles (5 km) from Quin, medieval banquets are held nightly during the summer, while at nearby Craggaunowen Castle (sixteenth century) there is a museum, and a reconstruction of a Bronze Age 'crannog' or lake dwelling. Also displayed is the 'Brendan', a replica of a sixth-century boat which sailed across the Atlantic in 1976 and 1977.

Kilrush

Cill Ruis (Peninsula Church)

Pop. 2,740 (urban district).

Tourist information office (seasonal): Tel. (065) 51577.

Kilrush, chief marketing centre of south-west Clare, is the third largest town in the county. Its fine harbour has been developed into Ireland's first west coast marina and has berthage for a large number of yachts.

Recreational facilities include golf (9), tennis, and there are some pleasant woodland walks on the east side of the town. A local heritage centre interprets the history of the area, including that of Scattery Island (see below).

Around Kilrush

A mile (2 km) to the south, Cappagh Pier is the berthing place of the vessels that ply

between Kilrush and Limerick. From the pier a fine coast road curves south-eastwards by the water's edge for 2½ miles (4 km), providing good views of Scattery Island and across the Shannon estuary. Scattery Island, 2 miles (3 km) out from Kilrush, is the site of a sixth-century monastery founded by St Senan. The principal remains are of five churches and a well-preserved round tower 115 feet high.

From Killimer there is a car ferry to the north Kerry shore at Tarbert; this is a great convenience to motorists as the first bridge across the Shannon is at Limerick city. Departures from Killimer are hourly on the hour, and from Tarbert hourly on the half-hour. In the graveyard at the ruined Killimer church can be seen the grave of Ellen Hanly, whose tragic death inspired Gerald Griffin's novel, *The Collegians*. (See Limerick city.)

Kilkee

Cill Chaoidhe (Church of St Caoidhe)

Pop. 1,448.

Tourist information office (seasonal): Tel. (065) 56112.

This west coast family resort is built around a crescent-shaped sandy beach, guarded on either side by low cliffs and protected from the Atlantic by a reef called the Duggerna Rocks. Kilkee offers safe bathing at all stages of the tide.

Things to do

The long sandy beach fronts the town, and there is bathing also at several coves and rock pools. Kilkee is a noted skin-diving centre. Good brown trout fishing on the River Creegh and the Cooraclare River, which also hold salmon and sea trout in autumn; there are several brown trout lakes within easy driving distance, and good sea fishing off the coast. Other recreations include golf (9), tennis, squash, pitch and putt, table tennis and other entertainments, and an amusement park. The Sweeney Memorial library, built with the aid of a legacy from an emigrant, is an impressive building and houses a range of library facilities.

Walks

The most enjoyable walk (distance 2½ miles/ 4 km) is from the west end. Starting at Edmund's Point, one soon comes to the Duggerna Rocks, a natural barrier that breaks the fury of the Atlantic. Further on, the Amphitheatre, with tier upon tier of seat-like rocks, is a favourite place for open-air concerts. Here also are the Pink Cave and Lion Head Rock, and further on the Puffing Hole. Near by are the Diamond Rocks, Intrinsic Bay and Lookout Hill (more than 200 feet above the sea, with a far-reaching view on clear days). One can either return from here to the town by road, or continue past Bishop's Island which has the remains of St Senan's Oratory. A little inland is what was once Fooagh chalybeate spa. Further on there is the Mermaid's Tunnel, the Sailor's Grave, and Castle Point, a fine vantage point for extensive views of the coast away to Loop Head.

From the east end, another enjoyable walk (distance 5 miles/8 km) is by Blackrock, the Elephant's Teeth, Burns' Cove, George's Head, Chimney Bay and Hill, into Farrihy Bay and Corbally village, returning by road to Kilkee.

Around Kilkee

The best way to explore the coast near Loop Head is to go first to Doonaha village (4 miles/6km to the south), birthplace of the famous Irish scholar, Eugene O'Curry, and on to Carrigaholt, a little Irish-speaking village on the Shannon shore. Then go west to the remarkable natural bridge of Ross and on to Moneen church, where 'The Little Ark' is preserved (at one time it was used for celebrating Mass). South 1½ miles (2 km) of Moneen is Kilbaha village, from where it is 3 miles (5 km) west to Loop

Head, the most westerly extremity of Clare. An isolated section of cliff standing off the head is known as 'Diarmuid and Grania's Rock' and the intervening channel is called 'The Lover's Leap'. This is where Cuchulainn, according to tradition, leaped from the mainland to the rock to escape the unwelcome attentions of a lady.

The road northwards from Kilkee passes (at 6 miles/10 km) the village of Doonbeg, where the Cooraclare (or Doonbeg) River enters the sea. Doonbeg Castle, now in ruins, was a fortress of the MacMahons and later of the O'Briens.

Lahinch

Leacht Ui Chonchubair
(O'Connor's Cairn)

♈♈♈ Pop. 511.

ℹ Tourist information office at Cliffs of Moher (Liscannor) (seasonal): Tel. (065) 81171.

Lahinch, fronted by a fine sandy beach fringing Liscannor Bay, is a popular resort for bathing and surfing, and has two 18-hole golf courses. Near the beach is an entertainment centre with a modern ballroom, cinema, theatre, café, seawater swimming pool, children's pool and playground, games room and tennis courts.

Ennistymon

Inis Diomain (Diman's River Meadow)

♈♈♈ Pop. 1,039.

Ennistymon is an attractive holiday centre on the main Ennis–Lisdoonvarna road, 2½ miles (4 km) inland from Lahinch. The town is in a wooded valley beside a cascade on the River Cullenagh. Boating, dancing, tennis, cinema and other recreations are provided, and there is good brown trout fishing on the Cullenagh River and the Dealagh River (about 2 miles/3 km away).

Around Lahinch and Ennistymon

The small fishing village of Liscannor is midway between Lahinch and the Cliffs of Moher. In the village are the remains of a castle built by the O'Connors but later wrested from them by the O'Briens. Near by in Castle Street is the house in which John P. Holland (1841–1914), inventor of the submarine, was born. St Macreechy's church, a ruin a mile (2 km) east of Liscannor, has interesting features. Glahane shore, west of the village, is a popular bathing place.

Three miles (5 km) west of Liscannor are the Cliffs of Moher, one of the outstanding features of the county. Rising sheer above the sea to nearly 700 feet and extending about 5 miles (8 km) along the coast, they provide magnificent views—especially from O'Brien's Tower at the northern end (where the cliffs reach their maximum height of 668 feet), and from Hag's Head (400 feet) at the southern end. O'Brien's Tower, a circular structure, was erected in 1835 by Cornelius O'Brien. The visitor information centre is open from mid-May to October, with literature, refreshments and car park. On a clear day the Aran Islands are visible from the cliffs. On the road from Liscannor to the cliffs is the very elaborate St Bridget's Well and the O'Brien monument (1853).

Going southwards from Lahinch, 2 miles (3 km) north-east of Milltown Malbay, is the ruin of the fifteenth-century Kilfarboy church. Two noted Claremen—Andrew MacCurtain (died 1749), hereditary bard of the O'Briens, and Michael Comyn (died 1760), also a distinguished poet and scholar—are buried here in graves which cannot now be identified. There is also a holy well dedicated to St Joseph.

At Spanish Point, 2 miles (3 km) west of Milltown Malbay, is a small resort with golf (9) and a good sandy beach. The Silver Strand at Freagh, 2 miles (3 km) to the north, is also a good bathing place. Spanish Point is so named because of the Spaniards who were buried here after the wreck of their Armada ships along this coast. One of the ships was wrecked on the reefs to landward of Mutton Island (2 miles/3 km) offshore, can be visited by currach hired in the fishing village of Quilty. More than a thousand men were lost, and many of their bodies were carried by the tide to Spanish Point.

Lisdoonvarna

Lios Duin Bhearna

(Enclosure of the Gap-Fort)
Pop. 648.

Lisdoonvarna, Ireland's premier spa and a popular holiday resort in its own right, is in the hilly Burren country of north Clare. Only 5 miles (8 km) from the sea, the town is surrounded by an interesting district with varied scenery. The Lisdoonvarna waters are sulphurous and chalybeate (iron) springs, all of which contain the valuable therapeutic element of iodine.

Much of the efficacy of the waters—especially the sulphur water—is ascribed to their radioactive properties. The principal sulphur spring is at the south side of the town, while the principal iron springs are on the north side. At the Spa Centre are sauna baths, sun lounge, showers, restrooms and a café, together with facilities for beauty therapy and massage.

Recreations include pitch and putt, dancing, bathing at Doolin Cove (5 miles/ 8 km), trout fishing on Lickeen Lake

Lisdoonvarna Spa

(7 miles/11 km) and other centres. There is a ferry to Inisheer on the Aran Islands from Doolin harbour during the season. Lisdoonvarna is a well-known centre for traditional music and dancing, and its September festival is very popular.

Around Lisdoonvarna

In the district is a complex system of limestone caves and underground waterways, some of which have not yet been fully explored (these caves are dangerous and must only be entered with a guide).

The most popular walks are the 'Bog' road and the 2-mile (3 km) circular walk via the Spectacle Bridge. Another objective is Ballynalacken Castle, a fifteenth-century O'Brien stronghold 3 miles (5 km) to the north-west. The most popular drive (distance 28 miles/45 km) from Lisdoonvarna is that by the coast and around Black Head to Ballyvaughan, returning by the Corkscrew road through the hills of the Burren, now a national park.

The word Burren means 'great rock' and the region is described by geologists as 'karst', after a similar tract of country in Slovenia. It is a strange lunar-like region of bare carboniferous limestone, occupying some 100 square miles near the towns of Lahinch, Ballyvaughan, Ennistymon, Corofin and north and north-west of Lisdoonvarna. Below the scarred surface of the Burren is the most remarkable assemblage of diverse types of flora in Ireland, and spectacular caves, streams, potholes and 'turloughs' (seasonal lakes). There are many misty legends surrounding this area, with its abundance of antiquities dating from prehistoric to medieval times. Poulnabrone Dolmen, a megalithic monument dating from about 2,500 B.C., is a noted Burren feature.

Two miles (3 km) south-east of Ballyvaughan is Aillwee Cave in one of the most beautiful parts of the Burren. The cave was formed millions of years ago and is now developed to allow guided tours

Poulnabrone Dolmen

into the mysterious underworld. Entry is through the award winning visitor centre, built into the hillside, which is open daily from March to October and at winter weekends.

At the foot of Abbey Hill, 6 miles (10 km) east of Ballyvaughan is Corcomroe Abbey (Cistercian), founded by King Donal O'Brien in 1182. The abbey church is in good preservation and its interesting features include the sculptured tomb of the founder's grandson, King Conor O'Brien (died 1267).

Kilfenora is 5 miles (8 km) south-east of Lisdoonvarna. In the town is the Burren Display Centre designed to help the visitor appreciate the history and environment of the Burren region, open daily from mid-March to October. Kilfenora was formerly the episcopal see of Kilfenora diocese. The cathedral dedicated to St Fachnan, is a small building with a square tower. The nave has been adapted for use as the Church of Ireland parish church. In a field about 50 yards to the west is an elaborately sculptured high cross.

Six miles (10 km) east of Kilfenora is another early church site at Killinaboy, where there are ruins of a church and the stump of a round tower. Two miles (3 km) further on, Corofin village lies in pretty country near the shore of Lough Inchiquin, a well-known beauty spot and trout lake (numerous other lakes in this district also have trout and coarse fishing). On the north shore of Lough Inchiquin are the ruins of Inchiquin Castle (1459), for long the seat of a powerful branch of the O'Briens. The village houses the Clare Heritage Centre which has as its main attraction an exhibition entitled 'Ireland West 1800–1860'.

Three miles (5 km) north-west of Killinaboy was another important O'Brien stronghold, Lemaneagh Castle. The remains are of a tall oblong tower dating from about 1480 and attached to it a seventeenth-century high-gabled house of four storeys. In 1651 Conor O'Brien died here of wounds received in defending the Pass of

Inchicronan against the Cromwellians, who then captured and garrisoned the castle. Conor's widow, Maire Rua (O'Mahon), afterwards married a Cromwellian officer and so saved the lands for her son.

Three miles (5 km) south of Corofin, Dysert O'Dea is the site of an early church founded by St Tola. There is also a Romanesque Church and round tower (twelfth century). A victory here for the O'Briens in 1318 halted the Norman conquest of Clare.

Killaloe
Cill Dalua (Dalua's Church)

👪 Pop. 1,033.

ℹ️ Tourist information office (seasonal): Tel. (061) 376866.

K illaloe has a fine situation on the west bank of the River Shannon, where it emerges from Lough Derg and narrows again on its way to the sea at Limerick. The town, which is connected with the village of Ballina (County Tipperary) by a bridge of thirteen arches, is the centre of a beautiful and historic district. As well as being a fishing centre for Lough Derg, Killaloe is a popular cruising, sailing and water skiing centre. Boats are available for hire on Lough Derg. A river bus provides a 1½ hour pleasure cruise out of Killaloe during the season. A new interpretative centre on Lough Derg has recently opened in the town.

History
Killaloe was the site of a church founded in the sixth century by St Lua, and later this place was the royal seat of the Dalcassian kings. In 1276 the town was taken by the Norman, Thomas de Clare. Patrick Sarsfield, on his famous night ride from Limerick to intercept the Williamite siege-train at Ballyneety (1690), forded the Shannon at Killaloe. (See Limerick city and around Tipperary town.)

Points of interest

The Cathedral (Church of Ireland) is believed to have been built in 1182 by Donal O' Brien, on the site of an earlier church; it was restored in 1887. It consists of nave, choir and transepts, with a heavy square central tower. A richly carved Romanesque doorway, blocked up on the outside and forming a recess internally, is the most noteworthy feature: it is said to have been the entrance to the tomb of King Murtagh O'Brien of Munster (died 1120). Near by is the shaft of a cross bearing a runic and ogham inscription of about A.D. 1000. St Flannan's oratory, in the church-yard of the cathedral, is a small early church with a high-pitched roof of stone and a door with two curiously carved capitals.

Beside the Catholic church is St Molua's Oratory. This was removed from Friar's Island in the Shannon before the island was submerged during the construction of hydroelectric works.

Around Killaloe

Lough Derg, 25 miles (40 km) long and 2–3 miles (3–5 km) in average width, is the largest and most southerly of the Shannon lakes. Its deeply indented shores, hilly background and many islets give it a varied and beautiful setting. The road north from Killaloe along the west shore of the lake has fine views of the lake itself and the hills on either side. After a mile (2 km) the road passes the large fort of Beal Boru ('Pass of the Tributes'), from which King Brian Boru (926–1014) took his title; near by stood Brian's palace of Kincora. Further on, along the road to Scariff, the rocky hill called Cragliath was in fairy legend the habitation of Aoibheall, banshee of the Dalcassians; a wild glen in the hills is said to be the site of her palace.

Beyond Tinarana Bay the road rounds the shoulder of Caher Mountain (758 feet) and runs west to Tuamgraney, 10 miles (16 km) from Killaloe. In this village is the tower of an O'Grady castle and a well-preserved church that incorporates the remains of the original pre-Romanesque building.

A mile (2 km) further north, the angling centre of Scarriff is charmingly situated near the shore of Scarriff Bay, one of the prettiest parts of Lough Derg. Some streams with brown trout flow into Scarriff Bay, notably the River Graney which flows from Lough Atorick through Lough Graney and Lough O'Grady (Lough Atorick has numerous small brown trout, while the other two lakes are more noted for pike).

Five miles (8 km) north-east of Scarriff is Mountshannon, a favourite haunt of anglers for the mayfly season on Lough Derg. A chain of islands lies along this part of the shore, and there is a large area of shallow water suitable for trout (the record Irish brown trout, 30½ lb, was caught here). Boats are available for angling and lake trips, and there is a bathing place on the lakeshore. With the recent improvement in the harbour it has become a popular sailing centre.

About 1½ miles (2 km) from Mount-shannon and nearly a half-mile (1 km) from the mainland is Inis Cealtra (also called Holy Island). Here St Caimin founded a monastic settlement in the seventh century and on the site today are the remains of five churches, a round tower 79 feet high, a drystone structure known as 'The Cottage', and a peculiar building called the 'Anchorite's Cell', which may have been used as a place of self-mortification by some of the early monks. There are also three or four enclosures of earth and stone (one of them called the 'Saint's Graveyard'), three large sculptured crosses, cross-inscribed slabs of the eighth to twelfth centuries, and many socketed stones which may have been bases for other crosses. Inis Cealtra suffered much from the ravages of the Danes in the ninth and tenth centuries, and the settlement was restored by Brian Boru. It is presently undergoing another restoration.

Six miles (10 km) west of Scarriff, Feakle is a secluded village on the southern slopes of the Slieve Aughty Mountains. There is some very pretty scenery in this area, particularly at Lough Graney which lies among the hills 4 miles (6 km) north of the village. The poet Brian Merriman (*c*.1749–1805) lived at Lough Graney, where he had a small farm, and wrote there his famous 'Cuirt an Mheadhoin Oiche' (The Midnight Court), first published in 1800; he died in Limerick and was buried in the family grave at Feakle. The Merriman Society holds an annual Summer School at a Clare centre.

Six miles (10 km) south-west of Feakle, the coarse-fishing centre of Tulla lies in a district of little lakes. There are interesting limestone caves called the 'Toumeens' at Kiltanan, 2 miles (3 km) away.

At Parteen, 5 miles (8 km) south of Lough Derg, is the dam which was constructed in 1925–1929 to harness the River Shannon for the generation of electricity— the first and largest hydroelectric project in Ireland. From the intake building beside the dam, a canal (or head race) 7½ miles (12 km) long cuts through low flanking hills on the right bank and carries a great part of the river's volume to the power station at Ardnacrusha (average yearly output of 350 million kilowatt hours). From the station another canal (the tail race) a mile (2 km) long leads the water back to the Shannon above Limerick city.

Tipperary

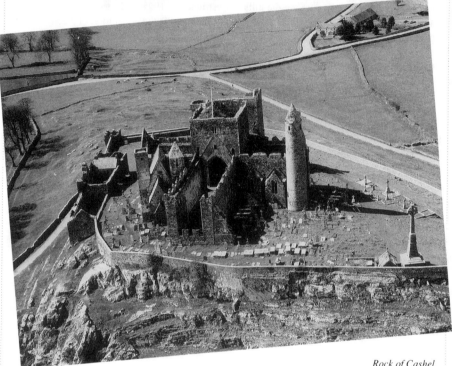

Rock of Cashel

Tipperary, Ireland's largest inland county, has richly varied scenery in its hills and mountains, its plains and river valleys. In the south are the Galtee Mountains, the Knockmealdowns and the isolated height of Slievenamon. Keeper Hill is the highest point among the various groups of hills in the north. The middle of the county is a broad plain, through which the River Suir flows from north to south; and from this plain the rich land of the Golden Vale extends westwards into County Limerick. Apart from its scenery and its excellent facilities for pastimes such as angling, golf, mountain climbing, caving and hunting, Tipperary offers the opportunity of seeing important antiquities such as the magnificent ruins on the Rock of Cashel.

Clonmel

Cluain Meala (Honey Meadow)

Pop. 14,481 (municipal borough).

Tourist information office (seasonal): Tel. (052) 22960.

Clonmel is set in fertile land and superb scenic surroundings along the north bank of the River Suir. Clonmel is one of the largest inland towns of Ireland, the administrative capital of the South Riding of Tipperary, the centre of the cider industry and an important horse-breeding and greyhound area.

Things to do

There is golf (18), horse-racing, greyhound racing, pony-trekking, trout fishing on the Rivers Suir, Nire, Tay and Anner, tennis, swimming, and cinemas. The County Museum in Parnell Street, in addition to a collection of over 10,000 items, has a permanent art display.

History

A settlement seems to have existed at this important crossing of the Suir even before Danish times. Edward I granted a charter to the town, which was walled and fortified in the fourteenth century. A stronghold of the powerful Anglo-Norman Butler family (who became earls of Ormonde), it was besieged and taken in 1516 by the Earl of Kildare. In 1650 the garrison gave Cromwell stiff resistance.

Charles Bianconi, from Como near Milan, who settled here, became mayor of Clonmel and gave Ireland a transport service—the 'Bianconi cars'—which began by running from Clonmel to Cahir in 1815 and by 1843 had a hundred vehicles in use. Hearn's Hotel was the starting point and today visitors can see the original clock which timed the system. Laurence Sterne, one of the giants of eighteenth-century literature, was born at Clonmel in 1713. Anthony Trollope served here for a time with the post office.

Points of interest

A well-preserved portion of the old town wall partly encloses St Mary's Protestant church, and the West Gate (rebuilt in 1831) is still intact. Number 19 Main Street was once a bishop's palace, and in its rafters in 1880 were discovered letters signed by Oliver Cromwell—relics from his forces' occupation of Clonmel in 1650. The Main Guard, said to have been built to a design

by Christopher Wren, is a massive structure which was built to house the main guard of the garrison; on the front wall are the arms of Clonmel and those of the Palatinate of Ormonde (which was founded in the fourteenth century, and became extinct in 1715).

The Town Hall contains the corporation regalia, including sword, silver maces and the mayor's gold chain, to which each holder of the office contributes a link. St Mary's Catholic church (nineteenth century) has a magnificent ceiling and an elaborate high altar. St Mary's Protestant church (nineteenth century), built on the site of a fourteenth-century church, incorporates part of the earlier building; it has a striking octagonal tower and some interesting interior features. The Franciscan Church, in Early English style, is a nineteenth-century restoration on the site of a thirteenth-century foundation; much of the tower belongs to the earlier structure, and among its interior features are remains of some of the old tombs.

Around Clonmel

The banks of the River Suir provide pleasant riverside walks, and Clonmel is an excellent centre for climbing and exploring the fine scenery of the Comeragh and Knockmeal-down Mountains and the Suir and Black-water valleys.

Two roads, one on either side of the Suir, run east from Clonmel, giving many fine views of the river valley and the mountain background. From the town to within about 1½ miles (2 km) of Carrick-on-Suir, the river is the boundary between Counties Tipperary and Waterford. At 3 miles (5 km) on the north bank is the demesne of Newtown Anner, and on the opposite bank are the ruins of Tickinor Castle and Derrinlar Castle. Kilsheelan village on the north bank, takes its name from an ancient church of St Sheelan, of which there are some remains. On the south bank, rising high on the hill slopes, is the beautiful demesne of Gurteen le Poer, once the home of Richard Lalor Shiel (1791–1851).

Kilsheelan

About a mile (2 km) east of Kilsheelan is the keep of Poulkerry Castle, bombarded and taken in 1650 by the Cromwellians. Kilcash, at the foot of Slievenamon, 4 miles (6 km) to the north-east, has the remains of an ancient church with a Hiberno-Romanesque doorway.

The village of Ardfinnan, 9 miles (14 km) south-west of Clonmel, is in a wide expanse of the Suir valley where the river cuts a gorge through low hills. In 1186 the Earl of Morton, afterwards King John of England, built a castle here that remained an important stronghold until it was taken by the Cromwellians in the seventeenth century. One of the square corner towers has been partly restored.

Five miles (8 km) south-east of Ardfinnan, Newcastle lies beneath the Knockmealdown Mountains on a southerly bend of the Suir, near the mouth of the beautiful Nire River valley which rises eastwards in the Comeragh Mountains.

Six miles (10 km) south-west of Ardfinnan, Clogheen is at the northern end of the famous Vee Road, which climbs a zig-zag course to the Knockmealdown Gap (1,114 feet above sea level) and then descends to Lismore and Cappoquin (County Waterford). This road has a series of magnificent views. About 3 miles (5 km) south of Clogheen, it passes above Bay Lough, a small tarn backed by steep mountain sides. Collenleigh Gardens at Clogheen admits groups by prior arrangement.

Ballyporeen, to the west of Clogheen, is the village which was visited by President Reagan to trace his Irish roots.

At Coolagarranroe, 3½ miles (6 km) north of Ballyporeen on the road from Clogheen to Mitchelstown, are the Mitchelstown Caves. These contain some of the finest examples of natural subterranean formations in Ireland. There are two groups of caves—the Old or Desmond Cave (where the 'Sugan Earl' of Desmond, with a large price on his head, took refuge in 1601), and the New Cave which was discovered in 1833. A rope or ladder must be used to enter the Desmond Cave, one of whose two vast chambers is the largest in these islands. A guide conducts visitors through the New Cave, a complex cavern of magnificent passages and chambers 1½ miles (2 km) in length. The caves are open to the public every day.

Two miles (3 km) north-east of the caves Burncourt House was one of the finest of the gabled houses or castles built in Ireland in the Elizabethan-Jacobean period. Built about 1640 by Sir Richard Everard, the house is said to have been burned down by Lady Everard to prevent its occupation by Cromwell, who passed this way on his approach to Cahir. The walls are topped by 26 gables and several tall chimneys; the stone corbels projecting between the top windows of the longer sides of the house were evidently designed to support defensive galleries of timber.

The Galtee Mountains rise immediately north of the Mitchelstown Caves to their highest point on Galtymore (3,018 feet). On this southern side of the range there are many easy routes to the summit peaks from the Mitchelstown– Cahir road which runs on the lower slopes. Steeper ascents and rock climbs can be made above the five tiny lakes lying in corries on the northern (Glen of Aherlow) side of the range.

Carrick-on-Suir
Carraig na Siuire (The Rock of the Suir)

Pop. 5,145 (urban district).

i Tourist information office (seasonal): West Gate. Tel. (051) 40726.

This picturesque town on the most beautiful stretch of the River Suir is partly in County Tipperary and partly in County Waterford.

Things to do
Golf (9), tennis, fishing for brown trout, hill walking in the foothills and climbing in the Comeragh Mountains where many peaks are over 2,000 feet. There is a heritage centre on the main street.

Points of interest
The southern suburb of Carrickbeg, a place of winding hilly streets, is connected by two bridges with the main part of the town. Carrick Castle, an Elizabethan fortified mansion in excellent preservation, is the only one of its kind in Ireland. This place was one of the principal seats of the Butlers, earls and later dukes of Ormonde, who played a major part in British government in Ireland for four centuries. The castle is said to have been built specially by 'Black Tom Butler', the 10th Earl, to receive his cousin Queen Elizabeth, but her visit was never made. Dermod O'Hurley, the Archbishop of Cashel who was martyred in Dublin in 1584, sought sanctuary in Carrick Castle but was arrested there despite the protests of the Earl. There are guided tours on request and the house is open to the public during the season.

Behind the Elizabethan structure is the square keep of a previous Butler castle (fifteenth century).

Around Carrick-on-Suir
In a gap of the hills 6 miles (10 km) north of the town, Ahenny is noted for its two beautifully sculptured high crosses in the old graveyard; part of a third cross is embedded in the soil at the northern end of the graveyard. Lough Coumshingaun, a noted rock-climbing centre 10 miles (16 km) from Carrick and 2 miles (3 km) west of the Dungarvan road, is surrounded by a horseshoe of cliffs rising to the highest peak of the Comeragh Range (2,597 feet).

Cahir
Cathair Dhuin Iascaigh
(Fortress of the Dun abounding in Fish)

Pop. 2,118.

i Tourist information office (seasonal): Tel. (052) 41453.

Ahenny Cross

This busy market centre straddles the River Suir at the eastern end of the Galtee Mountains, where the Dublin–Cork and Limerick–Waterford roads meet.

Things to do

Good fishing for trout and salmon on the Suir; the Aherlow River, which joins the Suir above the town, also has good trout fishing. Cahir is an excellent centre for hill walking and climbing the Galtee Mountains. Hunting, beagling and golf (9) at Cahir Park. Ireland's first railway museum (under development) is open to the public.

Points of interest

The rocky islet in the river here was recognised from very early times as a natural vantage point, and the ancient *Book of Lecan* records the destruction of a fort on it in the third century; in later times Brian Boru (926–1014) had one of his residences here. Cahir Castle (mainly fifteenth century), a splendid structure, now fully restored, was the largest of its period in Ireland. It has a massive keep, high enclosing walls, spacious courtyards and a hall, and is now an architectural interpretative centre. A guide service is available from June to September each year.

Built in 1142 on the ancient site by Conor O'Brien, Prince of Thomond, this castle came into the hands of the Anglo-Norman Butlers in 1375. The Butlers of Cahir sided with the Irish in the Elizabethan Wars, and in 1599 Elizabeth's deputy, the Earl of Essex, took the castle after a short siege in which the walls were widely breached by the English artillery. In 1647 the castle was surrendered to the Parliamentary commander, Lord Inchiquin, by the guardian of Lord Cahir, George Mathews.

Mathews also surrendered the castle to Cromwell in 1650 without firing a shot. Two years later the long war ended officially with the signing of articles in Cahir Castle.

Cahir Park, with its broad richly timbered lands on the banks of the Suir, south of the town, is a pleasant place with tree-lined paths.

Swiss Cottage, built in 1812, over a mile (1½ km) outside the town on the Ardfinnan road, was designed as a fishing and hunting lodge for Lord Cahir by John Nash, the famous Regency architect. It has been restored and is open to the public during the season.

Cahir Castle by night

Around Cahir

At Tubbrid, 5 miles (8 km) south of Cahir, a plaque dated 1644 over the entrance to the ruined mortuary chapel commemorates Fathers Eugene O'Duffy and Geoffrey Keating, who are buried there. O'Duffy is best remembered for his metrical satire in Irish on the pluralist Myler MacGrath, Protestant Archbishop of Cashel (the poem was written about 1577). Dr Keating, born near Tubbrid about 1570, was a fearless preacher who was forced to flee for his life after a sermon drew upon him the enmity of a local family of high standing; as an outlaw, he took refuge for some years in the Glen of Aherlow. Among his literary works is a history of Ireland down to the English invasion, *Foras Feasa ar Éirinn*. A modern tombstone with inscriptions in Irish and English stands over his grave.

The great Motte of Knockgraffon, a prominent landmark 4 miles (6 km) north of Cahir, is said to have been the coronation place of the Munster kings before the seat of the dynasty was moved to Cashel. When the Anglo-Normans first came to the district they made Knockgraffon their headquarters, and the motte was probably built by them on a pre-existing earthwork to command the important ford here across the Suir. Adjoining the motte is the ruin of a sixteenth-century castle of the Butlers, and in the old graveyard near by are the remains of the church where Father Geoffrey Keating preached the sermon which led to his being outlawed.

From Cahir, the road to Tipperary town winds around the eastern end of the Galtee Mountains, and runs north-west past the beautiful and fertile Glen of Aherlow (on the left), spread grandly between the Galtees and the long wooded ridge of Slievenamuck. This secluded glen, once an important pass between the plains of Counties Tipperary and Limerick, was the scene of many ancient battles and later became a frequent retreat of dispossessed and outlawed Irishmen. The statue of Christ

Glen of Aherlow

the King (16 feet high) was erected in 1950. A fish farm in the glen is open daily to visitors.

At the head of the glen, near the village of Galbally (County Limerick), are the ruins of Moor Abbey. This Franciscan foundation was established in the early part of the thirteenth century by the King of Thomond, Donagh Cairbreach O'Brien. The ruined church, the only part of the monastery to survive, dates from the fifteenth century. After its confiscation in the sixteenth century, Moor Abbey was used as a fortress during the Elizabethan Wars, and was burned by an English cavalry force in 1569. The church consists of a nave and chancel, divided by a tall belfry tower that is the most striking feature of the building. Also noteworthy are winding stairs in a turret at the south-west angle of the nave, leading to the wall-tops.

A few miles south of Bansha village Diarmaid O Riain (Darby Ryan, 1770–1855) was born, author of the famous satire 'The Peeler and the Goat'. A bilingual monument marks his grave in Bansha cemetery.

Tipperary

Tiobrad Arann (The Well of Ara)

Pop. 4,783 (uban district).

Tourist information office: (Community office). Tel. (062) 51457.

Tipperary town is a dairy-farming centre north of the Slievenamuck Hills, in the fertile Golden Vale which extends across the County Limerick border.

Things to do

Golf (9); fishing for brown trout on the River Ara and some miles to the south on the Aherlow River; Tipperary (formerly Limerick Junction) racecourse is 2 miles (3 km) north-west of the town, and the

Scarteen Black and Tans (foxhounds) hunt the district. Tipperary is a good centre for climbing and hill walking on the Slievenamuck Hills and Galtee Mountains. The Canon Hayes Recreational Centre includes a swimming pool, tennis, racquets, hockey and other activities. There is a signposted walking tour of the town.

History

At the end of the twelfth century King John built a castle here, beginning the Anglo-Norman settlement from which the town grew. Later an Augustinian friary was founded. No town walls were built, though Edward II made a grant for that purpose, and the place was burned by the O'Briens in 1339. The district suffered greatly in the Desmond Wars, and in a report of 1598 Tipperary was listed as 'waste'.

John O'Leary (1830–1907), the Fenian leader and journalist, and his sister Ellen (1831–1889) the poetess and helper in her brother's patriotic work, were born in Tipperary town. The area figured prominently in the Land League agitation in the late nineteenth century, when the tenants of Mr Smith Barry established a temporary settlement called 'New Tipperary' outside the town; the scheme was unsuccessful and was later abandoned. Muintir na Tire, a now widespread movement for the development of rural life, was founded in Tipperary by Father J. M. Hayes in 1931. There is a statue of another famous Tipperary Fenian (Charles Kickham of Mullinahone) in the town.

Points of interest

St Michael's Catholic church, a limestone building in Gothic style, has a beautiful west door, fine lancet windows in the east and west gables and a graceful arch separating nave and chancel. All that survives of the thirteenth-century Augustinian Abbey is the chancel arch, which stands on the property of the Irish Christian Brothers; in the same grounds are the ruined Abbey Schools, a foundation of Erasmus Smith

(1611–1691) who obtained large tracts of confiscated land in County Tipperary and used his wealth to found grammar schools and lectureships in Ireland.

Around Tipperary

The motte of a Norman motte-and-bailey castle, on a sandhill just outside the town on the north, is a well-known landmark; the outline of the bailey can still be traced. Liam Dall Ó hIferanain, a leading eighteenth-century Gaelic poet, was born near the village of Lattin, 5 miles (8 km) west of Tipperary. Emly village, 3½ miles (6 km) further west, was formerly the cathedral town of the diocese of Emly, now incorporated with the archdiocese of Cashel. A rude ancient cross in the cemetery beside the Catholic church is said to mark the grave of St Ailbhe, first Bishop of Emly, who founded a monastery here.

At Soloheadbeg, 4 miles (6 km) north of Tipperary, the first shot in the resumption of the Anglo-Irish War after the 1916 Rebellion was fired in January 1919. There is a memorial to this event at Solohead Cross. At Donohill crossroads, a short distance north of Solohead, is a good example of a Norman motte.

Four miles (6 km) further north is Cappawhite village, on the southern edge of the Slievefelim Mountains. This is an extensive area of elevated moorland, with Mauherslieve (1,783 feet) as its centre and Keeper Hill (2,279 feet) lying between Mauherslieve and the Silvermine Mountains at the north-west corner of the area. In the winter of 1601 the northern armies under O'Neill and O'Donnell made a celebrated forced march across these hills on their way to join their Spanish supporters at Kinsale. Keeper Hill is famous as the camping ground of Patrick Sarsfield's men on their way to intercept the Williamite siege train at Ballyneety in August 1690. A map of the route of 70 miles (113 km) taking in Counties Clare, Tipperary and Limerick can be obtained in the tourist information offices.

Among the people of this area many traditions survive of the rapparee Eamonn Ó Riain, celebrated in the Irish song 'Eamonn a' Chnuic' (Ned of the Hill). Born at Athshanboe, near Upperchurch, Ó Riain is said to have been a Jacobite officer who took to these hills after the Treaty of Limerick (1691) and preyed on the English planters in north Tipperary. In a ravine on the side of the mountain that rises behind Cappawhite is a small cave, now over-grown and partly collapsed, which is said to have been his retreat. He was murdered for reward by a kinsman at Foilaclug, and the reputed site of his grave is at Curraheen, near Hollyford village. Tradition also claims that Ó Riain himself was the author of 'Eamonn a' Chnuic' and other songs of which the best known is 'Bean Dubh a' Ghleanna' (Dark Lady of the Glen).

Ballysheeda Castle, a well-preserved circular keep on the hillside a mile (2 km) north of Annacarthy village, was once a stronghold of the O'Dwyers of Kilnama-nagh. In wooded surroundings on the plain beneath the south-eastern tip of these hills is the pretty village of Dundrum (good brown trout fishing). Killenure Castle, 3 miles (5 km) away on the Cashel road, was another O'Dwyer fortress; it consists of a large rectangular building of three storeys, with circular towers at each angle. Two of these towers are incorporated in a modern dwelling.

The road eastwards from Tipperary to Cashel crosses part of the undulating lime-stone plain called the Golden Vale, one of Ireland's richest pasture lands. Six miles (10 km) from Tipperary is the ruin of Thomastown Castle, birthplace of the Capuchin 'apostle of temperance', Father Theobald Mathew (1790–1856); he is commemorated by a statue at the adjoining Thomastown crossroads.

Two miles (3 km) beyond Thomastown is the village of Golden, built across the River Suir. On a rocky islet in the river is the ruined keep of Golden Castle. Athassel Abbey, on the west bank of the river 1½ miles (2 km) to the south, was founded for Augustinian canons by William de Burgh at the end of the twelfth century. This once extensive establishment was richly endowed by the de Burghs, many of whom were buried here. Among them was the 'Red Earl' of Ulster, Richard de Burgh, who retired here from the world and died in the abbey in 1326. The ruins consist of the abbey church, cloisters and some of the monastic buildings.

Cashel

Caiseal Mumhan (The Stone Fort of Munster)

Pop. 2,473 (urban district).

Tourist information office (seasonal): Town Hall. Tel. (062) 61333.

Most visitors to Cashel come to see the ecclesiastical remains on the famous Rock of Cashel which dominates the town on the north, but there are other points of interest, and Cashel is also a good centre for exploring the surrounding country. Salmon and trout fishing is available on the River Suir, and the district is also fine hunting country.

Brú Ború Heritage Centre features folk theatre, music, art and craft exhibitions by the local branch of Comhaltas Ceoltoiri (Ireland's premier cultural movement for promoting the Irish language and culture). Near the Rock there is also a folk village of thatched dwellings which is open to the public.

The GPA Bolton Library houses a rare and beautiful collection of books and manuscripts, some 12,000 titles.

The Rock of Cashel

This is a remarkable outcrop of limestone rising 200 feet above the plain and crowned with its magnificent group of ruins; it is one of Ireland's great historic sites.

The rock was the seat of Munster kings from about 370 until 1101, when King Murtagh O'Brien granted it to the Church.

Cashel Folk Park

St Patrick, on visiting it in 450, baptised King Aengus and his brothers here. Brian Boru was crowned King of Munster at Cashel. On its grant to the Church in 1101, the rock was dedicated to 'God, St Patrick and St Ailbhe'. Cormac's Chapel, erected by the King-Bishop who reigned 1122–1138, was consecrated in 1134 before a great gathering of the nobles and clergy of Munster. The first cathedral was founded in 1169, but nothing of it now remains. In 1495 Gerald, Earl of Kildare, burned the cathedral because, as he afterwards explained to Henry VII, he thought the archbishop was inside! Queen Elizabeth appointed the pluralist Myler MacGrath to the see in 1571. Archbishop Dermod O'Hurley, appointed by the Pope in 1581, was martyred in Dublin three years later.

Cormac's Chapel, a building unique in Ireland, has two towers rather like transepts at the junction of the nave and small chancel, storeys of blank arcading within and without, string-courses and a barrel vault with transverse arches. Although the chapel has features of European origin, its high-pitched roof of stone and the corbel principle are distinctively Irish in conception. In the south wall the doorway has a carved stone tympanum (depicting a huge beast being attacked by a centaur) and billet moulding—both uncommon in Irish architecture. The eccentric position of the chancel, to the south side of the axis of the nave, is a curious feature of the plan. A stone sarcophagus preserved in the chapel was at one time regarded as the tomb of King Cormac himself, but it does not belong to the chapel or to his period; its elaborate carving identifies it as eleventh-century work. When found, the coffin contained the Cormac Crosier, now in the National Museum in Dublin.

The Cathedral is a cruciform building with a central tower and at its west end a massive residential castle three storeys high. Its high-set lancet windows are characteristically thirteenth century. The wrought work of the chancel windows is in yellow sandstone, contrasting with the limestone of the rest of the building. In the south wall of the choir are the piscina and sedilia recesses and beside them the inscribed wall-tomb of Archbishop Myler MacGrath. The transepts each have two chapels on their east sides, Cormac's chapel abutting on the south transept. The central tower of the cathedral is approached by winding stairs off the south transept, rising by 127 steps to the summit roof walk.

The fifteenth-century Hall of the Vicars Choral is seen on entering the modern gateway at the head of the inclined way which approaches the rock enclosure from the south. This building, an extensive structure in two parts of two storeys each, housed laymen or minor canons appointed to assist in chanting the cathedral service. St Patrick's Cross, in the green inside the entrance gate, is a unique form of Irish cross. When complete it formed a cross enclosed in a frame without the usual ring around the intersection of the shaft and transom. On both faces are high-relief figures: on the west that of Christ Crucified and on the east a figure which may be that of St Patrick. The cross, carved originally from one large block of stone, probably dates from the eleventh century. It is 7½ feet high and is inserted into a base which may have been the coronation stone of the Munster kings. The Round Tower is a perfect specimen 92 feet high, built mainly of sandstone; the doorway is 12 feet above ground level.

Other points of interest

Near the base of the rock (approached by Chapel Lane) is the Dominican Friary. This was founded in 1243 by Archbishop MacKelly, who became its first prior, but most of the ruin dates from about 1480 when it was rebuilt after a fire. The beautiful thirteenth-century east window is a special feature. About a half-mile (1 km) west of the rock is the Cistercian Hore Abbey (1266), a daughter house of Mellifont in County Louth. Quirke's Castle, opposite the City Hall, is named after a family of printers who occupied it in the nineteenth century. The lower part is now a shop, but the upper storey shows typical crenellated battlements and gargoyles of the fifteenth century.

A cross commemorating the famous Archbishop Croke stands in a space which in medieval times was the milk market. The ornamental fountain at the south-west end of the main street commemorates the services of Dean Kinane in connection with the extension of the railway to Cashel in 1904. The Deanery, formerly the palace of the Protestant archbishops, is a beautiful specimen of eighteenth-century domestic architecture; it is now a hotel.

Behind the Christian Brothers' schools is the house known as Alla Eileen, once the home of Michael Doheny (1805– 1863), Young Irelander and author of *The Felon's Track*, which tells the story of his participation in the Rising of 1848. Here Gavan Duffy, Meagher, Kickham, Smith O'Brien and other leaders of the period frequently met.

Around Cashel
Longfield House 5 miles (8 km) north of Cashel, was the residence of Charles Bianconi (1786–1875), who gave Ireland its first regular transport system, the 'Bianconi Cars'. He is buried beside the Catholic church at Boherlahan, where a large monument in the form of a Romanesque-style chapel stands over the family vault. The authoress Margaret Power, afterwards Lady Blessington (1789–1869), was born at Knockbrit, 6 miles (10 km) west of Cashel.

At Ballydoyle near Cashel, Vincent O'Brien the famous horse trainer has his establishment, where many classic winners were trained.

Fethard
Fiodh Ard (High Wood)

♟♟♟ Pop. 982.

This little town was important in medieval times as an Anglo-Norman settlement that later became a corporate town. An Augustinian priory was in existence here until its suppression in the sixteenth century. In 1376 Edward I granted certain revenue rights to the corporation to wall the town, and a similar grant was made by Henry IV. In 1650 Cromwell appeared before the walls with his army, and after a short resistance the town surrendered on honourable terms.

Points of interest
There are some well-preserved remains of the priory buildings on the site of the Augustinian foundation, and also a number of fine tombs of the sixteenth and seventeenth centuries. Rectangular keeps of three castles (probably fifteenth century) still remain, including that of Fethard Castle at the centre of the town. Considerable remnants of the old town walls and their flanking towers are also to be seen. Some restoration work is being undertaken.

Around Fethard
A mile (2 km) west of Lisronagh village is Donaghmore Church, a good example of Hiberno-Romanesque architecture with a fine, elaborately carved west door. Kiltinane Castle, on a rock overhanging the Glashawley River 3 miles (5 km) south-west of Fethard, is said to have been built by King John. Granted to Philip of Worcester in 1215, it passed in the fourteenth century to a branch of the Butlers. This castle was battered by Cromwell's cannon in 1649, but it was later rebuilt and is still occupied.

A few miles south-east of Fethard, Slievenamon (2,368 feet) is a prominent conical mass at the western end of a range of low hills running eastwards into County Kilkenny; from its summit there is a superb view over a wide expanse of country. Its ancient name was Sliabh na mBan Feimhinn (The Mountain of the Women of Feimhinn), called after the fairy women of the surrounding territory who are said to have enchanted Fionn and his Fianna warriors. Another legend tells how Fionn decided to choose as his bride the first woman to reach him in a race to the summit, where he was seated. The winner was Grainne, whose later exploits with the hero Diarmuid are famous in Irish legend.

The village of Mullinahone, 10 miles (16 km) north-east of Fethard, is best known for its associations with the writer and patriot Charles Joseph Kickham (1828–1882). The house where he lived in Fethard Street is marked with a plaque, and a Celtic cross stands over his grave beside the Catholic church. Kickham's finest novel, *Knocknagow*, is based on rural life in this part of County Tipperary. The bleak windswept village of Ballingarry, high on the southern slopes of the Slieveardagh Hills 8 miles (13 km) north of Mullinahone, was the scene of the abortive rising of the Young Irelanders in 1848. The rising ended after a short attack on the home of the Widow McCormick (4 miles/6 km to the north), which had been occupied by a force of police.

Thurles

Durlus Eile (Strong Fort of Ely)

Pop. 6,683 (urban district).

A well laid out town built across the River Suir near the northern end of the plain of Tipperary, bounded by the Silvermine and Devil's Bit Mountains to the north-west and the Slieveardagh Hills to the south-east. The visitor here is offered rich and varied scenery. Thurles is the cathedral town of the archdiocese of Cashel and Emly.

Things to do

There is brown trout fishing near the town on the Suir and its tributaries; Thurles racecourse is 1½ miles (2 km) west of the town; golf (18), 1½ miles (2 km) south of the town; two packs of foxhounds hunt the district; there is greyhound racing twice weekly.

History

Named from the fortress of the O'Fogartys that stood here in ancient times, Thurles receives little notice in historical records until 1174, when Strongbow's Anglo-Norman army was heavily defeated here. Later the Anglo-Normans established themselves in the district and built a castle at Thurles to command the crossing of the Suir. The Carmelite priory founded by the Butlers in 1300 was suppressed in 1540 and granted to the Earl of Ormonde, James Butler. In 1850, the Synod of Thurles was the greatest gathering of the Catholic Church in Ireland since 1642. Another important historical event took place in Thurles in 1884, when the Gaelic Athletic Association was founded at a meeting in Hayes' Hotel. The GAA has since become one of the largest amateur sports organisations in the world. The Centenary All-Ireland hurling final was held in Thurles in 1984 to mark the occasion.

Points of interest

The Catholic Cathedral (1875), was begun as an extension of the previous plain building on the site of the Carmelite foundation of 1300. A fine Romanesque-style building, its square campanile 125 feet high is a landmark for many miles around. At the farther end of the façade, isolated from the main building, is a circular baptistery. Marble is used very effectively for much of the interior decoration. Perhaps the most

Devil's Bit Mountain

artistic features are the altars, beautifully inlaid with marbles of various colours. The apse also has rich marble decoration and a tessellated floor. Off this is a recess serving as a mortuary chapel, where on the floor a mosaic figure with a surrounding epitaph marks the burial-place of Archbishop Croke (1824–1902), whose active interest in Ireland's struggle for independence made him a national figure. He gave warm encouragement to athletic pastimes and was the first patron of the Gaelic Athletic Association.

Two rectangular keeps, the remnants of castles erected by the Butlers, still stand at Thurles: Bridge Castle, at the western end of the bridge across the Suir; and Black Castle, near the Square.

Around Thurles

On the west bank of the Suir, 4 miles (6 km) south of Thurles, stands Holycross Abbey, which was fully restored as part of European Architectural Heritage Year 1975. After standing roofless for over 200 years it is now in use as a parish church. Founded originally in 1168 for Benedictines by the King of Munster, Donal O'Brien, the abbey was transferred to the Cistercians about 1182. A particle of the True Cross was enshrined in the abbey, and Holycross became one of the most frequented places of pilgrimage in Ireland. Suppressed in 1536, the abbey was made over in 1563 to the Earl of Ormonde, but through the protection of the Butler family the monks remained at Holycross down to the seventeenth century. Much rebuilding was carried out in the first three centuries of the abbey's existence, so that little of the original work remains.

The church consists of nave with aisles, transepts with side chapels, and chancel with a square tower supported on pointed arches over the intersection. One of the most remarkable features is the beautiful window-tracery, particularly in the east and west windows

Holycross Abbey

and the window in the south transept. On the Epistle side of the high altar is the reconstructed sedilia of beautifully carved black marble, regarded as one of the most perfect works of its kind in Ireland. The floor of this is a tombstone bearing an incised cross. On the architrave are four panels containing shields with armorial bearings. Above these are highly decorated slabs and over them a canopy of beautiful design. Also in the chancel are the O'Fogarty and Purcell tombs.

The north transept and its two chapels are groined and each has a three-light window, pointed and decorated. On the north and west walls of the transept are traces of a fresco representing three men stag-hunting. A mural stairway leads from the north end to an apartment over the chapels. The south transept has also two side-chapels, separated by a narrow passage with an elaborately groined roof supported by a double row of twisted columns. This passage is believed to have been a shrine for the exposition of the relic.

The cloister has two entrances from the south aisle, one Hiberno-Romanesque and the other Gothic. The chapter house door-way, leading from the cloister, has a unique form of double arch in which the upper and lower parts join in the centre to form the keystone. Another group of ruined buildings, including the abbot's quarters, lies between the cloister and the river bank. Remains of the ancient gateway and enclosing wall of the abbey also stand.

There is an information office within the abbey which is open daily. A guide book is available from tourist information offices.

There are many other remains of churches and castles in the Thurles area, many of the sites having both church and castle in close proximity. At Leigh, 6 miles (10 km) east of the town, the ruins of two churches stand on the site of the sixth-century Monastery of Liathmore, founded by St Mochoemog. One of these

is a small building with high-pitched roof, a round-headed east window (restored) and a partially restored west door; the other larger ruin is of a Romanesque church with some Gothic features inserted later. In the chancel of this larger church are a number of tomb slabs, one of them bearing a sculpture of Christ Crucified.

On the north-west side of the Slieveardagh Hills, 4 miles (6 km) south of Urlingford (County Kilkenny), are the ruins of Kilcooley Abbey. This was founded as a daughter house of Jerpoint (see Thomastown, County Kilkenny) by King Donagh O'Brien in 1200. The remains are of the abbey church and some of the monastic buildings—as well as a dovecote which may belong to the period of lay occupation after the monastery's suppression in the sixteenth century (when the property was given to the Butlers by the English Crown). The east end of the church was rebuilt in the fifteenth century, and chancel and transepts are particularly well preserved. The east window, of six lights, shows some very elaborate tracery. In the chancel are several interesting sculptured tombs and monu-mental slabs. The north transept (by which the visitor enters) has an ancient font with interlaced carving. The end wall of the south transept is panelled and decorated with sculptures. Over the fine Gothic door in this wall are carved the Crucifixion, St Christopher carrying the infant Jesus over a river symbolised by fishes, and lower down a figure of a bishop with a censing angel overhead. To the left of this doorway is a pointed-arch recess containing a piscina and crowned by an ornamental finial.

In an island in Littleton bog outside Thurles was found the Derrynaflan Hoard in 1980, now in the National Museum in Dublin. The site of the find was that of an ancient monastery reputedly founded by St Ruadhan of Lorrha.

Templemore
Teampall Mor (Great Church)

👪 Pop. 2,188 (urban district).

Templemore lies on the plain beneath the western slopes of the Devil's Bit Mountain. In the 70-acre town park (part of the former Carden demesne) are the remains of Templemore Abbey and Black Castle. Also in the park are a large lake and swimming pool. There is good fishing for brown trout on the upper reaches of the River Suir near the town, and the lake in the town park holds pike, roach, perch and tench. The North Tipperary Foxhounds hunt the district. Nine-hole golf course.

Ireland's Gardai (police force) are trained here in what was the old British (later Irish) army barracks now completely refurbished as a modern Garda training college.

Around Templemore
Devil's Bit Mountain (1,577 feet) is named from the remarkable gap in this highest peak of the range west of Templemore. Legend has it that the devil (rather than a glacier), finding the 'Bit' unpalatable, spat it out and that it fell on the plain to the south to form the Rock of Cashel. Near the eastern entrance to the gap is a cylindrical castellated tower called 'Carden's Folly'. One of the Cardens, John, a JP and deputy lieutenant of the county, attempted to abduct Eleanor Arbuthnot of Rathronan near Clonmel in 1854. The attempt failed and Carden's infatuation earned him two years in Clonmel gaol.

Three miles (5 km) south of Templemore is a one-time seat of the Purcells, Loughmore Castle. This is a sixteenth-century rectangular tower with a larger and much later house and tower-like wing attached. Nicholas Purcell, an officer in King James's army and one of the signatories of the Treaty of Limerick (1691), came from Loughmore.

A prominent landmark two miles (3 km) south-west of Templemore is Barna Castle, a circular keep of five storeys rising to 60 feet. Surviving features include a spiral stairway leading to the battlements, from which there is a very fine view. At Drom, 4 miles (6 km) south-west of the town, are the remains of a church, and on high ground near by is an ancient ring fort. This place is traditionally the site of the Synod of Rathbreasail, held in 1111.

The small town of Borrisoleigh is 6 miles (10 km) south-west of Templemore, near the eastern end of the pass that carries the Thurles–Nenagh road between the Devil's Bit and Slievefelim Mountains. About 2 miles (3 km) to the north-west is Glankeen, where St Cuilan founded a monastery in the seventh century. There are some remains of the later church of Glankeen, with an inscribed table-tomb of the de Burghs inside the ruins.

Nenagh
Aonach Urmhumhan (Fair of Ormonde)

👪 Pop. 5,531 (urban district).

ℹ️ Tourist information office (seasonal): Connolly St, Nenagh. Tel. (067) 31610. Fax (067) 33418.

This busy town, the chief town of north Tipperary, is in a fertile plain bordered on the south by the Silvermine Mountains and on the west by the Arra Mountains.

Things to do
In the Nenagh River there is good trout fishing. There is golf (18), pitch and putt, tennis, squash and an indoor heated swimming pool. Nenagh has an interesting heritage centre which is housed in the octagonal Governor's house at the old County Gaol. A genealogical service is provided there.

Nenagh Castle

Points of interest

Nenagh Keep, the finest of its kind in Ireland, formed part of a larger castle built about 1200 by Theobald FitzWalter, ancestor of the Butlers of Ormonde. About 100 feet high and 53 feet across the base, the keep was originally incorporated in the curtain walls of the castle, at the northern angle. Its topmost portion was reconstructed in 1860. Some of the original interior features remain, including winding stairs in the thickness of the wall which gave access to the upper floors and the roof.

In an old graveyard in the town stand some remains of Nenagh's Franciscan Friary—mainly the east gable, with its three small lancets. Founded in the thirteenth century, this is said to have been one of the greatest Franciscan establishments in Ireland. It was suppressed in the sixteenth century, but the friars were again in occupation when the buildings were destroyed by Cromwell in 1650.

Around Nenagh

South-east of the town, less than a mile (2 km), are the ruins of the church of Tyone Abbey, founded by one of the Butlers in the thirteenth century for Augustinian canons. Toomevara village, 7 miles (11 km) east of Nenagh, has the ruins of a four-teenth-century Augustinian priory church.

Six miles (10 km) south of Nenagh, Silvermines village lies at the foot of the Silvermine Mountains (highest peak Knockaunderrig, 1,609 feet). At various periods as far back as the fourteenth century the mines here were worked for their silver-bearing lead. The most recent working was by the Canadian firm Mogul, who mined underground from 1966 to 1983. From a nearby hilltop the panoramic view of Lough Derg is worthwhile.

Six miles (10 km) north of Nenagh, Dromineer on Lough Derg is a good trout fishing centre and a popular resort with local people for picnics, boating and swim-ming. There is also lake cruising and yachting based in Dromineer. On the shore of Lough Derg at Terryglass (Ireland's tidiest town in 1983) is the ruin of a towered keep of the Butlers. Lorrha village, 5 miles (8 km) north-east of Terryglass, is the site of a sixth-century monastic foundation of St Ruadhan, which was destroyed by Norsemen under Turgesius (see around Mullingar, County Westmeath). The ancient site is now occupied by the ruins of a thirteenth-century church of the Dominican priory founded in 1269 by Walter de Burgh. The *Stowe Missal*, a national treasure, is thought to have been written in Lorrha in the late eighth century. Some 3½ miles (6 km) from Lorrha, Redwood Castle (Norman thirteenth century) is being restored.

The village of Cloughjordan, 10 miles (16 km) north-east of Nenagh, was the birthplace of Thomas MacDonagh (1878–1916), poet and a signatory of the Proclamation of the Republic in 1916. About 7 miles (11 km) further north is the hill of Knockshigowna, named after the fairy queen Una who was the legendary guardian spirit of the O'Carrolls. From the summit there is a panoramic view of the surrounding country.

Roscrea
Ros Cre (Crea's Wood)

👪 Pop. 4,378.

This prosperous town owes its origin to the monastery founded here in the seventh century by St Cronan.

Things to do
Golf (9), hunting with the Ormonde Foxhounds, handball, tennis. Roscrea is a good centre for climbing and walking in the Devil's Bit and Slieve Bloom Mountains.

Points of interest
St Cronan's Abbey was a twelfth-century Augustinian priory founded on the site of the ancient monastery of St Cronan, where the mid-eighth-century *Book of Dimma* (in Trinity College, Dublin) originated; only

the west gable and belfry survive. The west door is a good example of Hiberno-Romanesque, and forms the entrance to the grounds of the modern Protestant church. Just inside the enclosing walls of these grounds, and beside the public road, is the partly restored St Cronan's Cross. The round tower, near the abbey ruins, is in good preservation, though about 20 feet of the original upper part is missing; its present height is about 60 feet.

The remains of a fifteenth-century Franciscan friary are partly incorporated in the Catholic church of St Cronan. The tall square belfry of the ancient building is still standing, and its supporting arches provide an attractive entrance to the modern church. Roscrea Castle (now under restoration) dates in its present form from the thirteenth century. The remains are of a rectangular gate-tower and two other towers, as well as part of the curtain walls. The gables and chimneys which top the gate-tower were added in the seventeenth century. In the castle yard is Damer House built *c*.1715 and restored by the Irish Georgian Society. The house contains a magnificent carved wood staircase, an elegant carved stone doorway, paintings, furniture and local heritage exhibits, and a genealogical service. The house and castle are open to the public all year round. In 1990 a new Georgian planned garden was opened at the house, planted as it would have been in the eighteenth century.

Around Roscrea
Two miles (3 km) east of Roscrea is Mona Incha Abbey, variously attributed to St Cronan, St Canice or St Ciaran. It is on a site formerly surrounded by a lake which was drained in modern times. The principal remains are of a church with Romanesque features and later Gothic insertions and additions. In the Timoney Hills and Cullaun districts, some miles south-east of the town, is a remarkable group of nearly 300 standing stones spread over 120 acres.

Waterford

Newtown Cove, near Tramore

Counties Waterford, on the south
coast, combines many kinds of
beauty in its scenery. Much of the
north and centre of the county is mountainous, including the Comeragh range with its
fine lake corries; the rest consists mainly of
gentle hills and valleys. The coastline is a
series of rugged headlands, cliffs and sand-
fringed bays; Tramore is the best known of
several attractive resorts. On the north and
east the county is bordered by the pleasant
River Suir; in the west the Blackwater valley,
with its flanking hills and numerous wooded
stretches, provides the finest river scenery
in Ireland. The River Blackwater rises in
County Kerry and flows eastwards through
Cork and Waterford, turning southwards at
Cappoquin to flow into Youghal Bay by a
narrow estuary 15 miles (24 km) long. The
most beautiful part of the river is in County
Waterford—from near Fermoy (County
Cork) past Ballyduff, Lismore and Cappoquin to Youghal. Historic Waterford city,
the holiday attractions of Tramore, the
Early Christian remains at Ardmore, Lismore
and its castle above the Blackwater—these
are some of the places to include in your
itinerary of this pleasant county.

Waterford City
Port Lairge (Lairge's Landing-Place)

Pop. 40,345 (Waterford *city* CSO
1991 figures).

Tourist information office:
41 The Quay. Tcl. (051)75788.
Fax (051) 77388.

American Express:
Harvey Travel Ltd, 4 Gladstone St,
Waterford.
Tel. (051) 72048. Fax (051) 79721.

Post Office:
The Quay, Keyser St, Waterford.
Tel. (051) 74321. Open: 9.00 – 18.00.

Parking regulations: Disc parking.

Railway Station/Bus Depot:
Plunkett Station, The Bridge,
Waterford. Tel. (051) 73401.

Car Hire: Avis Rent a Car Ltd,
Waterford Airport. Tel. (051) 70170.

Bicycle Hire: Wright's Cycle
Depot Ltd, Henrietta St, Waterford.
Tel. (051) 74411. Fax (051) 73440.

Murphy's Toys & Cycles, 68 Main St,
Dungarvan, Co. Waterford.
Tel. (058) 41376.

Dates of principal cultural events/
festivals:
Waterford International Festival of Light
Opera (September).

Waterford has a fine situation on
the south bank of the River Suir,
which opens into the estuary of
Waterford Harbour some miles to the east
(after receiving the waters of the Rivers
Nore and Barrow). A bridge joins the city
with the suburb of Ferrybank on the
northern bank. The main seaport of the
south-east, Waterford has a considerable
shipping trade with British and European
ports; its important industries include
bacon and meat processing, furniture-
making, ironfounding, electrical products,
steel castings, pharmaceutical products.
Waterford Glass is now the largest crystal
factory in the world. Factory tours are
possible by appointment with the management or the Waterford tourist office.

Things to do

There is golf (18) at Newrath, Waterford,
and 8 miles (13 km) away at Tramore (18).
Waterford Foxhounds and Gaultier Foxhounds hunt the district. Greyhound racing
twice weekly, and frequent horse-racing
meetings at Tramore, sailing, tennis, squash,
horse-riding and pony-trekking.

There are guided walking tours of the
city available and there are also daily cruises
on the river during the season. Bus Éireann
operates a series of day tours from Waterford and Tramore.

The Theatre Royal, established in 1876,
features regular professional theatre and a
light opera festival in September. There are
also cinemas and dance halls.

Garter Lane Arts Centre has a permanent
art collection and provides a programme of
theatre, music, art and craft exhibitions.

History

Waterford became important in 853, when
the Danes established a settlement here
called Vadrefjord. The colonists were later
Christianised, and one of their later leaders,
Reginald, is said to have built Waterford's
Reginald's Tower in 1003. For centuries
there was strife between the Waterford
Danes and the Irish of the surrounding
country, but the Danes kept possession
until the Anglo-Norman invasion. In 1170
Strongbow and Raymond le Gros took the
town, and Strongbow later strengthened
his position by marrying at Waterford the
daughter of Dermot MacMurrough, King
of Leinster.

Waterford became second in importance
only to Dublin among Anglo-Norman
strongholds, and it remained in fact an
English colony down to the nineteenth
century. In 1171 Henry II reputedly landed
here to take possession of Ireland. King
John granted Waterford its first charter in
1205, and again visited the town in 1210.
In 1487, when the pretender Lambert
Simnel was crowned in Dublin, Waterford
remained loyal to Henry VII, and ten years
later another pretender Perkin Warbeck

was repulsed at Waterford and pursued to Cornwall by the citizens. In gratitude, King Henry gave the city 1,000 marks and conferred on it the title *Urbs Intacta Manet Waterfordia* (which still appears on the city arms).

In the sixteenth century the citizens refused to accept the English King's supremacy in religion, while still acknowledging their loyalty in temporal matters. This led to the withdrawal of the city's charter and the fining or imprisonment of members of the Corporation. In 1649, Cromwell was forced to abandon his siege of Waterford, but in the following year the city was taken by Ireton. James II was received here on his way to Kinsale after the defeat at the Boyne in 1690, but soon afterwards the city surrendered on honourable terms to William III.

In the eighteenth century Waterford enjoyed a period of economic development initiated by the industrialist Thomas Wyse. The much-prized old Waterford glass was produced between 1783 and 1851.

The Old City Walls
Waterford was walled by the Danes in the ninth or tenth century and by the Anglo-Normans in the thirteenth and later centuries. Much of the old Viking wall still remains, as well as parts of the Norman fortifications—principally near the railway station, the Mayor's Walk and Castle Street (where there are some of the old defensive towers).

Reginald's Tower
This ancient fortification, a circular building with a conical roof and walls ten feet thick, stands at the eastern end of the Quay. Erected in 1003 as part of the Danish defences, the tower was occupied by Strongbow in 1171. Henry II imprisoned Fitzstephen here, and the tower was later used as a mint by order of King John. During the many sieges of Waterford the tower was an inevitable target, and its walls still

Reginald's Tower

bear the scars of cannon. In 1819 it was converted into a prison, and passed into the hands of the Corporation in 1861. In the tower today is a very interesting exhibition of Corporation archives and civic regalia.

Church Buildings
The Church of Ireland Christ Church Cathedral stands on the site of that built by the Danes about 1050. In 1773 the ancient church was replaced by a new cathedral, which was enlarged in 1891, and a steeple was later added to the western end. St Olaf's Church (eleventh century) is near the City Hall and is also of Danish origin. The Normans rebuilt the Danish structure, and in 1734 the Norman edifice was restored by Bishop Milles. The pulpit and bishop's throne are of finely carved black oak.

The French Church (or Grey Friars), off the Quay, was originally a Franciscan foundation, built in 1240 by Sir Hugh Purcell and richly endowed by Henry III. After the sixteenth-century suppression of the monasteries, it was granted to the Walsh family. A century later the disused church was given as a place of worship to a colony of Huguenot refugees, who remained in possession until the building was abandoned in 1819. The principal features of the ruin are the central tower and a fine east window.

Waterford

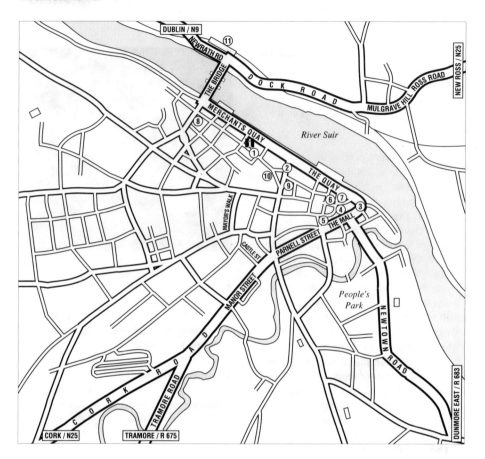

1. George's Street
2. Barronstrand Street
3. Reginald's Tower
4. City Hall
5. Christ Church Cathedral
6. St Olaf's Church

7. French Church (Greyfriars)
8. Dominican Friary (Blackfriars)
9. Holy Trinity Cathedral
10. St Patrick's Church
11. Plunkett Station

A t the city's heritage centre in Greyfriars, artefacts discovered from the excavation of the Viking and early Norman periods are on display.

In Arundel Square is the Dominican Friary (or Blackfriars). Founded in 1226, this was one of the oldest Dominican houses in Ireland. In 1541 the priory was suppressed, and in 1599 it passed by grant of Queen Elizabeth to Sir Anthony St Leger. The square tower of the church is the only significant remnant.

In Barronstrand Street is the Catholic Cathedral, a building on classic lines completed in 1796. Its richly decorated interior has a high vaulted roof resting on Corinthian pillars. Among the treasures preserved in the cathedral are an ancient crucifix (1620), two silver chalices (1646 and 1722), six silver candlesticks (1751) and a gold monstrance (1869).

St Patrick's Church in George's Street provides a genealogical service.

Other points of interest

On the Mall is the City Hall, an imposing though plain-fronted building erected in 1788. On display in the council chamber are the uniform, sword and battle flag of the Irish Brigade carried by Thomas Francis Meagher at the Battle of Fredericksburg. Also displayed is the old American Union flag with 34 stars. A magnificent old Waterford glass chandelier hangs in the chamber.

A few minutes' walk from the City Hall is the Courthouse (1849), a substantial building in Ionic style; from its grounds there is access to the People's Park, a tree-shaded recreation ground.

In St John's College, a seminary founded in 1871, the extensive library contains rare books and manuscripts. Mount Sion School (1803), was the first school of the Irish Christian Brothers Order.

On the Mall the Bishop Foy Palace by Waterford architect Terence O'Reilly is used as Corporation offices.

Distinguished Waterford Citizens

Perhaps no other Irish city outside Dublin has produced a greater number of distinguished people than Waterford. Among them were:

Luke Wadding (1588–1657), historian and philosopher. Educated at Lisbon and ordained there in 1613, he was President of the Irish College in Salamanca, and founder of the Irish College of St Isidore in Rome. Himself the author of many volumes, he presented to St Isidore's 5,000 printed works and 800 manuscripts. He gave material and moral support to the Confederation of Kilkenny, and was instrumental in the sending of Rinuccini as Papal Nuncio to Ireland.

The Jesuit Fathers Luke, Peter, Ambrose and Michael Wadding—all natives of Waterford and cousins of Luke Wadding— were also famous scholars with European reputations.

Dr Peter Lombard (1554–1625). Studied at Oxford and Louvain. Provost of Cambrai Cathedral.

Dr Thomas Walsh (1580–1654), Archbishop of Cashel. Imprisoned by the Cromwellian general, Ireton, he was later transported to the Continent; he died in Spain at Compostela.

T homas Francis Meagher (1823– 1867), called 'Meagher of the Sword'. Born in a house on the Quay (now the Granville Hotel), Meagher became a member of the 'Young Ireland' Party and a founder of the Irish Confederation. He was sentenced to death for his part in the 1848 Rising. He escaped to America and later fought in the Civil War, becoming brigadier-general. He was appointed Governor of Montana shortly before his accidental drowning in the Missouri River in 1867.

William Vincent Wallace (1814– 1865), composer of *Maritana* and other popular operas. Charles John Keane (1811– 1868), the famous actor, was also born in Waterford.

Around Waterford

Inland from the city 9 miles (15 km) west is Portlaw. This small manufacturing town on the River Clodagh was a flourishing centre of the cotton industry in the nineteenth century. Adjoining the town is Curraghmore, seat of the Marquis of Waterford and one of the most beautiful demesnes in the country. In the grounds is an interesting shell house and some fine bronze statuary. The grounds are open on Thursday afternoons only in summer, and also on Bank Holiday Mondays.

Fifteen miles (24 km) south-west of Waterford is the attractive village of Kilmacthomas, built on the steep slopes on either side of the River Mahon. The celebrated Gaelic poet Donnchadh Rua Mac Conmara (died 1814) lived here for some years; his grave is in the Catholic churchyard at Newtown, 2 miles (3 km) north-west. Another noted poet of the period, Tadhg Gaelach O Suilleabhain (died 1800), also lived at Kilmacthomas and is buried at Ballylaneen, 3 miles (5 km) to the south on the Bunmahon road. Riobard Weldon (died 1914), poet of the Decies

Dunmore East

district, was born about 4 miles (6 km) west of Kilmacthomas, near Mahon Bridge. His grave in Kilrossanty graveyard, a few miles south of Mahon Bridge, is marked by a headstone inscribed in Irish.

West of Kilmacthomas rises the fine range of the Comeragh Mountains, with many peaks over 2,000 feet. The highest point, Fascoum (2,597 feet), is above Coumshingaun, a mountain tarn hemmed in on three sides by steep cliffs which provide excellent rock-climbing. Crotty's Lake, a tarn north of Coumshingaun, is named after a highwayman who is said to have used a small cave overlooking the lake as a hiding place. He was hanged in 1742.

Tour of Waterford coast

The tour is begun by taking the road east from the city to Passage East (7 miles/11 km). This old-world village, at the foot of a steep hill overlooking the head of Waterford Harbour, was fortified at one time to command the passage of shipping in the river. There is a good view from the hill behind the village, but the best viewpoint in the area is Cheekpoint Hill, 2 miles (3 km) north of the Waterford road. From the summit there is a wonderful panorama.

Visitors may explore the Wexford shore of the harbour by taking the passenger ferry from Passage East across to Ballyhack (average crossing time 10 minutes). On the road from Passage to Dunmore East are the ruins of Geneva Barracks, which live in the memory through the ballad 'The Croppy Boy'. A colony of goldsmiths and silversmiths from Geneva were invited here in 1785. The barracks were to serve as workshops and accommodation for a Protestant colony that never arrived. It was later used by the British military, then as a prison for the 1798 insurgents or 'croppies' as they were called. Further on is Woodstown Strand with a beautiful sandy beach.

Nine miles (14 km) south-east of Waterford city is Dunmore East, a popular summer retreat, picturesquely situated at the mouth of Waterford Harbour. The bay

LEGEND has it that Irish monks invented whiskey, learning of distillation from the perfumers of the Orient. They called their discovery *Uisce Beatha* (the water of life) and to this day the finest of whiskey is distilled by the Irish.

A visit to the Jameson Heritage Centre in Midleton, Co. Cork will take you right to the heart of this cherished tradition.

You are invited to take a two-hour tour of the Centre - it's a beautifully restored 18th century, self-contained industrial complex, unique in Britain and Ireland. Delight in the fully-operational water wheel and be amazed by the copper pot still of 130,000 gallons, the largest in the world.

An audio-visual presentation, available in six languages, breathes life into the Irish whiskey legend.

After the history comes the tasting. Relax in the atmosphere of a traditional Irish pub and sample Ireland's finest whiskey. *Sláinte.*

Lose yourself in the charm of another age - the Jameson Heritage Centre with its craft and coffee shops is located on the main Cork/Waterford road which links the ferry terminals of Rosslare and Ringaskiddy. We're open from 10.00am to 4.00pm, May to October. Telephone John Callely at 021-613594 or fax 021-613642 for information.

JAMESON The Spirit of Ireland

Dunmore East, Co. Waterford

Enjoy travelling through
Ireland's Timeless Beauty

In Ireland we've a unique way of welcoming our visitors, wishing them well and helping them on their way.

At Jet, this Irish welcome is only the beginning of a special relationship. As soon as you drive into a Jet service station you'll notice the difference:-

We offer you the highest quality petrols, including 95 and 98 Octane Unleaded and all at the lowest prices.

You'll find friendly, helpful service to smooth your way and while the Jet Customer Attendant seeing to your car, you c enjoy the convenience our Jet Shop.

Our Jet Shops are specio designed with the motorist's needs in mind. offer everything from snacks and magazines the best touring map in Ireland. All in a han one stop-shop.

This is all just part of our Jet Customer Co Programme. So enjoy yo motoring experience in Irela under Jet Customer Care.

JET ///
We care and it shows

Dunmore East

on which the village stands is divided by projecting headlands, broken into cliffs and coves.

To the north is Creadan Head and in the south the high promontory known as the 'Black Knob', beneath which is 'Merlin's Cave'. In the extreme south of the peninsula is Swines Head, and facing the village from the Wexford side of the harbour is the conspicuous Hook Head with its lighthouse. Early in the nineteenth century Dunmore was a station for the packets which carried the mails between England and the south of Ireland. It is noted today as a sea fishing and curing station, and there is excellent sea angling for visitors.

Tramore
Tra Mor (The Great Beach)

👪 Pop. 5,999.

ℹ Tourist information office (seasonal): Tel. (051) 81572.

Tramore, 8 miles (13 km) south of Waterford city, is one of Ireland's most popular seaside resorts. Situated on a hillside overlooking Tramore Bay, it has a fine promenade and a sandy bathing beach 3 miles (5 km) long.

Things to do
Apart from the beach, popular bathing places are the Pier, Guillameen Cove and Newtown Cove. There is golf (18) a mile (2 km) away, and two miniature courses nearer the town. Special facilities for children at Tramore include a 50-acre amusement park with a miniature railway, paddle steamer, boating lake, marina, adventure island, etc. There are good facilities for tennis, boating, surfing, wind surfing, sea angling and dancing, and Tramore Races are a popular event in the Irish sporting calendar, particularly the traditional festival meeting in August.

At Celtworld, the legends and myths of Celtic magic and mystery are brought to life with the aid of modern technology in this new and exciting entertainment.

Tramore

Walks to points of interest

1. Along the promenade and beach to the Burrows, a succession of sandhills about a mile (2 km) long to the east of the town.

2. Along the Doneraile walk to Doneraile Cliffs which run south from the town and border the bay on the west. There are grassy slopes down to the edge of the cliffs, from which there are fine views. The Metalman erected to warn shipping is further along the coast.

A little further west are two good beaches, Garrarus Strand and Kilfarasy Strand.

3. Along the Waterford road to the Metal Bridge, then to the left along the Glen road to Kilbride (church ruins, old castle and earthworks). Knockeen dolmen is a mile (2 km) to the north.

4. Fennor to Dunhill (castle and church ruins); near by are a dolmen and ogham stone.

Around Tramore

A small holiday resort with a good sandy beach is Annestown, 6 miles (10 km) west of Tramore on the Dungarvan road. The seventeenth-century Dunhill Castle, once a stronghold of the Power family, stands at the northern end of a narrow valley running from Annestown Bridge to Dunhill.

Five miles (8 km) west of Annestown is the little fishing village of Bunmahon. This has a fine sandy beach. On either arm of the bay jagged cliffs rise to nearly 200 feet, and there are also interesting rock formations. Near by at Gleann an Earbaill is the site of the first modern college of Irish, founded in 1835 by a pioneer of the Irish language revival, Philip Barron.

Also with a good sandy beach is Stradbally, 5 miles (8 km) west of Bunmahon. There are cliff walks and little sandy coves near by. The land adjoining the beach is a part of the Woodhouse demesne that is open to the public.

Dungarvan

Dun Garbhain (Garvan's Fort)

👪 Pop. 6,920 (urban district).

ℹ️ Tourist information office (seasonal): Tel. (058) 41741.

D ungarvan, administrative centre for the part of the county outside Waterford city, is situated on Dungarvan Harbour, with the Comeragh and Monavullagh Mountains to the north. A causeway and bridge across the River Colligan connect the town with its Abbeyside suburb. Dungarvan is a busy marketing centre and has a leather-processing works.

Things to do

Though the town itself has no beach, there is a good sandy beach on the Cunnigar Peninsula. The River Colligan has brown trout and occasional salmon and sea trout; there is sea angling in the bay and specially equipped boats are also available for shark and general deep sea angling. There is golf (9) near Clonea, 3 miles (5 km) to the east, and tennis courts in the town. West Waterford Foxhounds and the Dungarvan Harriers hunt the district. The Touraneena Heritage Centre, 9 miles (15 km) north of the town, features period domestic and farm appliances, including a restored blacksmith's forge.

History

A tribe called the Deise, from Meath, settled in this area in the third century, and eventually extended their sway over much of the county. The area is still known in Irish as 'na Deise' (the Decies). Dungarvan was formerly called Achadh Garbhain (Garvan's Field), after the seventh-century saint who founded a monastery here. During the Anglo-Norman invasion the town was an important port and military centre. During the wars of 1641 it was besieged several times; in 1649 the town surrendered to Cromwell, and the church and castle were destroyed.

Points of interest

Beside the river at the eastern side of the town are the remains of Dungarvan Castle, originally built by King John in 1185 though much altered at later periods. The massive circular keep is surrounded by fortified walls with an arched gateway; in the enclosure are the remains of a British military barracks. Some remains of the old town walls are to be seen in the Dead Walk. The Holed Gable, in the churchyard, is a curious structure perforated with a number of circular openings whose origin remains a mystery.

In Abbeyside are the well-preserved ruins of a thirteenth-century Augustinian priory. Its square tower, resting on groined arches, is now used as a belfry for the adjoining church. Below a window in the ruins is a tomb inscribed 'Donald McGrath, 1490'. Abbeyside Castle (or McGrath's Castle) is believed to date from the twelfth or thirteenth century; only the west wall remains.

Around Dungarvan

Three miles (5 km) east is the popular little resort of Clonea, with an excellent sandy beach and nearby golf (9). At the junction of the Clonmel and Cappoquin roads, 2½ miles (4 km) north-west of Dungarvan, stands a limestone monument commemorating the celebrated coursing greyhound Master McGrath, who won the Waterloo Cup three times between 1868 and 1871 and was beaten only once in a career of 37 courses.

North of Dungarvan via Ballymacarbry is the Nire Valley, which runs deep into the heart of the Comeragh Mountains. It is an area of unspoilt beauty and is noted for pony-trekking; guides are available for both novice and proficient riders.

Five miles (8 km) south of Dungarvan is Ring, an Irish-speaking village with a language college. On the road from Dungarvan and at Ring itself there are fine views of the coast and surrounding country. There is good safe bathing at sandy beaches

Ardmore

near by. A mile (2 km) from Ring is Bally-nagaul, an old-world village where Irish is still the everyday language. Its little harbour shelters the boats of the fishermen-farmers of the district. Further east is the more recent fishing harbour at Helvick Head, a remarkable promontory rising to 230 feet and providing good views. Mine Head, 6 miles (10 km) to the south, is another vantage point for coastal views.

Ardmore

Ard Mor (The Great Height)

Pop. 343.

Tourist information office (seasonal): Tel. (024) 94444.

Ardmore, on Ardmore Bay, is an attractive little resort with a long sandy beach and a language college. It is renowned for a fine group of ecclesiastical remains, on the site of a seventh-century settlement founded by St Declan.

Points of interest

St Declan's Oratory is a very small early church with high-pitched gables and a lintelled west door with inclined jambs. The upper parts of the side walls and gables are of modern reconstruction. In the south-east angle of the building is a grave ascribed by tradition to St Declan.

The Round Tower, 97 feet high, is one of the most perfect of its kind. Each of the four storeys is marked on the outside by projecting string courses and slight rebates. The round-headed door is high above ground level, while a unique feature of the interior are the projecting stones carved into grotesque heads.

The Cathedral includes work of various periods and styles from the tenth century to the fourteenth. It consists of nave and chancel, divided by a beautiful pointed arch supported by semi-columns with sculptured capitals. The lower levels of the north wall in both nave and chancel show some early work, of large irregular stones set with a small amount of mortar. On the inside of this wall are panels which were probably filled with frescoes. There is an altar tomb (fifteenth century) in each side wall of the nave, and a curious opening in the north wall of the chancel leads to a passage in the thickness of the wall. The most remarkable feature of the building, however, is the external arcading of the west gable—two rows, one above the other, of round-headed panels filled with sculptured figures like those on the ancient high crosses.

About a half-mile (1 km) east of the main group of ruins, standing close to the cliff edge, is Temple Disert. There is the west gable, south side wall and part of the east gable of a large church. The eastern part appears to be of much later date (possibly fourteenth century) than the western end. There is a rude west window and a flat-headed south door with a curious keystone and a relieving arch.

A short distance west of Temple Disert is St Declan's Holy Well, and on the beach beneath the village is the glacial boulder called St Declan's Stone.

Around Ardmore

There are many pleasant walks, both inland and along the fine cliffs. A favourite excursion is to Monatrea, a picturesque spot 5 miles (8 km) to the west; it has a good bathing beach.

Cappoquin

Ceapach Chuinn (Conn's Plot of Land)

 Pop. 920.

This quiet market town lies beneath the southern slopes of the Knockmealdown Mountains and at the head of the tidal River Blackwater estuary. The surrounding country is well wooded and very beautiful, especially along the

Blackwater valley westwards to Fermoy (County Cork).

Things to do

There is good fishing for sea and brown trout in the Blackwater estuary at Cappoquin, and brown trout fishing on tributary streams. Cappoquin is also one of the best coarse fishing centres in the country, and holds a number of Irish records for roach and dace. Boating on the Blackwater is popular, and the West Waterford Foxhounds and the Dungarvan Harriers hunt the district.

Two miles (3 km) south of Cappoquin, Affane on the east side of the Blackwater was the birthplace of Valentine Greatrakes (1629–1683). Called 'the Stroker', he gained a great reputation for curing disease by stroking the parts affected. While on a visit to England, Greatrakes treated many people there and was invited to Whitehall Palace by Charles II. His grave in the Church of Ireland cemetery at Affane is on the right of the path leading to the church door.

Many picturesque houses overlook the Blackwater, including Dromana House which stands in an extensive demesne 4 miles (6 km) south of Cappoquin, on the east bank. The mansion is on the site of Dromana Castle, and there are some slight remains of that ancient seat of the Fitzgeralds of the Decies. This property passed by marriage in the seventeenth century to the Villiers family (later Villiers-Stuart). Henry Villiers-Stuart, himself a Protestant, was the candidate of the Catholics in the famous County Waterford election of 1826, and his victory paved the way for the Catholic Emancipation Act of 1829. South of the demesne is the neat village of Villierstown.

About 7 miles (11 km) south of Cappoquin the River Blackwater is joined by its tributary the River Bride, and the valleys of both form a delightful region to explore. Other places of interest on this stretch of the river are mentioned under Youghal, County Cork.

Three miles (5 km) north of Cappoquin, in the foothills of the Knockmealdown Mountains, is Mount Melleray Abbey, founded by the Cistercians in 1831 when they were expelled from Brittany. This hallowed, beautiful and peaceful spot is visited by thousands every year.

Lismore
Lios Mor Mochuda
(Mochuda's Great Enclosure)

Pop. 703.

Tourist information office (seasonal): Community Office. Tel. (058) 54855.

Lismore is on the south bank of the Blackwater, 4 miles (6 km) from Cappoquin. There is salmon, sea and brown trout fishing, though permits are required from the secretary of the Lismore estate. Golf (9).

The Lismore Heritage Centre in the Town Hall provides an entertaining cinematic presentation of the history of Lismore and the area around it, during the season.

History
In the seventh century St Carthach founded a monastery here that became one of the renowned universities of Europe. It reached the zenith of its fame in the eighth century under the direction of St Colman, when there were 20 sites of religion or learning within the monastic city. During the Danish incursions the city was often plundered, and in the eleventh and twelfth centuries it was destroyed four times by fire. Henry II marched to Lismore from Waterford to receive here the submission of many Leinster and Munster chiefs. The monastic city was finally destroyed by Raymond le Gros in 1173.

Points of interest
Incorporating the fabric of one of the early churches is the Protestant Cathedral, which has many inscribed slabs and curious figures within its walls. The modern Catholic Cathedral, dedicated to St Carthach, is in Romanesque style and has a beautiful altar and campanile. St Carthach's Holy Well is in the private grounds near Lismore Castle, but the enclosure it is in is open to the public each year on the Pattern Day (14 May). Standing majestically on a cliff overhanging the Blackwater is Lismore Castle, built by King John in 1185 and believed to occupy the site of St Carthach's monastery. The castle was much extended in later centuries, and became the episcopal residence until it was granted to Sir Walter Raleigh by Myler Magrath. In 1602 it passed to Richard Boyle, whose son Robert, the celebrated chemist whose name lives in 'Boyle's law', was born in the castle. In 1753 the estate became the property of the Duke of Devonshire. The castle gardens are open to the public from May to September.

Around Lismore
Five miles (8 km) south of Lismore is the quiet little town of Tallow, on the Glenaboy River near where that stream joins the

Lismore Castle

River Bride. In the seventeenth and eighteenth centuries this was a busy place with several thriving industries. The sculptor John Hogan (1800–1858) was born here. Tallow Hill (592 feet), less than a mile (2 km) north-east, has fine views. A half-mile (1 km) west of Tallowbridge village is the ruined keep of Lisfinny Castle, an ancient fortress of the Fitzgeralds.

Six miles (10 km) west of Lismore is Ballyduff, a quiet village on the Blackwater. Two miles (3 km) to the west of it, in the demesne of Mocollop House, are the ruins of another Fitzgerald stronghold—Mocollop Castle.

Among the tours that can be made from Lismore are:

1. The Blackwater valley to Youghal.

2. The valleys of the Blackwater and the Bride through beautiful country via Ballyduff to Fermoy returning by Castle-lyons (abbey ruins), Conna (old castle), Tallow and Tallowbridge.

3. The 'Vee' road across the Knock-mealdowns, Mitchelstown caves, and the picturesque Araglin valley.

Galway

Eyre Square

Galway is a large county divided into two contrasting regions by the expanse of Lough Corrib. To the west, lying between the lake and the Atlantic, is Connemara—a region of superb scenic grandeur dominated by the rocky mountain range known as the Twelve Bens. Connemara has inspired many famous paintings, and a tour of the district is a memorable experience. A great many of the inhabitants are Irish speakers, and much of the ancient Gaelic culture is preserved. The sturdy Connemara pony is particularly prevalent in the coastal area west from Spiddal and in the district lying between Oughterard and Clifden; the Connemara Pony Show is a popular annual event. East of Lough Corrib, a fertile limestone plain extends to the Galway-Roscommon border and the River Shannon. Galway city with its seaside suburb of Salthill lies south of the lake. It is an important tourist centre and a gateway to the scenic areas of the county.

Galway City and Salthill

Gaillimh (Gailleamh's Place)

Pop. 50, 842 (Galway *city* CSO 1991 figures).

Tourist information office: Victoria Place, Eyre Square, Galway. Tel. (091) 63081. Fax (091) 65201.

High Street, Galway city

Galway Airport (seasonal):
Tel. (091) 55252.
Salthill (seasonal): Tel. (091) 63081.

American Express:
John Ryan Travel, 1 Williamsgate St,
Galway. Tel. (091) 67375/6/7.
Fax (091) 63674.

Post Office: Eglinton St, Galway.
Tel. (091) 62052. Open 9.00 – 18.00.

Parking Regulations: Disc parking.

Railway Station/Bus Depot:
Ceannt Station, Galway.
Tel. (091) 64222 (train).
Tel. (091) 63555 (bus).

Car Hire: Avis Rent a Car,
Galway Airport. Tel. (091) 68901.

Budget Rent a Car, Ballygar, Co. Galway.
Tel. (0903) 24668.
Tel. (091) 66376 (Galway Airport).

Capitol Car Hire. Tel. (091) 65296.
Galway Airport: (091) 52028.

Johnson & Perrott Ltd, Higgins Garage,
Headford Rd, Galway. Tel. (091) 68886.

Bicycle Hire: Europa Bicycles,
Hinter's Building, Earl's Island, Galway.
Tel. (091) 63355. Fax (091) 63355.

Round the Corner Bicycle Hire, Queen St,
Galway. Tel. (091) 66606.

Dates of principal cultural
events/festivals: Galway Races (August
bank holiday weekend), Galway Oyster
Festival (September).

Galway is situated near the head of
a large bay, and is the principal
city of Connacht. The streets and
buildings of this ancient town have many
interesting features, and its position on the
fringe of the western Gaeltacht (Irish-
speaking area) makes it the obvious gateway to Connemara, an entrancing countryside where the ancient language and
customs of Ireland are preserved.

Galway Hooker off Inishbofin

Things to do

Sea angling and shark fishing, sailing, surfing, tennis, greyhound racing and horse-riding. Rowing boats may be hired for trips on the River Corrib, and on Lough Corrib a water bus provides daily trips during summer. Day and half-day tours to nearby scenic areas are available. The celebrated Galway Races, a five-day festival meeting at the end of July or beginning of August, attract racegoers from all over Ireland and Britain, while the Galway Oyster Festival also draws many visitors; the city is *en fête* for a whole week at these times.

An impressive ceremony is the annual Blessing of the Sea, which takes place at the beginning of the herring season. Another sight which enthrals visitors to Galway may be seen—in season—from the Salmon Weir bridge over the River Corrib. The waters of Lough Corrib plunge over the weir in a sheet of flashing foam, and just below the weir hundreds of salmon are clearly visible on the bed of the river waiting to leap upriver. The short Corrib River, which gives the salmon their only access to the 68 square miles of the lake, is a famous fishing water.

Salthill, the seaside suburb of Galway, stretches west from the city along the shore of Galway Bay; it is one of Ireland's leading resorts. There is good bathing, golf (18), tennis, dancing, sailing, amusements, band concerts and other attractions; the Leisureland entertainment complex provides a wide range of all-weather activities.

Galway became the centre of Irish language theatre with the founding of An Taibhdhearc in 1928.

Regular ferry services operate to the Aran Islands from Rossaveal, Doolin and Spiddal. There is also an air service to all three islands from Galway airport.

History

A town existed here from the earliest times, and may have been the city of Magnata mentioned by Ptolemy. According to the *Annals of the Four Masters* (1632–1636), a fort was erected here in 1124 by the Connachtmen. From 1232, when Richard de Burgh took the city and made it his residence, Galway became a flourishing Anglo-Norman colony. Among its settlers were the families who were later known as the '14 Tribes of Galway'—the Blakes, Bodkins, Brownes, D'Arcys, ffrenches, Kirwans, Joyces, Lynches, Morrisses, Martins, Skerrets, Athys, Deans and Ffonts.

The settlers guarded themselves against intercourse with the native Irish, and a by-law of 1518 ordered 'that neither O nor Mac shall strutte ne swagger thro' the streets of Galway'. The native clans, however, made many successful raids on the city, a practice reflected in the inscription which was once to be seen over the west gate: 'From the fury of the O'Flahertys, good Lord deliver us.'

Galway's first charter was granted by Richard II in 1484, an event which was celebrated by a Quincentennial year in 1984. A fountain was erected to mark this special year in Galway's history. In 1651 the city surrendered, after a siege, to Parliamentary forces under Sir Charles Coote; again in 1691 the city surrendered to Williamite troops under General Ginkel.

The city was long celebrated as an educational centre, and in the sixteenth century it had the most renowned classical school in the country. For centuries, too, Galway traded extensively with Spain and the town acquired some Spanish features, notably in the architecture and in the dress and manners of the people.

Points of interest

In Eyre Square is the Ó Conaire monument, sculptured by Albert Power, R.H.A.; Padraic Ó Conaire was a great Gaelic writer of the early twentieth century. Also in Eyre Square is the Browne Doorway, a relic of Spanish architectural influence, and at the north corner is a memorial to the 1916 patriot Liam Mellows. The square itself is landscaped as a memorial garden to US President John F. Kennedy.

In Lombard Street the Church of St Nicholas, founded by the Normans in 1320, is remarkable for its unique triple nave. Columbus is said to have prayed here before setting out for America, a tradition supported by the fact that a Galway man named Rice de Culvy accompanied him on his great voyage. Near the church is the site of the Old Jail, of which a window and a closed-up Gothic door remain. Set in the wall is a death's head and cross-bones in black marble, erected in 1624, with the inscription: 'This memorial of the stern and unbending justice of the chief magistrate of this City, James Lynch Fitzstephen, elected mayor A.D. 1493, who condemned and executed his own guilty son, Walter, on this spot.'

At the corner of Shop Street is Lynch's Castle, a fine old mansion (1320) which was the residence of the Lynch family; it is now a bank. Near the Fish Market is the Spanish Arch, which leads on to Spanish Parade. This space was once a favourite promenade of the Spanish merchants and their families. Close by is the Claddagh, said to be the oldest fishing village in Ireland. In the days when Galway was a Norman town, this section was where the Irish lived. Famous for its Claddagh ring of two hands clasping a heart, it had at one time a population of 8,000. The old thatched cottages have now been replaced by modern houses.

The University College, founded in 1845, is a Tudor-Gothic building beautifully situated outside the city, close to the banks of the River Corrib. In the college library are the minutes of Galway Corporation from 1485 to 1818, a map of the city in 1640, and many rare books. The college is a centre of Gaelic culture and many of its students are native Irish speakers who take their degrees in Irish. Summer courses in the English language are held for foreign students from June to September.

Situated off Market Street, in Bowling Green, is the home of Nora Barnacle, wife of James Joyce. A memorial plaque was unveiled on the building in 1982, the 100th anniversary of Joyce's birth. The house is open to the public.

Around Galway

West from Galway city the road lies close to the shore of Galway Bay, passing through Salthill to Barna, a picturesque little spot with an excellent bathing beach, namely, the Silver Strand. Spiddal, in the heart of an Irish-speaking district, is a charming little holiday resort with a fine sandy beach. Bathing, boating and shore fishing are attractions.

The route continues through Inverin, where Connemara marble is processed commercially; and runs north-west to Costelloe, site of the national headquarters of the radio service for Irish-speaking areas. The coastline here is greatly indented and fringed by numerous islands, while inland lies an extraordinary maze of rocks, lakes, moors and sandy beaches. Beyond Costelloe a road on the left leads to Carraroe, which stands on the peninsula between Cashla Bay and Greatman's Bay. At the mouth of Kilkieran Bay are Lettermore and

Lynch's Castle, Galway city

Galway

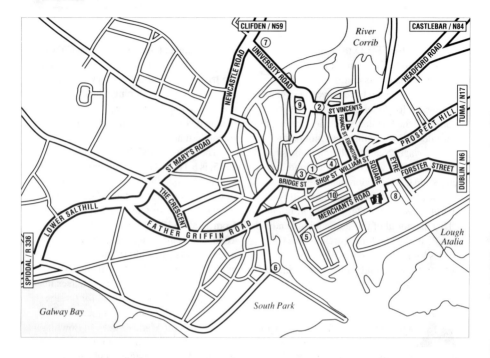

1. Market Street
2. Salmon Weir Bridge
3. St Nicholas Church
4. Lynch's Castle
5. Spanish Arch

6. The Claddagh
7. University College Galway
8. Ceannt Station
9. Catholic Cathedral
10. An Taibhdhearc Theatre

Gorumna Islands, which are connected to the mainland by bridges.

The Aran Islands

Oileain Arann (Islands of Ara)

👪 Pop. Inishmore 848, Inishmaan 236, Inisheer 255.

ℹ️ Tourist information office (seasonal): Kilronan. Tel. (099) 61263.

Thirty miles (48 km) out to sea from Galway lie the three Aran Islands, home of the sturdy fisherfolk immortalised by the playwright J. M. Synge in *Riders to the Sea* and *The Aran Islands*. The life of this remarkable community has also been portrayed in the film 'Man of Aran'.

The three islands—Inishmore (7,635 acres), Inishmaan (2,252 acres) and Inisheer (1,400 acres)—are rugged and barren. Through unremitting toil the islanders have made soil from sand and seaweed to provide sustenance for their livestock. From these meagre acres and the surrounding sea they wrest their livelihood. Some fishermen still use currachs, boats made of laths and tarred canvas.

The everyday language of the islanders is Irish, and their songs and stories enshrine much of Ireland's folklore and culture. They used to spin and weave their own clothing; almost every man wore a bainin (a white homespun coat of great durability), and many wore the variegated woollen belt called a crios. For footgear they used the pampootie, a hide shoe without a heel.

Apart from their great interest for the traveller and the antiquarian, the islands offer a fascinating holiday. There is excellent bathing and interesting walks. Kilronan, on Inishmore, is the main town of the islands and the terminus of the boat service from the mainland.

Points of interest

The antiquities of Aran include several ancient stone forts and a great number of Early Christian churches and other monuments. Most impressive of the stone forts is the great Dun Aengus on Inishmore. It is semicircular, resting on the edge of a perpendicular cliff rising 300 feet out of the ocean. Dun Aengus may originally have been fully circular, the other half having fallen into the waters below as the cliff-face eroded. The fort now consists of an inner court 150 feet across, surrounded by a wall 20 feet high and 18 feet thick at the base. This great wall has three walls built against each other, the innermost one being about 8 feet high, the middle one about 14 feet, and the outer 20 feet. Outside is another rampart with its accompanying *chevaux de frise*, a defence formed by sharp-pointed stones set closely together. Surrounding this is yet another rampart of which little remains. The outer fortification encloses an area of 11 acres.

Other forts: Dun Eoghanacht, near Kilronan, is built on a ridge overlooking Templebrecan. Near the village of Oghil is Dun Oghil, a small but excellently preserved fort. Dubhchathair, on the southern cliffs of Inishmore, 2 miles (3 km) west of Killeany, may be the oldest of the Aran forts. On Inishmaan, crowning the highest point of the island, is the finest specimen of a stone fort remaining in Ireland—Dun Conor. Cathair na mBan is on Inisheer. The only perfect clochan (ancient stone dwelling) is Clochan na Carraige on Inishmore.

Many early Christian hermits settled on the islands, and the sites of several churches may be distinguished. Teampall Breachain (the Church of St Brecan) on Inishmore dates from the ninth century; Teampall Mhic Duach at Kilmurvey is another early structure. Nearer Kilronan is Teampall an Cheathrair Alainn, 'the Church of the Heavenly Four'—Saints Fursey, Conall, Berchan and Brendan of Birr. Teampall Chiarain, the monastery of St Ciaran, is about half-way between Oghil and

Kilronan. Teaghlach Einne, the house of St Enda, is near Killeany village; this was the most important of the island's religious settlements, but most traces of the churches have disappeared under drifting sands. Also at Killeany is the primitive church, Teampall Bheanain (this saint was a contemporary of St Patrick, and his successor at Armagh). The church is one of the smallest in the world: 10¾ feet by 7 feet.

Among the antiquities of Inishmaan is the little early oratory of Cill Cheannannagh. Inisheer has two ancient churches and some remains of Teampall na Seacht n-Inghean ('the Church of the Seven Daughters').

Lough Corrib

Lough Corrib is drained by the short River Corrib on which Galway city is built. With a length of 27 miles (43 km) and a width of up to 7 miles (11 km) the lake covers 68 square miles: it is of very irregular outline, narrowing at one point to a little strait which connects the northern and southern

parts. In the north-west a long arm of the lake runs up to Maam, between the hills of the Joyce Country. Dotted with numerous islands, Lough Corrib is mostly shallow, but soundings of 150 feet have been taken at the northern end. The lake provides excellent fishing for salmon, trout, pike, perch and eels; mayfly fishing for trout is particularly good. Annaghdown, Cong, Cornamona, Clonbur and Oughterard are ideal centres for this lake, as is Greenfield on the east shore near Headford.

Two miles (3 km) up the Corrib River from Galway (on the right) is the ruin of Menlough Castle, an ivy-covered castellated mansion on the river bank. From Menlough a canal leads to the lake. Close to the south-eastern shore, a mile (2 km) further north, are the marble quarries of Anglihan, which yield a fine-quality black stone.

North-west of the lake are the hills of the Joyce Country, backed by the summits of the Partry range. The high ground along

Lough Corrib

the west shore contrasts with the flat fertile tract on the east side. At Annaghdown, close to the east shore, about 5 miles (8 km) from the southern end of the lake, are the ruins of a castle and an ancient church, once the seat of a bishopric founded by the O'Flahertys on the site of a monastery where St Brendan the Navigator is said to have died. A popular family trip in summer is to travel by waterbus from Woodquay, Galway, to Annaghdown pier.

A few miles north-west, in the narrow part of the lake where the shores are only a half-mile (1 km) apart, is the ferry of Kilbeg (or Knock). Further north, on the right, is Annaghkeen Castle, while close to Oughterard on the opposite shore may be seen the tower of Aughnanure Castle, a stronghold of the O'Flahertys. The castle has been restored and is now open to the public. The lake now expands, and there are delightful views towards Maam which include the summits of the Maamturk and Partry Mountains.

This part of the lake is studded with islands, the most notable being Inchiquin, Inishdoorus and Inchagoill. The last named of these may be reached in a hired boat from Oughterard, Cong or Galway; there are interesting ecclesiastical remains on the island, including a small ancient church called Templepatrick. It has a nave measuring 18 feet by 12 feet, and a simple doorway with inclined jambs and a lintel. The second and later church, Teampall na Naomh, consists of a nave and chancel and is an interesting example of Hiberno-Romanesque: the doorway has three recessed arches, the outer ornamented by a series of sculptured heads and the centre by a chevron band.

Touring from Maam Cross

As a glance at the map will show, Maam Cross is a meeting point of several of the roads that traverse the different parts of Connemara.

The route from Oughterard to Maam Cross (10 miles/16 km) lies through coun-tryside that presents an amazing variety of bog, moorland, lake and mountain scenery. Southward from the cross a road runs through lake-strewn moorland to Screeb Lodge and Gortmore. At Gortmore the road on the left leads to Rosmuc, where the author and 1916 leader Padraic Pearse studied the Irish language (his cottage here is open to the public).

Pearse's cottage, Rosmuc

Beyond Gortmore the route follows the shore of Kilkieran Bay to Carna, situated on one of the many creeks which indent this wild coastline. Carna offers sea angling and excellent fishing for sea trout, and for brown trout in the neighbouring lakes. In Lough Skannive there are two islands closely resembling crannogs (fortified lake-dwellings). Off the coast near Carna is the small St MacDara's island, where there is a beautiful stone-roofed oratory. Boatmen passing this island dip their sails three times in honour of the saint. A three-day festival, Feile Mhic Dara, is held every July in Carna. It features currach and hooker (traditional rowing and sailing craft) racing, also sea angling competitions, art and craft exhibitions and Irish dancing.

On the journey from Maam Cross to Recess (8 miles/13 km) is some of the best scenery in Connemara. The road skirts the shores of Lough Shindilla and Lough Oorid, with the Maamturk peaks on the right and the Twelve Bens looming majestically ahead. This latter group of mountains, the dominant feature of the Connemara landscape, occupies a circular area 6 miles (10 km) across; on the south and east they are bounded by a chain of lakes. The most prominent peaks are Benbaun (2,395 feet), Bencorr (2,336 feet), Bencollaghduff (2,290 feet), Benbreen (2,276 feet), Derryclare (2,220 feet), Bengower (2,184 feet), and Muckanaght (2,153 feet). Their conical form is the most striking feature; the precipitous slopes are beautifully coloured by lichens and mosses.

Recess, set among superb lake and mountain scenery, is one of the choicest beauty spots of Connemara. On one side is Glendalough Lake and on the other Derryclare Lough. North of Derryclare, Lough Inagh stretches along the glaciated valley of Glen Inagh, separating the Twelve Bens from the Maamturk Mountains. Recess is a well-known angling resort and has green marble quarries.

The road from Recess to Clifden runs beneath the shadow of the Twelve Bens and along the shore of Ballynahinch Lake. The lake has some wooded islands and on one of them is a ruined stronghold of the O'Flahertys. On the southern shore is Ballynahinch Castle, now a hotel, and long the residence of the family whose fortunes

Roundstone

are depicted in Charles Lever's novel, *The Martins of Cro Martin*. A member of this family was the philanthropic 'Humanity Dick' Martin, founder of the Royal Society for the Prevention of Cruelty to Animals. The area is noted for the excellence of its salmon and sea trout fishing.

From Recess a road on the left runs to Cashel, another good angling centre, at the head of Bertraghboy Bay. Near Toombeola are some remains of a fifteenth-century Dominican abbey founded by the O'Flahertys. From here the road runs south, with fine coastal views, to the quiet little resort of Roundstone. Around here the naturalist will find much to study, including the beautiful foraminiferous beach at Dog's Bay.

At the Franciscan monastery, there is a small bodhrán making industry. The bodhrán is an 18 inch one-sided drum made from goatskin treated by a traditional process.

Behind Roundstone rises Urrisbeg (987 feet), worth climbing for the view of the lake-dotted country to the north and the fine seascape in other directions. On the slopes of Urrisbeg are some unusual plants, including *Erica Mediterranea*. Another

Ballynahinch

rare heath, *Erica Mackaiana*, is found a few miles away on the shores of Craggamore Lake. On the shore of Mannin Bay, on the way from Roundstone to Clifden, is a coral strand composed of myriad bleached fragments of corallines interspersed with smooth rocks.

Clifden

An Clochan (The Stepping-Stones)

Pop. 896.

Tourist information office (seasonal): Tel. (095) 21163.

Clifden

The main town of Connemara, Clifden is an ideal centre for exploring the glorious scenery of the region. The town nestles on the edge of the Atlantic with a superb background of mountains. There is excellent bathing within about a mile (2 km) from the town; boating, riding, game and sea fishing, are available, and there is an 18-hole golf links southwards at Aillebrack near Ballyconneely about 8 miles (13 km) from Clifden. Clifden is the centre of Connemara pony breeding and the annual Connemara Pony Show in August is very well known.

Walks and points of interest

1. Walk by Quay Road to beach through castle grounds (marine view), returning by Cloghanard (3 miles/5 km).

2. Leave town by bridge east of waterfall and climb hill; fine view of lake, sea and moor at Dooneen, and even more spectacular one from the top of Cnoc Athy (400 feet). Continue walk to join main Clifden–Galway road (4 miles/6 km).

3. Walk by Sky Road and Cloghanard, keep left past the castle by Belleek to the beaches at Eyrephort; return Scardaun. This walk provides a magnificent view of sea, rugged coastline and islands. From Scardaun Hill (500 feet) range after range of mountains are seen to the east (8 miles/ 13 km).

4. Leave Clifden by Ardbear road. A worthwhile sight in the season is at Weir bridge, where vast numbers of salmon stand against the current. Keep right at Errislannan and Boat Harbour beaches, and return by northern shores of Mannin Bay to Derrygimla. On return journey, a road to the right leads to Lough Fadda, a haunt of wild birds; close by are the remains of the first Marconi transatlantic wireless station. The airmen to make the first non-stop Atlantic flight, Alcock and Brown, landed here in 1919; a memorial near by records this historic event (10 miles/16 km).

5. Walk by Streamstown to Claddaghduff, including at Streamstown a visit to the Connemara marble quarries. Near the water's edge at Doon is the ruined Doon Castle. Keep left at Fountain Hill to the beaches, and then continue along the coast to the beaches at Omey. Interesting ruins at Omey are the seventh-century college and church of St Fechin. Return by Claddaghduff Road (18 miles/29 km).

Further afield from Clifden, 7 miles (11 km) to the north-west, the little fishing village of Cleggan is the gateway to Inishbofin and its neighbouring islands. Inishbofin is ideal for an interesting out-of-doors holiday: its attractions include remarkable cliff scenery, good beaches, sailing, sea angling, and much of interest to antiquarians, geologists and naturalists.

The road from Clifden to Letterfrack (9 miles/14 km) first runs north through a

Near Moyard

good bathing, mountain climbing and hill walking, and the village is an angling centre for the streams and loughs of the neighbourhood. Short-distance gravelled walks have been laid leading from Letterfrack to Diamond Hill (1,460 feet) giving superb views of sea, mountain and lake *en route*. This area is now part of the Connemara National Park covering almost 4,000 acres. A visitor centre is open throughout the year depicting various features of the park.

North-west of Letterfrack is Tully Cross and Renvyle, where the coast scenery is unrivalled: almost the whole northern shore of the Renvyle Peninsula and the coast eastwards to the Little Killary is fringed with beautiful sandy beaches. A superb coast drive is to Salruck and Lough Fee. Salruck has lovely views of the Killaries—the little and greater bays—and of the mountains rising sharply from the shores. There is a rent-an-Irish-cottage scheme in Tully Cross.

The road north-west from Letterfrack passes the foot of Diamond Hill and

shallow valley, then east to the pretty village of Moyard where there is a good view over the landlocked Ballinakill Harbour. Letterfrack is a quiet village in beautiful surroundings, with fuchsia hedges demonstrating its mild climate; there is

Connemara National Park, Letterfrack

Near Leenane

crosses the Dawros River to enter the beautiful Pass of Kylemore. Here are the three Kylemore lakes, all famous angling waters, and above them the nineteenth-century castellated mansion Kylemore Abbey, now a girls' school run by the Irish Benedictine Dames. The nuns also run a pottery and restaurant.

Keeping on, the Maamturk mountain range soon comes into view, and Lough Fee is seen to the left after Lough Nacarrigeen. The road then begins to follow the southern shore of Killary Harbour, a magnificent fjord-like arm of the sea which runs inland between steep mountains for about 10 miles (16 km). Particularly striking are the enormous walls of Mweelrea (2,688 feet) and the huge form of Bengorm (2,303 feet) rising from the farther shore.

Near the head of the Killary is the village of Leenane, an angling resort and an excellent centre for the mountain climber. North 2½ miles (4 km) from Leenane, in County Mayo, is Ashleagh

Waterfall. The Joyce Country, an area extending east from Leenane, to Lough Corrib and Lough Mask, takes its name from the Joyces who settled there in the thirteenth century and whose name is still common in the district. Much of its delightful scenery can be enjoyed in this itinerary: Leenane–Lough Nafooey–Finny– shore of Lough Mask–Clonbur–Cong– shore of Lough Corrib–Cornamona–Maam– Maam valley–Leenane (50 miles/81 km). From Maam the return journey may be varied by taking the route via Maam Cross–Recess–Glen Inagh–Leenane; this adds 25 miles (40 km) to the round trip.

Tuam

Tuaim (A Burial-Place)

👪 Pop. 4,109.

ℹ️ Tourist information office (seasonal): Mill Museum. Tel. (093) 24463.

Tuam, the chief town in the northern part of this region, originated in the sixth-century religious settlement founded by St Jarlath. Tuam is a convenient angling centre, and has a golf course (18), pitch and putt and tennis.

Points of interest
The twelfth-century St Mary's Cathedral (Church of Ireland) has been largely rebuilt, and only the chancel remains of the ancient structure; the chancel arch is a magnificent specimen of Norman architecture. The Cross of Tuam is in the Market Square; its base carries inscriptions in memory of O'Hoisin (a twelfth-century abbot of Tuam) and of Turlough O'Connor, King of Connacht.

Around Tuam
Two miles (3 km) north is Bermingham House, headquarters of the Bermingham and North Galway hunt, a Georgian residence whose interior has fine plasterwork and furniture; it is open to visitors on weekday afternoons. The district west of Tuam towards Cong and south Mayo is the site of the Battle of Southern Moytura, fought between the legendary Tuatha De Danann and the Firbolgs about 1000 B.C. This may account for the large number of sepulchral tumuli and stone circles which have been discovered in the region.

The Mill Museum in Shop Street is an operational corn mill and mill wheel forming with related exhibits the first industrial museum in the west.

Twelve miles (19 km) south-west of Tuam on the Galway road is the village of Claregalway, near which are the ruins of a Franciscan abbey built by John de Cogan in 1290. It was one of the most beautiful of its kind in the country. The church consists of nave, choir, north aisle and transept, surmounted by a graceful tower, of which parts remain in good state of preservation. The arches under the tower are particularly beautiful, as are the windows and arcades. The old castle near by, with its massive square tower, was built by the de Burghs.

Seven miles (11 km) south-east of Tuam is the ruined Abbey of Knockmoy (Cistercian), beautifully situated on a small lake. It was founded in 1189 by Cathal O'Connor, King of Connacht, whose tomb is preserved within the ruins.

Ballinasloe
Beal Atha na Sluagh
(The Ford-Mouth of the Hosts)

Pop. 5,793 (urban district).

Tourist information office (seasonal): Tel. (0905) 42131.

This was an important place in ancient times. Today it is a thriving marketing town, famous for its horse, cattle and sheep fairs—especially the great October Fair. The castle here bears witness to the former military importance of the town. There is tennis and golf (18) about 2 miles (3 km) away and the town is a noted centre for coarse angling.

Around Ballinasloe
At Clontuskert, 3½ miles (6 km) to the south, is a ruined Augustinian abbey built around the fifteenth century on the site of an early monastery; ancient inscriptions are still legible on the tombstones within its precincts, and near by is a holy well. Seven miles (11 km) from Ballinasloe on the Athenry road is the ruined Franciscan Abbey of Kilconnell, founded in 1400 by Liam O'Kelly. The nave, choir, side aisles, south transept, and some of the cloisters and domestic apartments, are perfect. A slender tower rises gracefully from the intersection. This is Gothic architecture of a high order, an interesting feature being the number of inscriptions and coats of arms that decorate the stonework.

Tourist information office (seasonal): Tel. (0905) 73939.

About 2 miles (3 km) south-east from Kilconnell is Aughrim village, near which in 1691 was fought the Battle of Aughrim between the armies of James II and William—the Irish supporting James under General St Ruth (who was killed in the battle) and the English under General Ginkel. Aughrim museum contains many mementos of the famous battle, ancient household utensils, stone axes and archaeological 'finds' from the district.

Close to the banks of the Shannon, 13 miles (21 km) south-east of Ballinasloe, is Clonfert, where a monastic settlement was founded originally by St Brendan the Navigator in 563. The doorway of the present church is an outstanding example of Hiberno-Romanesque decoration, featuring an amazing variety of motifs, foliage, animal heads and human heads.

In the south-eastern end of the county, 20 miles (32 km) from Ballinasloe, Portumna is well known as a fishing centre and marina for Lough Derg and the Shannon and has golf (9) and tennis. Outside the town are the imposing ruins of Portumna Castle.

Clonfert Cathedral

Portumna Forest Park is one mile (2 km) from the town on the Ennis road. This wildlife sanctuary of one thousand acres borders Lough Derg and has a laid-out nature trail and many lovely forest walks.

Loughrea

Baile Locha Riach (Grey Lough Town)

Pop. 3,360.

Loughrea is a pleasant market town prettily situated on the northern shore of the small Lough Rea. De Burgh, realising the strategic importance of the site, built a castle here about 1300; he also endowed a Carmelite priory, of which some remains may be seen near the town centre. Near the cathedral, by the lakeshore, is the restored south-east gate, which houses a diocesan museum. The cathedral itself has outstanding examples of stained glass by Michael Healy, Evie Hone and other Irish artists. There is golf (9), tennis, boating, sailing and fishing on Lough Rea. The famous Galway Blazers hunt this area.

Around Loughrea

Many crannogs (ancient stockaded islands) have been discovered on the lake, and souterrains are a common feature of the surrounding countryside. East of the town, on Monument Hill, there is an ancient stone circle, and at Bullaun (3½ miles/ 6 km) is the well-known Turoe Stone. The sculpturing on this stone is an excellent example of La Tène art and is believed to date from before the first century B.C. Excavations at the nearby ring-fort of Feerwore (beside which the Turoe Stone once stood) have revealed much evidence of habitation between 100 B.C. and A.D. 100.

North-west 12 miles (19 km) from Loughrea is Athenry. The Dominican priory founded here in 1241 was an important house of the Order; in 1644 it had a brief revival as a university, but the buildings were soon to be destroyed by the Cromwellians. Interesting features are the rows of lancet windows in the nave and choir, the tomb recesses, the mural tablet in Latin, French and English (1682), and the large tomb of Lady M. Bermingham (1779) which occupies the centre of the chancel; the north transept has a beautiful arcade with trefoil-headed niches. Other points of interest at Athenry are the castle (1238), the market cross and part of the old town walls.

Between Athenry and Galway city is the pleasant town of Oranmore, at the head of a creek that forms part of Galway Bay. The castle was built by the Earl of Clanricarde. The Galway Bay Sailing Club is situated here at Renville with boats for hire and tuition given.

One of the largest ancient stone forts in south Galway is Caherdrineen, 2½ miles (4 km) south-east of Oranmore. The road from Oranmore to Gort passes through Clarinbridge, venue of the annual Galway oyster festival in September, and Ardrahan village, where there are remains of a round tower and a church. West of Ardrahan is the seaport village of Kinvara, near which Dunguaire Castle offers a nightly medieval banquet, music and entertainment to visitors in the season.

Gort, 15 miles (24 km) south-east of Loughrea, in the southern part of the county, was the residence of a seventh-century King of Connacht, Guaire; the foundations of his palace may still be traced. Many of the streams around Gort run into caves in the limestone—of particular note is the Beagh River, which flows from Lough Cutra and runs in and out of the rock in several places.

About 2 miles (3 km) south of Gort is the Lough Cutra demesne, while to the north of the town is Coole Park, once the residence of one of the Abbey Theatre's founders, Lady Gregory. Coole was a rendezvous of many famous Irish writers and several of W. B. Yeats's poems evoke its woods and lakes. The demesne is now a national forest and wild life park and open daily. It includes a very famous tree called the 'Autograph Tree' which bears the initials of such famous visitors to Coole House as George Bernard Shaw, Sean O'Casey, Oliver Gogarty, John Masefield, Augustus John and Douglas Hyde, the first President of Ireland.

i Tourist information office (seasonal): Tel. (091) 31436.

Four miles (6 km) north-east of Gort is Ballylee Castle. Yeats bought this tower, Thoor Ballylee, and spent summers there in the early 1920s. It was restored in 1956 and is open daily to visitors from May to September. An audio-visual presentation traces the history of the tower and the Yeats connection.

About 3 miles (5 km) south-west of Gort are the round tower and cathedral of Kilmacduagh. The cathedral is a fourteenth- or fifteenth-century rebuilding of an earlier church; outstanding features are the flamboyant windows in the south chapel, the altar tomb of the O'Shaughnessys, and the fifteenth-century doorway in the south wall. Of the abbey buildings, the church is well preserved. To the north-east of the cathedral are some ruins of Teampall Owen, which consisted of a nave and chancel. Near by is a castellated block two storeys high, which may have been a bishop's residence. The round tower, restored in 1879, is a fine specimen 112 feet high. It leans about 2 feet out of the perpendicular.

Mayo

Downpatrick Head

The County Mayo coastline, from Killary Harbour to Killala Bay, has a wonderful succession of views— of sandy beaches, cliffs, rugged headlands and islands. Prominent features are the holy mountain of Croagh Patrick and

Achill, the largest island off the Irish coast. Inland, too, the landscape is remarkably varied, with mountains rising from level plain or moorland or forming colourful backgrounds to islet-studded lakes. Mayo's attractions include unspoilt holiday resorts, angling, sailing, climbing and golf.

Westport
Cathair na Mart
(The Stone Fort of the Beeves)

👪 Pop. 3,688 (urban district). ·

ℹ️ Tourist information office:
The Mall. Tel. (098) 25711.
Fax (098) 26709.

Westport lies on an arm of Clew Bay, a superb expanse of island-dotted sea framed by mountain ranges. This is a unique town in that it was designed to the plan of James Wyatt, the well-known architect of the Georgian period. The Mall, with its lime trees lining both sides of the Carrowbeg River, is a charming thoroughfare. The Westport neighbourhood was the setting of many novels by George A. Bermingham (Canon Hannay), who was once Church of Ireland rector here.

The town is well known as a sea fishing centre and its annual festival attracts many visitors. There is bathing at many nearby beaches and a championship golf course (18).

One mile (2 km) from the town is Westport House, home of the Marquess of Sligo. It is a fine Georgian mansion designed by Richard Castle with additions by James Wyatt, and the contents include English and Irish pictures, silver, Waterford glass, and exhibits of historical interest. The house is open from mid-May to mid-September. In the woods is a late English style church with a beautiful interior. Three miles (5 km) north of Westport is the sailing centre at Glenans, Rosmoney.

The Clew Bay Heritage Centre depicts the maritime history of the area and local

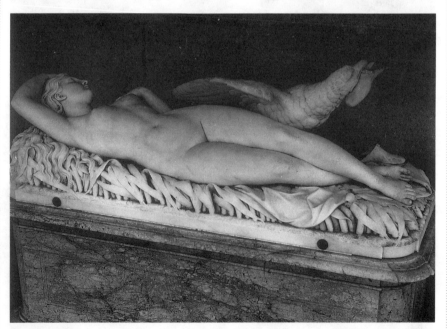

Sleeping Beauty, Westport House

Clare Island

history and traditions. It also provides a genealogical service.

South from Westport

Croagh Patrick, an isolated cone-shaped mountain rising 2,510 feet from the shore of Clew Bay, is one of the most conspicuous features of the west of Ireland landscape. From the summit is a magnificent panorama of coast, islands and mountains. This is Ireland's holy mountain, where the national apostle St Patrick spent the forty days of Lent in the year 441 in prayer and fasting for the people of Ireland. A national pilgrimage to Croagh Patrick takes place on the last Sunday of July each year. Thousands of people, some barefoot, climb the mountain, and Mass is celebrated in a little oratory at the summit.

There are fine views across Clew Bay along the road from Westport to Louisburgh. A point of interest is the fourteenth-century Murrisk Abbey. Two miles (3 km) further on, Lecanvey is a pleasant little place with fine bathing beaches.

Twelve miles (19 km) from Westport, Louisburgh is a pleasant fishing village with fine sandy beaches near by and angling in the neighbourhood and a rent-an-Irish-cottage scheme. A new road south- eastwards to Killeen crossroads (about 6 miles/10 km) gives access to Carrownisky Strand, a beach of golden sand that stretches for several miles. There is salmon and trout fishing on the Carrownisky River and some nearby lakes.

At the mouth of Clew Bay, Clare Island covers about 4,000 acres and has a small population. There is a ferry service to the island in summer from Roonagh Point, near Louisburgh. This was the home in the sixteenth century of the celebrated Grainne Uaile (Grace O'Malley), sea queen of the west. Her exploits have formed the basis of several historical novels, the best known being William O'Brien's *Queen of Men*. Grainne was the daughter of Owen O'Malley, Chief of the western islands, on whose death she made herself ruler of the district which surrounds Clew Bay. Her feats of war earned her the name 'Grainne of the Heroes'. Tradition hands down an unusual item of her marriage contract with MacWilliam Oughter, her second husband: the alliance was to last a year, after which it could be dissolved by either party saying to the other 'I dismiss you.' Grainne took advantage of the year's alliance to garrison all MacWilliam's castles with her own followers. At the end of the year, as MacWilliam was entering Carrigahooley Castle, Grainne ended the alliance by crying from inside 'I dismiss you!' Her body lies today in the island's thirteenth-century abbey: her massive square castle has served as a coastguard station and later as a police barracks.

The mountainous peninsula of south-west Mayo, lying between Clew Bay and Killary Harbour, has much of the characteristic beauty of Connemara. Two roads run through the peninsula to Leenane in County Galway. The main road, south from Westport, passes through the Erriff valley, with the Partry Mountains on the right and the Sheefry Hills on the left. The alternative route runs from Louisburgh between the Sheefry Hills and the Mweelrea Mountains to Delphi (it was so called by Lord Sligo because of its similarity to the home of the Greek oracle), a beautiful spot among the mountains 9 miles (14 km) from Leenane; a mile (2 km) north of it is Doo Lough, a long sheet of water with mountains rising steeply from both shores.

Achill Sound

North from Westport

The route from Westport to Achill (27 miles/ 43 km) follows the east and north shores of Clew Bay. Eight miles (13 km) from Westport, Newport is a picturesque little place sheltered by the mountains and fronted by the bay. It is a freshwater angling resort, and the geologist will be interested in the numerous drumlins in the immediate neighbourhood. The road then turns west across the short Burrishoole River, which drains Lough Furnace and Lough Feeagh. Lough Feeagh stretches for 3 miles (5 km) between the mountains, with Buckoogh (1,935 feet) to the east and Bengorm (1,912 feet) to the west.

Two miles (3 km) beyond Newport are the ruins of the fifteenth-century Burrishoole Abbey (Dominican), where the central tower of the cruciform church remains and there are some good pointed arches. Near by is Carrigahooley Castle, the stronghold of Grace O'Malley

where she dismissed her husband. Three miles (5 km) before reaching Mulrany, Rossturk Castle is seen on the left.

On the narrow isthmus that joins the Curraun Peninsula to the mainland is Mulrany, a picturesque resort with special appeal to those in search of an out-of-doors holiday. There is a good bathing beach and sports available include tennis, golf (9), boating and fishing. The climate is exceptionally mild, and fuchsia and Mediterranean heather flourish. The main route onwards to Achill Island skirts the north shore of the mountainous Curraun Peninsula; the southern road (via Curraun) has very fine seascapes.

Achill Island

i Tourist information office (seasonal): Courthouse. Tel. (098) 45384.

Achill, joined to the mainland by a bridge, is the largest island off the Irish coast.

Shaped like an inverted L, the island is 15 miles (24 km) long and 12 miles (19 km) across at its widest point. The surface is almost completely covered with heather and three great mountains rise in the north, west and south—Slievemore (2,204 feet), Croghaun (2,192 feet) and Minaun (1,530 feet). A feature of particular interest to visitors is the shark-fishing industry on the island.

At the bridge from the mainland is the village of Achill Sound, the main shopping centre of the island. There are facilities for bathing, boating and fishing, and excursions by motor or sailing boat can be made along the coast and to other nearby islands. Deep sea fishing is also available, with porbeagle shark providing exciting sport.

Achill Sound is a good centre for exploring the less frequented southern tip of the island. This can be done on the road which runs southward along the sound to Kildownet Church, which has a square-headed doorway and splayed windows. A

mile (2 km) further on is a rectangular stone-roofed keep of the O'Malleys. This drive may be continued around the coast to Dooega.

Keel is a charming resort with a magnificent 2-mile (3 km) sandy beach that curves away to the base of the impressive Minaun Cliffs, which fall 800 feet sheer to the sea at one point. The cliffs have been carved by the waves into some striking forms; the Cathedral Rocks are a particularly remarkable sight. Keel village is on a curving south-facing bay, sheltered on the north by Slievemore Mountain and on the west by Croghaun. A superb view can be had by walking a little way up the slopes of Slievemore, and the ascent of Minaun Mountain may also be made from here. There is fishing for brown trout at Keel Lough.

Two miles (3 km) beyond Keel is the old-world village of Dooagh, also facing south and sheltered on the north and west

Keem Bay, Achill Island

by the great bulk of Croghaun Mountain. Keem Bay, 3 miles (5 km) westward, is a beautiful inlet with a fine sandy beach sheltered by the steeply rising Moyteoge Head. From Dooagh or Keem one can climb Croghaun, which occupies the western end of the island and has a magnificent view from the summit. On the seaward side the mountain ends in a 4-mile (6 km) line of superb cliffs. At its highest point it drops suddenly to the ocean in a vast precipice of almost 2,000 feet (it is unwise to approach too near the edge, as the cliff-face curves inwards at some places). These cliffs, and others on Achill, were the last haunts of the golden eagle in these islands.

On the island's north shore, Dugort is another popular resort nestling at the base of Slievemore Mountain. The more modern part of Dugort, known as 'The Settlement', was founded in 1834 by the Rev. E. Nangle, a Protestant clergyman who erected schools and an orphanage and established a printing press.

Boats and experienced boatmen may be hired in the village for the trip to the Seal Caves which extend far into the cliffs under Slievemore. The mountain itself is a mass of quartzite rock, with dark rifted slopes occasionally relieved by shining masses of mica. There is a good view from the summit, though less extensive than from Croghaun. At the eastern base of the mountain between Dugort and Keel, is the site of the old village of Slievemore, near which are some antiquarian remains—a cairn, dolmens, stone circles, small tumuli and the remains of an old church. On the opposite side of the road is St Colman's Well.

A feature of Achill is the number of small villages scattered throughout the island. At the northern end, surrounded by three little lakes, is the hamlet known as The Valley. Midway between Achill Sound and Dugort is Cashel, while Sraheens is a cluster of houses near the south-east coast. Dooega village, at the mouth of a valley on the west side of Minaun Mountain, is a

picturesque seaside place with good beaches; it is a convenient starting point to climb the mountain or the Minaun Cliffs.

The Mayo Coast
(north of Achill)

From Mulrany the road runs north along Bellacragher Bay, with a fine view of Blacksod Bay as it approaches Castlehill. On the right is the curving range of the Nephin Beg Mountains, with Cushcamcarragh (2,343 feet), Glennamong (2,067 feet), Nephin Beg (2,065 feet) and Slieve Car (2,369 feet) rising in succession from south to north. Two miles (3 km) further on is Ballycroy, an angling resort in the heart of a desolate area; beyond it a road on the left descends to Duna Castle, a fortress of Grace O'Malley.

Crossing the Owenduff River the road turns inland through uninhabited countryside to Bangor Erris, angling centre for the Owenduff River and Carrowmore Lough. The road from Bangor to Belmullet passes the lough and soon after enters the ravine of Glencastle, where there is the ancient fortress of Dun Domhnaill. Belmullet is the key to the windswept Mullet Peninsula, which extends northward to Erris Head and tapers away southward to Blacksod Point. There is golf (9) 3 miles (5 km) from the town, and the district has good fishing. Elly Bay, between Belmullet and Blacksod, has fine beaches. The area is a favourite with birdwatchers.

Five miles (8 km) from Belmullet on the peninsula are the remains of a fine castle at Doonamo Point, with a great wall (200 feet long and 18 feet high at some points) that stretches across the neck of the headland and encloses three clochans and the remains of a circular fort. The trip from Belmullet to Blacksod Point (13 miles/21 km) gives a good idea of the extraordinary outline of the peninsula: its west coast, exposed to Atlantic storms, is completely denuded of vegetation; while its east coast overlooks the landlocked inlet of Blacksod Bay.

Off the peninsula are the Duvillaun Islands, the Iniskea Islands, Inishkeeragh, Inishglora and Eagle Island. On Inishglora are the remains of a sixth-century monastery founded by St Brendan, and an ancient burial ground.

The north coast of County Mayo, embracing some of the finest cliff scenery in Ireland, may be explored via the road from Belmullet to Killala through Belderg and Ballycastle. At Glenamoy Bridge a road on the left runs north 9 miles (14 km) to Portacloy, a charming little harbour between high cliffs. Benwee Head (829 feet) on the west forms an immense cliff with fine coastal views. About 1½ miles (2 km) offshore are the Stags of Broad-haven, seven precipitous rocks which rise 300 feet from the sea and form the most dramatic feature of all coastal views in this region.

On either side of Portacloy the coastal scenery is magnificent—a succession of headlands, cliffs, creeks and miniature fjords. A splendid walk of 3 miles (5 km) goes across the headland to Porturlin, near which are some striking rock formations. Most remarkable of these is The Arches, which can be rowed through at half-tide in good weather; it is about 30 feet high at the entrance, above which the cliff-face towers to a height of 600 feet.

Beyond Glenamoy Bridge, the road lies through the seemingly endless moors of the Barony of Erris, one of the least populated regions in Ireland. To the left are the rugged headlands of the northern coast; to the right a chain of heatherclad hills that gradually increase in height towards Belderg. The splendid coast to the west of Belderg may be explored on foot or by boat. The outstanding sight here is Moista Sound, a narrow chasm enclosed by vertical cliff-faces which seem almost to touch, hundreds of feet overhead. At Ballycastle thatched cottages may be rented for holidays.

At Ceide Fields near Ballycastle, turf cutting has in recent years revealed the oldest intact field system in existence. The Stone Age landscape of regular fields, dwelling areas and megalithic tombs has been preserved since the bog grew over it 5,000 years ago. Turf cutting to date has only exposed over 200 acres of the find but archaeologists estimate that the total area of the system is about 4 square miles.

About 5 miles (8 km) to the north of Ballycastle village is Downpatrick Head. Near the head there are some puffing holes, and the detached rock of Doonbristy bears witness to the force of the Atlantic. At Palmerstown, a road on the left leads to the thirteenth-century Rathfran Abbey (Dominican).

About 3 miles (5 km) further on is Killala, on the bay of the same name. The cathedral here was rebuilt about 1670, but the Gothic doorway on the south side is older. Near by is a round tower which was struck by lightning and subsequently repaired, and in the churchyard is an elaborate souterrain. The bishopric at Killala, which is believed to have been founded by St Patrick, was once held by the pluralist Myler Magrath. At Killala Bay in August 1798, a French force under General Humbert landed to assist the Irish insurgents. They took Killala, Ballina and Castlebar, but were defeated a few weeks later in County Longford at Ballinamuck. The book *The Year of the French* by American novelist Thomas Flanagan is based on the Humbert invasion. It was later turned into a television series.

Instead of following the direct route from Killala to Ballina, a slightly longer road near the coast brings one to the remains of Moyne Abbey (on the left, at 2 miles/3 km); this has a graceful fifteenth-century tower and almost perfect cloisters. About 2 miles (3 km) further on, in a dell overlooking the River Moy, is Rosserk Abbey (Franciscan, fifteenth century); it also has a fine tower and well-preserved cloisters.

Ballina
Beal an Átha (Mouth of the Ford)

👪 Pop. 6,563 (urban district).

ℹ️ Tourist information office (seasonal): Cathedral Street. Tel. (096) 70848.

The largest town in Mayo is Ballina, an angling centre on the River Moy. The Moy is excellent for salmon and trout and nearby Lough Conn has equally good fishing; golf (9) and hunting are other attractions. Near the modern Catholic cathedral are the remains of a fifteenth-century Augustinian friary, and near the railway station is the Dolmen of the Four Maols—marking the grave of four foster-brothers who murdered their tutor Ceallach, a sixth-century bishop of Kilmore-Moy. The Maols were hanged by Ceallach's brother at Ardnaree, on the opposite side of the river.

Eight miles (13 km) west of Ballina is Crossmolina, on the River Deel near the north shore of Lough Conn; it is a good centre for fishing this famous lake. Further south, Pontoon is another angling resort picturesquely situated between Lough Conn and the smaller Lough Cullen. Both lakes offer fishing, and boats and boatmen are available for hire.

Castlebar
Caislean an Bharraigh (Barry's Castle)

👪 Pop. 6,071 (urban district).

ℹ️ Tourist information office (seasonal): Tel. (094) 21207.

Castlebar, the county town, is in the heart of the limestone plain country. The pleasant tree-lined

Mall is the focal point of this thriving commercial centre, which has its own small airport.

Things to do
There is tennis, golf (18) and free fishing in small lakes near the town; a children's swimming pool, tennis and squash and a small sports complex. At Clydagh Bridge just 2 miles (3 km) from the town there is a lovely forest walk.

History
Castlebar, which received a charter from James I in 1613, was captured by the Confederate Irish in 1641. The town figured prominently in 1798, when Humbert's French forces routed the English under General Lake—an engagement known to history as the 'Races of Castlebar'. John Moore, who for a week was President of the Provisional Republic of Connacht in 1798, is buried in a plot beside the memorial on the Mall. Margaret Burke Sheridan, world famous soprano, was born in Castlebar. There is a plaque to her memory in the Mall.

Around Castlebar
On the Foxford road, there is a well-preserved round tower at Turlough. Five miles (8 km) further on, Straid was the birthplace of Michael Davitt (1846–1906), founder of the Irish Land League. Straid Abbey was founded for Franciscans and transferred in 1252 to the Dominican Order; there are some remains to be seen. The Michael Davitt National Memorial Museum (open during the tourist season), erected near the ruins of the abbey, houses a collection of documents and photographs relating to Davitt and the Land League. Fifteen miles (24 km) from Castlebar, Foxford is a sizeable town with an important woollen industry. Situated at a fordable point of the Moy River, Foxford was the key to the Barony of Tyrawley; and Cromwell's Rock is said to mark the spot where his army crossed the river. Admiral William Browne, founder of the Argentine Navy,

was born in Foxford. Foxford Woollen Mills includes an interpretative centre featuring the history of the mills and their methods of production.

The road south from Castlebar to Claremorris (golf 9) is across a level region known as the Plains of Mayo. At Balla St Mochua built a church and sank two wells.

About 3 miles (5 km) beyond Balla a road on the right leads to the village of Mayo, where there are some remains of an abbey. Founded in the seventh century by St Colman, the abbey later became the seat of a famous university. There is a legend that Alfred the Great studied at Mayo and that one of his sons is buried here. Twenty-five miles (40 km) south-east of Castlebar, via Claremorris, is the village of Knock.

Knock

i Tourist information office (seasonal): Tel. (094) 88193.
Knock Airport (Horan International), Kilkelly. Tel. (094) 67247.

Knock was the scene of an apparition of the Blessed Virgin Mary, Saint Joseph and Saint John in 1879. The little church and basilica (the largest church in Ireland) at Knock are visited each year by many thousands of pilgrims. It was the focal point of Pope John Paul II's visit to Ireland in 1979. A new addition is the Chapel of Reconciliation where pilgrims can find peace and relaxation in an atmosphere of prayer and repentance.

Horan International Airport is called after Monsignor Horan, the local parish priest, whose vision was of Knock as an international pilgrimage centre to which pilgrims could come by air from overseas. The airport was opened in 1986. There is also a folk museum in Knock which features the significance of the Church in the lives of our forefathers.

Ballinrobe

Baile an Rodhba (Town of the Robe River)

Pop. 1,270.

Ballinrobe, on the Robe River near the eastern shore of Lough Mask, is a good angling centre for this lake and Lough Carra. There is tennis, golf (9), horse-riding, forest walks and a racecourse. About 2 miles (3 km) south-west of the town is the great stone fort of Cahernagollum and further on is the Killower cairn.

Around Ballinrobe

On the road to Castlebar, 3½ miles (6 km) beyond Partree a road on the right leads to the largely restored Ballintubber Abbey. This consists of a cruciform church with nave, transepts and choir. The main doorway (early Gothic) is surrounded by a lofty gable, and the nave is lighted by eight early pointed windows. Over the altar are three blocked windows of Norman design with double dog-tooth moulding. The monastic buildings are at the end of the south transept; and in a chapel to the south of the choir there is an elaborate altar tomb with a row of figures on the pediment. This abbey was founded in 1216 by Cathal O'Connor, King of Connacht, for Canons Regular of the order of St Augustine. Despite the wrecking of the place by the Cromwellians, Ballintubber has been in almost uninterrupted use as a place of worship up to the present day.

Recent archaeological investigation of the monastic precincts has uncovered much of interest, including the guesthouse where pilgrims were received.

The return to Ballinrobe from Ballintubber may be made via Carrownacon and Ballygarries, the route lying near the eastern shore of Lough Carra. Near Carrownacon, on a promontory in the lake, is Moore Hall, birthplace of the novelist George Moore, whose ashes are buried beneath a cairn on

Ballintubber Abbey

Castle Island in the lake. Ruins of several churches and castles lie along the wooded shore of Lough Carra, which is noted for trout and coarse fish.

West of Ballinrobe is Lough Mask, 10 miles (16 km) long and 4 miles (6 km) broad, and connected with the larger Lough Corrib by an underground river. The lake is noted for large brown trout. The western shore is bounded by the Partry Mountains, with the Irish-speaking village of Tourmakeady beneath them. On the eastern shore, 4 miles (6 km) from Ballinrobe, is Lough Mask House—once the residence of Captain Boycott and scene of an episode in the Land League struggle which gave a new word to the English language. On the island of Inishmaan are the ruins of a church built by St Cormac in the sixth century and enlarged in the twelfth century.

Six miles (10 km) from Ballinrobe is the village of Cong, on the isthmus between Lough Mask and Lough Corrib. Cong is an excellent centre for the splendid fishing on both lakes, and tennis and boating are also available. Ashford Castle, a former residence of the Guinness family, is now a hotel. Among antiquities at Cong are an inscribed stone cross (fourteenth century) in the village street. The ruins of an Augustinian abbey stand close to Ashford Castle. This abbey was founded in 1128 probably on the site of a seventh-century settlement of St Fechin. Here Roderick O'Conor, the last High King of Ireland, died in 1198 after spending the last fifteen years of his life in monastic seclusion.

The famous processional Cross of Cong, now in the National Museum at Dublin, is a masterpiece of religious art; it was discovered in a chest in the village early in the last century. Made of oak plated with copper, and decorated with beautiful gold filigree-work of Celtic pattern, its function was to enshrine a portion of the True Cross. It was made at

Inishbofin, off the Co. Galway coast

Bunratty Castle, Co. Clare

Gallarus Oratory, Co. Kerry

Spanish Arch, Galway

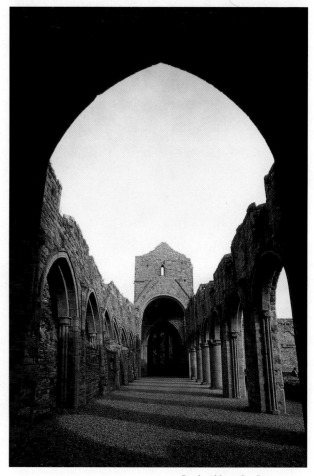

Boyle Abbey, Co. Roscommon

Adare village, Co. Limerick

Coliemore Harbour and Dalkey Island, Co. Dublin

Roscommon in 1123 for the cathedral of Tuam, by order of Turlough O'Conor, and later brought to Cong by his son Roderick. The famous film 'The Quiet Man' was shot in the Cong countryside.

The underground steam connecting Lough Corrib and Lough Mask is accessible at a number of points, and the descent to the 'Pigeon Hole' is particularly recommended. Between Cong and the Neale lies the Plain of Southern Moytura, a prehistoric battlefield where the legendary Tuatha De Danann inflicted the first great defeat on the Firbolgs. Seven years later the Firbolgs were completely crushed at the Battle of Northern Moytura near Sligo. These two battlefields have thrown much light on the history of megalithic monuments.

Sligo

Lake-isle of Innisfree, Lough Gill

Within a small area County Sligo has a fine variety of mountain, lake and coastal scenery. In the west of the county the Ox Mountains form a background to the coastal plain, while north of Sligo town the landscape is dominated by steep-sided and flat-topped limestone hills. The coast is mainly low-lying and is fringed by sandy beaches and low cliffs. Near Sligo town, in beautiful Lough Gill, can be seen the lake-isle of Innisfree immortalised in Yeats's poem. There is a 65-mile (105 km) signposted tour of the Yeats country featuring many of the places referred to in his poetry. Another beauty spot in the county is Lough Arrow, with its islets and encircling hills. For the holidaymaker in Sligo there are seaside resorts such as Inniscrone and Strandhill,

golf at Rosses Point and other centres, excellent lake and river angling, hill climbing and many other interesting activities.

Sligo Town

Sligeach (The Shelly River)

Pop. 17,297 (borough).

Tourist information office: Temple Street. Tel. (071) 61201. Fax (071) 60360.

Sligo, well situated on the wooded plain of the Garavogue River between Lough Gill and the sea, is north-west Ireland's most important town. Surrounded by a beautiful and interesting

Garavogue River in Sligo town

region, it is an excellent holiday centre. Except on the seaward side, Sligo is encircled by mountains.

What to do

Game and coarse fishing in many lakes and rivers. Golf at championship courses at Rosses Point and at Strandhill (18); boats for hire; pitch and putt and tennis. Conducted walking tours around town in summer. A signposted town trail commences from the tourist office. Theatre and cinemas.

History

In ancient times this was a place of strategic importance, as all traffic on the western coastal route between north and south forded the river here. The ford was guarded by a fortress whose site may still be traced near the bridge that spans the narrowest part of the Garavogue. Sligo was plundered by Norse pirates in A.D. 807, but did not become really important until 1245 when it became the residence of the Earl of Kildare, Maurice Fitzgerald. His castle played a prominent part in the Anglo-Irish struggles

of the thirteenth century, and was later a bone of contention between rival clans— notably the O'Conors and O'Donnells. The town was taken by Sir Frederick Hamilton in 1641, and four years later fell to the Cromwellian forces.

Points of interest

In 1252 Maurice Fitzgerald founded Sligo Abbey for the Dominican Order. In 1414 it was destroyed by fire and rebuilt; the present ruinous condition dates from the sack of Sligo in the rebellion of 1641.

The ruins consist of a nave and choir with a central tower. On the south wall is a fine mural monument (1623) to O'Connor-Sligo, depicting the kneeling figures of himself and his wife. The nave still has three arches on the south side and the north wall, in which is the elaborate altar tomb (1616) of the O'Creans. The tower is supported by lofty arches and has a groined roof. The cloisters (on the north side of the nave) are almost perfect on three sides, in each of which are 18 arches of beautiful workmanship.

Sligo

1. Grattan Street
2. Yeats Memorial Building
3. Sligo Abbey
4. Town Hall

5. Courthouse
6. MacDiarmada Station
7. Co. Sligo Museum

The most ancient of Sligo's churches is the seventeenth-century St John's Church. Adjoining it is the nineteenth-century Catholic Cathedral, a fine building in Romanesque style.

In the County Library, Sligo Museum has an interesting collection of exhibits, including a section on Yeats. The Art Gallery located in the Yeats Memorial Building houses a valuable collection of oils, watercolours and drawings by Jack Yeats, J. B. Yeats the elder, George Russell (AE), and other modern Irish artists. The Sligo Family Research Society in the museum provides a service for those interested in their genealogy. Other notable buildings are the graceful Town hall (1864) in the Italian Renaissance style, the Courthouse (1878), and the Gillooly Memorial Hall (1903).

Around Sligo

About 5 miles (8 km) long and 1½ miles (2 km) wide, Lough Gill rivals Killarney for sheer natural beauty and is also a region of considerable historic interest. It lies in a basin surrounded on three sides by wooded mountain slopes, and is connected to Sligo town by a 2½-mile (4 km) stretch of river that is lined by beautiful woods and lawns. On the north bank of this stretch is the old demesne of Hazelwood. In Hazelwood forest there is a unique collection of wooden sculptures dispersed on the forest trails which commence at the car park and picnic site. Opposite Hazelwood, near the south bank, is Cairns Hill, which is surmounted by two cairns, two cashels and a stone circle. The western cairn is 456 feet around the base, and has a 12-foot high rampart. Close to the hill is the holy well of Tobernalt with a rude stone altar that was used for worship in penal times (the shrine is the scene of a pilgrimage on the last Sunday of July). From the 'Scenic Road' east of Cairns Hill there is a fine view of 'The Narrows', a channel formed by the little island situated where the river issues from the lake.

In the lake itself the most prominent islands are the beautiful wooded Cottage Island, which has the ruins of an ancient church, and the larger Church Island, where there are remains of a church said to have been founded in the sixth century by St Coman. Near the south-eastern shore of the lake is the tiny island of Innisfree, which W. B. Yeats immortalised in his most widely known lyric. On the south shore near Cottage Island is Dooney Rock, which has a good view of the lake. The name of this rock has been celebrated by Yeats in his poem 'The Fiddler of Dooney'. There is a lovely nature trail and lakeside walk at Dooney.

North of Lough Gill is a pleasant region of small limestone hills and ferny glens, and the road through Colgagh to Dromahair is the best way of seeing the district. Four miles (6 km) from Sligo, near Fermoyle, is the immense megalithic tomb of Leacht Con Mhic Ruis (The Stone of Cu, son of Ros). It stands on a hill south of the road, and is a large sub-rectangular enclosure with smaller chambers at the east and west ends. Only one of the original three trilithon entrances to the small chambers is still complete. From the tomb there is a fine view of the Lough Gill area and of the coast.

West of Sligo town the main natural feature is the Hill of Knocknarea (1,078 feet), whose summit has fine panoramic views. Take the road that leaves Sligo by John Street; at 2 miles (3 km) a left turn leads to Carrowmore, a low hill possessing the largest group of megalithic remains in these islands—dolmens, stone circles, and cairns with sepulchral chambers, some dating to 4000 B.C. An information/ exhibition centre is open to the public during the season. Near by at Cloverhill is another sepulchral monument with carvings thought to be Bronze Age. About 2 miles (3 km) further on is Knocknarea. On the summit of the hill is a gigantic cairn known as Miscaun Meadhbh (Maeve's mound), traditionally considered to commemorate

Benbulben

Queen Maeve of Connacht who flourished in the first century of the Christian era. The cairn is 630 feet around the base; the slope to the crown is 80 feet and the diameter on top is 100 feet.

On the south-west of the hill is the Glen of Knocknarea, a deep chasm nearly a mile (2 km) long and only 30 feet broad, bounded on each side by steep cliffs and overgrown with trees and shrubs that spring from every crevice in the rock. At the foot of Knocknarea is the seaside resort of Strandhill, 5 miles (8 km) from Sligo town. There are two long sandy beaches and facilities for surfing, golf (18). Strandhill is the location of Sligo Airport. On the shore north of the village is the ancient church of Killaspugbrone (Church of Bishop Bronus), named after a follower of St Patrick.

Five miles (8 km) north of Sligo town, and linked to it by a bus service, is the holiday venue and touring centre of Rosses Point which has a widely known championship golf course (18), and Sligo Yacht Club. Coney Island is a half-mile (1 km) offshore. To the north across Drumcliffe Bay is Lissadell, and a fine sandy beach runs for about 3 miles (5 km) beneath the cliffs west of the village. Near by are the Dartry Mountains, where the most prominent summits are Truskmore (2,113 feet), Benbulben (1,730 feet) and King's Mountain (1,527 feet). The curious outline of Benbulben is a predominant feature of all views in this region.

The road from Sligo to Bundoran (22 miles/35 km) is a magnificent drive along the coast. At 5 miles (8 km) is Drumcliffe, situated on the river that drains Glencar Lough into the sea. A monastic establishment was founded here in 574 by St Columba; there is a fine ancient sculptured cross by the roadside with a particularly good panel depicting Adam and Eve. Close by is the lower portion of a round tower, the only one in County Sligo. In the little churchyard at Drumcliffe is the grave of W. B. Yeats, the great Irish poet who died in France in 1939 and whose remains were re-interred here in 1948.

Near Drumcliffe at Cuildrevne, the famous 'Battle of the Books' was fought in 561 between the followers of St Columba and St Finian. Finian had lent a psalter to Columba, who made a copy from it. Finian claimed the copy, and the dispute was submitted to the King of Ireland, who gave the succinct judgment: 'To every cow its calf, and to every book its copy.' Columba had recourse to arms, and 3,000 men were killed in the battle.

From Drumcliffe a road to the left skirts the north shore of Drumcliffe Bay. A short distance beyond the village of Carney is Lissadell demesne; the house and gardens are open to the public on summer afternoons (except Sunday). Here were born the poetess Eva Gore-Booth and her more famous sister Constance, who became Countess Markievicz and who took part in the 1916 Rising. Both were immortalised in a poem by Yeats, who was a frequent visitor to the house. On the shore near by are some slight remains of Dunfore Castle, and a little further on are the remains of a cashel with souterrains, a dolmen and a stone circle. Near the small village of Raghly at the head of the bay is Ardtermon Castle, former seat of the Gore family. The coast here has some extra- ordinary subterranean channels into which the tide rushes with tremendous force, and further north the havoc wrought in this region by drifting sands becomes very apparent; many acres of land and a number of houses have been buried under an accumulation of sand. Near Streedagh are the ruins of the ancient Abbey of Staad, consisting of part of a small church attrib- uted to St Molaise. Three large vessels of the Spanish Armada foundered on the strand at Streedagh and 1,100 bodies were washed ashore. Under certain tidal conditions the remains of a galleon can occasionally be seen. There is a small commemorative park to those who lost their lives in the shipwrecks.

The Sligo–Bundoran road is rejoined at Grange, a village beneath the flat-topped mass of Benbulben, the summit of which has a fine view of coast and countryside. There is much to interest the geologist here, and the mountain is famous among botanists for its rare flora (including

Arenaria ciliata and *Saxifraga nivalis*). Benbulben is known in legend as the place where the hero of the epic love tale 'The Pursuit of Diarmuid and Grainne' met his death while taking part in a boar hunt on the slopes of the mountain.

At Mullaghmore a boat may be hired for the trip to Inishmurray Island, 4 miles (6 km) north-west of Streedagh Point. The island—an almost barren area a mile (2 km) long by a half- mile (1 km) across—takes its name from the patron saint of the diocese of Killala, Muireadach. Viking pirates plundered the monastery and devastated the island in 807. The main attraction today is the island's remarkable collection of antiquities. The great cashel—a wall of uncemented stones—encloses a group of ruins that are the most characteristic example of a primeval Irish monastic establishment. Here also are three beehive cells, three altars and the well of St Molaise. The rounded cursing stones are the subject of a legend which claims that nobody has ever succeeded in counting them correctly twice in succession, though there are only about 40 in all. Outside the cashel, the most interesting object is Teampall Mhuire, also called Teampall na mBan ('Church of the Women').

Back on the mainland about 4 miles (6 km) beyond Grange is the neat village of Cliffoney—while one mile (2 km) away is the hamlet of Creevykeel, site of a mag- nificent court cairn. From Cliffoney a road on the left runs along a promontory bordered by sandhills to Mullaghmore, a sheltered little resort with a superb beach, a harbour and good sea fishing. Mullaghmore is a very popular sailing and boating centre.

About 7 miles (11 km) north of Sligo in the Dartry Mountains is Glencar Lough, stretching eastwards for 2 miles (3 km) along a valley which has some of the love- liest scenery in Ireland. Near the eastern end of the lake are two fine waterfalls—the uppermost making an unbroken leap of 50

Glencar Lake

feet and providing a real thrill for the sightseer when the wind blows strongly from the south. Near the waterfalls is the Swiss Valley, a wooded ravine formed by a giant landslip from the cliffs.

Inniscrone

Inis Eascrach Abhann (Watershed Island)

 Pop. 633.

nniscrone is a popular resort with a 3-mile (5 km) sandy beach, on the shore of Killala Bay in west County Sligo.

Things to do

The surf bathing here is excellent. Saltwater and other medicinal baths are available at two well-equipped bath houses. There are facilities for golf (18), tennis, dancing, sea fishing in the bay and river fishing on nearby waters. There are many pleasant walks in the neighbourhood.

Around Inniscrone

A few miles from the resort is Castle Firbis, a ruined stronghold of the renowned Gaelic poets and annalists, the Mac-Firbises. It was a member of this learned family who compiled the fourteenth-century *Book of Lecan*, now in the Royal Irish Academy library in Dublin.

The main road north-east from Inniscrone runs along a wide coastal plain to Easkey, a little seaside place on the Easkey River. Some rare flowers may be seen along the banks of the river, which has good fishing. Other recreations here are boating, surfing, tennis and dancing. In the vicinity are numerous forts and a large dolmen supported by four square pillars. This territory was the ancient patrimony of the O'Dowds and MacSweeneys, whose ruined fortresses still stand along the elevated parts of the coast. On the roadside just beyond Easkey is the remarkable Split Rock, an Ice Age erratic boulder with a deep fissure.

few miles further on, Dromore West is a village picturesquely situated on the wooded banks of a river rushing down from the Ox Mountains. There is a pretty terraced waterfall near by. On the right beyond Dromore rises Knock-along (1,786 feet), the highest peak of the Ox Mountains. At Templeboy, a road leads left to rugged Aughris Head, a prominent feature of the coast.

The next village *en route*, Skreen, was once an important religious centre and is said to have had seven churches. Near by is a fine well surmounted by a monument with a Latin inscription which translates as 'Eugene McDonnell, vicar of this place, had me erected 1591'. North of Skreen is the ruined Castle of Ardnaglas, originally occupied by the O'Dowds and later by the MacSweeneys.

At the mouth of the Owenmore River is Ballisodare. The river, which is famous as a salmon fishery, here falls over shelving rocks and forms a picturesque series of rapids; on the left bank are the ivy-clad ruins of a small seventh-century abbey founded by St Fechin of Fore.

The Hawk's Rock near Coolaney

South Sligo

Collooney is on the Owenmore River, 7 miles (11 km) south of Sligo town. Its strategic importance made this locality the scene of several important battles. In 1798 a skirmish occurred at Carrignagat, in which Humbert's French troops, who had landed near Killala to support the Irish rebellion, defeated a force of militia. The general's aide-de-camp Captain Teeling displayed remarkable bravery in the fighting, and a monument to him stands on a rocky hill near the Collooney–Ballisodare road. In earlier times this region saw clashes between rivals of the O'Conor clan, and in 1599 the country between Collooney and Boyle was the scene of a battle in which Red Hugh O'Donnell's forces routed the English under Sir Conyers Clifford.

South-west of Collooney is Coolaney, where a picturesque bridge spans the Owenbeg River. Near by are the remains of Moylough Castle, a former stronghold of the O'Haras; their modern demesne is at Annaghmore, about 3 miles (5 km) east of Coolaney on both sides of the Owenmore River. Many rare shrubs flourish in the grounds, where there are also the ruins of an old fort surrounded by a deep fosse.

Ballymote, 7 miles (11 km) south of Collooney, is a thriving business town, with golf (9), tennis. Ballymote offers some of the best coarse fishing. It is an ancient place that takes its name from a large motte that is still to be seen about a mile (2 km) west of the town. There are remains of a Franciscan friary, where the celebrated *Book of Ballymote* (now in the Royal Irish Academy) was compiled in 1391. The castle built in Ballymote in 1300 by the 'Red Earl' of Ulster, Richard de Burgh, was later occupied by Turlough O'Connor (King of Connacht), the MacDonaghs and Red Hugh O'Donnell. In the rebellion of 1641 it was taken by the Irish, and held out until 1652 when it fell to the combined forces of Ireton and Sir

Charles Coote. The ruins, covering a considerable area and flanked by six towers, give a vivid impression of the castle's defensive strength.

About 2 miles (3 km) south-west of Ballymote is Templehouse Lough, on the shores of which is the demesne of Temple House. In the grounds are extensive ruins of a fourteenth-century house of the Knights of St John. Seven miles (11 km) south of Ballymote, on the main Boyle– Ballina road, is the village of Gurteen from which Lough Gara may be reached at about 2½ miles (4 km) along the road to Boyle. On the western shore of the lake are the well-preserved ruins of Moygara Castle, a stronghold of the O'Garas.

About 2½ miles (4 km) further on, near Monasteraden, is the most famous of the many holy wells in the region dedicated to St Attracta. It is enclosed on three sides by walls, on one of which is sculptured a figure of the crucified Christ. On the top of the wall is a row of those curious rounded stones to be seen at Inishmurray, Toomour and other places in County Sligo.

Taking the road west from Gurteen the number of Raths and Cashels in the vicinity suggest the area was well populated in early historical times and this is borne out by an important archaeological find at Knock na Shee, about 4 miles (6 km) north-west of Tubbercurry, near Laragh village. After 5 miles (8 km) a turn leads to the village of Bunnanadden, where there are fragments of an old castle and church. A little further on is Tubbercurry nestling at the foot of the Ox Mountains. It remains unspoilt and some of the best traditions of Irish culture are preserved here. There is tennis, fishing, walking and climbing.

Ten miles (16 km) west of Tubbercurry the road skirts the northern shore of Lough Talt. This lake is beautifully situated high among the Ox Mountains and provides good brown trout fishing.

Starting again from Ballymote, but this time going eastwards, about 4 miles (6 km)

Lough Arrow

away (to the left of the Boyle road) is Keash. Here there are some extensive caves, the entrances to which are on the side of Keshcorran Hill (1,188 feet). This hill is frequently mentioned in early Irish literature. It is said that Cormac Mac Airt, an illustrious King of Ireland, was born here and nurtured by a she-wolf in one of the caves. According to legend, Diarmuid, the lover of Grainne, is said to have lived at Keash and to have set out from there on the ill-fated boar-hunt that ended at Benbulben. The name Keshcorran is derived from a legendary De Danann harper, Corran, to whom the district was granted as a reward for his musical skill.

The summit of Keshcorran commands a good view of the surrounding countryside, and the caves in the escarpment of the hill are of great archaeological interest; excavations have uncovered numerous bones of animals extinct in Ireland, such as the bear, reindeer and arctic lemming. Habitation layers have also been found, with remains and implements from early Christian times.

A battle was fought in this neighbourhood in 971, when the Ulstermen routed the men of Connacht with great slaughter. According to the *Book of Ballymote*, those who fell were interred at Easpaig Luidhigh, which has been identified as the old church of Toomour near Kesh. The 'Grave of the Kings' may be seen close to the church.

Further east, Castlebaldwin is near the northern shore of Lough Arrow, a lake with many islands which forms a striking contrast to the bleak surrounding hills.

Two miles (3 km) beyond Castlebaldwin the road passes on the left the demesne of Hollybrook which runs between the road and the lakeshore. Hollybrook (or Ballyhely) was the scene of the romantic adventures of Willy Reilly and his 'Colleen Bawn', celebrated by William Carleton's novel. About 1½ miles (2 km) beyond Hollybrook is the ancient church of Aghanagh, one of the first erected in County Sligo. Near Ballinafad, on an arm of Lough Arrow, are the ruins of a castle built in the reign of James I. In 1642 it surrendered to the Irish rebels and ten years later was occupied by Sir William Taaffe.

Beyond Ballinafad are the Curlew Hills, scene of many military encounters. The highest summit is only 860 feet, but the hills gain importance from their sudden elevation and their position across the route north to Sligo. In 1497 there was an engagement here between O'Donnell of Tirchonaill and MacDermott, Lord of Moylurg. O'Donnell's forces were defeated and lost their *Catach* (or Battle Book), a copy of the psalms made by St Colmcille and treasured by the O'Donnell family. It was said to ensure victory if carried around the army three times before going into battle. Two years later O'Donnell invaded the MacDermott territory and recovered the book (it is now in the Royal Irish Academy). An even more celebrated battle took place in the Curlews in 1599, when Red Hugh O'Donnell and Brian O'Rourke defeated the English under Sir Conyers Clifford.

The road from Ballinafad to Boyle crosses the Curlews, and there is a fine view from the highest point of the ridge. To complete the exploration of the county, turn left at Ballinafad along the road which runs between Lough Arrow and Lough Key. Beyond Corrigeenroe the route turns north-east to Kilmactranny, north of which is the prehistoric battlefield of Northern Moytura where the legendary Tuatha De Danann finally defeated the Firbolgs around the fourteenth century B.C. The battlefield is a bleak tableland about a mile (2 km) square, strewn with heaps of stones. There are a few dolmens, one of them (at Carrickglas) in a very good state of preservation.

From Kilmactranny a road on the left leads across the plain of Moytura to Ballindoon on the eastern shore of Lough Arrow. Inside the ruins of a fourteenth-century Dominican abbey there is an interesting monument (1737) to Terence McDonough, 'The Great Counsellor'. A few miles from Ballindoon is the great Cairn of Heapstown, which may be a Bronze Age monument marking the grave of a high king.

Along the way to Ballyfarnon (County Roscommon) the pretty Lough Skean is passed on the right. Here the road turns left and ascends a river valley between the plateau of Moytura and the Sligo-Leitrim mountains. This route was used by St Patrick on his first journeying west of the Shannon. Beside the little village of Geevagh is a huge dolmen and there are numerous caves in the hills. The road then meets rising ground and, forking to the right at Drummacool, crosses the upland to Ballintogher. There is an old castle here, and to the north is the ruined church of Killery and its ancient burial ground.

Leitrim

Lough Rinn House, near Mohill

County Leitrim extends for over 50 miles (81 km) from the County Longford border to Donegal Bay, where it has a coastline of 2½ miles (4 km). It is divided into two parts almost wholly separated from one another by an expansion of the River Shannon, Lough Allen. The area north of the lake is mountainous, reaching its highest point of just over 2,000 feet on the Sligo border, north of Glencar Lake. East of Lough Allen is another mountainous area in which Slieve Anierin (1,922 feet) is prominent. South of the lake is an area of little hills interspersed with many lakes. Leitrim is a county of fine lake and mountain scenery and of good angling waters, with many attractions for the climber, the walker and the cyclist.

Dromahair
Druim Dha Eithiar
(The Ridge of the Two Air-Demons)

Pop. 353.

Dromahair is a quiet village on the River Bonet near the south-east shore of Lough Gill. It is surrounded by a picturesque and historic region which was once the territory of the warlike O'Rourkes. There is a signposted tourist trail of the village.

Points of interest

On the river bank is the Old Hall, built by Sir William Villiers in 1626. It adjoins the ruins of Breffni Castle, once a stronghold of the O'Rourkes and the place from which in the twelfth century Dervorgilla, wife of Tiernan O'Rourke, eloped with the King of Leinster, Dermot MacMurrough. Outlawed by the neighbouring chiefs, Dermot applied for assistance to Henry II of England. Henry refused, but declared that his vassals were at liberty to undertake the venture. MacMurrough's invitation was eventually accepted by the barons of south Wales, and in 1169 a body of Anglo-Normans established themselves at Wexford. So began the Norman invasion of Ireland.

On the opposite bank of the river are the ruins of Creevelea Abbey (Franciscan), founded in 1508 by Margaret, wife of Owen O'Rourke. Close by are the remains of an ancient church which may have been founded by St Patrick, who spent some time at Dromahair.

Around Dromahair

Near the village is O'Rourke's Table, a flat-topped height covered with fern and moss. From the top one may survey the scene of Moore's poem, 'The Valley Lay Smiling Before Me', in which he describes the emotions of Tiernan O'Rourke on discovering the infidelity of Dervorgilla.

On the northern shore of Lough Gill 4½ miles (7 km) from Dromahair stands Parke's Castle, a fortified seventeenth-century manor house which has recently been restored. It is an interpretative centre for the national monuments of the North-West. The Castle is open to the public in summer months and has an audio-visual theatre and guided tours.

Manorhamilton

Cluanin Ui Ruairc
(O'Rourke's Little Field)

 Pop. 1,031.

Manorhamilton, at the meeting of four mountain valleys, is surrounded by the striking limestone ranges peculiar to this region. The steep hillsides, narrow ravines and fertile valleys of the neighbourhood offer a superb variety of scenery. In the town itself the chief object of interest is the ruined baronial mansion built in 1638 by Sir Frederick Hamilton.

Around Manorhamilton

A fine excursion is to Glencar Lough (8 miles/13 km). The direct road at first runs south-west, but it is best to follow the by-road north-west to Lurganboy, an attractive village among beautiful scenery. Rejoining the main road at Shanvaus, the route then follows the mountain valley which leads to Glencar. Glencar Waterfall, beside Glencar Lough was immortalised by W. B. Yeats in his poem 'The Stolen Child'.

Another delightful drive is to Lough Melvin. The road ascends the Bonet valley, passing after 5 miles (8 km) Glenade Lough which is situated in a deep glen between towering mountains (Truskmore and Cloghcorragh are both over 2,000 feet). The road then reaches the coastal plain at Park and bears right towards the pretty village of Kinlough, on the northern shore of Lough Melvin.

Celebrated for its salmon and trout fishing, Lough Melvin has several small islands, on one of which are the ruins of Rossclogher Castle. On the mainland near by is the ruined Rossclogher Abbey. A captain in the Spanish Armada named De Cuellar is said to have taken refuge in the castle after being wrecked on the Sligo coast.

The route back to Manorhamilton lies between the south shore of the lake and the hills, of which the most striking is Aghabohad Mountain—rising from the water's edge to a height of 1,346 feet. About 8 miles (13 km) from Kinlough the road turns sharply right, near the ruins of Rossinver Church. Near by is a holy well associated with St Mogue. The road then crosses the hills at a height of 700 feet and descends to Manorhamilton.

Another worthwhile excursion from Manorhamilton is to Upper Lough Macnean, which lies among the mountains of Counties Leitrim, Cavan and Fermanagh. The road runs eastward along a valley between high mountains; the lake comes into view about a mile (2 km) from Glenfarne.

Near the Fermanagh border, about 6 miles (10 km) north of Glenfarne, is the village of Kiltyclogher, near which was born one of the leaders of the 1916 Rising, Sean Mac Diarmada. In the village square is a memorial to him, a statue by Albert Power, R.H.A.; the pedestal carries the names of Leitrim men who died in the War of Independence.

Drumshanbo
Druim Sean-Bhoth
(The Ridge of the Old Huts)

👫👫 Pop. 622.

Nestling beneath the Slieve Anierin and Arigna Mountains this pleasant little town, situated at the southern end of Lough Allen, is an angling resort.

An annual festival, An Tostal, with emphasis on Irish music, singing and dancing is held in Drumshanbo each year. A heritage centre in the market house reflects the area's special links with narrow-gauge steam trains, coal-mining, and also features local folklore.

Around Drumshanbo
One of the three great Shannon lakes, Lough Allen, is 7 miles (11 km) long and 3 miles (5 km) broad. There are some small islands in the lake, which is surrounded on almost every side by bleak mountains. On the eastern side rises the Slieve Anierin Range, with the prominent summits of Slieve Anierin (1,922 feet), Bencroy (1,707 feet) and Slievenakilla (1,793 feet). There are

other hills to the north, while those on the west rise over 1,400 feet.

Slieve Anierin is of particular interest to the geologist because it is rich in the remains of a particular group of extinct marine animals dating from 275 million years ago.

The circuit of Lough Allen may be made from Drumshanbo by following the route which skirts the eastern shore of the lake to Dowra, a little town on the boundary of Counties Cavan and Leitrim. This road hugs the lakeshore, crossing a number of streams which rush down from the overhanging mountains. At Dowra it crosses the River Shannon (only a few miles from its source) and continues south-west to Drumkeeran.

On the island of Inismagrath, near the northern end of the lake, are the ruins of a church said to have been founded by St Beoy. At Tarmon, near the west shore, are the ruins of a church believed to have been founded by one of the O'Rourkes.

A mile (2 km) further on, the road enters County Roscommon, with the Arigna Mountains prominent on the right. The district around Lough Allen is noted for its veins of coal and iron, and Arigna is one of the few places in Ireland where coal was mined.

Carrick-on-Shannon
Cara Droma Ruisg
(The Weir of the Marshy Ridge)

👫👫 Pop. 1,984.

ℹ️ Tourist information office (seasonal): Tel. (078) 20170.

Carrick-on-Shannon is the county town of Leitrim. The Shannon is navigable to a short distance above the town, as is the strait westwards to Lough Key near Boyle. Carrick-on-Shannon was incorporated as a borough by James I in 1613, and sent two members to the Irish Parliament until the abolition of the franchise.

The Shannon at Carrick

Things to do
Carrick-on-Shannon is a centre for river cruising and boating with trout and coarse fishing in the Shannon and the neighbouring lakes. Tennis and golf (9) are other attractions.

Points of interest
The Costello Chapel at Main Street is reputed to be the second smallest chapel in the world. It was erected in 1877 as a mausoleum for Edward Costello and his wife who lie in coffins sunk in the floor and covered in a glass frame.

Around Carrick-on-Shannon
The road to Dromod crosses the Shannon at Jamestown. This small town incorporated by James I was the scene of a synod in 1650 and also of a successful raid by Sarsfield during the Jacobite wars. It was formerly a walled town. The Shannon here forms a loop and is crossed again at Drumsna, a village in the midst of beautiful scenery. Moving on, the landscape is brightened by the many small lakes which are an outstanding feature of this region. On the right the Shannon expands into Lough Boderg and Lough Bofin; a road to the right, 2 miles (3 km) beyond Aghamore, leads to the wooded promontory of Derrycarne which projects into Lough Boderg. Around the ford at this spot a skirmish took place between the troops of James II and William of Orange.

On the shores of Lough Bofin is Dromod, formerly noted for its ironworks. About 2 miles (3 km) south is Roosky, at the point where the Shannon emerges from Lough Bofin. From Dromod the road north to Mohill passes Lough Rinn, a pretty lake between high banks. The attractive demesne of Lough Rinn House (formerly the residence of the 3rd Earl of Leitrim) is now an important visitor centre, with an arboretum, attractive gardens and walks. It is open to the public during the summer months. In the town of Mohill is a remnant of an important monastery founded in 608 by St Manchan.

Carrigallen to the east of Mohill has a new community theatre, the Corn Mill, which has superb facilities and provides regular entertainment.

Interior, Lough Rinn House

Northwards 7 miles (11 km) from Mohill is Fenagh, on the northern shore of the little Fenagh Lough. A monastery founded here by St Columba later became famous as a divinity school under the presidency of St Killian. The ruins are of a Gothic church and have several interesting features, including an east window of unusual design.

Three miles (5 km) north of Fenagh is Ballinamore, on a pleasant site in a region of little hills and lakes, with the Slieve Anierin Mountains rising grandly in the north-west, golf (9). Lough Garadice, a beautiful lake with sailing and good coarse fishing, is 3 miles (5 km) to the east.

The heritage centre located in the county library provides local genealogical information. Ballinamore is at the other end of the canal now being developed to Ballyconnell, County Cavan.

At Castlefore, 3 miles (5 km) west of Fenagh, was a bardic school conducted by the Ó Duibhgeannains. Cuchoigriche

(Peregrine) Ó Duibhgeannain, one of the celebrated Four Masters, was born here. Two miles (3 km) further on is Lough Scur, one of whose islands has the ruined Castle John—an Elizabethan structure frequently besieged by the O'Rourkes. Another island contains the remains of a square fortress said to have been used as a prison. Lough Scur also has a number of crannogs (prehistoric lake dwellings).

Fenagh Abbey

Roscommon

In Lough Key Forest Park

Roscommon is an inland county where the main attraction is the beauty of island-dotted lakes. Much of the county is level plain, bogland and river meadow—broken with low hills and many lakes. The highest point (1,385 feet) is on the County Leitrim border in the north; also prominent are the Curlew Hills (867 feet) in the north-west and the Slieve-bawn Hills (864 feet) in the east. The county's eastern boundary is formed by the River Shannon and its lakes.

Roscommon

Ros Comain (Coman's Wood)

Pop. 1,363.

i Tourist information office (seasonal): Tel. (0903) 26342.

Roscommon, the county town, is an important road junction and a good touring centre. It mainly occupies the southern slopes of a gentle hill, and took its name and origin from St Coman, who founded a monastery here in early Christian times.

Things to do
Among the recreations available are fishing, boats for hire, tennis, horse-racing and golf (9); there is an indoor swimming

Roscommon Abbey

pool, a gymnasium for indoor sports and cinema.

Points of interest

Roscommon Abbey was founded in 1253 by the King of Connacht, Felim O'Conor. The principal ruins are a church, 137 feet long and 23 feet wide, with a northern transept in which is an aisle separated by four pointed arches. Over the main entrance is a beautiful window, with an architrave decorated with pinnacles. In the choir is a tomb which is said to be that of the founder; at the base are eight sculptured figures representing ancient gallowglasses, early Irish soldiers.

Standing impressively on the hillside, Roscommon Castle was originally built in 1268 by the Lord Justice of Ireland, Sir Robert D'Ufford; four years later it was captured by the Irish and razed to the ground. Rebuilt about 1280, the castle was later the subject of many sieges. During the Parliamentary wars it was held for the King by Sir Michael Earnley, but in 1652 it surrendered to the Cromwellians, who dismantled it. The ruins occupy a large quadrangular area with a tower at each angle; two similar towers project from the eastern wall to protect the gateway. These towers appear to have been connected with the inner court, containing the state apartments. The Old Jail in the Square once had a female 'hangman'.

Around Roscommon

On the road north-west to Castlerea, it is worth diverging to the right at 8 miles (13 km) to visit the castle at Ballintober. This was the chief seat of the O'Conors of Connacht, and figured in the Tudor, Parliamentary and Williamite wars. The ruins form a quadrangular enclosure, defended at the angles by polygonal towers which resemble those of Caernarvon Castle. The upper stories had windows and were

Roscommon Castle

obviously habitable. The curtain walls were nearly six feet thick at the height of the inner court, but much thicker at the foundation. Flights of steps led to the banquette below the parapet and a broad fosse surrounded the whole structure.

The town of Castlerea, 19 miles (31 km) from Roscommon, is prettily situated on a wooded reach of the River Suck. There is golf (9), tennis, and in the People's Park are sports grounds and a swimming pool. Castlerea was the birthplace in 1815 of Sir William Wilde, father of the celebrated dramatist and wit, Oscar Wilde. Just west of the town is Clonalis House, the home of the late O'Conor Don, twenty-fourth in direct descent from the last high king of Ireland, who abdicated after the Anglo-Norman invasion of 1169. The nineteenth-century mansion, open to the public on certain days from May to September, has a number of historical mementos. Around Castlerea the country is gently undulating: two small local lakes are Lough O'Flynn (6 miles/10 km north-west) and Lough Glinn (5 miles/8 km north-west).

On the other side of Roscommon town, 5 miles (8 km) south-west on the Ballygar road is the village of Athleague; a mile (2 km) north of it is an interesting sculptured stone at Castlestrange which belongs to the early Iron Age. In an ancient graveyard at Fuerty, 4 miles (6 km) from Roscommon, two early gravestones mark the site of a Patrician foundation conferred to Justus, baptiser and tutor of Ciaran of Clonmacnois.

The road from Roscommon to Athlone (20 miles/32 km) runs close to the western shore of Lough Ree and provides a delightful drive. Six miles (10 km) outside the town is Knockcroghery (The Hangman's Hill), so called from an elevated mound east of the village which was once an execution place. Knockcroghery was once noted for the manufacture of clay-pipes. On the left beyond the village is Galey Bay, near the shore of which stands the fourteenth-century Galey Castle. Out in the lake is the island of Inchcleraun (see County Longford).

At Lecarrow, a road on the left leads to Rindown Castle, standing on a rocky promontory projecting into the lake. This was built about 1214, but an earlier fortification may have occupied the site because the promontory is mentioned as Rinn-duin (The Point of the Fort) in the Annals of the Four Masters under the date 1156. The thirteenth-century building was in the form of a P, the tail of the letter being occupied by a banqueting hall and the head by a massive tower. Near by are the remains of a watch-tower, protected by a broad ditch and a long wall with defensive towers. For a time this castle was in the hands of the Knights Hospitallers, and is sometimes called St John's Castle; it is an interesting example of medieval military architecture.

Beyond Rindown the lake extends to its greatest breadth, and there is a fine view across the water to the wooded shores on the Leinster side.

Boyle
Mainistir na Búille
(The Monastery of the Pasture River)

👨‍👩‍👧 Pop. 1,859.

ℹ️ Tourist information office (seasonal): Courthouse. Tel. (079) 62145.

One of the chief towns of County Roscommon, Boyle has a pleasant position at the base of the Curlew Hills and on the north bank of the River Boyle, which connects Lough Gara and Lough Key. It is a good touring centre, with golf (9), tennis, and river and lake fishing. Launch trips and boats for hire at Lough Key.

Points of interest
The ruins of the Cistercian Abbey stand close to the river on the north side of the town. This was founded by Abbot Maurice

The River Boyle

O'Duffy in 1161, and was closely associated with the great abbey of Mellifont (County Louth). It was suppressed in 1569, but the ruins still convey an impression of the original splendour of this richly endowed foundation. The chief feature is the cruciform church, where the nave, choir and transepts are in good preservation.

Around Boyle

Two miles (3 km) north-east of Boyle in the Rockingham Demesne is Lough Key Forest Park, where facilities for visitors include a fully serviced caravan park and camping area, a shop and restaurant, boating, cruising, fishing, picnic sites and children's paddling pool, with nature trails and walks in the surrounding forest grounds. On an island in Lough Key are the ruins of the Abbey of the Trinity, founded by the White Canons.

Lough Key Forest Park

East of Lough Key, near the river course to Carrick-on-Shannon, is the picturesque hamlet of Cootehall. Here were compiled the *Annals of Lough Ce*, now preserved in Dublin at the Trinity College Library. Along the river bank near the lake is the ruined Church of Asselyn.

At the southern end of the Arigna Mountains, 4 miles (6 km) north-east of Lough Key, is the village of Keadue where the last of the Irish bards, Turlough O'Carolan, spent the last years of his life. He is buried near by in the ancient cemetery of Kilronan, close to the shore of Lough Meelagh. There are coal mines in the area of Arigna village, and the roads leading from there over the hills to Geevagh (in County Sligo) have magnificent views.

Midway between Boyle and Ballaghaderreen, Lough Gara is a good trout lake that is also abundantly rich in archaeological material. Finds include 338 crannogs, 31 dug-out boats and many implements and ornaments. On the right of the road, westward from Boyle, is one of the largest dolmens in Ireland: the tablestone, 15 feet by 11 feet, was formerly supported on five upright pillars.

Nine miles (14 km) from Boyle, Ballaghaderreen is near the head of the Lung River which empties into Lough Gara east of the town. Behind rises the chain of sandstone hills that stretches north-east to the shore of Lough Key. There is good coarse fishing in this area on the Breedogue and Lung Rivers. An interesting monument 3 miles (5 km) from the town is the Four Altars, where mass was celebrated in penal times. There is golf (9) convenient to the town.

Eight miles (13 km) south-west of Boyle is Frenchpark, where the rectory was the birthplace of Douglas Hyde, father of the Gaelic League and first President of Ireland. The Douglas Hyde Interpretative Centre, which depicts Dr Hyde's life and times, is open to the public in the summer months. Close to the village

French Park

are the remains of the thirteenth-century Dominican Cloonshanville Abbey, built on the site of an ancient church attributed to St Patrick.

Six miles (10 km) south-east of French-park is the hill of Rathcroghan, where the ancient palace of the kings of Connacht stood. In pre-Christian and early Christian times this place was a royal capital, and many of the kings who reigned at Tara were crowned here. Rathcroghan is associated with Queen Maeve of Connacht, whose deeds are celebrated in the *Tain Bo Cuailgne*—'The Cattle Raid of Cooley'. There are many small raths in the townland, Rathcroghan itself being a large central mound with its features largely affected by cultivation. A short distance south is an enclosure called Roilig na Ri (Burial Place of the Kings), which has several small tumuli. Here, according to tradition, are buried Conn of the Hundred Battles and the three Tuatha De Danann queens who, according to legend, gave their names to Ireland in prehistoric times—Eire, Fodhla and Banba. A little

further on is a smaller enclosure, where a tumulus with a remarkable red sandstone pillar marks the grave of Dathi, the last pagan monarch of Ireland.

About 3 miles (5 km) south of Rathcroghan is Carnfree, the traditional inauguration mound of the O'Conors. Standing on a lofty eminence, it consists of a small mound of earth and stones about 8 feet high and 40 feet around. The inaugural stone now stands in front of Clonalis House.

Three miles (5 km) south-east of Rathcroghan, Tulsk was once a place of importance that figured prominently in the battles waged around this region. In 1406 O'Conor Roe erected a castle here; for a long time it was one of the strongest in the province, and was garrisoned by the Earl of Kildare when he led his forces into Connacht in 1499. In 1443 a Dominican abbey was founded at Tulsk by Phelim O'Conor, and it continued to flourish until the reign of Elizabeth.

Six miles (10 km) north from Tulsk is Elphin, which has been the seat of a bishopric for more than 1,500 years. St

Patrick founded a religious establishment here and placed St Assicus over it as first Bishop. This monastery flourished for generations and attained great repute as a centre of learning. About a mile (2 km) north-west of Elphin is Smith Hill, which may have been the birthplace of Oliver Goldsmith: one account states that he was born here in the house of his grandfather, who was curate of Elphin at that time.

Seven miles (11 km) from Elphin on the Dublin–Castlebar road is Strokestown, a nineteenth-century market town adjoining a spacious demesne in which stands a fine mansion. Strokestown Park House has been restored and is now open to the public during the summer season. It is proposed to open a Famine museum at the house within the next year or two. The town was laid out for Maurice Mahon who was created Lord Hartland in 1800. To the east of the town is the low range of the Slievebawn Hills, worth climbing for the extensive view over the plains of Roscommon and the River Shannon. Strokestown is noted as a coarse fishing area: there are 65 lakes near by, there are boats for hire, with tennis and horse-riding available, and forest walks near by. There is evidence of an early civilisation in and around Strokestown, particularly at Clonfree, Clonfinlock and Ardkillen. The famous Ardkillen Brooch which is now in the National Museum originated at Ardkillen in County Roscommon. There are also several crannogs of great antiquity in and around this area. At Slieve Bawn Co-operative Handcraft Market in the town the ancient handcrafts of Ireland are kept alive. A wide range of home-made souvenirs and crafts are on display. At the Strokestown Craft Centre a thoughtfully designed cobblestone courtyard is surrounded by workshops and display windows. Visitors are welcome.

The former Church of Ireland St John's Church is now the County Heritage Centre, which houses an interpretative display on pagan Celtic society in pre-Christian Ireland, with emphasis on the monuments at Rathcroghan and on the epic tale of the *Táin Bó Cuailgne*. The centre also offers a family research service.

Down

Helen's Bay

Down, one of Ireland's most fertile counties, is remarkable for its many low, beautifully cultivated hills. In striking contrast is the granite mass of the Mourne Mountains in the south, where Slieve Donard rises from the sea to 2,796 feet, Slieve Croob (1,755 feet) tops another group of hills in the centre of the county. In the east, the Ards Peninsula forms a barrier between the sea and the almost land-locked Strangford Lough. Bangor, Donaghadee, Newcastle and Warrenpoint are some of the fine resorts that line the beautiful Down coast; they are linked by good roads that closely follow the winding shore. County Down has many important historic sites and ancient monuments, together with attractions for the sportsman, the climber, the walker and the sightseeing tourist. The county includes the part of Belfast that lies east of the River Lagan (see pages 414–24).

Holywood
Ard Mhic Nasca
(The Height of the Son of Nasca)

Pop. 9,500.

337

This is a small residential town beside Belfast Lough, 6 miles (10 km) from Belfast. There is a coastal path to Bangor and Groomsport (12 miles/19 km).

Things to do
There are bathing beaches beside the town, golf (18), tennis and yachting plus brown trout fishing in Holywood Reservoir.

History
A church was founded here in the seventh century by St Laserian (whose mother was called Nasca). Later the Normans changed the name to Sanctus Boscus ('holy wood'). In 1572, a Franciscan monastery standing on the site of St Laserian's church was burned by Sir Thomas O'Neill to prevent its occupation by Elizabethan soldiers.

Points of interest
On the monastery site, at the northern end of the town, some remains of a later church may be seen. At the main crossing in the town centre stands the only maypole in Ireland, which is sometimes danced around on May Day, and there is the statue of 'Johnny the Jig' playing for the dance at the roadside and a Norman motte.

Around Holywood
Much of the 7½ miles (12 km) of the road east to Bangor is flanked by wooded estates. In the seaside suburb of Cultra is the Ulster

Cottage at the Ulster Folk and Transport Museum

Folk and Transport Museum, on 136 acres with its own railway station, exhibition halls and reconstructed farmhouses, schools, churches and mill. The Museum which traces the vernacular of the Ulster architecture of the common people (not the milords of the 'big house') from the early eighteenth century onwards, is to many one of Ireland's main and most sympathetic tourist attractions. Unlike many other similar projects, the isolated houses and the small village which is growing, gradually, into a small Ulster town have all been rebuilt, stone by stone, in natural settings which echo their original environments. The school, the courthouse, the rectory and the church look as if they have always been there, as does the row of houses called Tea Lane, and the weavers' cottages and the flax and spade mills. Turf fires glow in the grates. Traditional farming methods are practised throughout the seasons, whilst across the busy Bangor/ Belfast road the transport section includes everything from pennyfarthing bicycles to vertical take-off planes, each with an Ulster link.

Helen's Bay is a popular little bathing place backed by a 9-hole golf course. Near the pretty village of Crawfordsburn is the Crawfordsburn Country Park which extends for about a mile to the coast. There is an enjoyable 3-mile (5 km) walk along the coast from here to Bangor and in Crawfordsburn village, still in business, stands Ireland's oldest coaching inn.

Bangor
Beannchar (Peaked Hill)

Pop. 48,000.

Though now principally a dormitory town for Belfast, this is one of the largest and best-equipped seaside resorts in Ireland. It is built around the sandy bays of Bangor and Ballyholme, near the entrance to Belfast Lough. The town is well laid out with fine promenades, gardens, parks and recreation grounds. It is noted as a shopping centre.

Things to do

The resort has a seafront stretching for 3 miles (5 km) and a good beach of 1½ miles (3 km) at Ballyholme on the eastern outskirts. There is a leisure centre (for indoor sports), a heated indoor swimming pool and a thirties-style sea pool, a children's zoo, ice-rink, bowling alley, boats for hire, trips round the bay, chartered skippered sea fishing, summer theatre, open-air band concerts, visitor mooring at the spanking new marina, regattas to watch from beside the Ballyholme and the Royal Ulster Yacht Clubs. Bangor Castle has a heritage centre. There are two 18-hole golf courses and four more near by, plus brown trout in Ballysallagh Reservoir. The corbelled stone tower house on the seafront, once (1687) a customs house, now provides tourist information.

History

Bangor had its beginnings in the monastery founded about 555 by St Comgall. It became one of the most celebrated of Ireland's monastic schools, attended by thousands of students from Ireland, Britain and the rest of Europe. Many Bangor missionaries carried Christianity to the peoples of central Europe—notably St Columbanus (who founded monasteries at Anegray, Luxeuil and Bobbio), and St Gall (the apostle of Switzerland, who founded the monastery that became the nucleus of the Swiss town and canton named after him). The Bangor monastery was destroyed by Danes in 824. St Malachy, a twelfth-century abbot of Bangor who later became archbishop of Armagh, rebuilt the church about 1120. In 1469 the monastery was taken over by the Franciscans, who occupied if for nearly 150 years until the friary and its lands were given by James I to Sir Thomas Hamilton (afterwards Viscount Clandeboye). Much of the stone of the old monastery was used

by the new owner and his Scottish settlers in building a Protestant church on the site in 1617. The church there today is still called the Abbey Church.

Around Bangor

The immediate neighbourhood has many pleasant walks—a favourite being that via the Marine Gardens to Strickland's Glen, a pretty spot running inland from Smelt Mill Bay, a mile (2 km) west of the town (the return may be made by bus from the landward end of the glen). This walk can be extended by continuing west along the shore to Carnalea (1¾ miles/3 km from Bangor) or Helen's Bay (4 miles/6 km), from either of which one can return by rail. Other popular walks are to the old-world village of Groomsport (3 miles/5 km to the east), and to Orlock Head (about 1½ miles/ 2 km further), which marks the entrance to Belfast Lough. At Groomsport in 1689 the advance army of William III—10,000 men under the command of General Schomberg—landed from 70 transports.

At Grey Point on the coast in the leafy suburbs near Helen's Bay is Grey Point Fort, a restored coastal gun site guarding

Helen's Tower

339

the entrance to Belfast Lough through both world wars. Inland and just south of the main Belfast/Bangor road is Clandeboye, the wooded demesne of the Marquises of Dufferin and Ava, with Helen's Tower (built in 1858 in honour of Helen, Lady Dufferin, granddaughter of the playwright Richard Brinsley Sheridan, and author of the popular ballad 'The Irish Emigrant'), dominating the skyline. A sadder replica was later constructed at Thiepval on the Somme battlefield in France, where 6,000 men of the Ulster Division who had been recruited from all over Ireland, many of whom had drilled at Clandeboye, were killed or badly injured in 1916.

Donaghadee
Domhnach Daoi (Church of St Diach)

 Pop. 4,000.

This is a popular seaside resort with a small sandy beach and a good harbour, fronting the Irish Sea near the entrance to Belfast Lough. Beside the harbour is a yachting marina.

Things to do
As well as the beach, motor boats are available for trips along the coast or to the three Copeland Islands (popular picnic spots a few miles offshore). There is golf (18), tennis, bowling and putting, and brown and rainbow trout angling at Portavoe reservoir 2 miles (3 km) north-west. During the summer sea-angling boats depart from the pier, morning and afternoon. There is a noted bird observatory on Cross Island, one of the Copelands group (contact the RSPB).

Points of Interest
The Church of Ireland parish church (1641) occupies an elevated situation; its spire, added in 1833, is a prominent landmark. Behind the town is a large prehistoric mound called 'The Rath'. Now a public park, it is crowned by a castellated building,

called 'The Moat', which was built as a magazine for the explosives used in making the harbour. South of the town is the Cable Station, terminal of a cross-channel telegraph and telephone link.

The splendid lighthouse is by Sir John Rennie, noted for his design of the Eddy-stone Light. For many years the Port-patrick (Scotland)/Donaghadee ferry was the most usual approach to the Belfast area and visitors included Peter the Great of all the Russias (purchasing horses for his armies), James Boswell (writing), John Keats (spying), Daniel Defoe (spying), Franz Liszt (who brought his piano) and the ageing Wordsworth (who also kept a diary). Grace Neill's in the High Street, now a pub and once an Inn, claims to have served most of them and Brendan Behan.

Around Donaghadee
South of Donaghadee is the Ards Peninsula, a tongue of land about 20 miles (32 km) long and on average 5 miles (8 km) wide. A fertile area of numerous little hills, it fronts the sea on the east and encloses on its western side the large sea-inlet of Strang-ford Lough. The lough was called Strang-fjord by the Danes because of the violent tides that rush through its narrow entrance. It contains many islands which are the haunts of countless birds, and is note-worthy for the number of castle and monastic ruins around its indented shore. To ornithologists the lough is a site of major international significance; home, during the winter months, to enormous flocks of water birds escaping the Arctic cold. Look out for flocks of brent, greylag and white fronted geese, the terns breeding on the islands, the skeins of duck, the oyster catchers, curlew and redshank on the mudflats. Raptors stall and stoop over the rocky shore.

There are several little resorts and fishing villages on the 40 miles (64 km) of coastal road around the peninsula. Two miles (3 km) south of Donaghadee is Millisle village, a popular family resort.

Mount Stewart

Ballycopeland Windmill, a mile (2 km) west of the village, is preserved as an ancient monument, one of two surviving working windmills in Ireland. Five miles (8 km) south of Millisle, along a road with good coastal views, is Ballywalter village with its beaches and good sea fishing. Ballyhalbert, the next village, is on a wide bay that terminates on the south in Birr Point, the most easterly place in Ireland. Beyond the important fishing village of Portavogie is Cloghey, on a beautiful sand-fringed bay with a golf course (18) adjoining. Kirkistown Castle, erected here in 1622 by Roland Savage, has been much altered and modernised at various times. High up on its northern face are set two remarkable carved stone heads similar to the one on Shane's Castle near Antrim. Kearney, almost on the tip of the peninsula, is a nineteenth-century fishing village now in National Trust care.

The most southerly town on the peninsula is Portaferry, in a magnificent setting looking out on the narrow strait connecting Strangford Lough with the sea. There is a car ferry from here to Strangford, on the further shore. At Portaferry, Queen's University (Belfast) has a marine biology station and there is a sea water aquarium with over 70 marine species, all native to the lough, in view. Charter boats take divers to the many wrecks outside the lough mouth and sea anglers after huge skate and tope (both protected species) inside the lough, or cod, ling and pollack outside. In a private demesne beside the town are the ruins of Portaferry Castle, a large rectangular structure built to guard the entrance to the lough by the Anglo-Norman family of Savage. North of the town is a hill rising to 340 feet, which has a fine view over the lough and the surrounding country.

The road along the western shore of the peninsula reaches, after 11 miles (18 km), the village of Greyabbey, called after a Cistercian abbey that was founded in 1193 by Affreca, wife of John de Courcy and daughter of King Godfred of

Man. The extensive ruins are mainly those of the abbey church and refectory; there are many interesting features, including the fine west door. Greyabbey village has interesting antique shops.

Not far from Greyabbey the road to Newtownards passes the extensive demesne of Mount Stewart, a National Trust property with gardens, open to the public, noted for their mythological statuary. The dodos, dinosaurs and satyrs carved on the instructions of Lady Londonderry, referred to her pet names for politicians of the 1920s. The Temple of the Winds is a Greek-style 'folly'. Mount Stewart was the birthplace in 1769 of Lord Castlereagh, who as chief secretary for Ireland, secured the passage of the Act of Union in 1800.

Newtownards

Baile nua na hArda
(New Town of the Heights)

👫 Pop. 21,000.

Newtownards is a noted shopping centre and stands at the northern end of Strangford Lough, on the direct road from Belfast to Donaghadee. A busy marketing and industrial town, much of its trade was connected with the linen industry.

History

In medieval times, Newtownards was a small village clustered around the Dominican priory founded in 1244 by Walter de Burgh. The present town, with its streets built at right angles around a huge central square, originated with the seventeenth-century plantations.

Points of interest

In Court Street is the ruined nave of the Dominican Priory, with beautiful pillars and semicircular arches. The tower, of much later date, was erected by the Montgomerys when the building was used for Protestant worship. The vault of the Stewart family of Mount Stewart is in the southeast corner. Also in High Street is a cross erected in 1636, incorporating fragments of an ancient cross which stood on the same base and which was smashed during disturbances in 1653. The small chamber inside the cross served as a police cell. The Town Hall, overlooking the market place, is a stone building erected in 1765.

Newtownards has a leisure centre and flying lessons and pleasure flights are available at the Ulster Flying Club, based at the small airfield south-east of the town.

Around Newtownards

The ruins of the fifteenth-century Movilla Abbey, outside the town on the east, stand on the site of the sixth-century monastery and school founded by St Finian. Movilla's greatest pupil was St Colmcille (or Columba), whose dispute with Finian over the copy he had made of his Psalter brought the historic judgment of King Dermot: 'To every cow her calf, and to every book its copy.' Colmcille's refusal to abide by this led to the disastrous 'battle of the books' at Cuildrevne (County Sligo); afterwards, Colmcille did penance in exile in Scotland. Some inscribed grave slabs of the tenth to thirteenth centuries are built into the walls of the abbey ruin.

One and a half miles (2 km) from Newtownards, to the west of the Comber road, is Scrabo Hill (540 feet)—a remarkable formation of red sandstone and basalt. The hillside is a country park, and on it is Scrabo Tower, erected in 1857 as a monument to the 3rd Marquis of Londonderry.

There is golf (18) at Scrabo, and at Kirkistown (18), home to one of the north's motor racing circuits.

Five miles (8 km) from Newtownards on the Belfast road is Dundonald village. The great mound here is probably of sepulchral origin; about a mile (2 km) east of the village is a fine dolmen called the 'Kempe Stone'.

Just south of the village of Comber, a pleasant village with antique shops and sea trout in the Enver River, is Castle Espie Centre, run by the Wildfowl and Wetlands Trust with hides for viewing a unique collection of waterbirds. You can also view them from the comfort of the coffee bar.

Ten miles (16 km) south of Newtownards is Mahee Island in Strangford Lough. This is approached from the mainland by two causeways via Reagh Island, and contains fine remains of the fifth-century monastery of Nendrum founded by a disciple of St Patrick, St Mochaoi. The Bell of Nendrum, found here and now in Belfast Museum, is of the type used in Patrick's time. At the entrance to the island is the ruin of a castle built about 1570, which retains some interesting features. Part of the island is laid out as a 9-hole golf course.

On Sketric Island, about a mile (2 km) further south, are the ruins of one of the many castles built by the Anglo-Normans around the shores of this lough. Oyster beds have recently been established here. White Rock beside Sketric is a yachting centre.

Downpatrick
Dun Padraig (St Patrick's Fort)

Pop. 8,250.

Downpatrick, a quiet market town, is on hilly ground beside the low-lying marshy land of the Quoile River valley. North of the town there are picnic areas with rudd and bream fishing, old quays, innumerable water birds and fine trees. There is a visitor centre at the Quoile Pondage, downstream of the town, where the river meets the lough, next to a seventeenth-century castle beside the freshwater nature reserve. The Ulster Harp National is held at the charming racecourse which has horse races throughout the year. Just past the racecourse the vast Bally-dougan Mill is being restored as an industrial archaeological feature. There is a railway preservation society and steam

train rides are on offer on summer weekends. There is golf (18) just north of the town and at Bright Castle (18) 5 miles (8 km) south-east.

History
In early times this place was known as Rathceltchair (from Celtchair, a hero of the legendary Red Branch Knights). St Patrick, who landed in 432 at nearby Saul, converted the chieftain Dichu and may have founded the original church at Downpatrick. After Danish raids, the church was rebuilt in 1138 by the Archbishop of Armagh, St Malachy O'Morgair. The name Dun-da-leathghlas (fort of the two broken fetters) was also in common use in 1177, when the town (then the royal seat of MacDonlevy) was taken by the Anglo-Normans under John de Courcy. De Courcy made his headquarters here, and later added the name Patrick to the shortened form 'Dun' in honour of the national apostle. The town was sacked in 1316 by Edward Bruce and again in 1528 by Lord Deputy Grey, who also destroyed the cathedral. Although Downpatrick's importance has waned in modern times, it is still the administrative centre of the county which was named after it.

Points of interest
The Church of Ireland Cathedral, by the prominent height of Rathceltchair at the western edge of the town, was completed in 1826. It incorporates some parts of the twelfth-century cathedral, as well as features

Reputed burial place of St Patrick, Downpatrick

of later date. Outside the building on the east, stands a cross pieced together from ancient fragments. In the churchyard is a granite boulder inscribed with a cross and the name PATRIC; this was placed here in more recent times to mark the reputed burial place of St Patrick. The whole area around the cathedral, with its many elegant buildings, is undergoing conservation and architectural restoration.

In front of the Old County Gaol—now the Down County Museum with a small St Patrick's heritage exhibition, local artefacts and refurbished cells telling stories of crime and deportation—was where Thomas Russell, a founder of the United Irishmen, was hanged in 1803; he was buried in the parish churchyard. On a hillock outside the town on the north-west is the great Mound of Downpatrick, one of the largest in Ireland. This was increased in 1177 for de Courcy, who built his castle on it.

Around Downpatrick

On the shores of Strangford Lough, 6 miles (10 km) north of Downpatrick, is the port of Killyleagh, the shore crowded with small craft. On a hill beside the town is Killyleagh Castle (1850), which incorporates two circular towers of a seventeenth-century building. The original castle on the site

Memorial church of St Patrick, Saul

was erected by de Courcy. Killyleagh was the birthplace (marked by a plaque) of Sir Hans Sloane (1666–1753), the physician and naturalist whose collections of natural history, antiquities, books, manuscripts, coins, etc. formed the nucleus of the British Museum. The stile referred to in Lady Dufferin's ballad, 'The Irish Emigrant', is at the entrance to the graveyard beside the town, where she met the bereaved husband whose grief inspired her to write the verses.

Three miles (5 km) from Downpatrick, on the further bank of the River Quoile is Inch Abbey. It is approached from the town by crossing the Quoile Bridge and taking the first turn on the left off the Belfast road. This was a Cistercian abbey founded by de Courcy about 1180 for monks from Furness Abbey in England—in atonement, it is said, for having destroyed a monastery at Erenagh, 3 miles (5 km) south of Downpatrick. An Irish monastery previously on the Inch site was destroyed by Norsemen in 1002.

Two miles (3 km) north-east of Downpatrick is Saul, where St Patrick landed in 432 to begin his Irish mission. In the barn of Dichu, chieftain of the district, Patrick celebrated his first Mass in Ireland, and eventually he died in the church built on land granted to him by Dichu. In later centuries the church was destroyed several times by Danes and others; some fragments of the old buildings remain.

On the height above the village is the little memorial church of St Patrick (Church of Ireland), a modern structure of Mourne granite. The Shrine of St Patrick, a mile (2 km) further west on the prominent hill of Sliabh Padraig (415 feet), is a place of pilgrimage. A granite figure of the saint stands on the summit, and on a terrace lower down the hillside is an altar where Mass is celebrated annually.

Saul was the birthplace of the scholarly Franciscan, Aodh Mac Aingil (1571–1626), who was consecrated Archbishop of

Armagh in Rome in 1626 but died while preparing to leave for Ireland.

About 1½ miles (2 km) north-east of Sliabh Padraig is the interesting ruin of Raholp church, founded by one of Patrick's disciples, St Tassach. At Struell, 1½ miles (2 km) south of Saul, are St Patrick's Wells, which down to recent times were a popular pilgrimage place. These wells, like many others throughout Ireland, are believed to have been places of pagan worship which Patrick blessed and dedicated to Christianity. The buildings—a ruined church, drinking well, eye well and bath houses for men and women—are very ancient. Some preservation work has been carried out and the wells and one of the bath houses are cared for as ancient monuments.

East of Downpatrick, the circuit of the Lecale Peninsula is an interesting part of the coastal tour of County Down.

Strangford village, 9 miles (14 km) from Downpatrick, is on the western shore of the strait connecting Strangford Lough with the sea. There is a car ferry to Portaferry on the opposite shore (see page 341). Outside Strangford on the west is the large demesne of Castle Ward, where the grounds were landscaped in the eighteenth century and recently re-created. There are good gardens, a barn theatre, a collection of wildfowl, a Victorian laundry and an eighteenth-century summerhouse. The house itself is an unusual construction, part classical and part Strawberry Hill Gothic. Close by are two fifteenth-century castles, and in the farmyard is a craft centre and a silversmith. The grounds are open to the public daily, and the house during the summer months (except Tuesdays). North of the demesne, Audley's Castle is one of the best-preserved and most beautifully situated tower houses in the north, guarding the Strangford 'narrows'.

Five miles (8 km) south of Strangford is Ballyhornan, a tiny resort with two sandy beaches, on the way to Ardglass. Killard Point, between the beaches, is a nature reserve. Close by is Kilclief Castle, a square keep in good preservation.

Ardglass

Ard Glas (The Green Height)

 Pop. 1,300.

This pretty village has a fine harbour which has made it an important fishing port. Ardglass herrings are famous, and the harbour is the scene of much activity during the season. Prawns are nowadays as important a product as herring.

Points of interest

In medieval times this was a town of great importance, and remains of seven castles are still to be seen. Traces of earthworks on the hill called the Ward of Ardglass (the 'Green Height' which gives the village its name) are probably the remains of the fort of the Anglo-Norman, Jordan de Saukeville, where King John stayed on his visit here in 1210.

Beside the harbour is Jordan's Castle, the best preserved of the ancient buildings. It consists of a square tower of four storeys (the lowest one vaulted); at each of the two front corners is a square turret, one of which was used as a dovecote. This building, believed to have been a merchant's fortified residence and store, was defended by Simon Jordan against Hugh O'Neill in 1598. In 1911 it was repaired by Francis Joseph Bigger, who renamed it 'Shane's Castle' and housed in it an interesting collection of antiquities (Shane O'Neill occupied the Castle of Ardglass in the sixteenth century). The building is now preserved as an ancient monument.

Two of Ardglass's oldest castles— King's Castle and Queen's Castle—were reconstructed in the nineteenth century into a mansion called King's Castle.

Annexed to the old tower called Horne Castle are the fragmentary remains of a terrace of eighteen vaulted compartments with rooms above. This range of fortified buildings is said to have been the warehouses and dwellings of an English trading company established here in the early fifteenth century; they now form the club house of the golf club (18). Near by are two small towers of later date, called Cowd Castle and Margaret's Castle.

Around Ardglass

The fifteenth-century ruin of Ardtole Church is on a height overlooking the sea half a mile (1 km) to the north. Killough, a little fishing port 2 miles (3 km) to the west, is an old-world village of one long street lined with sycamores. St John's Point, 2 miles (3 km) to the south, forms the eastern horn of the wide Bay of Dundrum. St John's Point Church, half a mile (1 km) north of the lighthouse, is a very early structure whose west door has the inclined jambs and single-stone lintel typical of the churches built in Ireland before the introduction of the arch.

The road westwards from Killough passes close to the bay, with its extensive sandy beaches and sandhills. Beyond Tyrella beach the road turns north-west to round the narrow Inner Bay of Dundrum. Near the head of the inlet is Clough village, where there are remnants of a late medieval castle on the motte of a previous structure. Just north of Clough is the tiny village of Seaforde with a butterfly house, maze and nursery in the grounds of the big demesne.

Four miles (6 km) north of Newcastle is Dundrum, noted for its twelfth-century castle—a circular keep inside irregular curtain walls, surrounded by a rock-cut fosse. There are continuous mural chambers in the wall of the top storey. This castle probably followed the lines of the ancient palisaded fort called Dun Rudhraidhe (Rory's Fort), which occupied the site in early times. The ancient manuscript 'The Book of the Dun Cow' tells of a feast given in the fort by Bricriu of the Venomous Tongue to King Conor Mac Nessa and the Red Branch Knights. The Norman castle, said to have been built by John de Courcy for the Knights Templars, was the object of frequent attacks in later times.

A good example of the megalithic dolmen is at Slidderyford, 1½ miles (2 km) south of Dundrum. Opposite is Murlough Nature Reserve, 700 acres of sand dunes with a National Trust information centre.

There is often mention in Irish writings of the three 'tonns' or waves of Ireland. One of these was Tonn Rudhraidhe in Dundrum Bay. In stormy weather and with the wind in certain directions, the sea produced a melancholy roar which was believed to forebode the death of kings and chieftains.

Newcastle

An Caislean Nua (New Castle)

👫👫 Pop. 6,250.

O ne of the main seaside resorts in Northern Ireland, Newcastle is beautifully situated at the western end of the great sandy beach that fringes Dundrum Bay. The great bulk of Slieve Donard fills the skyline behind the town.

Things to do

Newcastle is a well-known golfing resort, with two 18-hole courses, including the world-famous Royal County Down Club, on the sandy peninsula running north from the town. Bathing is provided on the extensive beach fronting the town, and there is also an open-air swimming pool. Boats and fishing tackle can be hired at the harbour. The recreation grounds in Castle Park have tennis courts, putting green, miniature golf course (9), bowling green, boating lake and a children's aquatic playground Tropicana near by. There are halls for concerts and dancing. Open-air entertainments are organised in the holiday season. There are salmon and sea trout in the Shimna River.

Around Newcastle

Two miles (3 km) north, at Bryansford, is Tollymore Forest Park. Here there are many planned walks varying in length from one to eight miles (2–13 km), along the Shimna River and on the mountainside. There is

Newcastle and the Mourne Mountains

also a natural history museum and refreshment facilities. Near by is the Tollymore Mountain Centre. Not far away at Maghera are the remains of a once important monastery. The ruins include a large church and the stump of a round tower, and fragments of early grave slabs were found in the surrounding graveyard. The village is a good base for pony-trekking in the Mournes, through the forest parks and along the breezy strands. Further north, Castlewellan is a quiet little town in attractive country between the Mourne Mountains and the Slieve Croob group. Castlewellan Forest Park has one of the best arboreta in these islands, several planned walks for visitors, an aviary, trout fishing and elegant Queen Anne-style farm courtyards.

South of Newcastle, Donard Cave (1¼ miles/2 km away), can be entered by boat at high water. A short distance further south, beside the coast road, is Maggie's Leap, a remarkable fissure in the cliff about 6 feet wide and 90 feet deep (care should be taken in approaching the edge). Bloody Bridge, a

mile (2 km) distant on the coast road, is named after a massacre which took place in the wars of the seventeenth century. Opposite the old bridge is a picnic site, a starting point for coastal and mountain walks.

Extending south-westwards for nearly 15 miles (24 km) are the Mourne Mountains. This is an excellent area for the climber and walker, and the roads that encircle it and lead through gaps in the hills also make it easily accessible by car or bicycle. The Mourne group was formed of granite thrust upwards through the older Silurian rock, and has numerous peaks of over 2,000 feet—mostly in the north-east, where Slieve Donard towers nearly 3,000 feet above the sea at Newcastle. Most of the rivers rising in the Mournes flow southwards to the sea, but the largest—the Bann—winds a long course northwards to Lough Neagh and eventually to the Atlantic near Coleraine.

There is fine scenery along the coastal road from Newcastle to Warrenpoint, and in the valleys among the hills. Many of the

Castlewellan Forest Park

peaks are worth climbing for the magnificent views from the summit. Slieve Donard is easily ascended in about two hours from Newcastle—by following the route of the old tramway from near the harbour to its terminus at the granite quarry, and continuing over the spur called Thomas's Mountain. On clear days the view ranges from Donegal to Wicklow and across the sea to Scotland and the Isle of Man. Other favourite destinations for walkers are Lough Shannagh and the large artificial lakes of Silent Valley (now accessible by car and equipped with tea rooms, parkland and information centre), Ben Crom and Spelga.

Kilkeel

Cill Chaoil (Narrow Church)

Pop. 6,050.

This little port is the headquarters of a large fishing fleet. Another local industry is the quarrying and dressing of Mourne granite—a fine-grained stone that takes a high polish and is much used in building. The town is also a quiet seaside resort with a good sandy beach, and is frequented by anglers for the salmon, sea and brown trout fishing on nearby rivers. There is golf (9) in Mourne Park, and recreational facilities on the esplanade.

Around Kilkeel

Kilkeel is a good centre for exploring the Mournes and the coast of south Down. About a mile (2 km) north-east of the town is a fine dolmen with a large capstone.

Annalong, 6 miles (10 km) north of Kilkeel, is another pretty coastal village with an attractive little harbour with a slipway, narrow streets and a restored water-powered corn mill. Behind the corn mill is a herb garden, and behind the whole village the patchwork of tiny fields, each separated from the other by stone walls, climbs up the side of craggy Slieve Binian.

South-west from Kilkeel the road passes a large ringfort with a chambered megalithic tomb near by and after 5 miles

Kilkeel Harbour

(8 km) reaches Greencastle, which has the massive rectangular keep of a Norman castle built to guard the entrance to Carlingford Lough.

Some miles west of Kilkeel the main road runs close to the shore of Carlingford Lough, giving fine views of this inlet flanked by the Mournes and (on the south side) the Cooley Mountains.

Ten miles (16 km) west of Kilkeel, on the northern shore of the lough, is Rostrevor, a health resort noted for its mild climate. The village is sheltered on the north and east by timberclad hills which give good views of the lough; a favourite viewpoint is the granite boulder Cloghmore ('Big Stone'), perched about 900 feet up on a spur of Slievemartin (1,597 feet). This stone, which weighs about 40 tons, was, according to legend, thrown by a giant from the further shore of the lough; in fact, it is a glacial erratic carried by the ice from the north.

About a mile (2 km) north of Rostrevor, in the valley of the Kilbroney River which is called the 'Fairy Glen', are the remains of Kilbroney Church. This was founded by St Bronach, a sixth-century nun; a shrine has been erected near by at St Bronach's

Well. St Bronach's Bell is in St Mary's Church, Rostrevor.

An oblelisk beside the road to Warrenpoint commemorates Major General Ross, who died from a wound received while leading the British attack on Baltimore (Maryland) during the American War of Independence; a few weeks previously he had captured Bladensburg and burned Washington, including the White House, eating the dinner abandoned in President Madison's dining-room before he himself fled.

Warrenpoint
An Pointe (The Point)

Pop. 4,800.

This popular resort and increasingly successful container shipping port, with spacious streets and tree-lined promenade, is beautifully situated on land projecting from the northern shore of Carlingford Lough.

Things to do
The lough shore is shingly but there are open-air seawater baths. There is golf (18),

tennis, bowling and putting, and other amusements. Row boats and wind-surfing boards (plus tuition) are available for hire, and there are pleasure boat trips in the lough. There is a ferry to Omeath, an active yacht club and prospects for sea angling, particularly for tope in late summer. Boats can be chartered at Greencastle.

Around Warrenpoint

The surrounding district can be explored on foot and from all parts there are beautiful views of Carlingford Lough, with the Mourne and Cooley Mountains rising from its shores. There is an ancient ringfort called Rathturret (1½ miles/2 km) and a dolmen at Burren (2½ miles/4 km). Warrenpoint is also an excellent touring centre for the Mournes and south Armagh, and the ferry to Omeath on the County Louth shore offers a convenient way to reach the Cooley district.

About 1½ miles (2km) from Warrenpoint by the bank of the Newry River, can be seen the original Narrow Water Castle on a rock connected with the shore by a causeway. John Sancky built this original castle here in 1560; the new castle, which now houses an interesting art gallery, was built by the Duke of Ormonde in 1663 on the hill above.

Newry

An tIur (The Yew Tree)

🚶🚶 Pop. 19,400.

This cathedral town and port is in a hollow among hills at the head of the Newry River estuary. The town is intersected by canals built in the early eighteenth century, now disused for commerce but stocked with fish and they are a venue for international angling contests. The inland canal was the very first to be constructed in the British Isles. The Town Hall (half in County Down, half in County Armagh) actually spans the Clanrye River. Evidence of the town's mercantile past can

be noted in the names of the streets: Buttercrane Quay, Sugar Island, Sugarhouse Quay and the associated warehouses. Newry Golf Club (18) is just south of the town.

History

From ancient times Newry was important because of its position at the 'Gap of the North'—the main crossing between the hills into Ulster from Dublin and the south. A Cistercian abbey founded here in 1153 by the King of Ireland, Maurice Mac-Loughlin, was burned only five years later. After 1177 de Courcy built a castle here, which was destroyed by Edward Bruce in 1315, rebuilt and again destroyed by Shane O'Neill in 1566.

The confiscated lands of Newry later came into the possession of Nicholas Bagenal, who converted the abbot's house into a residence for himself, rebuilt the castle and erected a Protestant church. He was succeeded as Marshal of the English army in Ireland by his son Henry, who was killed in 1598 in the Battle of the Yellow Ford. James II's forces under the Duke of Berwick set fire to the town when retreating before the Williamite army in 1690.

Points of interest

The Catholic Cathedral in Hill Street has some good stained-glass windows. The Church of Ireland St Patrick's Church in Church Street has part of the sixteenth-century tower, with the arms of Nicholas Bagenal who built it in 1578. This is the first post-Reformation Protestant church in Ireland.

In Newry Museum rests the table used by Lord Nelson on board HMS *Victory*. A restored eighteenth-century room with period furniture came from 19 Upper North Street in the town. The associated Arts Centre is the base for The O'Casey Theater (*sic*) Company, founded by the playwright's daughter Shivaun and the venue for travelling art exhibitions. The statue in the pedestrianised shopping area is that of John Mitchel, republican author of *Jail Journal*. From 9 a.m.–6 p.m., Tuesday–Friday you can visit the Victoria Bakery in Castle Street to watch the baking of Ulster's traditional breads.

Around Newry

Many places of interest in County Armagh are easily visited from Newry, which is also a convenient centre for the Mourne District.

Ten miles (16 km) from Newry on the Downpatrick road is Rathfriland village, perched on a steep hill. Here the Magennises, chiefs of Iveagh, had their main castle, which was destroyed in the wars of 1641. The Reverend Henry Boyd (1750–1832), translator of Dante, was vicar of Rathfriland. Ballyroney, 3 miles (5 km) to the north-east, was the birthplace of Samuel Neilson, United Irishman and editor of the *Northern Star* (see page 426); and of the novelist Mayne Reid (1818–1883). Reverend Patrick Brontë (or Prunty), father of the novelist sisters, was born in 1777 at Ballynaskeagh, 5 miles (8 km) north-west of Rathfriland on the Banbridge road. This and a number of other places in the area connected with the family are well signposted as The Brontë Homeland Drive. This district was also the home of Helen Waddell, modern medievalist, scholar and novelist (author of *Peter Abelard*, *The Wandering Scholars*). Her grave is at Magherally, near Banbridge.

There is a good run of late season grilse and fine brown trout to be seen from the many-arched stone bridge at Katesbridge, over the Bann, or at the weir at Hazelbank. Signposted off the Rathfriland to Ballynahinch road is the strikingly elegant Legananny Dolmen silouetted against the skyline.

East of Rathfriland, beyond the tiny village of Kilcoo, the road passes beside Lough Island Reavy. At Drumena, beside this lake, is a good example of an ancient stone cashel or fort with a souterrain that is preserved as an ancient monument.

Banbridge

Droichead na Banna (The Bann Bridge)

 Pop. 9,650.

This busy market town and light industry centre is named after the bridge which carries the Dublin–Belfast road across the River Bann. The main street is unusual in that the central part of its surface is cut at a lesser gradient than the sides. There is a statue in Church Square of Captain Francis Crosier (1796–1848), a native of Banbridge who was second-in-command on the voyage during which the North-West Passage was discovered.

There is golf (12) 1½ miles (3 km) north-west of the town and brown and rainbow trout fishing in Corbet Lough and Loughbrickland Lake near by.

Around Banbridge

The remarkable ringfort called Lisnagade, 3 miles (5 km) south-west, is the largest of a series of forts which defended the 'Dane's Cast'—a line of earthworks along the boundary of the ancient kingdoms of Ulaidh and Oriel. A fine section of this rampart can be seen in the demesne at Scarva, on the County Armagh border, 4 miles (6 km) south-west of Banbridge. Scarva was the rendezvous of William III's armies before they marched to the Boyne in 1690. A mock battle at Scarva recreating William's victory over James is an important feature of the Orangemen's annual celebrations each July.

Dromore

Druim Mor (Great Ridge)

 Pop. 3,100.

At Dromore the Dublin–Belfast road crosses the River Lagan. The old stocks in the market square are still occasionally used for imprisoning

Hillsborough, fort and lake

local brides and grooms before a wedding. There is a lively horse fair on the last Saturday in September.

History
A monastery was founded here by St Colman about 600, and the town was for long the ecclesiastical capital of the diocese of Dromore.

Points of interest
The High Cross of Dromore, erected by a successor of St Colman in the ninth or tenth century, formerly stood in the Market Square; in 1887 the remaining fragments were incorporated in a restoration of the cross, which was re-erected on its present site beside the bridge over the Lagan. The Protestant Cathedral dates from the seventeenth century; it has the traditional pillow-stone of St Colman and the tombs of two famous bishops of the diocese—Jeremy Taylor, who ruled the diocese along with that of Down and Connor from 1661 to 1667; and Thomas Percy, author of *Reliques of Ancient Poetry*, who was bishop from 1782–1811. The great Norman earthwork, Dromore Mound, is a quarter mile from the town.

Hillsborough

Pop. 1,200.

Hillsborough is named for Colonel Arthur Hill who built the seventeenth-century fort which stands in the fine park beside the town. William III is said to have spent a night in this fort on his way to the Boyne in 1690. The Church of Ireland parish church is a handsome Gothick (*sic*) building erected in 1774. Hillsborough Castle, once the Hill family seat, was the official residence of the Governor of Northern Ireland; there is an agriculture research farm in the demesne. There is trout fishing in the demesne lake. Sir Hamilton Harty, the musician, was born in Hillsborough, where his father was organist of the fine gothic parish church. The village has many fine examples of Georgian architecture, in particular the market house. It is a growing antiques centre.

Seven miles (11 km) west of Hillsborough is Moira village; a battle fought here in 637 between the High King of Ireland and the King of Ulster is the subject of a poem by Sir Samuel Ferguson. Between Hillsborough and Moira, Kilwarlin

Moravian church (built by a refugee Greek nobleman) has a landscaped model of the battlefield of Thermopylae in the grounds.

Ballynahinch

Baile na hInse
(Town of the River-meadow)

Pop. 3,700.

Ballynahinch is a thriving market town in pretty countryside which, because of its many low rounded hills, has been likened to a basket of eggs. These hills are known to geologists as drumlins, glacial deposits of boulder clay on a surface broken by rocky hummocks. South-west of the town the land rises into the more rugged Mid-Down group, topped by Slieve Croob (1,755 feet). Trout fishing in a beautiful setting is available on Montalto Estate Lake, where the County Down Staghounds meet.

History

The Battle of Ballynahinch in 1798 was the last stand of the United Irishmen in the north. The British troops of General Nugent occupied the town under cover of darkness. The battle began with a discharge of cannon at dawn on 13 June and the military were being scattered by a charge of pikemen when the untrained insurgents misinterpreted a bugle call and fled. The youthful heroine Betsy Grey, who fought with the insurgents in the battle, was overtaken outside the town by a party of yeomanry and killed. Her grave is in Ballycreen townland, 3 miles north-west of Ballynahinch.

Around Ballynahinch

The Spa, 2 miles (3 km) south, is a little inland resort with iron and sulphur springs, now disused. It has a golf course (18). Near the village of Loughinisland, 7 miles (11 km) south of Ballynahinch, are the ruins of three ancient churches on a lake-islet connected to the mainland by a causeway. The middle church—the oldest—appears to date from before the thirteenth century, but its architectural features are destroyed. Over the door of the southernmost of the buildings (called

Gardens at Rowallane

MacCartan's Church, from Phelim MacCartan who is said to have built it) is the inscription 'PMC, 1636'. This church, however, appears to be a remodelling of a structure already existing at that date. The largest building (to the north) was used at one time by both Catholics and Protestants, who held services in it at different hours until about 1718.

At the crossroads beside the northern end of the lake stood the house which was the Buck's Head Inn kept by Andrew Lemon—and called 'Andy Lemon's' in the ballad about Thomas Russell, 'The Man From God-Knows-Where'. Russell read the proclamation of Emmet's rising in 1803 from the capstone of the dolmen which still stands by the now widened roadside.

Six miles (10 km) north-east of Bally-nahinch is Saintfield, the scene of an engagement in 1798 in which Munro's insurgents defeated a force of yeomanry. Near Saintfield are the very fine gardens at Rowallane, which are open to the public.

Francis Hutcheson (1694–1746), father of the Scottish school of philosophy, was born at Drumalig, 4 miles (6 km) north-west of Saintfield.

Armagh

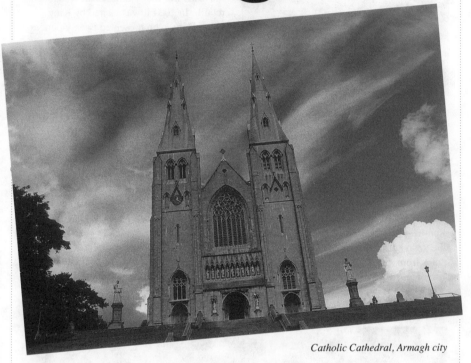

Catholic Cathedral, Armagh city

rmagh, like Down and Monaghan which adjoin it, is a county of gentle hills—the land becoming more hilly towards the south, where Slieve Gullion rises to 1,893 feet. Around Richill and Loughgall in the north is a rich fruit-growing area, which has earned for Armagh the title of 'The Garden of Ulster'; it is noted for Bramley apples, garden plants and jam. Lurgan and Portadown were important centres of the linen industry. This area was the scene of many events in the epic literature of ancient Ireland. In history it also holds an important place, and the ancient city of Armagh—in prehistoric times the seat of Ulster kings—has been Ireland's ecclesiastical capital for 1,500 years.

Armagh
Ard Macha (Macha's Height)

Pop. 12,700.

rmagh is an interesting town with an air of quiet dignity. Its well laid out streets are dominated by the two cathedrals standing on adjoining hills. There are many fine houses of the Georgian and Regency periods, and excellent wrought-iron work is to be seen in gates, signbrackets, etc. The Mall, once a race-course right in the city, tree lined and green swarded, is the perfect place to break a journey, to stroll or to watch a local cricket match. The city is currently undertaking an ambitious, sympathetic and lengthy

The Mall, Armagh

regeneration plan to present its past more readily to the visitor.

History
Armagh was probably named after the warrior Queen Macha, who about 300 B.C. built as her royal residence the great fort Eamhain Macha, west of the hill on which the town later grew. The cathedral city dates from A.D. 443, when St Patrick established his primatial see on the hill called Ard Macha, granted to him by a local chieftain called Daire. Patrick also founded a monastic school at Armagh, which became a great centre of learning. The importance of the place attracted plundering Danes and others, and during five centuries the town was many times destroyed and rebuilt. In 1004 it was visited by King Brian Boru, who presented twenty ounces of gold to the church; and in 1014 Brian and his son Murrough, both killed in the Battle of Clontarf, were buried here. Between 1014 and the Anglo-Norman invasion of 1170 Armagh reached its fullest brilliance, and in 1169 the last Irish high king, Ruari O'Connor, founded in Armagh a professorship 'for all the Irish and the Scots'. In 1556 the town was reduced to ruins by Shane O'Neill to prevent its occupation by the English, and in 1642 it was again destroyed by Phelim O'Neill.

The Church of Ireland Cathedral occupies the traditional site of the church built by St Patrick. It is a plain, well-proportioned building in perpendicular Gothic style, with a battlemented

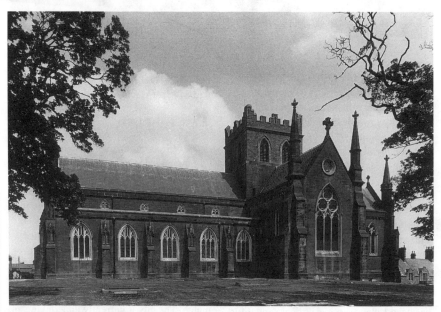

Church of Ireland Cathedral, Armagh

tower rising from the intersection of the nave and transepts. The building in its present form is mainly the work of restorations in the eighteenth and nineteenth centuries. Outside the north transept is a tablet marking the reputed site of Brian Boru's grave.

Monuments inside include a statue by Roubiliac of Sir Thomas Molyneaux (1661–1733) and effigies of some former archbishops. The north transept, now used as a vestry, has seventeenth-century memorials of the Caulfields, Earls of Charlemont, and the transept and crypt hold a collection of pre-Christian stone figures one of which, bare breasted, is referred as an effigy of Queen Macha. Another clutching its left shoulder may commemorate Conall Cearnach, a warrior of Ard Macha thrown from his chariot. The colours of the Royal Irish Fusiliers, and a French standard captured at Ballinamuck by the Armagh militia in 1798, are hung in the church. The cathedral library (1711), the first public library outside Dublin, contains an annotated copy, in Swift's hand, of *Gulliver's Travels*.

The Catholic Cathedral stands imposingly on a hilltop site, approached by a long series of steps with terraces. Erected in 1840–1873, in Decorated Gothic style, it has a fine west front with tall twin spires. The inside walls are completely covered with mosaic, including medallions of the saints of Ireland. Marble is also extensively used, and the altars, rood screen and marble pulpit are of particular interest. The red hats of the cardinal archbishops of Armagh hang in the cathedral. The statues flanking the doorway are those of the Primates, Crolly and McGettigan, during whose incumbencies the cathedral was built. Ara Coeli, the archbishop's residence, is near by.

Points of interest

At the northern end of the Mall (a pleasant green, lined partly by Georgian houses) is the attractive Courthouse designed by Francis Johnston (1761–1829), who was

Planetarium

born in Armagh. The Royal School in nearby College Hill was founded by Charles I in 1627. Across the road is the entrance to the Observatory, established by Archbishop Robinson in 1791. The domed Planetarium, in the grounds of the observatory, gives public shows daily and has a Hall of Astronomy with a telescope for public use. The building at the south end was the gaol. The Sovereign's house at the north-east corner comprises the museum of the Royal Irish Fusiliers.

The County Museum is in a little classic-style building on the east side of the Mall; the exhibits include a fine collection of bronze weapons and implements. A beautiful example of a Georgian town house is number 36 Scotch Street (now a bank).

The Protestant Archbishop's Palace, built for Archbishop Robinson, now the Council Offices, is approached through the palace demesne—which now incorporates a golf course (18)—from Priory Road. The chapel is a worthy example of the work of its designers, Thomas Cooley and Francis Johnston. In the demesne are the ruins of a thirteenth-century Franciscan friary and the stables have been restored to some of their former glory as a heritage centre with a focus on matters equestrian. In Navan Street, west from Ogle Street, are the old buildings of Drelincourt's School, erected in 1740.

The game of road bowls, peculiar to Cork and Armagh, is played on the roads around the city on summer Sundays. Competitors hurl, underarm, a heavy metal ball along the roadways, the winner being he or she who takes the least throws. Wagers can be heavy.

Around Armagh

Two miles west is Eamhain Macha. This is an elliptical earthwork that encloses a gigantic mound which has the appearance of a tumulus and may be the burial place of Queen Macha, who founded it about 300 B.C. Eamhain was the seat of the Ulster kings for 600 years until King Fergus Fogha was defeated by the Collas and his palace destroyed in A.D. 332. In the first century A.D., under King Conor Mac Nessa, Eamhain was the headquarters and training school of the Red Branch Knights, whose prowess is celebrated in many legends. The 16-acre mound—once Macha's Palace and her hospice where she sheltered the sick and where Deirdre of the Sorrows met Noisi, her lover, and where Cuchulainn demonstrated his prowess—was, archaeologists now know, the site of a vast 100 B.C. conical construction of concentric circles of wooden posts, which once built, was burnt ceremoniously to the ground. An interpretative centre is planned near by. The surrounding countryside has also been rich in archaeological finds, the locations of many of which are referred to in tourist information available at Navan.

Eight miles (13 km) west of Armagh is Tynan, noted for its ancient crosses. The village cross, 13½ feet (4 m) high, has been partly broken and restored. There are three other crosses in the Tynan Abbey demesne, and a smaller plain cross in the old churchyard at Eglish. Three miles (5 km) to the south, on the boundary with County Monaghan, is Middletown, near which are the remains of Rathtrillick (ancient earthen fort) and of Ardgonnell Castle.

ichill, with its seventeenth-century Dutch gabled manor house and Loughgall, also with a gable manor house—now a government agricultural centre—both 5 miles (8km) north-east, are deep in orchard country and are at their best in apple blossom time (May/June).

About 2 miles (3 km) north of Armagh is Beal an Atha Buidhe (The Yellow Ford), on the River Callan. This is celebrated for the battle here in 1598, when the army of Sir Henry Bagenal was defeated by Hugh O'Neill. O'Neill afterwards allowed the English garrison of the fort at Blackwaterstown (a few miles to the north-west) to march out and go unmolested to Newry. The fort at Charlemont, further north, was erected by Lord Mountjoy in 1602. It changed hands several times in the wars of the seventeenth century, after which it was garrisoned by English soldiers down to 1859. It was demolished in 1921.

Nine miles (14 km) north of Armagh, beyond the village of Loughgall, is Ardress House (open to the public). A seventeenth-century building with Georgian additions, Ardress has fine plasterwork by Michael Stapleton. Six miles (10 km) north-west of Ardress, at Bond's Bridge, is The Argory, another National Trust house still lit by a gas plant installed by the Sunbeam Acetylene Gas Company in 1906.

Portadown
Port an Dunain
(Landing Place of the Small Fort)

🚻🚻 Pop. 21,350.

rosperity came to Portadown first with the building of the Newry/ Lough Neagh canal in the 1730s and later with the growth of the linen industry and as the north's main rail junction. Now it is a town of light industries, of interest mainly to anglers in pursuit of massive catches of roach and bream from the River Bann.

Things to do

Recreational facilities at Portadown include a bowling green, golf (18), and fishing on the Bann and its tributary the River Cusher. Midway between Portadown and Lurgan is Craigavon Water Sports Centre, an artificial lake of 178 acres providing sailing, canoeing, water-skiing, wind-surfing and sub-aqua diving. The lake is stocked with rainbow trout and has a sandy beach. There are facilities for disabled anglers. Just out of the town is Oxford Island with its nature reserve on the shores of Lough Neagh. Water birds, particularly great crested grebes, herons and overwintering ducks are of great interest to the ornithologist. There is a marina at Kinnego.

Around Portadown

The little village of Maghery, situated where the River Blackwater enters Lough Neagh, is 8 miles (13 km) north-west of Portadown. It is an angling centre and boats are available for trips on Lough Neagh. About a mile (2 km) offshore is Coney Island, a wooded islet which is said to have given its name to the New York resort. The island is now a nature reserve, reached by boat from the slipway at Maghery and the property of the National Trust. At The Birches, 5 miles (8 km) north-west of Portadown, on Lough Neagh shore, are the remains of the ancestral home of General 'Stonewall' Jackson of American Civil War fame.

Nine miles (14 km) east of Portadown (M1 exit 13) lies Peatlands Park with a narrow gauge railway and exhibits describing the extraction of peat (turf) and its role in both industrial and rural society plus the importance of preserving the natural environmental wealth of peat bogs.

Lurgan

An Lorgain (The Strip of Land)

 Pop. 21,000.

Lurgan with its broad main street based its prosperity on the linen industry, as did all the old towns in this part of Ulster, and textile manufacturing is still important to the economy.

Things to do

Lurgan Golf Club's course (18) adjoins the public park where there are tennis courts, a putting green and a bowling green. There is a good sandy beach at Lough Neagh, about 2 miles (3 km) north of the town; boating on the lough is another popular pastime at Oxford Island and Kinnego marina, areas with excellent bird watching facilities. There is also some carp, bream, roach and perch fishing in Lurgan Park Lake in the centre of the town. Near by, at Turmoyra (Craigavon), there is an artificial ski slope and golf with (18), (9), par 3 and a 12-hole pitch and putt course.

History

In the early years of the seventeenth century, this district was taken from the O'Neills and given to William Brownlow, who planted it with his English followers and founded the nucleus of the town. The colony was destroyed by Sir Phelim O'Neill in the wars of 1641 and was not rebuilt until twenty years later. It was destroyed again by the army of James II, but soon after the defeat of James in 1690 it was restored. Some years later the local linen industry was established.

Beside the town is Brownlow House, erected in 1836 by Charles Brownlow, first Lord Lurgan. A subsequent holder of the title was the owner of the famous greyhound 'Master McGrath'. Brownlow House is now the headquarters of the Imperial Grand Black Chapter of the British Commonwealth (cognate with the Orange Order) and the grounds have become a public park.

Three and 5 miles (5/8 km) east of Lurgan, the villages of Waringstown and Moira have some of the most attractive houses in the north and two ancient Protestant churches with beautiful interior workmanship, this district having been colonised by Huguenot and Flemish weavers in the eighteenth century.

James Logan, one of the founders of Pennsylvania, was born in Lurgan in 1674; he became chief justice and later governor of the colony. George W. Russell (AE), the poet and economist, was born in William Street in 1867.

Craigavon

Planned for a population of 180,000 joining Lurgan and Portadown, the new town of Craigavon is still waiting for people to arrive. A bold experiment in new town planning, the visitor may see it as an inter-linked series of numbered roundabouts, distant large buildings and occasional housing estates.

Things to do

The two 'balancing' lakes which help to drain the surrounding flatlands provide a series of water-based sports referred to under Lurgan and Portadown, as are the golf and dry ski slope facilities.

Tanderagee

Toin re Gaoith (Windswept Bottomland)

 Pop. 2,200.

Agriculture and linen-weaving were the chief industries of this town, which is pleasantly situated on the River Cusher, 2 miles (3 km) from where it joins the Bann. The Cusher has fishing for brown trout and perch, and there is a golf course (18) in the demesne of Tanderagee Castle, now a potato crisp factory which welcomes visitors.

History

Tanderagee was for centuries the chief seat of the O'Hanlons, who built the first castle there. Under the plantation of James I the family was dispossessed and Tanderagee given to Captain Oliver St John. In the wars of 1641 the castle was recaptured and destroyed by the O'Hanlons. The most

celebrated member of this family was Redmond O'Hanlon who became leader of an outlaw band with headquarters at Slieve Gullion in south Armagh. For ten years he was a thorn in the side of the English, and levied exactions in Armagh, Down and Tyrone. He was murdered for reward by his foster-brother in 1681.

Around Tanderagee

Two miles (3 km) to the south-west is the little village of Clare, beside the pretty wooded glen of the Cusher River.

Five miles (8 km) south of Tanderagee is Poyntzpass. It is named after Lieutenant Charles Poyntz, who commanded the Elizabethan soldiery opposing a body of Hugh O'Neill's forces in an engagement at the pass here between County Armagh and County Down. In Drumbanagher House demesne, 2 miles (3 km) to the south, are the remains of the earthworks called 'Tyrone's ditches', thrown up by Hugh O'Neill in his war against the English.

Six miles (10 km) south-west of Tanderagee, on the Newry road, is the little town of Markethill. Near Markethill is Gosford Forest Park, in the demesne of the second, and nineteenth-century, Gosford Castle. The planned walks, many designed by Dean Swift during his stay on the estate, give panoramic views of south Armagh.

Keady

An Ceide (The Flat-topped Hill)

 Pop. 2,000.

This is a market town in a district of little hills south of Armagh, within easy reach of good trout and coarse fishing.

Around Keady

In a pretty valley 2 miles (3 km) north-east is the village of Tassagh, where an ancient burial ground and a group of three double-ringed forts may be seen. In the heart of the Fews, the picturesque hill country

Slieve Gullion Forest

south-east of Keady is the village of New-townhamilton, named after the man who founded it in 1770. The old coach road from Dublin came this way and the hills and dense woods of the district sheltered many an outlaw, including the famous Redmond O'Hanlon (see page 360). Clay Lake, 1½ miles (2 km) south of Keady, has 120 acres of perch, pike and rudd fishing.

About 6 miles (10 km) to the south are the remains of the prehistoric fortification called The Dorsey, an earthwork originally oval in shape and extending at least 1¼ miles (2 km) east and west. It is now much broken by cultivation and by roads.

Three miles (5 km) north-west of Newry, County Down, is Bessbrook, founded by a member of the Quaker family of Richardson to house the workers of the linen-spinning mills which were practically the only industry of the town. Derrymore House near by was built in 1780 by Isaac Corry, last chancellor of the exchequer in the Irish parliament. Here, in 1800, Corry and Castlereagh drew up the Act of Union.

About a mile (2 km) to the south is Camlough village, beneath the northern slopes of Camlough Mountain (1,389 feet). In the valley between this mountain and Slieve Gullion lies Camlough Lake, a well-known beauty spot with excellent pike fishing. The little Catholic church at Cloghoge, 4 miles (6 km) south-east of Camlough, is a beautiful example of modern Irish-Romanesque architecture. A conspicuous feature of the south Armagh landscape is Slieve Gullion (1,893 feet), rich in legendary associations. On the summit is one of two burial places consist-ing of a chamber and entrance passage, with the remains of a cairn which covered it. On the eastern slopes are the interesting ruins of the two Killevy churches (one tenth, the other fifteenth century) on the site of a fifth-century nunnery, in use till 1542. The most striking feature is the massive lintelled doorway of the earliest church. The Slieve Gullion area is now a forest park with scenic drive.

Further south, on the Armagh–Louth border, is Moiry Pass, the scene of many bloody conflicts between invaders and defenders of Ulster. Hugh O'Neill held the pass for five years against the English until his defeat by Lord Mountjoy in 1601. Mountjoy then built Moiry Castle (now a ruin), 2 miles (3 km) south of Jonesborough. In this district also is the Kilnasaggart Stone, a pillar stone bearing incised crosses and an inscription in old Irish.

West of Jonesborough is Forkhill village, beautifully situated in a pass between the hills. Peadar Ó Doirnín

(1704–1768), the celebrated Gaelic poet, was schoolmaster here and is buried near by at Urney graveyard.

Crossmaglen, in the south-west corner of the county near the Monaghan border, is a small market town with a very spacious square. There are some interesting ancient ringforts and other antiquities in the neighbourhood, and within a few miles are several small lakes which hold brown trout and coarse fish. There is golf (18) 4 miles (6 km) north of the village and a small thatched cottage folk museum at Mullaghbawn midway to Camlough.

Monaghan

Rossmore Monument, the Diamond, Monaghan

County Monaghan is remarkable for the great numbers of its little hills. Only a few rise higher than 1,000 feet, but from many points there are good views over the well-tilled, undulating countryside, with its lakes set here and there between the hills. Like County Cavan, Monaghan is well known to the coarse fishing enthusiast, but there is an ever increasing variety of activity holidays. The lace-making tradition of County Monaghan still thrives in both Carrickmacross and Clones. Monaghan formed part of the ancient territory of Oriel, and was known as the McMahon country because of the dominance of that powerful clan.

Monaghan
Muineachain (Little Hills)

Pop. 5,754 (urban district).

Tourist information office: Market House. Tel. (047) 81122.

Monaghan is the county town and a thriving agricultural centre. The early monastery founded here was plundered in 830 and 931, but continued to exist until 1161. In 1462 Phelim MacMahon founded, on the old site, a Franciscan friary which was suppressed by the English in the following century. When James I made the

TO THE MEMORY OF HENRY CRAVEN JESSE LLOYD, LATE LIEUTENANT OF THE 47TH REGT. AND OF THE NATAL MOUNTED POLICE, SON OF LIEUTENANT-COLONEL JESSE LLOYD, OF BALLYLECK, IN THIS COUNTY, WHO FELL FIGHTING AT ISANDULA, SOUTH AFRICA,

Lloyd Monument, St Patrick's Cathedral, Monaghan

town a parliamentary borough in 1613, it was inhabited mainly by retired members of the English garrison of Sir Edward Blayney, who had erected a fort here a few years previously.

An imposing landmark at the southern approach to the town is St Macartan's Cathedral (Catholic), a nineteenth-century Gothic Revival building with a slender spire. Other notable buildings are St Patrick's Church (Church of Ireland) of Regency Gothic design (1836), the St Louis Convent, the modern County Hospital and the Market House (1792). The town has a park and a children's swimming pool.

The St Louis Heritage Centre located at the convent is open to the public and depicts the history of the St Louis Order in Ireland. The Monaghan County Museum and Art Gallery exhibit archaeological, historical and artistic displays.

Lathlurkin Old Church, rebuilt in 1790, served as pro-cathedral until 1892. A barn-like church, it is situated in a graveyard on the Castleblayney road. Market Cross (1714)

at the Old Cross Square, may have been the cross to which proclamations were affixed.

Charles Gavan Duffy (1816–1903), founder of the *Nation* newspaper and of the Young Ireland Party, was born in Dublin Street; he later became Prime Minister of Victoria, Australia.

Around Monaghan

Adjoining the town is Rossmore Forest Park comprising 692 acres. The park is set among low hills and small lakes and has many pleasant forest walks. On the Castle-blayney road about half a mile (1 km) from the town is the birthplace of General Don Juan MacKenna, a famous soldier of Chile who died in Buenos Aires in 1814.

Glaslough village is 7 miles (11 km) north-east of Monaghan, with the beauti-fully timbered demesne of Glaslough House near by which is also an equestrian centre. A few miles west of there is Emyvale, in the heart of a picturesque, well-wooded district. Lough Emy, near the village, is noted for the number of its wild fowl and swans.

Four miles (6 km) north-west of Monaghan is Tydavnet, named after St Damhnait (Dympna), daughter of a sixth-century King of Oriel. Her relics are preserved at Gheel in Belgium, where her pagan father pursued her and killed her.

Clones
Cluain Eois (Eos's Meadow)

👪 Pop. 2,093 (urban district).

This is an important agricultural centre beside the Fermanagh border in the western part of County Monaghan.

In early Christian times it was the site of a monastery founded by St Tighearnach, who died here in 548. There are some slight remains of a later abbey and a well-preserved round tower. An ancient sculptured Celtic Cross stands in the centre of the town. Clones crochet lace, once widely exported, is still made in the area and a permanent exhibition of Clones lace may be viewed at the Diamond.

Around Clones
The River Finn, which flows east and south of Clones, is a brown trout river; it also has pike and perch, and many of the lakes in the district are good coarse fishing waters. There is a 9-hole golf course. Two miles (3 km) east of the town is Aughnakillagh, birthplace in 1870 of one of the leaders of the 1916 Rising, James Connolly. Newbliss, 5 miles (8 km) east of Clones, is a quiet village in a beautiful district of hills and wooded slopes. Annamakerrig House, where the famous theatre, radio and television producer Sir Tyrone Guthrie lived, was bequeathed by him to the nation on condition it was run as a home for those who live by the arts, including writing. It is now a thriving writers' and artists' community.

Ballybay
Beal Atha Beithe
(Ford-Mouth of the Birch)

👪 Pop. 530.

Ballybay is a progressive town set among low-lying hills on the shores of Lough Major, head-water of the Dromore River, a tributary of the River Erne. There is excellent coarse fishing in the neighbourhood, particularly for bream.

Lough Major, on the Castleblayney road, has also been developed as a trout lake.

Around Ballybay
Six miles (10 km) west is Rockcorry, lying beside a chain of lakes. This was the birthplace of John R. Gregg (1868–1948), pioneer of the Gregg system of shorthand. South-west of the village is one of the country's beauty spots, the Dartry Estate, with its woods, lakes and forest walks. Two miles (3 km) west of Rockcorry, in the old graveyard at Edergole, a slab bearing the MacMahon arms and a Latin inscription marks the grave of Bernard and Ross MacMahon. Ross succeeded his brother as bishop of Clogher in 1737, and again as archbishop of Armagh in 1747.

Carrickmacross
Carraig Mhacaire Rois
(The Rock of the Wooded Plain)

👪 Pop. 1,688 (urban district).

Carrickmacross is an attractive town with a spacious main street, in the southern part of County Monaghan; there is coarse fishing in the lakes near by. The exquisite Carrickmacross lace, which gained the town a great reputation, is still for sale at a local convent. Some slight traces remain of the castle built by the Earl of Essex, on the site now occupied by the St Louis convent.

Lough Muckno

Around Carrickmacross

At Tiragarvan, 1½ miles (2 km) to the west, are some interesting limestone caves.

Near the County Louth border, 7 miles (11 km) north-east of Carrickmacross is Inniskeen village, the site of a sixth-century monastery founded by St Deagh. There is a local history museum situated in the church. Patrick Kavanagh, poet and novelist, was born and is buried in the area. There is a burial vault or chapel of the MacMahons of Farney (erected 1672). A cross bearing the MacMahon arms and an inscription dated 1729 is embedded in a wall near the graveyard. A mile (2 km) from Inniskeen is Channonrock. This was the acknowledged boundary mark of the Norman Pale and the MacMahon territory of Farney.

Castleblayney

Pop. 2,027 (urban district).

Castleblayney is named after Sir Edward Blayney, who received a grant of land here from James I. The town is built on ground sloping up from the western shore of Lough Muckno, the largest and most beautiful of Monaghan's lakes and a well-known coarse fishing water. There are boats for hire, sailing, horse-riding, tennis, golf (9) and forest walks. In the grounds of Lough Muckno Leisure Park stands Hope Castle; the ill-omened Hope Diamond derived its name from the family which lived in the castle. The leisure park is set on 900 acres of wooded country with facilities of many kinds available.

Cavan

The Derries, Lough Sheelin

Cavan, the most southerly of the Ulster counties, is greatly diversified in surface. Its highest point is Cuilcagh Mountain (2,188 feet), in the mountainous projection of the county which reaches north-westwards between Counties Leitrim and Fermanagh. Ireland's longest river, the Shannon, has its source on the southern slopes of Cuilcagh. Most of the county is undulating land, with low round hills and myriad lakes. The River Erne, rising in Lough Gowna and flowing northwards through the centre of the county, spreads itself in a maze of small sheets of water separated by promontories and islands of every shape and size. Many of the Cavan lakes are very beautiful and offer first-class coarse angling.

Cavan

An Cabhan (The Hollow Place)

🚶 Pop. 3,332 (urban district).

ℹ️ Tourist information office: Farnham Street. Tel. (049) 31942.

Cavan, the county town, is in a pleasant district of low green hills. In ancient times it was the seat of

Killykeen Forest Park

the rulers of east Breifne, the O'Reillys. Their main residence was on Tullymongan Hill, on the outskirts of the town.

Of the Franciscan Friary founded in 1300 by Giolla Iosa O'Reilly, only the belfry tower remains. A plaque on the wall commemorates Owen Roe O'Neill, the victor of Benburb, who was buried in the chancel of the friary in 1649.

Things to do

There is golf (18), tennis, excellent angling for trout and coarse fish and a sports centre. Cavan Crystal produces 32 per cent lead crystal glass in the traditional mouth-blown and handcut fashion. Factory tours are available.

Around Cavan

Shantemon Hill, 3 miles (5 km) north-east, was the ancient inauguration place of the O'Reilly chiefs. About 3 miles (5 km) north-west is the fine demesne of Farnham House, and a few miles beyond on an island in

Lough Oughter is Clough Oughter Castle, a thirteenth-century O'Reilly fortress. This castle remained in the possession of the O'Reillys until the plantation of Ulster in the early seventeenth century. On the outbreak of the Rising of 1641 it was seized by Colonel Myles O'Reilly. William Bedell, Protestant Bishop of Kilmore, was held prisoner here for a time (1641–1642). The castle has been in ruins since it was taken by the Cromwellians in 1653. At Butlersbridge on the Annalee River there is coarse fishing with boats for hire.

There is an interesting folk museum at Cornafean which is open to visitors and which has about 3,000 items depicting the rural life-style from the 1700s up to the present. It is styled the 'Pighouse Collection' after the original building in which it was housed.

At Kilmore, about 3 miles (5 km) west of Cavan, the Protestant cathedral has a Hiberno-Romanesque vestry door that was brought from the old monastery on Trinity

Island in Lough Oughter. In the graveyard is the sculptured tomb of Bishop Bedell, the first translator of the Old Testament into Irish. On the west side of Lough Oughter is Killeshandra, almost surrounded by little lakes.

Four miles (6 km) north of here, at Kildallon lived the ancestors of Edgar Allan Poe. Killykeen Forest Park 8 miles (13 km) west of Cavan has 600 acres of woodlands with swimming, boating, fishing, nature trails and forest walks.

Beside the County Longford border 13 miles (21 km) south-west of Cavan is the little town of Gowna, beside beautiful Lough Gowna—source of the River Erne. Lough Gowna is a good coarse fishing lake.

Virginia

Achadh Lir (Lir's Field)

Pop. 699.

This little town is on the northern side of beautiful Lough Ramor, with its wooded shores and many islets. There is bathing at a sandy stretch of lakeshore beside the town and rowing boats can be hired for boating and fishing. The coarse fishing, for pike, perch, rudd and bream, is very good. There is a 9-hole golf course in a picturesque setting overlooking Lough Ramor.

Around Virginia

Murmod Hill (666 feet), 1½ miles (2 km) north, is a fine vantage point for views over the lake and surrounding country. At Cuilcagh Lough, 3 miles (5 km) north-east of Virginia, is the site of Cuilcagh House where Dean Swift began writing *Gulliver's Travels*.

The poetess Charlotte Brooke (1740–1793) was born at Rantavan, outside the village of Mullagh, 6 miles (10 km) east of Virginia.

The little town of Ballyjamesduff, celebrated in song by Percy French, is built

on the slope of a hill south of Lough Nadreegeel. William James, a native of this town who emigrated to America in 1789, was the grandfather of the philosopher William James and the novelist Henry James.

In the south of County Cavan is the pretty village of Mount Nugent, near the shore of Lough Sheelin—a well-known trout fishing lake in which the county borders of Cavan, Meath and Westmeath meet. Boats are for hire and there is an interesting crafts centre in the village.

Cootehill

An Mhuinchille (The Sleeve)

Pop. 1,487.

This town in east Cavan, lying between the Annalee River and its tributary the Dromore, is called after the family who founded it in the seventeenth century. There is coarse fishing on Dromlona Lake, boats for hire, and there are forest walks at Bellamont and Dartry. Thomas Brady (1752–1827), a field-marshal of the Austrian Army who became a privy councillor of Austria and Governor of Dalmatia, was born at Cootehill. The Irish-American authoress Mrs Sadlier (1820–1903) was a native of the town.

Around Cootehill

At Cohaw, 3 miles (5 km) away on the Shercock road, is a fine prehistoric tomb of the court cairn type. Shercock overlooks Lough Sillan—noted for its large pike and as the place where the largest horns of the extinct Giant Irish Deer have been found.

Kingscourt, a little town 8 miles (13 km) south-east of Shercock, has modern industries based on the rich gypsum deposits of the area. In the nearby Cabra demesne is the wishing-well featured in the song 'Doonaree', located at Dun-a-Rí National Forest Park, set in an area of outstanding beauty, part of which is maintained for public recreation and amenity.

At Bailieborough, 8 miles (13 km) west from Kingscourt, the Catholic church has notable stations of the cross by George Collie, R.H.A. At Killinkere, 6 miles (10 km) further south-west, is the reputed birthplace of General Phil Sheridan (1831–1888), a commander-in-chief of the US Army.

Belturbet

Beal Tairbeirt (The Ford of the Surrender)

Pop. 1,228.

A market town on the east bank of the River Erne, midway between the waters of Lough Oughter and Upper Lough Erne, Belturbet is an ideal coarse fishing centre. A two-hour river cruise is available during summer months.

Around Belturbet

The site of an abbey founded by St Colmcille is at Drumlane, 4 miles (6 km) to the south via the village of Milltown. The ruins, beautifully situated between Drumlane Lake and Derrybrick Lake, are of a fourteenth-century church and a round tower 45 feet high. On the Annalee River, 9 miles (14 km) south-east of Belturbet, is the pretty village of Ballyhaise, where there is an agricultural college. Canning, the English statesman, spent his early years here. There is good trout fishing on the Annalee.

Seven miles (11 km) west of Belturbet near the Fermanagh border is a well-known coarse fishing centre, Ballyconnell. According to tradition, it is named after Conal Cearnach, a first-century hero of the Red Branch Knights, who was killed here by the men of Connacht in revenge for the slaying of their king. Above the village rises Slieve Russell (1,331 feet), providing extensive views.

Work is in progress to open the canal between Ballyconnell and Ballinamore, County Leitrim. When completed in 1995, the Shannon and Erne will be again inter-navigable, providing the longest navigable waterway in Europe.

Nine miles (14 km) north-west of Ballyconnell, between Slieve Russell and Cuilcagh Mountain, is the village of Swanlinbar, once famous for its mineral springs. The only road connecting the north-western extremity of County Cavan with the rest of the county climbs steeply up to 1,100 feet in Bellavally Gap between Cuilcagh Mountain (2,188 feet) and Benbrack (1,652 feet). On the western side of the gap is Glangevlin, a wild glen hemmed around by mountains. Here, on the western slope of Cuilcagh Mountain, the River Shannon has its source—known as the 'Shannon Pot'. The mountains of this range provide interesting climbing and ridge walking.

North of Glangevlin the county border takes in part of Upper Lough Macnean, which County Cavan shares with Counties Leitrim and Fermanagh. Lower Lough Macnean, about a mile (2 km) further east, is in County Fermanagh, except for a small area near the village of Blacklion.

Monument to Cathal Bui Mac Giollghcheannaigh, Blacklion

Fermanagh

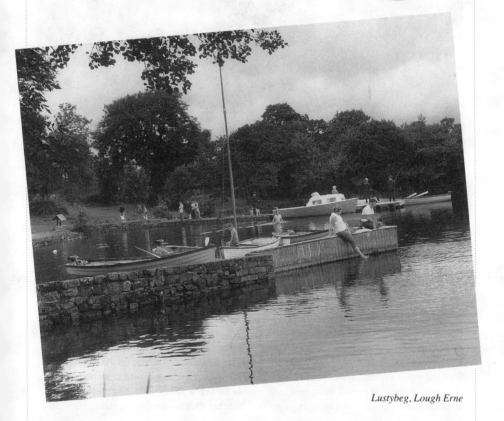

Lustybeg, Lough Erne

The most remarkable natural feature of County Fermanagh is the River Erne, which winds through the centre of the county. It expands into two extensive lakes, Upper and Lower Lough Erne, both of which have many islands. Some level land borders the river and lakes, but the rest of the county is hilly—rising to 2,188 feet in Cuilcagh Mountain on the County Cavan border. In the north-west Fermanagh touches the shore of Lough Melvin, and set among hills on the western border are Upper and Lower Lough Macnean. The limestone hills of west Fermanagh contain many interesting cave systems, and with the exception of County Clare is the most notable area in Ireland for the speleologist. This is a county with many attractions for the visitor: boating, bird watching and fishing on the 'lakeland of Ulster', climbing, interesting monuments, and throughout the county the charm of good scenery and pleasant towns and villages.

Enniskillen

Inis Ceithleann (Cathleen's Island)

👪 Pop. 10,450.

Lough Melvin

Enniskillen, the county town, is beautifully situated between two channels of the river joining Upper and Lower Lough Erne. In recent years, with the rapid expansion of cabin cruiser fleets on the two lakes and the superb angling, it has become a bustling holiday town.

Things to do

Vessels of all sizes may be hired for lake cruising and angling; guided boat trips are also available. There are facilities for bathing and golf (18) (9) (9), and Enniskillen is a convenient base for exploring the county—much of which can be visited in the course of tours by road around the lakes. There is a swimming pool and facilities for many indoor sports in the riverside Lakeland Forum. Pleasure flights and flying lessons are available through the flying club based at St Angelo Airport. Guided walks and tours concentrating on environmental

attractions are offered through the Tourist Information Centre near the Forum, as are pony-trekking and further active pursuits. The Ardhowen Theatre on the east side of the town has a magical lakeside setting and is the venue for exhibitions and professional touring theatre companies and musicians.

History

In ancient times Enniskillen was a stronghold of the Maguires, the ruling family of Fermanagh; their lands were confiscated early in the seventeenth century and granted to Sir William Cole. The town, incorporated by charter of James I in 1613, was settled by English families. In the wars of 1641 it was held for some time for the royalists, but finally surrendered to the Parliamentary forces of Sir Charles Coote. In 1689 Enniskillen was one of the principal strongholds of the English and Scottish settlers in Ulster, and attacking Jacobite forces were repulsed several times.

Points of interest

Beside the river is Enniskillen Castle which now houses both the county and regimental museum. Little remains of the old castle except a seventeenth-century turreted gateway and the foundations of the fifteenth-century Maguire castle which previously occupied the site. Inside the Castle Keep behind the Water Gate are two museums, the County Museum and that of the two famous Inniskilling Regiments, the Dragoons and the Fusiliers, which fought at Waterloo and the American War of Independence. The Church of Ireland Cathedral has part of the original seventeenth-century tower and has a good set of chimes. The regimental colours of the Royal Inniskilling Fusiliers hang in the choir. In Darling Street the Catholic church, a well-proportioned modern Gothic building, has a stained-glass window representing the founder of Devinish Abbey, St Molaise.

Other notable buildings are the Presbyterian Church, the Methodist Church and the Town Hall. A brass plate inside commemorates Captain Oates of the 6th Inniskilling Dragoons who walked out into a blizzard to save others on Scott's tragic return journey from the South Pole in 1912. A statue in the little public park on Fort Hill (above the east bridge) commemorates General Sir Galbraith Lowry-Cole, who fought in the Peninsular War and later became Governor of Cape Colony.

The old Buttercrane Market has been restored and reopened as a centre of craft workers and craft shops.

Around Enniskillen

By the lakeshore of the town is Portora Royal School, established in 1618 by charter of James I. Oscar Wilde was a pupil here, as also was Samuel Beckett, of *Waiting for Godot* fame, and Rev. Henry Francis Lyte, composer of 'Abide with Me'.

Most of the existing buildings date from 1777. Near by is the ruin of Portora Castle, built about 1618 by Sir William Cole. Bordering the town on the east is the well-wooded demesne of Castle Coole, now a National Trust property open to the public. The house was designed by James Wyatt and has plasterwork by Joseph Rose.

Circuit of Lower Lough Erne

Two miles (3 km) north of Enniskillen, Devenish Island—reached by ferry from Trory off the Kesh road every day except Monday in summer months—in Lower Lough Erne has a fine group of ecclesiastical remains on the site of a sixth-century monastery founded by St Molaise. The most remarkable building is a round tower nearly 85 feet high; this is noted for the fineness of its masonry and for its sculptured ornanent which is unusual in round towers. St Molaise's House is a remnant of a small rectangular oratory. Teampull Mór (Great Church) 80 feet long by 23 feet wide is also extensively ruined but there is a deeply splayed round-headed window in the south wall and near by a tomb of the Maguires.

Further up the hill is the latest of the buildings, St Mary's Abbey; there remains

Devenish Island

a quadrangular tower, part of the north wall of the choir, and a spiral staircase. Near the foot of the stairs is a stone with a Latin inscription dated 1449, which is probably the date the abbey was built. There is a good pointed doorway in the north wall. South of the abbey stands an unusual type of high cross, with the Crucifixion carved on the eastern face. (The shrine of St Molaise, now in the National Museum in Dublin, was made to contain a copy of the gospels. It is a small box of bronze plates of worked silver, with gold filigree and other ornamentation.)

On White Island—reached by ferry from Castle Archdale, near Kesh, every day except Monday in summer months— north of Devenish, are the ruins of a small church with Romanesque features; inside are seven strange sculptured figures of a very early period. Their identification continues to cause disputes among archaeologists, as both pagan and early Christian features are visible. Eight miles (13 km) north of Enniskillen is Killadeas, an angling, boating, sailing and cruising centre with a splendid view of the lake, where boats may be hired to visit Inismacsaint across the lake, where there are the ruins of an ancient church. At Killadeas Church are some curiously carved stones believed to date from the seventh or eighth century.

Four miles (6 km) further north is Castle Archdale Country Park and marina in a wooded demesne beside the lake. Here are caravan and tent sites, restaurant, fishing, boats for hire and nature trails. Pony-trekking and pony and trap hire can be arranged at nearby Drumhoney Stables. There is an exhibition illustrating the role of the site as a wartime flying boat base in the Battle of the Atlantic. Patchwork, tapestry, basketry, spinning and weaving courses are offered at Ardress Craft Centre near by. Kesh Bay and Lustybeg Island have bathing facilities and holiday chalets. Continuing north, 2 miles (3 km) beyond the village of Kesh is a road forking to the left which crosses Boa Island. This Island

is 4 miles (6 km) long and connected with the mainland by bridges; near the west end of the island at Drennan, there is a strange, double-faced statue of a very early period. Back on the mainland, the entrance gate to the ruined Castle Caldwell is reached after 4 miles (6 km). At the gate stands the 'Fiddle Stone', with an inscription referring to the fate of an eighteenth-century fiddler:

On firm land only exercise your skill,
That you may play and safely drink your
  fill.

Some distance further west the lake narrows into the River Erne, flowing past Belleek on the County Donegal border, where sluice gates control the level of the lake. Belleek is known for the lustrous parian chinaware produced in its pottery. The pottery has a gift shop, exhibition centre and café, and guided tours of the silent, skilled world of the potters are on offer. The village is the most downstream port of call and marina for tourists on boats from any of the eight hire cruiser companies— all of which also hire day boats or sailing dinghies (the Fermanagh cruiser bases are at Lisnarick, Lisbellaw, Blaney, Bellanaleck, Kesh, Enniskillen and Killadeas). Its riverside chalets are a mecca for game anglers fishing Lough Erne and Lough Melvin and pike anglers fishing the two Lough Macneans.

The main road from Belleek to Enniskillen runs close to the southern shore of the lake, and has fine views. About a mile (2 km) east of the road, 12 miles (19 km) from Enniskillen, are the ruins of Tully Castle, standing near the shore of Sand Bay. This castle, built by Sir John Hume, was burnt by Rory Maguire in a 1641 massacre.

Near Derrygonnelly is the entrance to the Lough Navar forest recreation area, at the top of cliffs 900 feet high. There is a 10-mile (16 km) scenic drive to the spectacular panorama from the Viewpoint.

Six miles (10 km) north-west of Enniskillen is Monea Castle, built early in the seventeenth century by Malcolm Hamilton, Rector of Devenish. Monea is one of the best-preserved examples of the plantation castles which were erected in that period.

A t Boho, 7 miles (11 km) south-west of Monea, is a complex cave system of labyrinthine passages through which a stream courses. Only for experts, the cave can be traversed from the stream inlet to where it emerges into the open air. Coolarkan Cave, on the north side of Belmore Mountain near Boho, also engulfs a surface stream. The very large chamber of this cave is worth visiting. The most famous of these potholes is Noon's Hole, which has been explored to a depth of 250 feet. In addition there are numerous dry caverns in the district. Those on the slopes of Knockmore, west of Derry-gonnelly, have shown signs of human habitation.

Other points of interest in the lower lake area

Five miles (8 miles) south of Belleek, Garrison has a fine situation at the eastern end of Lough Melvin; it is an angling centre for this lake, most of which is on the County Donegal side of the border. The lake has a good run of spring salmon and it holds three genetically distinct sub species of wild trout (sonaghan, gillaroo and ferox), as well as big brown trout and char, another salmonid, all with very distinct appear-ances and feeding habits. From Garrison, which has an outdoor pursuits centre with dormitory accommodation and sports facility hire—just by the small beach—it is 13 miles (21 km) south-east to the border village Belcoo, between Upper and Lower Lough Macnean. There are good views of these lakes and the surrounding hills on the way.

Monea Castle

Circuit of Upper Lough Erne

As Lower Lough Erne widens out from Enniskillen it becomes more and more the province of the game angler. Around the town and south into Upper Lough Erne the main magnet is non-salmonid or 'coarse' angling, i.e. roach, bream, perch and hybrids which have a great attraction for competitive match anglers. Several Five-Hour World Match Records have been broken in these waters. Whilst Lower Lough can be toured by waterbus from the Round O in Enniskillen, the Upper Lough waterbus is based at the Share Centre, Smith's Strand, 4 miles (6 km) south of Lisnaskea.

Upper Lough Erne is a maze of waterways spreading around numerous islands and peninsulas. From Enniskillen the visitor should take the Belcoo road for 1½ miles (2 km), then branch left along the road leading to Belturbet. The road passes between Knockninny (630 feet) on the left, 11 miles (18 km) from Enniskillen, and Molly Mountain (930 feet) on the right. On the summit of Knockninny (St Ninnidh's Hill) are three cairns, and near by are two dolmens. There is a fine view from the summit. Also at Knockninny are the ruins of a castle of the Maguires.

Two miles (3 km) further south is Derrylin village beyond which a road to the left drops down to the bridge which uses Trasna Island as a stepping stone across the lake. On reaching the eastern shore, a series of by-roads lead to Newtownbutler, 6 miles (10 km) to the south-east. Near this village the Protestants of Fermanagh won a victory over Jacobite forces in 1689. Crom Castle, seat of the Earl of Erne, stands in a beautifully wooded demesne, open to the public through the National Trust, 3½ miles (6 km) to the south-east. Here also are the ruins of the older castle, erected in 1611. In the grounds near by is an ancient yew tree, said to be the largest in Ireland.

Six miles (10 km) north of Newtownbutler is the neat little town of Lisnaskea. This takes its name (Lios na Sceithe: the fort of the thorn tree) from the tree under which the Maguire used to be inaugurated. The fort is locally called 'the Moat'. Also

Florence Court

here are the ruins of Castle Balfour, erected by Sir James Balfour about 1615 and re-fortified by General Ludlow in 1652. The folklife museum started by a publican and displaying an extraordinary variety of bygone goods and chattels, has been relocated in the town library. There are other small fascinating folk and family collections in the Olde Barn in Lisbellaw and the Glen Heritage Centre in Tempo. The Share Centre on the shores of the Lough, south of Lisnaskea, is remarkable for providing accommodation and water-based sporting activities for both the disabled and able-bodied.

At Aghalurcher, near Lisnaskea, are the remains of a church which was enlarged and beautified by the Maguires in 1447. In a barrel-vaulted chapel on the north side of the church is a carving of a bishop which perhaps represents the founder of the ori-ginal church here, St Ronan. Many sculptured monuments of the seventeenth and eighteenth centuries are in the church and graveyard.

Four miles (6 km) from Lisnaskea on the way to Enniskillen, a road on the left leads to the beautifully wooded island of Bellisle (private property), which is con-nected to the mainland by a bridge. This island, formerly called Ballymacmanus, is the site of a monastery in which Cathal Maguire, Archdeacon of Clogher, compiled the monumental Annals of Ulster in the fifteenth century.

Other points of interest in the upper lake area

About 9 miles (14 km) south-west of Ennis-killen is the Earl of Enniskillen's beautiful demesne, Florence Court, which has now become a Forest Park. The Georgian man-sion has fine plasterwork (by Robert West) and an art collection. In the demesne is the parent tree of the Florencecourt Yew which is now found in many parts of the world.

Three miles (5 km) west of Florence Court is Fermanagh's best-known cave system, Marble Arch. Here the Cladagh River issues from a complex cave system, part of which can be explored only by boat. There are some large chambers and gal-leries, with the underground river flowing beside water-eroded rocks. It is fed by

Marble Arch Caves

streams which run down the northern slopes of Cuilcagh Mountain (2,188 feet) and disappear underground through pot-holes on reaching the porous limestone rock. The principal stream is the Monastir, while other feeder streams go underground near it at Cat's Hole and Pollasumera. Guided tours (daily March to October/ 1½ hours) past stalactites and stalagmites and including the underground boat trip are organised at the visitor centre, complete with café and lecture room, well sign-posted on the Marlbank Scenic Loop Road, Florence Court. Since the tours are under-ground, bring a sweater and sensible shoes, and since they are very popular, ring ahead (Tel. 036 582 8855) to check availability, particularly at weekends.

Most towns and many villages through-out Northern Ireland have tourist informa-tion centres, well signposted, and run by local Councils in association with the Northern Ireland Tourist Board. In border areas many will carry tourist information on attractions both sides of the border. Otherwise contact the Northern Ireland Tourist Board, St Anne's Court, 59 North Street, Belfast BT1 1NB, Tel. (0232) 231221.

Dunluce Castle.

Take it all in.

Make sure Northern Ireland is part of your holiday plans this year. Go North and experience all the wonders for yourself.

A cruise on the Fermanagh Lakes. A hill walk in the Sperrins. Breathe in the beauty of the Giant's Causeway. The Mountains of Mourne. The green Glens of Antrim.

Touch the history of Derry. Of Armagh's Cathedral city. And the warmth of the people.

Golf. Fishing. Sailing. Horse-riding. Activities awaiting discovery in idyllic surroundings. Superb restaurants. Pubs and live entertainment. You're really spoilt for choice.

And don't forget to visit Belfast. A city steeped in history with a fine tradition of culture, crafts, sports and business.

16 Nassau Street, Dublin 2. Freefone: 1-800-230 230. Tel: (01) 679 1977.
St. Anne's Court, 59 North Street, Belfast BT1 1NB. Tel: 0232-231221.

The Grianan of Aileach, Co. Donegal

The Blowers and Cutters of Tyrone are guided by a 200 year old tradition that lays down a rigorous discipline. It applies to the creation of each original work of art that is a piece of Tyrone Full Lead Irish Crystal. Drawn from the fire, blown by breath, cut by hand: <u>no flaws are ever tolerated.</u> Each piece is perfect, or it returns to the fire in which it was born.

Tyrone Crystal
HANDCRAFTED IN IRELAND
AT KILLYBRACKEY, DUNGANNON, CO. TYRONE

UNFLAWED · UNCHANGED · UNMISTAKABLE

TYRONE CRYSTAL, KILLYBRACKEY, DUNGANNON, COUNTY TYRONE.
Telephone: (08687) 25335 • RoI 08 08687 25335 • Intl +44 8687 25335
Fax: (08687) 26260 • RoI 08 08687 26260 • Intl +44 8687 26260

Donegal

Tranarossan

onegal, the most northerly county in Ireland, extends along much of the north-west coast. It is a region famous for its scenery—with a beautiful, much-indented coast, great areas of mountains, deep glens and many lakes. All kinds of rock, from cave-riddled limestone to complicated mixtures of igneous rocks, make up the foundations of the county; and it is this that gives so much variety of form and colour to the scenery. There are many important antiquities and historic sites in the county, and the island retreat of Lough Derg is one of Ireland's most celebrated holy places. The entries for this county follow, in general, a south-north direction.

Bundoran
Bun Dobhrain
(Mouth of the Dobhran River)

Pop. 1,458 (urban district).

Tourist information office (seasonal): Tel. (072) 41350.

ne of Ireland's main seaside resorts, Bundoran has a fine situation on the southern shore of Donegal Bay, with the Sligo-Leitrim mountains behind it to the south and the hills of Donegal across the bay to the north. The strand, a fine sandy beach fronting the promenade, has at either end a range of cliffs carved by the waves into fantastic shapes.

Things to do

Waterworld, a new watersports centre on the beachfront (open during summer months), features a spiderslide and a wave-pool. Other recreations include golf (18) at a superbly situated championship course, putting, tennis, horse-riding, sea and river fishing, carnival amusements, children's indoor entertainment, dancing and hotel cabaret.

Around Bundoran

The many beauty spots of south Donegal, north Sligo and north Leitrim are within easy touring distance. In the immediate area there is much of interest that can be seen on foot, and these are a few of the possible walks:

1. By the promenade to Rogey and along the cliffs of Aughris Head to Tullan Strand. Rock formations at Aughris Head include the 'Fairy Bridges', the 'Puffing Hole' and the 'Wishing Chair'. Tullan Strand, a magnificent sandy beach, is backed by Finner sandhills.

2. Along the cliffs west of the town. A feature in the cliffs is the 'Lion's Paw Cave'. Near Bundrowes (2 miles/3 km) a small roofless tower called Cassidy's Folly stands by the sea's edge. Michael Ó Cleirigh, chief of the Four Masters, began his journeying at Bundrowes in 1627. A castle built here in the fifteenth century by O'Conor Sligo was frequently contended for by the O'Donnells.

3. To Finner Church ruin, about a mile (2 km) from Bundoran on the Ballyshannon road. On the hilltop, about 200 yards to seaward, is the now prostrate pillar stone called 'Flaitheartach's Stone', named after a fairy chieftain in local legend.

4. Southwards to the pretty village of Kinlough (2 miles/3 km), at the western end of Lough Melvin in County Leitrim. This route passes near the little sulphur

well at Ardfarna, a mile (2 km) from Bundoran.

Ballyshannon

Beal Atha Seanaigh
(The Mouth of Seanach's Ford)

 Pop. 2,573.

The largest town in south Donegal, Ballyshannon is built on the steeply rising banks of the Erne, where the river becomes tidal.

Points of interest

In the estuary just below Assaroe Falls lies the islet Inis Saimer. Here, according to tradition, Partholan landed from Scythia about 1500 B.C. to make the first colonisation of Ireland. At one time the princes of Tir Chonaill had a dwelling on the island. Flaherty O'Muldory, founder of Assaroe Abbey, died here in 1197.

On the north side of the town is a beautiful rounded knoll called Mullaghnashee. Now occupied by St Anne's Protestant church and graveyard, it was the site of a royal palace in early times. Aodh Rua (Red Hugh), father of the famous Queen Macha, was buried here around 300 B.C. after drowning at Assaroe Falls. Conall Gulban, great-grandfather of St Colmcille, lived at Mullaghnashee when St Patrick visited the palace. Beside the path to the south of the church is the grave of the poet William Allingham, who was a native of Ballyshannon; a plaque in the Mall marks the house where he was born, and Allingham Bridge is named after him.

The ford Ath Seanaigh from which Ballyshannon takes its name is 300 yards above the town bridge. Seanach was a fifth-century warrior who was slain on the south bank here by Conall Gulban.

Around Ballyshannon

About a mile (2 km) upstream from the town is the Erne hydroelectric power station and a great artificial lake of 1,000

Rossnowlagh

acres. A mile (2 km) north-west of Bally-shannon are fragments of the ruins of the once famous Cistercian abbey of Assaroe, founded in 1184. In the graveyard are many ancient headstones, including that of Abbot O'Cuinn (died 1669). About fifty yards away, on the bank of the Abbey River, is the grotto-like Catsby Cave, where Mass was celebrated in the penal days. In the rock of the grotto are a rough-hewn altar and two basin-like hollows believed to have been a baptismal font and a holy water stoup.

At the Watermillwheels Abbey, Assaroe, there are two restored mill buildings featuring waterwheels. There is also a display area with an audio-visual pre-sentation of the legacy of the medieval Cistercians. Outside Ballyshannon on the Sligo side there is a factory that won awards for handcrafted porcelain. On the Bally-shannon–Belleek road there is a Celtic weave factory where intricately designed porcelain basketweave is handcrafted and handpainted.

Rossnowlagh
Ros nGabhlach (The Forked Headland)

This little seaside resort is situated on the beautiful coast north of Ballyshannon. Its magnificent beach fronts a wide expanse of level sward hemmed around by gentle hills.

Things to do
Recreations include bathing, surfing, water-skiing, sea and river fishing. Also golf (18) at Murvagh (5 miles/8 km).

Around Rossnowlagh
The striking modern Franciscan Friary, which houses the museum of the County Donegal Historical Society, has gardens and shrines that are worth a visit.

Interesting rock formations are to be seen along the base of the cliffs that run from the southern end of the beach. About 2 miles (3 km) away in this direction are the ruins of Kilbarron Castle (thirteenth or fourt-eenth century), standing on a rocky promon-tory. Built by the hereditary historians of Tir Chonaill, the O'Sgingins, the property passed by marriage to the O'Clery family who were historians and tutors to the O'Don-nell lords. Michael Ó Cleirigh, chief of the Four Masters, was born here about 1580.

Further north, the remains of the fourteenth-century Kilbarron Church are visible, on the site of the original church of St Barron which was founded about 545.

The village of Ballintra, 4 miles (6 km) from Rossnowlagh, is in an area of little rounded hills known geologically as drumlins. In Brownhall demesne beside the village, the Blackwater River flows through a series of caves (the 'Pullans') with fine dripstone formations. A few hundred yards east of the village, at Aghadullagh Old Mill, the same river forms a pretty waterfall in a leafy hollow and then courses along the bottom of a remarkable 60-foot deep chasm.

A half-mile (1 km) south of Ballintra, a flat, rectangular mound of earth and stones known as Racoo is the site of a monastery founded by St Patrick about 440. 'The seven bishops of Rath Cunga' are mentioned in the litany of Aengus Ceile De. Two miles (3 km) south-west of Ballintra is the remarkable ancient fort of Ard Fothadh (also known as McGonigle's Fort). It has an earthen rampart about 20 feet high and 870 feet around. Inside is a beehive-shaped mound 20 feet high and 190 feet around, which was found to contain a small chamber that is believed to be the burial-place of a sixth-century king, Hugh McAinmire (after whom this southern part of Donegal is called Tirhugh).

Donegal Castle

Donegal Town
Dun na nGall
(The Fortress of the Foreigners)

👪 Pop. 2,242.

ℹ️ Tourist information office (seasonal): Tel. (073) 21148. Fax (073) 22763.

Donegal town is a thriving market town at the head of Donegal Bay. It is an excellent touring centre because of its position where the three main roads from Derry, west Donegal and Sligo converge. An important place from ancient times down to the early seventeenth century, Donegal was the chief seat of the princes of Tir Chonaill, the O'Donnells.

Things to do
Recreations include swimming at several nearby venues, sea and river fishing, golf (18) on a championship course at Murvagh, boating, pony-trekking and tennis; indoor amusements include cinema and dancing.

The Donegal Craft Village outside the town caters for craft workers ranging from ceramics to jewellery-making to poster design and is open to the public all year. A town tourist trail has been signposted through the most interesting parts of Donegal town; guidebook from tourist information office.

Points of interest
The imposing ruin of Donegal Castle, which can be visited, stands on the bank of the River Eske. In 1505 the old castle which stood here was rebuilt by Red Hugh O'Donnell and became the O'Donnells' main stronghold. The structure was much altered by Sir Basil Brooke, who was granted the castle in 1607. Its main feature is a massive rectangular gabled tower with two bartizan turrets. Attached to the south side is a fine Jacobean wing.

In the Diamond is the Four Masters Memorial, a 25-foot high obelisk on which are carved the names of the Four Masters. St Patrick's Memorial Church of the Four Masters, completed in 1935, is of Barnemore red granite quarried locally.

Around Donegal

The interesting though slight ruins of the fifteenth-century Franciscan friary, Donegal Abbey, stand beside the estuary of the River Eske, a short distance south of the town. There are the remains of some very graceful Gothic windows, and thirteen of the cloister's little arches still stand. The abbey was founded in 1474 by Nuala, wife of Red Hugh O'Donnell. From here originated one of the monumental literary works of Ireland, the *Annals of the Four Masters*. Brother Michael Ó Cleirigh, chief of the annalists, was attached to the abbey. The annals were written in the period 1632–1636.

About 5 miles (8 km) north-east of Donegal town is Lough Eske, in an exquisite setting of tree-fringed shores and an embracing horseshoe of mountains. On its shores are the wooded estates of Ardnamona and Lough Eske Castle. The 6-mile (10 km) circuit of the lake gives a succession of very colourful views.

By following the little Corabber River on foot for 2 miles (3 km) into the hills from the northern end of Lough Eske, one reaches the pretty waterfall of Eas Dunan. Two miles (3 km) further north is Lough Belshade hemmed around by rugged mountains which rise in cliffs for several hundred feet above the lake.

Seven miles (11 km) north-east of Donegal is Barnesmore Gap. Once the haunt of highwaymen and robbers, it extends for about 3 miles (5 km) between flanking mountains. Its wild appearance is relieved by the heath of the slopes and the green banks of the little Lowerymore River which winds beside the road.

There is also very fine scenery along the roads leading north and north-west

from Donegal into the Bluestack Mountains. Eglish Glen, 7 miles (11 km) to the north, is between Banagher Hill (1,268 feet) and the main Bluestack group. A few miles further north-west is Sruell Glen, with the 'Grey Mare's Tail' waterfall.

West of Donegal, the little town of Mountcharles (4 miles/6 km) has a fine situation on a steeply rising hill (from whose summit there are good views over Donegal Bay). There is a sandy beach within a mile (2 km) of the town, and good fishing on the Eany Water and nearby mountain lakes. Mountcharles is noted for its hand-embroidery work; Mountcharles freestone, used for building and ornamental purposes, is quarried near by. Mountcharles is also noted as the birthplace of the well-known Irish writer, Seamus MacManus. The district is identified with his writings. Many pleasant hours may be spent exploring the beauties of the coast and the neighbouring hills and glens. Carnaween Mountain (1,713 feet) is worth climbing for the view; it rises above the pretty Diseart Glen, 8 miles (13 km) to the north. North-west about 4 miles (6 km) from Mountcharles is the pretty village of Frosses. In the Catholic churchyard here a Celtic Cross marks the grave of the Belfast poetess and patriot, Ethna Carberry. She was the first wife of Seamus MacManus, who is now interred in the same grave and under the Celtic cross that he erected to her memory many years before.

The tiny fishing village of Inver lies at the mouth of the Eany River, 4 miles (6 km) west of Mountcharles. There is good bathing and sea and river fishing. The site of a sixth-century church built here by St Naul is now occupied by the ruin of a comparatively recent church. In the graveyard is the grave of Thomas Nesbitt, inventor of the gun-harpoon for whaling, who was born near Inver in 1730.

Four miles (6 km) beyond Inver is the village of Dunkineely. It is convenient to the River Oily (salmon) and other rivers and mountain lakes holding brown trout;

sea fishing is also available. From Dunkineely a long narrow strip of land juts out
into the sea between Inver Bay and
MacSwyne's Bay. There are many fine
views from the road along this peninsula,
which ends in St John's Point. On the
western shore, 1½ miles (2 km) from
Dunkineely, are the remains of the old
castle of the MacSwynes of Banagh.

Lough Derg
Loch Dearg (The Red Lake)

This lonely lake surrounded by
moorland and heathery hills is
famous for its pilgrimage of St
Patrick's Purgatory.

History
A very early legend tells that St Patrick, by
spending forty days of prayer and fasting
in a cavern on an island in the lake, expelled
the evil spirits who had infested the cave.
In the Middle Ages the legend of the cave
and its marvels spread throughout Christen-
dom, and men of high rank came on pilgrimage to Lough Derg from many parts of
Europe. Throughout the centuries the
pilgrimage has continued to flourish, even
in the worst times of oppression, and the
rigorous exercises are still performed by
thousands of pilgrims each year.

The Pilgrimage
The pilgrimage takes place to Station
Island, a half-mile (1 km) from the shore
and less that an acre in extent. Its buildings
include two modern churches and hospices
for the accommodation of pilgrims. The
'Penitential Beds' are the remains of the
stone cells or oratories of the early monks.

The pilgrimage takes three full days,
on each of which only one meal—of dry
bread and black tea—is allowed. Water
may be taken at other times. Pilgrims must
go barefoot during their time on the island,
and the penitential exercises include the
saying of prescribed prayers at St Patrick's
and St Brigid's crosses and while making

Fishermen tending their nets at Killybegs

the circuit of the basilica and of each penitential bed. A vigil is kept in the basilica
the first night.

During the pilgrimage season from
1 June to 15 August, only pilgrims are
allowed on the island. Information can be
had from the Prior, Lough Derg, County
Donegal.

Around Lough Derg
Five miles (8 km) to the south is the quiet
town of Pettigo, lying in a hollow amid
low hills and well known as the gateway to
Lough Derg. The little Termon River flows
through the town and forms the border
here with Northern Ireland.

One and a half miles (2 km) from the
town is the sixteenth-century Castle
Magrath. The Magraths were hereditary
guardians of the monastery at Lough Derg.
The notorious Myler Magrath, holder of
many bishoprics under Queen Elizabeth
and James I, was of this family. Not far
from the castle, at Aughnahoo, is the house
where John Kells Ingram, author of the
ballad 'Who Fears to Speak of '98', was
born in 1823.

In Templecarn graveyard, 3 miles
(5 km) north of Pettigo, is a well-preserved
bothog or Mass shelter, used in Penal times.
In Tawlaght townland near by are the
remains of a large oval cairn, erected over
a now exposed rectangular chamber about

25 by 12 feet. A half-mile (1 km) south-west of this cairn is a dolmen, and close to this a large number of embedded stones that mark an ancient burial-place. The townland name (believed to mean 'a plague burial-place') may be derived from these graves.

A fine view on every side is had from the top of Drimawark Hill, 2 miles (3 km) north-east of Pettigo.

Killybegs
Na Cealla Beaga (The Little Churches)

 Pop. 1,632.

Killybegs is one of Ireland's most important fishing ports but it has also much to offer as a tourist centre. It is situated on a fine natural

Slieve League

harbour and is gaining a reputation as a water sports centre.

Things to do

There is sea and river fishing, sub-aqua diving, tennis and dancing; there is a magnificent bathing beach at Fintragh (2 miles/ 3 km west). The Killybegs International Sea Angling Festival is held in August.

Points of interest

The arrival of the fishing fleet is a sight not to be missed: seagulls swarm around the pier as the fish are unloaded from the trawlers. Visitors may also see around the hand-tufted carpet factory whose products are world famous.

Inside St Mary's Church there is a remarkable old carved slab which is believed to commemorate Niall Mor MacSuibhne of Banagh. On the western shore of the bay are the slight remains of a Franciscan friary built by the MacSwynes family of Banagh.

Around Killybegs

There is very fine scenery in the immediate vicinity of Killybegs, especially along the coast. Carntullagh Head, which can be reached by rowing across the harbour, and Drumanoo Head 3 miles (5 km) to the south, should both be visited. There is an extensive view from the top of Crownarad Mountain (1,621 feet) 3 miles (5 km) to the west.

The picturesque village of Kilcar, 8 miles (13 km) west of Killybegs, is a centre of the Donegal handwoven tweed industry. Hand-embroidery, knitting and other cottage industries also flourish in this district. At Muckross Head, 2½ miles (4 km) south of the village, there are cliffs and caves which can be visited at low tide. Here also is the fine sandy beach at Traloar, lying beneath the steep slopes of Croaghmuckross (916 feet).

The village of Carrick, 3 miles (5 km) north-west of Kilcar, is a starting place for the ascent of Slieve League (1,972 feet) and for exploring the magnificent cliff scenery of the adjoining coast. Beyond

Teelin village, 2 miles (3 km) south of Carrick, a mountain track leads up over Carrigan Head to the secluded Lough O'Mulligan and to the cliffs of Bunglass, which rise sheer out of the water to a height of 1,024 feet. The view from the point named 'Amharc Mor' (the great view) is among the most magnificent in Donegal. Experienced climbers may go further ahead along the cliff edge to 'One Man's Pass', a narrow ledge with a precipice of more than 1,800 feet on one side dropping sheer down to the sea, and on the other an almost equally precipitous escarpment falling down to a lonely tarn. From there it is not far to the summit of Slieve League, where there is another magnificent view.

The excursion can be extended along the coast to the lovely crescent beach of Trabane, near which can be seen Doon Fort and a fine dolmen.

Glencolumbkille

Gleann Cholm Cille (St Colmcille's Glen)

Many houses dot the slopes of this glen, which runs back in between the hills from Glen Bay, in surroundings at once peaceful and strikingly picturesque. On the north side rises the cliff of Glen Head. The coast here has splendid rock scenery, and there is a beautiful beach. There is a tenacious tradition that Bonnie Prince Charlie spent some time here.

A popular holiday destination for families, Glencolumbkille lies in the heart of the Irish-speaking area of south Donegal. It is named for St Colmcille who had his retreat house here, and many relics remain from that time.

Things to do

Bathing, sea and river fishing and tennis are available, with dancing and hotel entertainment.

Points of interest

Glencolumbkille is rich in monuments dating back to pre-Christian times. There

Glencolumbkille

are portal dolmens, souterrains and cairns from the Bronze Age and as far back as five thousand years ago. They number over forty in all.

Adjacent to the holiday village lies a remarkable folk village, where there are four cottages representing different periods in Irish life and containing furniture and utensils of the period. There is also a craft shop where souvenirs and handcrafts made in the local co-operative are on sale. An Irish language and culture centre is located here which comprises an art gallery, tradi-tional music archive, archaeology informa-tion centre and an Irish language school for adults.

Around Glencolumbkille

On the Ardara road is the spectacular Glengesh Pass, where the road rises to 900 feet and then plunges in steep descent to the valley below.

Nine miles (14 km) south of Glen-columbkille is Malinmore, a pretty holiday spot with a fine beach. The cliff scenery along the shores of the bay is impressive, and the hinterland covers some charming scenery. There is a large number of pre-

historic tombs around Malinmore, including a fine horned cairn called Cloghanmore.

On the little island of Rathlin O'Birne, about 2 miles (3 km) off the coast, are some antiquities associated with the sixth-century saint Hugh MacBric. The waters around this island are among the best fishing grounds off the Donegal coast.

Ardara

Ard Rath (The Rath Heights)

 Pop. 685.

Ardara is one of the most attractive villages in Donegal and is set in a wide valley where the Owentocher River enters Loughros More Bay. It is an important centre for the manufacture of Donegal homespun tweeds, and many are engaged also in other crafts such as hand-knitting, hosiery and hand-embroidery. Visitors may see these articles being made. There are many brown trout lakes in the area.

Around Ardara

A long narrow peninsula extending from the town separates the two bays of Loughros More and Loughros Beg, the shores of which offer opportunities for many enjoyable excursions. Maghera Caves, Essaranks Waterfall and the Slieve-tooey Mountains, all to the west, can be included in a day's outing; another enjoy-able excursion is to Loughros Point (6 miles/10 km) which has beautiful views of both bays.

The road northwards from Ardara crosses the Owenea River and then passes through a wild tract of country studded with lakes. The twin holiday villages of Narin and Portnoo are beautifully situated at the foot of low sheltering hills on the southern shore of Gweebarra Bay. Narin has a magnificent beach 1½ miles (2 km) long and a golf course (18). Iniskeel Island has an ancient church ruin and can be reached on foot at low tide. On Dunmore

Head, west of Portnoo, there are fine views and two ancient ring-forts. A massive ancient circular fort of stone, in a good state of preservation, can be seen on an island in Lough Doon, 1½ miles (2 km) south of Portnoo; there is also a large dolmen at Kilclooney (3 miles/5 km).

On the much indented shore of Dawros Bay, 3 miles (5 km) south-west of Portnoo is the quiet little resort of Rosbeg. There is excellent bathing on a sandy beach and fishing for brown trout is available on the lakes of the district.

Glenties

Na Gleanntai (The Glens)

Pop. 914.

Glenties, several times the winner of the award for Ireland's tidiest town, is picturesquely situated where two glens converge. It is a thriving village with a knitwear, hoisery and glove-making industry, and its wooded surroundings contrast sharply with the ruggedness of much of the nearby countryside. At Glenties the River Owenea is joined by the Stracashel River, both of which are angling waters; several nearby lakes have good trout fishing.

At St Conal's Museum and Heritage Centre in the town, which is open in summer, themes featured include Donegal railways, landlordism and the archaeology of the area. Each year in August a Summer School is held in memory of Patrick McGill, author and 'naavy' poet who was born in Glenties in 1889.

Around Glenties

The view from Aghla Mountain (1,961 feet) is particularly fine; it is 5 miles (8 km) north-east of the town. Between here and the Glenfin road lies Lough Finn, a long narrow lake with Fintown village at the north-eastern end.

A legend associated with Lough Finn tells how the warrior Fergoman was

attacked beside the lake by a wild sow whose litter he had thoughtlessly killed. Lacerated by the sow's tusks, Fergoman raised a cry for help. His sister Finna, who was on the same side of the lake, heard the echo of the shout from the cliffs on the opposite shore. She swam across the lake, only to hear her brother's voice from the side she had left. So she crossed and recrossed, until the dying shouts of Fergoman so overwhelmed her with grief that she sank in the middle of the lake and drowned. Hence this was called the lake of Finna.

From Fintown the road continues through Glenfin (the valley of the Finn) to Ballybofey and Stranorlar. The road runs high above the river for several miles, giving fine views of the valley and the mountain folds rising beyond it to the south. The pretty Salmon Leap at Cloghan Lodge, 10 miles (16 km) beyond Fintown, is worth seeing. A short distance south of it is the Glebe House, where the founder of the Irish Home Rule Party, Isaac Butt, was born in 1813.

The Rosses

Na Rosa (The Headlands)

Tourist information office (seasonal): Dungloe. Tel. (075) 21297.

The district known as the Rosses is a remarkable tract of more than 60,000 acres of rock-strewn land,

The Rosses

intersected by streams and dotted with numerous little lakes. It extends from Gweebarra Bridge to the south as far as Crolly Bridge in the north. It offers an incomparable wealth of unspoilt mountains, rivers, lakes and beaches.

The 'capital' of the Rosses, Dungloe, is a lively and thriving town with a population of about 900. During the August Bank Holiday weekend each year the 'Mary from Dungloe Festival' is held in the town. On the coast to the south-west of it is a geological curiosity known locally as the 'Talamh Briste' (broken earth)—a narrow chasm over a quarter-mile (0.4 km) in length but only a few yards wide. Not far from this fissure is Crohy Head, where there are some fine cliffs and interesting caves. Beneath the head is the pretty Maghery Bay, with a perfect strand for bathing and some fine rock scenery on the north side of the bay at Termon. On the peninsula north of Maghery village is the ancient ruined church of Templecrone.

Five miles (8 km) from Dungloe is Burtonport, an important fishing village where more salmon are landed than at any port in Ireland or Britain. It is a popular centre for boating trips to Arranmore Island, which is 3 miles (5 km) offshore and has striking cliff scenery and some interesting marine caves. It also has a lake (Lough Shure) which has rainbow trout. The unique pearls known as 'The Four O'Donnell Pearls' are believed to have been hidden on Arranmore after the departure from Ireland in 1607 of their original owner, Red Hugh O'Donnell (they are now in private hands in London). Nearer the shore are many other islands, including Inishfree and Inish-MacDurn.

Three miles (5 km) north of Burtonport is Keadue Strand, at low tide providing a short cut to Kincasslagh village; near by is Donegal airport at Carrickfin. Cruit Island, a popular stopping place for tourists (with a 9-hole golf course), lies out in front of the village and is linked to the mainland by a bridge; to the north are the Stag Rocks

and the pretty Inishfree Bay. Eastwards some miles, the tiny village of Crolly is situated on the Gweedore River—which forms a lovely cascade as it tumbles over a rocky ridge a short distance from the village. This is where the famous Crolly dolls were made.

Just outside the village on the road to Dungloe is a glacial boulder of giant proportions known locally as Cloch Mhor Leim a tSionnaigh (the big stone of the leaping fox).

Bloody Foreland

The mainly Irish-speaking peninsula between Gweedore and Falcarragh culminates in the headland of Bloody Foreland, which takes its name from the warm ruddy colour of its rock in the setting sun.

In the Gweedore area are two small electricity generating stations, one of which is powered by handcut peat. The area is noted for game fishing and sea trout. To the east is another destination for anglers, Dunlewy, and from Dunlewy Lake a direct ascent can be made to the top of Errigal (2,466 feet)—the highest mountain in County Donegal. There are two summits, about 30 yards apart, connected by the 'One Man's Path'. From these there is a magnificent view that covers most of the mountains of Ulster and the rugged coast for miles to the west. A major attraction during the tourist season in Dunlewy is the Ionad Cois Locha (Lakeside Museum) which features a restored two-storey farmhouse, including farm museum, farm animal compound and craft exhibitions. To the north-east is Lough Altan, with Aglamore (1,916 feet) rising sheer from its waters, and on the east are the glaciated Derryveagh Mountains. To the south is the Poisoned Glen, a dark cliff-encircled corrie, and the distant heights of Slieve Snacht (2,240 feet).

The tiny village of Bunbeg, with its pretty harbour, is sheltered by cliffs at the mouth of the Clady River, 4 miles (6 km) west of Gweedore. There is good bathing in the open sea or at Magheraclogher Strand, an extensive sandy beach about a half-mile (1 km) from the village. Excursions can be made by boat to Gola, Innishinny and other islands, all of which have interesting rock and cliff scenery. From Bunbeg one can also explore the sandy shores and wild recesses of Bloody Foreland. Eastwards from Bloody Foreland is Gortahork, close to little Ballyness Bay with a sub-aqua centre. To the north of Gortahork is Falcarragh, the nearest point from which to climb Muckish Mountain (2,197 feet). Near the village is a giant stone which has given its name to the surrounding Cloghaneely district. It means 'MacKinley's stone', and tradition has it that on this rock a chieftain named MacKinley was beheaded by a Formorian ruler of Tory Island, Balor of the Mighty Blows. A red vein penetrating to the centre of the stone is declared to be the crystallised blood of the assassinated chieftain. Not far away in Myrath churchyard is a huge ancient cross which is said to have been hewn out of a single rock from Muckish Mountain and carried here by St Colmcille. Also in the Falcarragh area is Altan Lough, one of the wildest and loneliest mountain lakes in County Donegal.

Nine miles (14 km) from the mainland at Falcarragh is Tory Island, by far the largest of the islands in the area—so large that its form is clearly discernible from the shore. Visitors to Tory must be prepared for adventure, for it is not easy to land there in rough seas. Tory was a place of religion and learning from time immemorial until the reign of Queen Elizabeth, when the monastery founded by St Colmcille ceased to flourish. Antiquities on the island include the foundations of two churches, the stump of a round tower and an ancient tau cross. The present population of the island is about 200.

Horn Head

There are three popular resorts located on the sweep of Sheephaven Bay which terminates in the majestic cliffs of Horn Head. These are Dunfanaghy, Port-na-Blagh and Marble Hill; all have long beaches and holiday amenities.

One of the most rewarding excursions in the district is to Horn Head itself, a cliff rising straight out of the water to a height of more than 600 feet. The view is one of boundless Atlantic ocean, broken only by numerous islands and headlands, and inland of magnificent mountain ranges. Muckish and Errigal are prominent features in the panorama. The cliffs around the head abound in uncommon sea birds. The best view of the head is from Traghlisk Point on the east.

Another enjoyable excursion from the Horn Head resorts is to the peninsula and demesne of Ards, which has some of the most beautiful scenery in the county. Visitors may walk or drive through the grounds with the permission of the Capuchin Fathers, who have a monastery there.

Six miles (10 km) south of Dunfanaghy is Creeslough, standing on high ground overlooking an inlet that runs in off Sheephaven. From Creeslough trips can be made to Glen Lough (4 miles/6 km), a lovely lake with a fine mountain background, to Barnesbeg Gap (4½ miles/7 km) and to Lough Veagh.

On a strip of land running into the sea near Creeslough is the historic Doe Castle. Originally a fortress of the MacSuibhne family, who held it in the sixteenth century, it was the scene of many attacks by the rival clans of the north. A bridge now spans the rock-cut moat which was once guarded by a drawbridge and portcullis. In the graveyard adjoining (where a Franciscan monastery once stood) are the graves of many Donegal chieftains, including the tomb of the chief of the Clan MacSuibhne—MacSuibhne na Doe. On the slab of the grave embedded in the eastern wall is carved a cross bearing the MacSuibhne arms and a number of mythological figures.

Rosguill Peninsula

The Rosguill Peninsula is delight-fully situated between the bays of Sheephaven and Mulroy. The district is largely Irish speaking and the people have retained centuries-old skills in the various handcrafts. The short 'Atlantic Drive', which circuits the peninsula, is one of the finest scenic roads in Ireland.

Situated on an inlet of Mulroy Bay, Carrigart is a peaceful holiday resort which offers a range of activities which include bathing, riding, tennis and fishing. In the sandhills between Carrigart and Downings there are many prehistoric habitations or 'kitchen middens', where numerous Bronze Age objects have been found. At Meevagh are the ruins of a very old church, an ancient Latin cross and an ogham stone.

Three miles (5 km) from Carrigart is Downings, a pleasant resort that commands a superb view of the Ards Peninsula and has a good sandy beach. The handwoven tweed for which Donegal is famous may be inspected by visitors at the McNutts factory.

Less than a mile (2 km) from Downings is Rosapenna, a family resort well known for its beautifully situated golf course (18).

Fanad Peninsula

The Fanad Peninsula stretches north from Milford to Fanad Head and back down to Rathmelton. It has some of the most striking cliff scenery in Ireland, including remarkable examples of marine erosion. The 8-mile (13 km) Knockalla coast road offers a spectacular drive overlooking Lough Swilly and Inishowen. The Fanad Peninsula Scenic Tour is a 45-mile (72 km) signposted circuit of the peninsula through wonderful scenery.

At the head of Mulroy Bay is Milford, a tourist centre and angling resort in sur-roundings of great beauty. In the vicinity is the secluded Bunlin Glen, through which the little Bunlin Stream ripples on its way into Mulroy, forming in its course a pretty cascade known as the 'Golan Loop'. Close to Bunlin Bridge is a second waterfall, called 'The Grey Mare's Tail'. The 'Fairy

Downings

Glen' is another pleasant retreat on the shore of Mulroy. At Gortnavern, near Carrowkeel, 4 miles (6 km) north of Milford, is a dolmen with a capstone measuring 13 by 7 feet.

Another noted resort on this peninsula is Portsalon. It is situated on Ballymastocker Bay, on the western shore of Lough Swilly, and it has an 18-hole golf course. About 2 miles (3 km) from it are the spectacular rock-formed tunnels known as the 'Seven Arches'—some of which extend to 300 feet in length and measure 20 feet wide and 30 feet high at the entrance. At Doaghbeg the cliffs rise to a great height and a detached mass of rock forms the 'Great Arch of Doaghbeg', big enough to take a large boat. Murren Hill (754 feet) and Dargan Hill (570 feet) have splendid views across Mulroy Bay, Lough Swilly and the surrounding country. At the northern end of the peninsula, Fanad Head is a good vantage point.

Situated midway on the western shore of Lough Swilly is Rathmullan, a good headquarters for exploring this beautiful bay. Near at hand pleasant walks and drives can be had to Kinnegar Strand, Mill Bay, Lamb's Head Bay and Scraggy Bay in the north, and Cul Bay, Rathmullan Woods and Ray Bridge in the south. Croaghan (1,010 feet) and Crockanaffrin (1,137 feet) are good climbs, and further away the Knockalla Ridge may be walked.

At Rathmullan itself are the remains of a fifteenth-century Carmelite friary. Near the pier is an old fort, one of six Martello towers built in commanding positions on either side of Lough Swilly to protect the area from invasion by Napoleon. The resort has many historic associations. It was from here in 1587 that young Red Hugh O'Donnell was tricked into boarding a camouflaged merchant ship to sample wines; he was taken to Dublin Castle and held prisoner until his escape four years later. From Rathmullan also (in 1607), the earls of Tyrone and Tyrconnell fled with a company of friends and retainers to France.

'The Flight of the Earls' was followed by wholesale confiscations, and the plantation of Ulster with English and Scottish colonists. A 'Flight of the Earls' Heritage Centre, located in one of the Martello towers, traces the history of the period.

Six miles (10 km) south-west of Rathmullan is Rathmelton, a noted angling centre for the River Lennan and the lakes of the district. Pleasant walks can be enjoyed in the Lennan valley and by the shores of Lough Swilly. There is an extensive view from the summit of Carn Hill (797 feet), 4 miles (6 km) south of the town. Near the shore of Lough Swilly, 3½ miles (6 km) to the south-east is Killydonnell Abbey, a Franciscan friary founded by an O'Donnell in the sixteenth century. The ruins are in a good state of preservation. The Makemie Heritage Centre at Ramelton depicts the life and times of Reverend Francis Makemie who was born here and who established the first Presbyterian church on the American continent in Virginia.

Letterkenny

Leitir Ceanainn
(The Hillside of the O'Cannons)

Pop. 7,182 (urban district).

Tourist information office: Derry Road. Tel. (074) 21160. Fax (074) 25180.

Letterkenny, the chief town and ecclesiastical capital of County Donegal, overlooks Lough Swilly where the River Swilly drains into the lough. The Letterkenny Folk Festival brings together many European folk-dance teams every August. The Donegal Motor Rally takes place each June with Letterkenny as its base.

The town's main street is one of the longest in Ireland. St Eunan's Cathedral, a modern building in Gothic style, has round-headed doorways in the transept, much Celtic carving in the interior and richly decorated ceilings. The Donegal County Museum is located on High Road.

Things to do

Recreational facilities at Letterkenny include golf (18), pitch and putt, tennis, squash, cinema and dancing. Salmon and trout fishing is available on nearby rivers and lakes. A leisure centre has a swimming pool, sauna, jacuzzi and steam pool with plunge pool.

Around Letterkenny

Letterkenny is an excellent touring centre for north Donegal. There is a selection of routes across the interior of the county to the west coast, all of them passing through superb mountain scenery. The immediate neighbourhood of the town is highly picturesque, and from the elevated ground above it there are striking views of the southern shores of Lough Swilly, the winding River Swilly and the cultivated valleys which stretch away on every side.

Lough Swilly is a fjord-like arm of the sea that reaches inland for 25 miles (40 km) between the Peninsulas of Fanad and Inishowen. The shores have numerous sandy beaches and coves, cliffs and curious rock formations—all against fine mountain backgrounds. Into this sheltered inlet in October 1798 sailed the French battleship, *Hoche*, with Wolfe Tone and 300 Frenchmen aboard. It came, too late, to aid the United Irishmen in their long-awaited rising. The ship was captured, and Tone arrested and sentenced to death; he committed suicide in prison before the sentence could be carried out.

A few miles west of the town, Conwal Cemetery has the remains of an ancient church and many graves of great antiquity. This was a burial place of the O'Donnells, and the celebrated Godfrey O'Donnell (who wrested the chieftaincy from the O'Cannons) was buried here in 1258. Near by is Conwal Dun the ruin of a stone fort said to have been the O'Cannon stronghold; near by stands a conspicuous monolith.

There are some interesting tombstones in the graveyard of Conwal parish church.

About 2 miles (3 km) west of Letterkenny is Scarrifhollis, in ancient times an important ford on the River Swilly. Here in 1650, Irish forces under Bishop Heber MacMahon were defeated by the Cromwellian general, Sir Charles Coote.

The little village of Churchill, 10 miles (16 km) west of Letterkenny, is an angling centre near the beautiful shore of Gartan Lough. Gartan is celebrated as the place where St Colmcille was born in 521 and whose name is intimately associated with the history of Donegal. On the hillside west of the lake is a flagstone which is said to mark the place of the saint's birth; a modern Celtic cross has also been erected there. St Columb's house on the shores of Lake Garten was the home of landscape and portrait painter Derek Hill. The house contains a variety of antique art, furniture and William Morris textiles. The Glebe Gallery close by displays paintings by Derek Hill, also by Yeats and other Irish painters. House and galley are open to the public in summer.

The Colmcille Heritage Centre overlooking Lake Garten depicts the life and times of St Colmcille through the medium of silk and other materials; also the history of calligraphy (open to the public in season).

Situated on the banks of Lough Veagh in the vastness of the Derryveagh Mountains is the Glenveagh National Park of 25,000 acres, open all through the year; and Glenveagh Castle and gardens which are open at certain times in summer.

Seven miles (11 km) north of Letterkenny is another angling centre, Kilmacrenan. St Colmcille founded an abbey here, but the present slight remains are of a fifteenth-century Franciscan friary. Near by are the remains of an old parish church. Two miles (3 km) west is the Carraig a' Duin (Rock of Doon), a remarkable flat-topped eminence which was the inauguration place of the O'Donnell chiefs. At the foot of the rock is Tobar a' Duin (Doon

Well), visited by pilgrims who have faith in its curative properties.

Lurgyvale Thatched Cottage, Kilmacrennan and Farm Museum, a 150-year-old restored thatched cottage, is open to the public during the season. Guided tours are conducted during which butter churning, rope making and spinning may be observed.

From Kilmacrenan the main road north-west around the coast lies through Barnesbeg Gap, a wild and picturesque mountain pass.

Inishowen Peninsula

This peninsula, extending between Lough Swilly and Lough Foyle and tapering towards Malin Head (the most northerly point of Ireland), is mainly a mountainous region. Its most conspicuous summit is Slieve Snacht (2,019 feet) in the centre of the peninsula. A 100-mile (161 km) circular, scenic drive known as the 'Inis Eoghain 100' is signposted round the wild and beautiful landscape of the Inishowen

Peninsula. The whole area is an ideal holiday region, and several resorts offer good recreational facilities.

The main town of Inishowen is Buncrana, a popular seaside resort on the eastern shore of Lough Swilly with golf (9) and 4 miles (6 km) away at Fahan golf (18), tennis, cinema and dancing. A leisure centre open all year is equipped with swimming pool, sauna, jacuzzi and gymnasium. There is a Vintage Car and Carriage Museum which is open during the summer. A new visitor centre tracing the history of knitting and featuring traditional Irish styles, patterns and Aran stitches, and where practical instruction in the craft is given, is also open to the public in summer. Tullyarvin is a restored mill building on the Crana River in Buncrana. It houses a textile museum that represents 250 years of textile production.

Buncrana is sheltered on three sides by hills, including Slieve Snacht to the north-east. Near the Castle Bridge is the keep of

Sailing off Buncrana

the fifteenth-century O'Doherty's Castle, and close by the early eighteenth-century Buncrana Castle. Megalithic monuments in the area include a Bronze Age burial cairn, the remains of a stone circle at Crocahaisil, 2 miles (3 km) north of the town, and a dolmen at Gransha.

At Fort Dunree (near Buncrana) there is an exhibition centre at a restored coastal defence battery where 200 years of naval/military history are depicted in audio-visual display and guided tours in season.

Fahan is also the headquarters of the Lough Swilly Yacht Club. Little remains of the seventh-century abbey founded at Fahan by St Mura, but St Mura's Cross in the graveyard is a superb example of inter-laced stone-carving. Inch Island, near Fahan, is connected to the mainland by a bridge.

The most interesting relic of antiquity in Ulster, the Grianan of Aileach, is 7 miles (11 km) south of Fahan (via Burnfoot). This unique circular stone fort occupies the top of Greenan Mountain (803 feet), which commands fine views over the surrounding country, Lough Swilly and Lough Foyle. The enclosure is 77 feet across and the wall is 17 feet high and 13 feet thick at the base. The wall is terraced on the inside, and there are two passages running through the thickness of the walls near the entrance. Three circular embankments form outer fortifications. The Grianan was built about 1700 B.C. and was at one time the residence of the kings of Ulster—the O'Neills. The fort was restored in 1870, and a black line differentiates the original from the restored part above it.

The village of Clonmany, 11 miles (18 km) north of Buncrana is beautifully situated among sheltering hills; there is good bathing 2 miles (3 km) away, at the Priest's Pool. At Glenevin, a mile (2 km) from the village, the Clonmany River forms a pretty waterfall. There is an inter-esting souterrain at Rooskey (1½ miles/

2 km) and about 2 miles (3 km) to the east a dolmen with a massive capstone can be seen on the slope of Magheramore Hill. Rockstown Harbour (3 miles/5 km) is well known to geologists for its raised beach, which reaches a height of over 40 feet in places.

The hills stretching south-west of Clonmany to Dunree Head are of interest to climbers, and Dunaff Head has great cliffs which skilled climbers might scale in places. There is a magnif-icent view from the summit of the head (690 feet). A favourite place for excursions in this area is the Gap of Mamore, which passes at 800 feet above sea level between Mamore Hill and Urris.

Two miles (3 km) north of Clonmany is Ballyliffin, a secluded seaside resort in beautiful surroundings. Just to the north of it is the peninsula called the Isle of Doagh, where the splendid 2-mile (3 km) stretch of beach called Pollan Strand forms the western side. There is a magnificent view of the hills and the coast of the Malin Peninsula from the northern end of the beach.

Carrickabrahey Castle, in ruins, beyond the north end of the strand, was an ancient stronghold of the MacFauls and later the O'Dohertys.

The thriving little town of Carndonagh, about 2 miles (3 km) south of Trawbreaga Bay, is sheltered on three sides by hills. About a half-mile (1 km) west is the famous Donagh Cross (or St Patrick's Cross), probably the oldest low-relief cross standing in Ireland. There are some inter-esting monuments in the old graveyard near by. Other antiquities in the district include a souterrain of three chambers cut out of solid rock, at Collin; and a standing stone at Ballyloskey, on which is carved a large human figure.

Six miles (10 km) from Carndonagh is Culdaff, a secluded little village with an excellent bathing beach near by. The coastal scenery in this district is very fine. To the north-west a range of cliffs, rising to nearly 800 feet, runs from Glengad Head to Malin Head. Another range to the east runs for several miles to Inishowen Head. In the old church ruins at Cloncha, near Culdaff, is a beautifully carved slab with an inscription in archaic Scots Gaelic: 'Fergus MacAlian made this stone. Magnus MacOrriston of the Isles under this mound.' Outside the graveyard is the sculptured high cross of St Buadan, the arms of which are missing. At Carrowmore, the site of an ancient monastery, is a group of stone crosses. St Buadan's Bell, preserved in the church at Bocan, dates from about the ninth century. Also at Bocan are the substantial remains of a court cairn (called Laraghirrill Cairn or the 'Temple of Deen') and about a half-mile (1 km) from it are the remains of a stone circle.

Four miles (6 km) north of Carndonagh is the village of Malin, winner of the 1991 Tidy Towns Competition, and 8 miles (13 km) further on is Malin Head, the most northerly point of Ireland and a conspicuous

On the Atlantic Drive

landmark to sea-travellers on the north Atlantic. Though of no great height, the head has superb views of the neighbouring coast. Striking rock formations in this neighbourhood include Hell's Hole, a remarkable chasm into which the tide rushes with great force. The sandhills of Lagg, which are passed on the way to Malin, are among the largest on the County Donegal coast.

On the western shore of Lough Foyle is Moville, a popular Inishowen resort. The little town itself is an attractive place, and there is a charming variety of scenery inland and along the coast. Three miles (5 km) north of Moville is the pretty little seaside resort of Greencastle (with an 18-hole golf course), which has an excellent bathing beach. On a rock overlooking the entrance to Lough Foyle are the ruins of the castle after which the place is named. Built in 1305 by the 'Red Earl' of Ulster, Richard de Burgh, it was captured eleven years later by the forces of Edward Bruce. Later it fell to the O'Dohertys, who held it until the plantation of Ulster in 1608, when, with the rest of Inishowen it came into the possession of Sir Arthur Chichester. Near by is a fort with a martello tower (1810), now a hotel.

From Inishowen Head, 3 miles (5 km) beyond Greencastle, there is a fine view of the rocky coastline to the north-west and eastwards along the Atlantic shore of Counties Derry and Antrim and as far as the islands and coast of Scotland. Beneath the head is Shrove Strand, a favourite beach for bathers. A line of cliffs rising over 300 feet above the sea runs westwards from the head for several miles. Glenagiveny, called the 'Queen of the Inishowen Glens', runs inland from Kinnagoe Bay about 4 miles (6 km) west of Inishowen Head; it can be reached by road inland from Moville or Greencastle.

About 2 miles (3 km) north-west of Moville, at Cooley graveyard are the ruins of an ancient church, an unusual type of stone cross, and a small stone structure called the 'Skull House'. Outside the graveyard stands an ancient monolithic cross 10 feet high. It is without carving, but has a pierced ring and there is a hole through the upper part of the shaft which is a form of tomb identified with the graves of saints. St Finian is reputed to have been buried in this graveyard.

Other antiquities in the district around Moville include souterrains (of which there is an interesting example, hewn out of the solid rock, at Shrove), and a sweat house at Lecamy, 3 miles (5 km) from Moville. There are numerous ring-forts and some remains of megalithic tombs.

Lifford

Leithbhearr (The Half Cut)

 Pop. 1,478.

L ifford, the administrative centre of County Donegal, is on the eastern border, south of Letterkenny. It is separated by the River Finn from its larger neighbour, Strabane, in County Tyrone. The river is a good salmon river for spring fish. Lifford has the only greyhound racing track in Donegal.

History
Lifford was the site of an important castle of the O'Donnells, which was destroyed about the end of the sixteenth century. The place was soon afterwards fortified by the English, and in 1612 the town was granted a charter by James I.

Around Lifford
Raphoe is a thriving little town set in the heart of a fertile district where flax is grown. It owes its origin to St Colmcille, who founded a monastery here. Later it became a diocesan seat, and the monastery seems to have been converted into a cathedral about the ninth century. The present building is a plain Gothic structure with transepts built in 1702; the tower dates from 1738. Adjoining it is the ruined palace of the former bishops. Two miles (3 km) from Raphoe at Beltany is a stone circle 150 yards around, formed of 64 standing stones.

Ten miles (16 km) south-west of Raphoe, a bridge across the River Finn connects Ballybofey (on the south side) with Stranorlar on the opposite bank. The grave of Isaac Butt, 'father' of Irish Home Rule, is in the Protestant churchyard. Golf (18) available.

Tyrone

The Sperrin Mountains

One of the most beautiful of Ireland's inland counties, Tyrone has a fine variety of scenery—mountains and gentle hills, glens and river valleys, moorland and little plains. There is some low land bordering Lough Neagh in the east, and in the river valleys in the north-west; but the rest of the county is hilly, and towards the County Derry border in the north the land piles up in the 2,000-foot peaks of the Sperrin Mountains.

Dungannon

Dun Geannain (Gannon's Fort)

Pop. 8,300.

Dungannon is a busy marketing centre, with textiles, crystal glass and other industries.

Things to do

There is golf (18), greyhound racing and fishing on the River Blackwater for salmon, trout, pike, perch, bream, gudgeon, roach and tench. There is good rough shooting in many of the forests administered by the Department of Agriculture in the area. There are also organised tours of the Tyrone Crystal factory on the Coalisland road, where you can watch glass blowing and crystal cutting and purchase from the factory shop. Parkanaur, west of the town, is a pleasant forest park with an arboretum and a herd of white deer.

History

Dungannon was in former times the chief seat of the O'Neills, who carried on constant warfare against the English down to the seventeenth century. Their castle, which stood on Castle Hill at the top of the town, suffered many attacks and was frequently rebuilt until it was finally destroyed after the Battle of Benburb. All traces of it have disappeared.

In 1782 Dungannon was the venue of a historic convention of the Ulster companies of the Irish Volunteers, who paraded in the town and passed resolutions declaring Ireland's right to an independent parliament. The local Earl of Charlemont was the volunteers' leader, abetted by the Protestant Bishop of Derry.

Points of interest

The Royal School, founded by Charles I in 1628, is housed in a building erected in 1786 by Archbishop Robinson of Armagh. Adjoining the town is Northland House, formerly the seat of the Earl of Ranfurly. The town has attractive Georgian terraces.

Around Dungannon

Three miles (5 km) west is the village of Castlecaulfield. Here are the ruins of a Jacobean mansion erected in 1614 by an ancestor of the earls of Charlemont. Reverend Charles Wolfe, author of *The Burial of Sir John Moore*, was curate here from 1818 to 1821. In the main street of Donaghmore village, 3 miles (5 km) northwest of Dungannon, is an ancient stone cross which is a good specimen of early Irish sculpture. The Donaghmore Heritage Centre, 400 metres north of the high cross, is a converted national school dating from 1885.

At Coalisland, 4 miles (6 km) northeast of Dungannon, are coal deposits which have been worked at various times during the past 200 years.

Ballygawley, Clogher Valley

Augher Castle

Clay from the district has long provided raw material for brickworks.

Five miles (8 km) south-east of Dungannon is The Moy, a village on the River Blackwater with a wide tree-lined square. It was built in the eighteenth century by Lord Charlemont, on the plan of Marengo in Lombardy. Three miles/5km west of Moy is Benburb, where in 1646 the Irish army led by Owen Roe O'Neill defeated the English and Scottish forces of General Munro. The old castle ruin (called O'Neill's Castle) standing high above the Blackwater was the residence of the Wingfield family, erected on the site of the ancient O'Neill castle. From the grounds of Benburb Priory, where the Servite Brothers have their own hydroelectric power, an art gallery, an O'Neill Historical Centre and conference facilities, there is a fine view down the gorge in Benburb Valley Park to ruined Benburb Castle (1615). The river here attracts canoeists and anglers.

The Clogher valley in south Tyrone is a fertile well-wooded district extending 25 miles (40 km) from the border of County Armagh to the Fermanagh border. Caledon village, noted for its elegant cottages, was, during the wars of 1641, the headquarters of Sir Phelim O'Neill, who held Tyrone for several years against the English. Viscount Alexander, the British Field-Marshal, was born at Caledon in 1891.

The Grant Ancestral House at Dergina near Ballygawley, the farmhouse which was once the ancestral home of Ulysses Simpson Grant, 18th US President, has a collection of local artefacts.

At Errigal Keeroge near Ballygawley are the ruins of an ancient church and an interesting stone cross; and at Seskilgreen is a stone bearing remarkable late Stone Age sculpturing.

Old photographs of the Clogher valley and memorabilia of the Clogher valley railway are on show in the Display Centre in Fivemiletown. Further west along the Clogher valley is Augher village, north-west of which rises Knockmany (779 feet) where there is a Stone Age megalithic tomb with some stones sculptured similar to that at Seskilgreen. The village of Clogher, 2 miles (3 km) west of Augher, was the original cathedral town of the diocese (of which St Macartan, a disciple of St Patrick, was first bishop). The first Protestant bishop was the pluralist Myler Magrath, who continued to hold the Clogher see and other bishoprics after being appointed Archbishop of Cashel by Queen Elizabeth I. Rathmore fort, behind Clogher Cathedral, was the palace of the Airghialla and recent excavations have yielded important information about the Iron Age. William Carleton, the novelist, was born near Clogher at Prillisk in 1794 where his cottage is preserved, with some relics.

Cookstown

An Corr Chriochach (The Boundary Hill)

Pop. 7,650.

Cookstown, a centre of the bacon and sausage industries and an important market town, consists mainly of one tree-lined street nearly 1½ miles (2 km) long. A plantation town, it was named from Alan Cook, who founded it in the seventeenth century. The Convent Chapel has noteworthy examples of Irish ecclesiastical art.

Around Cookstown

South-east of the town is Killymoon Castle, a large castellated mansion designed by Nash and built at a cost of £80,000. The demesne is now the property of the Killymoon Golf Club (18).

Two and a half miles (4 km) south of Cookstown is Tullaghoge Fort, which in ancient times was the residence of the O'Hagans. They were justiciars of Tir Eoghain, and performed here the solemn inauguration of the O'Neills. The last ceremony was the inauguration of Hugh O'Neill in 1593. In 1602 the inauguration stone was destroyed by the Elizabethan General Mountjoy. Near Tullaghoge is

Loughry House, now a school of agriculture; some of Dean Swift's writings were penned here, on visits to the Lindesay family whose house it was.

Ten miles (16 km) east of Cookstown (via the village of Coagh, which has a fine dolmen), is Ardboe. This is where St Colman of Dromore founded a monastery in the sixth century. There are some remains of a much later church on this site by the shore of Lough Neagh. The Cross of Ardboe is perhaps the finest of the ancient high crosses in Ulster. It is 18½ feet high, with 22 sculptured panels filled with representations of scriptural scenes.

South-westwards in wild upland country, is the village of Pomeroy. At Altmore about 3 miles (5 km) further south, was born in 1810 General James Shields, a commander of the US Army in the American Civil War. He defeated his fellow countryman General 'Stonewall' Jackson and brought victory to the Union cause. Altmore Open Farm welcomes visitors.

Four miles (6 km) west of Cookstown on the Omagh road is Drum Manor Forest Park, with planned walks, wildfowl ponds, a shrub garden, a butterfly garden and a perfumed garden for the blind.

Close by at Wellbrook is an eighteenth-century beetling mill kept in working order by the National Trust.

The Beaghmore Stone Circles, a few miles further north and west, which are made up of a complex pattern of lines and circles, some aligned to the summer solstice, some not, are perhaps the North's most important archaeological find from this era.

Omagh

An Omaigh (The Sacred Plain)

Pop. 14,650.

Omagh, the county town, is in a wide valley among outlying hills of the Sperrin Mountains. At the town the Rivers Drumragh and Camowen join to form the Strule, which is noted for its now protected river pearl mussels.

The main buildings of the town are the twin-spired Catholic church, the Church of Ireland church and the Courthouse. The Convent Chapel has noteworthy examples of Irish ecclesiastical art.

Playwright Brian Friel (*Philadelphia, Here I Come* and *Translations*) and songwriter Jimmy Kennedy ('Red Sails in the Sunset', 'Teddy Bears' Picnic' and 'South of the Border Down Mexico Way') were born in the town. Visitors are welcomed at Lisnahoppin, a typical dairy farm, 3½ miles (6 km) south-east and there is golf (18) on the outskirts and another (9) at Fintona, 7 miles (11 km) south.

Around Omagh

At Camphill, 5 miles (8 km) north of Omagh, the Ulster-American Folk Park is an extensive open-air exhibition area consisting of 'Old World' and 'New World' cottages, illustrating the lives of northern Irish emigrants to the United States, including the ancestors of fourteen presidents and many frontier pioneers, soldiers and industrialists. It was endowed by the Mellon family whose cottage home is preserved. The dockside gallery and the emigrant ship transport the visitor to the land which the emigrants founded from the one they left behind.

The Ulster History Park, just north of the Folk Park, sets out the fascinating human history of Ulster from the arrival of the first primitive settlers in 7000 B.C. to the end of the seventeenth century, using examples of the built environment, from primitive skin-covered tent-like structures, through round towers and tiny churches to later complex fortifications.

There is excellent salmon, trout and roach fishing on local rivers. About 7 miles (11 km) north-east is Mullaghcarn (1,778 feet), which has extensive views from the summit. Between this hill and Curraghchosaly (1,372 feet) to the west,

Weaver's cottage, Ulster-American Folk Park

lies Gortin Gap which leads to the village of Gortin and the Gortin Glen Forest Park 2 miles (3 km) south of it, with scenic drive, lakes and deer reserves.

The pretty village of Plumbridge is at the mouth of a beautiful valley called Glenelly between the Sperrin and Munterlony Mountains. Sperrin village lies at the head of the glen, beneath the highest of the Sperrins (Sawel, 2,240 feet). At the Sperrin Heritage Centre visitors learn of the natural history of the area and how to pan for gold, or at least iron pyrites, in nearby streams. This fine mountain road then continues eastwards, climbing higher for some miles before dropping down to Draperstown (County Derry).

North from Omagh 10 miles (16 km) is Newtownstewart, where the River Mourne is formed by the junction of the Strule and the Glenelly; it is a well-known angling centre. South-west of the town is the Baronscourt demesne, in a picturesque valley between the hills. In Lough Catherine, one of three lakes on the estate, is an artificial island (or crannog) where excavations have yielded finds indicating periods of occupation from prehistoric times down to the Middle Ages.

Part of the estate is private but much is marketed with holiday cottages, pike fishing, water-skiing plus pheasant, rough and walk-up clay pigeon shoots available. Indeed the Sperrin Mountains are the best place in the North for this type of field sport and the state forests of Seskinore, Pomeroy and Dromore are recommended. Near by Newtownstewart Golf club (18) welcomes visitors.

Four miles (6 km) from Newtownstewart is Corick Glen, a beauty spot on the road to Plumbridge.

Strabane
An Srath Ban (The Fair River-Meadow)

Pop. 10,750.

Strabane on the River Mourne, is an agricultural town. A bridge across the River Foyle connects it with the County Donegal town of Lifford on the western bank of the river. There is golf (18) on the outskirts.

This was the birthplace of John Dunlap (born 1747), who in 1771 founded the first daily newspaper in the US, the *Pennsylvania Packet*, and printed the Declaration of Independence. He served his apprenticeship at Gray's printing press in Strabane, which is still in existence.

James Wilson, grandfather of President Woodrow Wilson, was likewise employed in the printing trade here before his emigration in 1807; his home at Dergalt on the Plumbridge road, open to the public, is still occupied by members of the Wilson family.

Another native of this district was Dr George Sigerson, the physician, scientist and poet. He was born in 1838 at Holy Hill, 3 miles (5 km) north-east of the town. The university colleges of Dublin, Cork and Galway, together with Queen's University in Belfast, compete annually in Gaelic football for the Dr Sigerson memorial cup.

Brian O'Nolan a.k.a. Myles na Gopaleen and Flann O'Brien, the surrealist Irish author of *At-Swim-Two-Birds*, was born in the town. A plaque in the Bowling Green square marks his birthplace.

Derry

The Diamond, Derry city

Derry is mainly a hilly county, with scenic hills, glens and river valleys. To the south the Sperrin Mountains, culminating in Sawel (2,240 feet), mass along the border with County Tyrone; in the north is the Atlantic coast, fringed with magnificent beaches of surf-washed sand. Derry city, on a commanding hill overlooking a broad tidal curve of the River Foyle, is an ancient and historic town. On the northern coast are the seaside resorts of Portstewart and Castlerock, and throughout the county there are numerous tourist attractions.

Derry
Doire (Oak grove)

Pop. 94,721 (Derry *city* 1991 CSO figures).

Tourist Office: 8 Bishop St, Derry BT48 6PW. Tel. (0504) 267284.

Post Office: 3 Custom House St, Derry. Tel. (0504) 362274.

Parking Regulations: Disc parking.

≣ Railway Station: Dukes St,
Waterside, Derry BT47 1DH.
Tel. (0504) 42228.

🚌 Bus Station: Foyle St, Derry BT48
6AP. Tel. (0504) 262261.

🚗 Car Hire: Eakin Bros, Maydown,
Derry. Tel. (0232) 860601.

Hertz Rent a Car, 173 Strand Road, Derry.
Tel. (0232) 360420.

🎭 Dates of principal cultural
events/festivals: Two Cathedrals Music
Festival (October).

The north's second city, straddling
the mouth of the River Foyle, Derry
to some, Londonderry to others,
has important shirt-making and chemical
industries and is undergoing massive new
investment in its harbour facilities. The
traveller, though, will focus on the left
bank and the seventeenth-century grid of
steep streets within the city walls.

Things to do
There is greyhound racing and the golf
clubs (18) and (9) are 1½ miles (2 km)
south of Derry. Salmon and sea trout fishing
is available within a few miles, on the
Faughan River. A licence from the Foyle
Fisheries Commission, 8 Victoria Road,
Derry, is required. A permit from the River
Faughan Anglers Association, 26a Carlisle
Road, is also required. Coarse fishing is
free. Ornithologists will be fascinated by
the bird life along the Foyle estuary. The
internationally renowned Field Day Theatre
Company premières its productions in the
Guildhall each September. The Orchard
Gallery also has an international reputation
for avante garde exhibitions and the fledgling
Foyle Valley Railway Centre will interest
train buffs. A cottage exhibition at Bally-
arnet, on the outskirts of the city, commemorates the landing there of Amelia Earhart,
the first woman to fly the Atlantic solo.

History
Derry dates from the foundation of a
monastery by St Colmcille (Columba) in
the year 546. Known then as Doire Calgaigh
(Calgach's Oakwood), the place was later
called Doire Cholmcille after the saint,
whose favourite monastery was here. The
growth of the monastic settlement and the
town around it made Derry a place of great
importance. Inevitably it also became a
prey for marauders, and from the ninth to
the eleventh century the town and churches
were ravaged may times by the Danes. In
1164 Abbot O'Brolchain, first bishop of
Derry, built the Tempull Mór (Great
Church) or cathedral on a site near the
ancient abbey church.

Derry was never occupied by the Anglo-
Normans, but from the latter part of the
twelfth century it was the scene of many a
struggle between Irish forces and invaders.
Not until 1600, however, did the English
gain a permanent foothold. In that year Sir
Henry Docwra landed a large force at
Culmore and took the town, which he
fortified with materials obtained by pulling
down the churches. In 1608 the young
chieftain of Inishowen, Cahir O'Doherty,
burned the town. He was defeated and
killed two months later, and his lands were
confiscated together with those of the
O'Neills and O'Donnells. Over 20,000
acres, including the borough of Derry,
were granted by James I to the City of
London. A large colony of Protestants was
imported and the walls fortifying the town
were completed in 1618. They founded the
present city and named it Londonderry, but
it is still called Derry by nearly all its
people.

In 1649 Owen Roe O'Neill made an
agreement with Sir Charles Coote, who
held Derry for the Cromwellians; as part of
the agreement, O'Neill came with his army
and relieved the city of a four months'
siege by royalist forces. The most famous
siege of Derry was, however, in 1689. The
garrison and inhabitants, including a large
number of Protestants who had fled there

Derry

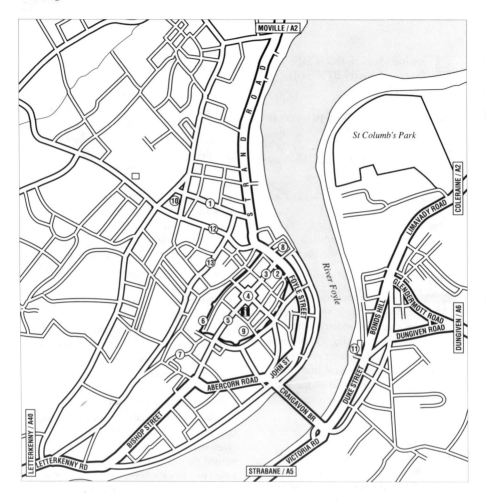

1. Great James Street
2. Bank Place
3. Shipquay Street
4. The Diamond
5. Bishop Street
6. City Walls
7. Long Tower Street

8. Guildhall
9. St Columb's Cathedral
10. St Eugene's Cathedral
11. Waterside Station
12. William Street
13. Rossville Street

from other parts of the north, were besieged in the city for 105 days. The invading Jacobite army threw a boom across the River Foyle at Culmore, preventing the approach of provision ships to the city.

Several thousand citizens perished from starvation and disease; sickness and exposure also took heavy toll of the besiegers. On 28 July the boom was forced by the ship, *Mountjoy*, one of an English convoy which then relieved the city. The Reverend George Walker, rector of Donaghmore, was the chief inspiration of the defenders during the siege.

Points of interest

The Old Walls, which are in an excellent state of preservation, are now laid out as a promenade. On them stand many of the cannon used during the sieges of the city. The largest of these, 'Roaring Meg', is near the Double Bastion; it played a prominent part in the great siege. The easiest access to the one-mile circuit, which may at times be obstructed by security activities, is from Bank Place, just inside the Shipquay Gate. The lifesize enigmatic cast-iron figures set around this promenade are modern, a comment by sculptor Anthony Gormley on the city's more recent turbulent past. The views out from the walls, at Bishop's Gate and Butcher's Gate, look over opposing political graffiti. Bishop's Gate, the most imposing of the four old city gates, is a triumphal arch erected in 1789 in place of the original. The other three are Shipquay Gate, Ferryquay Gate and Butchers Gate.

Shipquay Gate and Street

Guildhall, Derry city

In Shipquay Place is the Guildhall, a modern Gothic structure completed in 1912. The council chamber, furnished completely in Austrian oak, has a richly ornamented ceiling and a fine series of stained-glass windows illustrating events in the city's history. Among the treasures of the Corporation are an Andre Ferrara double-edged sword reputed to have belonged to Sir Cahir O'Doherty, and the mayor's chain and medal of office which were presented to the city by King William III.

Nearly opposite the Guildhall, Shipquay Gate gives access, first on the right to the O'Doherty Fort, a recently constructed local history interpretative centre, echoing to a certain extent its medieval original; and then straight ahead to Shipquay Street, the steepest business thoroughfare in Ireland. Hidden away half-way up the street, off to the right, is access to the Craft Village, devised as a showcase and living quarters for local crafts people. At the top of the hill is the Diamond, as town squares are called throughout the north.

407

Opposite Shipquay Street is Bishop Street, off which a turn to the left leads to the Protestant Cathedral (St Columb's). This is a plain Gothic building erected in 1628–1633 by the Honerable The Irish Society, a body of London merchants founded in 1613 by James I to administer the boroughs of Derry and Coleraine. The church has a fine spire which was rebuilt in 1802. In the vestibule is a mortarshell which fell in the churchyard during the siege. It contained a message bearing the terms of surrender offered to the garrison, but the reply was a defiant rejection. A large number of relics of the siege are in the Chapter House. The original eight bells of the cathedral were recast in 1929 and others added to bring the total to thirteen.

Outside the walls is the Catholic Church of St Columb, approached by Long Tower Street. This church, also known as the 'Long Tower', stands on the site of the ancient Tempull Mór (see page 405), the long tower of which stood until it was destroyed in the siege of 1689. Beneath the Calvary is a stone on which, according to tradition, St Colmcille used to kneel when praying. The Catholic Cathedral (St Eugene's), a well-proportioned nineteenth-century Gothic-style building, with a handsome spire, is at the head of Great James Street in the north-west end of the town.

Around Derry

Five miles east of Derry, Maydown, an industrial complex, has large chemical and synthetic textile plants, power station, tanker jetty, industrial training school and workers' township. Close by, at the pretty village of Eglinton, is the beauty spot called Muff Glen. The road through the glen continues southwards over Highmoor to the fine Ness Waterfall on the Burntollet River. This area is now the Ness Country Park, with signposted walks and picnic sites. Ballykelly village on the road to Limavady has a number of fine buildings constructed by the Fishmongers Company in the early nineteenth century.

Limavady

Leim an Mhadaidh (The Dog's Leap)

 Pop. 8,000.

History

This town, which dates from the seventeenth-century English plantation of Ulster, is named after an Irish settlement of the O'Cahans. This settlement was 2 miles (3 km) further south up the River Roe, at the place still called the Dog Leap. According to tradition, a dog belonging to a chieftain of the O'Cahans jumped the river here with a message in its collar which brought much needed help from the Dungiven branch of the family. A hill called the Mullagh, in the Roe Valley Country Park which extends along the river south of the town, is identified with the ridge Drumceatt— scene of the historic convention in 575 which determined the future of the kingdom of Scotland. The convention was attended by St Colmcille, who returned from Iona for the occasion. St Canice, who gave his name to Kilkenny and to Cambuskenneth in Scotland, was born at Drumramer, near Limavady, about the year 526. The Country Park has an exhibition centre.

The melody known as the 'Derry Air' was noted down in Limavady by Jane Ross in 1851 from an itinerant fiddler named MacCormick. Its author is believed to have been Rory Dall O'Cahan, a harper-composer of the sixteenth century. 'Peg of Limavady', the character in Thackeray's well-known poem, lived at an inn in Ballyclose Street. William Massey (1856–1925), one time Premier of New Zealand, was born and educated here.

Around Limavady

The Sampson Tower in Farlow Wood, a mile (2 km) west of the town, is an intriguing Gothic-style memorial to a local land agent. South of Limavady, the road to Dungiven follows the Roe valley and has many attractive views with the Sperrin

Magilligan Strand

Mountains as background. Northwards, the direct road between Limavady and Coleraine climbs to over 800 feet on the shoulder of a hill, offering a fine view of Lough Foyle and the Donegal Mountains.

A longer route to Coleraine follows the railway line along the beautiful coast by Downhill, passing beneath the basaltic cliffs of Binevenagh Mountain (1,260 feet). There is trout fishing in a small lake on the summit. This mountain, and the sandhills of Magilligan Strand which spread out beneath it, are interesting terrain for the botanist, ornithologist and entomologist.

The strand, over 6 miles (10 km) long, runs in a beautiful curve to the narrow mouth of Lough Foyle, where a Martello tower, relic of the Napoleonic wars, commands the view across Lough Foyle, with its huge population of migrating seabirds—an ornithologist's paradise—to Donegal. On occasions, a ferry service across the Lough to Greencastle is available.

At the eastern end of the strand is the quiet resort of Downhill. Here there was once a palatial castle, residence of Frederick Augustus Hervey (1730–1803), the eccentric Earl of Bristol and Protestant Bishop of

Derry. Hervey was a great traveller through the countries of Europe, where he is still commemorated in many a 'Hotel Bristol'. On the cliff-edge near the site of the castle is Mussenden Temple, now maintained by the National Trust, built by Bishop Hervey in 1783 to house a library and later dedicated as a memorial to his cousin. The temple, which is in excellent preservation, is a domed circular structure after the style of the temples of Vesta at Tivoli and Rome. It is believed to have been designed by Michael Shanahan.

A mile (2 km) east of Downhill is Castlerock, a resort fronting a fine sandy beach that runs about a mile (2 km) westwards from the mouth of the River Bann. There is an open-air heated swimming pool by the beach and a championship golf course (18), (9). Permits for fishing in the Bann (salmon, sea trout, trout, bream, roach, pike and perch) may be had from the Bann Fisheries, The Cutts, Coleraine. There is good beach fishing for bass along this coast in the summer months.

Just a mile (2 km) south of Castlerock, at Liffock crossroads, stands Hezlett House, a seventeenth-century thatched rectory with an unusual roof construction, now administered by the National Trust.

Four miles (6 km) south of Castlerock, on the old road between Coleraine and Limavady, is Sconce Hill (800 feet), crowned by the huge ancient fort of Dun Ceithern (called 'the Sconce'). This was a stronghold of the legendary Red Branch Knights.

Coleraine

Coil Raithain (Ferny Corner)

 Pop. 16,050.

Coleraine, on the wide River Bann, is a market and manufacturing town that has greatly increased in importance in recent years. The University of Ulster, on the northern outskirts, opened its doors in 1968. Though the town's ancient distillery has been merged with Bushmills, a small amount of this pale grain whiskey is still produced for local consumption. Mixed with four volumes of boiling water, cloves, cinnamon and a touch of sugar, it is recommended as a specific against winter's ills.

Things to do

Recreational facilities at Coleraine include tennis courts and bowling greens. Rowing on the Bann is a popular sport, and there is a public river sports centre at Ballysally, north of the university. Golf is within easy reach at Portrush, Portstewart (18) (18) (9) (9), Castlerock (18) (9) and Benone (9). The Riverside, an attractive on-campus theatre, has an imaginative programme of visiting professional companies and the university also operates a series of Talks and Tours during the summer months, tailored for the visitor and geared to the local environment. There is a marina and summer cruises on the Bann, a bird sanctuary, cinemas and an ice rink.

History

The name Coil Raithain is said to have been given to the place by St Patrick in the fifth century. Seven hundred years later Coleraine was referred to by St Bernard of Clairvaux as a 'city'. At one time the area between the Bann and the Foyle was called by the English the County of Coleraine, but when James I granted the whole area in 1613 to the London Companies, Coleraine was superseded by Derry as chief town. The suburb Killowen on the western bank of the river is named after the sixth-century monastery founded there by St Carbreus.

Around Coleraine

About a mile (2 km) south, on the eastern bank of the Bann, is the huge mound called Mount Sandel. This is believed to be the site of Dun Da Bheann, the royal palace of Fintan, ruler of this territory in the first century. Later it was the site of a castle built by John de Courcy about 1200. Originally Mount Sandel was a mesolithic site, and it has yielded more information about the Middle Stone Age (*c*.7000 B.C.) than any other site in Ireland.

The Lower Bann, which enters the sea 5 miles (8 km) below Coleraine, is a famous salmon river. Two miles (3 km) south of Coleraine is the salmon leap called The Cutts, near Castleroe (site of an old castle of the O'Cahans). The Bann eel fisheries are an important industry.

On the road to Maghera, 11 miles (18 km) south of Coleraine, is the small town of Garvagh, prettily situated in the foothills of the Carntogher Mountains. This was the birthplace of Denis O'Hempsey, a celebrated eighteenth-century harper who travelled Ireland for ten years and visited Scotland in 1745 where he played before Prince Charles at Holyrood. In 1792, at a great age, he attended the Harpers' Congress in Belfast. (See page 419.)

George Canning, born at Garvagh about 1730, was father of the George Canning who became Prime Minister of England in 1827.

On a hill slope 3 miles (5 km) south of Garvagh is the dolmen called Slaghtaverty (Leacht Abhartaigh: Abhartach's mon-

Marsh's Library, Dublin

Banduff beach, Co. Sligo

Pub, Co. Clare

Horseriding on the beach at Stracomer, Co. Donegal

Overleaf: Rothe House, Kilkenny

Blarney House, Co. Cork

Portstewart

ument). According to tradition, Abhartach was a malevolent dwarf who terrorised the people of the district enchanting women with his harp and magical powers. Finn McCool, creator of the Giant's Causeway, killed him, burying him upside down to stifle the sound of the harp.

Six miles (10 km) south-east of Garvagh, Kilrea is a well-known angling centre for the Lower Bann and lesser streams; there is also coarse fishing on small lakes near by, and three 9-hole golf courses.

Portstewart

Port Stiobhaird (Stewart's Harbour)

Pop. 5,300.

This fine resort is built around a pretty bay sheltered by rocky headlands. The novelist Charles Lever (1806–1872) was dispensary doctor here for some time, and many of the incidents related to his stories are said to have originated in this district.

Things to do

Portstewart is particularly noted for its bathing and golf. There are pools and coves beside the town and excellent bathing also from the surf-washed sands that run for nearly 2 miles (3 km) from the cliffs south of the town. For golfers there are two 18-hole courses—the strand course (6,784 yards) on the tongue of land between the River Bann and the Atlantic; and the town course (4,733 yards) which is beside the town on the east. Portstewart Golf Club also has a 9-hole course and there is another course (9) just east of the town. Other attractions include tennis, boating and sea fishing.

Magherafelt

Machaire Fíogaid (Rushy Plain)

Pop. 5,050.

This market town, a few miles from the north-western corner of Lough Neagh, was laid out on spacious

Springhill

lines by the Salters' Company of London, who came into possession of the district under the plantation of Ulster in the seventeenth century.

Around Magherafelt
The town is a convenient angling centre for the Moyola River, and there are pleasant runs by the shore of Lough Neagh and to other attractive spots in the neighbourhood including pretty Ballyronan marina. There is golf (18) 3 miles (5 km) north-east of the town.

Five miles (8 km) to the south on the Cookstown road is another market town, Moneymore; this was in the plantation territory of the London Company of Drapers. Just outside the town is Springhill (open to the public), a fine seventeenth-century house with attractive gardens and a costume museum. Five miles (8 km) north-east is Bellaghy which, besides having a fine Plantation bawn (fortified farmhouse), was the birthplace of the poet Seamus Heaney.

To the west is Slieve Gallion (1735 feet). On its eastern slopes, 3 miles (5 km) from Moneymore, is the pretty Carndaisy Glen. In the valley between Slieve Gallion and Fir Mountain (1,193 feet) is Lough Fea; this can be approached by an exhilarating mountain track across Slieve Gallion from the village of Desertmartin, 3 miles (5 km) west of Magherafelt.

North of Slieve Gallion, in a wide valley, is Draperstown, named after the London Company of Drapers, but still

known locally by its old name of 'The Cross'. From here roads branch in several directions through the mountains, offering many interesting scenic tours.

Maghera
Machaire Ratha (Plains of the Ring-fort)

This is an important junction on the main Belfast–Derry road, pleasantly situated at the eastern end of the Sperrin Mountains. It was the birthplace of Charles Thompson (1729–1824) who, as secretary to the first United States Congress, wrote out the Declaration of Independence. His brother, General William Thompson, commanded the third regiment of South Carolina in the War of Independence.

The ruined Maghera Old Church, an ancient structure said to have been founded by St Lurach in the sixth century, has a fine doorway with sloping jambs and a massive lintel which are sculptured with interlaced work and a representation of the Crucifixion. The Annals of Ulster record that this church was raided by the Norsemen in 832.

Around Maghera
Maghera is a convenient centre for fishing the Moyola and Claudy Rivers. Crewe Hill, near by, was the birthplace of Watty Graham, a local leader of the United Irishmen in 1798. He was hanged on a beech tree near the old church of St Lurach. Another Maghera United Irishman named Billy Cuddy, cut down by friends when half-hanged, was revived and smuggled to America. A mock funeral was held to deceive the authorities, and in the old graveyard of St Lurach's there is still a stone inscribed 'the burying place of William Cuddy'.

Four miles (6 km) north-west of the town on the eastern slope of Carntogher Mountain (1,521 feet), is the stone circle called Slaghtneill (Niall's Monument). Between Carntogher and Glenshane Mountain (1,507 feet), the road from Maghera to

Derry climbs steeply to 1,000 feet to enter Glenshane Pass. Beyond the pass the road descends the Roe valley to Dungiven.

Dungiven
Dun Geimhin (Fort of the Hide)

This is a small market town situated where the River Roe is joined by the Owenrigh and the Owenbeg, and surrounded by a horseshoe of hills. East of the town the peak of Benbraddagh (1,535 feet) rises steeply from the valley to the south lies the main range of the Sperrins and on the west are lesser hills with gentle slopes.

Things to do
Dungiven is a good angling centre for the River Roe (salmon, sea and brown trout). Within the Roe Valley Country Park the fishing is public (Foyle Fisheries Commission). Seawards of the town, most stretches are controlled by local angling clubs who will issue day permits to visiting anglers through tackle shops. The town is also a convenient base for climbing and walking in the Sperrins, and for exploring the glens which penetrate the hills to the south. There is good scenery in the immediate neighbourhood and along the Roe valley northwards to Limavady.

History
Dungiven was a stronghold of the O'Cahans down to the seventeenth century. Donal Ballagh O'Cahan, the last of the Dungiven chiefs, was imprisoned by the English in 1609 and died without a trial eight years later in the Tower of London. In the same year the confiscated lands at Dungiven were granted by James I to the London Company of Skinners.

Around Dungiven
Outside the town to the south, on a rock above the River Roe, are the ruins of an Augustinian Priory founded by the O'Cahans in the twelfth century and restored in 1397 by the Archbishop of Armagh. The remains are mainly of the chancel of the priory church, with a richly decorated arch. Beneath the arch is the finely sculptured altar tomb, the finest in Ulster, of a fourteenth-century O'Cahan chief, Cooey na nGall. The six kilted warriors, standing in niches below, were Scots mercenaries.

Beside the town is Dungiven Bawn, the remains of a fortified mansion, erected by the Skinners' Company in 1618. The castle itself has disappeared, but the surrounding bawn still remains. It has a defensive platform carried on arches—one of the largest of its kind.

Two miles (3 km) south-west of Dungiven is the ruin of Banagher Church, an ancient structure whose chief feature is a fine lintelled doorway which is square headed outside and round headed inside. Beside the church is a tiny structure in the form of the early oratories, with a high-pitched roof of stone. It is believed to be the tomb of the founder, St Muiredagh O'Heney; a curious figure is carved in relief on one side. A similar tiny building stands beside the ruin of Bovevagh Church, a few miles north of Dungiven.

The Irish patriot and man of letters, John Mitchel, was born in 1815 at Camnish, near Dungiven, where his father was minister of the Unitarian Church.

Antrim

Glenarm

County Antrim forms the north-east corner of Ireland, and a channel only 13 miles (21 km) wide separates Torr Head from the Scottish coast. Lough Neagh (the largest lake in Ireland or Britain) and the fertile valley of the Bann occupy the western part of the county, but the greater part of it is an irregular plateau of hills and uplands, dropping sharply to the sea on the north and east. Belfast, capital of Northern Ireland and a great port and industrial centre, is built where the River Lagan enters Belfast Lough, near the southern end of the county. On the east a magnificent coast runs north from Larne, curving round the base of steep headlands, between which the beautiful nine glens of Antrim open to the sea. Almost every bay along the coast is a link in a chain of fine holiday resorts. On the northern coast the Giant's Causeway is a celebrated natural wonder.

Belfast

Beal Feirste
(The Mouth of the Farset)

Pop. 303,000 (Belfast *city* 1991 CSO figures).

Tourist Office: St Anne's Court, 59 North St, Belfast BT1 1NB. Tel. (0232) 231221.

American Express: Alex M.
Hamilton Travel, 10 College St, Belfast
BT1 6BT. Tel. (0232) 322455.
Fax (0232) 328437.

Post Office: Donegal Square BT1.
Tel. (0232) 321532.
Castle Place BT1. Tel. (0232) 323740.
Shaftesbury Square BT2.
Tel. (0232) 326177.

Parking Regulations: Disc parking.
Clearway zone in city centre.

Railway Stations: Central Railway,
East Bridge St, all destinations except
Larne. Tel. (0232) 230310.
York St, Railway Station, boat train to
Larne. Tel. (0232) 235282.

Note: For backpackers, stations have no
left luggage facilities.

Bus Stations:
Great Victoria St. Tel. (0232) 320574.
Oxford St. Tel. (0232) 246485.

Car Hire: Avis, 69 Great Victoria
St, Belfast. Tel. (0232) 240404.
Carriageway Cars, 21 Holywood Road.
Tel. (0232) 652000.
Dan Dooley Kenning, 175 Airport Road.
Tel. (084 94) 52522.
Europcar Ltd, Sydenham Bypass.
Tel. (0232) 450904.
Hertz, Terminal Building, Belfast Airport.
Tel. (084 94) 732451.

Bicycle Hire: Bikeit, 4 Belmont
Road. Tel. (0232) 471141.
E. Coates, 108 Grand Parade.
Tel. (0232) 471912.
McConvey Cycles, 476 Ormeau Road.
Tel. (0232) 238602.

Dates of principal cultural events/
festivals: Belfast Folk Festival (September).
Belfast Festival (November).

The port of Belfast on the River Lagan is
the capital of Northern Ireland and the
second largest city in the country. Belfast
International Airport and Belfast City Airport
have, between them, flights to Amsterdam
and Paris and a dozen British cities.

Things to do
Belfast offers a wide range of recreation
and entertainments. There are facilities for
most major sports. The Lyric Players
Theatre, which specialises in Irish drama
and classics of the stage, is Northern
Ireland's 'National' theatre. The Arts
Theatre in Botanic Avenue specialises
mainly in musicals and modern English
and Ulster plays, the Group Theatre in
Bedford Street, in Ulster local comedies.
The Grand Opera House offers a splendid
range of touring opera, theatre, ballet and
music hall. The Old Museum Arts Centre
in College Square North is a home for
young experimental theatrical companies.
The Crescent Arts Centre concentrates on
community arts and the city's newest
theatre, The Golden Thread, on the Crumlin
Road, combines both approaches. The
Ulster Hall is the home of the Ulster
Orchestra. The Queen's Film Theatre,
University Square Mews, shows foreign
films and classics of the cinema. Shopping
is excellent.

The visual arts are catered for by the
Arts Council Gallery (touring
exhibitions) and the Ulster
Museum with its interesting collection of
Irish and contemporary art. The Orpheus
Gallery in York Street, the Old Museum
and the Fenderesky near the University
have adventurous approaches; the Tom
Caldwell and One, Oxford St, caters for
eclectic tastes whilst the Cavehill, Bell and
Ulster Arts Club galleries specialise in the
work of more traditional contemporary
Irish artists.
    The city's major cultural event, the
Belfast Festival at Queen's University is

Belfast

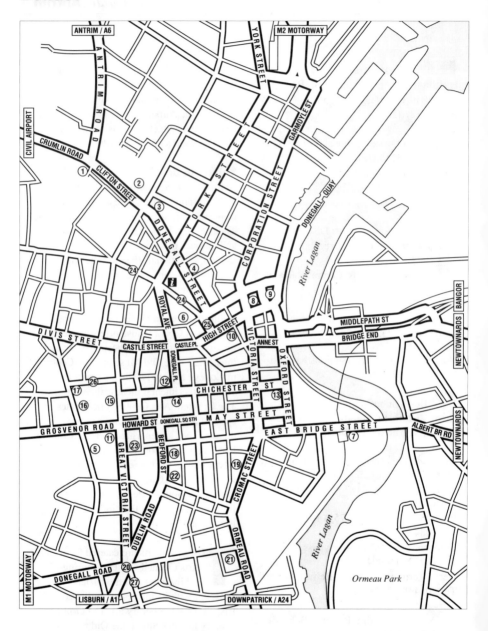

1. Carlisle Memorial Church
2. Clifton House
3. St Patrick's Church (RC)
4. St Anne's Cathedral (CI)
5. Gt Victoria St Bus Station
6. Old Presbyterian
   Oval Church
7. Central Station
8. Albert Memorial Clock Tower
9. Custom House
10. St George's Church (CI)
11. Grand Opera House
12. Linenhall Library
13. Royal Courts of Justice
14. City Hall
15. Municipal College
    of Technology
16. Royal Belfast Academical
    Institution
17. Christ Church (CI)
18. Ulster Hall
19. St Malachy's Church (RC)
20. Shaftesbury Square
21. Ulster Television
22. BBC
23. Crown Liquor Saloon
24. North Street
25. Bridge Street
26. College Square North
27. Botanic Avenue

Queen's University, Belfast

second only to the Edinburgh Festival in its range of cultural events.

There are ten 18-hole and five 9-hole golf courses within 4 miles (6 km) of the city centre, and several others within a short distance. There is yachting and sailing on Belfast Lough, and the city has a number of modern leisure centres with swimming pools and various sports facilities, also sauna baths. Facilities for various games are provided in the public parks.

The Crown Liquor Saloon, opposite the Grand Opera House, matches the victorian splendour of the work of the Opera House's architect, Frank 'Matchless' Matcham's gilt elephants and ambiguous chinoiserie in its elegant tile work, painted glass and mirrors, and finely carved snugs. It is preserved as a working pub by the National Trust. The Whitham Street Transport Gallery's exhibits (being moved to Cultra) include Old Maeve, the largest locomotive built in Ireland.

History

In ancient times Belfast was the site of a fort that commanded a ford on the River Lagan (near the present Queen's Bridge). John de Courcy destroyed the ancient fort soon after his invasion of Ulster in 1177,

and built a castle near by. This castle was in turn destroyed in 1316 by Edward Bruce, rebuilt and destroyed again several times in the next 300 years. During that time possession of the castle alternated between the O'Neills and the English. In 1574 Brian O'Neill, Chief of the Clannaboye territory that surrounded Belfast, was treacherously seized by the Earl of Essex during a banquet in the castle and put to death. The castle and the lands of Belfast came into the possession, 30 years later, of Sir Arthur Chichester, the Governor of Carrickfergus, who ruthlessly exterminated the inhabitants of the surrounding area and planted the lands with settlers from Devon and Scotland.

The Grand Opera House, Belfast

In the first half of the seventeenth century Belfast's import trade and its already established linen industry were encouraged by the Earl of Strafford, Lord Deputy of Charles I. He bought from Carrickfergus the monopoly on imported goods which that port had held. The linen trade got further impetus after 1685 from new methods introduced by Huguenot refugees. By the end of the century the population of Belfast had grown to 2,000—a four-fold increase since 1600.

Belfast's prosperity continued in the eighteenth century, but along with it was a growing resentment among the townsfolk against the English policy of repression in Ireland. Catholic and Presbyterian were united by their common disadvantages under the Penal Laws. The Society of the United Irishmen was founded in Belfast in 1791, and four years later Wolfe Tone, Samuel Neilson, Thomas Russell, Henry Joy McCracken and Henry Spiers climbed to McArt's Fort on Cave Hill and solemnly vowed never to cease their efforts until Ireland was independent. McCracken, who led the insurgents at the Battle of Antrim

in 1798, was hanged at Corn Market in Belfast's High Street.

Side by side with these developments went a cultural revival, and Belfast of the late eighteenth and early nineteenth centuries has been dubbed, because of its enlightenment, the 'Athens of the North'. Prominent citizens became patrons of learning and art, schools and libraries were established and great interest was taken in the language, literature and music of Ireland. An outstanding cultural event was the great Harpers' Congress of 1792.

Meanwhile, two brothers called William and Hugh Ritchie had founded a shipbuilding industry on the River Lagan in 1791, and during the nineteenth century this industry grew by leaps and bounds. In 1862, Harland and Wolff was founded, a firm that was to build some of the world's largest ships. New machinery and processes also helped Belfast to a position of supremacy in the linen industry, and in the nineteenth century the population grew from 25,000 to 300,000.

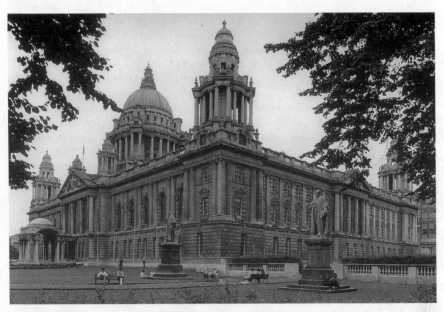

City Hall, Belfast

Incorporated as a borough in 1842, Belfast became a city in 1888. In 1920, when six of the Ulster counties were separated from the rest of Ireland by an Act of the British Parliament, the city became the capital of Northern Ireland.

Points of interest

Occupying a large area in the centre of Donegall Square is the City Hall, a Renaissance-style building of Portland stone completed in 1906 on the site of the old White Linen Hall. Each of the building's corners has a tower, and a graceful dome rises in the centre to 175 feet. Inside is the council chamber and other stately halls, with elaborate marble decoration. The statues outside are of Queen Victoria and prominent Belfast citizens; on the west side is a war memorial and garden of remembrance. At the east side of the City Hall is a sculptured group commemorating the victims of the *Titanic* disaster in 1912. This Belfast-built ship—the largest in the world at the time—struck an iceberg on her maiden voyage to New York, and sank with the loss of over 1,500 lives.

In Donegall Square North is the Linen-hall Library, originally founded in 1788 as the Belfast Society for Promoting Knowledge. It has a fine collection of books on the linen trade as well as books of general and recent historic interest. The society's first librarian was the scholarly Thomas Russell ('The Man from God-Knows-Where' of Florence M. Wilson's ballad). A prominent leader of the United Irishmen, Russell was hanged in Downpatrick in 1803 for his attempt to rally support for Emmet's Rising.

In College Square East, 300 yards west of the City Hall, is the fine building of the College of Technology. In the adjoining grounds is the Royal Belfast Academical Institution, whose pupils included two distinguished natives of Belfast: the scientist and inventor, Lord Kelvin (1824–1907), and the statesman and scholar,

Castlecourt Shopping Centre, Belfast

Viscount Bryce (1838–1922). Near by are the Assembly Buildings, headquarters of the Presbyterian Church in Ireland.

South of the City Hall, in Bedford Street, is the municipally owned Ulster Hall—scene of many a political meeting and a venue for cultural, social and sporting events.

About ¼ mile (0.5 km) east of the City Hall, in Chichester Street, are the Royal Courts of Justice, a massive building of Portland stone. Close by are the city markets, and to the north is the Custom House (completed 1857), which lies between Queen's Square and Donegall Quay. Near the Custom House is the Albert Memorial, commemorating Queen Victoria's consort, whose statue is in a niche high on the west side of the tower.

In High Street, a few yards away, is St George's Church (1812), with its fine classical portico. In early times this was the site of the 'Chapel of the Ford', rebuilt after the foundation of Belfast as the Corporation Church and pulled down in 1774. In St George's Churchyard the patriot McCracken was buried in 1798; about 130 years later his coffin was discovered during building operations and re-interred in Clifton Street cemetery. Clifton House, once the Poorhouse, is an elegant Irish Georgian building.

In Sugarhouse Entry, a narrow passage that ran between High Street and Waring

Street but destroyed by bombing during the Second World War, was the 'Doctor Franklin Tavern', where the leaders of the United Irishmen met under the name of 'The Muddlers' Club'. The home of the McCracken family in 1798 was in Rosemary Street, beside High Street and barely a hundred yards from the place where Henry Joy was hanged in Corn Market. The area between Corn Market and Donegall Place was where the Castle of Belfast stood until it was destroyed by fire in 1708.

Bridge Street, running north from High Street, leads to the street junction where a branch of the Northern Banking Company occupies the site of the Old Exchange— venue of the Harp Festival of 1792. Nearly opposite, on the corner of Waring Street and Sugarhouse Entry, stood the 'Irish Woollen Warehouse' of Samuel Neilson, a founder of the United Irishmen. The Home Front Heritage Centre (relics of the blitz), and the Royal Ulster Rifles Museum, stand in Waring Street. In Donegall Street were the offices of the *Belfast Newsletter* (now in Boucher Crescent), which has been published continuously since 1737 and is the oldest continuously published daily newspaper in these islands.

The Church of Ireland St Anne's Cathedral is a modern Romanesque building designed by Sir Thomas Drew. The three doorways of the west front are noteworthy for their recessed arches and tympanal sculptures. The nave is 85 feet wide and paved with Irish marble and Canadian maple. At the north-west corner is the chapel of the Holy Spirit and opposite it the baptistery, whose mosaic roof of 150,000 pieces of glass symbolises the Creation. In the nave is the tomb of the Unionist leader, Lord Carson. Adjoining the cathedral is the Ulster College of Art and Design.

In Upper Donegall Street the Catholic St Patrick's Church has a chapel beauti- fully decorated by the painter, Sir John Lavery, who was born near by in North

Queen Street and baptised in this church. On St Patrick's Day and other special occasions the Shrine of St Patrick's Hand is exposed for veneration in the church. This is a fifteenth-century reliquary shaped like a hand and forearm, containing a relic of the saint. Other churches of note are St Peter's Pro-Cathedral (Catholic) in Derby Street, which has an effective west front and graceful twin spires; St Malachy's (Catholic) in Alfred Street, which has some fine stucco work inside; the beauti- fully proportioned Carlisle Memorial Church (deconsecrated) in Carlisle Circus; and the Unitarian Church in Elmwood Avenue. Sinclair Seamen's Church, off Corporation Square, has a pulpit constructed from the bows, bowsprit and figurehead of the good ship, *Mizpah*, and port and starboard lights on the font. Rosemary Street First Presbyterian Church, built in 1783, has lunch-time concerts.

In the southern suburbs is the Tudor- Gothic building of Queen's University. Established in 1849, it was associated with the other Queen's Colleges of Cork and Galway until its incorporation as a separate university in 1908. Behind the university stands the Tuscan Doric building of the Presbyterian Theological College.

A short distance away, in the Botanic Gardens, are the Ulster Museum and Art Gallery, housed in a fine building designed by J. C. Wynnes and begun in 1923. Exhibits in the museum and gallery are changed periodically. Its main collections illustrate Northern Ireland archaeology, history, zoology, geology and botany. To many, the artefacts of the *Girona*, a Spanish galleas, wrecked on the north coast near the Giant's Causeway fleeing from the Armada's defeat, are the most beautiful and the most poignant. The inscription on a thin gold ring reads, 'no tengo mas que dar te' (I have nothing more to give you).

Among the industrial features of the city, the most extensive is the Port of Belfast, with its 7 miles (11 km) of quays

Ulster Museum, Belfast

approached by a deepwater channel from Belfast Lough. The city's maritime history is well illustrated in the paintings, sculpture and stained glass in the Harbour Office which can be visited by arrangement. Donegall Quay, on the River Lagan, is less than ½ mile (1 km) from the city centre; it accommodates cross-channel vessels. There are ambitious plans to regenerate and develop the whole Langanbank areas. The shipbuilding yards of Harland and Wolff include the largest shipbuilding dock in the world.

Belfast Parks

Among the city parks are:

Ormeau Park (137 acres), in the southeastern part of the city, well laid out and pleasantly wooded. A boulevard runs along the bank of the River Lagan, which bounds the park on the west. There are facilities for golf, putting, tennis, bowls, football and cricket.

The Botanic Gardens (38 acres), beside Queen's University, are open free every day until sunset. The grounds slope down to the River

Lagan. Features include the splendid curvilinear conservatories, the tropical fernery, the oak ground, flower garden, promenade, rockery, and rosary.

Musgrave Park (90 acres), in the southwest suburbs, has tennis courts, bowling and putting greens, and pitches for football, hurling, hockey and cricket. There is a fascinating collection of heathers.

Victoria Park (63 acres), in east Belfast, is formed from land reclaimed from the shore of Belfast Lough. There are facilities for bowls, tennis and putting, and a 20-acre saltwater lake for boating.

Falls Park (44 acres), is at the foot of the Black Mountain in the west end of the city.

Waterworks Park has fishing facilities.

Around Belfast

At Stormont, 5 miles (8 km) from the city centre, the Parliament Building occupies a magnificent site on rising ground in Stormont Park. Erected 1928–1932 at a cost of one and a quarter million pounds, the building was provided by the British Government to house the parliament and certain government ministries of Northern

Carrickfergus Castle

Ireland. It measures 365 feet by 164 feet, and rises in the centre to 92 feet. The main approach is a broad processional avenue ¾ mile (1 km) in length, rising gradually from the entrance on the Newtownards Road. An imposing statue of Lord Carson of Duncairn stands in front of the building.

About 4 miles (6 km) from the city centre is Cave Hill (1,188 feet), the most northerly of the chain of hills which curves around the city from the west. From the south-east (especially from the Antrim Road, about 2 miles (3 km) out from the city), the hill's outline bears a striking resemblance to a recumbent human profile—Napoleon's nose. From the hill itself, which is a great natural park, there are fine views over Belfast Lough.

On the eastern slopes is Belfast Castle, formerly a residence of the Earl of Shaftesbury and now owned by the city. The wooded grounds are open to visitors, and the castle is run as a restaurant.

On the slopes further north, Bellevue Gardens and the adjoining grounds of Hazelwood form a splendid mountain park. At Bellevue are the Zoological Gardens. There is a fine walk across Cave Hill from the southern end (approached by bus via Cavehill Road) and the walk may be continued for about 3 miles (5 km) to the bus terminus at Glengormley, or it may be shortened by rejoining the Antrim Road via the Sheep's Path or through Hazelwood or Bellevue Gardens.

On the highest peak of the hill, which drops on the eastern side in a cliff for several hundred feet, are the remains of earthwork of McArt's Fort (called after Brian McArt O'Neill, who was slain by Lord Deputy Mountjoy in 1601). This was where Wolfe Tone and the northern leaders of the United Irishmen met in 1795 and pledged themselves to Irish independence. In the face of the precipice beneath the fort are the five caves that give

423

the hill its name. The caves are at least partly artificial, but no evidence of their occupation has been found.

The pleasant hilly country near the city on almost every side gives many opportunities for excursions. On the west, extending southwards from Cave Hill, are several other peaks of over 1,000 feet—the highest being Divis Mountain (1,567 feet). The Castlereagh Hills, few of which rise higher than 600 feet, cover a wide area to the south and east.

There are also pretty places along the Lagan valley, now incorporated in the Lagan Valley Regional Park, which can be followed for up to 12 miles (19 km) by the riverside boulevards and towpaths. The 2-mile (3 km) walk along the towpath from Molly Ward's Lock at Stranmillis to Shaw's Bridge (near Malone Road bus route) is especially popular. About 1¼ miles (2 km) south of Shaw's Bridge is the Giant's Ring, a circular rampart nearly 200 yards across and averaging 15 feet in height. In the centre is a dolmen, beneath which were found the bones of a Stone Age burial. The rampart was originally built of unmortared stones, but in the course of time became covered with a layer of soil on which grass and furze now grow. The Ballylesson bus (from Great Victoria Street, Belfast) passes within half a mile (1 km), and there are signposts to guide visitors to the site. Near the River Lagan, at Upper Malone, Dixon Park has a large exhibition of roses from growers in many countries of the world. Nearer the Lagan are Barnet's Park, undulating and wooded, with Malone House and its art gallery and tea rooms in the grounds, and Clement Wilson Park. Wooded Belvoir Park, with its transit caravan park, and the headquarters of the RSPB, is also near by.

Carrickfergus
Carraig Fhearghais (Fergus's Rock)

Pop. 18,000.

Carrickfergus was at one time the main port in this part of Ireland, but its importance declined with the rapid development of Belfast from the seventeenth century onwards. The magnificent Norman Castle still dominates the port area where pleasure sailing, based on the extensive, well-equipped 300-berth marina, is replacing commercial maritime activities.

Things to do
There is a sailing school and sailing; other associated water-based sports, including sea angling, are the main attractions, but visitors in July/August should look out for the Medieval Banquets and Fairs associated with the Lughnasa celebrations and based around the castle. Derry author Brian Friel's acclaimed play, *Dancing at Lughnasa*, refers to the survival of related harvest customs in isolated areas in the west. There are marine gardens, a small beach, swimming facilities, a children's playground, golf (18) (9), bowls and tennis facilities. There is trout fishing in local reservoirs.

History
This town is said to be named after Fergus McErc, ruler of the ancient Dalriada territory in Antrim. He became the first Irish king of Scotland and drowned off the shore here when returning to Ireland. The castle of Carrickfergus was built in the period after 1180 either by John de Courcy, the first of the Anglo-Norman invaders of Ulster, or by his successor, Hugh de Lacy. In 1315 it was captured after a year's siege by the combined forces of Robert and Edward Bruce. After Edward's death in battle in 1318 the castle was retaken by the

English, who continued to hold it for 300 years except for occasional occupations by Irish and Scottish forces.

In the Parliamentary wars of the seventeenth century the castle and town changed hands more than once. In 1688 they were held by Lord Iveagh for James II, but were taken the following year by the Williamite General Schomberg. William III landed here on 14 June 1690, and a large stone at the harbour marks the place he stepped ashore. The town was taken and held for a short time in 1760 by a French expedition under Thurot, but the French force was defeated and Thurot killed in a battle with English ships off the Isle of Man. In 1778 Paul Jones entered Belfast Lough on the American ship, *Ranger*, and defeated the English naval vessel, *Drake*, after a sharp engagement off Carrickfergus. Carrickfergus Castle, probably the first real castle built in Ireland, is also one of the largest and best preserved in the country. It stands beside the harbour on a rocky peninsula which is enclosed by the curtain walls. The portcullis, with its ancient machinery, still exists in the double-towered entrance building at the landward end.

Inside are an outer and an inner courtyard which give access to the massive rectangular keep, nearly 60 feet square and 90 feet high. The keep had originally four storeys, but was later raised to provide a fifth. It contains the castle well and a dungeon. A notable prisoner here was Con O'Neill of Castlereagh, who escaped by means of a rope concealed in a cheese sent to him by his wife.

The first and second storeys are each divided into two rooms, but the third consists of one large apartment, 40 by 38 feet—the great hall of the castle. Relics of three cavalry regiments are housed in the museum in the castle keep.

Points of interest

The Church of Ireland Church of St Nicholas dates mainly from the seventeenth and eighteenth centuries, but the restored pillars of the nave belong to the end of the twelfth century, and part of the chancel dates from around 1305. In the north transept is a monument to Sir Arthur Chichester, Governor of Carrickfergus (died 1625). In the baptistery, a window commemorates St Nicholas in his role as Santa Claus, complete with reindeer and sledge.

There are few remains of the old town walls, principally the North Gate, restored in 1911. Near it was an inn kept by the forebears of Andrew Jackson (1767–1845), the US President whose father emigrated from here in 1765. The Andrew Jackson Centre, a reconstruction of an eighteenth-century cottage containing a small museum commemorating the US President's family links with the area, stands at Boneybefore, on the eastern outskirts. Of the old County Antrim Courthouse, erected about 1613, only the four walls remain. This was the scene of the trial of William Orr, the United Irishman who was hanged in Carrickfergus in 1797. His execution caused widespread resentment among the people, and 'remember Orr!' was the rallying cry of the northern insurgents in 1798.

Around Carrickfergus

About 2 miles (3 km) north-east of Carrickfergus in the ruined church of Kilroot, where Jonathan Swift held his first living between 1694 and 1696. This is also where Thurot's force landed in 1760. These are not the only literary associations: the Restoration dramatist, William Congreve, spent much of his childhood in the Carrickfergus castle where his father was a soldier, and the poet Louis Macneice spent his childhood in St Nicholas's rectory where his father was rector.

Whitehead

Ceann Ban (White Headland)

 Pop. 3,500.

This town, lying beneath sheltering cliffs where Belfast Lough opens into the North Channel, is a residential centre and seaside resort. It is of comparatively modern growth, and the only link with antiquity is a remnant of the sixteenth-century Castle Chester. A promenade runs along the sea front at the town, and walks have been built along the cliffs. Black Head, 1½ miles (2 km) north, has good views over Belfast Lough.

Things to do

The beach is pebbly but two sandy parts give safe bathing and paddling for children, there is also a seawater swimming pool at the promenade. The town is the headquarters of the County Antrim Yacht Club and of the Railway Preservation Society of Ireland, which runs a railway museum with working locomotives and, in the summer, steam train rides on the Portrush Flyer via Belfast to Portrush. Other recreations include golf (9) and (18), sea fishing, bowls, putting and tennis.

Around Whitehead

Dalway's Bawn, at Bellahill, 2 miles (3 km) west, is an excellent example, dating from 1609, of a fortified Plantation farmhouse with three flanker towers. Castle Dobbs, just south of Dalway's Bawn, was built in 1730 for Arthur Dobbs who became a governor of North Carolina.

Stretching north of Whitehead is the peninsula of Islandmagee, 7 miles (11 km) long and 2 miles (3 km) across at its broadest point. A fine range of basalt cliffs protects its eastern shore from the open sea; the most remarkable section of them, the Gobbins, are 5 miles (8 km) north of Whitehead. On one of the headlands sheltering Brown's Bay, a glacial boulder called the Rocking Stone is delicately poised. Not far distant is a dolmen known as the Druid's Chair. Cinerary urns and some ancient gold ornaments were among finds made at this site from time to time.

Islandmagee's greatest tragedy was the massacre of the inhabitants in 1642 by the garrison from Carrickfergus, who are said to have hurled some of their victims over the cliffs. Slaughterford Bridge which carries the road across a stream on to the peninsula at the southern end, is believed to commemorate the massacre. The inhabitants today are nearly all of Scottish and English extraction.

On the north of the peninsula, just south of the tiny resorts of Brown's Bay, Ferris Bay and Portmuck, in the front garden of No. 91 Ballylumford Road, stands, as it has done for at least 4,000 years, the Ballylumford Dolmen. The last witchcraft trials in Ireland (1711) took place on Islandmagee. There is a small farm museum on the Low Road.

The village of Ballycarry, ¾ mile (1 km) west off the coast road to Larne, has the ruins of the first Presbyterian church built in Ireland (1613). In the churchyard is the grave of James Orr (1770–1816), poet and United Irishman. A native of Ballycarry and a weaver by trade, Orr wrote verse for Samuel Neilson's patriotic Belfast paper, the *Northern Star*. After the 1798 Rising he escaped to America, but later returned to Ballycarry. His best-known song is 'The Irishman'. Another grave here bears the inscription, 'James Burns, born 1775', followed by a cryptographic verse in which the figures 1, 2, 3 and 4 represent the vowels a, e, i, and o; and 5 or 6 the letter *w*. Burns was also a 1798 insurgent, and returned to Ballycarry after a period in hiding. The Old Mill Glen near Ballycarry was the scene of a battle in 1597 in which Sir John Chichester was defeated and killed by the MacDonnells.

A few miles further north is Magheramorne, on the shore of Larne Lough. St Comgall (died 601), founder of the monastic school of Bangor, was born here. A soldier in early life, Comgall studied under St Finian of Clonard and St Ciaran of Clonmacnois. The monastery he founded became celebrated throughout Europe as a centre of learning.

Two miles (3 km) beyond Maghera-morne is Glynn, a pretty village at the mouth of a glen from which the Little Glynn River flows into Larne Lough. Even more picturesque is the tiny village of Glenoe, with its fine waterfall, 2 miles (3 km) south of Glynn near the head of the glen.

Larne
Latharna (Lahair's Territory)

👫👫 Pop. 18,000.

D ominated by the power-station chimneys of Kilroot and Bally-lumford, Larne is a town with several sizeable industries and a port which, in addition to its trading importance, is the crossing point for the car ferry services from Stranraer and Cairnryan in Scotland— the shortest cross-channel passage between Ireland and Britain. For many visitors, therefore, the town is the gateway to the Antrim Glens.

Things to do
As befits a cross-channel port, there are a number of camping and caravan parks close to the town. The maze at Carnfunnock Country Park, just north of the town, though modern, is intriguing. The Larne and District Historical Centre in Victoria Road re-creates turn-of-the-century rural life.

Golfers have a choice of 18- and 9-hole courses. There are bathing facilities at the promenade, and tennis, putting and other games are provided in two public parks.

History
The raised beach at the Curran, a long tapering gravel spit curving southwards from the town, has yielded many thousands of flint flakes and implements of the neolithic period, which are found only in this part of Ireland and provide the earliest evidence available of the presence of man in this country. On a map drawn by the Greek geographer, Ptolemy, in the second century A.D., the Islandmagee Peninsula is called Isa mnion Akron. This district was also well known to the Norse sea rovers, who used Larne Lough in the tenth and eleventh centuries as a base for their raiding expeditions.

Edward Bruce landed near Larne in 1315 with 6,000 men, to begin his three-year campaign in Ireland. The later history of the area, down to the mid-seventeenth century, is largely bound up with that of Olderfleet Castle (see below). In 1798, an insurgent force from Ballymena made an unsuccessful attack on the town. In 1914 Larne was the scene of the principal landing of arms from Germany for the Ulster Volunteers, to oppose the Bill for Irish Home Rule which had been introduced in the British Parliament.

Points of interest
At the Curran is Olderfleet Castle, now a ruin. The Norse sea rovers, whose name for Larne Lough was Ulfricksfiord (from which Olderfleet is derived), are believed to have built a castle on this peninsula. The present structure was, however, probably built by the Bissets, a Scottish family who settled here in the thirteenth century. On the arrival of Edward Bruce in 1315, the Bissets rallied to his support, and for this their castle and lands at Olderfleet were confiscated by the British Crown. In the sixteenth century the castle was held for a time by the MacDonnells, one of whom married a Bisset, but in 1569 it was granted by Queen Elizabeth to Sir Moyses Hill. James I restored the property to the Mac-Donnells, but later gave it to Sir Arthur Chichester. The castle was last occupied about 1641.

At the entrance to the harbour is a modern structure, 95 feet high, the Chaine Memorial Tower. On the lines of an ancient Irish round tower, it was built as a memorial to James Chaine, a County Antrim MP and a benefactor of Larne. He was buried in an upright position in a private enclosure overlooking the entrance to the lough, so that even in death he could still watch the passing ships.

The Antrim Coast Road

Extending northwards from Larne, the coast road is a very fine introduction to one of the most beautiful coastal areas in Ireland. Running close to the water's edge throughout its entire length of 25 miles (40 km) to Cushendall, the road has cliffs of basalt or limestone rising steeply above it. It provides a superb succession of views, with bays and sheltering headlands at almost every turn.

Four miles (6 km) north of Larne the road rounds Ballygalley Head (303 feet), off which on a rock in the sea are the remains of an ancient fortress, Carne Castle. Near by at the modern village of Bally-galley is Ballygalley Castle (now a hotel, complete with ghost in the Dungeon Bar), a fortified house built by James Shaw of Greenock in 1625. About 1½ miles (2 km) inland is the village of Carncastle, where the Catholic Church has a striking life-size statue of St Joseph and the Infant Jesus, executed in Portland stone by the Countess of Antrim.

Glenarm is a pretty village 12 miles (19 km) north of Larne on Glenarm Bay. The glen after which the village is named is one of the nine glens of Antrim, and runs southwards among the hills that rise to over 1,000 feet. Glenarm Castle, hidden among the trees, dates from 1636, but has been much altered. In the churchyard are remains of a fifteenth-century Franciscan friary built by the Bissets. Here Shane O'Neill's body was buried, with the exception of the head which was exhibited on a spike in Dublin Castle.

Three miles (5 km) beyond Glenarm, Carnlough has a fine situation on a crescent bay with a good sandy beach, at the mouth of one of the smaller Antrim Glens, Glen-coy. The limestone bridge over the main street was built for the Marquis of Londonderry to carry stone from the

Antrim coast road

quarries to the harbour, now a popular port of call for sailors. The Londonderry Arms was once owned by Winston Churchill. There are several cascades on the stream which flows through this glen. Behind Carnlough is a group of hills with several peaks over 1,000 feet. Knockore (1,179 feet) descends to the sea in steep escarpments, forming the bold headland of Garron Point (5 miles/ 8 km north of Carnlough). On a terrace on the headland's south side is Garron Tower, a castellated mansion built in 1848 as a residence for Lord Londonderry; it is now a secondary school. The school is the venue for the John Hewitt International Summer School which explores the radical literary tradition of the northern counties. Just off the point is the isolated chalk pinnacle called Cloghastucan, or the White Lady.

Into the next bay opens the most famous of the Antrim glens, Glenariff. The host village, in July, to the Feis na nGleann, the best known of the northern competitive festivals of Irish culture and sport, Water-foot (or Glenariff) stands at the mouth of the Glenariff River here at Red Bay. The boatyard here builds, sells and hires out for

Cushendall

sea fishing, small boats of traditional design. The glen stretches inland for about 5 miles (8 km) between steep mountain sides, on the lower slopes of which rises a multicoloured pattern of fields. The whole glen is now a forest park, which can also be approached from Parkmore on the Ballymena–Cushendall road. Here the little Glenariff River tumbles between thickly wooded banks, over pretty falls with names like Ess na Larach (the Mare's Fall) and Ess na Crub (the Fall of the Hooves). Paths have been built to give views of the falls and other features of the glen; care should be taken in traversing them, especially in wet weather.

North of Waterfoot the coast passes through the 'Red Arch' tunnel in the sandstone cliffs of Lurigethan (1,154 feet). Near by are the slight remains of Red Bay Castle, a MacDonnell fortress.

Cushendall

Cois Abhann Dalla
(The Foot of the Dall River)

This attractive little town near the northern end of Red Bay, where Glenaan and Glenballyeamon converge, is an excellent centre for exploring the Antrim glens. In the town is a quaint old tower, built as a lock-up for 'idlers and rioters', and until recently used as a dwelling. Bathing, boating, fishing and golf (9) are among the holiday amenities.

Around Cushendall

On the cliffs north of the town is the ruin of Layde Old Church, which has tombs of the MacDonnells. Two miles (3 km) to the west, on the slope of Tievebulliagh (1,346 feet), is the group of Neolithic stones called Ossian's Grave. Above the village soars Lurigethan, table topped, and steep sided.

In Glenballyeamon, which runs west from Cushendall, the remains of axe factories of the Neolithic period were discovered. At the south-western end of the glen is the highest of the Antrim Mountains, Trostan (1,817 feet).

Beyond Cushendall the main road crosses Glencorp, with Cross Slieve

(675 feet) to the right and Gruig Top (1,123 feet) to the left. At 1½ miles (2 km) the entrance to Glenaan is passed. Three miles (5 km) further on the road crosses the deep gorge of the River Dun by Glendun Viaduct and then traverses a plateau of moorland to Ballycastle.

Five miles (8 km) from Cushendall on the coast is Cushendun, at the southern end of a pretty sand-fringed bay with ranges of cliffs at either end. The whitewashed village houses were designed by Clough Williams-Ellis who created Portmeirion in Wales, for the first (and last) Lord Cushendun. The poet, John Masefield, was a frequent visitor to another house in the village, the Cave House, now a Catholic retreat, and approached only through a 60-foot cave. The Gloonan (from glúna the Gaelic for knees) Stone, opposite the Catholic church, has two hollows made, the story goes, by St Patrick's knees. Bathing and boating are among the holiday pastimes here, and in the sandstone cliffs to the south are many caves which can be visited by boat. When in spate the Dun River has good brown trout fishing; it also holds salmon and sea trout.

North of the village are the slight remains of MacDonnell's Castle. About half a mile (1 km) further north is the Cairn of Shane O'Neill (slain by the MacDonnells here in 1567), and beside it a large limestone monument that commemorates Sir Roger Casement (1864–1916) and other Antrim patriots. At a bend in the River Dun, about 150 yards west of the village, were found numerous flint tools embedded in distinct layers in the river bank—discoveries which threw much light on the chronology of the Stone Age in Ireland.

The main road to Ballycastle can be rejoined 3 miles (5 km) from Cushendun, but a more picturesque route runs on the steep seaward slopes of the hills to the north. This road has steep gradients and sharp bends, and should be attempted only by walkers or careful motorists; it is not suitable for heavy traffic or inexperienced cyclists. From it there are magnificent views of the cliffbound Antrim coast and across the North Channel to Scotland. Byroads lead off to Torr Head (the nearest point to the Scottish coast, 13 miles/21 km away), to Portaleen Bay on the south side of the head, and to Murlough Bay further north. This coast road joins the main road at Ballyvoy, 2½ miles (4 km) east of Ballycastle.

Ballycastle
Baile an Chaisleain
(The Town of the Castle)

Pop. 3,300.

Ballycastle is an attractive market town and the port for reaching Rathlin Island; it is noted for its Lammas Fair held over the summer bank holiday at the end of August and dating from 1606. It is also a well-known seaside resort. It is beautifully situated where Glenshesk and Glentaise converge at Ballycastle Bay. The town proper is 1½ miles (2 km) inland and is connected with the smaller seaside part by a broad tree-planted avenue. At the seafront a picnic site is a memorial to Guglielmo Marconi, the inventor of wireless telegraphy, who in 1898 made his first successful cross-water transmissions between Ballycastle and Rathlin Island.

At the Ould Lammas Fair

Things to do

There is a three-day festival of Irish music and dance, the Fleadh Amhran Rince, in the town in June, and the Ould Lammas Fair with its dulse (edible seaweed) and Yellow Man (hard crunchy toffee) immortalised in the song:

Did you treat your Mary Ann
To dulse and Yellow Man
At the Ould Lammas Fair at Ballycastle-O?

A plaque at 21 Ann Street commemorates the song's author, John McAuley. Ballycastle Museum, sited in the eighteenth-century courthouse, is devoted to the social history of the glens.

Ballycastle is a convenient centre for exploring the magnificent coast of north Antrim. There is an excellent sandy beach and other recreational facilities include boating, golf (18), tennis and bowls. There is good salmon, sea trout and brown trout fishing in the Margy, the Carey and the Glenshesk Rivers close to the town. Anglers fishing the right bank of the Margy should be alert for the golfer's cry of 'Fore'. Ballycastle is also the point of departure for Rathlin Island.

History

This area is rich in legendary associations, and for centuries it was the scene of much strife in which the MacQuillans, Mac-Donnells, Normans, Scots and English all played a part. In the eighteenth century the coal deposits in the area between the town and Fair Head were extensively worked.

Around Ballycastle

The remains of the old Franciscan foundation of Bonamargy Friary stand by the River Margy half a mile (1 km) east of the town. It is believed to have been founded by the MacQuillans about 1500 or earlier. After its burning by the MacDonnells and the Scots in 1584, it was restored by Sorley Boy MacDonnell. The remains include the church and some of the monastic buildings. Many of the

MacDonnells, including Sorley Boy and his son Randal, 1st Earl of Antrim, are buried in what was formerly the south transept, but was converted into a private mortuary chapel by Randal in 1621.

The Margy River is associated with the tragic legend of the Children of Lir, who were turned into swans by their jealous stepmother and made to spend 300 years on the turbulent Sea of Moyle (the North Channel). Another of the three great tragic tales of ancient Ireland tells of the fate of the three sons of Uisneach. Carrig Uisneach, on the shore near Ballycastle, is where they landed on their return from Scotland.

To the south of Ballycastle rises the prominent isolated mass of Knocklayd (1,695 feet). The circuit of the mountain makes an interesting tour of about 17 miles from the town. The road goes south through Glenshesk, with the wooded slopes of Knocklayd on the right. On the lower slopes of the hill are the ruins of an ancient church, known as the Goban Saer's Castle. (The Goban Saer in Irish folklore was the builder of many structures, including some of the round towers.) Five miles (8 km) south of the town, the road turns west between Knocklayd and Croghan (1,368 feet) towards the village of Armoy, where there is a round tower 35 feet high. Ballycastle Forest, on the slopes of Knocklayd, has a fine scenic drive.

There is pony-trekking in Ballypatrick Forest and an 'open farm', a 500-acre farm which welcomes visitors, at Watertop near Loughareema, the 'vanishing' lake. Six miles (10 km) east of Ballycastle is Fair Head (or Benmore), reached via the village of Ballyvoy. The head is the north-eastern extremity of Ireland, and rises for nearly half its total height of 626 feet in sheer cliffs of columnar basalt. From the summit past Lough na Cranagh, with its crannog or artificial lake dwelling, there is a magnificent view that includes Rathlin Island and the Scottish coast and islands; a fine view of the head itself is had from the 'Grey Man's (a legendary monstrous creature) Path', which

Carrick-a-Rede Rope Bridge

descends steeply to the base. Beneath the head on the east side lies Murlough Bay, its beautiful setting enhanced by the colourful vegetation on the sheltering cliffs.

Six miles (10 km) from Ballycastle by boat is Rathlin Island. The island's shoreline cliffs are the haunt of millions of sea birds. The Kebble National Nature Reserve at the West Lighthouse is home to the island's breeding colonies of kittiwakes, razorbills and puffins. Black guillemots breed on the chalk cliffs of Church Bay, and rare choughs may be spotted. There are native brown trout in the small lakes and massive ling and cod in the deep sea waters. There is a scuba diving centre. Stone Age axe heads found all over Europe came from Brockley, right in the middle of the island. There is an early Christian sweat house at Knockans between Brockley and the harbour. Bruce's Cave was the refuge of Robert Bruce, King of Scotland, and is traditionally the place where he found encouragement in the perseverance of a spider. Rathlin was ravaged by Norse sea rovers in 790, and later was frequently the prey of Scots and English. It was the scene

of three great massacres—one by the Scottish Clan Campbell and two by the English. In 1575 the MacDonnells sent their old people, women and children to the island for safety. The English fleet, however, sailed to the island and killed everyone on it, leaving the place uninhabited for many years. In 1617 a protracted lawsuit taken to decide if Rathlin was Scots or Irish was settled when an advocate pointed out that it had no snakes and was therefore Irish.

West of Ballycastle (¾ mile/1 km) is the scanty ruin of a MacDonnell stronghold, Dunaneanie Castle. The celebrated Sorley Boy MacDonnell died here in 1590. A few miles further west are the fragmentary ruins of another castle on Kenbane or White Head. On the shore here is Grace Staples Cave, with basaltic columns like those at Staffa in Scotland.

West of Kenbane, before you come to White Park Bay, a beautiful crescent of sand, backed by cliffs, are Carrick-a-Rede rope bridge, a salmon fishermen's bridge spanning an 80-foot (25m) chasm, and not for the faint-hearted, and picturesque

Whitepark Bay

Ballintoy Harbour. Much evidence of occupation by man from the neolithic period to the Iron Age has been found in this neighbourhood particularly at the caves in the bay. All this is well described on the one-mile-long (2 km) Whitepark Bay Nature Trail. Portbraddan, snug under the cliffs at the east end of the bay, has the smallest church in Ireland, 12 feet by 6½ feet.

On the coast 2 miles (3 km) west of Whitepark Bay the ruin of Dunseverick Castle stands on the rock which was the site of Dun Sobhairce (Sophairce's Fortress), mentioned in the Triads as one of the three great buildings of ancient Ireland. In the legends of the Red Branch Knights this was the home of Connall Cearnach, a hero of many exploits, who is said to have been in Jerusalem on the day of the Crucifixion, and to have been present at the laying of Our Lord in the tomb. The present slight ruins are of a castle probably built in the twelfth or thirteenth century by the Anglo-Norman de Mandevilles (later known by the Irish name of MacQuillan). This castle later came into the hands of the O'Cahans.

The Giant's Causeway

Clochan na bhFomhorach
(The Formorian's Stepping Stones)

This wonderful rock formation on the west side of Benbane Head, now a World Heritage Site, is one of the world's outstanding geological curiosities. All the features can be seen by following a 4-mile (6 km) cliff path.

Formation

The causeway was formed by the cooling of lava which burst through the earth's

Giant's Causeway

Dunluce Castle

crust in the Cainozoic Period, over an area extending from the Antrim coast to the island of Skye in Scotland. At this particular place the cooling of the lava resulted in the splitting of the basaltic rock into innumerable prismatic columns. Mostly they are hexagonal, but some are pentagonal and others have irregular numbers of sides. The cliffs consist of two beds of this columnar basalt separated by a red band of iron ore formed by the decaying of the surface of the lava between periods of eruption.

Points of interest

The three main sections are called the Little Causeway, the Middle (or Honeycomb) Causeway and the Grand Causeway. Various formations have been given names, such as Lord Antrim's Parlour, the Giant's Organ, the Lady's Fan, the Giant's Loom, the Wishing Chair, the Giant's Horseshoe, the Key Stone and numerous others. Beyond the amphitheatre is a bay called Port na Spania, where the Spanish Ship *Girona* foundered in 1588 in its flight after the defeat of the Armada. In the late 1960s, a team of Belgian divers brought up a fortune in doubloons, gold chains, jewels, cameos of the Roman Caesars, rings and crosses, as well as cannon and muskets. (This treasure is now on display in the Ulster Museum, Belfast.) Further east is an extension of the causeway, Pleaskin Head, which has a magnificent panorama of sea and coast.

From the Giant's Causeway Centre, with its audio-visual display, book shop, environmental presentations, hydroelectric tram replica, souvenir counter and tea rooms, a bus (National Trust) takes visitors down to the causeway. Refreshments and souvenirs are on sale. Boats can also be hired here for trips past the causeway and to the caves further west. These are Portcoon Cave, 450 feet long and 40 feet high, which has beautiful colouring; Leckilroy Cave, which cannot be entered; and Runkerry Cave, 700 feet long and 60 feet high. Beside the causeway a delightful school building designed by Clough

Williams-Ellis has been preserved as a School Museum of the 1920s.

Around the Giant's Causeway

Three miles (5 km) south is the little town of Bushmills, noted for its distillery which can be visited (the oldest licensed in the world) and for salmon and trout fishing on the River Bush. The Bush is one of the best game fishing rivers in the north. From the village to the sea the fishing is in private hands, but tickets are available from Dungarve Estates Ltd (tel. 026 57 31215). Permission to fish the river in the town and above rests with the management of the Bush Fishery, whose interest is primarily in the study of salmon biology. Permits for the most productive stretches are available at the Hatchery, Bushmills. Other permits are available at local tackle shops. Bushfoot Golf Course (9) is 1½ miles (2 km) north, about half a mile (1 km) from Portballintrae, a pleasant seaside village on a little sand-fringed bay. Sea fishing boats can be chartered at the tiny harbour or by contacting skippers listed in the appropriate tourist information bulletin.

On the coast 2½ miles (4 km) west of Bushmills stands Dunluce Castle, an impressive ruin perched on a seagirt rock. The ruins are mainly those of a Jacobean mansion, but two of the original four cylindrical towers remain from an earlier structure. Dunluce is believed to have been built about 1300 by Richard de Burgh, Earl of Ulster, but it was in the hands of the MacQuillans when it was wrested from them in the sixteenth century by the MacDonnells of the Isles.

In 1584, English forces took the castle from Sorley Boy MacDonnell after a nine- month siege. Sorley Boy succeeded in retaking it, and ultimately made peace with the English. His son Randal was made Viscount Dunluce and Earl of Antrim by James I. In 1642 the commander of the Scottish army in Ulster, General Munro, paid a friendly visit to

Dunluce with a party of his forces and was received with hospitality. Before leaving, however, he made Randal a prisoner and seized the castle. After this the building ceased to be a dwelling and fell into decay. The cave beneath the castle, which can be approached on a calm day by boat, was used by the defenders as a safe approach.

Portrush

Port Ruis (Peninsula Fort)

 Pop. 5,100.

Portrush, splendidly situated on a promontory which ends to the north in Ramore Head, is one of the leading seaside resorts in Northern Ireland.

Things to do

The town is a well-known golfing centre, with two 18-hole courses (including the Royal Portrush championship course) and a 9-hole par 3 course. Bathers have the choice of excellent sandy beaches, and there is an indoor holiday centre, Waterworld, on the harbour with flumes, saunas, jacuzzis, a café and a sea aquarium. Boating and sea angling are popular pastimes, and salmon and trout fishing is to be had within easy driving distance. The fossil ammonites, preserved, conserved and protected in the rocks below Landsdowne Crescent, and of great geological significance, are well described in the Portrush Countryside Centre. The large recreation grounds at the town have tennis courts, bowling greens and a putting green. Summer theatre and various other entertainments are held during the summer season.

Around Portrush

There is a bus service between Portrush and the Giant's Causeway. Many other places of interest can also be conveniently visited from the town, and there are fine walks on Ramore Head and along the coast on either side. About 2 miles (3 km) to the east are the cave-riddled limestone cliffs called the White Rocks. Most of the caves here are accessible only by boat, but the Cathedral Cave, 180 feet deep can be reached by a steep path from the road. Another favourite boat trip is around the rocky islands offshore, the Skerries.

The border with Derry is just outside Portrush on the west and south, and a few miles to the west is the popular Derry resort, Portstewart.

The Causeway Coast Lion Park at Benvarden, 8 miles (13 km) north-east of Portrush, is a reserve for African lions; there is an enclosed zoo to interest children.

In the Bann Valley, 14 miles (22 km) south-east of Portrush is Ballymoney, a market town with, on its western outskirts, Leslie Hill Historic Farm and Park with its attractive eighteenth-century farm buildings and pony and trap rides.

Ballymena

Baile Meadhaonach (Middle Town)

 Pop. 28,250.

Ballymena, in the pleasant valley of the River Braid, is an important borough with linen and other industries. It is situated in central Antrim at the convergence of many roads, which give ready access to all parts of the north-east of Ireland. The Saturday market dates back to 1626. Roger Casement went to school here.

Things to do

There are tennis courts and a bowling green in the town. Ballymena golf course (18) is 2½ miles (4 km) north-east at Raceview. The Rivers Main, Braid, Clogh, the Kells Water and other streams have salmon, dollaghan and trout. Sunday fishing is not encouraged on many sections. Fish farms at Stranocum and Movanagher may be visited.

History

Most of the town is built on land of the estate received by William Adair of Kinhilt, Scotland, from Charles I. About 1732 the Adairs and another family named Hickey introduced the linen industry, to which the town chiefly owes its development. In 1798 a body of United Irishmen held Ballymena for three days, after defeating British forces in a battle in the streets.

Around Ballymena

About ¾ mile (1 km) to the south is the ancient earthern fort Ballykeel Rath, on a hill with a fine view of the surrounding country. At Kells, 4 miles (6 km) further south, are remains of an ancient abbey. Connor village half a mile (1 km) east of Kells is the site of a fifth-century monastery founded by St Macnice, first bishop of Connor diocese. Edward Bruce's defeat of the Anglo-Normans here in 1315 initiated nationwide resistance to the invaders.

Eight miles (13 km) west of Bally-mena, Slemish Mountain rises prominently on the south side of the Braid valley. This was the scene of St Patrick's six-year captivity as a youth. The Shrine of St Patrick is a place of pilgrimage. There are now picnic sites and a scenic drive on the mountain. About 4 miles (6 km) north-west of Slemish, on the northern side of the valley, are the ruins of Skerry Church, the traditional site of a church founded by St Patrick himself. The barrel-roofed vault in

Slemish Mountain

the east end of the ruins was for centuries the burial place of the O'Neills of Clannaboye.

Two miles (3 km) north of Ballymena is the ruined church of Kilconriola, where a large souterrain was discovered in the graveyard. An ancient tombstone found at this site in 1865 can be seen in the porch of the Church of Ireland parish church in Ballymena. It bears the inscription, Ort do Degen: a prayer for the soul of Degen. Cullybackey village, 3 miles (5 km) north-west of Ballymena on the River Main, was the home of the Reverend William Arthur, who emigrated about 1820 and whose son, Chester Alan Arthur, was US President from 1881 to 1885.

Two miles (3 km) west of Ballymena, the Derry road passes Gracehill village, a Moravian settlement with a typical central square; this was founded about the middle of the eighteenth century. In the grassy cemetery, a path separates the graves of the men from those of the women, a custom still observed locally. The town's architectural importance is registered by its presence on the Europa Nostra lists.

Antrim
Aontroim (Elder Tree)

 Pop. 23,500.

Antrim, a manufacturing and marketing centre, is situated where the Six Mile Water enters the north-eastern corner of Lough Neagh.

History
The town was burned by the Scottish general, Monro, in 1643, and in 1798 it was the scene of a hard-fought battle in which the insurgents, led by Henry Joy McCracken, were finally routed; in this engagement the British military commander, Lord O'Neill, was killed.

Points of interest
The cottage in Pogues' Entry which was the birthplace of Alexander Irvine (author

of *My Lady of the Chimney Corner*) is maintained as a permanent memorial to the writer's parents. In Steeple Park, ¾ mile (1 km) north of the town centre, stands Antrim Round Tower. Dating from about the tenth century, the tower is one of the most perfect in Ireland. It is 92 feet high including the restored conical cap; the door is 9½ feet (3 m) from the ground.

Extending west from the town is Antrim Castle Demesne, along the shore of Lough Neagh. The gardens in these grounds were laid out by Le Notre, the distinguished French landscape gardener who designed the gardens at Versailles. There is an arts centre and theatre, Clotworthy House, in the gardens. A golf course (18) is on the lake shore, and trout fishing is available on the Six Mile Water and other convenient streams. Antrim Forum, a large indoor sports complex with two swimming pools, is beside the demesne. A pleasure boat provides cruises on Lough Neagh from the Six Mile Water marina.

Around Antrim
By far the largest lake in Ireland or Great Britain is Lough Neagh. It is 17 miles (27 km) long and 11 miles (18 km) broad, and has an area of 153 square miles. It is fed by numerous tributary streams—principally the Upper Bann, which enters it from the south—and is drained northwards by the Lower Bann. Several of the tributaries are good salmon and trout waters, with a run of dollaghan, a localised sub species of very large wild trout, in the autumn. There is also excellent pike, roach and bream angling, but fishing on the lake itself is not developed—except for the commercial netting of pollan (a fish sometimes called 'the Lough Neagh herring'), and perch and long lining for eels. The vast waters of the lake, and nearby small lakes, both called Lough Beg, are magnets for vast numbers of breeding and wintering waterbirds and therefore also for ornithologists, for whom the area is one of the most significant in these islands. The waters of

Lough Neagh and Ram's Island

the lake are supposed to have petrifying qualities because of the many examples of petrified wood found on the shores. This petrification was a process of gradual replacement of the wood fibre by silica in waters which flowed over the area at a very early stage in its geological history.

About 9 miles (14 km) to the south is Ram's Island, the largest island in the lake and a popular objective for boating trips. On the island there is the ruin of an ancient round tower. Wolfe Tone visited here in 1795, before his departure for America.

At the outflow of the River Bann from Lough Neagh, 11 miles (18 km) west of Antrim, is Toome Bridge. The town is a centre of the Lough Neagh eel fisheries, the largest eel fishery in western Europe. The eels spawn in the Sargasso Sea in the east Atlantic, and as tiny elvers take three years to return to the native rivers and lakes, where they take another twelve years to mature before taking that long journey down the River Bann and back out across the Atlantic. Toome is also a popular base for anglers after pike, bream

and roach in the Bann, the Toome Canal and Lough Beg (1½ miles/2 km to the north). The castle at Toome Bridge changed hands more than once in the wars of the seventeenth century, and was finally dismantled by the Cromwellians. In 1798 a body of insurgents, retreating from the Battle of Antrim, destroyed the bridge across the Bann to delay the crossing of the river by General Knox and his yeomanry.

Five miles (8 km) west of Antrim is Randalstown, a market town on the River Main, noted for its dollaghan fishing. Near by Shane's Castle demesne contains a narrow guage steam railway running along the shore of Lough Neagh, and the ruined tower of Shane O'Neill's Castle, at one time the headquarters of the O'Neills of Clannaboye. There is also a deer park, camelia house, café and nature reserve. South of the town is Randalstown Forest, a wildlife reserve. Four miles (6 km) south-west, just above the beach of Cranfield Bay, is the ruined Cranfield Church, probably thirteenth century. This church and a holy well about 100 yards (90 m) to the east were for centuries a popular place of pilgrimage.

Two miles (3 km) east of Antrim is Farranshane, birthplace of the United Irishman, William Orr, who was executed at Carrickfergus in 1797. Near Farranshane are the ancient earthen ring-forts of Rathmore (Great Fort) and Rathbeg (Little Fort). On Donegore Hill, a mile further east, is another ancient earthwork. This hill was the point to which the main body of insurgents withdrew after the Battle of Antrim in 1798. In the old graveyard of Donegore near by is the grave of the poet, Sir Samuel Ferguson.

On the Belfast road, 5½ miles (9 km) east of Antrim is Templepatrick, birthplace of one of the northern leaders of the United Irishmen, James Hope. Also at Templepatrick is Castle Upton, on the site of a twelfth-century priory of the Knights of St John; their refectory has been conserved. A family mausoleum designed by Robert Adam is open to the public, but Castle Upton (also by Adam) may only be visited by special arrangement.

At Crumlin near by there is an interesting collection of quail and exotic pheasants at Talnotry Cottage Bird Garden and Station 597 at Langford Lodge, a museum of the US 8th Army Airforce, stationed there during the Second World War.

Ballyclare, 12 miles (19 km) north-east of Antrim, is a busy market town with golf (18) on the Six Mile Water. Ballyeaston, 1½ miles (2 km) to the north, was the home of US President Andrew Johnson's grandfather, who emigrated about 1750.

Ballynure, 2 miles (3 km) north-east of Ballyclare, was the scene of the wake of William Orr, after his execution in 1797.

Lisburn
Lios na gCearrbhac
(The Fort of the Gamblers)

👨‍👩‍👦 Pop. 27,405.

This busy town in the Lagan valley owes its development mainly to the growth of the linen industry.

Things to do
Wallace Park contains tennis courts, bowling greens and cricket grounds. There is a golf course (18) near by, and reservoir fishing for trout; pike, roach and bream can be had on the River Lagan. The Maze, or Down Royal Racecourse is 4 miles (6 km) west of the town.

History
Linen manufacture was organised here under the direction of the Huguenot, Louis Crommelin at the end of the seventeenth century. Viscount Conway, who built a castle here in the time of Charles I, planted the town with English and Welsh settlers. The castle was besieged in the wars of 1641, and in 1707 both castle and town were accidentally destroyed by fire.

Points of interest
In the Market Square is a statue of General John Nicholson, who was killed in the siege of Delhi in 1857 and whose parents were from Lisburn. The Church of Ireland Cathedral, dating from 1623, has a conspicuous spire and is a good example of the Gothick (*sic*) architecture peculiar to the Plantation churches of Ulster. It contains a monument to the famous Jeremy Taylor (whose barn church, built in 1666, can be found at Upper Ballinderry), Protestant Bishop of Down and Connor, who died in 1667 and who is buried at Dromore Cathedral.

The Assembly Rooms in the square, now the Lisburn Museum, with special reference to the linen industry, have a domed clock and a handsome interior. A plaque in an external wall was rescued from the first house rebuilt after the great fire. Dated 1708, it warns the townspeople to be of good behaviour:

*This town was burned ye year before
People therein may be directed*

God hath judgments still in store,
And that they do not Him provoke
To give to them a second stroke.

Around Lisburn

The arts centre at Harmony Hill, towards
Belfast, is noted for its exibitions of the
work of Ulster artists. Lambeg village,
1½ miles (2 km) from Lisburn on the
Belfast road, has a well-equipped linen
research institute. This village gives its

name to the drums, beaten with canes,
which are a feature of parades of the
Orange Order.

On the slopes of White Mountain,
3 miles (5 km) north of Lisburn, are the
remains of Castle Robin, which dates from
the late sixteenth or early seventeenth
century. At nearby Hilden, the north's only
'real ale' brewery welcomes visitors and
runs an occasional summer beer festival.

Ten Scenic Tours

Powerscourt Waterfall, Co. Wicklow

These ten scenic tours are designed to help you get the most from your motoring holiday in Ireland—to show you the most beautiful scenery, and to introduce you to Ireland's many interesting cities and towns. Tour number 1 is a scenic tour which you can complete easily within 10 days—over 1,000 miles (1,610 km) altogether, and taking you through some of the most spectacular scenery in the country. The seventh tour is a 4-day tour of the West, taking you through the picturesque Connemara region. Tours numbered 2, 3, 5 and 9 are regional and can be made in 2 days or more. In addition there are 3 one-day tours numbered 4, 6 and 8, out of Dublin, Cork and Galway respectively. Tour number 10 is a detailed 5-day tour of Northern Ireland. As all 10 tours are circular you can commence at any point of the given routes. The daily distance covered is shown to the right of each tour heading, in miles (bold) and kilometres (italics). Included are maps of the 10 tours, with alternative routes indicated by broken lines. In the unlikely event of your meeting with any problem during your tour, just ask the first person you meet. He or she is bound to help.

1 Tour of Republic of Ireland
A 10-day tour over **1,000** miles *(1610 km)*, suggested starting point—Dublin.

Day One
Dublin–Tramore **118** *(190 km)*
Having seen Dublin's historic buildings and Georgian squares and having sampled its lively cosmopolitan atmosphere, you're on your way to Enniskerry, a pretty hillside village just 12 miles (19 km) south of the city. Near by you can visit the splendid Powerscourt Estate, with its gardens, deer herd and waterfall. Continue on through Roundwood to Glendalough and see the ruins of an Early Christian settlement in a beautiful wild setting of mountains and lakes. Your next stop, via Rathdrum, is Avoca, made famous by Thomas Moore's song, 'The Meeting of the Waters'. Southwards is the prominent holiday resort of Arklow, overlooking the sea. Onwards to Enniscorthy, with its old-world charm—just 33 miles (53 km) from the car ferry port of Rosslare Harbour—and then New Ross, with its twisting lanes and Dutch-type houses. When you reach Waterford, visit Reginald's Tower, built in 1003 by Reginald the Dane and containing a remarkable collection of the city charters from Tudor times on. Spend your first night at Tramore, a family resort with 3 miles (5 km) of sandy beaches.

Day Two
Tramore–Cork **73** *(117 km)*
After lunch leave for Cork, via Dungarvan, into Youghal, a popular holiday resort. Con-

Connor Pass on the Dingle Peninsula, Co. Kerry

tinue through the market town of Midleton to Cork. Enjoy the friendly atmosphere of Cork, built on the banks of the River Lee. Visit St Mary's Shandon, where the famous Shandon Bells are played on request, and admire the many fine public buildings.

Day Three
Cork–Killarney **94** *(151 km)*
Leaving Cork on the third day your first stop is Blarney Castle with its famous stone, said to impart the gift of eloquence to all who kiss it! Continue through Macroom, Ballingeary, Pass of Keimaneigh (2 miles/3 km from Gougane Barra National Park), Ballylickey, and into the beautiful holiday resort of Glengarriff. Then in a northerly direction you drive through Kenmare into Killarney, enjoying one of the finest scenic drives on the way. You'll find plenty to do in Killarney—pony riding, boating, and visiting islands and ancient abbeys. Drive around the 'Ring of Kerry', a brilliant 109-mile (176 km) scenic drive bringing you to Killorglin, Cahirciveen, Waterville, Sneem, Parknasilla, Kenmare, and back to Killarney.

Day Four
Killarney
It's worth spending a day in Killarney, setting out the next day for Galway.

Day Five
Killarney–Galway **156** *(251 km)*
On the fifth day your drive takes you through Abbeyfeale, Newcastle West, the lovely village of Adare, and into Limerick, 16 miles (26 km) from Shannon Airport, on the River Shannon, a graceful and historic city, featuring King John's Castle, the Treaty Stone and St Mary's Cathedral. Traditional medieval banquets can be enjoyed at Bunratty Castle (8 miles/13 km from Limerick), and Knappogue Castle (8 miles/13 km from Ennis). Continuing on you reach Ennis with its old abbey and the seaside resort of Lahinch, featuring excellent golf courses. You should make your next stop by the breathtaking Cliffs of Moher before driving to Lisdoonvarna,

Ireland's premier spa. Drive through the bare limestone hills of the Burren Country to Ballyvaughan, to Kinvara (medieval banquets at Dunguaire Castle), Clarinbridge and into Galway. Galway is the capital of the 'Western World' with its famous Spanish Arch and Church of St Nicholas, where, tradition holds, Columbus prayed before sailing to America.

Day Six
Galway–Westport **86** *(138 km)*
The next day your route through Connemara takes you to Moycullen, Oughterard, Recess, Clifden (capital of Connemara), Leenane, and Westport—on Clew Bay, with over 100 islands. Near by is the magnificent Westport House, with its gardens and zoo park.

The High Cross at Drumcliffe, Co. Sligo

Day Seven
Westport–Bundoran **96** *(154 km)*
Head north next day to Castlebar, Pontoon, Ballina and the family resort of Enniscrone. Enjoy a swim with the children before driving on to Sligo, where you can look around the thirteenth-century Franciscan Friary and the museum, situated in the county library. Head on via Drumcliffe (burial place of W. B. Yeats) to complete your day's driving at Bundoran.

Day Eight
Bundoran–Dunfanaghy **120** *(193 km)*
On the following day head further up the Atlantic coast through Ballyshannon to Donegal town, visiting the Franciscan Friary and castle. Drive through Dunkineely, Ardara, Glenties, Maas and Kincasslagh—noted for their cottage industries and Donegal tweed. Then by Annagry, Crolly, Bunbeg, Bloody Foreland, Gortahork into Dunfanaghy, nestling in a cosy inlet of Sheephaven Bay.

Day Nine
Dunfanaghy–Carrick-on-Shannon **110** *(177 km)*
Next day your tour takes you south via Port-nablagh to Letterkenny—Donegal's chief town. This is an excellent point from which to extend your drive, by taking the 'Inishowen 100', an extremely scenic trip around the Inishowen Peninsula, to Buncrana, Malin Head and Moville. Return to Letterkenny by Manorcunningham. Total mileage for the trip is over 120 miles (193 km). Continue south through the picturesque Finn valley to the twin towns of Stranorlar and Ballybofey, completing your round trip of County Donegal in Donegal town.

The next stage takes you to Ballyshannon and Bundoran in a southerly direction to Manorhamilton. Overlooking the town you'll see the picturesque ruin of Sir Frederick Hamilton's castle, built in 1638. Continue south through Drumkeeran, along the beautiful shores of Lough Allen into Drumshanbo. Drive on through Leitrim into Carrick-on-Shannon, an important cruising and angling centre.

Day Ten
Carrick-on-Shannon–Dublin **150** *(241 km)*
On the final day head for Cavan, travelling by Mohill, Carrigallen, Killeshandra and Crossdoney enjoying the lake scenery on the way. Continue to Bailieborough (9 miles/14 km from the important angling centre of Virginia) and into the attractive town of Carrickmacross. The last stage of your trip takes you to Drogheda, a historic town in County Louth. From Drogheda visit the prehistoric tombs at Newgrange, Knowth and Dowth. Drive on by Slane into Navan. Six miles (10 km) from here see the Hill of Tara, a former residence of Irish high kings. Complete your tour of the Boyne valley in Trim, rich in historical associations and ancient monuments, before returning to Dublin, via Black Bull, Clonee, Blanchardstown and the Phoenix Park.

2 East Coast Tour
Two circular tours—one north, the other south of Dublin—total **480** miles *(773 km)*.

Day One
Northern tour **190** *(306 km)*
Take the Navan road out of Dublin for Tara—site of a former royal acropolis, situated in an area rich in ancient monuments and historical associations.

Continue north to Navan, Donaghmore and Slane. Visit the Bronze Age cemeteries at Brugh na Boinne, King William's Glen, Mellifont Abbey and Monasterboice, before heading for Dunleer, Castlebellingham and Dundalk—an ideal base for exploring the surrounding countryside. If you wish you can travel further north to see the delightfully rugged little Carlingford Peninsula, taking you through Bally-mascanlon, Carlingford, Omeath, and back into Dundalk. Heading south you reach Castlebellingham, Clogher, Termonfeckin, Baltray, with its fine beach and golf course, and on into Drogheda, on the river Boyne. In Bettystown, further south, there's a long sandy beach linking up with Laytown, while further on is Julianstown. Following

Bective Abbey, in the Boyne Valley, Co. Meath

the coast enjoy a pleasant drive through Balbriggan, Skerries, Rush, Lusk, Swords and Howth, stopping to admire the magnificent views from the rocky hill of Howth. Return to Dublin via Sutton.

Day Two

Southern tour **290** *(467 km)*

Next day the southern tour takes you through Dun Laoghaire, Dalkey and Killiney—with its magnificent view over the bay from the Vico road—into Bray, one of Ireland's premier seaside resorts. Continuing, you reach Enniskerry, a pretty village beneath the Sugarloaf Mountain and near the beautiful Powerscourt Estate. The scenic mountain drive takes you to Glendalough, with its ancient ruins and picturesque lakes, passing through Glencree, Glenmacnass and Laragh. If you wish you can return to Dublin by Blessington, making a short but enjoyable trip, or keep south to Rathdrum, Avoca and Woodenbridge into Arklow, where you can enjoy a swim or go sea fishing.

Driving on through County Wexford takes you to Gorey, Courtown Harbour (seaside resort), Ferns, Enniscorthy and Wexford, which is 13½ miles (22 km) from Rosslare Harbour. These charming old towns are well worth a visit. Follow the coast through Rosslare, Duncormick, Arthurstown, and into New Ross.

From here take the road to Kilkenny, a cheerful town steeped in history. Visit the Kilkenny Design Workshops, Rothe House and Kilkenny Castle. Return to Dublin through Carlow and County Kildare towns of Athy, Kildare, Kilcullen and Ballymore Eustace, taking in the lake drive near Blessington and reaching the city via Brittas.

3 Lake-land Tour

This is a 2-day circular drive of about **150** miles *(214 km)*. This tour of Ireland's quiet heart offers a charm of a different kind in contrast to the coastal tours.

Day One

Athlone–Mullingar **84** *(135 km)*

The starting point is Athlone—'Capital' of the midlands. From here drive to Roscommon, visiting Hodson Bay and Rinndown Castle *en route*. Have a look around Roscommon Abbey. North-east of Roscommon is Lanesborough, a popular angling centre at the head of Lough Ree. Then visit the busy market town of Longford with its nineteenth-century cathedral. Move on to Edgeworthstown, which gets its name from the remarkable literary family.

Continue to Castlepollard, a good angling centre near Lough Derravaragh—featured in a tragic legendary romance, *Children of Lir*. See nearby Tullynally Castle.

Tullynally Castle, Co. Westmeath

Drive to Fore, with its ancient crosses and Benedictine Abbey, returning to Castlepollard and south via Multyfarnham to Mullingar—an important town and noted angling centre. Spend the night there.

Day Two
Mullingar–Athlone **65** *(105 km)*
Next day a westward drive takes you to Ballymore and to the Goldsmith country via Tang. Visit Lissoy and the Pigeons on the road to the pretty village of Glasson, passing the tower-like structure marking the geographical centre of Ireland. Return to Athlone.

From Athlone make an excursion to Coosan Point for a good view of Lough Ree, one of the largest Shannon lakes. Going downriver it's worth a visit to Clonmacnois, one of the country's most celebrated holy places, completing your tour in Athlone.

4 Dublin and Wicklow Mountains
This is a 1–day scenic tour of about 110 miles *(177 km)*.

Leave Dublin by the suburb of Rathfarnham, 4 miles (6 km) south of the city. The ruined building known as 'The Hell Fire Club' forms a prominent landmark on the summit of Mount Pelier, 4 miles (6 km) south of Rathfarnham. Drive via Glencullen, Kilternan and the Scalp into Enniskerry—one of the prettiest villages in Ireland. From here you can visit Powerscourt Estate and Gardens, which includes the highest waterfall in these islands.

Continue to Sally Gap, a notable crossroads situated between Kippure Mountain and the Djouce Mountain, where the road leads to Glendalough, by Glenmacnass and Laragh. Have a look around Glendalough, one of the most picturesque glens of County Wicklow, with extensive ruins of the sixth-century Irish monastery of St Kevin. Drive on through Laragh by the Military road to Rathdrum. Head south by the Vale of Avoca into Arklow, a popular holiday centre. From Arklow drive north to Wicklow, where you can admire the view over the bay.

Ashford is the next village on your route—close by the beautiful Mount Usher Gardens, with its countless varieties of trees, plants and shrubs. These gardens are open all year, including bank holidays, but closed on Sundays between September and May. Move on through the rugged Devil's Glen to Newtownmountkennedy, Delgany and into the attractive resort of Greystones, which retains the atmosphere of the former quiet fishing village.

Head back through Delgany to the Glen of the Downs, Kilmacanogue (from where you can climb the Great Sugar Loaf) into Bray. From this fine resort at the base of Bray Head, take the route to Killiney and the Vico road to Dalkey, enjoying the superb views of Killiney Bay. Follow the coast road to Dun Laoghaire and on into Dublin.

5 South-west Tour
This is a 2–day circular tour of about 430 miles *(692 km)* on main route.

Day One
Cork–Killarney **223** *(359 km)*
The suggested starting point is Cork—a charming city on the River Lee, excellent for shopping and offering first-class pubs and restaurants, with entertainment for every member of the family. Blarney Castle, with its famous Stone of Eloquence, is 5 miles (8 km) away. Visit there to kiss the stone before continuing to the old-world town of Kinsale. Drive on to Timoleague, where you'll see the remains of the once

largest friary in Ireland, to Clonakilty, Ross-carbery, Glandore, Union Hall and Skibbereen. Continue this exceptionally beautiful drive through Ballydehob, Schull, Toormore, Durrus and Bantry, into Glengarriff, visiting the Forest Park and Garinish Island, with its ornate gardens.

Afterwards take the 'Tunnel Road' to Kenmare or head west over the Healy Pass.

Some of the finest sea and mountain scenery in Ireland can be enjoyed on the next stage of the tour, around the 'Ring of Kerry'—through Sneem, Castlecove, Derrynane, Water-ville, Cahirciveen, Glenbeigh and Killorglin into Killarney. There are some lovely quiet beaches in this region—for example, Rossbeigh near Glenbeigh. Spend the night in Killarney.

Day Two
Killarney–Cork **200** *(322 km)*
From Killarney drive directly to Tralee or alternatively explore the Dingle Peninsula, the heart of *Ryan's Daughter* country. Places along the route are: Inch, Annascaul, Dingle, Ventry, Slea Head, Dunquin, Ballyferriter,

Murreagh, back to Dingle and on through Stradbally and Camp to Tralee, an unforgettable drive of breathtaking beauty.

Follow the coast from Tralee to Ardfert, Ballyheigue, Causeway, Ballyduff, Lisselton Cross Roads, Ballylongford, and Tarbert, where a car ferry operates to Killimer, County Clare. Drive through Foynes along the Shannon estuary via Askeaton to Limerick, an old and historic city, not far from Bunratty Castle, with its medieval-style banquets.

Having spent some time looking around Limerick, head back to Cork through Tipperary and Cashel, visiting the magnificent ruins on the Rock of Cashel—including a cathedral, castle, chapel and round tower. Enjoy the mountain views on the way to historic Cahir town and into Cork by Clogheen, Lismore and Fermoy, providing a splendid trip through the Knockmealdown Mountains.

6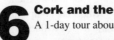
Cork and the 'Ring of Kerry'
A 1-day tour about **220** miles *(354 km)*

Lady's View, Killarney, Co. Kerry

Travel west from Cork via Ovens to Macroom. Turn off for Toon Bridge and Inchigeelagh, through the wild mountain scenery of the Pass of Keimaneigh into Ballylickey. Along the way you could visit Gougane Barra National Park which is just north of your route.

From Ballylickey enjoy the superb views of Bantry Bay *en route* to Glengarriff, from where you can visit the beautiful Italian gardens of Garinish Island. Head north to Kenmare through rugged mountains. Here your trip around the 'Ring of Kerry' begins—encircling the Iveragh Peninsula, which features Ireland's highest mountains, the Macgillycuddy's Reeks. Excellent views are provided over Dingle Bay to the north and the estuary of the Kenmare River to the south.

Travel south-west through Parknasilla and Sneem, into Caherdaniel, where you'll find excellent swimming and diving along the fine beach. Go north to the well-known resort of Waterville, continuing your tour by Cahirciveen, Glenbeigh and Killorglin, completing this exceptionally scenic trip in Killarney.

Your route back to Cork takes you through the Derrynasaggart Mountains to Macroom, turning off the main road for Dripsey and Blarney Castle, where you can stop to kiss the famous Blarney Stone.

7 West Coast Tour

This is a 4–day circular tour of about **523** miles *(842 km)* on main route.

Day One
Athlone–Limerick **94** *(151 km)*
Athlone is the suggested starting point for a tour of this richly varied region. From this impressive town south of Lough Ree you pass the early Christian site of Clonmacnois to the south and on to Birr, where the gardens of Birr Castle are open to visitors. Driving in a southerly direction you come to Nenagh, with its fine castle built about 1200. Continue via Portroe with lovely views over Lough Derg into Killaloe, a popular waterskiing centre. From here drive to O'Briensbridge, Ardnacrusha, and on to Limerick for the night.

Day Two
Limerick–Galway **144** *(232 km)*
Having seen the sights of Limerick, head for Bunratty Castle where medieval banquets

The Skelligs, off the Co. Kerry coast

are held, and visit the Bunratty Folk Park. Drive south-westerly from Ennis to the resorts of Kilrush and Kilkee, going north to Lahinch and around Liscannor Bay to the magnificent ruggedness of the Cliffs of Moher, reaching up to 700 feet. Move on to Ireland's premier spa, Lisdoonvarna, enjoying the remarkable 'Burren country', consisting of a desert of bare limestone hills which are a botanist's paradise in spring. Take the road from Lisdoonvarna through Black Head, Ballyvaughan, Kinvara and Clarinbridge into Galway. Discover Galway for yourself—its Church of St Nicholas, the Spanish Arch and the gathering of salmon (in season) under the Salmon Weir Bridge.

Salthill, Galway's fashionable seaside suburb, offers you top-class restaurants and hotels, pubs, discos, and many other forms of entertainment, including the amenities of the Leisureland complex.

Day Three
Galway–Westport **122** *(196 km)*
Next day start your tour of Connemara by Spiddal, Costelloe, Screeb, Gortmore, Carna, Toombeola, Ballynahinch and Glendalough. From Clifden you head northwards

to Tullycross and on to Leenane, on the corner of picturesque Killary Harbour. Drive northwards through the mountains of Louisburgh, in the shadow of Croagh Patrick. Stop in Westport, an important sea angling centre. Alternatively you can get from Leenane to Westport through the Joyce Country, taking you to Maam, Cong, Ballinrobe, Partry, Ballintubber, with its famous abbey, and into Westport.

Day Four
Westport–Athlone **163** *(262 km)*
The following day explore the beauties of Achill Island, taking the road to Newport, Mulrany, through Curraun Peninsula, Achill Sound, and on to Keel and Dooagh.

Return via Newport to Castlebar, visiting Clonalis House, then on to Claremorris, Ballyhaunis, Castlerea, Roscommon, and back to Athlone.

8 Galway and Connemara
This is a 1-day tour of about **160** miles *(257 km)*.

Travel north-west of Galway to the pretty village of Oughterard, with views of Lough

The Cliffs of Moher, Co. Clare

Corrib along the way. Continue through the rugged countryside of Connemara, dominated by the craggy peaks of the Twelve Bens, via Maam Cross and Recess into Clifden—the capital of Connemara.

From Clifden drive to Letterfrack and on to Leenane, at the head of picturesque Killary Harbour. Along the way you'll see the magnificent Kylemore Abbey.

Having left Leenane, turn off the main road for Louisburgh and Westport, passing Doo Lough and the lofty Croagh Patrick. In Westport you can visit one of Ireland's premier stately homes—Westport House, with its adjoining Zoo Park. Castlebar, principal town of County Mayo, is the next on your route, offering you a charming old-world atmosphere. Of particular note is the pleasant tree-lined Mall.

Return to Galway by Ballintubber, with its impressive Abbey, Ballinrobe and Headford.

9 Donegal and Yeats' Country

This is a 2–day circular tour, over **320** miles *(515 km)* on main route.

The Shannon, near Carrick-on-Shannon, Co. Leitrim

Day One
Carrick-on-Shannon–Carrigart **200** *(322 km)*
The popular centre of Carrick-on-Shannon—well known for cruising and coarse fishing—is the starting point for this tour. The first town on route is Boyle, 2 miles (3 km) from Lough Key National Park, with its numerous facilities, from boating to nature trails. Your drive will continue to

Collooney, entering the magical country of Yeats. Share his experiences as you drive through Ballysodare, Kilmacowen and Strandhill on your way to Sligo.

Sligo, a beautifully situated town, surrounded by mountains. Pay a visit to Sligo Abbey and the museum, situated in the county library. Follow the road through Drumcliffe (Yeats' burial place) to Grange and Cliffoney into Bundoran, a resort where you'll find enjoyment for all the family.

Begin your tour of Donegal from Bally-shannon, leading north to Donegal town and on to Killybegs by way of Mountcharles, Inver and Dunkineely. Following the coast to Glencolumbkille, a popular holiday centre, you are now in a part of Ireland's 'Gaeltacht' or Irish-speaking region. This area of Donegal is noted for its excellent crafts and the production of hand-made Donegal tweed. From Glencolumbkille head east to Ardara, Maas and Dungloe, a remarkable tract of rocky lakeland.

Drive north from Crolly to the lovely little fishing village of Bunbeg, along the coast to Gortahork and Dunfanaghy, with its lovely beaches and superb cliff scenery. Turn off at Creeslough for Carrigart, beautifully situated on Mulroy Bay. Spend the night here.

Day Two
Carrigart–Carrick-on-Shannon **120** *(193 km)*
From Carrigart there is a charming 12-mile (19 km) trip around the little Rosguill Peninsula, taking in Tranarossan Bay and Rosapenna. Continue south to Letterkenny via Milford.

Before driving south for Donegal town again, you could take a trip around the Inishowen Peninsula, an extra 129 miles (208 km) in all, giving unrivalled views, a top-class resort at Buncrana and some very interesting antiquities, such as the cross at Carndonagh. Complete your tour from Donegal by Ballyshannon, Bundoran, Kinlough, Manorhamilton, Killarga, Drum-keeran and along the shores of Lough Allen by Drumshanbo into Carrick-on-Shannon.

10 Tour of Northern Ireland

A 5-day tour about **377** miles *(609 km)*, suggested starting point—Belfast.

Day One
Belfast–Cushendall **51** *(82 km)*
After you have explored Belfast, go north on the M2 motorway, leaving it at exit 2 to take the A2 to the car ferry port of Larne (only 22 miles/ 35 km from Scotland) round the foot of the great chalk and basalt cliffs to the first villages of the Nine Glens of Antrim— Glenarm and Carnlough.Complete your first day comfortably at Cushendall, the capital of the Glens or at Cushendun.

Day Two
Cushendall–Derry **84** *(135 km)*
Your route now takes you over the Antrim moors to Ballycastle, one of County Antrim's most attractive seaside resorts. (From here you can visit beautiful Rathlin Island.) Onwards to Portrush, with recommended stops at Carrick-a-Rede rope bridge, White-park Bay, Dunluce Castle and the incredible Giant's Causeway. From Portrush your tour brings you by Portstewart, Coleraine, Downhill, Magilligan (Ireland's largest beach) and Limavady, into the historic city of Derry. There's much to see in this ancient city, including the City Walls and the graceful St Columb's Cathedral.

Day Three
Derry–Enniskillen **59** *(95 km)*
On the following day you reach Strabane, an agricultural market town on the River Mourne, before going south via Castlederg and Ederny to Kesh, on the shores of Lower Lough Erne. Head on by Boa Island to Belleek, with its famous pottery, completing your trip to Enniskillen by the south shore road.

Day Four
Enniskillen–Newcastle **106** *(171 km)*
On the fourth day your trip from Enniskillen to Armagh brings you by Fivemiletown and Aughnacloy. At Armagh it's worth seeing the two cathedrals, the Planetarium and the Mall. Continue on to Newry, enjoying the splendour of Slieve Gullion along the way. Head south-east by the popular resorts of Warrenpoint and Rostrevor on Carlingford Lough, making the final part of your journey to Newcastle along the coast, with the rugged Mountains of Mourne to your left.

Day Five
Newcastle–Belfast **79** *(127 km)*
On the final day your route takes you first to Downpatrick—traditional location of St Patrick's grave. From here you reach the pretty village of Strangford, where a car ferry takes you to Portaferry on the opposite side of Strangford Lough narrows. Head north by the shore of Strangford Lough, through the pleasant fishing village of Kircubbin into Greyabbey. Here you can explore the well-preserved Cistercian abbey founded in 1193. Continuing on to Newtownwards you'll have an opportunity to see the wonderful Mount Stewart Gardens, including the well-known Temple of the Winds. Complete your route back to Belfast via Bangor, with its large seaside marina, and the Folk and Transport Museum in the grounds of Cultra Manor near Hollywood.

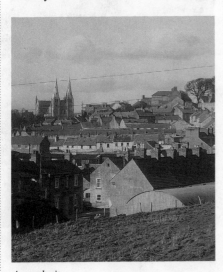

Armagh city

The Shannon Basin

Since this book is organised on a county-by-county basis, it is necessary to draw the reader's attention to the one great natural resource in Ireland which overflows all county boundaries. Rising in the Cuilcagh mountains in Co. Cavan, the River Shannon flows south through the flat limestone plain of central Ireland before finally opening out into a broad estuary below Limerick and flowing into the Atlantic between counties Clare and Kerry.

The Shannon is the longest river in Britain or Ireland and is a paradise for inland waterway enthusiasts. The 185 km stretch between Battlebridge, Co. Leitrim and Killaloe, Co. Clare, at the southern end of Lough Derg, is the principal navigable area of the river. The cruiser hire companies do not permit their boats to travel beyond these points.

This is the heart of the great river. And while the Shannon itself is a constant delight, it also opens up into a series of lakes, of which the two largest are Lough Ree and Lough Derg, 29 km and 39 km long respectively.

In all, the catchment area of the Shannon is over 15,000 square km or more than one-fifth of the entire area of Ireland. For the most part, it meanders slowly through the central plain. There are many villages and harbours along the way but very few large towns. Athlone, at the southern end of Lough Ree, is the biggest.

It is difficult to do justice in words to 'the broad majestic Shannon'. It is one of Ireland's great natural resources—and one, moreover, which is still quite unspoilt. No visit to Ireland is really complete without some time spent on its waters.

The Shannon Basin

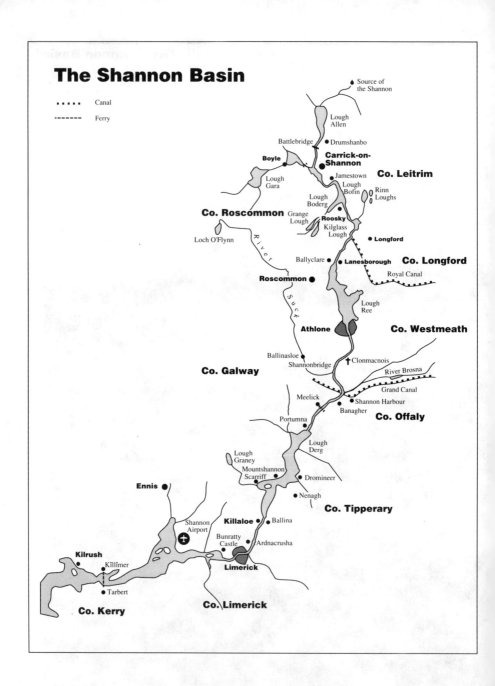

..... Canal

------- Ferry

Source of the Shannon

Lough Allen

Battlebridge ● Drumshanbo

Boyle ● **Carrick-on-Shannon**

Lough Gara ● Jamestown **Co. Leitrim**

Lough Bofin Rinn Loughs

Lough Boderg

Co. Roscommon Grange Lough **Roosky**

Kilglass Lough

Loch O'Flynn ● **Longford**

Ballyclare ● ● **Lanesborough** **Co. Longford**

Roscommon ● Royal Canal

Lough Ree

Athlone **Co. Westmeath**

Ballinasloe ● † Clonmacnois
Shannonbridge River Brosna

Co. Galway Grand Canal

Meelick ● ● Shannon Harbour
Banagher

Portumna ● **Co. Offaly**

Lough Derg

Lough Graney Mountshannon
Scarriff ● ● Dromineer

Ennis ● ● Nenagh

Shannon Airport **Killaloe** ● ● Ballina **Co. Tipperary**

Bunratty Castle ● Ardnacrusha

Kilrush **Limerick**

Killimer

● Tarbert **Co. Limerick**

Co. Kerry

454

Glossary

The following is an alphabetical list of archaeological, architectural and technical terms, common elements in Irish placenames, and a brief guide to the myths and historical events mentioned throughout this book.

A

Abbey Theatre
Famous Dublin theatre associated with Irish Literary Renaissance.

Act of Union
In 1800 the British Prime Minister William Pitt pushed through this Act, which dissolved the Irish Parliament—thereby transferring legislative control of Ireland to London and merging the Irish economy with that of England, although the Treasuries were only merged in 1817.

Aengus Ceile De
A member of the ascetic Culdee movement which flourished around A.D. 800, he wrote a poetical calendar of Irish saints.

Alto-relievo
Literally 'high-relief'—figures projected by at least half their thickness, from the background on which they are sculptured.

Anglo-Norman
The name given to a mixture of English, Norman and Welsh peoples who invaded Ireland during the twelfth century.

Annals of the Four Masters
One of the most important sources of early Irish church history and genealogy, compiled in the seventeenth century by four friars from the Franciscan friary near Donegal town.

Antae
Pilaster-like projections or extensions of the side walls of a building. (Singular: *anta*.)

Aonach
An assembly held on regular occasions, when the king and his subjects could meet to transact business. This was accompanied by games and horse-racing.

Aras an Uachtarain
Residence of the President of Ireland in Phoenix Park, Dublin.

Arcade
A series of arches employed as an architectural feature.

Architrave
A main beam resting on top of columns or moulded frames round window, doorway or arch.

Ar(d)
(Irish *ard*): a high place.

Asgard
Sailing ship from which arms for Irish volunteers were landed in Howth in 1914.

Ath
(Irish *ath*): ford—shallow place where river may be crossed. Ford of the Hurdles—translation of Irish name for Dublin.

B

Bailey
A courtyard or ward in a castle: see also motte-and-bailey.

Bally
(Irish *baile*): a hamlet or group of dwellings.

Baltimore, Sack of
North African pirate raid on town in 1631 described in Thomas Davis's poem.

Banshee
A female fairy figure who wails and shrieks before a death in a family to which she is attached.

Barrel-Vaulting
Simple vaulting of semicircular form, e.g. St Kevin's Church, Glendalough.

Bawn
(Irish *badhun*): a fortified enclosure attached to a castle, which besides being an outer defence, provided protection for cattle.

Beehive Cell
A small stone cell or hut shaped like a beehive, with stones in a circle piled on each other in corbel technique until they reach a point at the top.

Black Pigs Dyke
Ancient defensive earthwork in Ulster.

Bronze Age
2000 to 500 B.C.—the earliest metal-using period, lasting from the end of the Stone Age to the beginning of the Iron Age.

Bruidhean da Choga
The hostel of the innkeeper, Da Choga, west of the Shannon. In ancient Ireland people had a number of esoteric prohibitions placed upon them. One of the taboos of Cormac, son of Conchoban, who had been selected to succeed his father as King, was not to go with dry feet over the Shannon to visit Da Choga.

Brugh na Boinne
Legendary burial place of kings in Boyne valley.

C

Caher
(Irish *cathair*): a stone fort.

Cailleach Beara
(The Hag of Beara)—a character in Irish folklore.

Cairn
The mound of stones usually over a prehistoric grave.

Capital
The head of a column, often decorated, upon which a superstructure is supported.

Capstone
See Dolmen.
Carrig
(Irish *carraig*): rock.
Carton House
Residence of Dukes of Leinster.
Cashel
(Irish *caiseal*): a stone fort.
Catholic Confederation
Established in Kilkenny in 1642 and composed of the members of the Roman Catholic Party expelled from the Dublin Parliament. It virtually became a Catholic, pro-monarchist parliament backing the rebellion begun in 1641 and aiming at obtaining full civil rights for the Catholic majority in Ireland. It lasted until 1649 when Cromwell landed in Ireland.
Chancel (Choir)
The east end of a church reserved for the clergy and containing the High Altar.
Children of Lir
Legendary children, turned to swans.
Cist
A box-like grave of stone slabs; there is occasionally a covering mound.
Civil War
(1922–1923). Fought between the independent Irish Government established for 26 of 32 counties under the Anglo-Irish Treaty of 1921 (which had been ratified by the Irish and English parliaments) and those who, led by Eamon de Valera, opposed it.
Clerestory
An upper row of windows in a cathedral above the level of the aisle roofs.
Clochan
A beehive-shaped hut of dry (unmortared) masonry.
Columbarium
Pigeon house of ancient abbeys.
Comhaltas Ceoltoiri Eireann
Irish cultural institute founded to promote national music, song and dance.
Confederate (Wars)
Wars between the supporters of the Catholic Confederation (1642–1649) and the British Government in Ireland.
Confederation of Kilkenny
See Catholic Confederation.
Connradh na Gaeilge
Gaelic league—founded to promote use of Irish language.
Corbel
A projection from a wall, generally of stone, designed to support a weight.
Corrie
An extensive, deep, rounded hollow with steep sides, at the head of a valley, formed by erosion by the ice of a glacier; a cirque.

Court Cairn
A cairn with one or more gallery graves, opening off a court or courts for ritual purposes.
Crannog
An island, usually artificial, built in or at the edge of a lake, river or marsh, to provide an easily defended dwelling-place.
Croppy Boy
Name given to insurgents in 1798.
Cuchulainn
Legendary hero of Red Branch Knights.
Currach
A primitive type of boat made of tarred canvas (originally hide) stretched over a framework of laths.

D
Dáil
Lower house of Irish legislature.
Dalcassians
The people of the tenth-century Kingdom of Dal Cais in east County Clare who defeated the Norse at Limerick in 964. Brian Boru was a member of this tribal group.
Danes
Vikings from Denmark who first raided the Irish coast in 795 and established a settlement at Dublin in 841.
Deise
(Decies)—area of Co. Waterford settled by tribe from Co. Meath in third century A.D.
Derg
(Irish *dearg*): red.
Derry, Dare
(Irish *doire*): oak tree or wood.
Desmond (Revolt)
Second Anglo-Irish rebellion of the sixteenth century.
Diarmuid & Grania's Bed
See Druid's Altar.
Dissolution
Of the monasteries, in reign of Henry VIII.
Dolmen
The simplest form of megalithic tomb, consisting of three or more uprights supporting a heavy roofing stone, known as the capstone.
Druid's Altar
A type of megalithic chambered grave. Other popular names include: Diarmuid and Grania's Bed, Giant's Grave, Cromlech, Dolmen and many others.
Drum
(Irish *druim*): ridge, hillock.
Drumlin
An elongated hill or ridge of boulder clay, usually shaped like half an egg; it occurs in previously glaciated regions.
Dun
A fort

E

Eamhain Macha
Palace built by warrior Queen, Macha, *c*.300
B.C.; seat of ancient Ulster kings—training centre
for Red Branch Knights.
Esker
A long, narrow ridge, chiefly of gravel and sand,
which was once the bed of a stream flowing in
the ice of a glacier, usually at the bottom, and
was left behind when the ice melted.

F

Fairy Ring
See Lis or Rath
Feis
Assembly, Gaelic festival.
Feis Ceoil
Music festival
Fenian
The Irish Republican Brotherhood, also called
the Fenian movement, was founded in 1858, its
aim being the overthrow of the British
Government in Ireland. This group was called
after the legendary Fianna: see Fianna.
Ferdia
Legendary friend and foe of Cuchulainn.
Fert
(Irish *Feart*): grave.
Fianna
A possibly legendary band of roving warriors of
ancient Ireland who loved war and hunting. Their
leader was Fionn Mac Cumhaill (*Finn McCool*).
Fionn Mac Cumhaill
See Fianna
Fir Bolg
Legendary invaders of Ireland in pre-Celtic
times.
Fleadh Ceoil
Festival of ballad-singing and traditional music.
Formorians
Sea-rovers said to have inhabited Ireland in pre-
Celtic times.

G

GAA
Gaelic Athletic Association founded in 1884 to
promote Irish games.
Gaeltacht
A district, usually on the western seaboard,
where Irish is spoken as the vernacular.
Gallan
A standing, upright stone.
Gallowglass
A heavily armed foot-soldier serving in the Irish
armies during the fourteenth and fifteenth
centuries. Gallowglasses were originally Scottish
mercenaries.

Geraldine
Anglo-Norman family Fitzgerald
Goban Saor
Legendary builder in Irish folklore.
Grianan
Palace

H

High Cross
A tall cross of stone, usually with figure and/or
other carvings. They date from the eighth to the
twelfth century, and were probably used for the
religious instruction of the unlettered. The carvings
were probably originally picked out in colour.
Hill Fort
A fort whose defences follow a contour round a
hill to enclose the hilltop.
Huguenots
French Protestants who came to Ireland in the
seventeenth century to escape the religious
persecutions of Louis XIV.

I

Inch, Innis(h), Ennis
(Irish *inis*): island, river-meadow.
Irish Confederation
See Catholic Confederation.
Irish Land League
Founded by Michael Davitt in 1849 to protect
Irish tenants from eviction.
Irish Volunteers
Private army founded in 1913 to counterbalance
the 100,000-strong force of the Ulster Covenanters,
who were resisting the Home Rule about to be
granted to all Ireland.
Iron Age
The earliest iron-using period, lasting from the
end of the Bronze Age to the coming of
Christianity in the fifth century.

J

Jacobites
Adherents of King James II of England.
Joly Collection
Donated to the National Library by Robert Joly,
book collector (1819–1892).

K

Keep
A tower.
Ken
(Irish *ceann*): head.
Kil
(Irish *cill*): church, cell.
Kitchen-midden
Ancient habitation site, consisting of banks of
opening shells, often mixed with charcoal, and
various implements, etc.

Knights Hospitallers
A charitable brotherhood, caring for the sick in hospitals.
Knights Templars
Religious and military order of knights for the protection of pilgrims to the Holy Land.
Knight of Kerry
One of three members of the Fitzgerald family knighted by Edward III at the Battle of Halidon Hill (1333), though they probably held the titles by usage from an earlier date. The other two were the White Knight and the Knight of Glin.
Knock
(Irish *cnoc*): hill.

L
Lammas Fair
Famous fair held in Ballycastle, Co. Antrim, every late August.
Lambeg
Large drum beaten by canes—feature of Orange parades.
Lanert Window
Window with a pointed head.
Lis
(Irish *lios*): an earthen fort.

M
Martello Tower
A round tower a series of which was erected by the military authorities on the coast for protection against sea invasion by Napoleon, and named after a town in his native Corsica.
Mass Rock
Rock used during penal days in Ireland on which Mass was celebrated when the Roman Catholic religion was prohibited.
Milesius
Legendary pre-Christian invader of Ireland.
Moraine
Rock debris or fragments brought down by the movement of a glacier.
More
(Irish *mor*): great.
Motte-and-bailey
Early Norman earthen fortress. The motte was a high, flat-topped mound surrounded by a deep fosse or ditch, and crowned with a stockade, inside which was a wooden tower. The bailey was a large enclosure adjoining the motte at the lower level, likewise stockaded and surrounded by a fosse. Within it were situated various wooden buildings, including the troops' quarters.

N
Nave
The main body of a church from inner door to chancel; the western portion.

Neolithic (New Stone Age)
Covered the centuries from the end of the fourth millennium B.C. to the beginning of the second. This was the period of the first farmers and food producers, and was characterised by the use of polished stone axes, leaf-shaped flint arrowheads and usually round-bottomed pottery.
Norman (architecture)
Name for English Romanesque architecture in vogue in Ireland the twelfth century.
Nugent (Family)
Anglo-Norman family.

O
Ogham
Early form of writing or cypher having twenty letters formed of strokes drawn on either side of or crossing a central line. Ogham inscriptions are mostly found in southern Ireland and occur mainly on standing stones.
Oratory
A small church or chapel.
Ossory
Ancient kingdom of west Leinster.
Oughter
(Irish *uachtar*): upper.
Outlier
A mass of comparatively new rocks surrounded by older ones.
Owen, Avon
(Irish *abhainn* or *abhann*): river

P
Palatinate
Province of an important and generally notable personage—usually connected with an area in Germany.
Palatine
District around Adare and Rathkeale, Co. Limerick, where German refugees from French invasion of their homeland were settled.
Pale
The district centred on Dublin, and varying in extent, to which for some four centuries following the Norman invasion, English sovereignty was, in practice, limited.
Parliamentarian
Supporters of the English parliament which, from 1640, struggled against Charles I.
Parliamentary Wars
Fought between supporters of the Parliamentarians and the King, who was defeated at Naseby in 1645 and finally executed. The wars were then continued in Ireland under Cromwell.
Passage-grave
A tomb consisting of a burial chamber (or chambers) approached by a long passage.

Pattern
The festival of a patron saint, held on the traditional day of his death.
Penal Laws
Oppressive measures which were in force against Irish Catholics between 1695 and 1829.
Pikemen
1798 insurgents named after their main weapon.
Piscina
A basin for washing liturgical vessels in a wall-niche near, and south of, the altar.
Pluralist
A holder of more than one office at a time.
Portcullis
A sliding door in the form of a grid with points on the bottom and standing above a gate; it could be lowered in time of danger.
Poynings' Law
Law passed in 1494 which decreed that laws passed in Irish Parliament would only be valid when approved by English Privy Council.

Q
Quatrefoil Windows
Four-pointed or 4-leafed ornament on windows.
Queen Maeve of Connacht
Legendary Queen who initiated the Táin (the Cattle Raid of Cooley).

R
Rath
The rampart of an earthen fort; also the whole structure.
Rebellion of 1641
Began with an abortive plot to seize Dublin Castle and aimed at forcing the British Government to grant full civil and religious rights to the Irish. Terminated in 1652, two years after Cromwell's departure.
Rebellion of 1798
Often called the 'rebellion of the younger sons' because so many of the leaders came from leading Anglo-Irish, and even noble, families. Inspired by the French Revolution, it relied on military help from France, but broke out and was quelled before this arrived. When it did arrive it was too late and too little. The objective was an Irish Republic.
Reliquary
Receptacle for relics.
Rising of 1916
Armed rebellion of the Irish Volunteers and the Irish Citizen Army in Dublin on Easter Monday. Patrick Pearse declared Republic of Ireland. Leaders of Rising were executed.
Ros
Promontory, wood.

Round Tower
A tall, independently standing circular stone belfry cum refuge with a conical roof. Round towers generally date from the ninth to the twelfth century.
RDS
Royal Dublin Society.
Runic
A form of lettering practised in the Germanic world during the early historic period. Its rare occurrences in Ireland can presumably be attributed to the Vikings.

S

Seanad
Upper house of Irish legislature.
Sedilia
A set of wall seats on the south side of the chancel, intended for the use of celebrant, deacon and subdeacon. (Singular: sedile.)
Sept
In the old Irish system, a ruling family tracing its descent from a common ancestor; a clan.
Siamsa Tire
Folk theatre of Ireland.
Skerry
Rock.
Slieve
(Irish *sliabh*): mountain
Souterrain
An artificially constructed underground chamber.
Standing Stone
Dating from several different periods, the stones, set in the ground, functioned as boundary stones, burial markers or were part of cult beliefs.
Statutes of Kilkenny
Laws passed to prevent contact between Anglo-Normans and Irish.
Stone Circle
A ring of standing stones, often a Bronze Age ritual monument.
Stone Fort
A fort built of dry, unmortared masonry—Staigue Fort, Co. Kerry.
Stout
A strong dark beer with a rich creamy head. Made from barley, hops, yeast and water.
Striae
Scratches or narrow grooves worn on rock surfaces due to rock fragments being dragged over them by a glacier.
Sugan
Traditional type of rope-work used in the manufacture of furniture etc.

Sweat House
A stone house in which heat was generated so that a person would sweat inside it as in a Turkish bath.

T

Tailteann
See Aonach

Táin Bó Cuailgne
Cattle raid of Cooley—a famous legend of ancient Ireland.

Tau (Cross)
T-shaped (cross).

Teampall
Church.

Tène, La
Early Celtic art believed to date before first century B.C.

Termon Cross
Cross marking the boundary of ecclesiastical lands.

Tholsel
Town Hall, originally Toll House.

Tober, Tubber
(Irish *tobar*): well.

Tra
(Irish *traigh*): beach.

Transept
The side arms of a church, running north and south.

Tuatha De Danann
The Celtic gods who were worshipped by the pagan Irish.

Tully
(Irish *tulach*): hillock.

Tumulus
A prehistoric sepulchral mound, a barrow.

Turf
Name often used for peat in Ireland.

Turlochs
Intermittent lakes in limestone regions—sometimes called 'disappearing' lakes.

Tympanum
Space over a door between lintel and the arch; a carving on this space.

U

United Irishmen
Society founded at the end of the eighteenth century to bring Catholics and Protestants together in the cause of radical political reform and to do away with religious discrimination. When all moderate methods failed, they became the fathers of Irish republicanism: see also Rebellion of 1798.

Y

Yola
Dialect once spoken in baronies of Forth and Bargy in Co. Wexford.

Young Irelanders
A group of young men who joined O'Connell in his fight for the repeal of the Act of Union.

Persons Mentioned in the Text

Abercromby, Sir Ralph
Commander of British forces in Ireland prior to 1798 Rebellion who resigned after criticising the cruelty of the soldiers.

Alcock, Capt. John
who, with Lt. Arthur Whitten Brown, completed the first non-stop Atlantic flight when they crash-landed near Clifden, Co. Galway, in 1919.

Alexander, Field Marshal Viscount (1891–1969)
Born Caledon, Co. Tyrone. Supreme Commander of allied forces in Mediterranean theatre during World War II.

Allingham, William (1824–1889)
Poet, born Ballyshannon, Co. Donegal.

Ashe, Thomas (1885–1917)
Teacher and revolutionary, born Lispole, Co. Kerry; died in prison from forcible feeding while on hunger strike.

Bagenal, Henry
English commander defeated and killed in 1598 at the Battle of the Yellow Ford in Co. Armagh by forces of Hugh O'Neill.

Barry, Commodore John (1745–1803)
'Father of the American Navy', born Tacumshane, Co. Wexford.

Beatty, Sir Alfred Chester (1875–1968)
Mining engineer and philanthropist, left his collection of oriental manuscripts to the Irish nation.

Beckett, Samuel (1906–1989)
Dramatist, novelist and Nobel prizewinner, born in Dublin; lived most of his life in France and died in Paris.

Bedell, Bishop Wm (1571–1642)
Bishop of Kilmore and Ardagh, translated the Old Testament into Irish.

Beit, Sir Alfred
Owner of Russborough House near Blessington, Co. Wicklow, home of the Beit art collection.

Bellingham, Colonel Thomas
Aide-de-camp to King William III at the Battle of the Boyne.

Berkeley, Bishop George (1685–1753)
Born Dysart Castle, Co. Kilkenny, metaphysical philosopher.

Bianconi, Charles (1786–1875)
Born in Lombardy, founded first public transport service in Clonmel, Co. Tipperary in 1815; became Irish citizen in 1831.

Bigger, Francis Joseph (1863–1926)
Author and antiquary, born in Belfast.

Bond, Oliver (1760–1798)
Born in Ulster, founder member of the Society of United Irishmen in 1791; died in prison.

Boru, Brian (926–1014)
King of Munster and High King of Ireland, defeated the Danes at Clontarf in 1014; killed after the battle.

Boycott, Captain
Landlord of Lough Mask House near Ballinrobe, Co. Mayo, whose problems with the Land League introduced a new word into the English language.

Boyd, Reverend Henry (1750–1832)
Translator of Dante, vicar of Rathfriland, Co. Down.

Boyle, Richard (1566–1643)
English lawyer who became 1st Earl of Cork.

Boyle, Robert
Son of Richard Boyle, 1st Earl of Cork, celebrated chemist whose name lives in 'Boyle's Law'; born in Lismore Castle, Co. Waterford.

Brigid Saint
Founded an abbey in Kildare in the fifth century.

Brontë (Prunty), Reverend Patrick (1777–1861)
Born near Rathfriland, Co. Down, father of the Brontë sisters.

Brooke, Charlotte (1740–1793)
Author, born Co. Cavan; translated Irish poetry and songs into English verse.

Browne, Archbishop
First Protestant to occupy the See of Dublin.

Bruce, Edward
Brother of Robert Bruce, King of Scotland, who invaded Ireland in 1315, but was defeated and killed at the Battle of Faughart, Co. Louth, in 1318.

Bryce, Viscount James (1838–1922)
Jurist, historian and politician; born Belfast.

Burke, Edmund (1729–1797)
Born Dublin, political writer and orator; founded Trinity College Historical Society.

Butler, Black Tom
10th Earl of Ormond, built Carrick-on-Suir Castle, Co. Tipperary, for a visit by his cousin, Queen Elizabeth I, but she never came.

Butt, Isaac (1813–1879)
Barrister and politician, born Glenfinn, Co. Donegal; founded the Home Rule movement.

Byrne, Billy
Of Ballymanus near Aughrim, Co. Wicklow, an insurgent of 1798.

Callan, Nicholas Joseph (1799–1864)
Priest, scientist and inventor, born near
Dundalk, Co. Louth; Professor of natural
philosophy at Maynooth.

Carbery, Ethna (1866–1911)
Writer, born in Ballymena, Co. Antrim; wife of
Seamus McManus.

Carew, Sir George (c.1560–1629)
Elizabethan President of Munster.

Carleton, William (1794–1869)
Novelist, born near Clogher, Co. Tyrone.

Carroll, Paul Vincent (1900–1968)
Playwright, born Blackrock, Co. Louth.

Carson, Sir Edward (1854–1935)
Lawyer and political leader, born Dublin; leader
of the Ulster Unionists.

Casement, Sir Roger (1864–1916)
Patriot, served in British colonial service; later
leading revolutionary activist; hanged in 1916.

Casey, John Keegan (1846–1870)
Popular poet, born near Mullingar, Co.
Westmeath.

Castle, Richard (1690–1751)
German born architect (original name Cassels)
who came to Ireland in the 1720s and designed
many of the country's finest classical buildings.

**Castlereagh, Lord (Robert Stewart)
(1769–1822)**
Chief Secretary, he secured the passage of the
Act of Union 1800.

Chambers, Sir William (1723–1796)
Designer of the Examination Hall in Trinity
College, Dublin and the casino at Marino.

**Charlemont, Lord (James Caulfield)
(1728–1799)**
Born in Dublin, nationalist; commander-in-chief
of the Volunteers in 1780; opposed Union.

Chichester, Sir Arthur
Governor of Carrickfergus, died in 1625.

Chichester, Sir Francis
Round-the-world yachtsman on Gypsy Moth III,
built in Arklow, Co. Wicklow.

Ciaran Saint
Founder of Clonmacnois.

Clarke, Harry (1889–1931)
Stained-glass artist, born Dublin.

Collie, George (1904–1975)
Portrait painter, born Carrickmacross, Co.
Monaghan.

Collins, Michael (1890–1922)
Born near Clonakilty, leader of the Irish forces
in the War of Independence; killed in ambush.

Colmcille Saint (521–597)
Born Garton, Co. Donegal; founded a monastery
in Derry and on Iona.

Colum, Padraic (1881–1972)
Poet and dramatist, born in Longford.

Comgall Saint (d. 601)
Founder of a monastic school at Bangor, Co.
Down.

Comyn, Michael (1688–1760)
Poet, born near Miltown Malbay, Co. Clare.

Congreve, William (1670–1729)
Dramatist, born near Leeds; educated at Trinity
College, Dublin.

Connolly, James (1868–1916)
Socialist and union leader, born in Edinburgh;
executed in 1916.

Conolly, William
Speaker of the Irish Parliament; built
Castletown House in 1722.

Cooley, Thomas
Designer of the City Hall in Dublin.

Cornwallis, Lord
Commander of the British forces at the Battle of
Ballinamuck, Co. Longford, in 1798.

Crawford, William (1781–1861)
Politician, born Co. Down; formed the Ulster
Tenant Right Association.

Croke, Archbishop (1824–1902)
Born Ballyclough, Co. Cork; supporter of the
GAA and Gaelic League.

Crozier, Captain Francis (1796–1848)
Arctic explorer, born in Banbridge, Co. Down.

Cromwell, Oliver (1599–1658)
Lord Protector of England and leader of the
Parliamentary forces in Ireland, 1649–1650.

Curran, John Philpot (1750–1817)
Lawyer and nationalist, born Newmarket, Co.
Cork; opposed the Act of Union.

Curran, Sarah (d. 1808)
Daughter of John Philpot Curran and beloved of
Robert Emmet.

Davis, Thomas (1814–1845)
Poet and nationalist, born Mallow,
Co. Cork; co-founder of *The Nation* newspaper
in 1842.

Davitt, Michael (1846–1906)
Born Straide, Co. Mayo; founded the Land
League in 1879.

Dervorgilla
Wife of Tiernan O'Rourke, Prince of Breffni,
whose liaison with Dermot MacMurrough, King
of Leinster, caused the Norman invasion of
Ireland.

De Valera, Éamon (1882–1975)
Revolutionary, politician and President of
Ireland.

De Vere, Aubrey (1814–1902)
Poet, born Curragh Chase, Co. Limerick.

Dillon, John (1851–1927)
Nationalist, leading member of the Irish Party in
the House of Commons after the death of
Parnell.

Doheny, Michael (1805–1863)
Young Irelander, born near Fethard,
Co. Tipperary; helped to found the Fenian
movement in America.

Donnelly, Dan (d. 1820)
Boxer who defeated Cooper, the English

champion, in a famous fight at the Curragh in 1815.

Dowland, John (1562–1626)
Musician, born Dalkey, Co. Dublin; greatest lutenist of his period.

Duffy, Sir Charles Gavan (1816–1903)
Nationalist, born Co. Monaghan; founder with Davis and John Dillon of *The Nation*; Prime Minister of Victoria, Australia, 1871.

Dunlap, John (b. 1747)
Founded the first daily newspaper in the US in 1771; born Strabane, Co. Tyrone.

Dwyer, Michael (1771–1826)
1798 insurgent leader, born Co. Wicklow.

Edgeworth, Maria (1767–1849)
Novelist, born and educated in England but spent most of her life in Edgeworthstown (Mostrim), Co. Longford.

Edgeworth, Richard Lovell (1744–1817)
Landlord, inventor and father of Maria; born in Bath.

Edgeworth, Abbé de Firmont (1745–1807)
Cousin of Richard Lovell, confessor to Louis XVI of France at his execution in 1793.

Edgeworth, Michael Pakenham (1812–1881)
Botanist and author.

Emmet, Robert (1778–1803)
United Irishman and leader of the abortive rising in 1803, after which he was hanged.

Farquhar, George (1678–1707)
Dramatist, born Derry; educated at Trinity College, Dublin.

Ferriter, Pierce (c.1600–1653)
Poet and leader of the Irish in the 1641 Rebellion.

Ferguson, Sir Samuel (1810–1886)
Poet and antiquary, born in Belfast.

Finbar Saint
Founder of church and school in Cork in the sixth century.

Finian Saint
Founded a monastic school at Clonard, Co. Meath.

Fitzgerald, Lord Edward (1763–1798)
United Irish leader, died in prison of wounds received during his arrest.

Fitzgerald, Gerald (d. 1513)
Great Earl of Kildare, Lord Deputy for Ireland under Henry VII and Henry VIII.

Fitzgerald, Garret Og (1487–1534)
9th Earl of Kildare, died in the Tower of London.

Fitzgerald, George Francis (1851–1901)
Natural philosopher, born in Dublin.

Fitzgerald, Percy Hetherington (1834–1925)
Writer, sculptor and painter, born Fane Valley, Co. Louth.

Fitzgerald, Silken Thomas
10th Earl of Kildare, led the abortive rebellion for which he was executed at Tyburn.

Fitzmaurice, George (1878–1963)
Playwright, born Co. Kerry.

Foley, John Henry (1818–1874)
Sculptor, born Dublin.

Ford, Henry (1863–1947)
Born Ballinascarthy, Co. Cork; creator of the Model T.

Foster, John (1740–1828)
Last Speaker of the Irish House of Commons, born Collon, Co. Louth.

French, Percy (1854–1920)
Entertainer, songwriter and painter, born Co. Roscommon.

Gandon, James (1743–1823)
Born in London, designed the Custom House, Dublin City Hall and King's Inns.

Gilbert, Sir John (1829–1898)
Historian and antiquary, born Dublin.

Gilbert, Marie (Lola Montez) (1818–1861)
Adventuress, born in Co. Limerick.

Ginkel, General
Williamite general who defeated the Jacobites at the Battle of Aughrim 1691.

Goldsmith, Oliver (1728–1774)
Author, born Co. Longford; educated at Trinity College, Dublin.

Gore Booth, Eva (1870–1926)
Poet, born Lissadell, Co. Sligo; sister of Constance Countess Markievicz.

Grattan, Henry (1746–1820)
Patriot and orator, born Dublin; gave his name to Grattan's Parliament and opposed the Union.

Graves, Robert (1796–1853)
Physician, born Dublin; researcher in medicine.

Gray, Betsy (d. 1798)
Heroine of the insurgents at the Battle of Ballynahinch, 1798, where she was killed.

Greatrakes, Valentine (1629–1683)
Stroker or faithhealer, born Co. Waterford.

Grey, Lord Deputy
Commander of the English forces at the massacre of Smerwick Harbour, 1580.

Gregg, John R. (1867–1948)
Born Rockcorry, Co. Monaghan, inventor of Gregg Shorthand.

Gregory, Lady Augusta (1852–1932)
Playwright, co-director with Yeats and Synge of the Abbey Theatre; born Co. Galway, lived at Coole Park.

Griffin, Gerald (1803–1840)
Dramatist, novelist and poet; author of *The Collegians*; born Limerick.

Halpin, Captain Robert (1836–1894)
Born in Wicklow, laid transatlantic cable in
1866 as navigator on the *Great Eastern,* then the
largest ship in the world.

**Hamilton, Sir William Rowan
(1805–1865)**
Mathematician and astronomer, born Dublin.

Handel, George Frederick
Composer whose *Messiah* was first performed
in Dublin, 1742.

Hanly, Ellen
Her tragic death inspired Griffin's *The
Collegians.*

Hannay, Canon James (1865–1950)
Novelist under the pen-name George A.
Birmingham, born Belfast.

Harty, Sir Hamilton (1879–1941)
Musician, born Hillsborough, Co. Down.

Harvey, Bagenal (1762–1798)
Commander of the 1798 insurgents in Wexford,
born in Bargy Castle.

Hayes, Canon John M. (1887–1957)
Founded Muintir na Tire, the influential society
for rural community development; born Murroe,
Co. Limerick.

Healy, Michael (1873–1941)
Stained-glass artist and painter, born Dublin.

Healy, T. M. (1855–1931)
Politician and first Governor-General of the
Irish Free State, born Bantry, Co. Cork.

**Hervey, Frederick Augustus
(1730–1803)**
Bishop of Derry and Earl of Bristol.

Heuston, Sean (1891–1916)
Executed after the 1916 Rising, born Dublin.

Hoche, General Lazare (1768–1797)
French general who brought fleet to Bantry Bay
in 1796.

Hoban, James (1762–1831)
Architect of the White House, Washington,
D.C, born Callan, Co. Kilkenny.

Hogan, John (1800–1858)
Sculptor, born Tallow, Co. Waterford.

Hogan, Michael (1832–1899)
Bard of Thomond, born Limerick.

Holland, John P. (1841–1914)
Inventor of the submarine, born Liscannor, Co.
Clare.

Holt, Joseph (1756–1826)
United Irishman, born Co. Wexford.

Hone, Nathaniel (1718–1784)
Portrait painter, born Co. Dublin.

Hone, Evie (1894–1955)
Stained-glass artist, born Co. Dublin.

Hope, James (Jemmy) (c.1764–1846)
United Irishman, born Templepatrick, Co.
Antrim.

Hopkins, Gerard Manley
Poet, professor of Greek at the Royal University
of Ireland.

Humbert
French general who landed in Killala, Co.
Mayo, in 1798.

Hunt, John (1900–1976)
Medievalist, born Limerick.

Hutcheson, Francis (1694–1746)
Father of the Scottish school of philosophy;
born at Drumalig, Co. Down.

Hyde, Dr Douglas (1860–1949)
Scholar and first president of the Gaelic League,
later first President of Ireland; born Castlerea,
Co. Roscommon.

Ireton, Henry
Son-in-law of Cromwell, Commander of the
Parliamentary forces in Ireland on Cromwell's
return to England.

Ingram, John Kells (1823–1907)
Scholar and poet, born Co. Donegal.

**Jackson, General Thomas
'Stonewall' (1824–1863)**
Born near Portadown, Co. Armagh.

Johnston, Denis (1901–1984)
Playwright, born Dublin.

Johnston, Francis (1760–1829)
Architect, designed the GPO in Dublin; born
Armagh.

Joyce, James (1882–1941)
Poet, novelist and playwright, born Dublin.

Joyce, Patrick Weston (1827–1914)
Historian and music collector, born Glenasheen,
Co. Limerick.

Joyce, Robert Dwyer (1830–1883)
Physician and songwriter, brother of Patrick
Weston.

Kavanagh, Patrick (1904–1967)
Poet, born Inniskeen, Co. Monaghan.

Kean, Charles John (1811–1868)
Actor, born Waterford.

Keating, Geoffrey (c.1570–c.1650)
Poet and historian, born Co. Tipperary.

Keating, Sean (1889–1977)
Painter, born in Limerick.

Kelly, Captain John (d. 1798)
Leader of Wexford insurgents in 1798—'the
boy from Killann'.

Kelvin, William Lord (1824–1907)
Scientist and inventor, born Belfast.

Kennedy, John F. (1917–1963)
President of the United States 1961–1963.

Kettle, Tom (1880–1916)
Nationalist, born Co. Dublin; killed at the Battle
of the Somme.

Kevin Saint (d. 618)
Founder of Glendalough monastic school.

Kickham, Charles (1828–1882)
Novelist, born Mullinahone, Co. Tipperary.

Kyteler, Dame Alice
Reputed witch who lived in Kilkenny in the
fourteenth century.

Lake, General
Led the government forces against the 1798 insurgents.
Lane, Sir Hugh (1875–1915)
Art collector and critic, born Co. Cork.
Lavery, Sir John (1856–1941)
Painter, born Belfast.
Lawlor, John (1820–1901)
Sculptor, born Dublin.
Lecky, William Edward (1838–1903)
Historian, born Co. Dublin.
Ledwidge, Francis (1887–1917)
Poet, born Slane, Co. Meath; killed in the Great War, 1917.
Le Fanu, Joseph Sheridan (1814–1873)
Novelist and journalist, born Dublin.
Le Gros, Raymond
Norman knight, son-in-law of Strongbow.
Leinster, Dukes of
Principal branch of the Fitzgeralds, whose family seat was Carton House, Co. Kildare.
Lever, Charles (1806–1872)
Novelist, born in Dublin.
Logan, James (1674–1751)
One of the founders of Pennsylvania, born Lurgan in 1674. Emigrated 1699.
Lover, Samuel (1797–1868)
Novelist and painter, born Dublin.
Lucas, Charles (1713–1771)
Patriot, born Co. Clare.
Mahaffy, John (1839–1919)
Scholar and Provost of Trinity College, Dublin.
Malone, Edmund (1741–1812)
Shakespearean scholar, born Dublin.
Malachy, King (d. 1022)
High King of Ireland.
Malachy Saint (1094–1148)
Archbishop of Armagh, introduced the Cistercians to Ireland.
Mangan, James Clarence (1803–1849)
Poet, born Dublin.
Marsh, Archbishop (1638–1713)
Provost of Trinity College, Dublin, founder of Marsh's library.
Markievicz, Countess (1868–1927)
Born Constance Gore-Booth at Lissadell House, Co. Sligo, she was a sister of Eva Gore-Booth. Revolutionary and patriot, participated in 1916 Rising and later leading Sinn Fein activist.
Martin, Richard (Humanity Dick) (1754–1834)
Founder of the Royal Society for the Prevention of Cruelty to Animals
Massey, William (1856–1925)
Premier of New Zealand; born Limavady, Co. Derry.
Mathew, Father Theobald (1790–1856)

Apostle of Temperance, born near Cashel, Co. Tipperary.
MacAirt, Cormac
High King of Ireland in the third century A.D.
Mac Conmara, Donncadh Rua (1715–1810)
Gaelic poet, born Cratloe, Co. Clare.
McClure, Admiral Sir Robert (1807–1873)
Arctic explorer, born Wexford.
McCormack, John Count (1884–1945)
Operatic and concert tenor, born Athlone.
McCracken, Henry Joy (1767–1798)
United Irishman, born Belfast.
McCurtain, Andrew (d. 1749)
Born Co. Clare, hereditary bard of the O'Briens of Thomond.
McCurtain, Thomas (1884–1920)
Nationalist Lord Mayor of Cork, murdered in 1920.
Mac Diarmada, Sean (1884–1916)
Revolutionary, born Co. Leitrim; executed in 1916.
Mac Domhnaill, Sean Clarach (1691–1754)
Gaelic poet, born Charleville, Co. Cork.
McDonagh, Thomas (1878–1916)
Poet and revolutionary, born Cloughjordan, Co. Tipperary; executed in 1916.
McDonnell, Sorley Boy (c.1505–1590)
Chieftain of the Antrim McDonnells, 1st Earl of Antrim.
McGee, Thomas D'Arcy (1825–1868)
Writer and nationalist, born Carlingford, Co. Louth; Canadian politician.
McGill, Patrick (1889–1963)
Author, born Glenties, Co. Donegal.
McGrath, Myler (c.1523–1622)
Archbishop of Cashel and bishop of several other sees.
McKenna, Don Juan (1771–1814)
Chilean general, born Clogher, Co. Tyrone.
McMahon, Bishop Heber (1600–1650)
Bishop and general in the Irish Confederacy forces.
McManus, Seamus (1869–1960)
Poet, historian and novelist, born Co. Donegal; husband of Ethna Carbery.
MacMurrough, Dermot (1110–1171)
King of Leinster who invited the Normans to Ireland.
McNamara, Brinsley (1890–1963)
Writer, born Delvin, Co. Westmeath.
McSwiney, Terence (1879–1920)
Revolutionary, Lord Mayor of Cork; died in Brixton on hunger strike.

Meagher, Thomas Francis (1823–1867)
Nationalist, born Waterford, general in the Union army in the US Civil War.
Mellows, Liam (1892–1922)
Civil War leader of republican forces; executed 1922.
Merriman, Brian (c.1749–1805)
Poet, born Ennistymon, Co. Clare.
Mitchel, John (1815–1875)
Patriot, born Dungiven, Co. Derry.
Molyneaux, Sir Thomas (1661–1733)
Physician.
Molyneaux, William (1656–1698)
Philosopher and patriot.
Moore, Sir John
Commander of the government forces in Wexford, 1798.
Moore, John
President of the Provisional Republic of Connacht during the invasion by General Humbert.
Moore, George (1852–1933)
Novelist, born Co. Mayo.
Moore, Thomas (1779–1852)
Poet, born Dublin; friend of Lord Byron.
Mosse, Bartholomew (1712–1759)
Born Portlaoise, founded the Rotunda Maternity Hospital, Dublin.
Mountjoy, Lord (Charles Blount) (d. 1606)
Lord Deputy of Ireland, who commanded the Elizabethan forces at the Battle of Kinsale in 1601–2.
Mulchinock, William (1820–1864)
Wrote 'The Rose of Tralee'.
Murphy, Father John (1753–1798)
Leader of the 1798 Rising, born Ferns, Co. Wexford.
Murray, Thomas C. (1873–1959)
Playwright, born Macroom, Co. Cork.
Nagle, Nano (1728–1784)
Founder of the Presentation order of nuns, born near Mallow, Co. Cork.
Neilson, Samuel (1761–1803)
United Irishman, born Co. Down.
Newman, Cardinal John Henry (1801–1890)
Founded the Catholic University of Ireland, 1854.
O'Brien, William (1852–1928)
Nationalist MP and author, born Mallow, Co. Cork.
O'Brien, William Smith (1803–1864)
Nationalist, born Dromoland, Co. Clare.
O'Brien, Charlotte Grace (1845–1900)
Writer and social worker, daughter of William Smith O'Brien.

O'Byrne, Fiach MacHugh (1544–1597)
Chief of the O'Byrnes of Wicklow, defeated English forces under Lord Gray at Glenmalure in 1580.
O'Carolan, Turlough (1670–1738)
Last of the Irish bards, born Nobber, Co. Meath.
O'Casey, Sean (1880–1964)
Author and playwright, born Dublin.
Ó Cleirigh, Michael (1575–1643)
Chronicler, born Co. Donegal; compiled the *Annals of Ireland, 1632–1636*.
Ó Conaire, Padraic (1882–1928)
Gaelic writer, born Galway.
O'Connell, Daniel 'The Liberator' (1775–1847)
Born near Cahirciveen, Co. Kerry; achieved Catholic Emancipation in 1829.
O'Connor, Roderick (d. 1198)
Last high king of Ireland.
O'Connor, Thomas Power (1848–1929)
Journalist and politician, born Athlone.
O'Conor, Don
Title held by head of family in direct descent from last high king of Ireland. Family seat at Clonalis, Co. Roscommon.
Ó Crohan, Thomas (1856–1937)
Gaelic author, born on the Blasket Islands, Co. Kerry.
O'Curry, Eugene (1796–1862)
Scholar, born near Carrigaholt, Co. Clare.
Ó Doirnín, Peadar (1704–1768)
Gaelic poet.
O'Donnell, Red Hugh (c.1571–1602)
Earl of Tyrconnell, Co. Donegal.
O'Donoghue, Geoffrey (d. 1677)
Gaelic poet.
O'Growney, Fr Eugene (1863–1899)
Leader of the Irish language revival movement, born Co. Meath.
O'Hanlon, Redmond (d. 1681)
Leader of an outlaw band in the Slieve Gullion area of Co. Armagh.
O'Hempsey, Denis (c.1695–1807)
Harper, born Co. Derry.
O'Hurley, Dermot (1519–1584)
Archbishop of Cashel, executed 1584.
O'Leary, John (1830–1907)
Writer and Fenian, born Tipperary.
O'Leary, Ellen (1831–1889)
Poetess, sister of John.
O'Leary, Fr Peter (1839–1920)
Author, born near Macroom, Co. Cork.
O'Mahony, John (1816–1877)
Fenian, born Co. Limerick.
O'Malley, Grace, Grainne Mhaol (c.1530–1600)
Sea queen of the West.

O'More, Owen MacRory (d. *c*.1652)
Descended from the chiefs of Laois, leader in the Confederate army during the wars of the 1640s.

O'Neill, Hugh (1550–1616)
2nd Earl of Tyrone, born Dungannon, Co. Tyrone; last great leader of Gaelic Ireland, defeated by Lord Mountjoy at Kinsale, 1601.

O'Neill, Owen Roe (*c*.1590–1649)
Commander of the Irish forces in the Confederacy, victor at Benburb in 1646.

O'Neill, Sir Phelim (*c*.1604–1653)
Leader of the Irish forces in the north before Owen Roe.

Ó Rahaille, Aodhagán (1670–1726)
Gaelic poet, born Co. Kerry.

O'Reilly, Myles 'The Slasher'
Heroic defender of the bridge of Finea, Co. Cavan, in 1646.

Ó Riain, Eamon 'Ned of the Hill'
Gaelic poet and outlaw from Co. Tipperary.

Ó Riada, Seán (1931–1971)
Musician and composer.

Ormonde, Dukes of
Family seat was Kilkenny castle; 1st Duke was leader of the Royalist forces in the 1640s.

Orpen, Sir William (1878–1931)
Painter, born Stillorgan, Co. Dublin.

Orr, William (1766–1797)
United Irishman from Co. Antrim, hanged at Carrickfergus in 1797.

Orr, James (1770–1816)
Poet and United Irishman, born Co. Antrim.

O'Rourke, Tiernan
Prince of Breffni whose wife, Dervorgilla, eloped with Dermot McMurrough, causing the Norman invasion.

Osborne, Walter (1859–1903)
Painter, born Dublin.

O'Sullivan Beare, Donall (1560–1618)
After the defeat at Kinsale, led the famous march to Co. Leitrim in 1602.

O'Sullivan, Eoghan Ruadh (1748–1784)
Gaelic poet, born Co. Kerry.

O'Sullivan, Muiris (1904–1950)
Gaelic author, born on the Blasket Islands.

O'Toole, Saint Laurence (*c*.1130–1180)
Archbishop of Dublin at the time of the Norman invasion.

O'Toole, Luke
Leader of the Co. Wicklow O'Tooles during the 1641 Rising.

O Tuama, Sean (1706–1775)
Gaelic poet of the River Maigue district in Co. Limerick.

Palladius
Reputedly the first Christian missionary to Ireland in 430 A.D.

Parnell, Charles Stewart (1846–1891)
Patriot, the 'uncrowned king of Ireland', born Avondale, Co. Wicklow.

Patrick Saint (d. *c*.490)
Patron saint of the Irish, successfully introduced Christianity to Ireland.

Pearce, Sir Edward Lovett (1699–1733)
Architect, designed the Houses of Parliament, now the Bank of Ireland, College Green, Dublin.

Pearse, Patrick (1879–1916)
Educationalist, writer and revolutionary, born Dublin; executed in 1916.

Pearse, William (1881–1916)
Brother of Patrick, also executed in 1916.

Penn, Admiral Sir William
Governor of Kinsale in the seventeenth century.

Penn, William
His son, Clerk of the Admiralty Court in Kinsale and founder of Pennsylvania.

Petrie, George (1790–1866)
Antiquary, painter and musician, born Dublin.

Plunkett, Saint Oliver (1625–1681)
Archbishop of Armagh and martyr, born near Oldcastle, Co. Meath.

Power, Albert (1883–1945)
Sculptor, born Dublin.

Prior, Thomas (1682–1751)
Founder of the Royal Dublin Society, born Rathdowney, Co. Laois.

Prout, Father (F. S. Mahony) (1804–1866)
Humorist, author of *The Bells of Shandon*; born in Cork.

Purcell, Nicholas
Officer in King James II's army, signatory of the Treaty of Limerick in 1691.

Raftery, Antoine (*c*.1784–1835)
Gaelic poet, born Co. Mayo.

Raleigh, Sir Walter (*c*.1552–1618)
Elizabethan favourite who served and lived in Ireland; later executed for treason in London.

Redmond, John (1856–1918)
Political leader, leader of the Irish Party 1900–1918, born Co. Wexford.

Reid, Thomas Mayne (1818–1883)
Novelist, born Ballyroney, Co. Down.

Rice, Edmund Ignatius (1762–1844)
Founder of the Irish Christian Brothers, born near Callan, Co. Kilkenny.

Rinucinni, Cardinal Giovanni Battista (d. 1653)
Papal legate to the Confederation of Kilkenny from 1645 to 1649.

Ritchie, William and Hugh
Founded the shipbuilding industry on the River Lagan in Belfast.

Robinson, Lennox (1886–1958)
Playwright, born Douglas, Co. Cork.

Robinson, Sir William (d. 1712)
Architect of the Royal Hospital, Kilmainham, Dublin.
Rosse, 3rd Earl of (William Parsons) (1800–1867)
Astronomer who built the largest telescope of the time at Birr Castle.
Russell, George 'AE' (1867–1935)
Poet and painter, born Lurgan, Co. Armagh.
Russell, Thomas (1767–1803)
'The man from God knows where'; United Irishman, born Co. Cork.
Ryan, Darby (1770–1855)
Co. Tipperary satirist who wrote *The Peeler and the Goat.*
Sadlier, Mary Anne (1820–1903)
Novelist, born Cootehill, Co. Cavan.
Salmon, George (1819–1904)
Mathematician and theologian, born Cork.
Sarsfield, Patrick, Earl of Lucan (d. 1693)
Commander of James II's forces at the Siege of Limerick.
Schomberg, Duke of (d. 1690)
Commander of the Williamite forces at the Battle of the Boyne, where he was killed.
Shackleton, Abraham
Founded the Quaker School at Ballitore, Co. Kildare.
Shaw, George Bernard (1856–1950)
Playwright, born Dublin.
Sheares, Henry (1753–1798) and John (1766–1798)
United Irishmen, born Cork; executed in Dublin, 1798.
Sheehan, Canon Patrick (1852–1913)
Priest and novelist, born Mallow, Co. Cork.
Sheehy Skeffington, Francis (1878–1916)
Writer, born Bailieboro, Co. Cavan; a pacifist who was murdered in 1916.
Sheppard, Oliver (1865–1941)
Sculptor, born Cookstown, Co. Tyrone.
Sheridan, Philip H. (1831–1888)
Commander of the Union forces in the US Civil War, born Co. Cavan.
Sheridan, Margaret Burke (1889–1958)
Soprano, born Castlebar, Co. Mayo.
Sheridan, Richard Brinsley (1751–1816)
Playwright and orator, born Dublin.
Shields, General James (1806–1879)
General in the Union army in the US Civil War, born Co. Tyrone.
Shiel, Richard (1791–1851)
Dramatist and politician, born Co. Kilkenny.
Shiels, George (1886–1949)
Playwright, born Ballymoney, Co. Antrim.

Sigerson, George (1836–1925)
Physician, scientist and man of letters; born near Strabane, Co. Tyrone.
Simnel, Lambert
Pretender to the English throne, crowned Edward VI in Dublin, 1487.
Sirr, Henry Charles (1764–1841)
Town major of Dublin, arranged the capture of Lord Edward Fitzgerald in 1798 and of Robert Emmet in 1803.
Sloane, Sir Hans (1660–1753)
Physician and naturalist, born Co. Down.
Smith, Erasmus (1611–1691)
Used his wealth to found Erasmus Smith Grammar Schools in Ireland.
Spenser, Edmund (c.1552–1599)
Elizabethan poet who served and lived in Ireland.
Stephens, James (1825–1901)
Founder of the Fenians, born Co. Kilkenny.
Sterne, Laurence (1713–1768)
Novelist, born Clonmel, Co. Tipperary.
Stoker, Bram (1847–1912)
Novelist, author of *Dracula*, born Marino Crescent, Dublin.
Stokes, William (1804–1878)
Physician and pioneer of medical research, born Dublin.
Street, George Edward
Architect who restored Christ Church in the nineteenth century.
Strongbow (Richard le Clare) (d. 1176)
Leader of the Norman knights invited to Ireland by Dermot MacMurrough.
St Ruth, Charles
French general defeated and killed at the Battle of Aughrim, 1691.
Swift, Jonathan (1667–1745)
Dublin writer and dean of St Patrick's Cathedral.
Synge, John Millington (1871–1909)
Playwright, born Rathfarnham, Co. Dublin.
Taaffe, Nicholas (1677–1769)
General in the Austrian Army, born Co. Sligo.
Taaffe, Theobald (1639–1677)
Earl of Carlingford, commander of the Confederacy forces.
Talbot, Matthew (1856–1925)
Dublin working man, declared Venerable (Servant of God) in 1976.
Taylor, Jeremy (d. 1667)
Protestant Bishop of Down and Connor.
Teeling, Captain Bartholomew (1774–1798)
Born Co. Antrim, United Irishman; aide-de-camp to General Humbert, executed after Battle of Ballinamuck.
Thompson, Charles (1729–1824)
Born Maghera, Co. Derry; as secretary to US

Congress wrote out the Declaration of Independence.

Tone, Theobold Wolfe (1763–1798)
United Irishman; organised French invasion in support of 1798 rebellion; captured by British and committed suicide in prison.

Tuohy, Patrick (1894–1930)
Painter, born Dublin.

Waddell, Helen (1889–1965)
Writer and scholar educated in Belfast.

Wadding, Luke (1588–1657)
Franciscan scholar, born Waterford.

Walker, Reverend George
Born Co. Tyrone; he inspired Protestant defenders of Derry during the siege of 1689.

Wallace, William Vincent (1812–1865)
Composer, born Waterford.

Warbeck, Perkin
Pretender to the English throne, as Richard IV, supported by the mayor of Cork in 1492.

Ware, Sir James (1594–1666)
Historian and antiquary, born Dublin.

Wellington, Duke of (1769–1852)
Arthur Wellesley, field marshal; born Dublin. Victor of Waterloo.

Wentworth, Thomas (d. 1640)
Earl of Strafford—Viceroy of Charles I; recalled and executed, 1641.

Whaley, Buck (1766–1800)
Politician and eccentric, born Dublin.

Wilde, Sir William (1815–1876)
Surgeon and antiquary, born Castlerea, Co. Roscommon.

Wilde, Oscar (1854–1900)
Wit and dramatist, son of Sir William; born Westland Row, Dublin.

Wogan, Sir Charles (1698–1754)
Soldier of fortune, born Co. Kildare.

Wolfe, Charles (1791–1823)
Poet, born Co. Kildare.

Yeats, John B. (1839–1922)
Painter, born Co. Down.

Yeats, William Butler (1865–1939)
Famous poet and dramatist, born Dublin.

Index

Ardboe, Co. Tyrone, 401
Ardbraccan, Co. Meath, 170
Ardee, Co. Louth, 55, 183–4
Ardfarna, Co. Donegal, 380
Ardfert, Co. Kerry, 55, 233
Ardfinnan, Co. Tipperary, 262
Ardglass, Co. Down, 345–6
Ardgonnell Castle, Co. Armagh, 358
Ardhowen Theatre, Enniskillen, 372
Ardkillen, Co. Roscommon, 336
Ardmore, Co. Waterford, 277, 286–7
Ardnacrusha, Co. Clare, 259
Ardnaglas Castle, Co. Sligo, 323
Ardnamona, Co. Donegal, 383
Ardnaree, Co. Mayo, 312
Ardnurcher Castle, Co. Westmeath, 160
Ardpatrick, Co. Limerick, 248
Ardpatrick, Co. Louth, 182
Ardrahan, Co. Galway, 304
Ardress Craft Centre, Co. Fermanagh, 374
Ardress House, Co. Armagh, 358
Ards Peninsula, Co. Donegal, 337, 340, 390, 391
Ardscull Motte, Co. Kildare, 144
Ardsheelaun River, 222
Ardtermon Castle, Co. Sligo, 321
Ardtole Church, Co. Down, 346
Argory, The, Co. Armagh, 358
Arigna, Co. Roscommon, 18
Arigna Mountains, 328, 334
Arklow, Co. Wicklow, 103–4
  tourist information office, 10
Armagh, Co., 351, 355–62
Armagh, Co. Armagh, 355–8
  tourist information office, 19
Armoy, Co. Antrim, 431
Arra Mountains, 274
Arraglen, Co. Kerry, 51
Arranmore Island, Co. Donegal, 389
Arthur, Rev. William, 437
Arthurstown, Co. Wexford, 124
Arts Theatre, Belfast, 33, 415
Arva, Co. Cavan, 165
Ashbourne, Co. Meath, 172
Ashe, Thomas, 172, 231
Ashford, Co. Wicklow, 102
Ashford Castle, Co. Mayo, 59, 314
Ashleagh Waterfall, Co. Mayo, 301
Askeaton, Co. Limerick, 242, 245–6
Assaroe Abbey, Co. Donegal, 381
Assaroe Falls, Ballyshannon, 380
Asselyn Church, Co. Roscommon, 334
Assicus, St, 336
Assumption, Cathedral of the, Carlow, 138
Assumption, Church of the, Wexford, 120
Ath Seanaigh, Ballyshannon, 380
Athboy, Co. Meath, 173–4
Athboy River, 173

Athcarne Castle, Co. Meath, 177
Athclare Castle, Co. Louth, 185
Athenry, Co. Galway, 18, 54, 303–4
Athleague, Co. Roscommon, 333
Athlone, Co. Westmeath, 160–63
  tourist information office, 10
Athlone Castle, 160–61
Athlumney, Co. Meath, 57, 170
Athshanboe, Co. Tipperary, 267
Athy, Co. Kildare, 144
  tourist information office, 10
Attracta, St, 324
Auburn, Co. Westmeath, 163
Audhaven Theatre, Enniskillen, 33–4
Audley's Castle, Co. Down, 345
Augher, Co. Tyrone, 400–401
Aughnacliffe, Co. Longford, 166
Aughnakillagh, Co. Monaghan, 365
Aughnanoo, Co. Donegal, 384
Aughnanure, Co. Galway, 55, 297
Aughrim, Co. Galway, 303
Aughrim, Co. Wicklow, 111
Aughris Head, Co. Sligo, 323, 380
Augustinian Abbey, Adare, 243
Augustinian Abbey, Tipperary, 266
Augustinian Canons, 53
Augustinian Priory, Dungiven, 413
Australia
  Bord Fáilte office, 8
Avoca River, 111
Avonbeg River, 106, 109
Avondale, Co. Wicklow, 109
Avonmore River, 109
Awbeg River, 204
Axe-Factories, 46

B & I Terminal, North Wall, Dublin
  tourist information office, 12
Bagenalstown. *see* Muine Bheag
Baginbun, Co. Wexford, 123
Bailieborough, Co. Cavan, 370
Baily Lighthouse, 95
Balbriggan, Co. Dublin, 94, 178
Baldongan Castle, Co. Dublin, 94
Balla, Co. Mayo, 313
Ballagan, Co. Louth, 180
Ballaghaderreen, Co. Roscommon, 18, 334
Ballaghmore Castle, Co. Laois, 147
Ballina, Co. Mayo, 312
  tourist information office, 10
Ballina, Co. Sligo, 324
Ballina, Co. Tipperary, 257
Ballinacarriga Castle, Co. Cork, 214
Ballinacor Mountain, Co. Wicklow, 106
Ballinafad, Co. Sligo, 325
Ballinakill, Co. Longford, 165
Ballinakill Harbour, Co. Galway, 300
Ballinalee, Co. Longford, 166
Ballinamore, Co. Leitrim, 18, 330, 370

Saltee Islands, 122
Salthill, Galway, 290, 292, 293
  tourist information office, 15
Sampson Tower, Limavady, 408
Sand Bay, Co. Fermanagh, 374
Sandycove, Co. Cork, 210
Sandycove, Co. Dublin, 96, 97
Sarsfield, Patrick, 238, 257, 267
Saul, Co. Down, 343
Sawel, Co. Derry, 404
Scalp, the, Co. Wicklow, 101
Scardaun, Co. Galway, 299
Scariff, Co. Clare, 16, 258
Scarrifhollis, Co. Donegal, 393
Scarteen Black and Tans, 247, 266
Scarteen House, Co. Limerick, 247
Scarva, Co. Down, 351
Scattery Island, Co. Clare, 253
Schull, Co. Cork, 210
Scilly, Kinsale, 208
Sconce Hill, Co. Derry, 410
Scota's Glen, Co. Kerry, 232
Scott, Michael, 60
Scrabo Hill, Co. Down, 342
Scraggy Bay, Co. Donegal, 392
Screeb Lodge, Co. Galway, 297
Scullabogue House, Co. Wexford, 126
sea fishing, 41
sea trout fishing, 40
Seaforde, Co. Down, 346
Seal Caves, Achill, 310
Seanach, St, 230
Seanad Eireann, 3, 88
Seefin Mountain, Co. Kerry, 224
Seefin Mountain, Co. Limerick, 248, 249
Seirkieran, Co. Offaly, 152
Selskar Abbey, Wexford, 118, 120
Senan, St, 253
Seskilgreen, Co. Tyrone, 400
Seskinore, Co. Tyrone, 403
Seven Hogs, Co. Kerry, 230
Shalwy, Co. Donegal, 45
Shanagarry, Co. Cork, 206
Shanagolden, Co. Limerick, 245
Shanahan, Michael, 409
Shandon Church (St Ann's, C of I), Cork, 196
Shane O'Neill's Castle, Co. Antrim, 438
Shane's Castle, Co. Antrim, 341
Shane's Castle demesne, Randalstown, 438
Shanid Castle, Co. Limerick, 245
Shannon, Co. Clare, 252
Shannon Airport, Co. Clare, 237
  tourist information office, 15
Shannon Basin, 452–4
Shannon Callows, 152
Shannon Development, 9
  entertainment, 34
Shannon River, 3, 73
  hydroelectric scheme, 258, 259

in Co. Clare, 250, 257
in Co. Galway, 303
in Co. Kerry, 233, 234
in Co. Leitrim, 328, 329
in Co. Limerick, 236, 241
in Co. Longford, 164
in Co. Offaly, 150, 152
in Co. Roscommon, 331, 336
in Co. Westmeath, 156, 160
source, 367, 370
Shannonbridge, Co. Offaly, 153
Shantemon Hill, Co. Cavan, 368
Shanvaus, Co. Leitrim, 327
Shaw, George Bernard, 64, 80, 97, 304
Shee Almhouse, Kilkenny, 132, 133(p)
Sheefry Hills, Co. Mayo, 307
Sheehan, Canon, 203
Sheelan, St, 261
Sheephaven Bay, Co. Donegal, 390, 391
Sheep's Head Peninsula, Co. Cork, 211
Shehy Mountains, 213
Shelmalier, Barony of, 117
Shelton Abbcy, Co. Wicklow, 104
Shenick's Island, Skerries, 94
Sheppard, Oliver, 87, 117, 120
Shepperton Lakes, 209
Shercock, Co. Cavan, 369
Sheridan, General Phil, 370
Sherkin Island, Co. Cork, 210
Shields, General James, 401
Shillelagh, Co. Wicklow, 111
Shimna River, 346
Shippool Castle, Co. Cork, 208
shopping, 37–8
  VAT rebates, 38
showjumping, 40
Shrone Hill, Co. Cork, 211
Shrove, Co. Donegal, 396, 397
Siamsa Tire, 33, 231
Siamsa Tire, Tralee, 35
Sigerson, Dr George, 403
Silent Valley, Co. Down, 348
silver, 38
Silver Strand, Co. Clare, 255
Silver Strand, Co. Galway, 293
Silver Strand, Co. Wicklow, 103
Silvermine Mountains, 267, 271, 275
Silvermines, Co. Tipperary, 275
Sinclair Seamen's Church, Belfast, 421
Sion Mills, Co. Tyrone
  tourist information office, 23
Six Mile Water, Co. Antrim, 437
Skellig Islands, Co. Kerry, 74, 223, 224
Skerries, Co. Dublin, 93–4
Skerries, Portrush, 436
Skerry Church, Co. Antrim, 436–7
Sketric Island, Co. Down, 343
Skibbereen, Co. Cork, 209–10
  tourist information office, 15

Wicklow Sailing Club, 103
Wicklow Way, 42, 101
Wide Streets Commissioners, 58
Wilde, Oscar, 64, 80, 333, 373
Williams-Ellis, Clough, 430, 434–5
Wilson, James, 403
Windy Gap, Co. Kerry, 225
Windy Gap, Co. Laois, 147
'Wonderful Barn', Co. Kildare, 142
Woodbrook golf course, Bray, 99
Woodenbridge, Co. Wicklow, 104, 111
Woodfield, Co. Cork, 209
Woodhouse demesne, Co. Waterford, 284
Woodstock Castle, Co. Kildare, 144
Woodstock House, Co. Kilkenny, 135
Woodstown Strand, Co. Waterford, 282
Worth Library, Steevens' Hospital, 93
Wren, Christopher, 261
Wyatt, James, 306, 373
Wynnes, J. C., 421
Wynne's Folly, Co. Kerry, 225

Yeats, J. B., 92, 319
Yeats, Jack, 319
Yeats, W. B., 62, 64–5, 66, 80, 304, 316, 319, 321, 327
 grave of, 320
Yeats Memorial Building, Sligo, 319
Yeats Summer School, 66
Yeats Tower, Co. Galway, 15
Yellow Ford, Co. Armagh, 358
Yellow Steeple, Trim, 172
Youghal, Co. Cork, 205–6
 'Clock Gate', 58
 tourist information office, 16
Youghal Bay, Co. Cork, 277
Young Irelanders, 271

Zoological Gardens, Belfast, 423
Zoological Gardens, Dublin, 78